PENGUIN BOOKS

THE COMPLETE WOMAN'S REFERENCE BOOK

Although Mary Gostelow has masterminded *The Complete Woman's Reference Book*, she and her colleagues have been helped by a extensive team of specialists and organizations to provide accurate inside information on all that women – and men! – could possibly want to know.

Mary Gostelow is truly a woman of the 1980s. As a recent press article said: 'She talks authoritatively and fluently on any subject you name, ranging from cooking and travelling to economics and microprocessors. Her ambition is to explain the complexities of modern-day life in the simplest of terms to the thousands of her readers around the world.'

GW00507455

Mary Gostelow

THE COMPLETE WOMAN'S REFERENCE BOOK

Penguin Books

Penguin Books Ltd, Harmondsworth, Middlesex, England
Viking Penguin Inc., 40 West 23rd Street, New York, New York 10010, U.S.A.
Penguin Books Australia Ltd, Ringwood, Victoria, Australia
Penguin Books Canada Limited, 2801 John Street, Markham, Ontario, Canada L3R 1B4
Penguin Books (N.Z.) Ltd, 182–190 Wairau Road, Auckland 10, New Zealand

First published by Viking 1985
Published in Penguin Books 1986

Filmset in 9/10½ Monophoto Photina by
Northumberland Press Ltd, Gateshead,
Tyne and Wear
Printed in Great Britain by Hazell, Watson & Viney Limited,
Member of the BPCC Group, Aylesbury, Bucks

Contents

Introduction

Who is 'The Complete Woman'? Well, for the purposes of this book she is seventeen (or seventy-one), she lives in Helston (or in the Hebrides), she is tall/short, dark/fair and has no children or twenty grandchildren.

How ludicrous! It is obvious, of course, that there is no such person. 'The Complete Woman' is an amalgam of age, localities, ideas, interests and lifestyles. The unifying factor is simply that she lives in the United Kingdom. Too many books and magazines think that all life happens in London. *The Complete Woman's Reference Book* intentionally concentrates on the whole of England, Northern Ireland, Scotland and Wales. It tells you what you need to know in today's world. It is a basic information guide and a pointer to sources of further reading, organizations and ideas. Say, for instance, that you want to know why your car will not start – some simple explanations are suggested here. Say you want to understand what education is all about or you need to have a handy first aid book – this is it. The key to the *Reference Book* is the index. Turn to it first to find where the information is.

I had to draw the line somewhere and there are, deliberately, no hints on gardening or cookery. Both important topics are already amply covered and there was not room to do them justice here.

Much of the material applies both to men and women and many men have been involved in putting it together. However, all subjects are written from a woman's viewpoint.

It is exciting being a woman today. Some of us have a new freedom and perhaps combine family life with a job away from home. Yet it is, at the same time, a difficult period, one of conflict between tradition and change for the sake of change. *The Complete Woman's Reference Book* does not attempt to adjudicate – and deliberately leaves such emotive issues as religion and the nuclear debate to you, the reader.

I have been aware of the need for such an almanac for some time, and for many years my partner Wendy Lees and I have been compiling notebooks which formed the nucleus of this project. We have to thank Jenny Wilford for making us realize that we should expand our personal notebooks to share with you – and Diana Hastings, Janet Rae and Margaret Rice for contributing their own wide knowledge throughout the book.

My name is on the cover and I fed all the information into the word processor, but the concept and formulation have been a team effort masterminded by Sally Gaminara, Wendy Lees and myself. Without Sally and Wendy 'The Complete Woman' would not have had her reference book.

Welcome, therefore, to *The Complete Woman's Reference Book*. May it be as indispensable to your life as it is already to ours.

Acknowledgements

We should especially like to thank the following:

American Express; Berni Inns; Boots; British Airways; British Home Stores; British Telecom; Debenhams; Gleneagles Hotels; Lloyds Bank; Safeway Food Stores; Scottish Transport Group; Vauxhall-Opel.

We want, indeed, to give thanks to all those who realized the need for this book and helped to provide information and back-up support. They are too many to mention them all by name (some are mentioned in the text) and to those who are not listed below we still give our heartfelt thanks:

American Airlines; Frank Arnold; Asda and Elizabeth Knox; Association of British Launderers and Cleaners and Ruth Parkhouse; Barbara Attenborough Associates, Barbara, Clare and Nick Attenborough and Gill Hutcheon; The Automobile Association, John Douglas and Mark Hughes; Avis and Jim McGovern; Caroline Bailey; Frankie Bainbridge; Jennifer Baker; Barclay's Bank and Mike Dennely; Barratt Developments and Trevor Wiles; Peter Bates, Julia Camp and Pam Crawford and Gleneagles Hotels; Beefeater and Maureen Bown; Lotte Berk Studios and Gay Christie; British Caledonian, Dr P. J. C. Chapman and Hilary Christmas; British Insurance Association and E. J. Dewberry; British Pregnancy Advisory Service and J. L. Barton; British Rail and D. A. Marshall; British School of Motoring and C. Deacon; British Standards Institution and Judith Tabern; Brook Advisory Centres and Caroline Woodroffe; Building Societies Association, Mark J. Boleat and Tricia McLaughlin; Norman Challenor; Champagne Bureau, Malcolm McIntyre and Alison Pendree; Chubb and R. J. Pilgrim; Sir James Cobban, CBE, DL; Colour Me Beautiful and Mary Spillane; Commercial Union and Ray Morley; Commission for Local Administration in England and Wales and Neville Jones; Company Pensions Information Centre and M. J. Brown; Linda Cook; Ken Cook and Kate Moody (British Airways); Fleur Cowles; Department for National Savings and David Percival; Department of Health and Social Security, David Percival and Michael Brennan; Diners Club and Margaret Farquharson; Electrical Association for Women; Electricity Council and Michael King; European Commission for the Promotion of Silk and Rosalind Woolfson; Family Planning Association and Ronnie Goodchild; Federation of Master Builders and Max D. F. X. Winthrop; Flour Advisory Bureau and Gillian Niblock; Mike Fleetwood of Fleetwood Mac; Helen Galas; General Synod of the Church of England and Schools Secretary Geoffrey Duncan; Sheila Gilmore; Gin and Vodka Trade Association and Major General W. S. Cooper; Hampshire Constabulary, Chief Inspector Ian Fox and Terry Morris; Hampshire Fire Brigade and Chief Fire Officer G. Clarke, CBE;

Sheila Hart; Brigadier Mike Harvey; Health Education Council and Karen Waterman; Hertz and Brian Mackie; Homelink and M. R. Fitzsimmons; Independent Schools Information Service, Tim Devlin and Jane Capon; Industrial Society and Matthew Butler; Inner London Education Authority and Laurie Andrews; Institute of Chartered Accountants and Margaret Strong; Institute of Plumbing and Margaret Wickenden; Johnson & Johnson and Julie Rowan; Miriam Karlin; Cyril Kern; Kingsway Public Relations, Anne Dickinson, Jane Howard and Sheila Ritchie; Jenny Kirkpatrick; Lancome, Susi Jenkins and Sarah Jackman; Laurent-Perrier, Vicomte Bernard de la Giraudière and Martine Borgemeister; Law Society and Nicola Watkins; Law Society of Scotland; Jan Leeming; Helen Lees; Johnny Lees; London Coffee Information Centre and Susan Lake; Manpower Services Commission and Margaret Windle; Marks & Spencer; Mastectomy Association and Gillian Mann; Maxim's and Ralph Taylor; Meat Promotion Executive and Wendy Godfrey; Milk Marketing Board, John Friend and Freda Corin; Valerie Mitchell; Marjorie Mockler; Morrison's Bowmore Distillery, Tim Morrison and Brian Crook; Mothercare and Frances Ward; National Association of Funeral Directors and Pamela Maas; National Girobank and Philip Bryant; National Express and Alan Watkins; National Marriage Guidance Council and Stephen Saunders; Cecilia Norman; O1 Computers and Ken Blackman and his colleagues; Office of Fair Trading and J. K. Howell; Osborne and Kate Pulling; Panasonic and Caroline de Mancha Stevens; Sidney Pemberton and Sheila Stone (representing Vauxhall-Opel); Peter Dominic and Jean Crossley; Pifco and Susan Jowett; Alan Piper; Post Office and John Tylee; Rape Counselling and Research Project and Bernadette Manning; Debbie Rix; Helene Rogers; Amanda Ross; Royal Automobile Club and Derek Tye; Royal Ballet School and Penny Dane; Rufflette and Jackie Woodford; Russell & Bromley and Mary Bentham; Sainsbury's and Jane Lyon; Samaritans and the Rev. David Evans; Scottish Association of Citizens' Advice Bureaux; Scottish Consumer Council and Esme Walker; Scottish Information Office; Sealink and Alan Root; Sinclair Research, Bill Nichol, Mary Reinman and Liz Walker; Jill Skinner, Adrian Talboys and Safeway; Spar and R. F. Tuker; Spurhill Technical and John Baker; Tate & Lyle, Charles Runge and Dr M. L. Burge; Telecom Gold, Dr Peter Bury, Nigel Bell and Karen Langdale; Tesco and Ann Brown; Trades Union Congress and Mike Smith; Travel Press Services and Patricia Watson; Sheila and Melissa Tuffley; Typhoo and Celia Price; Van den Berghs, Rosamond Wilkinson and Doreen Hunt; Waitrose and Deborah Waring; WeightWatchers, Barbara Hardwick and Marie-France Newberry; Westco and Martin Freeman; *Which Computer?*, Nicky Trevitt and Jane Freeman; Derek Willson, David Orr and Margaret Stewart (British Telecom); Women's Gas Federation and Sue Pearson; Women's Press.

1 Your Money

The way you manage your money can make all the difference to your life. Perhaps you are a student wondering how to make your grant go further. Perhaps you need to borrow in order to buy a car, or you are wondering where to put your savings so that they give you the best return. Whatever your age and occupation, you should know about pension plans and insurance.

It is important not to be afraid of the subject of money or banks and other organizations. Remember, there are two kinds of money – yours and theirs; and banks are using your money to provide a service, a point about which they should be reminded from time to time.

Chip Shipley, Marketing Manager of Lloyds Bank Investment Department, defines finance as 'using their money to increase yours'. For the first part of this chapter he told me about money in terms of *investment* (how to look after and increase your money) and *borrowing* (who to borrow from and how to go about it). Before going into detail, however, you should be familiar with the terminology.

Terminology

Account – in investment terms, accounts are the periods into which the Stock Exchange year is divided. There are usually twenty-four fortnightly periods, depending on the incidence of public holidays (e.g. how long the Christmas break is).

Bargain – a deal on the Stock Exchange (*not* a cheap purchase or a good sale, just the transaction).

Bear – someone who expects share prices will fall: tends to be a seller hoping to buy back cheaper later on.

Blue chip – top quality share (ICI, Marks & Spencer, Shell). The name comes from the second highest denomination chip in a casino.

Bond – binding document or deed, nowadays frequently used to describe insurance company investment with tax advantages and some disadvantages.

Bonus issue – issue of fully paid shares to shareholders in proportion to their existing holding by capitalizing reserves.

Bull – an investor who expects prices will rise, often one who buys stock in the hope of a quick profit by selling before he has to pay up.

Capital gains tax (CGT) – a tax on profit made on selling goods, chattels, shares; maximum 30 per cent with an annual exemption subject to change.

Capital transfer tax (CTT) – tax on gifts of capital during lifetime or on death. There are exemptions and reliefs, subject to change.

Cash-flow account – a bank account that carries an automatic overdraft facility to help budget annual expenses on a monthly basis.

Chattel – a movable possession: anything that you own that is not alive and that can be moved.

Cheque card – a bank card guaranteeing payments of cheques up to £50 in value which are drawn properly and bear the card number.

Closing – buying or selling the same parcel of shares you dealt in earlier in the same account. Stamp duty is avoided because registration is not effected.

Collateral – security put up to back a loan.

Covenant – a promise: in financial terms, a promise in writing to pay over money regularly to another person or charity, usually for at least six years to a person, four years to a charity (see page 26).

Cum – prefix meaning 'with', attached to 'bonus', 'dividend', 'rights', etc., to denote that the transaction effected includes ownership of the item referred to.

Current account – a bank account with cheque book facilities, not normally interest-bearing, for everyday money transactions.

Deal – purchase or sale of stock or shares.

Debenture – frequently a bond issued by a company acknowledging indebtedness on which interest is payable until the principal is repaid. Often pledging specified assets as security.

Direct debit – a payment system used by major companies to obtain monthly or annual payments directly from an individual's bank account. It differs from a standing order (see below). With direct debit, the company through its bank charges whatever sum is required to meet your commitments. It is used for index-linked insurance premiums and for increasing subscriptions.

Dividend – a share of a company's profit distributed to shareholders proportionately to the number of shares they hold.

Equity shares – those shares which have the right to participate in the whole of the profits of a company after the prior claims of debentures, creditors and preference holders have been met. (Common parlance for ordinary shares.)

Ex div – abbreviation for deals done *without* the current dividend: commonly XD (similarly, ex rights, ex bonus).

Executor – someone who winds up the estate of a deceased person, distributing the assets in accordance with the will of the deceased (see Chapter 7).

Fixed interest – where the rate of interest paid on a loan or deposit is fixed and cannot be varied.

Flat rate – used to denote a rate of interest charged on a loan regardless of whether or not repayments are made (very misleading).

Gilts or **Gilt-edged** – usually British government securities (the name comes from nineteenth-century gilt-edged calling cards used by persons of the highest standing).

Gross – before tax has been deducted.

Grossing up – converting a net figure back to its gross equivalent by including the tax.

Index-linked (Indexation) – relating the price or value of something to changes in the cost of living. The government keeps a list of items of expenditure which most have to face – food, clothing, petrol, heating, lighting, rates, etc. – called the Retail Price Index or RPI, really the 'cost of living'. Each month this list is checked against the price of the goods on the list in the shops. Any changes in the larger items are noted and any change in the total bill brings about a change in the index. If RPI goes up by 1 per cent a month, so does the value of any scheme that is index-linked.

Insurance – financial protection against disasters such as death, fire, accident, flood, burglary, etc.

Jobber – middle-man in stock market transactions who links buyers with sellers.

Jobber's turn – difference between the buying and selling price of a share – the jobber's remuneration for bringing buyer and seller together.

Kaffirs – stock market jargon for South African gold shares.

Limit – price restriction set on Stock Exchange order. Purchaser or seller effectively advises his broker of the worst price he will accept.

Long – an investor is said to be 'long' in a share if he has bought more than he intends to keep.

Longs – British government stocks (gilt-edged) not redeemable within the next fifteen years.

Mandate – authority to a company to pay a shareholder's dividends directly into her bank account.

Mediums – British government stocks (gilt-edged) redeemable within five to fifteen years.

MIRAS – Mortgage Interest Relief At Source: new method of allowing house purchasers to pay interest net of basic tax relief (limited to loans of up to £30,000).

Net – used to denote payments or rates after standard rate tax has been deducted or allowed for.

Nominal value – the face value or *par* of a share as opposed to its market value.

Price/Earnings ratio (P/E ratio) – the number of years it would take at the current attributable earnings per share to meet the market price.

Scrip – short for 'subscription receipt', commonly any share certificate.

Short – an investor is said to be short if he sells more than he possesses of a stock.

Shorts – British government stocks (gilt-edged) redeemable under five years.

Stag – one who subscribes for a new issue in the hope of selling any allotted shares immediately for a profit, with no intention of holding the shares.

Standing order – instruction in writing to your bank to make regular payments to a third party or company.

Stockbroker – professional adviser on investments who acts as an agent and arranges purchases or sales of investments: only person allowed to deal with a jobber.

Top-up loan – where a building society will lend only, say, 80 per cent against property, a top-up loan from an insurance company can provide the extra against an insurance policy (often expensive).

Travellers' cheques – cheques drawn on leading international banks which guarantee payment.

Unit Trust – collection of investors who jointly own the investments held by the trust (see below).

Yield – the dividend or interest on a stock or share expressed as a percentage of the price paid for it (e.g. if a share has a nominal or par value of £1 and there is a 10 per cent dividend, but the share actually costs £2, then the yield is 5 per cent).

Zero rate bond – carrying no annual interest, only a bonus paid on maturity.

Saving Money and Investment

Investment can be safe or risky or anything between the two, so it is necessary to define safety and risk at each stage.

Effectively, you *lend* your money to a bank or other institution, and in return it pays you interest for the privilege of using your money until you need it again.

Why, you may ask, are there so many different rates of interest offered by banks, building societies, the National Savings Bank, finance houses and a host of others?

In every transaction there are always two factors to be considered:

● *Safety.* Banks are generally careful to lend their customers' money to companies and people who can reasonably be expected to pay it back over a comparatively short time. Banks have large reserves and are considered to be one of the safest places to leave your money. Finance companies, on the other hand, lend out the money they borrow from investors in hire-purchase contracts, from cars to double-glazing, without having the same knowledge of the borrower as the bank manager does of his customer. Accordingly, the bank does not have to offer such high rates of interest as the finance company because its deposit accounts are considered to be less risky.

● *Convenience* (theirs not yours!). If a bank, company or building society borrows money from you and you ask for it back tomorrow, they would not be able to do very much with the money or to plan ahead. Most institutions which borrow from the public, therefore, lay down the period of notice that they require before repaying the loan or deposit. The more time you are prepared to give them, the greater the interest rate you generally receive.

It does not, however, always work this way because the institutions may be expecting interest rates to go down shortly. So, expecting to borrow money more cheaply in the near future, they would not pay high rates for long periods in the present

DEPOSIT
ACCOUNT

A basic deposit account provides all customers with an easy and flexible method of saving. Any amount can be paid in at any time at any branch of the bank where the account is held. Interest, to be taxed at source, can either be added on to the balance to earn more interest or paid into a current account if you want to spend the interest. Although you can withdraw from your branch at any time, if you do not give seven days' notice you will lose seven days' interest (roughly about 10p for every £100 you withdraw).

SAVINGS BANK ACCOUNT

This has terms similar to those of a deposit account – i.e. you can put in and take out any amount, large or small, and the interest rate is usually the same. Because it is designed for small savers, however, a passbook is issued instead of a bank statement and you can withdraw up to £20 at any branch if this is produced. Larger amounts can be withdrawn at the branch where the account is held. The interest is added to the account. From the tax year 1985–6 this is *net* of basic rate tax.

SPECIAL SAVINGS PLAN

This is a scheme for those who wish to save on a regular monthly basis. It pays a higher rate of interest than a deposit account and offers preferential rates of interest on loans equivalent to the amount saved. There are two rules: you must save for at least twelve months and the minimum amount is £10 a month. The bank will, however, let you miss one payment per half year and you can make one withdrawal if you so wish: if you wish to make more, the manager may ask you to change to an ordinary deposit account.

EXTRA-INTEREST DEPOSIT ACCOUNT

Those wishing to invest larger sums which are not required for short-term needs can take advantage of this scheme which pays a higher rate of interest than a deposit account. You have to give one month's notice of withdrawal in writing and keep at least £2,500 in the account. You can elect to have interest paid monthly into a deposit or your current account, or added to the principal half yearly.

FIXED RATE DEPOSIT

If you have from £2,500 to £100,000 to invest this may be for you. You set the term in months to suit yourself – either 1, 2, 3, 6, 9, 12 or 18 months – and the rate of interest paid will vary with the period chosen. It is difficult to get out of this one before the time is up unless you can establish personal hardship, and you will need at least £10,000 invested if you want to choose the 1-month option. You will get money market rates for your deposit and these tend to be quite a bit higher than standard deposit rate.

BUILDING SOCIETIES

Rather like banks and finance houses, building societies' rates also vary depending on the size and stature of the society and on the period for which the investment is made. Generally, the larger societies pay lower rates than the smaller ones because investors think there is less risk with a large society (some of the smaller ones have gone bust).

Building societies offer a full range of time deposits, the rate of interest varying with the amount you deposit and the period of notice you are prepared to give. One important difference between the interest paid by the banks and the building societies is in the tax treatment. The banks always used to pay their interest on accounts gross and the building societies pay interest net of basic rate tax. Although they both now pay net of basic rate tax, there is still an important difference (see 'Tax' below).

Many building societies offer fixed period savings schemes, linked either to Save As You Earn or Family Bonds (see below). The principle remains the same: the longer you commit yourself, the better the return.

Several building societies, like banks, have cash-card schemes which allow you to withdraw money out of hours. Some building societies are also associated with Access. See also 'Building Societies', pages 67–9.

SAVE AS
YOU EARN

There are two schemes, the government scheme, which is index-linked, but which is being phased out, and the building society scheme which is not index-linked.

Both schemes require you to make sixty monthly payments before you receive the full benefit. They are 5-year savings plans with enough flexibility for you to miss a few months if times are hard: the period is extended by a month for each payment you miss. If you do cash the scheme in before the five years are up, you will receive a fixed, but lower, rate of interest and none at all if you do not stay in for at least one year. Should you wish, you can leave the money in at the end of the five years for a further two years and earn a tax-free bonus.

Anyone over sixteen can save on a regular basis with the government scheme, which is particularly attractive in times of high inflation. The minimum monthly contribution is £4, the maximum is £50, paid in sixty instalments. You can pay with a standing order on a National Savings Bank ordinary account, National Girobank or other bank account, or in cash at the Post Office. (Get details from your local post office.)

NATIONAL
SAVINGS
CERTIFICATES

At present, National Savings Certificates (in Northern Ireland, Ulster Savings Certificates) offer a guaranteed return entirely tax free. You buy certificates from post offices and banks and you will be given a holder's card.

In order to persuade you to stay invested the biggest cash bonus is paid at the end of the fifth year and the least at the end of the first. When you want to redeem your certificates (which you can do at any time) ask for a National Savings Certificate repayment form and pre-paid envelope at a post office. You can cash any number of £25 units and you will receive back that sum plus whatever increase is due. You should receive your money in about eight working days.

Notes

● You can give National Savings gift tokens which can be exchanged for National Savings Certificates or Premium Bonds or used to invest with the National Savings Bank. Tokens are available at the post office from £5 up.

● Index-linked National Savings Certificates are known as 'granny bonds', although anyone can buy them.

● See 'How to Choose', page 18.

NATIONAL
SAVINGS
BANK

Ordinary accounts pay a low rate of interest but it is completely tax free up to £70 interest a year. The rate of interest is 6 per cent if you keep £500 or more in your account for a whole year, otherwise you will receive 3 per cent.

The investment account is similar to a bank deposit account except that you have to give one month's notice, but the interest rate is generally higher than that of a bank term deposit account. You can get details of all National Savings plans from your post office. Children over seven can operate a National Savings account with an initial deposit of only £1. This is a good way to teach them about money management.

NATIONAL
SAVINGS
BONDS

● *Income bonds* pay an even higher rate of interest for the larger investor (£2,000 to £200,000), but remember there is a tax liability. You must give at least three months' notice (six months to avoid losing some interest). If the investment does not stay in at least a year then you could lose all your interest so check the penalties very carefully before you buy.
● *Deposit bonds* are available for those with a lump sum to invest – a minimum of £500 and maximum £50,000 in multiples of £50. They pay a premium rate of interest, without deduction of tax at source.

PREMIUM
BONDS

These cost a minimum of £5 for five units. There is no guaranteed interest whatsoever but you have a separate chance in weekly and monthly draws to win at least one of the 100,000 prizes ranging from £50 to £250,000. You can buy premium bonds at your post office or bank.

For children under sixteen, parents, grandparents and legal guardians can purchase bonds in the child's name and prizes are paid on behalf of the child to that purchaser who is then regarded as a trustee of the money.

HOW
TO CHOOSE

The most important piece of investment advice is *be honest with yourself*. If you are muddle-headed and lazy where money is concerned, do not pick an investment which requires concise, active and sophisticated management. Decide what your prime objective is. Remember that you cannot have it both ways: the highest rate of interest usually means the least safe or the longest fixed period or probably both. Remember the two kinds of money – yours and theirs – and it is *yours* we are talking about now.

If you are trying to save some money of your own, National Savings Certificates do not create any tax complications. Building society or bank interest payments are declarable by law so should appear on your tax return. Remember that although building society and bank deposit interest is net of basic, or standard rate, income tax, if your personal circumstances are such that you do not pay tax then you cannot get anything back from the taxman or the building society.

It is obvious that your *tax rate* determines which is the better investment, the bank deposit or the building society. This factor becomes even more important at the high end of the scale: for someone paying tax at 60 per cent things look very different. A building society paying 7 per cent net would yield only $2\frac{1}{2}$ per cent in net terms to the very high taxpayer. Even the National Savings ordinary account at only 3 per cent would be better, as would National Savings Certificates, with a completely tax-free return.

Every woman is an individual case but, on the whole, *high taxpayers should look for tax-free returns* and *lower or non-taxpayers should look for high interest rates compatible with their other objectives.*

Finally, some advice:

● Put your objectives in order of importance.
● Don't be greedy – but *do* look for the best returns.
● Think about when you are likely to want the money out.
● Don't invest for when you *might* want it out.
● Save if you can.
● Don't save long term on short-lived enthusiasm.

'RISK' INVEST-MENTS Investments cover a range of goods from antiques to artillery and from something to drink to stocks and shares. Anything which can be bought at a price with the hope of selling at a profit can be termed an investment.

Buying an investment does not, however, make you an investor. If you have no intention of parting with your purchase you are not truly an investor. Investment in risk enterprise should be unemotional and uninvolved, though it is easy to become attached even to stocks and shares!

Outside the stock market it is difficult to get unbiased advice, as most of the professionals are also dealers in their relevant subject. Unless you have substantial personal knowledge, do not invest.

If you are thinking of stocks and shares, on the other hand, you can obtain free impartial advice from a stockbroker or your bank manager. With recent changes in commission charges laid down by the Stock Exchange, however, it has become expensive to buy and sell shares and you would really need at least £20,000 to buy a selection of shares to reduce the risk of investment to a reasonable and acceptable level.

So, unless you do have that kind of money, why not think about a unit trust?

UNIT TRUSTS More like a co-operative than a company, a unit trust is effectively a group of investors whose combined investment is used to buy a selection of stocks and shares. The investment is made by a professional fund manager who will look after the investments daily, making whatever changes he thinks necessary. The cost of running the fund – generally about 1 per cent – is deducted from the dividends the fund receives on the investments before they are distributed to unit holders.

The unit trust into which you buy will probably have a portfolio of at least fifty different companies and may well have as many as eighty or ninety so that you are spreading whatever risk there might be. Instead of receiving a whole host of small dividends and company reports you have just one report and one lot of dividends (most, but not all, unit trusts pay dividends half-yearly). Unit trusts are controlled by the Department of Trade.

That is the good news. But the stock market can go down as well as up. There are some unit trusts that have not only failed to beat inflation but have actually lost money quite substantially over the past year. Will the market be all right when you want to sell? Clearly, if you want to invest in the stock market you should make sure that you have sufficient cash on deposit to meet not only your immediate needs but anything that you are likely to want cash for over the next year or two.

There are two kinds of unit trusts:

● *General Funds* are broadly based and are designed to meet a basic objective such as capital growth or income – or indeed a bit of both. Because they will tend to have widely spread investments they do not usually figure in the list of top performing unit trusts but, equally, you rarely see them at the bottom.

For someone who wants to invest in the stock market and does not have enough money to do so on a large scale, then a general unit trust would be the sensible way.

● *Specialist Funds* are much more specific, e.g. American Smaller Companies Fund, Medicare Fund, High Technology and so on. You can easily see that if you pick the right fund at the right moment you could do very well indeed – similarly, picking the wrong one could be disastrous.

With a specialist unit trust the fund manager undertakes to invest in a specific area or sector and cannot change just because he feels opportunities are better elsewhere. Some unit trust groups, like Lloyds, prefer to have slightly wider-based specialist funds to give the experts a little more room to manoeuvre (e.g. Lloyds Pacific Basin Fund, which could cover Japan, Australia or even the US). With such a wider-based fund you would not expect to see quite such dramatic performances (good or bad) as with a narrowly designed fund.

To sum up   ● General funds for a sensible approach – be prepared to invest for at least four or five years and keep a cash reserve.

● Specialist funds are more risky and perhaps more rewarding: there is a shorter time-scale. Be prepared to change even after only a year or so (these are only for the interested person who follows the financial news and can afford the 'downs' as well as the 'ups').

Borrowing Money

SPECIFIC OR AGREED
BORROWING

CREDIT OR IMPLIED BORROWING
OVER-BORROWING

It is no longer sensible to borrow as much as you can for as long as you can. In times of very high inflation when you could get tax relief on all sorts of loan interest it did seem a good idea, but single-figure inflation and tax relief limited to loans for house purchase and improvement make massive borrowing less desirable.

Why borrow at all? Strangely enough there are quite different reasons. It is too simple to say that you can then have something immediately rather than having to wait until you can afford it. Many people use borrowing almost like a form of saving (a contradiction in terms, if you like). Money saved for a 'special buy' can so easily be channelled elsewhere, so a loan is a sure way to get it. For many, borrowing is the only way to buy something large like a house or a car.

Note that all the information in this section refers to Lloyds Bank plc. While most banks provide similar services and will have much the same attitudes to their customers, it would be as well to check that your bank does offer the same facilities before committing yourself irrevocably to any big venture involving money – yours or theirs – as services and charges vary slightly between banks from time to time.

There are two main ways of borrowing: specific or agreed borrowing and credit or implied borrowing.

SPECIFIC OR AGREED BORROWING

This means, quite simply, that you come to an agreement with a bank, building society, insurance company or hire-purchase company to lend you a specific sum at an agreed rate of interest for a specific period with terms of repayment laid down.

Building society and insurance company loans are least varied in purpose and shape. Usually, but not always, a building society will lend specifically to help you buy or improve a home (see Chapter 2). This loan may well qualify you to offset the interest you pay on the loan against your income tax bill: there is at least one Finance Bill every year which often changes personal tax rates or relief so it is as well to check with your tax inspector. Nearly all other forms of borrowing are much shorter term.

The first place you should go to is your bank because it is likely to be the least expensive. If you have a temporary embarrassment or your budgeting has gone wrong, then provided you ask him first your bank manager will normally allow you to overdraw your current account. These days bankers, like everyone else, are keener to identify the different reasons for borrowing and if you really need a loan rather than an overdraft he will try and persuade you to take it.

With an overdraft you normally pay interest only on the amount you actually owe to the bank on a daily basis. Payments 'in' (pension, salary, dividends, etc.) would temporarily reduce the debt, although you would probably be spending them again in the course of the coming month. A loan account, on the other hand, has no connection with the balance on your current account. You could be in the position, say, of having £500 on your current account and owe £500 on your loan account and still be paying interest on this loan.

Most loan arrangements, from banks or finance companies, quote a rate of interest that will be charged annually on the amount borrowed. Very often these rates initially sound reasonable but in practice work out somewhat higher. The term 'flat rate' generally means that when you start off the loan, the interest is added to the amount borrowed and you reduce this monthly until it is paid off.

For example: if you borrow £1,000 over two years to buy a car at 10 per cent flat rate of interest, the bank or hire-purchase company would charge your loan account £1,000 plus £200 interest, i.e. £100 or 10 per cent for each year of the loan.

Look at the position half-way through. At the end of that first year you would have paid back 12 × £50; that is, £600 of the £1,000 borrowed. Even adding on interest for the full year you will still owe only £500, so the interest for the second year (at 10 per cent) ought to be no more than £50. By the end of the second year you will have repaid another £600 and the lender gets £50 more than he seems entitled to. The government is well aware how misleading this 'flat-rate' (Actual Percentage Rate – APR) practice is, and so by law lenders are obliged to quote the true rate in any contract or advertisement based on flat-rate figures (although, like health warnings on some cigarette packets, the print may be small and not easy to find).

Talk to your bank manager

Frankly, what *is* the best method to discuss borrowing money with your bank manager?

The bank manager's primary concern is always to get back the money he lends. He will want to be sure that you are both able to repay the money and intend to do so. He may insist on security, but that is not intended to be the source of repayment.

Banks are *not* reluctant lenders – far from it, that is where they make their money. Large companies often drive hard bargains and you, the individual, might be one of your bank manager's 'best bets'.

Bankers look for two things – security and a capacity to repay. It is essential that your bank manager can discern these two vital factors, either from the pattern of your existing bank account or the convincing argument you put to him. Clearly it is an advantage to have a track record of living within your means: if you are always overdrawn and get clear only when the manager gets cross, you will not look like a good bet for a large loan.

If an experienced financier does not think you can repay the loan, then you probably cannot easily do so and you might be better off without it. Hire-purchase companies, on the other hand, do not have the same knowledge of your financial affairs and therefore take a greater risk when they lend money and accordingly charge a much higher rate.

To recap, the salient features of specific or agreed borrowing are:
- house purchase and improvements – building society or insurance company
- house improvements down to overdrafts – try your bank first
- tell your bank manager the full story
- do not be misled by flat rates of interest.

For money for starting your own business, see Chapter 11.

CREDIT OR IMPLIED BORROWING

This could also be called 'impulse' or 'random' borrowing – in other words, all convenience borrowing such as accounts with shops, credit cards (see below) and charge accounts in general.

Unauthorized overdraft. Quite simply, do not do this if you want to maintain a good relationship with your bank. An unauthorized overdraft is a case of helping yourself to the bank's money without asking first. In practice it is simple to do: you merely draw cheques for more than you have in your account. If you hitherto have had a good track record with the bank your manager may well authorize the overdraft, but, equally, habitual borrowing in this way without asking may result in your cheques being bounced.

Your bank manager will probably also charge you a very high rate of interest for borrowing money without permission. The bank has responsibility for everyone's money: if confidence in the banks evaporated, everyone would try to take their money out, the banks would have to recall all loans and the entire financial structure would collapse.

Credit-rating and **credit-scoring** are two newish but increasingly important phrases, and as spending becomes more and more computerized your rating will become important. You need that good track record. Having a cheque card withdrawn by the bank or an unfavourable credit reference are extremely difficult to recover from.

If you cannot get credit the unco-operative company or trader concerned might have contacted a credit reference agency (also known as a credit reporting agency). This agency might have wrong information on you. You have the right under the Consumer Credit Act to know this, and also to see the agency's relevant file (this will cost you £1). If you want help, contact your local Citizens' Advice Bureau or look at the booklet 'Refused Credit? Your Right to Know What Credit Reference Agencies are Saying about You' from the Office of Fair Trading.

To recap:
- If you need money talk to your bank manager first – a good old-fashioned overdraft is likely to be the cheapest source of money although banks sometimes like to steer their customers towards personal loans which you pay off at an agreed monthly rate over so many years (an overdraft is more flexible than a personal loan).

● Show the bank manager – and yourself – how and when you can repay.

● Never *never* borrow money from a back-street loan shark, however desperate you are. As a rule of thumb, the 'postal loans' you see advertised are invariably more expensive than a bank loan or a direct credit or hire-purchase deal.

● Remember to protect your credit rating!

OVER-
BORROWING

If you find yourself burdened with debts – perhaps you have taken on too many loans and credit contracts – do the following:

● Set out your total monthly commitments against your total monthly income.

● Work out the bare essentials that you must pay each month – obviously the mortgage or the rent is a high priority – and decide what you have left to pay your other creditors.

This is a far more rational method of dealing with a crisis than panicking and borrowing from Peter to pay Paul and this method should keep the bailiffs from the door. Debt, after all, is only credit gone a bit wrong and everyone would rather have half a loaf than none at all. It is expensive to take people to court: building societies, incidentally, are particularly understanding and you should ask if you can lengthen the terms of your mortgage or just repay capital for a while and suspend payments of interest.

You cannot always foresee trouble in meeting commitments. **Shelagh Salter**, chairperson of the Welsh Consumer Council, says: 'The single most important cause of consumer debt today is a sudden unexpected drop in income such as that which is caused by redundancy, short-time working, illness, a death in the family or marriage break-up.'

If you do get into trouble go to your local Citizens' Advice Bureau.

Banks

CHOOSING A BANK
GETTING CASH
COVENANTS

OTHER SERVICES
NATIONAL GIROBANK

CHOOSING
A BANK

All the big banks offer a more or less comparable service. The advantage of joining one of the big banks is their wide range of facilities plus the important fact that it is easier to cash a cheque away from home.

If you do not already have a bank account you may go to a bank that is recommended by a relative or a friend – or you may simply go to the one that is most convenient for you. You may decide you want a bank with a person (in the form of a manager) to whom you can talk. Bank managers spend a lot of their time out of the office so try to make an appointment well in advance and let him know what it is you want to talk about: do not be secretive.

If you want a bank exclusively for women, you will have to be within reach of Edinburgh – the Ladies' Branch of the Royal Bank of Scotland.

Ladies' Branch
Royal Bank of Scotland
142 Princes Street
Edinburgh EH2 4EQ
031–226 2895

Here are the main headquarters of the largest banks:

Bank of Scotland
The Mound
Edinburgh EH1 1YZ
031–229 2555

National Westminster Bank plc
41 Lothbury
London EC2P 2BP
01–606 6060

Barclays Bank plc
54 Lombard Street
London EC3P 3AH
01–626 1567

Royal Bank of Scotland
42 St Andrew Square
Edinburgh EH2 2YE
031–556 8555

Lloyds Bank plc
71 Lombard Street
London EC3P 3BS
01–626 1500

Trustee Savings Bank
3 Copthall Avenue
London EC2P 2AB
01–588 9292

Midland Bank plc
Poultry
London EC2P 2BX
01–606 9911

Whichever bank you choose, the procedure is more or less the same. You will be sent a statement so that you can check your balance. It is important to fill in amounts, dates and purchases on your cheque stubs as the statement records only the cheque number and amount.

Perhaps one of the most valuable services the bank provides is secrecy. Your affairs are strictly between you and the bank and, generally, may not be disclosed to a third party without your permission or unless there is a court order.

GETTING
CASH

Most banks are open Monday to Friday 9.30 to 3.30 (some branches are also open Saturday mornings 9.30 to 12 noon and some Scottish banks have extended hours to 4.45). You can cash a cheque for any amount (as long as you have it in the account) at your own branch, and for up to £50 a day at any other branch of your bank. You will need to show your cheque card when presenting the cheque: try to keep your cheque book and cheque card separately so that a thief cannot so easily use your account.

The following banks will also cash cheques on accounts at other banks (shown in brackets) without charge: cheques from other banks are cashed at a small charge.

- Bank of Scotland (Co-op, National Westminster, Royal Bank of Scotland, TSB Scotland and Yorkshire. All banks except NatWest, £1 between 3.30 and 4.45 p.m.)
- Lloyds Bank (the National Westminster Group).
- Midland Bank (Clydesdale Bank and Northern Bank).
- National Westminster (Bank of Scotland and Ulster Bank).
- Royal Bank of Scotland (Bank of Scotland).

You can also get money from cashpoint dispensers around the country, some of which are open twenty-four hours a day. By inserting your personal card and keying in a special number you can get up to £100 daily: it is less expensive to get cash this way than by writing a cheque (e.g. most banks charge 29p for a cheque, and 16p for cashpoint). You may also be able to get details of your account and key in requests for cheque books and statements. You will get full details of your cashpoint's operation from your bank. *Never* keep a written note of your cashpoint card number with the card.

Note   You can also get cash from building societies, which keep longer hours. Some building societies also have cashpoint facilities.

COVENANTS   A covenant is a bargain made by one person with another. If you make a promise to pay money regularly to another person or body such as a charity or church, provided first that you have paid tax on the money and second that the person to whom you pay the money pays less than the standard rate of tax or none at all, some or all of the tax you paid can be reclaimed by the recipient.

You can do all the paperwork required yourself but you have to follow strict legal wording, which differs in Scotland. The trust department of your bank or your accountant can do all the necessary work involved with a covenant.

If you covenant to a charity, provided the payment is out of income, the charity can reclaim all the tax you have paid on that money. Normally covenants are drawn up to run for seven years although a change in the tax law means that covenants for charities are now sometimes drawn up for only four years.

The most common form of covenant is from parents to students. If you covenant money up to the limit of the personal allowance of someone over eighteen, the student can reclaim the tax deducted from the income you are giving away. (If the child's income from earnings or other sources has already used up the allowance then there is nothing to claim back.) The Inland Revenue will require you to certify that you are making the payments and will want to see a copy of the covenant. Although you may be paying higher rates of tax, a private person is allowed to reclaim only the basic rate tax under covenanted payments. The person reclaiming tax needs specific forms from the tax office: in the case of a recipient under eighteen, the refund will go to the parents unless they instruct the taxman to pay it into a bank or building society account in the student's name.

Perhaps the most important point to understand is how covenants can be used to gain a tax advantage while making a parental contribution towards a student's upkeep. Courses generally run for three or four years and the covenant is usually drafted for a minimum of six years. The covenant is a legal promise and is legally enforceable by the child upon the parent. The Inland Revenue is merely a party to the covenant provided the child does not endeavour to reclaim tax when no payments were made. You can stop the covenant once the child ceases to be a student and the parental obligation ends.

There are many other applications of covenants: to grandchildren, to elderly parents as well as to charities. You should consult your bank's tax department or your accountant before starting in one of these specialized areas.

OTHER SERVICES

Your bank can provide you with *travellers' cheques*, a Eurocheque encashment card and travel insurance (see also Chapter 17). And, in an emergency, cash can be sent to you anywhere in the world – the larger the bank, the quicker the money will get to you.

Budget or cash-flow accounts are specially designed by the banks to help you budget. By listing all your annual expenses (rates, heating, gas, insurance, etc.) and dividing them into monthly amounts the bank will automatically allow you to pay the bills when due while the monthly payments into the account will spread your costs over the whole year.

All the large banks provide a wide range of ancillary services ranging from *business advisory counselling* to *trusteeship* and *tax planning*. They will certainly help you *make a will*, even act as executor and trustee of your estate and advise you on insurance matters, *manage your investments* for you and help you provide for a *private pension* if appropriate.

Many of these additional services are provided at what the banks consider to be a commensurate fee. Initial service is often free but full utilization of these extra services is not, so it would be sensible to inquire the cost before you start.

You can also *deposit* such articles as wills, bonds, policies, boxes and parcels with the bank. The bank can help with *powers of attorney* and with *redirection of mail* – you can always give your bank's address rather than that of your home. They will also take responsibility for *standing orders* – regular payments of all kinds.

NATIONAL GIROBANK

National Girobank is different from all the other banks mentioned above in that it does not have its own branches. It operates via ordinary post office counters and there is, therefore, no 'friendly' bank manager.

You can cash cheques for up to £50 at either of two post offices of your choice. If you are eighteen or over you can also apply for a cheque card which enables you to draw up to £50 from virtually any post office – or up to £100 from the post office named on your cheque card. You can pay in at any post office (or by post, using Freepost, courtesy of Girobank).

All household service bills (electricity, gas, etc.) come with a Girobank payment slip attached. If you have a Girobank account you can settle such bills without incurring postage charges.

As a personal account holder with Girobank you can open a deposit account offering an attractive rate of interest. If you are eighteen or over you can apply for a personal loan of up to £5,000, a bridging loan to assist with house purchase or a Flexiplan account to help spread the cost of bill-paying.

Girobank travellers' cheques are issued in conjunction with Thomas Cook. Girobank postcheques are especially useful when travelling: they can be cashed, in local currency, at many post offices overseas.

There is no charge for personal transactions as long as the account is not overdrawn, but there is a small charge for business accounts.

You can get details of Girobank from your post office or from:

> National Girobank
> Freepost
> Bootle
> Merseyside GIR OAA

Cards

TERMINOLOGY   SPECIFIC FEATURES
ALL ABOUT CREDIT CARDS

TERMINOLOGY

Cardholder – the person who is authorized by the owning company to use the card.

Card transaction – the purchase of goods or the obtaining of services or cash advances against the use of the card.

Floor limit – each shop or other outlet has an agreed limit with the credit card company: if you want to buy something for more than this amount the trader (or whoever) will telephone the company for authorization.

Principal cardholder – a cardholder in whose name a card account is maintained.

ALL ABOUT CREDIT CARDS

All the cards mentioned below allow you to pay for things and to get cash both at home and when you are overseas. Generally anyone over eighteen can apply for a card.

Their *advantages* include:
- they allow you to 'get now, pay later'
- if you are careful, you can get several weeks' interest-free loan

- they save you having to carry round a lot of cash
- when travelling overseas, you do not have to worry about different currencies – or the problems of having enough cash with you.

The *disadvantages* include:
- they encourage you to overspend
- if you want a refund on an item, you will not be given cash but generally a credit note to your card company.

There are three main types of credit card:
- *Bank credit cards* (Access and Visa – for details see below). These cost nothing to get. You will be given a 'credit limit' on the total you can spend. If you pay in full each month (unless you draw cash) no interest is charged on credit: if you choose to pay a smaller sum, interest is charged but there may be a short interest-free period.
- *Charge cards* (American Express, sometimes known as Amex, Diners Club). You pay an enrolment fee and an annual sum (about £22.50). Cards can be used with ordinary cheque books to get cash at some banks. There is no limit or interest on the amount you spend provided you pay in full at the end of the month. High spenders are particularly invited to take out a gold card – see below.
- *Gold cards* (American Express Gold Card, Barclays Premier Card, Midland Gold Mastercard). You need to be earning at least £20,000 p.a., there may be a joining fee and you will pay an annual sum (about £40). You can get larger sums of cash and overdrafts at lower interest rates.

How do you use a card?

Apart from shop cards (see below) – which you can use only in the shop or one of the shops of that group – you can usually use a card wherever you see the identifying logo. You may find, however, that you cannot use the card in some departments of a shop (e.g. groceries in a department store).

When you hand over your card, an assistant will make a print of it on a duplicated slip. One copy will be given to you and another sent to the credit card company. The amount involved will appear on your next statement.

Warning!

- It is better not to use a card:
(a) if you can get interest-free or low-cost credit elsewhere (unless you pay the card bill in full)
(b) to pay your rates (paying by monthly instalments is interest free)
(c) if you can buy an identical item somewhere else for a cash at a lower price
(d) if you can get a discount paying cash.
- When you hand over your card in a shop or restaurant, try not to let it out of your sight. It has been known for a card to be taken out of the customer's sight, and for the next statement to include all types of extra meals.
- Remember to take the card away with you after each transaction: if

you forget it and go back to reclaim it, you may find that it has been legally cut in half.

● Check every statement carefully. Did you really buy £27 worth of petrol or was it only £7? Has something extra been added? If you think you have cause for complaint, contact the credit card company immediately (look at the references on the statement).

● Hotels, in particular, have a habit of writing in 'late charges' (e.g. if they did not add your telephone bill to the main bill) so there might be a difference between what you signed and the amount shown on the statement. This is not the card company's fault: complain if necessary to the hotel concerned.

● Do not miss a payment: if you do, your card might be 'blacked'. If you know you are going to be away for any length of time either plan beforehand to 'run the card down' or send the card company a post-dated cheque with a covering note.

● If you lose your card tell the police immediately and contact the credit card company which will have 24-hour answering facilities. You must confirm the loss in writing.

● In theory you are liable if someone else uses your card, but if you report the loss immediately you should not have to pay. To cover yourself, check whether loss of your cards is included in your insurance policy.

Card Protection Plan insures cards up to a total of £250. You put security stickers on your cards, luggage labels, etc., to warn the prospective thief. In case of loss you immediately call a 24-hour 'action line'. Details from:

Card Protection Plan
88–92 Earls Court Road
London w 8 6 eh
01–938 1041

SPECIFIC
FEATURES

Access

Application forms are available from any branch of Bank of Ireland, Clydesdale, Coutts, Lloyds, Midland, National Westminster, Northern, Royal Bank of Scotland or Ulster Bank, or by post from:

Lloyds Bank plc
Access Department
PO Box 35
Southend on Sea ss9 9 7bb

The card will be issued free. You will be allocated a credit limit normally in the £400 to £1,000 range: you can ask for this to be changed.

Your statement will be sent monthly and you can pay off completely or make a minimum payment of 5 per cent (or £5) of the sum involved. If a sum is not settled within twenty-five days of the statement date interest of 1¾ per cent per month is charged. (This can vary.)

The main advantage is that it costs nothing to 'belong' to Access and if you settle immediately you will not be charged interest. You can use the card in over 180,000 places in Britain and nearly 4 million around the world (look for Eurocard or Mastercard signs as well as Access). All cardholders can get up to £100 per day at any bank displaying the Access sign.

The main disadvantage is that with limited credit you cannot rely on the card in case of an expensive emergency.

Emergency phone number if your card is lost or stolen: 0702–352233.

American Express   Application forms are available from any American Express office or by post from:

> American Express
> PO Box 63
> Edward Street
> Brighton
> West Sussex BN2 1YE

The enrolment fee is £15 and the annual fee £22.50. You pay a further £12.50 if someone else has a card on your account. There is no credit limit.

The monthly statement should be settled in full as soon as you receive it – in practice, within fifteen days – or, after sixty days, you might find yourself liable for 'liquidated damages'.

The main advantage of Amex is that with no credit limit you can cope with an expensive emergency. You can use it in nearly 70,000 places in the UK and ten times that number world-wide. In Britain you cannot use it for cash but if you present it with your cheque book you can draw up to £50 per day at any branch of Lloyds on your current account, or up to £100 in any 7-day period from any American Express office (you can also get a further £400 in travellers' cheques). There are also special travel and holiday facilities (see the booklet 'Cardmember Rail: American Express Exclusive Breaks, Exciting Events' from any Amex office or main British Rail station).

The American Express Gold Card offers extra facilities, including cheque cashing up to £1,000 a week (in the UK – higher overseas) at American Express offices and Lloyds Bank. The Gold Card is especially attractive to business people and the annual fee is £50: the joining fee of £20 is waived for current cardmembers. Details from:

> Gold Card Membership
> PO Box 88
> Brighton
> West Sussex BN1 1YZ

Emergency phone number if your card is lost or stolen: 0273–696933.

Diners Club   Application forms are available from Diners Club outlets and from branches of the Bank of Scotland, Coutts, Isle of Man, National Westminster and Ulster Banks or by post from:

Diners Club
Kingmead
Farnborough
Hants GU I 4 7SR

You pay an enrolment fee of £15 and a yearly fee of £22.50 (annual fee for an extra card on the account is £12.50). There is no credit limit.

As with American Express, payment should be made in full when you receive your monthly statement or, 'after a time', you will be charged 'a service charge' of 2 per cent per month.

You can use the card at 43,000 places in the UK and at over half a million world-wide. By presenting the card with your cheque book you can draw cash from your current account at any of the banks mentioned above. You can, overseas, draw up to US $1,000 a day from a Diners Club office (handling charge 4 per cent).

Their insurance policy, Cardcare, ensures that:

● if you charge air tickets to your card you get free personal accident insurance

● if you charge purchases to your card abroad you get free insurance for them on your way home

● if you charge enough of any items to your card you get free overseas travel insurance (covering accident, loss, medical expenses and theft).

Emergency phone number if your card is lost or stolen: 0252–516261.

VISA
(including
Barclaycard
and Trustcard)

Application forms are available from any Allied Irish, Bank of Scotland, Barclays, Cooperative, Trustee Savings Bank or Yorkshire Bank or by post from:

Barclaycard
Freepost
Northampton NN I I YG

The card is issued free and you will be allocated a limit normally in the £200 to £1,000 range (you can ask for this to be changed).

Your statement will be sent monthly and you can pay off completely or make a minimum payment of 5 per cent of the sum involved. If a sum is not settled within twenty-five days of the statement date, interest of 1¾ per cent per month is charged. (This can vary.)

Like Access it costs nothing to 'belong' and if you settle immediately you will not be charged interest. You can use the card at 184,000 places in Britain and nearly 3.5 million world-wide. You can draw any amount of cash (up to your credit allowance) at any of the banks mentioned above (1 to 1.2 per cent interest). With Barclaycard you can get cash from special dispensers. Abroad, you can get up to £100 per day at any bank displaying the Visa sign (1¾ per cent interest).

The main disadvantage is that the limited credit may not cover you in an emergency.

Emergency phone number if your card is lost or stolen: 0604–21288.

Gold Cards
(see above)

Inquire at any bank or travel office in a scheme. You will probably pay a special enrolment fee and an annual amount of about £40.

Monthly statements should be paid in full.

You can use a Gold Card wherever the related 'ordinary card' is acceptable. There is no pre-set limit on credit and you can generally overdraw up to £7,500 without asking. You can draw large amounts of cash from banks, travel offices or hotels in the scheme and you can use some cash dispensers.

Shop cards
(Boots,
Debenhams,
House of Fraser,
and so on)

Many chains and other groups of shops issue these. Apply to any shop in the chain for an application form. There is no charge for the cards but you will probably have a credit limit.

How you pay depends on what type of account you have with the shop:

Budget account – you pay a certain amount each month so that you can buy things up to more than that amount (say, up to thirty times what you have paid). A few accounts pay interest if you are in credit but usually the store concerned is getting your money interest free.

Monthly account – at the end of each month you are sent a bill, which you should settle by the date specified (generally towards the end of the next month).

Option account – each month you pay either the full amount or a proportion of it. Unlike a bank credit card, you might be charged interest from the date of purchase rather than date of statement.

In some cases, you have up to two months' interest-free credit. It is also an advantage to have a shop card when the shop does not take credit or charge cards (e.g. John Lewis, Marks & Spencer).

If your card is lost or stolen telephone the credit department of the shop concerned as soon as possible.

Discount cards

These are not credit cards. Instead of the trader paying a percentage on each transaction to the card company, he lets you have a discount.

Countdown, with over 1.5 million holders, has exclusive discounts of up to 15 per cent off normal prices at over 18,000 places. As well as cash transactions, Countdown can be used for discounts on shopping and by telephone for air fares and holidays annually. Details from:

Countdown
88 Earls Court Road
London W8 6EH
01–938 1041

or Belfast 0232–249777.

Telephone cards

See Chapter 4.

Insurance

For years insurance companies have been trying to persuade women of the need to insure themselves – with, apparently, very little success. Single girls may want to know why, with no dependants, they should fix up life insurance early; the answer is that it is cheaper if you do it early. Married women, particularly those not in paid work, often feel they are not worth insuring. If you are divorced it is important that you insure your ex-husband's life as well as your own if he is helping to maintain the children and you are relying on his income.

Insurance baffles a lot of people and there is a mighty array of insurance products on offer, but the fact remains that if you want basic protection it is necessary to know what some of the terms mean.

TERMINOLOGY

Actuary – the specialist who applies mathematical probabilities to the statistics on which your insurance is based.

Adjuster – an independent professional who negotiates loss settlements for the insurer.

Agent – someone who advises you on a policy; an agent may be employed by one insurer or act independently.

Annuity – a form of assurance that, rather like a pension, guarantees a definite sum of money to be paid at regular intervals to the holder for the rest of her life.

Assurance – arrangement by which something is promised or guaranteed; usually refers to a life insurance, which is the term used here.

Assurer (or assurance company or life office) – organization providing the assurance.

Broker – an intermediary who gives advice on and can arrange insurances and place them with insurance companies or underwriters (a broker must be registered with the Insurance Brokers' Registration Council).

Claim – request by the policy-holder (or her representative) for payment under the policy.

Co-insurance – cover on one risk provided by a number of separate insurers.

Consequential loss (or 'business interruption') – insurance which covers loss of earnings of a business after a fire or other specified damage.

Constructive total loss (or 'write-off') – a damaged vehicle which would cost more to repair than it was worth before the damage occurred.

Cover note – confirmation of cover issued for a limited period pending the issue of a policy and, where applicable, a certificate of insurance.

Deferred annuity – type of annuity which is paid for by the policy-holder over an agreed period of time before the annuity is due to start.

Endorsement – amendment to an insurance policy, thereafter becoming an integral part of it.

Endowment insurance – life insurance policy which provides a sum of money at the end of an agreed period of time or on the prior death of the life insured.

Endowment maturity date – agreed point in time when the sum insured (plus bonuses if the policy is with-profits) will be paid on the survival of the life insured.

Exception – disclaimer (part of a policy disclaiming liability from specified events or perils).

Excess – the first part of a loss, which the insured agrees to pay.

Fidelity guarantee – insurance against loss arising from dishonesty of persons holding positions of trust.

Immediate annuity – a form of life insurance, like a pension, which provides for a sum of money to be paid at regular intervals to the policy-holder (a capital sum is the means of purchase).

Indemnity – principle by which the policy-holder shall be put in the same financial position after a loss as she was in immediately before it.

Insurable interest – you, as policy-holder, have an insurable interest if the insured event would involve you in financial loss.

Insured – person who has an insurance policy (also called policy-holder).

Insurer – an organization which provides insurance.

Knock for knock – agreement in which each insurer pays for what has happened to its policy-holder's car, regardless of who was to blame (providing the policy covers 'own damage').

Level premium – premium paid by a policy-holder for a policy does not ordinarily change other than at the request of the insured. (All types of life policies can be calculated at a level or fixed premium.)

Life fund – pool of money into which all life insurance policy-holders' premiums are paid and from which all benefits are paid back.

Lloyd's – an insurance market. Members of Lloyd's personally add their names to a syndicate which insures risks. Lloyd's policies are issued in the syndicate's name and members pledge their personal wealth to pay losses arising.

Low cost endowment – form of with-profits endowment assurance guaranteeing payment if the assured dies before the policy matures: used to back some mortgages.

Maturity date – agreed date when a policy comes to an end and no further payments are required.

No claim discount – a reduction from a motor renewal premium when there has been no claim during the previous years.

Policy – document which proves written evidence of the contract between the policy-holder and the insurer.

Policy-holder – see Insured.

Premium – amount payable by the policy-holder for the insurance cover given.

Proposer – you, when you wish to take out insurance.

Reinstatement – after a loss, *either* the restoration of the sum insured to the original figure *or* the repair or replacement of the damaged property to a condition the same as but not better than it was originally.

Reinsurance – the system by which an insurer or underwriter shares part of the risk with other insurers.

Renewal – a date for continuation of a policy and on which the payment of a premium is due.

Renewal notice – a statement requesting payment of a premium for a further period, normally a year.

Schedule – the part of a policy form that states details relevant to the individual policy.

Subrogation – after payment of a claim the insurer can take over a policy-holder's legal rights against a third party.

Term insurance – type of insurance policy which provides that an agreed sum be paid in the event of death within a set number of future years (5, 10, 15, etc.).

Underwriter – one who examines the particulars of a risk and decides whether or not to accept it and, if so, the terms of acceptance and the premium to be charged.

Whole life policy – life insurance policy under which the sum insured is payable on death at any time.

Without profits – no profits on policy, just a sum assured at maturity; the premiums are therefore much lower.

With-profits – form of endowment assurance where assurance companies invest premiums and pay out profits on maturity in addition to guaranteed sum.

LIFE INSURANCE (Assurance)

Life insurance, like joint bank accounts, can be an awkward subject for many married couples. Most men think they are going to live for ever but every married woman should find out exactly what she would be left to bring up her family on if he were to have a fatal heart attack or fall under a bus. People often think they are well insured when they are not – and with inflation you should increase the amount regularly anyway.

Life insurance can benefit your family and yourself. With a life insurance policy:

● You agree to pay a fixed premium at regular intervals for an agreed number of years.

● During this time your life is insured and your family is protected to the extent of the sum insured (i.e. the amount to be paid in the event of your death during the term of years of the policy).

● If the policy is an endowment insurance and you live until the maturity date, you will receive the sum insured, and the profits or bonuses if the policy is with-profits.

● If you have an annuity policy instead of receiving a sum insured at the end of the premium paying time, you will receive a pension which can be paid throughout your life.

Basically there are three types of life insurance policy: endowment, term and whole life (see 'Terminology' above). It is vital to decide clearly what you need and then look for policies that fit. Talk to someone who really understands what is best for you.

Help   You can get useful leaflets and a list of members of the Life Offices' Association (LOA) and the Associated Scottish Life Offices (ASLO). Contact:

> LOA/ASLO Information Centre
> Buckingham House (2nd Floor)
> 62–3 Queen Street
> London EC4R IAD
> 01–236 1101

For basic life insurance, contact your bank or make a direct approach to a reputable insurance company or a broker who is a member of the British Insurance Brokers' Association (look in the Yellow Pages).

In the event of any dissatisfaction which has not been resolved by writing to the life insurance company concerned, you can contact:

● If your policy is one where you pay the premium to a collector:

> Industrial Assurance Commissioner
> 17 North Audley Street
> London W1Y 2AP
>   01–629 7001
> or
> Belfast 0232–34121

● If the company is a member of the Life Offices' Association:

Life Offices' Association
Aldermary House
Queen Street
London EC4N ITP
  01–236 1101

Associated Scottish Life Offices
23 St Andrew Square
Edinburgh EH2 IAQ
  031–556 7171

HOUSEWIFE INSURANCE

When a family considers life insurance there is seldom any thought given to what would be the cost, in financial terms, of an accident which disabled the housewife. One estimate recently quoted her value at nearly £300 per week in terms of wages that would have to be paid were she not there ... All companies will insure the *life* of the housewife; not all companies will insure against *disability*.

Some companies have policies that are particularly attractive to women. Others say that all their policies are equally attractive to both sexes.

BUILDINGS INSURANCE

This should cover the structure, main fixtures and fittings and interior decorations against fire, theft, falling aerials or trees, floods or riots. Make sure you are covered for the full up to date cost of rebuilding. It will also cover your liability as house-owner for injury or damage to others on your property. It can also cover accidental damage for an additional premium. Most policies are index-linked so the sum insured goes up as rebuilding costs increase. You should also be covered where relevant for alternative accommodation.

For further explanation of such insurance see 'Buildings Insurance for Home Owners' from the British Insurance Association (address below).

HOME CONTENTS INSURANCE

Exact cover depends on what policy you have, but in general this should cover all interior fittings (including televisions and jewellery – more or less anything you would take with you were you to move) against the same kind of calamities as outlined above. Most policies are index-linked, and accidental damage to contents is included in many policies.

For further explanation of such insurance see 'A Guide to Home Contents Insurance' from the British Insurance Association (address below).

OTHER INSURANCES

- All-round cover. It is obviously easier if you can have one insurance policy that covers everything. Commercial Union's 'Golden Key' policy, to quote one example, covers fire, theft, breakages, accidents and death.
- If you need to insure against rain ruining your village fête, contact your local insurance agent.
- Car insurance is covered in Chapter 3.
- Insurance for travel and holidays is covered in Chapter 17.
- If you are taking your car abroad, again see Chapter 17.

Help

- Some small insurance companies are just as good as the large ones. Here are the headquarters of some nationally known larger companies:

Commercial Union Assurance
Commercial Union House
69 Park Lane
Croydon CR9 1BG
    01–283 7500

Eagle Star Insurance
1 Threadneedle Street
London EC2R 8BE
    01–588 1212

Guardian Royal Exchange
  Assurance Group
16–17 Royal Exchange
London EC3V 3LS
  01–283 7101

Legal and General Assurance Society
11 Queen Victoria Street
London EC4N 4TP
  01–248 9678

Norwich Union Insurance
Surrey Street
Norwich NR1 3NG
  0603–22200

Royal Insurance Group
1 Cornhill
London EC3V 4QR
  01–283 4300

● For *general information* and leaflets contact the British Insurance Association, which represents over 340 insurance companies transacting some 90 per cent of the world-wide business of the British insurance company market. Send s.a.e. to:

British Insurance Association
Aldermary House
Queen Street
London EC4N 1TP
  01–248 4477

● For information on *insurance brokers* contact (s.a.e.):

British Insurance Brokers' Association
130 Fenchurch Street
London EC3M 5DJ
  01–623 9043

● If you have a complaint about *Lloyd's* insurance first contact your broker and then, if still dissatisfied:

Lloyd's Advisory Division
6 London Street
London EC3M 7HA
  01–623 7100

● For main *insurance complaints* – see 'Ombudsman' in Chapter 5.

See 'Some Life Assurance Terms' and 'What is Life Assurance?' – s.a.e. to Life Offices' Association (address above).

Income Tax and Other Personal Taxation

PAYE
CAPITAL GAINS TAX
MARRIAGE AND TAXATION
CHILDREN

WIDOWED, SEPARATED/
DIVORCED AND AGE
ALLOWANCES
SAVINGS
CHARTERED ACCOUNTANTS

An eminent Law Lord, Lord Chorley, once said: 'It is every man's right to so order his affairs as to pay the minimum amount of income tax legally possible.' That goes for women too.

If you have extremely complex tax problems you may need an accountant, but most people find that with time and patience they can understand their own tax situation. It will help if you have at least some of these leaflets (available from your local tax office or PAYE Office):

IR 13 'Wife's Earnings Election'
IR 22 'Personal Allowances'
IR 29 'Income Tax and One-Parent Families'
IR 30 'Income Tax, Separation and Divorce'
IR 31 'Income Tax and Married Couples'
IR 32 'Income Tax – Separate Assessment'

Your liability for income tax is calculated as follows: GROSS INCOME (all your income added up) *minus* OUTGOINGS (allowable deductions such as mortgage or alimony payments) *equals* TOTAL INCOME; *minus* ALLOWANCES (such as those for a single person, a married man or for disablement) *equals* TAXABLE INCOME.

This taxable income is then taxed according to the rates determined each year by the Chancellor of the Exchequer.

It is up to you to claim all possible and legal outgoings and allowances as well as to declare all income.

PAYE
(Pay As
You Earn)

Most employees and some pensioners have income tax deducted before they are paid. You should receive a Notice of Coding whenever your tax circumstances change.

The taxman calculates your code by:
- Adding together your allowances and outgoings.
- Subtracting figures for untaxed interest, taxable fringe benefits such as a company car, and for tax owed from previous years.
- Dividing the result by ten.
- Adding a letter according to your circumstances (L for a single person or wife with earned income allowance, H for a married man or person with allowance for children, etc.).

CAPITAL
GAINS TAX
(CGT)

This is profit resulting from selling an asset which is not part of the trading stock of a business. If a business is run from home the exemption from CGT which private property normally has could be prejudiced if you have been seeking income tax relief on part of the running cost of the home.

MARRIAGE AND TAXATION

For most couples, marriage will result in a small reduction in their combined income tax. This is the effect of the replacement of the *single person's allowance* for the man by the larger *married man's allowance*. A wife has the same allowance as a single person provided she is earning at least that much (after allowable expenses) but it is called the *wife's earned income allowance*.

A married couple will be liable for *more* tax if:
● Both have capital gains, which added together exceed the allowable tax-free amount.
● They are both earning and the total is greater than (approximately – and liable to change) £24,000 after outgoings.

In the second case you can jointly ask to have the wife's earnings taxed separately. The larger the total income and the nearer to equality the earnings are, the greater the saving of separate taxation. 'Wife's earnings election' should not be confused with 'separate assessment' which is merely the apportionment of tax liability between a husband and wife and produces no overall saving.

If in doubt, ask your tax inspector or your accountant or see the leaflet 'Wife's Earnings Election' from your local tax office.

When fixing the date for your wedding, remember that the tax year runs from 6 April to the next 5 April. Unless your wedding takes place on 6 April – the first day of the tax year – you are treated as single for tax purposes for the whole of the tax year in which you marry.

A man receives a proportion of the married man's allowance depending on the fraction of the tax year remaining. If, therefore you will gain – on a tax basis – from being married, it is advantageous to have the wedding on or before 6 April. If, conversely, your tax position will suffer by your being married, leave the wedding until 7 April or after if you can.

CHILDREN

Children have their own single person's allowance, up to which amount they can receive income tax free. This can be from relatives but not parents; it must *not* be merely some part of the parents' income that has been diverted.

If you are looking after children and receiving maintenance payments it is advantageous to have an amount equal to or greater than their single person's allowance paid directly to them.

WIDOWED, SEPARATED/ DIVORCED AND AGE ALLOWANCES

● If you are widowed you will revert to the single person's allowance. A widow receives a *bereavement allowance* in the tax year in which her husband dies. This can be set against income (earned and investment) between the date of his death and the end of the tax year.
● If you are separated or divorced, you revert to the single person's allowance but you may be able to claim an *additional personal allowance* to help with the bringing up of children. If you receive enforced payments

(under a court order or separation deed) from your separated/former husband, he should deduct the tax before making the payments and you will not pay any tax on the amount received. You may, indeed, be able to reclaim tax if your total income is small.

● If you are sixty-four or over before the beginning of the next year there is an additional allowance which should be borne in mind, especially when investing any savings. The higher your total income, the less this *age allowance* becomes, down to the normal personal allowance level. It may be that tax-free investments (e.g. National Savings Certificates) give a better return than building society accounts.

SAVINGS

Building society interest, although paid without any liability to basic rate tax, is not regarded as having suffered taxes by the taxman. If you are below the tax threshold, therefore, you will not be able to claim back tax on building society interest. In these circumstances other types of deposit such as bank extra-interest accounts or the National Savings Bank would probably be more attractive.

Conversely, the higher rate taxpayer should bear in mind that building society interest will be grossed up to determine what extra tax is due. Supposing your husband is a 50 per cent taxpayer and that you keep £1,000 in a building society which pays 7 per cent interest. You would receive £70 interest p.a. but your husband would be assessed as if the interest was the 'grossed up' figure of £100; however, allowance would be made for tax at 30 per cent: he would therefore have to pay the extra 20 per cent, not of the £70 which you received but of £100 which was the gross equivalent. That is, he would have to pay £20 tax.

Help

Members of the Taxpayers' Society obtain free advice on taxation. Details from:

Room 22
Wheatsheaf House
4 Carmelite Street
London EC4Y 0JA
01–583 6020

Remember

1. If you are paying high rates of income tax:
● You can earn up to £70 (liable to change) interest tax free from the National Savings Bank.
● National Savings Certificates (in Northern Ireland, Ulster Savings Certificates) give tax-free interest.
● You can invest for capital gains rather than income; for example, in low-yielding government stocks ('gilts') which are getting close to their redemption date.
2. If you are paying very little or no tax but have some small investments from which the income is taxed at source, be sure to keep the evidence (dividend slips/tax credits). You should be able to claim repayment of tax.
3. A few random points:

● The interest on loans for home improvements of a permanent nature is an allowable outgoing so it is better to borrow for that purpose than for buying a car or diamonds or paying for a holiday.

● If you let a room or a house or flat you can deduct running expenses, including wear and tear, from the rent received.

● If you are self-employed, even part-time, a long list of business expenses may be allowable and can be subtracted from your business takings. Consult the lists published in the excellent *Which? Tax Saving Guide* published each March and in the *Tax Guides* published by Hambro and available in most libraries.

4. Finally, if you think that you have been incorrectly assessed for tax and cannot get satisfaction from your tax inspector, look at Inland Revenue leaflet I R 3 7 for appeals procedures.

The headquarters of the tax structure is:

Inland Revenue
London W C 2 R I L B
01–438 6622

CHARTERED ACCOUN-TANTS

If you do have complicated tax problems you may need a Chartered Accountant. He or she is experienced in all the minutiae of tax laws and can help with all the above problems as well as setting up in business, complying with the law, planning for profit, controlling costs, managing cash, raising finance, managing growth, buying, selling or merging, minimizing business tax, personal tax planning and personal and family finances.

To find a Chartered Accountant, write for a list of firms in your area (you can also write with any complaints) to:

Institute of Chartered Accountants in England and Wales
P O Box 433
Chartered Accountants' Hall
Moorgate Place
London E C 2 P 2 B J
01–628 7060

Institute of Chartered Accountants of Scotland
27 Queen Street
Edinburgh E H 2 I L A
031–225 5673

VAT

Value Added Tax (VAT) is a tax levied on most business transactions in the United Kingdom or the Isle of Man. Many categories of imports are also taxable.

There are various anomalies – children's clothing is not taxed but adults' is.

TERMINOLOGY

Exempt supplies – business transactions not liable to VAT (e.g. insurance, education, services of doctors and dentists, undertakers' charges).

Input tax – what everyone, regardless of whether or not he or she is registered for VAT, has to pay over and above the basic price on many goods and services. The marked price usually includes VAT where applicable.

Output tax – what someone who is registered for VAT charges over and above the basic price.

Taxable supplies – business transactions which are liable to VAT. These are taxed at *positive rate* (of standard 15 per cent) or *zero rate* (e.g. most foodstuffs).

HOW IT WORKS

● The supplier, once registered, adds 15 per cent (output tax) to all goods and services that are standard rated. He or she must keep all invoices of payments made which include (input) tax. At the end of three months output tax is balanced with input tax. If output tax is the greater, the balance is paid to the government (via the VAT-man). If input tax is the greater, the government (via the VAT-man) pays the supplier the difference.

● The average person who is not registered simply has to pay out (input) taxes every time he or she has a meal in a restaurant or buys petrol or a pair of shoes.

WHO REGISTERS AND HOW?

● You must register for VAT if turnover (of your existing business operation or one you have purchased) exceeds £20,000 p.a. or you anticipate turnover during the next year to exceed that amount.

● You may apply for exemption if most or all of your taxable supplies are zero-rated.

● You can apply for registration if your turnover is below £20,000 p.a.

● As a rule of thumb, if you have any choice about registering, it will be to your advantage to register if the goods and services you buy are mostly standard rated and those that you offer your customers are not. The reverse also holds – i.e. if the goods and services you buy are exempt or zero-rated and those that you offer your customers would be standard rated – because the price to your customers would go up (with no benefit to you), if you were to register.

● Many small traders find the operation of VAT records time-consuming and onerous.

If you want further information about registering for VAT ask to see your VAT officer at the local Customs and Excise office or see 'The Ins and Outs of VAT' and 'Should I be Registered for VAT?', from any VAT office or Customs and Excise.

National Insurance

TERMINOLOGY   TYPES OF CONTRIBUTION

TERMINOLOGY

Exception limit – self-employed people earning less than a certain amount are exempt from contributions (see leaflet NI208. 'National Insurance Contribution Rates and Earnings and Exception Limits').

Lower earnings limit – the minimum amount you have to earn to pay national insurance contributions (see leaflet above).

Working life – in national insurance terms, this is taken to mean the number of tax years from the beginning of the tax year in which you reached the age of sixteen up to the end of the one before you reach pension age (normally forty-four years).

TYPES OF
CONTRI-
BUTION

Class 1 – you and your employer must pay this on all your earnings between the lower earnings and upper limit levels. The amount you pay depends on the amount you earn – i.e. it is earnings-related. (See leaflet NI40 'National Insurance Contributions for Employed [Class 1]'.)

Class 2 – you must pay this if you are self-employed unless you are below the exception limit. Contributions are at a flat rate. You are not normally eligible for unemployment benefit. (See leaflet NI41 'National Insurance Guide for the Self-employed'.)

Class 3 – you can pay these, voluntarily and at a flat rate, to help qualify for benefits. (See leaflet NI42 'National Insurance Voluntary Contributions'.)

Class 4 – if you are self-employed and earning over a certain amount you may have to pay these earnings-related contributions as well as Class 2. (See leaflet NP18 'Class 4 National Insurance Contributions'.)

Notes

● If you have *more than one job* you will normally have to pay national insurance contributions in each one in which you earn a certain amount each week. If you pay more than the maximum contributions due in a tax year you will automatically get a refund from the DHSS.

● If you are *self-employed* and paying Class 2 contributions you are eligible for basic sickness, invalidity and widow's benefits and basic retirement and maternity and child's special allowance. You generally are not eligible for unemployment benefit or additional benefits (see leaflet NI41).

● If you are *sick*, entitled to *maternity allowance, invalid care allowance* or *unemployability supplement* or taking an approved course of *training* or if you have just left school and not yet started work, you are credited with contributions instead of having to pay them. (See leaflet NI125 'Training for Further Employment? How to Protect Your Right to National Insurance Benefits'.)

● If you are *staying at home* to look after children or someone sick or old you may be able to protect your rights to basic retirement pension by applying for Home Responsibilities Protection. (See leaflet NP27 'Looking after Someone at Home? [Home Responsibilities Protection]'; this and other leaflets can be obtained from your local DHSS or Job Centre.)

Pensions

STATE RETIREMENT PENSION   PERSONAL OR SELF-EMPLOYED
COMPANY PENSION SCHEMES   PENSION

STATE RETIREMENT PENSION

You normally become entitled to a state pension at the age of sixty (for men, sixty-five). This may be made up of a number of components:

● the flat-rate basic pension
● earnings-related additional pension
● graduated pension
● increased pension earned by postponing retirement or returning to work after retirement
● a small increase for those over eighty
● an increase for a child under sixteen (or nineteen if in full-time education)
● a husband can claim an increase in his pension if his wife is under sixty (and not earning more than the earnings rule limit).

Notes

● The *flat-rate basic* 'old age' pension is paid to you if you have paid or been credited with national insurance contributions for a sufficient number of full years out of your working life. For a full basic pension you should have paid contributions for nine-tenths of your working life. If you paid contributions for a lesser time than that the pension will be reduced in proportion. A married woman may get a basic pension through her own contributions or her husband's, whichever is the more advantageous to her.

● The state *earnings-related* pension is for employees whose employers do not run their own scheme. Employers must put their employees into one or the other. In the state scheme, contributions are made on earnings between the level of the state basic pension and a certain level, currently about seven times the amount of the basic pension. The amount of the earnings-related pension that will result depends on total contributions and is the subject of complicated calculations and regular revaluations to keep pace with average earnings. The eventual effect is likely to yield a total pension of about half the average earnings of a worker in industry for those who have made full contributions.

● The *graduated pension* was an earnings-related scheme operated by the state between April 1961 and April 1975. The benefits accrued by employed people during that period are still payable on retirement but, despite being increased in line with the cost of living in recent years, are so small as to be insignificant, being perhaps £1 per week or less.

● *If you do not retire* at sixty (sixty-five for men) your earnings-related pension will be increased when you eventually do retire. After sixty you do not have to pay contributions, and when you reach sixty-five (seventy for men) you will be paid your pension whether you retire or not.

● Many women who married before 1978 were allowed to opt out of the state earnings-related scheme and pay a lower rate stamp. This proved in many cases a false economy: the scheme is well worth joining and if you 'opted out' you are urged to reconsider the position.

COMPANY PENSION SCHEMES Employers are permitted to *contract out* of the state earnings-related pension scheme only if they establish an approved system which provides benefits at least as good. A typical attractive scheme might provide a pension of one-sixtieth of final pay (i.e. pay just before retirement) for each year of service.

● If you leave an employer after less than five years you may get your contributions back (but not what the company contributed). Depending on the rules of your scheme, if you leave after, say, five years and you are at least twenty-six, you get a *frozen* pension – the amount of pension to which you are entitled if you leave a job before retirement (although not usually available until you retire): the amount you get usually depends on the number of years you were in the job and what your final salary was. (See the Company Pensions Information Centre leaflet 'How Changing Jobs Affects Your Pension', address below.)

● If female employees die, most schemes provide some benefits in certain circumstances for the dependants (say, young children or elderly parents). If you are a widow and your husband had a scheme, in some instances his pension is paid after your death too as long as there are children below a certain age.

● With some schemes you can, at retirement, choose to take *commutation* – a tax-free cash sum in exchange for part of your private-scheme pension (which is taxed as earned income). The limitation on lump sums depends on the type of pension. Companies which offer these special schemes employ investment specialists who can invest the money tax-free so that you get a better return on your money than you would if you invested it yourself.

● In the case of *death before retirement* there are three kinds of benefit which a widow or dependant could receive:

(a) Refund of contributions, sometimes with interest at a modest rate

(b) Many schemes pay out a lump sum, sometimes a flat amount but generally a sum expressed as a multiple of the member's yearly earnings

(c) Some schemes pay a widow's pension, either based on the husband's earnings or on what his pension rate would have been. The maximum pension that can be provided is two-thirds of the husband's expected pension rate.

Notes   ● It is becoming more common for a pension to be paid to a widower when a woman dies and the same conditions apply as set out above. If *you* have a pension scheme and are married and/or have dependants, check what their benefits would be if you died before retirement.

● In the case of *death after retirement*, many schemes guarantee that the pension will continue for a certain number of years (often five) even if the holder dies within that time. The beneficiary may get a lump sum or a continuing pension until the end of that time. Some schemes automatically continue paying pensions to a widow or widower for her/his lifetime at a maximum of two-thirds of the rate the deceased would have received.

● It is generally possible to elect for an option. Someone with a pension of, say, £1,000 a year payable during his lifetime only could exchange this for a pension of, say, £800 payable to him and continuing at the rate of £400 if his wife is still alive when he dies.

PERSONAL OR   If your employer does not already have a scheme and will not co-operate
SELF-   in setting one up, you can think about belonging to a personal or self-
EMPLOYED   employed plan. This is open to anyone who works for herself or who
PENSION   is not a member of a company pension scheme. It is flexible: there is a wide choice of schemes and benefits built up continue to grow if you switch schemes or jobs.

If you are self-employed you will certainly have to meet all the costs of your pension but you can gain tax relief. Any part of your income set aside for your pension is exempt from tax up to a maximum of $17\frac{1}{2}$ per cent of your relevant earnings (more if you were born before 1934). At retirement you can take a tax-free cash sum in exchange for part of your pension.

Help   ● If you and/or your partner are part of any pension schemes, do take the trouble to find out exactly what your benefits will be. Ask your personnel officer or a trade union official (and see the booklet 'How to Understand Your Pension Scheme').

● If you want to understand exactly what pensions are all about see the excellent booklet 'Pensions for Women'.

The above leaflets and much other information are available from the Company Pensions Information Centre. Send a large s.a.e. to:

Company Pensions Information Centre
7 Old Park Lane
London W1Y 3LJ
01-493 4757

Family Income Supplement (FIS)

To be eligible, you must be in full-time work and bringing up children, at least one of whom must be under sixteen (or under nineteen if still at school), and total family income must be under a certain amount.

FIS is paid on top of earnings and it is tax-free. As well as benefit money the family is entitled to free school meals and milk, dental treatment and glasses and prescriptions.

To see if you are eligible for FIS, or to apply for it, go to your Citizens' Advice Bureau, local social security office or see leaflet FIS1 'Help for Families on a Low Wage' from your local post office.

Even if you are not entitled to FIS you may still have a right to some of these benefits if you are on a low wage:

● Free NHS prescriptions (children under sixteen, expectant and nursing mothers, those with some medical conditions, women over sixty). See leaflet P11 from your post office.

● Less rent and rates. See leaflet RR1 and claim forms from your local council.

● Free NHS glasses. See leaflet G11 from the post office or your optician.

● Free milk and vitamins. See leaflet MV11 from your post office or clinic.

● Free NHS dental treatment (generally all those under nineteen, expectant and nursing mothers). See leaflet D11 from your post office or dentist.

● Fares and expenses incurred for medical reasons. See leaflet H11 from the hospital.

There are many other benefits which are not dependent on your national insurance contributions: for a full list of these see leaflet NP41 from your tax or social security office.

DHSS leaflets can be obtained from the Citizens' Advice Bureau or Department of Health and Social Security office or by post from:

DHSS (Leaflets)
PO Box 21
Stanmore HA7 1AY

How to Get Financial Information

STOCK
EXCHANGE
INDEX
The *Financial Times* Index and business news (FT Cityline) provides information on the latest state of the London Stock Exchange Index and commodity markets with a summary of current business news.

You can get the latest Index information from any of the following British Telecom numbers:

01–246 8026
021–246 8026
051–246 8026
061–246 8026
0532–8026

TALKS AND
COURSES
Barclays Bank and Lloyds Bank will both send someone to talk to a group about how to manage money in general and your bank account in particular. Talks are free of charge and expenses are met by the bank concerned. Write to the public relations department at the head office of the bank concerned (for addresses see page 25).

One way to find your way around the maze of finance is to join a 'cash course'. One such, covering every aspect of money management for women, explores and explains the tax system, investment and saving schemes, bank services, foreign investments and property and how to find your way around the Stock Exchange, Lloyd's of London, the London Commodities Exchange, the Metal Exchange, the London International Financial Futures Exchange (LIFFE) and the Bank of England.

CASH (Capital and Savings Handling), runs a beginners' course once a week for six weeks. It is held either at the Stock Exchange itself or nearby. One-day courses are also offered on such topics as 'Taxation' and 'Planning to Start Your Own Business'. Brochure and full details of all courses from:

The Lady Wardington
The CASH Course
29 Moore St
London SW3 2QW
01–584 5245

PERSONAL
ADVICE
The Dorothy Genn Women's Financial Service is an independent comprehensive advisory service in direct association with financial institutions prepared to offer special facilities to women. The service offers advice on investment, insurance, pensions, taxation and mortgages, and on a number of allied subjects, provided by women lawyers, accountants, etc.

There is also a complete financial package specifically for women which includes a pension plan linked directly to a major building society pension fund.

Details of the service, and costs, from:

Dorothy Genn Women's
  Financial Service
Freepost
London N 2 2 4 BR
  01–889 9451

Other addresses Bank of England
London EC 2 R 8 AH
  01–601 4444
H M Treasury
London SW 1 P 3 AG
  01–233 3415

Royal Mint
London SW 1 W OEH
  01–828 8724

SUGGESTED *Money Which?*
  FURTHER 'Express Money' in the *Daily Express*
  READING 'Money Mail' in the *Daily Mail*
'Family Money-Go-Round' in the *Daily Telegraph*
Duncan, John, *How to Manage your Bank Manager*, David & Charles
Faulds-Wood, Lynn, *Cosmopolitan's Money Guide* Cosmopolitan
Fingleton Eamonn, and Tom Tickell, *The Penguin Money Book*, Penguin
McDonnell, Liz, *Money Matters for Women*, Collins
Tingley, Kenneth R., *Daily Mail Income Tax Guide*, Associated Newspapers
The Which? Book of Saving and Investing, Consumers' Association

Help ● If you want advice on housing or social security benefits, and you
live anywhere in the British Isles, write to (or telephone, 2.00–5.30 p.m.):

Citizens' Rights Office
1 Macklin Street
Drury Lane
London WC 2 B 5 NH
  01–405 5942

2 Your Property

If you are thinking of moving, you should take a deep breath now and realize that you are about to undergo what could be a nightmare. Moving is not fun. Anticipate the worst – and you might afterwards look back with relief that it was not as bad as you expected.

The more you know about all the details involved with your property the less devastating the whole process will be. Here are those details – with lots of ideas about people and organizations who might help.

Terminology

Before you think of moving, learn the language.

Completion day – the actual day (generally at a set hour) on which the keys are handed over and the property changes hands.

Completion statement – account of amount payable on completion (purchase price less deposit, plus/minus proportion of rates, ground rent, etc.).

Contract – agreement between buyer and seller binding both to completion. If you withdraw you are liable to a severe penalty.

Conveyance – the document which makes the buyer the owner of a house with unregistered title.

Deposit – the purchaser pays (to the vendor's solicitor) 10 per cent of the purchase price when contracts are exchanged.

Fixtures and fittings – the normal rule is that permanent fixtures (e.g. bathtub) and anything planted in the garden 'goes with the property' whereas anything that could easily be removed belongs to the seller and, if staying in the property, should be paid for.

Freehold – property where the owner has no obligation to pay any rent or charge to any landlord. There is no freehold in Scotland.

Gazumping – when a seller of property raises the agreed price (this is morally wrong but not illegal). Because there is no 'subject to contract' in Scotland, gazumping is unknown there.

Ground rent – annual rent for a long lease.

Leasehold – a landlord allows the use of land or property for a specified time, from a few weeks to thousands of years. If a tenant breaks the terms of the lease – which may include an obligation to undertake repairs – the landlord can sue or seek a court injunction to prevent subsequent infringement of the lease's condition. A lease does not automatically end at its timing: either party has to give notice of its intention to terminate it.

Leasehold exists only rarely in Scotland. The normal tenure is *feudal*, which means that the house-owner is the owner and that he cannot be put out at the end of a specified number of years. Ownership of the property is, however, subject to conditions laid down in the original Feu Charter and they can vary from one title to another. In practice, this sometimes means that, when planning house alterations, consent is needed not only from the local authority but also from the feudal superior. Anyone buying a house today does not have to pay the feu duty that was required until 1974 unless that old duty was 'unallocated', i.e. split between several houses by private arrangement between the owners without reference to the superior – this is something to look out for if you are buying a flat in a tenement.

Mortgage – sum of money lent over the long term for the purposes of property purchase.

Searches – inquiry forms sent to the local council, to the Land Registry and to the Land Charges Registry to check there are no possible obstacles to the purchase.

Title deeds – documents showing ownership.

Choices

LOCATION
ADDITIONAL EXPENSES

BUILD, BUY OR RENT?

LOCATION

Few people really have a tremendous amount of choice about where they are going to live. There are, admittedly, those with stars in their eyes who simply drive around the countryside admiring local views until they find somewhere that really suits them. There are some retired people who do not have any ties, and expatriates and others wanting second homes may find themselves without any geographical obligations.

Most people, however, are restricted by jobs, schooling and family ties. As far as jobs are concerned, unless a commuter really likes spending half the day getting to and from the factory or office, a radius of some fifty miles from the work-place is considered a maximum.

Look at a current map showing motorways, other roads and rail networks around the work-place. You need to be able to travel to and from work as quickly and easily as possible, and if you are going to commute during rush hours try 'test-runs' to the work-place at busy times from various likely locations.

Some people say it is a good idea to live to the east of your work-place. This way, if you are driving, you have the early morning sun behind you on your way in and the late afternoon rays behind you as you drive home.

Education is a major factor in choosing a home. If you opt for state schooling for your child this is a particularly important point to bear in mind (see Chapter 10).

Family ties work both ways. There are people who want to live as far away as possible from Aunt Mabel and there are others, conversely, who could not possibly be more than a hundred yards from mum.

ADDITIONAL EXPENSES

The purchase of a home is probably the largest investment you will make in your lifetime. Therefore, whether you are a first-time buyer or you have a property to sell – or you are merely exchanging one home for another – it is wise to remember that there are a number of expenses involved.

As well as the cost of the property itself, there are possible commissions to estate agents, advertising and surveyor's fees, solicitor's fees, stamp duty (a tax payable to the Inland Revenue on properties costing more than £25,000), recording dues, removal charges, possible readjustment of insurance, connection of utilities and so on.

All this is before you even set foot in your new home and begin thinking about gutting the kitchen. Even though you may have calculated all these sums in advance, you would be wise to add several hundred pounds to your budget as a precaution against 'hidden extras'.

BUILD, BUY OR RENT?

In England and Wales most people buy their homes, whereas in Scotland – according to a Scottish Office survey in 1981 – 54 per cent of householders rent from a public landlord and 36 per cent are owner-occupiers.

The reasons why many people like to buy rather than build include:

● There is a wide selection of existing property from which to choose.
● Planning laws do not encourage new building.
● From a time point of view, you will probably be able to move more quickly.
● Building a new house generally costs more (say, 20 per cent more) than buying an equivalent existing house.

Building a House

BUYING LAND
PLANNING PERMISSION
ARCHITECTS

BUILDERS
EXTENSIONS AND
IMPROVEMENTS

Before you start talking to architects and builders it is a good idea to get information on new house construction from (s.a.e.):

House Building Advisory Bureau
353 Strand
London WC2R 0HU
01–836 5263

National House Building Council
58 Portland Place
London W1N 4BU
01–637 1248

BUYING LAND Land for sale is advertised in the same way as property (see below). Some terms you might come across include: *registered land* – title is registered at HM Land Registry; *restrictive covenants* – restrictions applying to the use of land.

PLANNING PERMISSION This has to be obtained from the local council. Your solicitor or architect can help you with this – or you can deal with them directly.

ARCHITECTS You might prefer to buy ready-made architectural plans from which your builder can work direct. This saves the 10 per cent of the total cost price of the house which an architect can command.

If you need an architect and you do not already have one personal recommendation is often a good way to find one. Or you can contact the Clients' Advisory Service of the Royal Institute of British Architects. If possible, go to one of their offices (look in Yellow Pages) to see photographs of architects' work. Check that the architect you want to use is registered with the Architects' Registration Council, and try to visit examples of his or her past work. Can he or she produce references from past clients?

You should ask your architect to estimate costs and you should formalize the agreement in writing. Various ready-made contract forms are available that safeguard the consumer's interests – see the Joint Contract Tribunal's Minor Works Form, 1980 edition.

Your architect will:
● Draw up plans for your approval.
● Get them passed by the local planning committee.
● Get quotations from building contractors.
● Once you (as employer) and the chosen contractor have exchanged contracts, the architect will oversee the building.

Useful addresses

Architects' Registration Council
   of the United Kingdom
73 Hallam Street
London WIN 6EE
   01–580 5861

Royal Institute of British Architects
66 Portland Place
London WIN 4AD
   01–580 5533

Royal Incorporation of Architects
   in Scotland
15 Rutland Square
Edinburgh EH1 2BE
   031–229 7205

Royal Society of Ulster Architects
51 Malone Road
Belfast BT9 6RY
   0232–668846

Society of Architects in Wales
75a Llandennis Road
Rhydypennau
Cardiff CF2 6EE
   0222–762215

See 'Extending, Altering, Improving Your Home: Use an Architect', 'Some Advice on Getting it Built: Your Own Building' and 'Thinking of Building?', all from the Royal Institute of British Architects (s.a.e.).

BUILDERS Choose your building contractor with care and remember that the architect has no authority to guarantee what the builder will do.

Before you look for a builder, ask yourself:

- What do I want?
- How quickly do I want it done?
- How much do I want to pay?
- Will the work require an architect?

To find a builder, ask for personal recommendations or contact the Federation of Master Builders (address below). Check that any builder whom you are thinking of employing is a member of the federation. Check that he is insured. Can he produce references from past clients, architects and surveyors? Try and visit examples of his past workmanship.

Ask for an estimate of costs and, when you are satisfied, you should formalize the agreement in writing.

A builder's guarantee to protect customers from shoddy work by cut-price 'cowboys' has been approved by the Restrictive Practices Court. For a charge of 1 per cent of a contract's value, the Building Employers' Confederation will guarantee that unsatisfactory work costing between £500 and £25,000 will be completed or remedied.

If you need any information on building-related topics or if you need addresses of builders, contact:

Federation of Master Builders
33 John Street
London WCIN 2BB
   01–242 7583

Scottish Building Employers' Federation
13 Woodside Crescent
Glasgow G3 7UP
   041–332 7144

EXTENSIONS
AND
IMPROVE-
MENTS

Some of the most popular alterations to houses include the following (note that the outlay does not necessarily add much to the resale value of the total property):

- bathroom expansion
- double-glazing – heat savings are limited and it will be years before you recoup your outlay, but noise is substantially cut down
- extra rooms – separate rooms or buildings are not as attractive to potential purchasers as additional space incorporated into or attached to the main house
- garage(s) – while one garage does add to the value of the total property two or more garages do not
- garden improvement – the upkeep of your garden is very important. It can make or mar the sale of your house.
- kitchen expansion (see below)
- loft conversion
- nuclear shelter
- solar heating – depends on where you live and what the summer is like
- swimming pool – maintenance costs are high
- thermal insulation – may lower your fuel bill
- window replacements

For information on all house extensions contact:

National Home Enlargement Bureau
PO Box 67
High Wycombe
Bucks HP15 6XP
0494–711649

Kitchen extensions and rebuilding

A fitted kitchen, be it in a specially constructed extension or put into an existing room, is a major purchase which can amount to several thousand pounds. As a guide, you should invest about 10 per cent of the resale value of your home. If you spend less than 10 per cent you could be wasting money as the result may be dismissed by the intending purchaser as of little or no value.

Regardless of whether or not you later take responsibility for the theme of the kitchen (see Chapter 15) it is well worth while asking a reputable firm to do your kitchen. This is especially important if you have a small kitchen as space is all the more valuable. Check that the firm is a member of the Kitchen Specialist Association:

31 Bois Lane
Amersham
Bucks HP6 6BU
02403–22287

Your chosen firm will employ their own qualified joiners, plumbers and electricians: avoid any firm that simply offers 'Jacks-of-all-trades'.

The company should come and survey and quote (find out beforehand if there is a charge for this service). If you accept their terms, their designer should come and plan your ideal kitchen with you. He will be experienced in planning a kitchen that does not leave anything out, accommodates windows and doors, and has units that all fit *exactly* (if you buy individual items yourself, you are likely – despite quoted measurements – to end up with pieces that do not fit into the available space). He will also take your own wishes into account.

● Give consideration to the *flow* of kitchen preparation (usually, food storage to preparation area to sink to cooking area to eating area).

● Make sure all your existing appliances fit and take into account whether vertically hinged doors open to left or right.

● You will eventually need many more cupboards and electric points than you now anticipate, so incorporate them from the start.

After you accept the designer's plan, a made-to-measure kitchen takes about six weeks to manufacture. Actual installation (into an existing room) could take a minimum of two days.

For details of special shops that provide complete kitchen equipment and services, look up Yellow Pages under 'Kitchen Specialists' or go to your local department store.

Buying and Selling a House

ESTATE AGENTS
SOLICITORS
CONVEYANCING
SCOTLAND

SURVEYORS
FURTHER CHECKING
MOVING

The usual order of buying a house involves:
● Seeing an estate agent.
● Thinking about payment.
● Talking to your solicitor.
● Instructing a surveyor.
● Building estimates if necessary.
● Contract and completion.
● Moving.

ESTATE AGENTS

Estate agents do not have to be professionally qualified, although many are.

An agent advertises property publicly, within his own office or through a private list. He must give you certain information, including details of his charges, before you engage his services and he must declare any personal interest he has in the transaction, be it buying or selling a property. In the case of a sale, he should advise on the best method of sale, the right asking price and the best time to sell. (However, he is not legally required to visit any property concerned.) A property can be placed with more than one estate agent.

Sole agency means the job of selling the property is given to one agent only. If another agent sells the property, the vendor has also to pay commission to the 'sole agent'. Giving sole agency rights encourages but does not force the agent to give better service.

Sole selling rights mean that only that agent can sell the property. If the vendor sells privately he still has to pay commission to the agent. It is a good idea to consult your solicitor before giving an agent sole rights or sole selling rights – and to impose a time limit on the exclusivity.

The estate agent's sole responsibility is to the vendor not the purchaser. He is paid usually on completion of the sale. The vendor's solicitor hands over a percentage of the final sale price – the percentage was agreed when the vendor first contacted the agent. The sum includes all the agent's expenses. No sale usually means no money coming to the agent.

Because the agent is employed by the vendor he is not legally bound to point out a property's defects to potential purchasers although he must not make false statements. When a suitable property is found, the agent may ask the prospective buyer for an immediate 'goodwill' deposit although the buyer is not legally bound to pay this. If he does, and decides subsequently not to buy, his money must be returned unless he has signed a binding contract.

If you have any cause for complaint, contact the Trading Standards Officer at your local council (in Northern Ireland, at the Department of Economic Development). Under the Estate Agents Act 1979 the Director-General of Fair Trading can:

● Ban someone from engaging in estate agency work if he thinks that the agent is unfit to undertake such work.

● Warn the agent that if he continues to operate in certain undesirable ways he will be considered unfit and therefore banned.

To find an estate agent, or if you have any complaint, contact:

> National Association of Estate Agents
> Arbon House
> 21 Jury Street
> Warwick CV34 4EH
> 0926–496800

SOLICITORS If you need a solicitor ask a friend or some other professional person for recommendations – or look in the Solicitors' Diary in the library or the Legal Aid Solicitors List at the Citizens' Advice Bureau (the CAB may have its own solicitor whom you can consult free of charge). Alternatively, you can contact the headquarters of the Law Society (address below).

Your solicitor will be acting for you alone when advising you. In the case of property, your solicitor will:

● explain about planning permissions and by-laws;

- for leasehold properties, advise on clauses in the lease that might affect the new owner;
- send out searches;
- check on tenancy agreements;
- tell you how much you can borrow, from whom and how it is best done;
- explain which fixtures and fittings are included in the purchase price;
- hurry builders along if necessary;
- advise partners on the possible benefits of co-ownership (in the case of a death, the surviving partner still owns the property);
- cope with tax problems;
- advise about paying the right proportion of general rates and payment for coal in shed or oil in tanks;
- deal with all conveyancing, preparation and exchange of contracts and supervision of completion;
- give advice on moving in;
- offer help after the purchase (e.g. obtaining the legal receipt for the repayment of the seller's mortgage).

If you need help finding a solicitor, or if you have any problems, contact:

Law Society
113 Chancery Lane
London WC2A 1PL
01–242 1222

Law Society of Scotland
PO Box 75
26 Drumsheugh Gardens
Edinburgh EH3 7YR
031–226 7411

See 'Buying a House? See a Solicitor', Law Society.

CONVEY-
ANCING

Conveyancing is defined at the beginning of this chapter. In England and Wales, contracts are exchanged when the various searches and inquiries have been completed and purchase of the property usually becomes irrevocable at this point. A deposit, normally equal to 10 per cent of the purchase price, has to be paid to the vendor's solicitor. The house finally changes ownership some time – usually one month – after exchange of contracts.

If you want to avoid employing a solicitor and to do the work yourself you will save the solicitor's fees but you need to have a lot of time and patience and determination.

Before you decide to do any conveyancing yourself, you should carefully study: 'Buying or Selling Your Home: Questions and Answers about Conveyancing', from the Law Society and the books listed at the end of this chapter.

SCOTLAND   In Scotland, the sale or purchase of property is traditionally handled by solicitors from start to finish.

The main urban areas in Scotland have Solicitors' Property Centres where prospective purchasers can see listings of properties for sale in the area. Operated by member-solicitors, some of these centres may also handle viewing arrangements or show property. In the main, however, they act as information centres, sometimes with printed lists of available property.

Some of the largest centres are:

> Aberdeen Solicitors' Property Centre
> 40 Chapel Street
> Aberdeen AB1 1SP
>   (no telephone)

> Edinburgh Solicitors' Property Centre
> 81 George Street
> Edinburgh EH2 2JG
>   031–226 3891

> Solicitors' Estate Agency (Glasgow)
> 251 Kilmarnock Road
> Shawlands
> Glasgow G41 3JF
>   041–649 8899

An offer and acceptance constitute a binding contract in Scotland, whereas in England the agreement reached between selling agent and purchaser is 'subject to contract', which gives the purchaser time to seek legal advice.

Although some Scottish properties are offered for sale at a 'fixed price', the usual practice is for the seller to ask for 'offers over' a quoted sum. This results in the *blind-bidding system* whereby prospective purchasers submit bids for the property through their individual solicitors by a specified closing date. The system, while usually advantageous to sellers, puts a certain strain on purchasers who are never quite certain how much money to offer. They must, however, know when making the offer that they have the finance to meet the terms of that offer.

There is often little time lapse – sometimes a matter of hours – between the point when the purchaser makes the offer and the bargain is concluded: the practice of gazumping is therefore unknown in Scotland and deposits against purchase are uncommon.

Precise details of buying and selling a house in Scotland, including a scale of solicitors' fees for conveyancing and a list of all Solicitors' Property Centres, are available in 'Buying or Selling a House' from the Law Society of Scotland (address above). They also publish an annual *Directory of General Services Provided by Solicitors*, available in public libraries and Citizens' Advice Bureaux.

SURVEYORS   The surveyor specializes in all those professional matters concerning land, property and buildings which are not normally carried out by the architect and the solicitor.

The types of surveyor with whom you may come into contact include:

Chartered building surveyor who advises on alterations, building defects, extensions, renovations, improvement grants, maintenance, fire insurance and structural surveys on buildings.

Chartered surveyor who acts as agent or valuer for anyone buying, selling or letting a home.

Chartered surveyor estate agent who is often also a valuer (see below). He manages and surveys property, deals with planning applications and appeals and negotiates in property developments.

Valuation surveyor who values all types of land or property prior to purchase, sale or letting, and for investment, mortgage, rating, insurance, compensation or tax purposes.

You may be able to find a surveyor by personal recommendation or you can contact the information centre of the Royal Institute of Chartered Surveyors. Check that your surveyor has the initials FRICS or ARICS after his name: all chartered surveyors have to adhere to the code of conduct of the Royal Institute of Chartered Surveyors and carry full indemnity insurance. There is no set scale of fees: all fees are negotiable and must be confirmed in writing before any transaction.

Remember, when arranging for a survey in connection with a loan, that some building societies consider the surveyor's report confidential to the society. They will not tell you specific details of the survey and it is therefore often necessary to get a separate report for your own use. Since this could cost you two surveying fees, it is advisable to query both surveyor and building society in advance. If your building society does not offer you a copy of their report then try to make arrangements for a separate report from the same surveyor.

For information, contact (s.a.e.):

> Incorporated Society of Valuers and Auctioneers
> 3 Cadogan Gate
> London SWIX OAS
>   01–235 2282
>
> Royal Institute of Chartered Surveyors
> 12 Great George Street
> London SWIP 3AD
>   01–222 7000
> or
> 7 Manor Place
> Edinburgh EH3 7DN
>   031–225 7078

See   'Buying a Flat?', 'Buying a House?', 'Buying and Selling a House and How to Go about It', 'Structural Surveys of Residential Property' and 'What is a

Chartered Surveyor?', from the Royal Institute of Chartered Surveyors. 'Surveying Services: a Guide', Incorporated Society of Valuers and Auctioneers.

FURTHER CHECKING

Timber treatment and damp control

If the surveyor reports woodworm or other infestations, rot or damp, first try to discover whether the property is the subject of any guarantee in respect of previous treatment for such a problem. If it is not, go to reputable timber treatment and damp control specialists and consultants.

Things they will be looking out for include:

Rising damp. Found especially in houses built before 1900 – caused by moisture rising from the ground through capillaries in masonry and mortar and creating unhealthy living conditions and weakening wall structures; leads to timber decay.

Penetrating damp. Usually caused by faulty guttering and vertical pipes, broken roof tiles, unsatisfactory pointing or porous masonry allowing rain to infiltrate the structure of a property.

Condensation. Often mistaken for other forms of damp, this occurs when moisture-laden warm air meets a cold surface and releases moisture.

Woodworm. Wood-boring beetles attack timber in property. The most usual species found in Britain is the common furniture beetle (*Anobium punctatum*).

Dry rot (*Serpula/Merulius lacrymans*). Originating in wet or damp timber, this form of wood-destroying fungus can spread at an alarming rate to other timbers not necessarily affected by damp.

Wet rot. Timber decay by wood-destroying fungi, the most common of which is cellar fungus (*Coniophora cerebella*).

To get names of firms who can help you, see 'Firms Specializing in the Remedial and Curative Treatment of Timber in Situ' from the British Wood Preserving Association. (Addresses of these firms can be obtained from Yellow Pages.) For further information, or if you have any cause for complaint, contact (s.a.e.):

British Wood Preserving Association
150 Southampton Row
London WC1B 5AL
01–837 8217

Other checks

As well as professional checks, you might like to check the following:
1. Aspect
● in which direction does the house face?
● is the house surrounded by trees that might afford privacy in summer and none in winter?
● are there hills around which would obscure winter sun?
● is the house near a church (with clock or bells), pig farm, pub or school?
2. Damp

- is there a damp course?
- are floors, skirting boards, pointing, window surrounds, loft, etc., free from damp? (Apart from isolated patches in otherwise damp-free houses anything should be taken seriously.)

3. Electricity
- are there enough sockets?
- does the wiring seem suspect? (If so, contact the local electricity board.)

4. Heating
- ask to see it working.

5. Gas
- to which rooms, if any, is it supplied?
- does the system seem to be in good order?

6. Occupation
- has the house been standing empty for any length of time? If so, why?

MOVING

Before

As soon as you know when and where you are moving:
- Contact a removal firm (see below). Make sure the firm you choose knows exactly what is going to be moved where and when. Tell them if there are parking problems either end.
- Talk to your children's present head-teacher and ask advice about schooling.
- Have change of address cards printed and send them to anyone who might need them (e.g. credit card firms, your bank, anyone else who might send a bill to you after you move).
- Compile a comprehensive list of useful telephone numbers (e.g. milkman, plumber) for the new occupants.
- Think about whether you will need post forwarded after your move. The Post Office will do this for a nominal fee (see form P944G from your local post office).
- Check all goods to be moved are on your insurance and ask what the remover's liability is (he may not be able to take responsibility for the condition of items that you have packed for yourself).
- Shortly beforehand settle all milk, newspaper and other bills, and contact all services (e.g. gas board).

Removal firms

Removal firms are experienced in skilfully packing awkward objects. The average contents of a family home weigh around two tons and you might be surprised how many of your 'friends' are suddenly busy if you do decide to dispense with a removal firm, hire a van and do the job yourself.

You might decide to pack china and glass yourself. The removal firm will give you boxes beforehand.

If you want a list of removal firms in your area, send s.a.e.:

British Association of Removers
279 Gray's Inn Road
London WC1X 8SY
01–837 3088

On the day
- Catch the cat.
- Make sure everything is put away.
- Leave out a basket containing electric kettle, coffee or tea-bags, mugs, spoons, sugar, milk and biscuits (for you and removal men). Have plenty of sandwiches made.
- Clearly label anything you do not want moved (furniture you are leaving behind) or throw it away.
- When the removal men arrive, leave them to it. Do not try to interfere.
- At some point the electricity and gas services will arrive to read the meters.
- Probably at a set time the new occupants or their solicitor will arrive for the key. *Do not hand the key over until you have checked with your solicitor that their money has been cleared.*
- After the removal men have finished, check around the property and if necessary/possible clean up. You should leave the property after the removal men.
- You should arrive at the new property before the removal men (they will be driving a slower vehicle).
- Clearly label each room (e.g. 'Bedroom 1' on that door).
- When the van arrives, you should direct each item being carried into the house into a specific room.
- Do *not* attempt to unpack boxes until the removal men have left (you will be left the boxes for a few days).
- It is customary to tip the removal men (about £10 a head).
- Check that all services read their meters – otherwise you might be liable for the previous occupants' bills.
- Check that the previous occupants have left everything they promised.

After
- Arrange for milk, newspapers, etc., to be delivered.
- Telephone the local district council about refuse collection: if you live in a rural area with a fortnightly collection they might be able to arrange for a special pick-up of your moving debris.
- Introduce children to their new school.
- Check on the security of your new house and have the locks changed (see 'Protect your house', page 560).
- If you have moved to a completely new district, make arrangements to get on a doctor's list as soon as possible.
- Get on the lists of dentist, chiropodist and any other necessary professionals.
- Go to your local gas and electricity showroom to 'sign on' as the new subscriber of your property. Do likewise with British Telecom.

See
'Your Key to a Successful Removal' and 'Your Keys to Moving Abroad', from the British Association of Removers, and look at such magazines as *Exchange Contracts: the Magazine for Home-buyers* (for details of subscription rates, telephone 01–631 4092).

Paying for Your House

No one today is going to hand over suitcases of 'real money' for a house. The chances are that you will need a mortgage, usually undertaken by a building society. If you buy a house or flat before selling your previous home you may need an expensive bridging loan from the bank.

MORTGAGES

So that you know what building societies are talking about, here are the major types of mortgage:

Repayment mortgage – you pay interest on the long-term loan and pay the capital back in stages. With some mortgages the payments vary, with others they are constant for a year at a time; this is the most usual type of mortgage.

Endowment mortgage – another way of borrowing money for this purpose is through a loan linked to an insurance policy. You pay interest on the loan for the whole of the mortgage term: you also pay into an endowment policy. At the end of the pre-determined length of time this has grown large enough to pay all the capital of your loan in one go and leave you a tax-free cash sum. Such a mortgage costs more, and suits only the high-rate taxpayer.

Pension mortgage – linked to a pension plan. Such a mortgage would normally suit only the high salary earner or prosperous self-employed person.

If you have a mortgage do make sure you take out a mortgage protection policy or similar kind of insurance so that if the main earning partner should die, the mortgage can be paid off.

It is important to emphasize most strongly that there is no hard and fast rule, no best buy in mortgages. If you need advice you can talk to your bank manager, mortgage broker or a building society.

Mortgage brokers

The world of finance has become so complex and bewildering that prospective borrowers are finding that it can pay them to consult reliable 'middlemen' who know exactly what is going on.

A mortgage broker can:

- Advise a client on the best possible mortgage she can get.
- Find that mortgage for her.
- Assist with form-filling and liaison between the client and estate agents, solicitors and so on.

For details of mortgage brokers near you, contact the Corporation of Insurance and Financial Advisers (CIFA, formerly the Corporation of Mortgage Brokers):

6–7 Leapale Road
Guildford
Surrey GU1 4JX
0483–39121

The corporation will be happy to send a mortgage broker to speak to a group of not less than fifteen people.

BUILDING
SOCIETIES

If you need money for your house – if you need a mortgage – you will almost certainly, unless you are working with a mortgage broker, need a building society. (Banks also offer some mortgages.)

Building societies are distinct legal entities constituted under special Acts of Parliament. They are able to lend a large proportion of the purchase price of the property over a long period of time (typically twenty-five years).

Although building societies are sometimes prepared to lend the total value of the property, most borrowers would be expected to put some of their own savings into the purchase. You can generally borrow two and a half times your gross annual income. If it is to be a joint loan, the multiple might be two and a half times the higher gross annual income plus the other income. The difference between this figure and the purchase price of the property is met by the house-buyer.

When working out how much money you will need, remember to allow for solicitor's and other fees involved in house purchase.

Having agreed in principle to make a loan, the building society will, once advised of the property you are wishing to purchase, arrange for a valuation of that property.

Unless the valuation report is unfavourable, the society will then make an offer of an advance based on the valuation of the property or purchase price – whichever is lower. In the normal course of events the society will offer the amount initially indicated to the applicant, assuming of course that his or her income can support it and that the loan required is below the valuation.

Some common
questions

How long does all this take?
In England and Wales there are various legal procedures that have to be undertaken before a prospective buyer can exchange contracts on the property and these can take varying amounts of time. The purchaser's solicitor, for example, will inquire as to any local development which might affect the purchase of the property: searches may take quite a long time. In Scotland, however, where the whole system of sale and purchase is quicker, many building societies will take a verbal order for a property valuation either from the prospective purchaser or her solicitor and, if required, report back within twenty-four hours. Any prospective buyer requiring this kind of service, however, would be well advised to establish the size of loan in advance.

Does the fact that you are not married to your partner or that you are a
single woman make any difference?
It should make no difference whatsoever – as long as you are at least eighteen, the minimum age at which a mortgage loan can be given.

What happens if you cannot pay your mortgage because of illness or
redundancy?
Building societies will make loans only to people who they believe are able to keep up the necessary repayments. But circumstances do change and inevitably some people face financial difficulties. Societies are sym-

pathetic to borrowers whose circumstances have changed, but it is vitally important that home-buyers contact their building society as soon as they believe they are going to experience difficulty. The worst thing to do is to let arrears mount up without explanation because then the building society may not offer any help at all.

In the event of a temporary shortfall of income the society may well be able to put the mortgage on to an interest-only basis for a short time – although if the mortgage is a relatively new one this is not likely to have any significant effect on the repayment.

Supplementary benefit, which can, among other things, cover the interest on the mortgage, may well be available to a home-buyer who is not in employment so, in such circumstances, borrowers should contact their nearest office of the DHSS.

How do you know which building society to choose?
● Check that a building society has been designated by the government as having *trustee status*.
● Check also that the building society is a member of the Building Societies Association which has strict conditions for membership.
● Now that self-imposed restraints on competition have been removed, it is a good idea to 'look around' several societies to see which offers you the best deal.
● For a complete list of building societies see the Building Societies Association's 'Directory of Members' (s.a.e.):

> Building Societies Association
> 3 Savile Row
> London WIX IAF
> 01–437 0655

There are many building societies and the financial press frequently list them, quoting their interest rates. Here are the addresses of the national headquarters of some of the larger societies:

Abbey National Building Society
27 Baker Street
London WIM 2AA
  01–486 5544

Alliance Building Society
Alliance House
Hove Park
Hove
East Sussex BN3 7AZ
  0273–775454

Anglia Building Society
Moulton Park
Northampton NN3 INL
  0604–495353

Bradford & Bingley Building Society
PO Box 2
Bingley
West Yorks BD16 2LW
  0274–568111

Britannia Building Society
PO Box 20
Newton House
Leek
Staffs ST13 5RG
  0538–385131

Cheltenham & Gloucester Building
  Society
Cheltenham House
Clarence Street
Cheltenham
Glos GL50 3JR
  0242–36161

Dunfermline Building Society
12 East Port
Dunfermline
Fife KY12 7LD
  0383–721621

Halifax Building Society
PO Box 60
Trinity Road
Halifax
West Yorks HX1 2RG
  0422–65777

Leeds Permanent Building Society
Permanent House
The Headrow
Leeds LS1 1NS
  0532–438181

Leicester Building Society
Oadby
Leicester LE2 4PF
  0533–717272

National & Provincial Building
  Society
Provincial House
Bradford BD1 1NL
  0274–733444

Nationwide Building Society
New Oxford House
High Holborn
London WC1V 6PW
  01–242 8822

Woolwich Equitable Building
  Society
Equitable House
London SE18 6AB
  01–854 2400

See also 'Building societies', pages 16–17.

Suggested
further reading

'Building Societies and House Purchase', from the Building Societies Association.

Other Purchases

BUYING A HOUSE 'PACKAGE'   BUYING YOUR COUNCIL HOUSE

BUYING
A HOUSE
'PACKAGE'

To save endless trips to estate agents, solicitors and building societies you might consider contacting an organization which offers a total house package on a specific estate or site. There are many such firms: for details of their addresses and what they offer look in local and national newspapers for their advertisements.

Some packages offer homes complete with wall-to-wall carpeting and some kitchen goods. They guarantee 100 per cent mortgages (subject to income), pay all legal fees – and pay removal fees up to a fixed limit. Properties may also carry a warranty. These 'extras' may be included in the price, but they are not 'free'.

A package mortgage is usually two and a half to three times the purchaser's annual salary plus the partner's income. Repayment can be from as little as £25 per week, depending upon the amount borrowed and the location. But penalties for falling behind may be severe, and such houses are often difficult to sell, because prospective buyers will not take into account the 'extras' that were built into the original package price.

Such schemes often attract first-time house-buyers who would be well advised to consult their own solicitors before making a decision. As with building society mortgages, there is no discrimination against unmarried partners or against single women as long as they are eighteen or more and they have satisfactory financial status.

BUYING YOUR COUNCIL HOUSE

If you have been a 'secure tenant' for at least three years you can apply to buy your council house. You can buy jointly with up to three members of your family who are not themselves tenants of the property (for definitions see 'Guidance Notes Accompanying Tenant's Notice Claiming to Exercise the Right to Buy – Housing Act 1980', from your housing officer or Citizens' Advice Bureau).

Your house or flat will be valued at its open market value with vacant possession, less the value of improvements that you have paid for yourself – and as a secure tenant of three years' standing you will be allowed nearly one-third off that valuation. It is recommended that you have a survey; you will have to pay these fees and those of your solicitor. You can get a mortgage from a building society or from your landlord (the council). You can sell the house at any time – but if you do so within five years of purchase you have to repay some of your discount.

If you would like to know more about buying your council house, talk to your local housing officer (at the local council) and see 'The Right to Buy: a Guide for Council, New Town and Housing Association Tenants', published by the Department of the Environment and available from your local council or CAB.

Renting

RENTING PRIVATELY
COUNCIL HOUSE
ACCOMMODATION

LETTING PROPERTY

It is actually quite difficult today to find property that you can rent. Potential landlords are discouraged by the fact that if they let you in they may not be able to get you out. The law relating to rented property is very complex and you are wise to seek advice from a solicitor or your nearest Citizens' Advice Bureau before you become either a tenant or a landlord, since there are special rights and obligations for each.

RENTING PRIVATELY

● To find accommodation you should carefully check through newspaper and newsagents' advertisements, ask at estate agents and ask friends. Start in plenty of time – you may need it!

● If you want to know anything about the *Rent Act* or to query whether or not you are paying a fair rent, see the rent officer at your local council (or talk to the CAB). You can also get help from the Chartered Surveyors Voluntary Service. See 'Problems with Compulsory Purchase? Repairs? Rates? Rents?', from the Royal Institute of Chartered Surveyors (address on page 62).

● In the *private sector*, all tenants have the right of freedom from harassment; the right of a written lease and rent book if paying weekly; twenty-eight days' written notice to quit; no eviction without a court order and the right to wind- and rainproof property.

Protected tenants – generally those who do not have a resident landlord – also have security of tenure and the right to a fixed fair rent.

Within the private sector there is also the category of *shorthold tenancy* which is for a limited period of one to five years and gives the landlord the absolute right to regain possession at the end of the specified period.

● Your landlord has a duty to maintain the outside of the property and to provide essential services. If you have any cause for complaint, contact your CAB or a housing advice centre.

● If you have *any other housing problems* (building repairs, tenancy agreements, etc.), contact the CAB and see their 'Housing Problems? Building Repairs, Fair Rents, Tenancy Agreements and Rates'.

● *Notice to quit* must be served by a landlord on a tenant to end a *periodic tenancy*. A periodic tenancy runs, say, from month to month or week to week. When a house is let on a *fixed-term* basis, after that fixed term has run out a periodic tenancy comes into effect (the periods in this case being those for which rent was last payable under the fixed-term tenancy).

To be valid, a notice to quit must be in writing and must be given at least four weeks before the date it runs out. If the tenant does not leave the building, the landlord must get an order for possession from the court before he can lawfully evict him or her. A tenant who does not know if he has any right to remain in possession can obtain advice from a solicitor or the CAB or the housing aid officer, rent officer or rent tribunal officer.

COUNCIL HOUSE ACCOM-MODATION

● If you want to know about *council house accommodation*, talk to the housing officer at the local council (or talk to the CAB).

● There are *secure tenancies* within the public sector (e.g. the landlord is the local authority or the Scottish Special Housing Association [SSHA]). These tenants have:

(a) the right to buy

(b) right of succession of tenancy to spouses and members of the family, and

(c) security of tenure. To evict, the local authority must obtain a possession order on grounds of 'conduct' (e.g. rent arrears) or 'management' (major alterations to the house are planned, in which case the authority must show the court that alternative accommodation is being provided).

● If you are in council housing and you want to *move to another area*, you can do so with the Tenants' Exchange Scheme, details from your CAB or send s.a.e. to:

> Tenants' Exchange Scheme
> PO Box 170
> London SW1P 3PX

LETTING PROPERTY

● If you have *property you want to rent* you should check carefully on your rights. If you rent rooms in the house in which you live you become a resident landlord.

Talk to your solicitor or the CAB or see: 'Letting Rooms in Your Home'; and 'Letting Your Home or Retirement Home: a Guide for Homeowners and Servicemen Who Want to Let Their Homes Temporarily', Department of the Environment (Welsh Office). See also 'Reselling Electricity: a Guide for Tenants and Landlords', leaflet RE2 from the Post Office.

Further Information

SUGGESTED FURTHER READING

Broughton, David and Dryborough, John, *Surveying for Home-Buyers*, Penguin

Consumers' Association, *Raising the Money to Buy Your Home*
  The Legal Side of Buying a House
  Which? Way to Buy, Sell and Move House

Cutting, Marion, *A Housing Rights Handbook*, Penguin

Faulds-Wood, Lynn, *Cosmopolitan's Money Guide*, Cosmopolitan

Fingleton, Eamonn, and Tom Tickell, *The Penguin Money Book*, Penguin

Fry, Eric C., *Buying a House? A Guide to Finding Faults*, David & Charles

Joseph, Michael, *The Conveyancing Fraud* (available from 27 Occupation Lane, London SE18 3IQ)

Steele, Robert T., *Do-it-yourself Conveyancing: a Practical Guide to Handling the Legal Side of Buying and Selling a House*, David & Charles

Wright, Diana, *A Consumer's Guide to Mortgages*, Daily Telegraph

3 Your Car

Your car is a major purchase and requires a lot of consideration. On the whole, women are generally very unsure of what they are looking for and whether or not they are making the right decision in their choice of a particular car. So here is all you need to know about cars. What are the various parts? What should you look for when buying? How do you get the best price when selling? How much will all this cost?

This chapter reflects the knowledge of **Roger Bell**, a former editor of *Motor* magazine and now a freelance motoring journalist who specializes in car tests. He himself started racing 'at an age when some men retire' – in his late thirties – and he is especially concerned with problems women may face when buying, selling or driving a car.

Terminology

Aerodynamics – fancy word for streamlining. Air resistance greatly affects performance and economy above 60 m.p.h. Aerodynamic drag is expressed as a C_d (coefficient of drag) number – the lower the better.

Ammeter – dashboard instrument that measures the electric current being supplied to (or drained from) the battery.

Antifreeze – chemical concoction added to radiator water to prevent it from freezing in cold weather. Cars with air-cooled engines (e.g. vw Beetle, Citroën 2cv) do not need it.

Aquaplaning – dangerous condition caused by driving too fast on wet roads. Instead of breaking through water, tyres tend to skim over it like water-skis.

Backfire – explosion of fuel in the exhaust system. If it happens regularly, have exhaust, ignition and carburation checked.

Brake pads (and linings) – equivalent of a brake shoe on a bicycle wheel; the bit that applies friction on the brake disc (or drum). Like tyres, they wear out and need replacing from time to time.

Carburettor – instrument that vaporizes petrol, mixes it with air and feeds it to engine for burning.

Choke – device for making fuel/air mixture fed to engine extra rich to assist cold starting. Some cars have automatic chokes; others have manual ones.

Clutch – friction plates that disconnect the drive between the engine and gearbox. Plates are prised apart when you press clutch pedal.

Convertible – car with a soft top that can be folded back.

Coupé – sporty-looking car, usually with less room in the back than a saloon.

Detonation (usually called pinking) – explosive burning of fuel/air mixture in engine, detected by knocking or 'pinking' noise. Condition can eventually destroy an engine. Use higher octane petrol (i.e. move up a star rating) if persistent.

Diesel – special kind of engine, becoming more common in cars, that runs on DERV (Diesel Engine Road Vehicle fuel). Operates without usual ignition system to ignite fuel in engine. Diesels are economical but tend to be slower and noisier than petrol cars. DERV is also messy and smelly.

Dipstick – metal rod that measures the amount of lubricating oil in engine. Never let the oil level get too low: engine will seize solid without lubricant.

Distributor – electro-mechanical device that 'distributes' high-voltage current with split-second timing to sparking plugs to ignite petrol/air mixture in engine.

Electrolyte – solution of sulphuric acid and distilled water used in batteries. Never top up battery with tap water. Use distilled or de-ionized water.

Estate – van-shaped car with opening rear door, usually top hinged. More practical for load carrying than saloon, but maybe not so attractive.

Fastback – car with roofline that sweeps down at the back.

Flat spot – hiccup or hesitancy by the engine in response to pressure on the accelerator. It may mean that the car needs tuning. Consult a garage.

Fuse – safety device that protects electrical components from damage in the event of a short circuit or overloading.

Gasket – special sealing pad between two mating metal surfaces.

Gearbox – literally a box full of gearwheels that can be meshed (by the gearlever) four or five different ways to allow engine to function within its (limited) working range; also enables the car to go backwards.

Hatchback – cross between estate and saloon car, with rear door (or tailgate) and folding rear seats to increase luggage capacity.

Horsepower (usually expressed as brake horsepower, b.h.p.) – unit to measure an engine's output. A typical small engine develops 45 to 55 b.h.p., a small to medium-sized one 70 to 115 b.h.p. Big powerful engines can develop 200 b.h.p. or more.

Ignition system – those parts of a petrol engine concerned with igniting the fuel/air mixture inside the engine. Diesels do not need an ignition system.

Kickdown – means of changing down a gear on cars with automatic transmission by pressing the accelerator to the floor and thereby activating a switch.

MOT – Ministry of Transport (now Department of the Environment) annual safety test, demanded by law on all cars three or more years old.

Overdrive – extra high gear which allows the car to go fast (on a motorway, say), without the engine revving hard.

Oversteer – jargon for a skid caused by the tail of the car swinging wide. Can be corrected by steering into the slide.

Plug lead – cable that carries high-voltage current from distributor to sparking plugs. *Beware:* terminals can give a jolting electric shock if touched while engine is running.

Points – little metal pads that open and close rapidly in the distributor to trigger high-voltage current to sparking plugs. (Plug terminals are also known as 'points'.)

Power steering – engine-powered hydraulic system that assists the driver to turn the steering wheel. Fitted to most large, heavy cars. Offered as an option on many middleweights. Particularly beneficial for town driving and parking.

Quartz bulb – extra-bright headlight bulb that produces more white light than an ordinary tungsten bulb.

Radial ply – type of tyre with pliant radially-constructed sidewalls that help keep the tyre tread flat on the road when cornering. Most modern cars run on radials.

Radiator – multi-tubular air-cooled 'sandwich' which lowers the temperature of water (or antifreeze mixture) circulated round the engine to cool it. Usually positioned in the air stream just behind the front grille.

Rev counter (or tachometer) – dashboard instrument that indicates speed (in revolutions per minute) of the engine. Most have 2-digit calibrations to which two noughts should be added to get true reading (i.e. an indicated 40 is 4,000 r.p.m.).

Running in – initial period of restrained driving of new car to allow moving parts, particularly of engine and transmission, to bed in. Usually all that is necessary is to avoid using full throttle, pulling hard at low engine revs in a high gear and revving the engine too fast.

Running on – continued spluttery running of the engine after you have switched off. Can be caused by dirty plugs, dirty engine or dirty fuel – consult your garage if it persists.

Shock absorber (or damper) – device, usually tubular in shape, that stops ('damps') the car's suspension springs from bouncing up and down after the wheels have passed over a bump or depression.

Suspension – compliant mechanism that links the wheels to the body to soak up surface irregularities in the road.

Torque – the turning effort exerted by the engine; not to be confused with power (torque is what a cyclist applies to the pedal of a bike).

Torque converter – a special sort of coupling, fitted between the engine and an automatic gearbox, which can multiply (within set limits) the engine's torque output. It also acts as a clutch, engaging as the engine revolutions increase above tickover speeds.

Transverse engine – an engine placed across the car, not lengthwise. Most modern small cars have a transverse engine to leave more room for passengers and luggage.

Turbocharger – a turbine pump, driven by exhaust gases, which forces air under pressure (and thus more oxygen) into the engine so that it can burn more fuel to increase power.

Understeer – jargon for tendency of car to carry straight on when wheels are locked over by steering wheel. Usually caused by going too fast around slippery corners.

Abbreviations Car talk is riddled with jargon that is incomprehensible to most lay people. Most of it need not concern the average motorist but it is useful to be able to interpret the abbreviations often used in advertisements:

A/C – air conditioning (usually available only on expensive cars).

AH – air horn (usually loud and unsociable).

Alloys – lightweight alloy wheels which look good.

AT (or auto) – automatic transmission.

DHC (or DH or D/H) – drop-head coupé (i.e. one with a roof that can come back or be taken off).

EW – electrically-operated windows.

FHC – fixed-head coupé (i.e. one without a roof which comes off).

FI – fuel injection. Sophisticated way of feeding fuel to engine rather than sucking it through a carburetter.

FM – radio with VHF (Very High Frequency) reception; essential for stereo radio.

FWD – front-wheel drive. Most modern small cars have FWD, mainly because by 'packaging' the major mechanical parts at the front there is more room for people and luggage behind.

HP – usually hire purchase but it could mean horsepower.

HRW – heated rear window.

H/S top – hard and soft top (e.g. as fitted to a Triumph Stag).

LHD – left-hand drive. Cars with LHD can usually be bought cheaply as few people want to sit on the wrong side.

LSD – limited slip differential. Unless you are buying a powerful car you will not come across this device for limiting the wheelspin of the driven wheels when accelerating hard.

LWB – long wheelbase. A few 'top' cars are available in stretched form to give more passenger space between the wheel centres.

MOT – with current MOT test certificate.

OD (sometimes O/d) – overdrive, an extra long-legged cruising gear. Used to refer mainly to a switch-actuated electrically-engaged fifth gear. Many modern cars have 5-speed gearboxes, though, with top acting as an overdrive.

ONO – or nearest offer (an invitation to haggle).

OVNO – or very nearest offer (a warning not to haggle too much).

PBR – push-button radio.

P/X – part exchange.

QIS (or quartz) – quartz halogen lights, usually additional to the car's normal ones.

RHD – right-hand drive.

Spots – extra spot (long-range) driving lamps.

SR – sunshine roof.

TINTS – tinted glass.

VGC – very good condition.

WW (or wires) – wire-spoked wheels.

WW tyres – white-walled tyres.

Selling

You will get the best price by selling privately. Advertise in your local newspaper (if there is more than one, choose that with the best classified section). To reach a wider readership, advertise in *Exchange and Mart*. The specialist motoring press (*Autosport, Classic Cars, Motoring News*, etc.) is good for interesting cars like sports models or so-called 'classics'.

To save on advertising costs (especially if your car is not worth much), try placing a 'for sale' notice on the notice-board of local shops.

Another way to sell privately is through computer operations which, in return for a flat fee, will put buyers seeking your sort of car in touch with you. Contact:

Computacar
Western House
65–7 Western Road
Hove
East Sussex BN3 2JQ
  buying: 0203–778161
  selling: 01–903 8383

Unless you are part-exchanging your car for a newer one – a convenient method – do not sell direct to a dealer unless you are desperate for instant cash. His profit will be your loss. The value of your trade-in will vary from dealer to dealer: if he is anxious for your custom and thinks he can dispose of your old car easily he may be quite generous. Shop around. Get several quotes.

You are likely to get the poorest price at an auction – a high reserve price will probably mean no sale. Car auctions are used mainly by the trade and business houses as a quick and convenient means of car disposal.

Pricing

If you are selling privately, establish a realistic price from one of the consumer price guides (available at any good newsagent). Study advertisements for the same model of similar age and mileage. Pitch the price a little lower than a dealer would: his profit margin will take into account overheads and after-sales problems which will not concern you.

For cars less than two or three years old, mileage is likely to influence the value strongly. For older cars, the overall condition is more important.

Make sure the car is looking its best. Thoroughly clean it inside and out. It may be money well spent to have a scruffy youngster professionally valeted and the engine bay and wheelarches steam-cleaned (see 'Car Washing and Polishing' in Yellow Pages). Do not spend much money on old bangers: you are unlikely to get your money back.

A 'long' MoT certificate is a good selling point. If it is near termination, have the annual check-up done early to get a new 12-month certificate.

Dealing with buyers

● Have the right documents ready to show them:
(a) vehicle registration certificate (it used to be known as the log-book)
(b) MoT certificate (if the car is three or more years old)
(c) service and repair receipts (never throw these away)
(d) service record booklet (if it is up to date).
● Stand firm on your price – or something close to it – if you have had several encouraging phone inquiries.
● Remember to get the finance company's permission to sell the car if it is still subject to a hire-purchase agreement.
● Do not lie or mislead about any defects, even though it is the buyer who is at risk when purchasing privately.
● Do not give prospective buyers a test drive unless you are certain that either your insurance policy covers them or that their own does.
● Do not let the car out of your hands until you have cleared the buyer's cheque. Insist on a banker's draft (or cash) if they want an instant deal.
● Get the buyer to sign a receipt to indicate that the car is accepted and approved as seen (and tried, if appropriate).
● Remember to inform the Vehicle Licensing Office at Swansea (address on page 99) when the car has changed hands, using the tear-off slip on the registration document. Give the other main part to the buyer.

Buying

MAKING
A CHOICE

Selecting the right car – new or used – is no easy task as there are so many models to choose from. Purchase price will obviously be a deciding factor but, contrary to popular belief, it is rarely the main one. For all sorts of reasons, you may be able to raise more cash than you thought or, conversely, it might be better to pay less than you can actually afford.

Consider *all* the following points when thinking of buying a car:

1. *Usage.* If most of your motoring is done locally on short runs there is not much point in buying a large, fast car. Go for something that is nippy but also easy to park and manoeuvre. If you regularly cover long distances, comfort, quietness and an easy cruising gait are much more important than agility in the multi-storey.

2. *Type and size.*
- Decide whether you want a saloon with a conventional boot (best for security when you are carrying parcels, etc.), or an estate or hatchback with rear opening and folding seats (handier for carrying shopping or awkward loads and perhaps best if you have animals).
- Consider how many side doors you need. Opt for four if you frequently carry more than two adults: opt for two (for peace of mind) if you regularly carry young children in the back. Two-door models are a bit cheaper.
- If you fancy a sports car or coupé (exotic thoroughbreds apart) remember you are likely to sacrifice a lot of room and practicality for flashy looks and higher insurance premiums. There are many sensible sporty saloons and hatchbacks (like the Vauxhall Nova SR and Astra GTE) that handle and perform just as well as some sleek-looking sports cars.
- If you want a soft-top car with a folding roof, your options are strictly limited – though convertibles are making a comeback.

3. *Running costs.* Regard official fuel consumption figures as no more than a guide to a car's economy. Its overall consumption is likely to be poorer than, say, the m.p.g. figure at a steady 56 m.p.h. (90 k.p.h.) often quoted in advertisements.

Do not consider only the fuel consumption. You must also remember depreciation, insurance (the lower the group rating the better), spares and servicing.

4. *Specification.* Do not be too concerned with technicalities. It is results that count, so be wary of fancy-sounding sales talk about suspension design and engine torque figures.

A car with a small engine will not necessarily be more economical than a larger engined one. Engine size – expressed in so many ccs or litres (e.g. 1,600cc or 1.6 litres) – is only one of several criteria that affect performance and economy. The type of transmission (manual or automatic), the number of gears (usually 3, 4 or 5), the gear ratios, overall weight and air penetration (see 'Aerodynamics' above) all play their part.

A 1,300cc car driven well within its limits might give better economy than a hard-pressed 1,100. Remember, too, that some efficient, light-weight cars with small engines can accelerate much quicker than heavier cars with large engines.

If in doubt, find out from independent sources (*Which?*, AA test reports and the specialist motoring press like *Autocar*, *Car*, *Motor* and *What Car?*) what your short-listed cars will do, how they perform, whether the experts consider that they handle and stop safely, what they will do to the gallon and so on.

5. *Transmission*. There are two basic sorts, manual (with a clutch and gearlever) and automatic (with only two pedals and self-changing gears). In skilled hands, manuals can accelerate faster than automatics. Automatics are, however, sometimes quicker off the mark because no driver skill is required to make them perform smartly. You simply press the accelerator hard.

Automatic transmission makes driving in towns much easier but it tends to use more petrol than manual as it absorbs more power. For the same reason, an automatic has slower acceleration after initial getaway.

6. *Colour, trim*. When choosing a colour, remember that a light shade is more easily seen at night (but not necessarily in fog) and it is therefore safer than a dark shade. Remember too that black and white tend to show the dirt more than bright colours like red and yellow.

Light-coloured cloth trim looks good in a new car but it shows the dirt easily and cloth upholstery is difficult to keep in pristine condition – especially if you have small children scrambling in with muddy boots. Go for mid-shade patterned cloth if you want to be really practical.

When buying a car, look carefully at the equipment options. Work out whether the additional items offered on, say, the HLS (or GLS or SGL – such model nomenclature means different things to different manufacturers) is really worth the extra money to you. It might be cheaper to buy a lesser model in the range and fit only those extras and accessories that you want afterwards.

7. *The test run*. In the end only you can decide whether a car's looks and driving qualities are right for you. Make your test run as long as possible. Pay particular attention to seat comfort and adjustment, the position of the controls, the ease with which the controls work, how well you can see out, noise levels and heating and ventilation. Look for convenience details (stowage space inside, door locking, how the boot or tailgate is released, whether you can locate the switches easily in the dark and so on).

Consider hiring the car of your choice before buying it. You will get to know it much better over two or three days. Read as much as you can in the motoring columns of national newspapers and in magazines –

and look at *Which?*, which gives guidelines: sometimes you will see that the same car is a 'best buy' both new and second-hand.

On a used car (see below) you should also be on the alert for suspicious noises, vibrations, smells and other overt signs of wear (like a smoky exhaust).

BUYING A NEW CAR

Autocar and *Motor* both publish weekly price guides of all the cars sold on the British market. Remember that they are only guides, showing recommended retail price. They do not not take into account discounts which may vary from nothing to 15 per cent or more. Nor, in general, do they include 'on-the-road' extras like number plates, delivery charges (which may run into three figures) and the road fund licence.

Shop around. Find out what discounts are available on the listed prices from local dealers. Keep in mind that a trusted dealer with a good reputation can in the long term be worth more than a few pounds off elsewhere.

If you have an old car to sell (see below), find out its trade-in value. If business is slack a dealer might find it quite attractive. Calculate, however, whether you would be better off selling privately.

Chronic over-production has plagued the world's motor industry for some time, so in general terms it is a buyer's market. Haggle. It will not always work (especially if the car you want is in heavy demand). But have a go.

Watch out for special offers and incentives advertised in the local press (like no-interest credit, discounts and free weekend test drives). If the incentive sounds almost too good, ask yourself why. It may be because the car has a bad reputation and no one wants it.

The best time to register a new car is either at the beginning of the year or in August when the registration letter changes. A January 1985 car will be worth more than a December '84 one when you come to sell. Similarly, a B-registered car will be preferred by buyers to one with the previous year's A-prefix.

End-of-line cars that are about to be replaced by a new model can be excellent buys as they are likely to be heavily discounted to clear stocks.

When you order your new car you will be asked to sign a contract which details the model, delivery date and price. Because of the Supply of Goods Act, the deal is weighted in your favour – but if the price goes up between ordering and delivery you will probably have to pay the extra (or cancel) and you have no redress if the car does not arrive on the promised date. Remember that any delay between ordering and delivery could affect the value of the car you may be part-exchanging.

Teething problems are common on new cars. Keep a record of any faults so that they can be put right at the first free service (not as 'free' as it is usually described as you will have to pay for things like oil). The normal warranty on mechanical parts is twelve months unlimited mileage. Make sure you get any known problems fixed before the expiry date.

FINANCE   If you cannot pay the full asking price from your own funds (the cheapest way), you will have to borrow and borrowed money can be expensive. If you are lucky enough to have wealthy relatives try them first. Then try your employers.

A bank personal loan is usually easy to arrange. Provided your bank manager reckons you can afford the repayments he will probably consider lending you enough for a new car or he may allow you to run up an overdraft, which could be cheaper. Consider opening a bank loan account too: the amount you borrow is transferred to your current account from which you repay the loan with regular monthly instalments. Again, it may be a bit cheaper (ask your bank).

The norm for car hire-purchase, arranged through the dealer with a finance house, is 20 per cent down and three years to pay. At, say, 10 per cent interest that means a £5,000 loan would cost you £1,500 after three years.

Low (or zero) interest offers – usually made to shift slow-moving stock – can be attractive, but do not expect no-interest purchase *and* a discounted price. Dealers can be quite flexible about how they 'package' a special offer but they will not give ground in every direction nor will they necessarily be swayed by a cash offer as they get finance house commission on HP deals. Never forget that dealers are in business to make a profit.

If you have a life insurance policy you may be able to borrow money against it relatively cheaply. Ask.

If you are self-employed and use your car for business purposes, consider leasing or lease purchase. The big attraction is that there is no heavy initial outlay to deplete capital you may want for other things. And there are also tax concessions: get professional advice from an accountant.

BUYING
A USED CAR   In a good trading year, around 1.7 million new cars are bought in Britain, a large percentage of them by businesses. Four times as many used cars are sold each year. The chances are, therefore, that you will be looking at a used car rather than a new one, especially if you have less than £3,000 to spend.

Be wary of large, high-mileage luxury cars, particularly foreign ones that are a few years old. A low purchase price might make them look tempting on a dealer's forecourt but they are likely to be a cash-draining liability to keep on the road in decent running order. That is almost certainly why they are cheap: no one wants them.

Rust is the modern car's worst enemy. Mechanical parts can be replaced but serious corrosion of the body/chassis structure is a terminal disease. Beware of outwardly smart elderly cars that have black-painted bottoms and lower sills. In all probability, the 'protective layer' is camouflaging rotten metal.

There are several sources from which to consider buying a used car:

1. *Buying from a dealer.* If you buy from a dealer, try and make it a local one. The closer he is the more convenient it is for you to get your car serviced and repaired. He is more likely to bend over backwards for a

local resident (word gets around), than he is for a stranger. It is human nature.

Franchised dealers – those handling a specific make or makes – are likely to charge the highest prices for used cars. But they should also offer the best guarantee and after-sales back-up with properly trained mechanics. If only for peace of mind, the extra can be money well spent.

The after-sales service of a used-car dealer without garage facilities is unlikely to be so good. If the car is guaranteed, read the small print to find out what it covers. It may not be as all-embracing as you think. Perhaps the most encouraging thing about a short-term guarantee is that the dealer would not offer it if he thought the car was going to go wrong. The cost of the guarantee will be built in to the car's price, of course. You rarely get something for nothing in the car trade.

2. *Buying privately.* Expect to pay less for a car bought from a private owner than one bought from a dealer but remember the old maxim of *caveat emptor* (buyer beware). You are on your own if things go wrong afterwards. Jo Public can be far more dishonest and tricky to handle than the most unscrupulous dealer whose scope for 'exaggeration' (lying) will be tempered by various Acts of Parliament. In short, the product the dealer sells must be of 'merchantable quality'.

If you mistrust the seller do not buy his (or her) car. Even if you do – and obviously there are honest, trustworthy private sellers – take a friend along who knows the ropes, what questions to ask and, above all, what faults to look for.

You are in the best position to strike a good bargain if you have cash in your pocket. Many sellers are easily swayed by a bundle of ready notes and the thought of a quick, clean sale.

Make sure you get a receipt for your money from the seller and a signed declaration that the car (properly described and identified) is not subject to a hire-purchase agreement and that it is accompanied by the registration document and MoT certificate (if applicable). Such a declaration might just be useful if things go horribly wrong after purchase – provided the seller is not a fly-by-night professional crook.

Never buy from an individual selling from suspicious – or non-existent – premises. He could be a thief selling a stolen car. You, in turn, should be prepared to sign a declaration that you accept the car as seen and tried (if you did try it).

3. *Buying at an auction.* Unless you are a gambler in search of a bargain, be wary of auctions. If you do try your luck, go as a spectator (they are rather fun to watch) the first time, to learn the rules.

When you buy, try and get an expert who can mix with hard-nosed dealers to go with you. Auction houses, like private sellers, give you no after-sale guarantee. Nor do they allow you to test-drive the car first.

Note ● If you cannot call upon an expert friend to help you vet a used car, have it professionally inspected by the AA or RAC: the fee is modest in comparison to possible savings later on.

Motoring Costs

Cars are a terrible drain on the pocket and there is no such thing as cheap motoring. According to the A A's *Drive* magazine (November 1983) the least expensive form of ownership is provided by an elderly 'banger' that you can buy cheaply and then run into the ground before scrapping. It will cost you more to keep in a roadworthy condition than a younger car (and much more than a new one under guarantee) but it will not suffer much from depreciation – the biggest factor to take into account when assessing the running costs of a new or young used car.

If you do not use a car often it may well be cheaper, but not so convenient, to opt out of ownership altogether and hire a car only when you need one. If use is confined to, say, twenty-five weekends and a holiday fortnight, hiring could be cheaper than owning.

Whether you do 500 or 50,000 miles a year there are certain fixed-cost charges you cannot avoid.

DEPRECIA-TION

All new cars start to drop in value the minute they leave the showroom (some drop more than others). In general, large, expensive thirsty cars depreciate much faster than small, popular economy ones.

A typical £5,000 1,300cc family hatchback is likely to depreciate in retail value by up to £1,000 in the first year. As it gets older, the depreciation curve flattens out. That is why a young low-mileage used car in good condition can be a better buy than a brand-new one.

There are exceptions to the depreciation rule. Some 'enthusiast' cars (like the Triumph Stag) will hold their value if kept in good condition. They may even appreciate, but do not bank on it; very few cars actually increase in value.

INSURANCE

Never drive a car (yours or anyone else's) unless you have proper insurance cover.

These are the main types available:

Third party covers liability for injuries to other people, including passengers, and damage to their property when you have caused an accident.

Third party, fire and theft covers the above *plus* fire and theft.

Comprehensive covers all the above *plus* accidental damage to the car, accidents to yourself and your husband in your own car or someone else's, medical expenses incurred by you or your passengers as a result of an accident involving your car, loss or damage to personal effects in your car, up to about £100.

You must by law have some car insurance (normally the minimum is third party). If you are a terrible risk it may be the only cover you can get but try for something better – at least third party, fire and theft. Under this sort of policy you forfeit the right to claim on accident damage. Unless the car's value is low, go for fully comprehensive cover if you can get it. It is illegal to allow others to drive your car without insurance and you should always have the insurance certificate with you when you drive.

Your policy normally covers you while you are driving someone else's car but check beforehand. Check also that your policy covers use of your car for business purposes (if relevant).

Insurance premiums vary enormously according to your age, experience, claims record, where you live, the type of car you drive (a fast, expensive car will cost many times more than an economy runabout) and the type of cover you want. You can keep costs down by restricting comprehensive cover to yourself and perhaps one other named driver and by agreeing to pay the first part of any claim.

A typical premium for a good-risk driver with a 1,600cc saloon and full no-claims discount would be around £100. For a young bad-risk driver living in an expensive area (London) with a poor claims record it could be several times that amount.

A 'no-claim discount' rewards the policy-holder who has a proven claim-free insurance record. Although the scale of discount varies, most insurers offer 25 per cent for one claim-free year, rising in steps to 60 per cent or 65 per cent after periods of up to six years.

Insurance can be arranged through your normal insurer before buying. If you buy privately, make sure you have fixed up insurance before driving away. A good broker will arrange the best policy for your needs. Often your motor certificate covers any car owned by you so all you need is to telephone your insurer with details of the new vehicle.

See   'What You Need to Know about Motor Insurance' and 'When it Comes to the Crunch: Do You Know What to Do Next?', both from the British Insurance Association (address on page 39).

MoT   If your car is three years old or more you will need an annual Department of the Environment inspection to ensure it is roadworthy. Appointed garages do the job for a set fee.

PETROL   In a 10,000-mile year (average) a car that does thirty miles to the gallon will use £600-worth of petrol. Put another way, that is 6p a mile in fuel alone. Most modern cars with engines of 1,300cc or less are capable of doing forty miles to the gallon if driven with restraint. Expect much less if you nip around on short urban journeys.

ROAD TAX   Currently, this costs £90 annually regardless of what car you run. It is an offence not to display a current vehicle licence in the bottom left-hand corner of your windscreen.

SERVICING

Charges vary enormously from car to car. So does the cost of spare parts. It is best to consult one of the consumer guides (*Which?*, *Drive*) for detailed guidance. Labour – a major factor in assessing service costs – is likely to be at least £10 an hour. The longer the intervals between services and the shorter the time allocated to carry them out, the better.

Do not skimp on routine servicing of a new car. It could invalidate the warranty. With an older car, it might be worth trying a local non-franchised garage which may offer a more personal and flexible service.

Tyres, batteries, exhaust systems and brake pads/linings need replacing from time to time. Tyres, in particular, can be expensive.

EXTRAS AND ACCESSORIES

Cars are much better equipped now than they used to be. Top-of-the-range models may come with everything you want. Less expensive models probably will not.

If you fit after-market extras to your car, bear in mind that when you come to sell they probably will not make all that much difference to the value. It follows that extra equipment fitted to a used car you *buy* can make it a bargain.

Extras and accessories fall into five main groups:

1. *Comfort.* The range of equipment here is vast, ranging from woolly seat-covers to audio equipment. If you want stereo radio, you need a VHF set. The reception of good equipment can be ruined by poor fitting so you need professional installation.

Other possibilities include: opening roof (there are many different sorts on the market), extra sound-proofing and replacement seats.

2. *Convenience.* Such things as a roof-rack (restrict to short-term use if possible – see 'Taking Your Car Abroad', page 513), a tow-bar and additional instruments fall into this category.

3. *Performance.* Go-faster engine conversions are available for many cars but they tend not to justify their initial cost. Economy and reliability are also likely to suffer and your insurance premiums will probably increase. There *are* some worthwhile conversions on the market but in the main it is probably better to buy a quicker car than convert an existing one.

4. *Safety.* Safety experts strongly recommend carrying small children in a special safety seat (see 'Travelling with a Baby or Young Child' page 302). Also, consider rear safety-belts for adults if they are not already fitted.

If your car's fog lights are a bit dim, you can fit extra ones. Consider rear fog lights and a reversing light, especially for an older car, and an extra mirror (or mirrors) may make you feel more comfortable at the wheel in busy traffic.

5. *Security.* There are many different forms of anti-theft devices on the market – and with good reason: theft of (and from) cars is a growing problem and many cars are easy to break into. A simple, visible device is better than nothing at all, particularly as protection against 'joyrider' thieves.

Care and Attention

Unless you know what you are doing and have proper facilities and equipment, leave servicing and repairs to the professionals but do read the handbook (which should be kept in the car) for guidance on routine chores.

Know where to find things like the fuse box and oil dipstick. Checking the oil can be a messy job so keep a kitchen roll in the boot to handle the dipstick and oil filler cap. The check-out assistants at many self-service garages are quite likely to know less about your car than you do, so consult the handbook if you are in doubt about what grade of oil to use (the grade, incidentally, is much more important than the make).

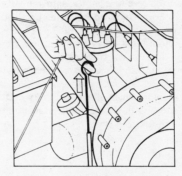

Check the oil level regularly, using the dipstick

Never let the oil level get below the bottom mark on the dipstick. Without an adequate supply of lubricant, the engine will seize.

Check brake and clutch fluid reservoirs

While you are under the bonnet, check the contents of the windscreen-washer bottle. Add proprietary anti-smear solution (or sachet powder) when topping up with water. Washing-up liquid will do but is not ideal as it tends to froth. Also keep an eye on the little container carrying fluid for the brake pipes (and maybe clutch mechanism too). If the level looks low, top up with fresh brake fluid (never water or ordinary oil) or get expert advice.

Many modern cooling systems are sealed and rarely need topping up but on older cars regularly check that you can see liquid (a solution of water and antifreeze, mixed three parts to one unless the handbook says otherwise) in the radiator header tank. *Never remove the cap of a hot engine* – you could be severely scalded. There is no need to flush out and refill every year (as in the past). Modern antifreeze helps prevent internal corrosion: if you have to top up regularly, do not forget to add more antifreeze to keep the solution strength up.

Some modern batteries need no maintenance though most will need topping up with distilled, not tap, water from time to time. The liquid should just cover the metal plates you can see through the top-up holes.

Check – or have checked – the tyre pressures at least once a fortnight and ideally once a week. Learn how to do the job yourself at a self-service garage. Apart from causing potentially dangerous handling, a partially deflated tyre will wear rapidly and unevenly. Do not forget the spare tyre: there is nothing worse than finding it flat when you need it to replace a punctured tyre.

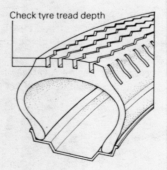

Check tyre tread depth

Keep a check on tyre wear. If the tread looks shallow (the legal minimum is 1mm), you probably need new tyres, and if there are any bald spots you *must* replace them.

Before submitting your car for its MoT test, go through the list of items on the form that you can check yourself: lights, screen-washer operation (an empty bottle could mean failure), wipers, tyre pressures, tyre wear and so on. It could save you the inconvenience and expense of a second test.

Other items to check regularly

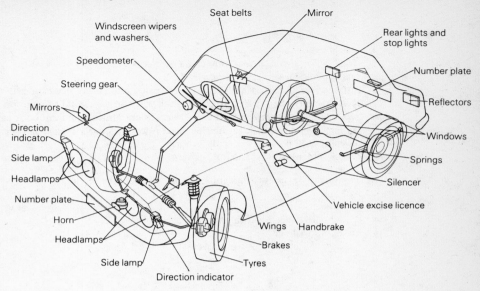

Seat belts

Mirror

Windscreen wipers and washers

Rear lights and stop lights

Speedometer

Number plate

Steering gear

Reflectors

Mirrors

Direction indicator

Windows

Side lamp

Springs

Headlamps

Silencer

Number plate

Vehicle excise licence

Horn

Headlamps

Wings   Handbrake

Side lamp

Brakes

Direction indicator

Tyres

Bodywork   Modern cars do not need to be cosseted in a garage. It is fine if you can keep your car dry under cover – and the windows protected from frost in winter – but corrosion is accelerated by warmth and moisture so it is probably best not to put a hot, wet car in a garage.

Wash the car regularly. The proper sequence, if you do not use a mechanical wash, is to do the horizontal surfaces first – roof, bonnet and boot – followed by the front, tail and flanks. Leave the wheels until last. Never clean with a dry cloth – it will scratch the paint. Polish twice a year if you can – and look out for rust spots while you are doing it (they spread rapidly if not treated).

Clean the windows inside and out regularly. Avoid domestic cleaners on the outside of the screen. Use soapy water and a leather – or a proprietary screen cleaner. Do not get car polish on the windows: it smears them. Change the wiper blades at least once a year.

If freezing temperatures are forecast you can save tiresome scraping and frozen hands in the morning by placing newspapers under the screen wipers (set them diagonally by switching off the ignition at the right moment).

First aid kit   Keep in a clearly labelled box (say an old large plastic ice-cream box):
- 6 triangular bandages (each with safety-pin)
- stocking or triangular bandage plus newspaper to make a neck collar
- prepared unmedicated sterile dressings:

      3 medium
      1 large
      1 extra large
- 10 individually wrapped adhesive plasters, assorted sizes
- 1 sterile eye-pad
- Gamgee Tissue cut into about 10 pieces, each about 30 × 20cm
- 2 cotton elastic or crêpe bandages 8cm wide
- roll of adhesive tape 2.5cm wide
- 6 extra safety-pins
- 1 pair strong scissors

Do not keep any sterile packs that are torn or damaged or have been opened.

See 'Car Accidents – First Aid', page 156.

Handy aids   If you want to be prepared for most eventualities, carry the following:
- blanket
- chamois leather
- de-icing aerosol (preferably with a scraper top)
- fire extinguisher
- glasses (spare pair and sunglasses)
- gloves (plastic)
- handbook
- jump leads (see below)
- map books
- paper towels, tissues and moist wipes
- personal requirements (e.g. spare tights, make-up, hairbrush – and soda water for removing spots)
- notepad and pencils (see 'Motor Accidents', page 549)
- red reflector triangle
- screen-washer liquid
- tools (screwdriver, spanners, pliers)
- torch
- tow-rope
- umbrella
- water repellent aerosol.

If the weather is bad or likely to become so, take the extra items suggested in 'Difficult Driving' below.

Faults and Breakdown: What to Do

STARTING PROBLEMS   SCREEN BREAKAGE
ENGINE OVERHEATS   MOTORING ORGANIZATIONS
PUNCTURES   COMPLAINTS

The old adage about prevention being better than cure is particularly relevant to cars. Regular servicing and inspection will minimize the risk of trouble. Even so, things do go wrong – and usually at the worst possible time and place. Here are some typical problems and guidance about how to tackle them.

STARTING PROBLEMS

Flat battery. If nothing happens when you turn the key, the battery is probably flat. Confirm this by trying the lights, which will look dim or not work at all.

● Either replace battery (but only if it is old and decrepit) or have the existing one recharged at a garage (usually an overnight job).

You can use another car's battery to start your engine with the help of a pair of *jump leads* (household cable will not do). Park so that the two batteries are as close as possible. Connect the leads between batteries one at a time in this order: plus (positive) to plus, minus (negative) to minus, placing them on the booster battery first. With the aid car's engine idling, operate the start motor of the 'dead' car. All being well it should start – and continue to run when the jump leads are removed. Disconnect immediately: provided there is no major fault with your electrics the battery will recharge itself on a longish run.

Other starting problems

● If the starter motor will not function when the lights are bright, perhaps the battery terminals need tightening. This is a spanner job: fingers will not do. It could also be something more serious like a defective starter motor. If the car has automatic transmission, wiggle the gear selector round in 'neutral' or 'park' and try again.

● If the starter motor turns the engine vigorously but it will not start, make sure there is petrol in the tank. Assuming there is then you probably have an ignition or fuel-feed fault that needs expert attention.

● If the car has been standing out in heavy fog or rain, try spraying water repellent (e.g. WD40, available from most garages) over the ignition system – sparking plugs, plug leads, distributor and coil. If dampness is 'shorting' the system, water repellent can effect an instant and magical cure.

ENGINE OVERHEATS

If you missed the tell-tale warning light or high temperature gauge reading you will smell it – and probably feel a reluctance to pull properly. The first thing to do is to *stop and switch off*. The next is to be patient and *let the engine cool down*. Do not remove the radiator cap to inspect the water level (you will be sprayed with hot steam if you do).

When the engine has stopped simmering:

● Carefully remove the radiator cap. If there is a lack of liquid inside, top with water (or, even better, antifreeze solution). Top up slowly, ideally with the engine ticking over. Engine blocks can crack like crockery if cooled quickly when very hot.

● If lack of water was the cause of the trouble, carry on. With any luck, no lasting damage will have been done – but do not bank on it. Engines made of light alloy (and many modern ones are) have a nasty habit of warping when overheated.

● If the *fan belt* (which usually drives the water pump) has broken, you may be able to carry on without it for a while on an open-road journey. Air rammed through the radiator should be sufficient to keep the engine cool. In stop-start driving, you will not get far before the engine overheats again.

Without a fan belt the alternator (or dynamo) will not charge the battery. Using a neck tie or pair of tights as a drive belt has been known to work as a get-you-home measure but do not rely on it.

PUNCTURES

If a tyre bursts at speed you will hear a bang and feel an alarming vibration. However unnerving *do not brake or swerve suddenly* towards the verge. It might make the tyre roll off the rim and put the car into an uncontrollable skid: worse still, the rim could dig in and roll the car over. Slow down and turn in gently and you should come to no harm.

Changing a wheel is not a difficult job – though some strength is needed to undo the wheel nuts. The best advice is to follow the instructions in the handbook or to proceed as follows:

● Locate and remove spare wheel, jack, jack handle (probably a long rod with a hook on the end) and wheelbrace (normally an L-shaped device with a hexagon socket on the end). If you know your car properly you will know where they are kept.

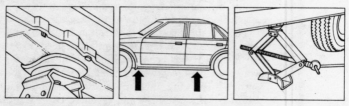

Typical wheel-change procedure

● Look underneath for body recesses to accommodate the jack head (this is where you really need the handbook).

● Wind up the jack so the head locates with the jacking-point closest to the wheel to be changed. Make sure the base is on firm ground and that the handbrake is on hard. As an added precaution, leave in gear.

● Before lifting the car on the jack, remove the trim (if there is one) from the wheel with suitable lever implement, then loosen nuts with wheelbrace.

● Turn anticlockwise to undo. If the nuts are very stiff, it may help if you let them cool down (if the wheels are hot), tap them with a hammer first, or try turning the brace with your foot. When you have loosened them slightly – in diagonal sequence, a bit at a time – jack up the car until the bottom of tyre is a couple of inches off the ground.

● Now remove the nuts completely, pull off the wheel and place the new one on the studs. Tighten nuts by hand then gently with wheelbrace before lowering and removing jack.

● Tighten nuts properly, a little at a time, in diagonal sequence (not 'round the clock').

● Wheelnuts do not need to be tightened with Mr Universe strength but have them checked later if you are not sure.

● Remember to get the punctured spare mended or replaced as soon as possible.

SCREEN
BREAKAGE

Laminated screens, safer in an accident, will not shatter as easily as so-called *'toughened'* glass screens, which occasionally shatter with a terrific bang. If it happens, you should have sufficient vision through the fractured glass to pull up safely. Do not punch your fist through the screen: although the fractured granules are not razor sharp the bits might fly into your eyes and would probably cut your wrists and knuckles.

If you cannot get help fairly quickly from one of the motoring organizations or if there is no screen-replacement specialist nearby, knock out the shattered screen, ideally on to a sheet of something – anything – to prevent the bits going all over seats and into the heater ducts. Wear gloves or a protective roll round your hands to do it. With all the windows shut and the heater full on, it is quite possible to drive without a front screen as a get-you-home emergency but beware of bits blowing into your eyes from around the screen edges – it is difficult to get rid of all the glass remnants. Wear glasses if possible.

MOTORING
ORGAN-
IZATIONS

Membership of a large motoring organization such as the AA or the RAC provides peace of mind whenever you use your car. Sooner or later, no matter how new and reliable your car, something will go wrong and leave you stranded. This is where they can help.

When your car breaks down away from home, the AA/RAC will come to your aid – twenty-four hours a day, 365 days a year. All you have to do is telephone one of the breakdown information and service centres (the numbers are listed in the members' handbooks) or call from one of the roadside telephones. The emergency telephones on motorway hard shoulders are connected to the nearest police control room, from where your problem would be passed on.

You should always carry your membership card with you as you will need to quote your membership number to obtain help. Normally a patrol vehicle will be with you within an hour but it may be necessary to wait a little longer if bad road or weather conditions have put undue strain on the service.

Patrols are trained and equipped to undertake minor roadside repairs, and usually will be able to get you on the move again quickly. Major repairs, however, are needed in 25 per cent of cases and cannot be attempted at the roadside. In these circumstances the patrol will arrange

– at the organization's expense – for your car to be towed to their nearest appointed garage.

The relay service is an optional addition to the breakdown service and is well worth considering if you travel long distances. The inconvenience of breaking down hundreds of miles from home and then finding that a garage will take several days to repair your car is considerable. Relay will help to ease the frustration. If prompt local repair cannot be carried out, you, your family and your car – even a caravan or boat if on tow at the time – will be transported to your home or anywhere else of your choice in the UK mainland.

The other optional addition is Home Start, which has proved very popular. Since the normal class of membership does not entitle you to assistance at home, Home Start will help you out of trouble in your own driveway on a frosty morning if your car suffers a flat battery or frozen radiator.

Technical advisers can offer you assistance on almost everything related to the garage trade, the motor industry, motor accessories and components, vehicle maintenance and so on. They can help in disputes with garages, and staff engineers can rigorously inspect a second-hand car for you.

The AA's and RAC's expertise and buying power enables them to offer special insurance schemes and preferential rates to their members. Motorists travelling to Europe can take out a comprehensive package offering emergency assistance, travel insurance and emergency credit facilities. Both organizations will take up claims on behalf of members (contact the legal department of the relevant organization). Headquarters are based at:

Automobile Association
Fanum House
Basingstoke
Hants RG2 1 2EA
0256–20123

Royal Automobile Club
RAC House
Landsdowne Road
Croydon CR9 2JA
01–686 2525

Also: National Breakdown
Freepost
Bradford BD12 0BR
0274 671299

COMPLAINTS

● If you want to complain about a *garage or dealer*: check whether they belong to one of the following organizations and contact the customer services manager at the nearest/relevant place. These associations share a joint code of practice for the motor industry which covers sale of new and used cars, warranties and accuracy of mileage reading and repair and servicing.

Motor Agents' Association
(MAA)
201 Great Portland Street
London W1N 6AB
01–580 9122

Scottish Motor Trade Association
(SMTA)
3 Palmerston Place
Edinburgh EH12 5AF
031–225 3643

Society of Motor Manufacturers and Traders (SMMT)
Forbes House
Halkin Street
London SW I X 7DS
01–235 7000

● In case of complaints about *car body repairs*, you can contact:

Vehicle Builders' and Repairers' Association (VBRA)
Belmont House
Finkle Lane
Gildersome
Leeds LS 2 7 7TW
0532–538333

● If you are unhappy with a *tyre*, contact:

Tyre Manufacturers' Conference
90–91 Tottenham Court Road
London W I P OBR
01–580 2794

● If you want to complain about your actual *car*, write to the customer relations department manager:

Alfa Romeo (GB)
Geron Way
Edgware Road
London NW 2 6LW
01–450 9191

(*Audi, Volkswagen*)
VAG (UK)
Yeomans Drive
Blakelands
Milton Keynes MK I 4 5AN
0908–678121

(*Austin Rover, MG, Triumph*)
Austin Rover
PO Box 29
Oxford OX4 2XB
0865–778941

BMW (GB)
Ellesfield Avenue
Bracknell
Berks RG I 2 4TA
0344–80110

Citroën
Mill Street
Slough SL 2 5DE
0753–23808

Colt Car Co.
Watermere End
Cirencester
Glos GL 7 I LF
0285–5777

Daihatsu (UK)
PO Box 5
Poulton Close
Dover
Kent CT I 7 OHP
0304–213030

Datsun (UK)
New Road
Worthing
West Sussex BN I 3 3HD
0903–68561

Fiat Auto (UK)
Great West Road
Brentford
Middlesex TW8 9DJ
01–568 8822

Ford Motor Company
Beckett House
Chapel High
Brentwood
Essex CM14 4BY
0277–251100

Honda (UK)
Power Road
London W4 5YT
01–995 9381

Jaguar Cars
Browns Lane
Allesley
Coventry CV5 9DR
0203–402121

Mazda Cars
Mount Ephraim
Tunbridge Wells
Kent TN4 8BS
0892–40123

Peugeot Automobiles UK
PO Box 122
Whitley
Coventry CV3 4GB
0203–306500

Porsche Cars GB
Richfield Avenue
Reading
Berks RG1 8PH
0734–303666

Renault UK
Western Avenue
London W3 0RZ
01–992 5322

Rolls-Royce Motors
Crewe
Cheshire CW1 3PL
0270–255155

Saab (GB)
Fieldhouse Lane
Marlow
Bucks SL7 1LY
06284–6977

Talbot Motor Company
PO Box 25
Humber Road
Stoke
Coventry CV3 1BD
0203–452144

Toyota (GB)
The Quadrangle
Redhill
Surrey RH1 1PX
0737–68585

(Vauxhall, Opel)
Vauxhall Motors
PO Box 3
Luton
Beds LU2 0SY
0582–21122

Volvo Concessionaires
Lancaster Road
Cressex Estate
High Wycombe
Bucks HP12 3QE
0494–33444

Car Hire

Sometimes it just does not make sense to own a car – if you live in the centre of a town and walk to work, for example, or if you have good public transport or a friend who likes nothing better than chaufferring you around. But perhaps you want to get out of the city for a weekend or you want to escape . . .

What to do Car hire is simple. All you do is ring the local number of a car-hire company (Yellow Pages) and make a reservation. Even though you can sometimes get a car immediately it is always worthwhile booking in advance to avoid delays, and at some times of the year there may be a shortage of vehicles.

The large nationwide companies allow you to order a car from any-where in the UK (or overseas) and drop it off anywhere (there might be an extra charge if you do not return it to your pick-up point). Rental rates depend on the type of car.

When you make your reservation the company will want to know your name, what type of vehicle you wish to rent and for how long, and how you intend to pay. Most accept major credit cards. A 'deposit' must be authorized by the relevant company but is not charged to your account. If you pay by cheque the same amount is required on 'deposit'. There is no objection to cash but form-filling will take a little bit longer (about ten minutes): you must provide a personal reference, which has to be checked, and cash renters are photographed as a simple safety precaution – just occasionally would-be thieves 'rent' rather than going to the trouble of stealing a car!

Most offices are open from at least 8.30 a.m. to 6 p.m. during the week and half-day Saturday. Arrangements can be made to pick up out of hours for a small additional charge and some airport locations are open twenty-four hours. When you go to collect the car, the company will note licence details while you supply name, address and occupation.

When you are shown the car you should make sure any dents, etc., are noted by the company's representative. Ask where emergency flasher, lights and dimmer switch and windscreen wipers are. You are given the keys and document folder – and away you go.

The headquarters of car-hire companies can be found under 'Car Hire' in Yellow Pages.

Your Driving

LEARNING TO DRIVE   ADVERSE CONDITIONS
BEFORE WINTER COMES

LEARNING TO DRIVE Some people are lucky and can pass the driving test with no professional help. Others – including many women – are not instantly at ease with the mechanics and controls of a car.

It is important to have a *qualified* driving instructor: do not ask a friend to give you lessons in her spare time. Good driving lessons are expensive especially if you fail to pass your test at the end of the programme. The

British School of Motoring (BSM) sets out to give each of its pupils the most professional grounding in the art of safe driving: their driving instructors helped launch the official driving test and were among the first driving examiners.

BSM's service includes an individually tailored course of instruction. They recommend when you should apply for a driving test (well in advance) – and this gives you an end objective. The best way to learn is to take two lessons per week planned all the way up to the driving test. BSM offers credit facilities to spread the cost to suit your personal budget. When you pass the test (with at least ten lessons) you may be entitled to a discount on your first year's car insurance premium.

For details of all BSM's services, contact your local branch or:

British School of Motoring
81–7 Hartfield Road
London sw19 3tj
01–540 8262

BEFORE WINTER COMES

(RAC recommendations)

● Make sure the battery is in good condition and fully charged: many of the items needed in difficult driving conditions (windscreen wipers, heater, etc.) are electrically operated.
● Check all tyres – including the spare. They should have a minimum of 1mm tread depth in a continuous band over at least three-quarters of the tread width and around the full circumference.
● Check strength of the antifreeze in the radiator. Make sure that you use the proportions of antifreeze and water as recommended by the car's manufacturer and do not use antifreeze containing alcohol.
● Put windscreen antifreeze (not engine antifreeze) in the windscreen-washer reservoir.

ADVERSE CONDITIONS

As the law requires, switch on dipped headlights in all unpleasant driving situations – fog, rain, mist and snow. Sidelights are hardly ever appropriate. Remember that *being seen* is at least as important as seeing and this is the main reason for headlights.

In really adverse conditions, it is a good idea to make sure that, as well as your 'usual accessories' (see above), you have the following in the car (not the boot):

● lantern torch with flashing dome
● red triangle
● waterproof clothing
● wellington boots
● sweater
● thick socks
● blanket
● shovel and hand tools
● a good ice-scraper
● can of spray de-icer
● length of rope.

Slippery roads

Heavy rain, falling leaves and snow make road surfaces dangerous. Stopping distances may be doubled or trebled. Directional stability of the car is threatened.

- To get moving on a slippery surface you may need a higher gear than usual to stop wheels spinning.
- To prevent skids, avoid sudden action of accelerator, brakes, gear change, steering wheel, clutch.
- Gentle braking takes a greater distance to stop the vehicle, so look well ahead and anticipate changes of speed.
- Wait until a hill is clear rather than risk being stopped half-way up when it may be impossible to restart. Select the gear to take you all the way up rather than risk losing speed with a gear change.
- Accelerate lightly when making a turn (anything more may cause skidding).
- On wet roads in very cold weather listen for the 'swish' of the tyres through the water. If it stops you are probably on black ice.

Fog   If you have special fog lights – there is no scientific evidence that yellow lenses increase visibility – they should be in pairs and will give the best illumination if focused about four metres ahead of the car. Fog lamps may be used only in fog and when snow is falling; and if the headlights are switched off, *both* fog lamps must be on. It is advisable also to fit a pair of rear fog lights which must not be wired so that they illuminate when the brakes are applied.

When driving in fog:
- Take extreme care. The fringe area of fog is always thin but it usually thickens rapidly, so slow down enough to allow for this beforehand.
- Keep to known routes if possible and, if you have a choice, turn only at traffic lights.
- Keep the driver's window open – sometimes danger can be heard before it is seen.
- Do not overtake.
- Drive within the limit of your lights: if you are in a built-up area street lights might dazzle, so lower the sun visor.

Notes
- Lead in all petrol available in Britain puts lead compounds into the atmosphere, whence they can reach the body by various means (breathing, via crops). A cumulative poison, lead is thought to be a cause of brain damage in young children. For further information, contact:

> Campaign against Lead in Petrol (CALIP)
> 68 Dora Road
> London SW 19 7MM
> (no telephone)

- If you misplace your driving licence, contact:

> Driver and Vehicle Licensing Centre
> Swansea
> SA99 1AA
> 0792-782341

You should also always inform the DVLC of any change of address so they can keep their records up to date.

● If you are stopped by police on a public highway, *for whatever reason*, and cannot produce the required documents, i.e. driving licences, insurance, etc., you will be given a form which will tell you what documents they need to see and five days in which to take them to the police station of your choice. If you fail to do this you will have committed the offence of failing to have the documents at the time you were stopped.

● Disabled drivers – see page 582.

Further Information

Suggested further reading

Department of Transport, *Driving*, HMSO

Hosken, M.J., *Sensible Driving: the Logical Basis of Everyday Motoring*, David & Charles

Jolly, Ken, *Driving Made Easy*, Penguin

Spencer, John, *Questions of Motoring Law*, Hamlyn

4 Cameras, Computers and Communications

Technology is *not* a dirty word – and it should not be offputting. This chapter is a simple guide to the technological advances that most of us are aware of and an indication of what is going to happen in the near future.

The Camera World

Suppose you ask a photographer what camera you should buy and you receive the reply, 'What you need is a nice SLR with TTL metering, automatic with aperture priority and manual override, standard, tele-photo and wide-angle lenses and preferably a macro zoom, and of course a dedicated flash with bounce and zoom ...' Is this just a mouthful of pretentious jargon? No. It is a sort of shorthand for describing the important features of cameras and their accessories. Even absolute beginners can take advantage of devices which a few years ago were technological wonders and which now are available for under £20 – if only they know how to ask for them.

Before you buy, therefore, read through the glossary of camera terms below.

TERMINOLOGY

Aperture – the size of the hole that lets the light through to reach the film, usually expressed as f4, f5.6, f8, etc. (the larger the number, the smaller the hole).

Aperture priority – a feature of some automatic cameras; the aperture is decided first and the shutter speed varies automatically to control the light.

Autofocus – Camera which measures the distance to the subject nearest it and focuses itself. Only recently widely available.

Automatic camera – one which measures the light reaching it from the subject and adjusts the exposure accordingly (not autofocus unless also so described).

Exposure – the amount of light reaching the film, which depends on both the aperture and the shutter speed (time).

Film speed – described by an ASA number (e.g. 64, 100, 400); the higher the number, the less light is needed to give a good picture.

Film types: *black and white* – for black-and-white prints; *colour negative* – for colour prints; *colour reversal* – for colour slides (transparencies).

Flash: *automatic* – when correctly set, should deliver the right amount of light to give a well-lit picture by detecting the light coming back from the subject and cutting itself off at the right time; *bounce* – a unit with a swivelling head so the flash can be reflected off a wall, for example, on to the subject; *dedicated* – made for a specific model of camera; *electronic* – emits a brief bright light, powered by a battery (rechargeable or ordinary) which does not use up bulbs; *zoom* – can be set for use with a variety of lens types.

Format – the size of the piece of film which the light reaches when you take a picture: it varies from 'tiny' (in the disc film) through '110' (1.1cm across), '35mm' (35mm long), '2¼' (2¼ins. square, favoured by many professionals) to many inches across in 'plate' cameras.

Instamatic – name given to a range of ordinary simple cameras.

Instant cameras – pioneered by Polaroid, these produce a finished print in seconds or minutes (not to be confused with Instamatic, above).

Lenses – many cameras, especially the more expensive ones, have inter-changeable lenses. The standard lens usually sold with the basic body of a camera can thus be replaced by: a *wide-angle* lens which includes more of the view around you in the picture, making it look further away and – beware! – sometimes more boring or sometimes more distorted; a *telephoto* lens which makes subjects look closer; a *zoom* lens, offering a continuous range of effects such as those above; a *macro* lens, which allows the camera to focus very close to the subject in order to fill a picture with a small object (e.g. a piece of jewellery).

Shutter speed (time) – controls, with aperture, the amount of light reaching the film.

SLR camera – Single Lens Reflex camera, usually 35mm, the most popular of the versatile, compact and more expensive cameras. When you look through the viewfinder, you are looking through the camera's own lens at the same picture that will fall on the film when you press the shutter.

TTL lightmeter – measurement of the light actually coming through the lens, thus affording a more exact method of getting the right exposure in both manual and automatic cameras.

BUYING
A CAMERA

There are various factors to be considered before even setting foot in a photographic shop. Individual requirements should not be allowed to be pushed to one side by an over-zealous sales assistant, and it is a good idea to know beforehand what you want.

These are some of the questions you should ask yourself:

1. Do you want the camera for:
- holidays and other special occasions?
- specific jobs (e.g. photographing jewellery?)
- general photographs?
- creative photography?

2. Bearing in mind that the larger the negative size the crisper the quality of the picture, do you want a camera that:
- produces miniature negatives (disc camera)?
- produces slightly larger negatives (pocketable oblong camera)?
- produces larger negatives (single lens reflex)?

3. How complicated a camera do you really want? Are you thinking of:
- an inexpensive 'point and shoot' model?
- a 'semi-intelligent' point and shoot model which may have automatic focus and automatic/semi-auto film loading and rewinding, etc.?
- an 'intelligent' camera which has a program to do it all for you, with the added facility of being able to control exposure time, focal length, and even to create special effects?

4. How often, in all honesty, will you carry the camera with you? Will it be:
- always in your pocket or handbag?
- rarely used, so that portability is not really a problem?
- used for specific occasions where camera accessories are required (e.g. lenses, flashguns, tripod etc.)?

5. Bearing in mind how much you plan to use the camera, are you prepared to pay:
- under £50?
- £50 to £100?
- over £100?

Remember that some cameras do not always come complete with lens; this and other accessories can add substantially to the price.

Armed with this basic but invaluable information you should look through a couple of specialist magazines (e.g. *Amateur Photographer* and *Camera Weekly*) to get an idea of what is available and what the price structuring is. You will find that there is not really much difference price-wise from one company to another and that you basically 'get the camera you pay for'. You should therefore go to a maker with a wide range of easy-through-advanced equipment (e.g. Canon, Minolta, Olympus, Pentax) and one that has good after-sales service.

TAKING BETTER PHOTO-GRAPHS

No camera, however automatic, is completely fool-proof and it can't in any case select the subject matter of your pictures. So if you are unhappy with your results, the faults could be technical or artistic – or both.

Do read the instruction book, even if you have had the camera for some time. It may actually make more sense to you after you have tried the camera and made some mistakes. With a new camera try practising without a film at first.

Here are some faults and their possible causes:

● *Fuzzy pictures* can result if you haven't focused to the correct distance, or if you haven't held the camera still while pressing the shutter. Practise keeping yourself and the camera steady when you squeeze the shutter button. In poor light you need longer times so look for a wall or chair to rest the camera on.

● *Strange colours* can result if the film is old or has been allowed to get very hot. Don't leave a camera or film in the hot sun on a beach or in a car. They can also be due to wrong exposure (see below) because although factory colour processing goes some way towards correcting exposure errors the colour may suffer.

● *Over-exposed* (too light) and *under-exposed* (too dark) final pictures – and vice versa if you are looking at the negatives – can be caused if:

(a) the film speed, ASA number, shown on the film box was not set correctly on the camera and on the flash unit if used.

(b) one of the batteries on which many cameras rely to run their exposure meters and other functions is flat or low. Use the battery check button occasionally if your camera has one.

(c) the time or aperture or both were wrongly set. On simpler cameras this would be a wrong setting of the sunny/cloudy switch.

● *All-black* final pictures (all-clear negatives) may mean:

(a) you sent an unused film to be processed

(b) the film was not properly loaded in the camera and never came out of its cassette

(c) the shutter did not open (faulty camera)

(d) in flash pictures, the flash setting on the camera (usually X for electronic flash, M, P or V for other kinds) was wrongly set or was knocked into the wrong position

(e) in older cameras, the lens cap may have been left on!

● *All-white*, or nearly, final pictures (all-dark or black negatives) mean that far too much light has reached the film. This can result from opening the camera with the film exposed to light, or from some older types of airport X-ray or, unusually, if the shutter is stuck open.

● *Flash pictures* can show special problems. People in such photographs often have chalk-white faces and red eyes. A 'bounce' flash correctly used can cure these effects. If you don't have one, another bright light in the room or the light from a window can help, or it may be possible with some cameras to mount the flash away from the camera.

On most cameras you need to set a slow speed to use flash, perhaps one-sixtieth of a second, or make a special time setting for flash. If you forget to do this you will probably get a black picture.

● *Flat, dull and uninteresting* photographs. Try:

(a) getting closer to the subject.

(b) having something in the foreground of a picture of distant scenery.

(c) avoiding the midday sun – go for early morning and the hour before sunset to get more interesting and richer colours.

(d) *not* to photograph people while they are facing the sun. Try having the sun over their shoulders and lighting their faces with flash. You can use flash outdoors to 'fill in' shadows.

(e) *not* to 'pose' people every time but take them when they are not looking. If children are too aware of the camera at first they will soon get used to it and stop concentrating on it, especially if they have something more interesting to do.

(f) looking for striking colours and interesting textures. You may want to get a close-up device. All but the simplest cameras can be fitted with some sort of attachment to enable you to take greatly magnified pictures.

● If you become really interested, join your local camera club.

The Computer World

TERMINOLOGY

UNDERSTANDING COMPUTERS

BUYING A COMPUTER

WORKING WITH YOUR
    COMPUTER

LOOKING AFTER YOUR
    COMPUTER

SHOPPING BY COMPUTER

From microwave ovens to video recorders to personal computers ... new technology is changing the way we work, the way we are entertained and, in short, the way we live. Computers or products run by them are showing up in the classroom, on store counters and in cars. Appliances of just one decade ago already have an old-fashioned look about them.

The technological advances being made today should be seen as one of the advantages of living in these times. Already 10 per cent of British households have invested in a computer for home use. They have decided that the way to control the technology revolution is not to fight it but, rather, to understand what is happening and the benefits computers might hold for them.

Tempted by the inexpensive equipment designed for the man and woman in the street, the British have been particularly keen on acquiring personal computers for home use. Britain, in fact, tops the world in per capita ownership of computers. The Economist Intelligence Unit's latest research report on the topic shows that computers are likely to be found in 50 per cent of households in the UK by 1987.

If you have not yet joined their ranks – or if your computer has been closeted away since shortly after its purchase – read this section carefully. First some computer terms are explained and then ('Understanding Computers') the fundamentals of a computer system are defined and suggestions are given so that you can gain from the new technology.

TERMINOLOGY   Do not be put off by the large number of specialized words and phrases – you will learn them as you need them. The manual that comes with the computer will explain all the terms you need to know, as well as describing how to use the machine.

Baud rate – the number of bits (see below) per second which the computer can transfer from one place to another via a telecommunications network.

Bit – basic unit of information storage in a computer, derived from 'binary digit'.

Byte – eight bits; the smallest unit of information with any real meaning, representing a number or character.

Chips – the building blocks of the computer: its 'brain' is a building block called the central processing unit (CPU) and each computer company has a different formula for its building block.

Computer – although technically this is only the CPU and chips connected to it, the term generally refers to the whole 'machine'.

Cursor – the moving pointer – perhaps a short horizontal line or a solid block – that tells you where you are 'working' at the moment.

Database management – allows you to organize information held in the computer.

Disk drive – although most home computers use tape recorders, some larger models and all business computers store and use information on plastic disks operated by a disk drive.

Floppy disk (diskette) – a flexible magnetic storage device like a small record in a sleeve (which is not removed).

Footprint – the space occupied by a computer or terminal on a desk or other flat surface.

Hardware – the mechanical, electronic and plastic physical construction of a computer.

Heads – as in record player terminology, these delicately balanced items in each disk drive 'read' the disks.

Input/output (i/o) – input is information you feed in; output is the information fed to you by the computer.

K – a measure of storage capacity (short for kilobyte): 1K equals 1,024 bytes.

Languages – systematic means of communication whereby humans can communicate with computers: Basic (Beginner's All-purpose Symbolic Instruction Code) is the most popular language for home computers.

Memory – the part of the computer which stores information.

Modem or modulator/demodulator – a facility that enables you to attach your computer to a telephone line for electronic data transmission.

Operating system – the program that co-ordinates the entire system (one of the most popular is Control Program for Microcomputers, CPM).

Program – list of instructions to the computer telling it how to execute a task. See also 'Software'.

Qwerty – typewriter layout (from the top left-hand row of letters) for most keyboards (in Germany Y and Z are transposed).

RAM (Random Access Memory) – part of the computer's memory reserved for filling by the user.

ROM (Read Only Memory) – computer's static knowledge base built into the machine.

Software (or programs) – the instructions by which a computer operates: *applications* software do the work; *systems* software keep the computer in check.

User-friendly – term used by marketing people to denote ease of use of equipment or programs by non-specialists.

VDU (Visual Display Unit) – the screen, i.e. TV set or monitor, used in conjunction with the computer.

UNDER-STANDING COMPUTERS

Hardware and software

Simply put, a home computer is a general purpose machine (hardware) whose tasks are defined by specific programs or sets of instructions (software). The hardware is to computing what a turntable is to record playing. Continuing the analogy, the software is like the records played on a hi-fi (although, unlike records, all software cannot be played on all computer models).

Because the available software determines what your computer can do, careful computer customers must take a good look at the software programs which are available for any particular computer before deciding which computer system to buy – hence the expression 'hardware sales are software led'.

Increasingly simplified software means that computers can now be used by those who have no knowledge of programming.

Nuts and bolts

The brain of a computer – including a mass of circuit chips and connections – will rarely be seen by the user (unless your interest grows to include the details of what makes it run). The brain is responsible for reading the software, directing the hardware and processing all results, whether it is your move in a game of chess or your tax reports.

The computer is accessed through a keyboard, usually in a very similar configuration to that of a standard typewriter. Computer keyboards vary cosmetically from the membrane type, which are flat and touch sensitive, to plastic moving keys. To make computers user-friendly, a number of computer keyboards list commands in English. This eliminates the need for some typing and saves time.

In order to know what you have typed into the computer and to see its response a video display terminal is essential. Depending on the model, the display unit can be a special dedicated monitor or a standard home television.

The system will also use a cassette recorder or a disk drive (see 'Storage' below); if it is to function as a word processor, it will need a printer as well.

All this may seem rather alarming, but if you already have a TV set and a tape recorder, you have all that is needed to operate a home computer, at least to start with. (Business computers are more sophisticated.)

Storage To carry out your planned applications on the computer, you will need to use pre-programmed software. This will be stored in one of three ways:

1. *Cassette tapes* – a cassette recorder is attached to the computer by special leads.

2. *Floppy disks* – very thin slices of plastic packaged in a sturdy sleeve, playable on a disk drive.

3. *ROM cartridges* – a more recent storage development which features speed in loading and needs only to be plugged into a porthole built into the computer itself or an attachable interface.

Personal computers Software for personal computers generally falls into three categories:

1. *Business* software can be used to manage a company or a household. The many spreadsheet programs available enable you, for example, to forecast what effect a rise or fall in one budget item will have on others.

2. *Educational* programs can work on anything from developing reading skills for five- to seven-year-olds to helping you brush up on foreign language phrases before a holiday abroad. More emphasis is now being placed on good quality educational software as the positive results of introducing young children to computers are assessed. In addition to holding children's attention, computers have infinite patience and their three-dimensional graphic capabilities can convey concepts quite clearly.

3. *Games* might be arcade style (Pac Man, for instance) or adventure types where the player must surmount obstacles to meet a goal or discover the solution to a riddle. Many popular board games such as scrabble and backgammon have also been programmed for computer play, offering a ready opponent at any time. One of the most popular games is flight simulation, which imitates a real-life situation and 'puts you in the cockpit'.

You can use your personal computer for the following:
- word processing
- preparing tax returns
- managing home finances
- monitoring lights, heating, appliances
- tutoring your children
- playing games
- communicating with larger information databases

If you think that a personal computer with the right software could serve a useful purpose in your household, the task of finding the right model arises. What should you look for?

BUYING
A COMPUTER

Before shopping it is important to determine your budget. Read computer magazines and get advice from anyone you know who has a computer or works with one. Get hold of a copy of *Which Micro?* (home computers) or *Which Computer?* (business micros) – see page 110.

Decide just how much hardware and software you will need to get started or to do what you want the computer to do. This will be your *system* (your minimum requirements): price all the alternatives which fulfil your system description. For example, will a small home computer with a cassette recorder and 5K of memory do, or will you need 64K plus with disk drives?

Ask yourself, too, if you want your computer to be portable – and do you want it to tie in with any existing equipment? You may also at this stage, or later, wish to purchase a printer in order to make hard copies (on paper) of your programs or other data: a printer will enable you to edit programs away from the computer and record data or send letters or reports.

Do not be intimidated by the staff at a computer store or counter – even if they seem to speak a foreign language. If you do not understand, say so.

Consider the *independent support system* for any model you are thinking of buying. This includes not only the hardware and software which is available, but also magazines, books and newsletters which cover the machine and user groups that bring people together to share their experiences and expertise.

Review the guarantees behind the computer you choose. These should include both a manufacturer's guarantee and a servicing guarantee. Who are the service company? Are they guaranteed by the manufacturing company? If they are not part of that company itself are they in a position to become uninterested/uninvolved at any time? Make sure there is good *local* support when (not if) something goes wrong: it is no good buying a machine if you live in Anglesey and you need to talk to someone in London every time the machine and you have 'language problems'.

LOOKING
AFTER YOUR
COMPUTER

Inevitably, things will go wrong.
● Try to keep your computer as clean as possible. Air-conditioning and heating have a particularly nasty habit of fouling up the heads of the disk drive. When the machine is not in use, whenever possible close the flaps over the (empty) disk drives and cover the whole machine (with plastic not cloth).
● You should clean your computer heads from time to time. This is a simple operation that takes only a few minutes: you need something like 'Safe-clene' (follow its clear instructions – you can buy it from a computer shop) and a set of 'Floppiclene' disks. If you use the machine regularly, get into the habit of cleaning both heads every ten days or so – if you leave it until the head announces it is dirty (whenever your monitor reads 'B/dos' or similar) you will lose whatever you were working on at that point.

**WORKING
WITH YOUR
COMPUTER**

A computer will do exactly what it is told but only when given specific instructions. You will find that computer languages are not interchangeable: you cannot start a program in one computer language and continue it in another. You cannot use a language which the computer does not recognize. It can only manipulate data and instructions which you input by using the instructions/rules which have been built into it or specifically defined (e.g. language cards). It will not be able to make any logical or independent assumptions or steps and therefore must receive clear and specific instructions to operate as required.

The computer manual will be your chief guidebook: refer to it continually.

As with any other relationship, if you put in enough time and communicate clearly you should soon understand each other. In this relationship, however, it must be you who rules the computer and not vice versa.

Help
- Take an evening class (ask your library or local education authority).
- Consider one of the classes run by *Cosmopolitan* magazine.
- Contact a member of the Federation of Microsystems Centres: you can get local addresses via:

> National Computing Centre
> Oxford Road
> Manchester MI 7ED
> 061–228 6333

- General information can be obtained from:

> Computing Service Association
> Hanover House
> 73–4 High Holborn
> London WCIV 6LE
> 01–405 3161

- Advice on buying a home computer can be found in *Which Micro?*, which lists the various models available according to price, together with such information as suitable use (home, education, business), amount of RAM and languages available.

Which Computer? guides the business user through the jungle of business micros, from the popular Apple II to the IBM PC, and features a regular business computer guide listing packages (computer plus applications software) and where to buy them.

The Communications World

THE POST OFFICE RADIO TELEPHONES

TELEVISION TELETEXT AND PRESTEL BUYING HOME ENTERTAINMENT

THE POST OFFICE

With certain exceptions, the Post Office has a monopoly over the delivery of letters but not of parcels. Neither class of letter delivery guarantees time of delivery. Braille or talking books and other articles for the blind can be posted free as long as no personal message is included. Letters – apart from those to the Queen or Members of Parliament or to Business Reply and Freepost addresses – must be pre-stamped or franked. Attempts to evade postage (by using old stamps) could make you liable for a maximum of twelve months' gaol. In principle first-class letters arrive more speedily than second class but this seems to depend on the routes.

Tips for speedy delivery

- Use envelopes of post office preferred (POP) size – not smaller than 90 × 140mm ($3\frac{1}{2}$ × $5\frac{1}{2}$ ins.) and not larger than 120 × 235mm ($4\frac{3}{4}$ × $9\frac{1}{4}$ ins.). Increasingly, mail is electronically sorted out but any envelope outside these sizes is diverted to one side and dealt with manually, which is slower.
- Write the name and address of the sender as legibly as possible on the back of the envelope.
- Use the postcode. Already it speeds up mail to some areas and increasingly it will speed up delivery nationwide. For a free booklet 'Using Postcodes in Business Systems' write to the Post Office's main headquarters, address below.

Compensation fee post gives compensation in the event of loss or damage.

Special services

Data-Post inland and international (services to Northern Ireland available only to contract holders): guaranteed overnight delivery at home and generally overseas. For details, ask the telephone operator for Freefone Data-Post.

Expresspost, a same-day courier service, is often used by banks, hospitals and other organizations. For details, ask for Freefone 2333.

Intelpost is facsimile transmission of documents and drawings to any point around the world. For details, ask for Freefone Intelpost.

Recorded delivery is useful if you want to make sure that a letter is received, as the recipient has to sign for delivery.

Registered letter service gives extra security and careful handling *en route* and compensation in the case of loss of damage.

Special delivery is often thought to get letters from one point to another more quickly: in fact if you are sending a letter from central Edinburgh to central London it might take longer by special delivery than by ordinary first-class mail.

For details of the above, see the Post Office's leaflet 'How to Send Things You Value through the Post'.)

Email (electronic mail or mailboxing) is being increasingly used by individuals and business. I can take my portable machine – a small computer and a modem which fits over any telephone – around the world with me and send messages back to my office. I have my own private 'mailbox' and those with similar access to the system can get through to me instantly.

I am working with Telecom Gold, operated in Britain by British Telecom International. Details from:

> Telecom Gold
> 60–68 St Thomas Street
> London SE1 3QU
> 01–403 6777

Complaints
- If a letter is lost or damaged you may be able to get compensation (up to £17.00) if you can prove that it was actually posted (you can get a certificate proving postage when you post anything over a post office counter).
- If you want to complain about a lost or damaged item ask at the post office for the form 'Inquiry about a Missing or Damaged Letter or Parcel' and send it, completed, to the local head postmaster. If you are dissatisfied with his reply refer it to the regional postal director.
- If you feel you have cause for complaint about another matter, you can contact your local post office advisory committee (ask your Citizens' Advice Bureau or look in the telephone directory) or:

Post Office Users' National Council
Waterloo Bridge House
Waterloo Road
London SE1 8UA
01–928 9458

Post Office Users' Council
for Northern Ireland
22 Great Victoria Street
Belfast BT2 7PU
0232–242240

Post Office Users' Council
for Scotland
Alhambra House
45 Waterloo Street
Glasgow G2 6AT
041–248 2855

Post Office Users' Council
for Wales
2 Park Grove
Cardiff CF1 3BN
0222–374028

The main headquarters of the Post Office are:

> 33 Grosvenor Place
> London SW1X 1PX
> 01–235 8000

RADIO Now, with so many local stations (BBC and independent) as well as the BBC's national radio programmes, the choice is wider than ever. If you don't have a receiver capable of giving you FM stereo you are missing the best sort of radio reception. It may be that you live in one of the areas that do not pick up a satisfactory signal, or that your home is in the 'shadow' of a hill. In these cases you will probably have to do with FM mono or the poorer quality of AM, but ask your local radio retailers what their experience is of the signal strength. For good VHF reception on fixed equipment such as hi-fi tuners and music centres, the BBC recommends the use of an outdoor aerial, particularly for stereo.

Tables of frequencies of FM stations in (MHz) and of frequencies (in kHz) and wavelengths of AM stations for all BBC national and local radio stations are found in the *Radio Times.*

● Radio suffers in that newspapers do not give full accounts of what programmes are available. If you are a keen BBC Radio listener, however, there are two weekly BBC publications to which you should turn:

1. *The Listener* contains transcriptions and discussions of what you might have heard. Details from:

> 35 Marylebone High Street
> London W 1 M 4 A A
> 01–580 5577

2. The *Radio Times* tells you what is available during the following week (address as above): make sure you buy the correct regional issue.

● BBC Local Radio provides a local news-and-information service around the country. The headquarters of BBC Local Radio is at:

> The Langham
> Portland Place
> London W1A 1 A A

● To find details of your nearest *independent radio* station, ask at the library or look in the telephone directory.

● Anyone who has ever spent any time overseas knows what accurate and marvellous information is provided by the *BBC World Service*. If you have a short-wave radio and do not mind unusual hours for listening you can pick up transmission in parts of Britain (the 5 a.m. news broadcast is the best means of finding out what is going on in the outside world).

The World Service is interested in information on new British products, processes and inventions. The address to write to is:

> BBC World Service
> Bush House
> Strand
> London WC2B 4PH
> 01–240 3456

● If you are interested in learning about how to become a *ham* (someone interested in amateur radio), contact:

Radio Society of Great Britain
Alma House
Cranbourne Road
Potters Bar
Herts EN6 3JW
0707–59015

● *Citizens' band* is becoming more popular. For information write to:

Citizens' Band Association
16 Church Road
St Mark's
Cheltenham
Glos GL5 1 7AN

● *Radios for the disabled* – see 'Disabilities', page 581.

TELEPHONES   Modern telephones now come in a wide range of styles and colours, and application of the microchip has brought great sophistication to a whole variety of facilities.

All new telephones are now fitted with a special 'jack plug' which slots into special sockets mounted on the wall; so you can change phones as often as you like, and move the instruments you have from room to room, wherever the sockets have been fitted. If you haven't already got the new type of sockets, British Telecom will install them for a small fee – get in touch with your local area telephone sales office.

Most phones can now be rented or bought. Of the British Telecom range the cheapest to buy is Slimtel – a one-piece phone that incorporates a memory that stores the last number called and re-dials it at the touch of a button. 'Top' of the range is the Sceptre 100, an advanced electronic press-button phone with a ten-number memory which can store frequently used numbers and dial them for you at the press of a single button. Sceptre's visual display acts as a 24-hour clock, and automatically times any call made. You can see these and other models at 'phone shops' thoughout Britain.

An answering machine can mind the telephone if you are out or too busy to answer it. These range from inexpensive 'answer only' units which do not record messages, to versatile machines which allow you to check messages no matter where you are by ringing up and using a remote-control 'bleeper'.

Notes   ● You can put a receiver down on an *incoming* call (from within Britain) or unplug the telephone and pick up another extension, or plug in again without cutting off the caller. The person who made the call is, of course, paying for all the 'waiting time' until you pick up again.

● *Telemessages* can be sent by telephone or telex up until 10.00 p.m. (7.00 p.m. Sundays and Bank Holidays) for delivery in a distinctive yellow envelope to anywhere in the UK the next working day. The service also operates to and from the USA. They are printed on headed notepaper, and can also be delivered in a range of 'special occasion' cards.

Making a call within the British Isles

● You can dial anywhere in the British Isles. Locally dialled and long distance calls have different codes for the same place. Look in the front of the relevant telephone directory or code book.

● It is obviously advisable to telephone at cheaper rate times if you possibly can. Avoid telephoning on Monday to Friday 8 a.m. to 1 p.m. Try to make all business calls after 1 p.m. and personal calls between 6 p.m. and 7 a.m. and any time over the weekend.

● By dialling direct you are charged by unit. If you make your call via the operator (dial 100) you are charged by three minutes or part thereof: if you want details of charges for operator-connected inland and overseas calls dial 100 and ask for Freefone 2500.

Making a call away from home

● The new style *blue payphones* being installed by British Telecom are generally much easier to use and get jammed far less often. You insert money before you dial the call and get any unused coins, but not change from partially used coins, back at the end. There is no 'beep beep' tone at the beginning of the call so the person to whom you are speaking need not know you are in a call box.

● You may be lucky enough to be able to use a *cardphone*. Special cards are required and are available from John Menzies and railway buffets.

● Amongst the many marvellous inventions making communicating so easy nowadays, British Telecom, Racal and other companies offer *car radiophones* and *radio paging* devices.

● If you are unable to force money into an unwilling old-style public callbox, you can *reverse charges* through the operator (which is expensive).

● Another way of avoiding using coins is to have a *telephone credit card* which gives you a special number. You can simply dial the operator and ask for your required number, quoting your telephone credit card number. One big advantage of this system is that you can call from anywhere any time, regardless of whether or not you are carrying any money. It also enables you to 'charge' a call if the calls from your home telephone number are paid for by someone else.

The main disadvantage is that this is an expensive way of making a call: each time you use the card you incur usual operator-assisted charges plus a 22p fee (25p if using a call box) and there is also a standard 50p rental per quarter.

Making a call overseas

● Check (from your telephone directory or operator) if you can dial direct. This is much less expensive than going via an operator.

● The cheap time is not the same as for inland calls. Expensive time is Monday to Friday 8 a.m. to 8 p.m.

● If you can dial direct from Britain dial:

010 + country code + area code (but omit the first zero) + number.

● Note that each country's exit dialling code is different. If you are

overseas and dialling back to Britain you need that country's exit code +
the British country code (44) + area code (but omit the first zero) +
number.

● Service 800 is an international 'reverse charges' and is especially
useful for business purposes. To find out more about service 800,
telephone 01–628 3751.

● International text transmission by telex often reaches its destination
almost instantly; the printout produced is admissible in a court of law.

Help   ● To help pay your telephone bill you can save with telephone stamps,
available in units of £1 and £5 from the post office. When the amount
of the bill is greater than the value of the stamps held, you must pay
the excess in cash or by cheque; if you are in profit the excess will be
returned as stamps on a new card. (However, it is probably more sensible
to save the money in a way that earns interest.)

● If you want to complain about any telephone matter, contact your
local British Telecom area office. (Look in the front of your telephone
directory for the relevant Freefone numbers.) They will let you have a
copy of British Telecom's code of practice, which gives details about the
complaints procedure. Most problems are sorted out at the local level but
they can be taken to an independent complaints panel or even to
arbitration.

The headquarters of British Telecom is at:

> 81 Newgate Street
> London EC I A 7 A J
> 01–356 5000

TELEVISION
BBC

The British Broadcasting Corporation (BBC) is an enormous and complex
organization with tremendous power. It controls television and radio
services (including the foreign-beamed World Service), transmits Open
University and schools' educational programmes and it has its own
publications.

The main headquarters is:

> British Broadcasting Corporation
> Broadcasting House
> Portland Place
> London W I A I A A
> 01–580 4468

Regional headquarters (all addresses should be preceeded by 'BBC, Broadcasting House'):

> *Northern Ireland*
> 25–7 Ormeau Avenue
> Belfast BT2 8HQ
> 0232–244400

Scotland
Queen Margaret Drive
Glasgow GI2 8DG
041–339 8844

Wales
Llantrisant Road
Llandaff
Cardiff CF5 2YQ
0222–564888

● If you want to be in an *audience* send a list of preferred programmes and dates and number of tickets wanted (and s.a.e.) to:

BBC Ticket Unit
London WIA 4WW

● If you want to query your reception or another *technical* matter contact Engineering Information at the Portland Place address above.
● If you want to comment and/or congratulate somebody or something write to the head of programme correspondence at Portland Place.
● If you want to send in *scripts or ideas*, have them clearly typed on one side of the paper and send them:
(a) to the scripts editor, drama (radio) or the scripts editor, light entertainment (radio) at Portland Place.
(b) to the head of television script unit at:

BBC Television Centre
Wood Lane
London WI2 7RJ

● If you want to know more about BBC *publications* – which are often extremely good value, send s.a.e. to:

BBC Publications
PO Box 234
London SEI 3TH

● For the Open University – see Chapter 10.

ITV   Independent television consists of individual companies serving their own regions. Five of these companies produce programmes which are networked, that is, transmitted to other regions. Main contact points of these companies (telephone numbers only) are:

Anglia Television
(Norwich)   0603–615151

Border Television
(Carlisle)   0228–25101

Central Independent
Television (Birmingham)   021–643 9898

Channel Television
(St Helier)   0534–73999

Grampian Television
(Aberdeen)   0224–646464

Granada Television
(Manchester)   061–832 7211

HTV Wales
(Cardiff)   0222–590590

Scottish Television
(Glasgow)   041–332 9999

Television South (TVS)
(Southampton)   0703–34211

Television South-West (TSW)
(Plymouth)   0752–663322

Thames Television
(London)   01–387 9494

Tyne Tees
Television (TTTV)
(Newcastle upon Tyne)   0632–610181

Ulster Television
(Belfast)   0232–228122

Yorkshire Television
(Leeds)   0532–438283

and

Channel 4 Television
(London)   01–631 4444

London Weekend
Television (London)   01–261 3434

TV-am
(London)   01–267 4300

● You can find out what is going to be on your screen by looking at the relevant regional edition of *TV Times*, published weekly by:

> Independent Television Publications
> 247 Tottenham Court Road
> London WIP OAU
> 01–636 3666

● If you want to submit scripts to independent television, send them direct to a company (not to the Independent Broadcasting Authority).

Complaints ● If you have any complaints about explicit sex or violence, etc., shown on television, contact:

National Viewers' and Listeners' Association
Ardleigh
Colchester
Essex CO7 7RH
0206–230123

● If you have any complaints about ITV, either contact the local station concerned or write to:

Complaint IBA
The Director of Television at IBA
Independent Broadcasting Authority
70 Brompton Road
London SW3 1EY
01–584 7011

● If you have any complaints about Channel 4, either write to the Independent Broadcasting Authority (above) or to:

Channel 4
60 Charlotte Street
London W1P 2AX
01–631 4444

● If you are unhappy with the working or servicing of your television (or radio), the relevant trade association is:

Radio, Electrical and Television Retailers' Association (RETRA)
57–61 Newington Causeway
London SE1 6BG
01–403 1463

TELETEXT
AND PRESTEL

Teletext broadcasts written information on the television screen. You need a set that's designed to receive teletext, but watching it is free. You summon the appropriate 'page' by keying in on a remote-control keypad.

BBC's teletext (on BBC1 and BBC2) is called Ceefax: the teletext on ITV and Channel 4 is Oracle. Both offer continuous items on everything from current news to recipes.

Because teletext is visual it is especially useful for those who are hard of hearing. For further information on such special services contact:

Royal National Institute for the Deaf
105 Gower Street
London WC1E 6AH
01–387 8033

Oracle Teletext
Craven House
25–32 Marshall Street
London W1V 1LL
01–434 3121

Ceefax
Room 7059
BBC Television Centre
Wood Lane
London W12 7RJ

British Telecom's viewdata service is called Prestel. The display is on your television screen, but the information is relayed via the telephone line. You pay for the 'call' and, in many cases, a fee to those supplying that information. Prestel relays news and other material to you but you can also 'talk' to it via a remote-control keypad. You can use it for shopping from home, for instance, or for paying bills.

● For information, dial the operator (100) and ask for Freefone Prestel Sales.

Homelink   With Homelink – a joint venture of the Bank of Scotland and Nottingham Building Society – you can use your own television set to shop, pay bills, see your bank account, transfer funds between bank and building society, make travel reservations, take part in auctions and play games.

You are given a small console called a 'home deck' that is plugged into the aerial socket of your television set. For many subscribers this is provided free of charge. When you press buttons on your console the signals go through your television set, down your telephone line, into a national network of computers – and back to you in the same way. There are many different security procedures which mean that your records are 'safe' from infiltrators.

To find out more, contact any branch of the Nottingham Building Society or contact:

Homelink
Nottingham House
5–13 Upper Parliament Street
Nottingham NG1 2BX
0602–419393

BUYING HOME ENTERTAINMENT   Television is almost taken for granted today.

When buying you should ask yourself:
● Do I want a fixed or portable set?
● Do I want remote control?
● Do I need a set that will take Homelink or one of the other communications systems?

Television

Video   A video cassette recorder (VCR) enables you to do the Saturday afternoon grocery shopping while recording the England v. Scotland match so that you can watch it at your leisure. It also enables you to record that match watching *Jamaica Inn* on another channel. And, if you have a portable video camera, it enables you to make 'films' with sound and show them when you want, via your television screen. You can also buy or rent commercially recorded video-tapes of films and other material.

Perhaps somewhat surprisingly, many people who have videos find they watch less rather than more television. Having the power to choose what you are going to watch means that you record only things which really interest you.

If you are thinking of buying a video cassette recorder, specific features to bear in mind include:

● If you want to make your own 'films', you need a system with a camera. Make sure that it and the power pack are easily portable.

● Increasingly, today, most systems use V H S format: if you buy Beta format (e.g. Sony) you may not be so readily able to borrow tapes from friends.

Recorded music Most of us want to listen to music of one kind or another. We may be happy with reasonably good reproduction at an economic price, in which case a 'music centre' is probably the best buy. Some of us aspire to greater and greater faithfulness of sound reproduction and want to build up a high-fidelity (hi-fi) system, at much greater expense. And on to the market in the last few years has come the revolutionary 'compact disc' which, allied to digital recording, has set new standards in realism as well as hiss- and crackle-free reproduction.

Music centres. From £100 upwards, music centres comprise a package of FM stereo and AM radio, cassette tape player and record player. The loudspeakers ('speakers') are included and are best set away from each other to enable the stereo effect to be heard. Apart from the speakers, the components may come in one unit or a stacking set of separate units.

Hi-fi. Those in search of perfect sound from records or tapes are probably never going to be satisfied but, for the enthusiast, the quest is the thing and gives enormous pleasure to those who undertake it. A hi-fi system includes a tuner and amplifier, record deck and tape deck, as well as speakers. Any one of these parts can cost hundreds of pounds, so before embarking on the purchase of a hi-fi system you should take plenty of expert advice, though you may find it conflicting. The magazine *What Hi-Fi?* will give you an idea of the choices and prices available.

Compact discs. Many of the drawbacks of conventional records and tapes have been overcome with the advent of a small (about 5 ins. or 12 cm) disc which is played without the familiar needle; it uses a laser beam to track over the surface. Thus it cannot wear and should be free from unwanted surface noise. CDs are one-sided and contain up to seventy minutes of playing time. Special equipment is needed to play them, costing from less than £200 to over £1,000; in addition to which good speakers are obviously desirable to take advantage of the quality of recording. The discs themselves cost about £10, and the players can offer a variety of pre-programmable options, for example picking out certain tracks from an album.

Further Information

Suggested
further reading

CAMERAS

Busselle, Michael, *A Pocket Guide to Photography*, Octopus

Calder, Julian and John Garrett, *The 35mm Photographer's Handbook*, Pan

COMPUTERS AND COMMUNICATIONS

Chandor, Anthony, *The Penguin Dictionary of Microprocessors*, Penguin

Consumers' Association, *The Which? Guide to Hi-fi*
The Which? Home Computer, Video and Audio Guide

Fox, Barry, Richard Maybury and Tim Smith, *A Pocket Guide to Video*, Octopus

Graham, John, *The Penguin Dictionary of Telecommunications*, Penguin

Huws, Ursula, *Your Job in the Eighties: A Woman's Guide to the New Technology*, Pluto Press

Laferty, Peter, *Introduction to Computing*, Windward

There are many paperback guides to home computers, each dealing with a particular model of computer.

5 Some of Your Rights

LEGAL INFORMATION
CONSUMER INFORMATION

FURTHER INFORMATION

The more you know about the law, the more you know your rights and what you can and cannot do. The legal rights of the consumer are of vital importance to everyone.

As a result of compiling this information I have learned, for instance, from the Office of Fair Trading (one of the many organizations whom I have to thank for help with this chapter), what to do with unsolicited catalogues or Christmas stickers sent through the post, and to whom to complain if a new dress comes to pieces at the first wearing.

This chapter is backed up by some other rights included elsewhere in the book: you can find what you need to know by looking in the index. Rights relating to marriage, separation, divorce, widowhood, old age and death, for instance, are covered in Chapter 7 (Lifecycle) and your rights at work are in Chapter 11 (Your Job). Main financial rights are in Chapter 1 (Your Money) but entitlements for child and mother are in Chapter 9 (Your Child), your rights regarding property and cars are, similarly, in Chapter 2 (Your Property) and Chapter 3 (Your Car). Depending on the issue, you might alternatively find what you want in Chapter 10 (A Guide to Education) or Chapter 17 (Travel).

Legal Information

TERMINOLOGY

REGIONAL DIFFERENCES

First, you need to know what legal people are talking about:

TERMINOLOGY

Civil law – protects one individual from another. If you buy faulty goods from a shop and the trader refuses to satisfy you, civil law enables you, the unhappy purchaser, to sue in the courts (see 'Sale of Goods Act' below).

Common law – not legalized by an Act of Parliament, but something which has been built up on court cases over the years (e.g. the provision of services 'in a proper and workmanlike manner').

County courts – where disputes between citizens (with no crime involved) are heard, before a judge.

Criminal law – this discourages behaviour which can harm the country as a whole (e.g. drunkenness or theft). A prosecution is brought by the police. Deliberate fraud, sharp practice and selling bad food are criminal acts (see 'Trade Descriptions Act' below); so are careless driving and parking offences.

High Court – all major non-criminal cases are heard by one of the three High Courts, Chancery, Family or Queen's Bench, which have jurisdiction over what goes on in magistrates' courts. If it sits on cases referred from a magistrates' court, the High Court temporarily becomes the *Divisional Court.*

Magistrates' courts – more than 98 per cent of all criminal cases are heard in such courts. They deal with the less serious criminal cases, some domestic matters and – outside London – licensing applications. Specially chosen magistrates deal with juvenile offenders.

Statutory law – any law contained in Acts of Parliament (e.g. Trade Descriptions Acts, which are criminal, and Sale of Goods Act, which is civil).

REGIONAL
DIFFERENCES

Law in the UK is both diverse and complicated. England and Wales are governed by the same Acts of Parliament. Sometimes Acts cover Scotland as well (e.g. Sale of Goods Act); sometimes there are separate sections within an Act (Unfair Contract Terms Act) and sometimes there is a separate Scottish Act (Food and Drugs [Scotland] Act).

Scottish differences. Instead of magistrates' courts there are sheriff courts for both criminal and civil cases. Important civil cases go to the Court of Session: important criminal cases to the High Court of Justiciary and minor criminal cases to the district courts. 'Barristers' are known as 'advocates' and 'maintenance' is called 'aliment'.

Help

If you want – or need – to know more about a matter of law, you can contact a solicitor or go to your Citizens' Advice Bureau.

Rights for Women offer free legal advice sessions:

> Rights for Women
> 374 Grays Inn Road
> London WC1X 8BB
> 01-278 6349

The organization Release has a twenty-four-hour nationwide service to help with urgent problems: phone 01-603 8654

The Citizens' Advice Bureau offers free confidential advice and help on all problems including consumer affairs, education, employment, family matters, health services, housing and legal services. You can get help with filling out your income tax and if you need a solicitor for any reason that, too, can be arranged.

To find your nearest Citizens' Advice Bureau look in the main telephone directory (telephone beforehand to see when they are open). The national headquarters is at:

> National Association of Citizens' Advice Bureaux
> 110 Drury Lane
> London WC2B 5SW
> 01-836 9231

or

Edinburgh 031–557–1500
Belfast 0232–43986

● You can also contact (s.a.e.):

Legal Action Group
28a Highgate Road
London NW5 1NS
01–485 1189

● If you are accused of shoplifting, moral support and practical advice can be obtained from:

Crisis Counselling for Alleged Shoplifters (CCAS)
c/o NCPC
London NW4 4NY
01–202 5787

● If you want to know what magistrates do – or if you would like to become one – contact (s.a.e.):

Magistrates' Association
28 Fitzroy Square
London W1P 6DD
01–387 2302

See   'Justices of the Peace: How They Are Appointed and What They Do', from the Magistrates' Association.

Consumer Information

ADVERTISING AND SALES
  PROMOTION
CODES OF PRACTICE
COMPLAINTS
THE CONSUMER
DELIVERY OF GOODS
DEPOSITS
DOORSTEP AND HOSTESS
  SELLING
EQUALITY
ESTIMATES AND QUOTATIONS
EUROPEAN ECONOMIC
  COMMUNITY
FOOD AND DRUGS ACT
GUARANTEES
INDUSTRIAL TRIBUNALS

LOCAL GOVERNMENT
MAIL ORDER
MANUFACTURER'S LIABILITY
MARKET RESEARCH
NEIGHBOURS
THE OMBUDSMAN
PRICES
RECOMMENDED RETAIL PRICES
REFUNDS
SALE ITEMS
SALE OF GOODS ACT
SECOND-HAND GOODS
SERVICES
SEX DISCRIMINATION
SEXUAL HARASSMENT
SHOPPING

STANDARDS
TRADE DESCRIPTIONS ACTS
TRADING STAMPS

TRADING STANDARDS OFFICER
UNSOLICITED GOODS ACT
WEIGHTS AND MEASURES ACTS

ADVERTISING AND SALES PROMOTION

Advertising is controlled by the following different codes of practice:
● *The British Code of Advertising Practice* covers everything but radio and television advertising. Advertisements should be decent, honest, legal and truthful. Some advertising (e.g. alcohol, medical and slimming products, smoking) is strictly controlled.
● *The British Code of Sales Promotion Practice* controls the use of children in promotion, and what is and should be meant by all those 'free prizes' or 'reduced offers'.
● If you are not happy with advertising or sales promotions coming under the above codes of practice, contact:

Advertising Standards Authority (ASA)
2–16 Torrington Place
London WC1E 7HN
01–580 5555

● Radio and television advertising fall under the control of the Independent Broadcasting Authority (IBA). Their code pays particular attention to alcohol and health and strictly governs the use of children and noise and fear. If you think you have cause for complaint contact:

Independent Broadcasting Authority
70 Brompton Road
London SW3 1EY
01–584 7011

CODES OF PRACTICE

These are rules for members of an association to follow. Some codes (but not all) have the approval of the Office of Fair Trading. There are codes for the suppliers of goods and of services. All codes provide a redress procedure when you are dissatisfied which is often faster and more satisfactory than going to a solicitor or to court. Leaflets explaining the main codes are available from:

Office of Fair Trading
Field House
Bream's Buildings
London EC4 1PR
01–242 2858

To show he supports his code of practice a trader usually displays his association's symbol on his premises and on printed material. Before coming to an arrangement on such diverse things as, for instance, double-glazing, dry-cleaning, electrical repairs, funerals and photography, check that the supplier adheres to his association's code of practice.
● If you have cause for complaint, contact the relevant headquarters

of the association to which the purveyor belongs. If you still are dissatisfied you could contact the trading standards officer.

COMPLAINTS

● If you have *bought* something that you are not happy with, stop using it and take it back to the shop (if you can) as soon as possible. Take a receipt or proof of purchase if you have one but if you do not, do not worry – the trader does not require you to have a receipt. Ask to see the person in charge. If you are not satisfied with the outcome, go to the Citizens' Advice Bureau or a consumer advice centre or contact your local trading standards officer.

You might decide to take the matter to court.

(a) England and Wales: Small Claims at the county court. Get a copy of 'Small Claims and the County Court' from your CAB.

(b) Northern Ireland: county court. Get a copy of 'Small Claims – the New Procedure in Northern Ireland' from your CAB. If you lose the case there will normally be no costs involved other than initial fees.

(c) Scotland: Scottish Summary Cause in the sheriff courts. Consult your CAB before starting such a case.

Note

● If more than the amount covered by small claims procedures is involved, it is generally advisable to see a solicitor before thinking of any court cases.

● If you have a *hygiene* complaint report the matter without delay to the environmental health officer at your local council.

● In the case of a *nationalized industry* there is always a special consumer or consultative committee, addresses from the telephone directory or CAB.

● If you have a complaint against any item in a newspaper or magazine, regardless of whether or not it concerns you, first write directly to the editor. For complaints about television programmes, see pages 118–19.

If you are not happy with the editor's response, write to the Press Council enclosing a copy of the relevant offending item (you must lodge your complaint within three months of its publication). Contact:

The Press Council
1 Salisbury Square
London EC4Y 8AE
01–353 1248

THE
CONSUMER

● The *Consumer Credit Act 1974* means that most businesses which offer hire or credit must be licensed by the Office of Fair Trading. If you feel you have been unfairly treated in some way, contact your area trading standards officer. Courts have the power to reopen credit agreements which they consider extortionate.

● The *Consumer Safety Act 1978* enables the Secretary of State for Corporate and Consumer Affairs to require goods to be labelled with, for instance, warning symbols, instructions for use or lists of ingredients. He can also quickly ban the sale of dangerous goods.

● Earlier Acts relate to the reduction of the risk of death or personal injury (e.g. safety of domestic heating items, children's nightdresses, etc.).

Note   ● It is a criminal offence to sell items new or second-hand which do not comply with the regulations.

Associations   ● If you want to know what is going on and to have access to independent testing of a whole variety of products, subscribe to *Which?*, the monthly magazine of the Consumers' Association.

Details of *Which?*, and its related publications, from (s.a.e.):

> Consumers' Association
> 14 Buckingham Street
> London WC2N 6DS
> 01–839 1222

● The *National Consumer Council*'s job is to persuade the government to change its policies or introduce new ones to better the lot of consumers. It also induces public services to give better value for money and to be more responsive to the needs of users. Their publications list includes such useful work as 'New Rights for Tenants' and 'Getting Around: the Barriers to Access for Disabled People'. Full list of publications from (s.a.e.):

> National Consumer Council
> 18 Queen Anne's Gate
> London SW1H 9AA
> 01–222 9501

> Northern Ireland Consumer Council
> 176 Newtownbreda Road
> Belfast BT8 4QS
> 0232–647151

> Scottish Consumer Council
> 314 St Vincent Street
> Glasgow G3 8XW
> 041–226 5261

> Welsh Consumer Council
> Oxford House
> Hills Street
> Cardiff CF1 2DR
> 0222–396056

● If you want to join a local *voluntary consumer group* (or to get details of starting one) contact:

> National Federation of Consumer Groups
> 12 Mosley Street
> Newcastle upon Tyne NE1 1DE
> 0632–618259

DELIVERY OF GOODS

Sometimes when goods are sent to you by, say, a delivery company, you are asked to sign a receipt of delivery note that is also a statement of satisfaction. Unless you have actually examined the goods and found them to your liking, it is a good idea to sign that the goods have been received but that you have not yet had time to check them.

DEPOSITS

A deposit – which reserves goods or services – is legally binding. If you change your mind the trader could be entitled to keep your deposit – he could even sue you for up to the full amount of the goods or work and, sometimes, for compensation for other work turned away.

DOORSTEP AND HOSTESS SELLING

'Direct selling' covers both items sold at Tupperware parties and by unsolicited 'doorstep' sales.

If you are invited to a Tupperware-type party the hostess should make clear to all guests the nature of the event. All sales leaflets must show the company's name and address. If you order any items, you have two weeks in which to change your mind and get full deposit refund – assuming that the firm adheres to the relevant code of practice.

Unsolicited salespeople should carry identification cards. If you are uneasy about someone, ask to see their card and remember the number, which you can later relay to the Direct Selling Association (this applies also to telephone sales, in which case ask for the number of their card).

● If you are not happy with any direct selling experience contact:

> Direct Selling Association
> 44 Russell Square
> London WC1P 4JP
> 01–580 8433

EQUALITY

The *Equal Pay Act 1970* determines that a woman doing the same job as a man is entitled to equal pay. If you think you have cause for complaint you should take it to an industrial tribunal (see below).

The *Equal Opportunities Commission* (EOC) was established in 1975 to monitor the Equal Pay Act and the Sex Discrimination Act (see below).

The EOC will send literature and give advice on how to take your case to an industrial tribunal or court. They will send you a form to fill in with details of your complaint. They can assist you with the initial stages of your case and can give full financial backing.

You can contact the main office of the EOC at:

Overseas House
Quay Street
Manchester M3 3NH
 061–833 9244
or
Chamber of Commerce House
22 Great Victoria Street
Belfast BT2 2BA
 0232–242752

Caerwys House
Windsor Place
Cardiff CF1 1LB
 0222–43552

249 West George Street
Glasgow G2 4QE
 041–226 4591

ESTIMATES
AND
QUOTATIONS

An *estimate* is what someone suggests a service might cost but he does not have to stick to it: a *quotation* is a price given to which the supplier must stick.

Most suppliers (e.g. car repair people) find it difficult to assess beforehand exactly what a complex job will cost. They prefer to quote a basic sum with a rider that this does not include anything else they might discover while doing the job.

You should always ask for an estimate or quotation to be put in writing, properly itemized. If you accept an estimate, make sure that it is agreed in writing that the supplier has to ask your permission to exceed a certain sum. You should also, where relevant, insert a completion date into the contract.

EUROPEAN
ECONOMIC
COMMUNITY
(EEC)

Clear concise details of how the EEC affects you are set out in the *Reader's Digest* book mentioned at the end of this chapter.

Some points of interest to a British citizen include:
● You should be able to travel within the EEC with only an identity card, but since Britain does not issue these you will either need a full or visitor's passport or, for a cross-Channel shopping trip, a temporary identity card (see your travel agent).
● You can live and work in another EEC country without a work permit but you must have a valid full passport endorsed with the words 'Holder has the right of abode in the United Kingdom'. Once abroad, you should register with the local police. For your social security and pension rights see DHSS leaflet SA29.

FOOD AND
DRUGS ACT

Under this 1955 Act it is illegal to sell food that proves unfit for human consumption, to describe food falsely, to mislead people about a food's nature, quality (including nutritional value) or to interfere with a food or drink by adding or removing any substance that might make it injurious to health.

All pre-packaged foods must be labelled with a complete list of ingredients (including water if more than 5 per cent), in descending order of weight. They must have a date mark of some kind or another, e.g. 'Best before ...' or 'Sell by ...'.

Premises and sales staff must be and must look clean (cut fingers, for instance, should be covered).
● If you think you have cause for complaint take the offending item as soon as possible to the environmental health officer at your local council (in Northern Ireland, the district council; in Scotland, the Environmental Health Department of the district council).

GUARANTEES

A guarantee is the manufacturer's warranty. When you buy something check the guarantee carefully.
● It would be worthwhile signing it if, for instance, a replacement television set is offered for the next five years.
● Read carefully to see if you would be liable for labour costs or postage.
● If the guarantee offers satisfaction only for, say, the next six months

you would be better off not signing the guarantee but complaining, if necessary, to the seller.

- Some services (e.g. woodworm treatment) may also offer guarantees.
- If you do sign and send off a guarantee, keep your part carefully together with proof of purchase (e.g. credit card slip) and date.
- Regardless of whether or not you signed a guarantee, the negligent manufacturer of an item is liable for unsafe goods (see 'Manufacturer's Liability').
- Remember too that under the Sale of Goods Act it is the *seller* who is responsible for the goods – even if you have signed a manufacturer's guarantee. While the guarantee may be helpful, you still have full protection under the Act irrespective of whether you signed the guarantee or not.

INDUSTRIAL TRIBUNALS

An industrial tribunal can hear such cases as those of maternity pay, racial and sexual discrimination and unfair dismissal. For a detailed list of the working of the tribunals and what their jurisdiction covers, see the *Reader's Digest* book mentioned at the end of this chapter.

If you think you have cause to approach an industrial tribunal you should go, as soon as possible, to your union or to a Citizens' Advice Bureau or Jobcentre to get the relevant application forms.

LOCAL GOVERNMENT

If you think you have been unjustly treated by a council or water authority you can approach the local ombudsman (see 'Ombudsman').

MAIL ORDER
Notes

- When you order from a brochure or catalogue which says 'subject to price fluctuations' (or similar) you are bound to pay the current price.
- If you are sent something unsolicited through the post – a mail order catalogue or a book from a book club – such items become your property
(a) after six months if the sender has made no effort to come and collect them
(b) or thirty days after you have contacted the sender and he has made no effort to come and collect them.

1. All the big mail order *catalogue* companies are members of an organization whose code of practice provides for prompt delivery dates, return of unwanted or faulty goods and for customer service.
- If you have any cause for complaint contact:

> Mail Order Traders' Association
>   of Great Britain (MOTA)
> 25 Castle Street
> Liverpool L2 4TD
> 051–227 4181

2. If you are unhappy with mail order *book clubs*, contact:

> Mail Order Publishing Association
> 1 New Burlington Street
> London W1X 1FD
> 01–437 0706

3. If you send away for something through a *newspaper or magazine* you should be able to get compensation from the publication if it takes part in the 'Mail Order Protection Scheme'.

Always keep a careful note of what you sent off for, when, to whom, how much you sent and where you saw the advertisement. Remember that 'allow two weeks for delivery' invariably means 'allow a minimum of six weeks': if you want the goods only within a specific period you should write clearly on the coupon or order form 'Delivery by ... is essential' and initial it.

● If you have not heard anything from the supplier, at least twenty-eight days after you sent your money off (and within two months of that date) send the publisher of the publication concerned a clear letter (preferably typed) telling him what you ordered, from whom and when and with what payment.

4. If you do not want to receive unsolicited mail you can apply to have your name and address deleted from the lists circulating within the direct mail industry by writing to:

Mailing Preference Services
Freepost 22
London WIE 7EZ

MANUFAC-
TURER'S
LIABILITY

● Although the retailer is responsible for compensating the consumer for faulty goods, if you have been injured or your property damaged the manufacturer may be liable.
● It does not matter if the injured party was not the purchaser of the faulty item.
● It makes no difference whether or not the purchaser signed the item's guarantee.

MARKET
RESEARCH

It is infuriating to discover that someone with a clipboard 'finding something out' is really a doorstep salesman. Unsolicited telephone calls can also be a nuisance.

The Market Research Society suggests that you should always ask to see the authorized identity card of such intruders. Similarly, ask a telephone caller what his card number is. If there is any problem, contact the Market Research Society:

15 Belgrave Square
London SWIX 8PF
01–235 4709

NEIGHBOURS

Sometimes 'neighbourliness' can go wrong. Here are a few problems that may arise.
● *Who owns what?* Disputes over boundaries do occur. If you think you have cause for complaint:
(a) Establish your rights. If you *know* you own the small strip of grass in front of your house and the next door one, park your car on it.

(b) As a rule of thumb, the person who 'owns' a fence is the one who lives on the side of the fence posts. (*Note*: in Scotland, fences are usually mutual.)

(c) Check the deeds or lease – if your property is mortgaged write to the deeds administration department at the head office of your building society and ask to see your deeds.

● *Trespass*. Anyone who comes into or on to your property without your permission is trespassing and you are entitled to ask them to leave. In a serious matter you would take legal action in the civil courts asking for an injunction or compensation (this is not 'prosecution').

Note: there is no law of trespass in Scotland and if you wish to prevent people using your land you must apply for an interdict (injunction).

● *Continued annoyance*. Many people have rowdy parties or visitors from time to time and even the most placid dog occasionally has to bark. If the matter continues, try at all costs to avoid taking legal action: if you do, you might get compensation but more possibly an injunction (or interdict) prohibiting the neighbours from continuing with the annoyance. (See also 'Noise Control', page 448.)

In the case of a barking dog, a possible remedy is to throw a bucket of water over it – but do wait until the owner is out of the way.

THE OMBUDSMAN

An ombudsman (from the Swedish word for agent or representative) is a watchdog. If you have a complaint about the administration of a health authority, local council or central government department and you cannot get satisfaction after complaining to them, you can ask an ombudsman to help you.

Health Ombudsman. If you feel that you have been let down by any part of the National Health Service or that you have been treated unjustly (e.g. delays in admission or wrongful detention in psychiatric hospitals) you can follow this procedure:

● Complain first to the relevant health authority (ask the local community health council or, in Scotland, the local health council for the address and ask for help with your letter).

If you are not satisfied with the health authority's reply, write direct to the Health Ombudsman, whose office is:

Church House
Great Smith Street
London SWIP 3BW
01–212 7676

Insurance Ombudsman. If you have a difficult dispute with your insurance company, the Insurance Ombudsman can try to settle it (but *only* if the insurance company is in the Insurance Ombudsman scheme: ask the company, your broker or a Citizens' Advice Bureau).

If you feel you have cause for complaint you should:

(a) Write to the manager of the branch or office that issued your policy and explain why you think you have been unfairly treated.

(b) If you are still dissatisfied, write to the chief executive of the company at its head office (the address is on your policy).

(c) If you continue to be dissatisfied you can either take legal action or contact the Insurance Ombudsman: if in doubt, see your broker, a solicitor or your CAB and note that the ombudsman cannot deal with a dispute while it is subject to legal proceedings.

(d) To contact the Insurance Ombudsman you must write or telephone within six months of the date when the company gives you its final decision on your dispute:

> Insurance Ombudsman Bureau
> 31 Southampton Row
> London WCIB 5HJ
> 01–242 8613

Local Ombudsman. He can investigate complaints that injustice has been caused by a fault in the way that something has been done (or not done) by a local council or water authority.

If you feel you have cause for complaint you should follow this procedure:

(a) Ask the council (or water authority) to look into your complaint.

(b) If you are not happy, ask a councillor (or member of the authority) to help.

(c) If you are still not happy, complain in writing and ask a councillor (or member of the authority) to send it to the Local Ombudsman or send it yourself, direct to the Local Ombudsman at:

> 21 Queen Anne's Gate
> London SW1H 9BU
> 01–222 5622

or

| *North of England* | 29 Castlegate
York YO1 1RN
0904–30151 |

| *Scotland* | 5 Shandwick Place
Edinburgh EH2 4RG
031–229 4472 |

| *Wales* | Derwen House
Court Road
Bridgend
Mid Glam CF31 1BN
0656–61325 |

Parliamentary Ombudsman. If you think you have been unfairly treated by a central government department (failure to reply adequately to correspondence, slowness, bias, etc.) you can follow this procedure:

(a) Complain first to the central government department concerned.

(b) If you are not satisfied, explain your problem to an MP and ask him to refer it to the Parliamentary Ombudsman. (It does not have to be your own MP although it usually is: the Member will need a written explanation of what the dispute is about and you should present all written evidence.)

(c) Although the Parliamentary Ombudsman can start an investigation only if he is asked to do so by an MP, you can write to him direct: his address is the same as that of the Health Service Ombudsman (above).

See   'Which Ombudsman?' from HMSO or from any of the offices above.

PRICES   The prices of certain goods must be displayed at the point of sale – e.g. food and drink in restaurants, cafés, pubs; petrol; meat, fish, cheese, fruit and vegetables. The prices of milk and butter are controlled. There are complicated regulations dealing with recommended prices and bargain offers. If you think you have any cause for complaint, contact the trading standards officer.

RACIAL DISCRIMINATION   See pages 352–3.

RECOMMENDED RETAIL PRICES   It is illegal for shops to compare their prices with manufacturers' recommended retail prices (RRP) for beds, carpets, electrical (and other powered) domestic appliances, furniture and for consumer electronic products.

REFUNDS   If you are dissatisfied with a purchase and want your money back:

● Do not be put off by a notice saying 'No refunds'. This is illegal.

● Complain to the seller not to the manufacturer. You may be able to get all your money back or a cash payment between what you paid for the goods and their reduced value.

● You can accept replacement or repair but the trader is not obliged to offer anything except cash compensation.

● You are not bound to accept a credit note for faulty goods: you might find the credit has a time limit and, anyway, if you eventually want your money back it might be difficult to get it.

● You have the right to include in your claim any additional expenses such as travel or return postage.

● You will not be entitled to anything if you examined the faulty item in the shop and were aware of the handicaps or if the seller specifically pointed them out to you.

● You will not be entitled to refund, either, if you simply changed your mind.

- If you were given a faulty item as a gift, the donor (who bought the thing) should make the complaint.
- You have an extra right if you bought the goods on credit – you can ask for your money back from the credit supplier (finance house, some credit card companies) instead of the shop.

SALE ITEMS
- These are covered by the Sale of Goods Acts (see below): they must be of merchantable quality and perform the tasks for which they were made.
- A shopkeeper must not offer anything for sale at a marked-down price unless it was on offer at the old price for at least twenty-eight consecutive shop days in the last six months.
- It is an offence for the shopkeeper to suggest in any way that the price of an item is less than it really is.
- Bargain offers – comparing one price with another (e.g. 'worth £10 – our price £8') – are mostly illegal.

SALE OF
GOODS ACT
1979

This covers all sales from a trader, doorstep salesman. Tupperware hostess or mail order: it does not make any difference if the goods are bought with cash or credit.
The seller must:
- sell goods that are of merchantable quality, fit for the normal purpose;
- sell goods that are fit for the purpose he describes;
- sell goods that are as described.
If you are not happy, ask for a refund (see above). If you are still unhappy, contact the CAB.

SECOND-
HAND GOODS

These are still covered by the Sale of Goods Act if bought from a trader, but if anything goes wrong your right to compensation will depend on such factors as age and the original description of the item and the price paid.

SERVICES

The Supply of Goods and Services Act 1982 means:
- Protection for consumers provided by the Sale of Goods Act 1979 is now extended to goods supplied as part of a service, on hire or in part exchange. Goods must be of merchantable quality (e.g. taps must not leak), they must be fit for any particular purpose made known to the supplier and they must be as described.
- Unless anything more specific is agreed between customer and supplier, a person supplying a service must do so:
(a) with reasonable care and skill (e.g. a builder must provide a roof that does not leak)
(b) within a reasonable time (e.g. a shop should not take three months to repair your television)
(c) for a reasonable charge (e.g. a garage which does a minor job on a car must not make a sky-high charge for it).
These rights apply even if nothing is said or written down at the start

of your dealings with the supplier or if you have a written contract which does not mention them.

If you are not happy with a service you should first go back to the supplier. If you are not satisfied with the response contact your local trading standards officer or Citizens' Advice Bureau.

SEX DISCRIM-INATION

The Sex Discrimination Act 1975 states that it is illegal to discriminate on grounds of sex in the areas of advertising, consumer services (including housing, mortgages, banking and credit service), access to and use of cinemas and theatres, hotels, restaurants and pubs (but not private clubs), education and employment. It applies to women and to men. However, employers can give special treatment to women in connection with pregnancy and childbirth. In the area of employment, the Act is complemented by the Equal Pay Act 1970 (see 'Equality' above).

Some bodies (e.g. trades unions, employers' agencies, and the BBC) must *not* discriminate. The police, incidentally, have no powers to enforce this Act as it is not criminal law.

If you think you have cause for complaint, you can contact the EOC. It is a good idea to obtain from them (address on page 129) or from a CAB, a standard-form questionnaire. This will clarify matters and help you to decide whether to proceed – by going to an industrial tribunal if it is an employment complaint or to a county court in other cases. But be careful – in practice it is notoriously difficult to win a discrimination case.

● *Education*. If you or your children have been treated unfairly, complain first to the head-teacher or principal of the school or college. If you are still dissatisfied, write to the managers or governors involved (in Scotland, to the regional council), then to your local education authority and, as a near-to-last resort, write to:

Permanent Under-Secretary of State
Department of Education and Science
Elizabeth House
York Road
London SE1 7PH

Secretary of State
for Northern Ireland
Northern Ireland Office
London SW1P 3AJ

Secretary of State
for Scotland
Scottish Office
Edinburgh EH1 3TB

Secretary of State
for Wales
Welsh Office
Cardiff CF1 3NQ

● *Employment*. Complain first to the company's grievance director (if there is one) or to your union if you have one or go direct to an industrial tribunal (see above). You can also contact the Advisory, Conciliation and Arbitration Service (ACAS) at their head office:

11–12 St James's Square
London SW1 4LA
01–214 6000

and

Birmingham	021–643 9911
Bristol	0272–211921
Cardiff	0222–762636
Glasgow	041–204 2677
Leeds	0532–38232
Manchester	061–228 32222
Newcastle	
upon Tyne	0632–612191

On any point relating to the Act, you could contact:

National Council for Civil Liberties (NCCL)
21 Tabard Street
London SE1 4LA
01–403 3888

or

Scottish Council for Civil Liberties, Glasgow 041–332 5960
Incorporated Law Society of N. Ireland, Belfast 0232–469984
You can also contact your local MP or MEP.

SEXUAL HARASSMENT

Unfortunately, there are no legal remedies to protect you from sexual harassment as such. So you have to rely on your own strength of character. Joining up with other women in a similar predicament may help and reasonable retaliation is often the answer.

At work, it is a real problem if the sexual harassment comes from your employer. But even if you feel this forces you to leave your job, you cannot bring a claim for unfair (constructive) dismissal unless he has actually broken the contract of employment.

SHOPPING

● Remember, *a shopkeeper does not have to sell*. If asked to take the last item out of a shop window because you are interested in looking at it but possibly not in buying it – he is not obliged to.

● If you *order* something, the trader has to supply the goods 'within a reasonable time'. And if you had a written supply date and that is not kept you have a right to your money back and, possibly, compensation if you had to spend elsewhere.

● If you are given or sent a *free sample*, you are not entitled to a replacement if it does not work. If, however, the free sample is faulty enough to injure you, the supplier might be negligent.

See

'How to Put Things Right' (covering England and Wales) or 'Dear Shopper in Northern Ireland' and 'Dear Shopper in Scotland' from the Office of Fair Trading, address on page 126.

STANDARDS

British Standards are technical agreements, published in booklet form by the British Standards Institution (BSI).

There are over 8,000 standards, of which some 350 are for consumer goods. Not all standards are for products: those which have been tested and certified by the BSI Test House bear the kitemark (a B lying flat side down above an S in a V) as well as a standard number. Only motorcycle helmets sold for use on roads in the UK have to bear a kitemark by law.

If you are ever in a position to choose an item with the kitemark or an identical one without, in each case go for the one bearing the official BSI certification.

● Look out for some other BSI marks: paraffin symbol (two wavy lines, one above the other – displayed by shops selling Class 1 paraffin or kerosene); petrol stars; safety mark (pair of legs, forming the letters BSI, coming into a triangle – used on domestic gas equipment, electrical floodlights, etc.).

If you want to know more about the BSI send s.a.e. to the consumer education officer at:

British Standards Institution
2 Park Street
London W1A 2BS
01–629 9000

Publications are available at the BSI bookshop:

101 Pentonville Road
London N1 9ND
01–837 8801

● If you feel dissatisfied with something bearing the BSI's seal of approval you should first contact the retailer concerned. If you are still unhappy contact:

Certification and Assessment Department
British Standards Institution
Maylands Avenue
Hemel Hempstead
Herts HP2 4SQ
0442–3111

TRADE DESCRIPTIONS ACTS

Two Acts, 1968 and 1972, make it a criminal offence for goods and services, accommodation and facilities to be described falsely. If, for instance, a photograph on the label of a food packet is a gross exaggeration, that is an infringement of the Act.

Some goods (textiles, clothing) must be marked with country of origin. Any new goods carrying the name of a UK business must, if they were manufactured outside the UK, carry a clear indication of their real manufacturing country.

● If you are not happy with something you have bought or with a service, you can contact the local trading standards officer. You may eventually be entitled to compensation.

TRADING
STAMPS

Goods given in exchange for coupons, stamps or tokens must be of merchantable quality. If not, you are entitled to compensation.

TRADING
STANDARDS
OFFICER

The trading standards officer is based at county level. You can therefore contact him via your county council or regional council headquarters. In Northern Ireland this should be taken as 'the Trading Standards Branch of the Department of Economic Development'.

UNSOLICITED
GOODS ACT

Under this 1971 Act, if you receive an invoice for goods you have not ordered or have any complaint about unsolicited mail order material (see 'Mail Order' above), you should go to the trading standards officer. Corresponding legislation covering Northern Ireland was passed in 1976.

WEIGHTS
AND
MEASURES
ACTS

Two Acts, passed in 1963 and 1979, now mean that:
● Quantity of contents must be marked on most groceries and some other items (milk is one of the few exceptions). In the case of cheese, fish, meat and some other items, weights must at least be made known before a sale.
● Most pre-packed goods must be sold in prescribed quantities. When changeover from imperial to metric is taking place, both quantities must be given.
● In some instances an 'average' quantity is allowed: this is generally controlled by the packer.
● If you have any cause for complaint you should go to the trading standards officer.

Further Information

Useful Addresses

Since this is a free country and anyone should in theory be able to make contact with anyone else, here are some names and addresses not necessarily intended to be the recipients of complaints – but you should have them by you anyway:

Buckingham Palace
London SW1 1AA
01–930 4832

Home Office
London SW1H 9AT
01–213 3000

Central Office of Information
London SE1 7DU
01–928 2345

House of Commons
London SW1A 0AA
01–219 3000

Foreign and Commonwealth Office
London SW1A 2AL
01–233 3000

House of Lords
London SW1A 0PW
01–219 3107

Northern Ireland Office
London SWIP 3AJ
  01–273 3000

Scottish Office
Edinburgh EHI 3TB
  031–556 8400

Prime Minister
London SWIA 2AA
  01–233 3000

Welsh Office
Cardiff CFI 3NQ
  0222–825111

Suggested further reading

Many of the leaflets mentioned in this chapter are published by the Office of Fair Trading. You can get these from a local consumer group or by post from:

Office of Fair Trading
Field House
Bream's Buildings
London EC4 IPR
  01–242 2858

Borrie, Gordon and Aubrey L. Diamond, *The Consumer, Society and the Law*, Penguin
Consumers' Association, *A Handbook of Consumer Law*
  Which? Way to Complain
Coote, Anna and Tess Gill, *Women's Rights: a Practical Guide*, Penguin
Leder, M. J., *Consumer Law*, Macdonald & Evans
McGlone, Jean, *The Consumer's Handbook*, St Michael
Pritchard, John, *The Penguin Guide to the Law*, Penguin
Street, Harry (Consultant ed.), *You and Your Rights: an A to Z Guide to the Law*, Reader's Digest
Winstanley, Dr Michael and Ruth Dunkley, *Know Your Rights*, Independent Television Books

6 Medicine Chest

by Diana Hastings, SRN RCNT

WHAT TO DO IN AN EMERGENCY
A TO Z OF FIRST AID
MINOR MEDICAL CONDITIONS

SOME COMMON MEDICAL
   PROBLEMS
PUBLIC AND PRIVATE MEDICINE
FURTHER INFORMATION

There is no way this can be a *complete* first aid manual but I hope it will be useful for quick reference. You can learn some of the skills required by following the instructions below and, when applicable, practising on willing friends and relations.

The majority of accidents happen in the home and it is really important that you have a good first aid kit and know what to do in an emergency.

The second half of this chapter provides information and guidelines to help you cope with problems of home care. Perhaps you have a friend who is an epileptic: here you will find a basic description of what that problem is, what to do in the case of a fit, what to read and to whom to turn for further information and help.

'First Aid' is help given to the injured before professional help arrives. The term implies that 'Second Aid' is to follow. Calmly and sensibly applied, first aid may:

- save life
- prevent further damage to the casualty
- improve the condition of the casualty
- prepare for medical aid.

Notes
- Emergencies which do not necessarily involve people are dealt with in Chapter 19.
- References in parentheses in the next section refer to the 'A to Z of First Aid' which follows, pages 144–68.

What to Do in an Emergency

- Assess the situation in terms of the casualty and the cause and source of injury.
- Act quickly, calmly and quietly and in a methodical manner. *Do not panic*.
- Make sure neither you nor your casualty is in danger (e.g. from fire, flooding, electrical equipment plugged into the mains, escaped gas or oncoming traffic).
- If safe, examine and treat casualty where he is.

- Check:

(a) Is he *breathing?* If not, commence *artificial respiration* (see page 144).

(b) Is he *choking?* If he is, clear airway (see 'Choking', page 156).

(c) Is his *heart beating?* If not, commence *heart massage* (see page 162).

(d) Is he *unconscious?* If so, put him in recovery position (see 'Unconsciousness', page 167).

(e) Is he *bleeding heavily?* (see 'Bleeding', page 148).

- Cover, protect from cold but *do not* apply heat. Loosen tight clothing around neck, chest and waist. Do not remove clothing unnecessarily.

- Prevent any further accidents (e.g. control traffic, remove broken glass, etc.).

- Clear the crowd (if applicable). Other people will only hinder you and cause anxiety and embarrassment to the casualty. Advise him not to move and reassure him by being careful what you say. Listen to what he says and answer his questions tactfully. Do not question him unnecessarily: this will make him more anxious. Do not appear nervous. Work calmly and quickly – this will also reassure those around you.

- Get a bystander to telephone for an ambulance or doctor if this is necessary. Your message (preferably written) should say:

(a) where you are telephoning from (in case you are cut off).

(b) the site of the accident – its address and how to find it (give obvious nearby landmarks).

(c) the number of injured and the approximate age of the casualties.

(d) the nature of the injuries or any special problem such as a heart attack or someone having a baby.

- Do not hang up before the ambulance control officer, police duty officer or doctor does.

- While the telephone call is going on you should stay near the casualty. Watch and record any changes in his condition.

- Dress all wounds (see 'Bleeding', page 148). Immobilize all fractures (see 'Broken Bones', page 151).

- Prevent or minimize shock (see 'Shock', page 165).

- Do not give any food or drink and do not allow him to smoke.

- When medical help arrives, give an account of the accident or illness and the care that you have given.

- Give the ambulance or police authorities the casualty's property.

- You should also send a tactful message to the casualty's home stating what has happened and where he has been taken (unless this has already been done by the police).

- In the case of a minor accident that does not require medical assistance you can allow the patient to go home.

- If the casualty can be safely moved take him to a nearby house or shelter and wait for medical help to arrive.

- For minor injuries requiring hospital treatment arrange for transport by car.

- Remember – *never* send home anyone who has been unconscious even for a few seconds. Similarly, *never* send home anyone who is in shock.

Note ● The above assumes that there is only one casualty. If there are several you must decide which need urgent help. Tell casualties calmly but firmly to remain still until you can see to them. Give treatment first to those who might die from lack of rapid treatment (those who are not breathing, choking, unconscious, bleeding).

A to Z of First Aid

ABDOMINAL WOUNDS	FAINTING
ARTIFICIAL RESPIRATION	FIRST AID KIT FOR THE HOME
BITES AND STINGS	HEAD INJURIES
BLEEDING	HEART MASSAGE/CARDIAC
BLISTERS	MASSAGE
BROKEN BONES/FRACTURES	OBJECTS IN THE EAR, EYE OR
BRUISES	NOSE
BURNS AND SCALDS	POISONS
CAR ACCIDENTS	SHOCK
CHOKING	SPRAINS AND DISLOCATIONS
DRESSINGS AND SLINGS	UNCONSCIOUSNESS

ABDOMINAL WOUNDS
The abdomen is the area in the front between the chest and the hips. Any deep wound in this area can be very serious, not only because of bleeding you can see but also because the organs under the wound may be damaged or even protruding from the wound.

What to do ● Put the casualty on his back with his head to one side in case he vomits. Bend his knees up over cushions or coats to prevent the wound from gaping.
● If the abdomen has been pierced by a sharp object (e.g. a knife) *do not attempt to remove it*. You could cause even more damage.
● Put a clean – preferably sterile – dressing over the wound and secure with a bandage or adhesive strapping (see 'Bleeding', page 148).
● If some of the contents of the abdomen are actually protruding through the wound then cover them with a damp sterile dressing or damp clean cloth and keep in place with a loose bandage. *Do not attempt to touch them or put them back.*
● Minimize shock (see 'Shock', page 165).
● If the casualty becomes unconscious, place something soft underneath him to support the wound and put in the recovery position (see 'Unconsciousness', page 167).
● Arrange to transport your casualty to hospital as a stretcher case as soon as you can.

ARTIFICIAL RESPIRATION
● Act quickly.
● Put casualty on his back on a firm surface.

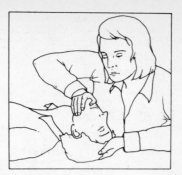 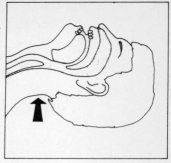

What to do • Make sure the airway is clear by bending the head back with one hand and pushing the jaw upwards with the other hand (this action lifts the tongue off the back of the throat).

• In this open airway position turn the casualty's head to the side. Hook your first two fingers and sweep around inside the mouth to remove any foreign matter (e.g. dentures, food, loose teeth or vomit). Do not waste time searching for hidden obstructions.

• Squeeze the nostrils together and open the casualty's mouth.

● Put your mouth completely over the casualty's mouth and blow hard enough to make the chest rise.

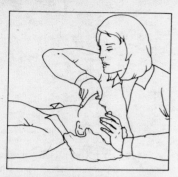

● Remove your mouth and watch the chest fall. Take in another breath without waiting for the chest to deflate completely. Then continue at 16 to 18 breaths per minute for adults (for children and infants, at a gentle 20 breaths per minute).

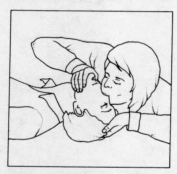

● Mouth to nose breathing: hold the mouth closed with your thumb and breath into the nose.

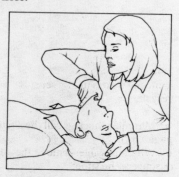

- Casualty breathes out while you hold his mouth open and take another breath ready to continue at the same rate as above.
- Continue until casualty breathes and then place him in the recovery position (see 'Unconsciousness', page 167) or until a doctor tells you to stop because the casualty is dead.

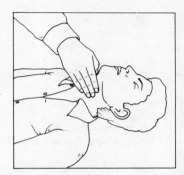

- After the first 4 breaths and every two minutes you must check the pulse in the neck (the carotid pulse) to check that the heart is beating. If there is no pulse and the casualty remains a pale colour then the heart has stopped and the oxygen you are breathing in cannot reach the casualty's brain because there is no circulation. You must therefore start heart massage in conjunction with artificial respiration (see 'Heart Massage', page 162).

BITES AND STINGS

Animal bites

Animals have sharp pointed teeth and harbour germs in their mouths. When they bite they inject these germs deep into the tissues of the body. Any bite which breaks the skin needs prompt attention.

What to do
- Wash area well with soapy water for at least five minutes. Dry and cover with a sterile unmedicated dressing.
- If bleeding is severe, dress wound and use direct pressure (see 'Bleeding').
- Get medical advice.

Stings

Someone who is highly sensitive to insect stings may collapse and become very ill.

What to do
- Minimize shock or call the doctor or get to hospital *quickly* (see 'Shock', page 165).
- Where possible, remove the sting with clean fingers but do not force or squeeze the sting.

● If the sting is in the mouth, throat or tongue, *call for medical help immediately*. Be ready to resuscitate casualty if necessary.

● Stings near the eye should be treated with a cold compress.

● If there is a lot of swelling of the mouth, place the casualty in the recovery position (see 'Unconsciousness', page 167) and give him ice to suck. Get medical advice.

● For immediate relief of pain and irritation gently rub on some anti-histamine cream or a pain-relief spray especially for stings. (Do not use in eye, mouth or tongue.)

● Alternatively, immerse the area in cold water or apply a cold compress (see 'Dressings and Slings' page 157).

● Stings which become increasingly painful and inflamed over the next few days may be infected so get medical advice.

BLEEDING   The adult body contains approximately six litres of blood and the rapid loss of even a litre threatens life.

● *Arterial bleeding* is bright red; blood spurts out in time with the heart-beat.

● *Venous bleeding* is darker red; blood gushes out.

● *Capillary bleeding* just oozes out.

What to do   **Minor cuts** can be washed under running cold water. Apply a little anti-septic cream and a plaster.

Severe bleeding (following a deep cut or laceration): act quickly – you must restrict the blood flow to the wound and allow clots to form.

● Apply direct pressure for ten minutes unless there is an object embedded in the wound. Do not remove object (see *Indirect pressure*, below).

● If possible, raise the injured limb unless you suspect a broken bone (see 'Broken Bones', page 151).

● Lie casualty down in a comfortable position.

● Cover the wound with a sterile unmedicated dressing or clean cloth and bandage firmly but not so tight as to stop circulation (if fingers or toes go blue the bandage is too tight).

● If bleeding continues, put more dressings on top and bandage again. *Do not remove original dressings* as this may disturb the clot.

● Leave the part at rest and elevated. Observe for any further bleeding.

● Minimize shock (see 'Shock', page 165).

Note   ● Transport to hospital.

In the case of road or gardening accidents or any other accident which leaves a deep or dirty wound, always seek medical advice as protection against tetanus may be required.

Indirect pressure. If severe lacerations prevent direct pressure being used, arterial bleeding can be stopped by applying pressure to the artery *under the arm*. Slide your fingers under the casualty's arm between the muscles and press upwards and inwards, pushing the artery against the bone.

On the artery *in the groin*, feel for the pulse and press it against the rim of the pelvis with your fist or the heel of your hand. *This method is used only in the last resort* and apply pressure only for ten minutes. Repeat as often as necessary until bleeding stops.

Note   ● Never apply a tourniquet.

Bleeding from the ear

This may occur when a fractured skull has been sustained (see 'Head Injuries', page 161) or when an eardrum has ruptured, perhaps as a result of pushing an object into the ear or by falling while water-skiing or diving or being too close to an explosion.

The casualty may suffer pain inside the ear, deafness and a moderate flow of blood from the ear.

What to do   ● Put the casualty in a half-sitting position with his head on one side (towards the injured side, to allow the blood to drain out).
● Cover the ear with a clean and sterile unmedicated dressing and keep it in place with a bandage.
● *Never plug the ear:* if you stop the blood from draining, the pressure may build up within the ear.
● Minimize shock (see 'Shock', page 165).
● Transport to hospital.

Bleeding from the mouth

Bleeding from this area may be severe because of the rich blood supply and the very thin skin covering the vessels. Injuries are usually caused by the casualty's teeth cutting into the tongue, lips or lining of the mouth during blows to or falls on the face.

What to do   ● Tell the casualty to sit down.
● Put a towel round his shoulder with his head forward, over a bowl, and inclined a little towards the injured side.
● Give casualty a cloth to hold to his mouth.
● Tell the casualty to spit out any blood.
● When bleeding has stopped advise him not to take any hot drinks for the next twelve hours.
● Advise him not to rinse out his mouth as this will disturb the clot.
● If bleeding persists for more than twenty minutes or the wound is large and gaping, transport to hospital.

Bleeding from a tooth socket

This may occur as the result of accidental loss of a tooth or tooth extraction.

What to do   ● Tell the casualty to sit down.
● Put a towel around his shoulders and bend his head forward, over a bowl, inclined to the affected side to allow blood to drain out.

- Hold a thick pad of dressing or a clean handkerchief on to the socket – *do not put it into the socket.*
- Get the casualty to hold the pad there and then to bite down on to it for 10 to 20 minutes. He will find it less tiring if he rests his jaw in cupped hands with elbows on the table.
- Ask him to spit out any blood in the mouth but try to keep the pad in position.
- Carefully remove pad: if still bleeding, replace with a clean pad.
- When bleeding has stopped, advise him not to take any hot drinks for the next twelve hours.
- Advise him not to rinse out his mouth or he will disturb the blood clot.
- If bleeding persists or recurs get medical or dental advice.

Internal bleeding

Bleeding into a space in the abdomen with no outward signs may be caused by disease, a blow or crush injuries. There may be no pain but a rigidly firm abdomen and rapidly developing shock (see 'Shock', page 165). If there is a chest injury and the casualty is conscious, sit him up and incline to the affected side. If he is unconscious, put in recovery position on the affected side (see 'Unconsciousness', page 167).

What to do
- Casualty needs a blood transfusion – *he must be sent to hospital at once.*
- Meanwhile minimize the shock (see 'Shock', page 165).
- Keep him at rest, lying down with legs raised, head low and turned to one side.
- Cover with a blanket or jacket – avoid weight on the abdomen by placing a small table or chair over the abdomen and putting the covering over it.

Nose bleeds

What to do
- Sit casualty with head slightly forward over a bowl, a towel round his shoulders. Loosen any tight clothing around the neck.
- Tell him to breathe through his mouth.
- Tell him to pinch the soft part of his nose firmly for five minutes (be ready to take over if it becomes tiring for him). Wrap a piece of ice in a handkerchief and place over the nose. (Do not pinch the nose if bleeding was caused by a blow as it may increase the damage.)
- Tell him to spit out any blood in his mouth and not to swallow it as this may make him feel sick or vomit.
- Release pressure after five minutes. If bleeding has not stopped, repeat treatment for another five minutes.
- When bleeding has stopped, tell him to avoid blowing his nose for at least four hours so as not to disturb the clot. Give him a piece of material or large handkerchief to hold under his nose, this will absorb spots of blood collecting on the end of his nose, causing irritation and a desire to blow the nose clear.

- Seek medical advice if bleeding has not stopped in thirty minutes or if bleeding recurs within thirty minutes.
- *Never* plug the nose with cotton wool or anything else.

Severe vaginal bleeding

This may be due to heavy menstrual bleeding, a miscarriage or internal injury so ask the casualty the following questions:

(a) Are you menstruating at the moment?
(b) Have you got severe cramps or any pain?
(c) Are you pregnant?
(d) Have you sustained any injury?

Remember the answers so that you can report all facts to the doctor if it is necessary to call one.

What to do

- If possible get the casualty to a place where she can have privacy. If this is not possible get some form of screening around. Give her a sanitary dressing if one is available or a clean towel to place over the entrance of the vagina.
- The casualty will feel most comfortable lying down on her back with her head and shoulders supported and knees raised and back supported with blankets or pillows – this will help relax muscles in the abdomen.
- If you are sure it is only menstrual cramp then give one or two of the casualty's own pain-killing tablets.
- If you think she is miscarrying phone for a medical adviser (see also 'Miscarriage', page 212).
- If the bleeding is severe and the casualty looks shocked then arrange for transport to hospital.

BLISTERS

Blisters are bubbles which form on skin damaged by burns or friction. They are caused by fluid from the tissues called serum which leaks into the damaged area, just underneath the skin. When they heal the new skin forms at the bottom of the blister underneath the bubble of serum. The serum is reabsorbed and the outer layer of skin peels off.

There is no need to burst the blister: if you do you will just increase the risk of infection. Apply a dry dressing over the blister to protect it.

BROKEN BONES/ FRACTURES

The word 'fracture' is a term used to describe a broken bone. You should suspect a fracture if there has been a blow or crush injury followed by pain. The casualty may not be in *severe* pain but will complain of some pain.

Look for the following signs:

- Can he move the limb on his own? (If not, then the bone is probably broken – do *not* try to move the bone for him.)
- Is the limb swollen and lying in an unnatural position or deformed in any way? (If the answer is yes the bone is broken.)
- Feel very gently over the suspected fracture: you will find it is tender and that there is an irregular knobbliness compared with the other, normal, limb. The site may be discoloured (red and/or bruised).

● If you have any doubt about whether or not the limb is broken *treat it as if it is broken*. It is not easy to tell if a bone is broken, and the only way to be certain is by X-ray, which will be done at the hospital.

What to do   ● The most important part of the management of the casualty is to make sure that you do not move the broken limb and in so doing cause more pain and tissue damage or even push the jagged bone through the skin – this will have very serious consequences.

● If a bone *is* protruding, control the bleeding (see *Indirect pressure*, page 148) and apply a ring pad (see 'Dressings and Slings', page 157).

● Control any severe bleeding immediately (see 'Bleeding', page 148).

● Tell the casualty not to move and treat him where he is.

● Cover any open wound with a light dry dressing.

● Immobilize the injured part.

(a) Immobilize the joints above and below fracture site. This will prevent movement of the broken bone.

(b) Secure the injured part to a suitable part of the casualty's body with bandages, e.g. a fractured arm to the chest wall, a fractured leg to the good leg (move the good leg to the injured one and not the other way round).

(c) If you have to move an arm or a leg into position to immobilize it then do it slowly and carefully. Tell the casualty to relax as much as he can. Support the whole limb in both your arms and hands then move it smoothly into position.

Immobilizing a fractured thigh

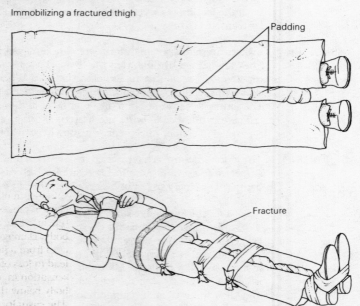

Padding

Fracture

● Never move an elbow: bandage the arm to the body in the position in which it is found.

(d) Putting pads between the hollows will be more comfortable and make the splinting more effective.

(e) Then apply wide bandages: put them round the limbs very carefully without too much disturbance and *do not* bandage over the fracture site. Bandages should be firm but not tight and tied with reef knots or bows on the uninjured side (see diagram, page 152).

(f) If the fingers or toes are blue the bandages are too tight.

● Minimize shock (see 'Shock', page 165).

● Do not give anything by mouth as the casualty may need an anaesthetic.

● Get the casualty to hospital as soon as possible.

TYPE OF BROKEN BONE	HOW TO IMMOBILIZE FRACTURE	SPECIAL PROBLEMS
Skull	Not required	Blood or clear fluid oozing from from ear or nose, cover with dressing and secure with light bandage. If conscious, incline head to injured side. If unconscious, place in recovery position on injured side (see 'Unconsciousness', page 167)
Lower jaw	Place a pad under the jaw and hold in place with a bandage tied on top of the head	Maintain casualty's airway
Cheek bone and upper jaw	Not required – hold a cold compress over site	
Spine	Do not move. Place rolled-up clothing along both sides of the trunk for support. Cover with a blanket and wait for medical aid	The chain of bones which form the backbone are called vertebrae and they form a canal through which runs the spinal cord of nerves which control movement and sensation throughout the body. Damage to the spinal cord from a jagged bone can lead to loss of power or sensation in all parts of the body below the injured area. The casualty may even be paralysed

TYPE OF BROKEN BONE	HOW TO IMMOBILIZE FRACTURE	SPECIAL PROBLEMS
Neck	Make a collar (see 'Dressings and Slings', page 157)	As for a fractured spine
Ribs	Sometimes feels more comfortable with arm on the injured side supported in an arm sling (see 'Dressings and Slings', page 157)	
Upper arm, forearm, wrist and hand	Soft pad under arm, carefully move forearm and arm across the chest. Hand should reach opposite armpit – pin the sleeve to the clothing or use a sling. If elbow is painful keep it in the position in which it is found and immobilize the casualty	
Collar bone	Soft pads under armpit. Put injured limb gently across the chest. Fingertips should almost rest on the opposite shoulder. Support with sling or pin sleeve to casualty's clothing (see 'Dressings and Slings', page 157)	
Pelvis	Two wide bandages around the pelvis, overlapping each other. Put padding between legs. Make a figure-of-8 around ankles and feet to keep them together. Bandage knees together	A severe fracture may have damaged the bladder or the urinary passage making the casualty want to pass urine. Advise him not to pass water if he can possibly help it until he has been seen by a hospital doctor
Thigh and leg	Bring good leg alongside injured leg. Bandage feet and ankles together then bandage knees together. One bandage should be below the fracture and one around the thighs	
Foot	Protect with a folded blanket or a small pillow tied around the foot and ankle	

BRUISES Bruises are collections of blood caught under the skin. They are purple or blue at first and in time turn green or yellow.

Severe bruises

Severe bruising can result, for instance, after a fall from a height. There may be no sign of a cut or a broken bone but there may be signs of swelling and bruising to the chest and upper arm that could contain as much as a litre or more of blood which has escaped from many blood vessels damaged by the fall.

Treatment is as for internal bleeding and shock (see 'Bleeding', page 148).

Minor bruises

If a small area is involved, apply a cold compress (see 'Dressings and Slings', page 157).

BURNS AND SCALDS

What to do

- Immerse the burnt area in – or place under – running cold water for ten minutes or until the pain ceases.
- Do not remove burnt clothing.
- Cover with a clean or sterile dressing.
- Except for small skin surface burns, all casualties should receive medical treatment.
- Prevent or minimize shock (see 'Shock', page 165).
- Do not prick blisters.
- Never put grease or oil on the burn.
- If the casualty's clothes are on fire get him on the ground at once with the burning part uppermost, then smother the fire with a blanket

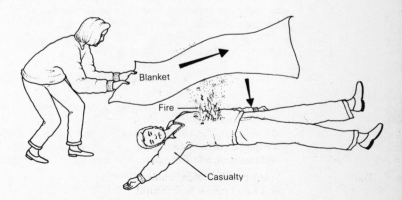

or thick cloth. Protect the face by bringing the blanket down, making sure you fan the flames away from the face and down towards the feet. Use the blanket as a shield between you and the flames. *Do not roll the casualty round on the floor* as this would burn him all over (however this might be the last resort for someone who is on his own and on fire, see page 567).

CAR
ACCIDENTS
– FIRST AID

First see 'Motor Accidents' in Chapter 19.
● Turn off ignition, lights and radio.
● No smoking.
● Look for casualties: inside cars for small children thrown behind seats or under luggage and anyone who may have been thrown clear.
● Do not move or pull casualties from vehicles unless surroundings are dangerous – e.g. fire.
● Instruct someone to telephone for emergency services.
● Ask bystanders to:
(a) direct traffic
(b) set up warning triangles or signal with torch about 200 yards either side of the accident.
● Light the scene using the headlights of your own car placed sideways off the road (if it must remain on the road leave hazard lights flashing).
● Check casualties' airways are clear and that they are breathing (if not, try artificial respiration, see page 144). Check heartbeat (see 'Heart Massage', page 162).
● Establish level of consciousness and put the unconscious in the recovery position (see 'Unconsciousness', page 167).
● Check for severe bleeding and control it (see 'Bleeding', page 148).
● Minimize shock (see 'Shock', page 165).
● If in no immediate danger from surroundings treat all fractures and large wounds before moving (see 'Broken Bones', page 151, and 'Bleeding', page 148). If position is dangerous, immobilize injured parts and move casualties carefully. Do not move casualties unless their lives are in danger from fire, water or gas.
● Use your common sense. Treat all casualties and their injuries in order of priority to the best of your ability.

CHOKING

● Slap the casualty smartly between the shoulder blades with the heel of the hand up to four times. If the casualty is a baby, grasp the ankles firmly in one hand – hold him upside down and slap firmly between the shoulder blades.
● If this does not work then apply four abdominal thrusts:
(a) standing behind him, put one arm around his abdomen and clench your fist in the middle between the navel and the breastbone
(b) grasp your fist with the other hand
(c) pull both hands towards you with a quick upward and inward thrust from the elbows so that you dislodge the obstruction.
● Give artificial respiration if necessary (see page 144).

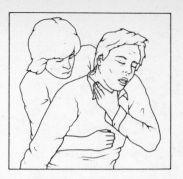 

DRESSINGS AND SLINGS

Cold compress
Soak a towel in cold water, wring out and apply. Repeat as it becomes warm.

Collar for suspected broken neck
Fold a newspaper longways to a width of about 10cm and insert into the leg of an old stocking. Place around the neck and tie the loose ends together at the front.

Ring pad (for an embedded object)

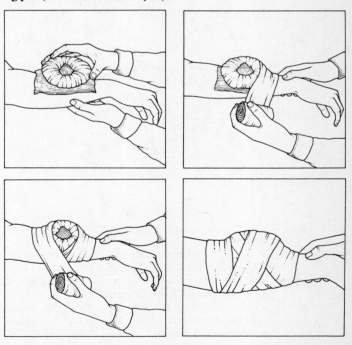

Holding opposite corners of a large handkerchief or similar piece of material, fold it diagonally and wrap it around two or three fingers; secure the ends to make a ring pad. Place this over the embedded object. This is then held in position with a bandage.

Roller bandages

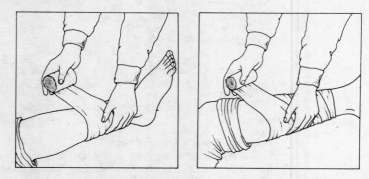

● *Straight*: start at the bottom of the limb and work upwards, covering each layer by two-thirds.

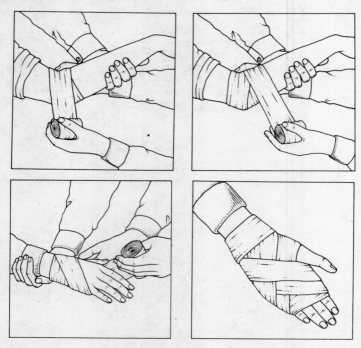

● *Round a joint*: make one straight turn around the joint, then one above then one below, covering one half of each turn as you bandage. Secure above the elbow or knee.

● *Hand*: start at the wrist, one straight turn, then up to the fingers, down across the palm, diagonally across the back of the hand.

Slings

Sling for broken collar bone

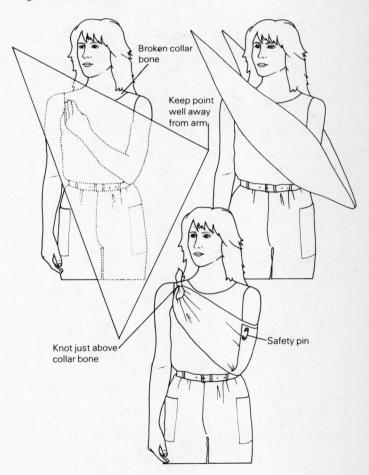

Broken collar bone

Keep point well away from arm

Knot just above collar bone

Safety pin

Sling for broken arm

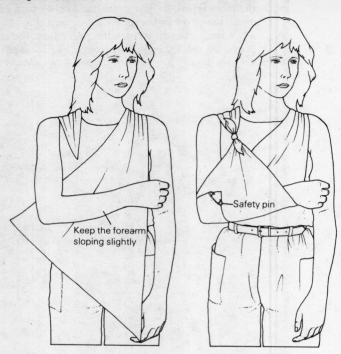

Keep the forearm sloping slightly

Safety pin

FAINTING

Feeling faint
- Ensure a supply of fresh air.
- Sit casualty in a chair and put head between knees.
- When colour returns, allow the casualty to sit up.

Fainting
- If the casualty has collapsed, get him on to the ground with feet raised on a chair or small table.
- Loosen tight clothing round the neck and chest.

FIRST-AID KIT FOR THE CAR

See Chapter 3.

FIRST-AID KIT FOR THE HOME

- antiseptic cream
- cotton wool
- assorted plasters
- adhesive dressing strip
- roll of adhesive tape 1cm wide
- packet of white gauze

- 2 triangular bandages (for slings or holding dressings in place), each with safety-pin
- prepared unmedicated sterile dressings:
  3 medium
  2 large
- 2 × 8cm cotton crêpe bandages (for supporting limbs)
- 16 safety-pins
- 2cm and 14cm cotton bandages (for holding dressings in position)
- gauze (for dressing grazes and wounds)
- packet of paper tissues
- sharp scissors (*only* to be used for first aid)
- tweezers (for removing splinters)
- a first aid manual

No antiseptic lotions have been included in this list as it is safer to clean cuts and grazes with soap and water and use antiseptic cream. Solutions are harmful if made up too strong and become dangerous if they are kept too long.

HEAD INJURIES

- If the casualty is unconscious (see 'Unconsciousness', page 167), send for an ambulance.
- Be careful not to twist the casualty's neck in case it is injured.
- Carefully dress any wounds to protect the skull and brain from infection.
- If there is bleeding from nose or ear lie casualty on that side to allow blood and fluid to run clear. *Never plug with cotton wool*, just cover with a clean dressing.
- Every half-hour:

(a) shine a light into his eyes and watch the pupils contract (this is the normal reaction to light). If one pupil is a small black dot and does not alter in size and the other is normal, this means the casualty's condition is getting worse – the brain is being compressed and the nerve controlling the pupil reaction is being squashed. If the pupil becomes paralysed, dilating into a large black circle, and the other pupil is normal, this means pressure has built up even further.

(b) Check the pulse rate. If the normal pulse (70 to 80) becomes slower and slower, full-bounding but slow, this means that the part of the brain governing the heartbeat is inhibited by compression. His condition is worsening.

(c) If the casualty is conscious at first but complains of headaches, he may go through the levels of responsiveness (see 'Unconsciousness', page 167) until a coma develops. If he is asleep you will have to wake him every thirty minutes to check his level of consciousness: he may drift from sleep to unconsciousness without you knowing due to increasing pressure in the skull which is compressing the brain.

- The brain controls such functions as the heartbeat, breathing, temperature regulation and blood pressure. It cannot function if it has been compressed – your casualty will die. He needs *urgent medical attention*.

Concussion

This is unconsciousness following a knock on the head or jaw: the brain has been shaken up and the casualty must go to hospital.

HEART MASSAGE/ CARDIAC MASSAGE

Once the heart has stopped beating you have only four minutes before the brain, deprived of circulating blood and therefore oxygen, becomes damaged.

Heart massage

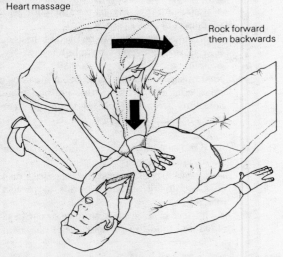

Rock forward then backwards

What to do

• The casualty must be on his back in the same position as for artificial respiration, on a hard surface.

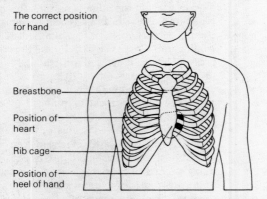

The correct position for hand

Breastbone

Position of heart

Rib cage

Position of heel of hand

• The heart lies behind the breastbone, slightly to the left. When the breastbone is depressed it pushes down against the front of the heart. This pushes the heart back towards the backbone.

• Because the backbone is a large rigid structure and he is lying on a firm surface the heart is now compressed between these two surfaces and the blood in the heart is forced out into the circulation.

● When you release the pressure, the heart and chest resume their usual shape and size and the heart fills with blood.

● When you repeat this procedure regularly you are making an artificial heartbeat which pumps the blood around the body. (If you attempt heart massage with your casualty on something soft like a mattress the heart is not compressed enough.)

● Kneel beside the casualty leaving enough room for you to be able to lean forward with outstretched arms over the middle of the chest.

● Quickly feel for the top and lower end of the breastbone. Find its middle point and then place the 'heel' of one hand mid-way between this point and the lower end of the breastbone.

● Place the second hand over the first. Keep your fingers and palms off the chest: this reduces the risk of cracking the ribs.

● Press the breastbone down by rocking your body forwards and keeping your arms straight. The breastbone will sink as much as 5cm under pressure and this is quite normal.

NB *Never practise this on a conscious person or on anyone with a beating heart.*

● Relax the pressure by rocking back and letting the breastbone rise to its normal position but leaving your hands in position and repeat until you have given fifteen compressions. Then move to the casualty's head and re-open airway; give two breaths of mouth-to-mouth resuscitation.

Artificial respiration and heart massage

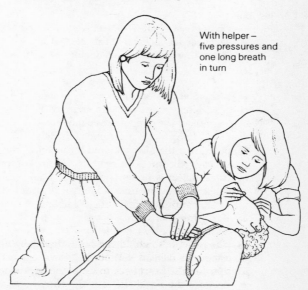

With helper –
five pressures and
one long breath
in turn

● For an *adult casualty* repeat at the rate of 60 per minute (1 per second), always with 15 compressions to two mouth-to-mouth.

● For a *child casualty*, reduce pressure and use only one hand at 100 compressions per minute. For small children and infants use only two fingers at 100 compressions per minute. Still use 15 compressions to two mouth-to-mouth.

● Heart massage is always done in conjunction with artificial respiration either on your own or with someone else. If resuscitation is being carried out with someone else, the heart must not be compressed at the same time as the other first aider is breathing into the lungs.

● The casualty's colour should improve. Continue until the heartbeat and pulse have returned.

● Check the pulse every three minutes. Stop resuscitation while pulse is checked.

● As soon as the heartbeat returns, stop compressions but continue mouth-to-mouth until breathing is restored.

● Continue to check the pulse every three minutes.

● When breathing is restored, place in recovery position (see 'Unconsciousness', page 167). Continue to check casualty's pulse and respiration rate. Observe him carefully until he regains consciousness.

MOUTH-TO-MOUTH RESUSCI-TATION

See 'Artificial Respiration', page 144.

OBJECTS IN THE EAR, EYE OR NOSE

Ear
● Do not try to remove object – you may push it further in.
● Turn casualty's head to the affected side to see if it drops out.
● If not, then take him to a doctor or hospital.

Eye

What to do
● If the object is on the pupil or is sharp, do not try to remove it but cover with an eye pad or clean dressing. You may need to cover the other eye to prevent the damaged one moving. Get to hospital quickly.
● Object lying loose under one of the lids:
(a) pull down the lower lid and if the object can be seen remove it with the moistened corner of a soft handkerchief or a wisp of cotton wool
(b) if the object is under the upper lid, ask casualty to look down and pull upper lid downwards and outwards over the lower lid.
(c) if pain continues apply an eye pad and see the doctor.
● If anything corrosive is splashed or spilled into the eye:
(a) wash out quickly with plenty of cold water
(b) take care not to wash liquid into the other eye
(c) cover with a clean cloth
(d) seek medical advice.

Nose

Beads or small toys may be pushed up the nose by children.

What to do
- Do not attempt to remove objects.
- Get your casualty to breathe through the mouth and take him to a doctor or hospital.

POISONS
1. Look for signs:
- burns around the mouth
- unusual sleepiness
- rapid deep breathing
- stomach pain
- vomiting or retching
- diarrhoea
- convulsions
- red face.

2. Look for evidence of what has been taken. Keep it, and a specimen of any vomit.

3. If breathing or heart stops, see 'Artificial Respiration', page 144, or 'Heart Massage', page 162.

Note
- Do not contaminate your own mouth with the poison.
- Do not try to make him vomit if a corrosive poison has been taken.
- If lips or mouth show signs of burning, cool and dilute by giving milk or plain water to drink.
- *Get medical help immediately.*

Gas poisoning

What to do
- Turn off gas and get your casualty out into the fresh air.
- If breathing has stopped, see 'Artificial Respiration', page 144.

SHOCK
There are two main sorts of shock:

Primary or emotional shock is when the casualty feels faint almost immediately. It is a nervous response to injury or emotional upset: it is not serious and recovery is quick.

Traumatic shock follows severe blood or fluid loss and extreme pain or fear. It is a serious condition and *can lead to death*. A badly shocked casualty may show the following:

(a) he may be pale or ash grey, cold, clammy and sweating
(b) breathing may be weak, shallow and fast or yawning and sighing
(c) his pulse rate will be fast, weak and sometimes irregular
(d) he may be thirsty, feel sick and vomit
(e) he may be restless, faint and giddy
(f) his speech may be slurred, as may his thoughts and reactions
(g) unconsciousness may develop.

- Your role is *not* to treat for shock – this can be done only in a hospital. You should *prevent* or minimize shock worsening by adequate first aid.

To prevent or minimize shock

- Stop bleeding (see 'Bleeding', page 148).
- Reassure and comfort the casualty. Talk calmly and answer his questions sensibly.
- Treat him where he is – unless it is dangerous for you or for the casualty.
- Lie him down, keep head low and feet slightly raised. Support them on a rolled-up jacket or coat. Keep the patient on his side in case he vomits or becomes unconscious (see 'Unconsciousness', page 167). Elevating his feet increases the blood circulation to the heart and the brain.
- Loosen tight clothing around neck, waist and chest to help him breathe more easily. Do not overexpose him.
- Your patient is pale because the blood vessels in his skin have contracted and hold very little blood. If he is now heated these vessels become larger and fill up with blood to provide a pink skin colour – this blood is drawn from the heart and brain which need it urgently.
- Cover him with a blanket if he needs protection from cold, rain and wind.
- Relieve pain and discomfort (e.g. dress wounds and burns and immobilize fractures – see 'Broken Bones', page 151).
- Even if he is thirsty, *do not give him a drink* as he may need an anaesthetic at the hospital. Fluid can remain in the stomach of an injured person, only to be vomited up later and possibly choke him.
- Allow *no alcohol* and *no smoking*: they have the same effect as too much heat by drawing blood away from the brain and heart.
- Remove to hospital as soon as possible.

SPRAINS AND DISLOCATIONS

Joints are places where bone joins bone so that movement can take place. Muscles and strong ligaments keep them in position.

Sprains

A sprain is a stretching and tearing of ligaments around a joint when it is suddenly wrenched. There is pain and tenderness around the joint which will swell and be followed by bruising. A sprain often resembles a fracture – if in doubt, treat it as a fracture.

What to do

- Elevate the injured limb with the casualty sitting or lying in a comfortable position.
- Carefully remove any covering and apply a cold compress.
- Apply a thick layer of cotton wool and secure with a bandage (see 'Dressings and Slings', page 157).

Dislocations

This is when the ligaments are torn and a bone has been pulled out of its normal position. This results in severe or even sickening pain at or near the joint and the casualty may be unable to move the affected joint, which looks deformed. There will be swelling, and later bruising, over the injured site.

What to do
- Never try to correct a dislocation.
- Put the joint at rest by supporting it in a sling or immobilizing it with bandages (see 'Dressings and Slings', page 157).

UNCONSCIOUS-
NESS
There are stages through which a casualty passes when going from consciousness to unconsciousness, called levels of responsiveness:
1. Responds normally to questions and conversation.
2. Answers only direct questions.
3. Responds vaguely to questions.
4. Obeys commands only.
5. Responds only to pain (e.g. pinching the earlobe or back of hand).
6. No response at all.

What to do
The unconscious person should be put in the recovery position. This prevents swallowing the tongue or choking on blood or vomit. Call an ambulance.

- *Recovery position*

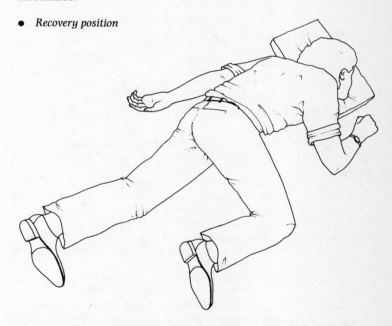

Ensure the casualty is lying on his back:
- Kneel down beside the casualty.
- Turn his head towards you and tilt it back, keeping the jaw forward in the open airway position.
- Place his arm nearest to you by his side and place his hand under his buttock.
- Bring the other arm over the front of the chest.

- Holding the leg furthest away from you under the knee or ankle, bring it towards you and cross it over the other leg.
- Hold his head with one hand and with the other hand hold him by his clothing over the hip furthest from you. Roll him quickly towards you. Support him on his side against your knee.
- Gently roll him on to the ground. Make sure his airway is open.
- Bend his uppermost arm so it supports his upper body.
- Bend the uppermost leg at the knee to bring the thigh well forward to support the lower body.
- Gently pull the other arm out from under the casualty. Leave it lying parallel to the casualty to prevent him from rolling on to his back.

Minor Medical Conditions

ABDOMINAL PAIN	EYES
COLDS	FAMILY MEDICINE CHEST
CONSTIPATION	FEVERS – RAISED TEMPERATURES
COUGHS	IMMUNIZATION
CRAMP	SORE THROAT
DIARRHOEA	VOMITING
EARACHE	

Notes
- *Signs* are things that you see, e.g. rashes.
- *Symptoms* are things that you feel, e.g. sore throat.

ABDOMINAL PAIN

There are many different types of pain all with different causes and it takes a doctor to diagnose and treat the problem. There are, however, a few simple guidelines to help you decide when to call the doctor:
- if the pain is severe and getting worse
- if the patient is ill
- if any other symptoms develop (e.g. constipation, diarrhoea, fever, vomiting or he just feels ill).

If in doubt, always seek medical advice.

COLDS

Symptoms

Runny nose, sore throat, cough and maybe a raised temperature (37.5 to 38°C or 99 to 100°F), aching and generally feeling unwell.

A cold is a virus infection passed on by someone else. The nose runs with a clear liquid and later a thick yellow discharge. It lasts about 7 to 10 days.

There is no need to see a doctor unless more serious symptoms develop (e.g. deafness, earache, high temperature).

Babies: consult the doctor if not feeding normally or if more serious symptoms develop.

Treatment
- Adults: two soluble aspirin or paracetamol every four hours.
- For a *sore throat*: dissolve the aspirin in warm water and gargle before swallowing.
- For *raised temperature*: plenty of fluids. It will not matter if the patient does not eat for a couple of days.
- For thick yellow *discharge*: steam inhalation – add 1 tsp of vapour rub or a few menthol crystals to one pint of steaming (not boiling) water. Put a towel over the head and the bowl, inhale for ten minutes, three times a day.
- Children gradually build up resistance to infection and are not really troubled by uncomplicated colds except at night when they lie down and the discharge trickles down the back of the throat making them cough. Do not suppress productive coughs with cough mixtures. Put babies on their sides without a pillow and children sitting upright supported by pillows. If the cough is very irritating rub a little vapour rub on the chest. You can also use nose drops (two drops in each nostril before the child goes to bed – never use for more than four days in succession).

CONSTIPATION

Hard, infrequent bowel movement. Remember, not everyone has a bowel movement every day.
- Do not take laxatives unnecessarily: this just upsets the normal pattern.
- Do eat plenty of fruit and high-roughage foods.
- Taking more fluids may also help.

Constipation is sometimes a symptom of other illnesses (see your doctor), but over-concern about bowel movements may even cause constipation.

COUGHS

This is a reflex action which prevents food or mucus from entering the air passages and causing infection. To suppress it with cough mixture can cause more harm than good. Treat with a steam inhalation (see above).

Coughing may be caused by infection of the lower air passages producing a dry cough. Treat it with a sedative linctus (which can be bought from the chemist) and with steam inhalation.

Consult the doctor if
- The cough produces yellow or green mucus.
- Coughing continues for up to two weeks after the cold has gone.
- There is any chest pain or shortness of breath.
- The cough produces blood.
- You or the patient are worried about the general condition.

CRAMP

This is a sudden, painful involuntary contraction of a muscle or group of muscles – it can happen to athletes and to those who take no exercise.

Some people swear that a cork in the bed prevents cramp in the middle of the night. Others say that eating a small amount of ordinary salt cures cramp.

If you get cramp, straighten the affected part and gently massage the muscles. If you get a lot of cramps, consult your doctor.

DIARRHOEA Loose, runny stools with colicky cramp-like pain in the stomach – may be preceded by vomiting. It may be due to sudden change in diet, too much eating and drinking, virus or bacterial infections.

Treatment
- Eat nothing.
- Drink clear fluids only (e.g. water or squash).
- Take kaolin mixture (from the chemist)
  - Adults: 1 tbs every two to three hours.
  - Children: 1 tsp every two to three hours.
- Rest for forty-eight hours (most attacks diminish within that time).

Call the doctor if
- The patient does not feel better within forty-eight hours.
- The pain becomes continuous.
- The patient is a baby under six months old.
- The attack follows a trip to a foreign country.
- The patient is having repeated attacks.

EARACHE
- A common cause is middle ear infection – *otitis media* – which usually follows another infection.
- Toothache from the lower back teeth may be felt in the ear.
- A sore throat may produce pain in the ear.
- Mumps may cause earache.
- A cold wind on the ears may produce earache.

Because there are so many causes it is wise to see the doctor (if there is a discharge from the ear see the doctor at once).

See also 'Objects in the Ear', above.

EYES **Black eye** – this is bruising around the eye. Unless the eye itself has been injured or the patient has been unconscious there is no need to see the doctor.

Conjunctivitis – inflammation of the inside of the eyelids, caused by an infection or allergy. In the former case give your patient his own flannel, towel, etc. See the doctor for a suitable eye ointment.

Stye – infection of an eyelash root (common cause is dandruff). Apply heat to the eye – a cloth soaked in hot salted water. See the doctor for antibiotic ointment.

See also 'Objects in the Eye', above.

FAMILY MEDICINE CHEST
- soluble aspirin and junior aspirin – for headaches, colds, sore throats. etc.
- paracetamol mixture – for relief of pain or fever in children
- kaolin mixture – for diarrhoea
- ephedrine nose drops – for runny noses in children
- Phenergan syrup – sedative for children
- sedative cough mixture – for painful or dry coughs (not those caused by common colds)

- menthol crystals – to make steam inhalations
- vapour rub – to make steam inhalations or rub on chests for dry coughs and blocked noses
- throat lozenges – for sore throats
- antiseptic cream – for septic spots and sores
- calamine lotion – for dabbing on rashes, bites and stings
- antihistamine cream – for bites and stings
- paper tissues
- thermometer
- eyebath
- 5ml dosage spoon

Note
- *Do not* give medicines prescribed for one member of the family to anyone else.
- Dispose of any leftover medication once treatment is completed.
- See your chemist for advice about medicine.

See
'First Aid Kit for the Car', Chapter 3.
'First Aid Kit for the Home', page 160.

**FEVERS –
RAISED
TEMPERA-
TURES**
- Put the patient to bed in light cotton nightwear and keep him cool
- Give plenty of fluids
- Adults: two soluble aspirin or paracetamol every four hours
- Children: junior aspirin or Panadol Elixir as prescribed
- Babies under one year: see your doctor.

If the patient is not better within forty-eight hours, consult the doctor.

	Celsius	Fahrenheit
Normal temperature	36.2° to 37°	97° to 98.4°
Slightly raised	37° to 38°	98.4° to 100°
High temperature	38° to 39.5°	100° to 103°
Greatly raised (inform doctor)	39.5° upwards	103° upwards

**IMMUNIZA-
TION**
Here are suggested times for immunization: you can fill in the dates your child has the immunization, and note any side-effects. Descriptions of the immunizations follow.

Diphtheria, tetanus and **whooping cough** are usually given as a triple injection or, if you prefer, only the vaccines against diphtheria and tetanus can be given. Diphtheria is now very rare, largely due to immunization. Tetanus is a serious disease which can be prevented by immunization: if your child gets a deep cut or dirty wound he will be given a booster dose unless he has had the triple vaccine or a booster tetanus during the last three years.

The vaccine against *whooping cough* will either prevent your child from

	3 MONTHS	5 MONTHS	9 TO 12 MONTHS	DURING 2ND YEAR	5 YEARS	10 TO 14 YEARS	15 TO 19 YEARS
Diphtheria	yes	yes	yes		yes		
German measles*						yes	
Measles				yes			
Polio	yes	yes	yes		yes		yes
Tetanus	yes	yes	yes		yes		yes
Tuberculosis†						yes	
Whooping cough	yes	yes	yes				

*Girls only: make a careful note if your daughter has had this disease.
†BCG, if not naturally immune.

getting whooping cough or at least make the illness less severe. It is a very unpleasant disease (see page 191) and there is not much that your doctor can do to ease the symptoms. There have been cases of children who have been brain damaged by the vaccine; these complications are rare but of course are very serious. Experts in Britain and the USA, however, feel that the risks associated with the vaccine are less than the risks associated with the complications of whooping cough, so they recommend that children should be immunized against it. If your child has had fits in the past it may be withheld – and if you are worried or have any doubts about whether or not to have your child immunized against whooping cough, talk to your doctor.

German measles (rubella) is given as a vaccine to girls between the ages of 10 to 14. Sometimes there is a slight rash, slightly swollen neck glands and (rarely) joint pains about the ninth day after the injection.

Influenza: there is now a vaccine available for the prevention of influenza but it is not routinely given to children.

Measles – just one injection is given at about thirteen months. Sometimes there are mild symptoms about 5 to 10 days after the injection.

Poliomyelitis vaccine is given by mouth and at the same time as the triple vaccine. Polio is a very serious disease and immunization against it is strongly recommended.

Smallpox – vaccination against this is no longer given as a matter of course as the disease is very rarely seen anywhere in the world.

Tuberculosis (TB) – this disease is passed on through infected milk or by someone who is suffering from it. Milk given to small children must be pasteurized or boiled to ensure that it is not infected. You should never allow your children to visit anyone who is suffering from TB unless they have been protected by BCG vaccine, given at 10 to 13 years following a negative tuberculin test.

Notes
- Triple vaccine is not given within 3 to 5 weeks of measles and German measles vaccines.
- If your child misses a triple vaccine dose there is no need to start the course all over again. The next dose gives adequate protection (ask your doctor for details).
- Polio vaccine is not given to children with diarrhoea or within three weeks of German measles or measles vaccine.
- If your child has not been well prior to or following any immunizations, tell your doctor.

See 'Immunization: a Few Moments' Discomfort for Years of Protection', Health Education Council.

SORE THROAT
- Often a *virus* which antibiotics will not cure – normally gets better in 4 to 5 days.
- *Tonsillitis*
(a) usually starts with a sore throat with pain on swallowing
(b) rise in temperature and feeling unwell
(c) it may be possible to see swollen tonsils with white spots on them
(d) the glands in the neck may be swollen – a normal response to infection
(e) the patient may need antibiotics – see a doctor.
- Alternatively, a sore throat may occur with a cold or flu – dry throat, pain on coughing, loss of voice.

Treatment
- Adults:
(a) Aspirin relieves pain and lowers temperature. Use soluble aspirin and gargle before swallowing, repeat every four hours. Paracetamol (swallowed) can be used instead of aspirin.
(b) Plenty of fluids.
(c) Food – if the patient feels like it.
(d) Steam inhalations (see 'Colds', page 169).
- Children:
Take junior aspirin or Panadol Elixir as prescribed on the packet. Gargle with aspirin if possible – if not, just swallow.

Consult the doctor if:
- Sore throat is getting worse after forty-eight hours.
- Patient complains of earache.
- Temperature rises above 39.5°C (103°F).
- You or the patient are anxious about his condition.

STOMACH PAINS   See 'Abdominal Pain' page 168.

VOMITING   Occurs when the stomach empties its contents suddenly as a result of:
(a) eating or drinking too much
(b) virus infection – usually stops within twenty-four hours and may be followed by diarrhoea.

Treatment
- Eat nothing.
- Drink small quantities of water every two hours.
- As vomiting stops, take a little solid food (e.g. dry biscuits, bread or breakfast cereals) and gradually return to normal diet.

Consult the doctor if:
- Your patient feels ill after vomiting.
- There is diarrhoea as well.
- There is stomach pain with vomiting.
- Patient vomits for more than twenty-four hours.
- A child is vomiting and has a raised temperature above 38°C (100°F).
- There is a history of a recent head injury.
- You are worried about his condition.

Some Common Medical Problems

ALCOHOLISM
ANXIETY AND DEPRESSION
ASTHMA
BACK PROBLEMS
CANCER
CYSTITIS
DIABETES
DRUG DEPENDENCY
EPILEPSY
FITS OR CONVULSIONS
GLUE SNIFFING
HEART ATTACK OR CORONARY THROMBOSIS
HYPOTHERMIA
INDIGESTION
INFECTIOUS DISEASES
MIGRAINE AND HEADACHE
PRE-MENSTRUAL TENSION
STROKES
SUNBURN
VAGINAL HEALTH AND DISCOMFORT
VARICOSE VEINS

ALCOHOLISM   One pint of beer, two measures of spirits, two glasses of port or sherry or two glasses of table wine all have roughly the same amount of alcohol in them.

Alcohol is absorbed into the bloodstream through the stomach wall. It circulates around the body and enters the brain. It is finally broken down in the liver and excreted in the urine.

The effect of
alcohol on the body

- It slows down the working of the brain.
- It makes you less rational.
- It impairs decision-making.
- It takes about three hours for the body to get rid of the alcohol in a pint of beer (this may happen at a slower or faster rate depending on your size and whether or not you have had anything to eat).
- One or two drinks make you less inhibited, the skin flushes and you become more sociable.
- Three drinks make your judgement slower and you may become giddy and unco-ordinated.
- Five to six drinks may make you experience blurred vision and loss of balance.
- After eight or nine drinks you may get double vision and loss of balance.
- Twenty drinks will probably make you unconscious.
- Large amounts of alcohol can cause death by stopping the breathing, usually preceded by unconsciousness.
- Prolonged habitual drinking damages the liver, stomach, heart and brain.
- An *alcoholic* starts by drinking excessively – any alcohol, including beer. This may be for social or business reasons or it may be to help cope with tension or worry. He (or she) may then go through a stage where alcohol is needed regularly and every excuse is made to get it. Eventually he may either be unable to stop drinking though rarely getting drunk, or he can go for long periods without drinking, but when he does it is to excess and until he becomes intoxicated.

To avoid becoming
an alcoholic

- Do not drink excessively.
- Drink only with food.
- Never drink alone.

Withdrawal
symptoms

If alcohol is withdrawn the alcoholic may get diarrhoea and vomiting, hallucinations, raised blood pressure, raised heart rate, fits, sweating – and possibly die through delirium tremens (DTs). This is a mental and physical state with acute restlessness and hallucinations which may last 4 to 5 days.

Help

- See your doctor.
- Talk to sympathetic friends and relations.
- Consult professional organizations such as:

Alcoholics Anonymous
PO Box 514
11 Redcliffe Gardens
London SW10 9BQ
01–352 9779

AA have branches throughout the British Isles: contact them for the nearest one. In Scotland you can contact:

Alcoholics Anonymous
50 Wellington Street
Glasgow G2 6HJ
   041–221 9027

Other professional organizations which can help are:

Drugs, Alcohol and Women Nationally (DAWN)
London Council of Alcoholism
146 Queen Victoria Street
London EC4U 4BX
   01–236 9770

National Council on Alcoholism
Hope House
Great Peter Street
London WIX 9HY
   01–222 1056

Scottish Council on Alcoholism
147 Blythswood Street
Glasgow G2 4EN
   041–333 9677

● There are also registered nursing homes which specialize in the treatment of alcoholism. You can contact:

Galsworthy House
Kingston Hill
Kingston-upon-Thames
Surrey KT2 7LX
   01–549 9861

Life-Anew Trust
Clouds House
East Knoyle
Salisbury
Wilts SP3 6BE
   074–783650

● Help is often needed by the alcoholic's family. Al-Anon Family Groups and Information Centre are linked to Alcoholics Anonymous and, like AA, have branches around the country. To find support locally, contact:

Al-Anon Family Groups and
Information Centre
61 Great Dover Street
London SE1 4YF
   01–403 0888

136 Ingram Street
Glasgow GI IEJ
041–552–2828

Churches and other organizations often offer special counselling services, for example:

> Family Support Unit
> Westercraigs Hostel for Alcoholics
> 21 Westlands Drive
> Glasgow G14 9NY
>   041–959 1679
>
> Turning Point (Helping Hand Organization)
> CAP House
> 9–12 Long Lane
> London EC1A 9HA
>   01–606 3947

See 'Facts about Alcohol' and 'Good Health? Advice on Sensible Drinking' from:

> Health Education Council
> 78 New Oxford St
> London WC1A 1AH

ANXIETY AND DEPRESSION

These are quite common conditions and may be exaggerations of a normal response to stressful situations, grief or bereavement.

Anxiety

This is a state of fear, a feeling of inner tension, a feeling that something unpleasant is about to happen. It can be a mild state of tension or nervousness or an overwhelming feeling of panic and terror. Some of the symptoms are: being unable to make decisions or to concentrate, restlessness, extreme irritability, sleeping badly, poor appetite and loss of weight.

If you – or someone you know – feel like this, consult the doctor.

Depression

It appears to be most prevalent among women who are housebound with young children and isolated from other adults, in women whose children have left home, those in the mid 40s to mid 50s age group and to those who lost one parent before they were six years old.

It can vary from a mild case of 'the blues' to a severe illness requiring hospital care. Some of the symptoms are: feelings of hopelessness, helplessness, indifference to friends, family or job, tiredness, loss of appetite, difficulty in sleeping or waking early or sleeping too much, an increase in alcohol consumption, lack of interest in sex, not enjoying activities that are usually enjoyed, physical pains and complaints and even thoughts of suicide.

If you – or someone you know – feel like this, consult the doctor.

ASTHMA

There is a narrowing and spasm of the air passages so that the patient wheezes and has difficulty in breathing out. It may be caused by an allergy or by nervous tension.

What to do when an attack occurs

- Reassure and calm the patient.
- Loosen tight clothing round the neck and chest.
- Position him with his back straight and limbs relaxed (e.g. sitting upright, leaning forward with head on his arms on the back of a chair or on a table).
- If he has medication allow him to use it.
- If he has several attacks one after the other, get medical advice.
- The Asthma Society has over eighty branches around the British Isles. You can get details of your nearest branch – and an information pack which includes a list of publications – from (large s.a.e.):

> Asthma Society
> St Thomas's Hospital
> London SE1 7EH
> 01–261 0110 (9.30 to 5.30)

See 'Asthma and Allergy', Asthma Society

BACK PROBLEMS

You do not have to be tall to have back problems at some time during your life. Many women 'put their back out' simply by lifting their baby out of the cot. It is important that you learn how to lift everything in the correct way. Try to bend at the knees rather than straight over from the waist. Correct posture is also very important. You should stand straight and tall without your back arched.

Sometimes backache can be caused by sleeping on a sagging bed. If your bed is not firm enough, try putting boards (or the ironing board) under the mattress – or, ideally, buy a new bed (see 'Orthopaedic Beds', page 451). If you have persistent or recurring backache go to your doctor.

If your back suddenly 'freezes' when you are at home try to get yourself on to your bed and lie still. If the problem is severe call the doctor.

Sadly, if you have ever had back problems you will be prone to them all your life.

- For general information contact:

> Back Pain Association
> Grundy House
> 31–3 Park Road
> Teddington
> Middlesex TW11 0AB
> 01–977 5474

See 'Back Complaint or Bed Complaint?' from Orthopaedic Bedding Design Centre (address on page 451).

CANCER

Breast cancer
If you find a lump in your breast the chances are that it is *not* anything

serious. But in case it is the sooner you do something about it the better.

Examine your breasts after your period or, if your periods have ceased, regularly once a month.

● *Breast test*
● Stand in front of a mirror, stripped to the waist. With your arms first by your side and then with your hands behind your head check for:

(a) any dimpling (a lump under the skin causes it to pucker)
(b) any change in shape
(c) nipples turned in or discharging (do not squeeze the nipples)
(d) veins standing out more than usual.

● Lie down in a comfortable position.

To examine the *left* breast:

(a) raise left arm behind your head
(b) with your right hand flat, fingers together, slide it above the nipple starting under the arm and moving across to centre of body – pressing to feel for lumps
(c) repeat below the nipple from the outside inwards
(d) slide your hand across the nipple
(e) feel for any lumps under the arm.

● To examine the *right* breast, repeat, using your left hand (right arm raised).

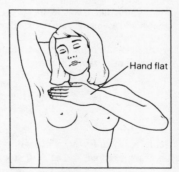

Breast self-examination

● If you want to have professional screening contact your medical insurance company or one of the Well Woman Clinics run by regional health authorities. To find the nearest clinic, look in the telephone directory or ask your local health authority. The headquarters of the Well Woman Clinics are at:

Well Woman Centre
Marie Stopes House
108 Whitfield Street
London WIP 6BE
01–388 0662

- If a lump is discovered and it is subsequently found to be malignant (cancer), then it will have to be removed surgically by *lumpectomy* – removal of the lump; or *mastectomy* – removal of the breast.

You should insist on taking part in the discussion and decision as to which operation you will have. Surgery of either type is usually followed by X-ray therapy or drug treatment.

MY MASTECTOMY
by Gillian Mann (courtesy of the Mastectomy Association)

I was thirty when I found a lump – it was not a complete surprise as I had had a growth removed from my back six months before.

Anyway, I went to the doctor and since he did not seem too concerned I went to my specialist who said 'leave it in my hands'. I did – and when I came round from the operation there he was by my bedside.

Apparently my reaction was unusual. I simply said 'thank you' and went back to sleep (many women, it seems, try to leap out of bed and attack the surgeon).

My surgeon was marvellous. He encouraged me to play badminton again. He said all the time 'it is up to *you*' and he really supported me.

My friends were marvellous too. There was one time, camping in the south of France, when my prosthesis swam out of my bikini and floated out to sea. One of the men with me swam out after it: it was a good thing everyone had a sense of humour.

It is so important that people are not scared by the word 'mastectomy'. People must realize that, if you are lucky, you can live a pretty healthy life afterwards and you should feel no different from other people.

- If you have had a mastectomy, you will gain information, comfort and general guidance from:

Mastectomy Association
26 Harrison Street
London WC1H 8JG
01–837 0908

They will send you information on how to get back to normal life as soon as possible and lists of stockists around the country of prostheses (artificial breast shapes) and mastectomy bras and swimsuits.

See 'Living with the Loss of a Breast: a Booklet for Mastectomy Patients', Health Education Council

Early detection of cancer
(from the American Cancer Association)
Consult your doctor immediately if any of the following signs and symptoms appear:
- *Any* sore that does not heal quickly, especially around the mouth.
- *Any* unusual bleeding or discharge from any natural body opening.
- *Any* painless lump, especially on breast, lips, tongue or soft tissues.
- *Any* persistent indigestion or unexplained weight loss.

- *Any* persistent hoarseness or cough or difficulty in swallowing.
- *Any* unexplained change in normal bowel habits.
- For advice and support contact:

> Women's National Cancer Control Campaign
> 1 South Audley Street
> London W1Y 5DQ
> 01–449 7532

- If you or anyone you know are found to have cancer, contact this support group:

> National Society for Cancer Relief
> 30 Dorset Square
> London NW1 6QL
> 01–402 8125

Cancer of the cervix (the neck of the womb)
- A *cytotest* can detect cancer of the cervix early.
- The doctor will do an internal vaginal examination and take a small sample (pap smear) – it is quite painless.
- It will be about two weeks before you hear the result. (Some clinics contact you only if the test shows an abnormality so ask about this before leaving the clinic or surgery.)
- You may be asked to go back for another test. Do not worry: the test picks up many things that are not cancer and they are easily treated.
- If it is an early sign of cancer then they will probably remove a small area about the size of your little fingernail. It will mean having an operation but it will not affect your sex life or your being able to have children.
- You will be asked to have regular pap smears just to keep an eye on you.
- As a matter of course, *all women, including those under twenty-five who have had intercourse, should have a smear at least every five years until they are sixty-five.*

Cancer of the womb
- Irregular bleeding after the age of thirty-five is probably due to hormonal changes and not cancer but it should be investigated.
- A more important sign is bleeding which occurs *after* the menopause.
- This cancer grows slowly so go to your doctor with the early signs.
- It can probably all be removed with a *hysterectomy* (removal of the uterus). This means that your periods will cease and you will not be able to get pregnant. However, it does *not* mean that you will lose your femininity, libido or that sexual intercourse will no longer be possible or that you will become fat.
- If the ovaries are removed as well (*bilateral oophorectomy*) then you may experience the signs and symptoms of the menopause.

CYSTITIS   This is an inflammation of the bladder lining.

Signs and
symptoms
- Stinging, burning or discomfort on passing water.
- You feel the need to pass water frequently but little water is passed.
- A dragging ache in your lower abdomen.
- Strong dark-coloured urine which may be blood-stained.

What to do
- Drink lots of water, milk or weak tea – drink at least half a pint every twenty minutes for the first three hours.
- Take 1 tsp of bicarbonate of soda dissolved in water – repeat every four hours.
- Keep warm, put a hot water bottle over your abdomen or between your thighs.
- Take two paracetamol – and repeat as necessary as stated on the packet.

To prevent further
attacks
- Drink plenty of water, milk or weak tea (three or four pints daily).
- Wash the genital area well with baby soap, using a special flannel which you should boil once a day – always wash and wipe from front to back.
- Use soft toilet paper.
- Use no bath oils, bubble baths, talcum powder, deodorants or anti-septic near the genital area.
- It is not necessary to bath every day – this may cause inflammation of the urethra. Use shallow and not deep bath water (a shower is better still).
- Before intercourse:
(a) you and your partner should wash with plain water
(b) use a special lubricant to prevent soreness and bruising (e.g. KY-jelly).
- Pass water after intercourse.

See   'Cystitis' from:

Health Education Council
78 New Oxford St
London WC1A 1AH

DIABETES   This is a condition in which the body is unable to regulate the sugar concentrations in the blood. Too much sugar accumulated in the blood-stream is known as *hyperglycaemia*; too little sugar is *hypoglycaemia*.

Hyperglycaemia develops slowly. The patient loses weight and becomes tired – he may even pass into a coma. As the situation deteriorates over several days he usually feels unwell enough to consult the doctor. When the condition is diagnosed and treated, he will have to remain on insulin injections or tablets for the rest of his life; and he must eat regular meals and stick to a special diet. If he forgets his drugs or does not stick to his diet his blood sugar will rise again. If he takes too much insulin or overexerts himself he will become hypoglycaemic. This affects the brain and if not treated it will lead to unconsciousness and possibly death.

Hypoglycaemia
- The patient may feel faint and dizzy or be staggering about like a drunk.
- He may be pale and sweaty.
- His pulse may be rapid, above 100.
- Breathing may be shallow.
- His limbs may shake and his level of responsiveness may deteriorate (see 'Unconsciousness', page 167).

What to do
- If patient is conscious and able to swallow give sugar lumps, or sugary drink or chocolate (this will raise the blood sugar level).
- If unconscious but breathing normally, place in recovery position (see 'Unconsciousness', page 167).
- Get patient to hospital immediately.
- Details of suggested diets and good cookbooks for diabetics can be obtained (s.a.e.) from:

> British Diabetic Association
> 10 Queen Anne's Street
> London WIM OBD
> 01–323 1531
>
> British Diabetic Association (Scotland)
> 8 Hillpark Loan
> Edinburgh EH4 7BH
> 031–336 7675

DRUG DEPENDENCY

Common causes for drug taking:
- Young people look for new and exciting experiences or they find themselves with others who are using drugs and they feel that they ought to join in.
- Someone, often a young person, has a problem which has grown out of all proportion and drugs seem to be the answer – they block out the problem for a while.

Drug dependency is mental and/or physical dependence on drugs which are taken continously or regularly in order to experience their pleasant effects and to avoid the unpleasant effects of withdrawal.

Amphetamines ('uppers') are stimulants. They make the user feel wide awake and full of life but, as the drug wears off, leave a feeling of depression and great tiredness so he takes another one to get back on to the high. This will eventually lead to mental and physical exhaustion. Amphetamines are addictive.

Barbiturates ('downers') are normally used as sedatives and when abused have an effect similar to that of alcohol. They make the user less inhibited:

he becomes talkative, excited, irritable and even trembles. Speech becomes slurred and he is unsteady on his feet. This is followed by drowsiness, confusion and – in cases where large doses have been taken – unconsciousness and coma. Barbiturates are addictive.

Cannabis makes the user feel relaxed and confident and may have a mild hallucinating effect.

Cocaine is often combined with heroin. It can be sniffed or injected and it appears to speed up such intellectual functions as making rapid decisions. It increases self-confidence and gives a euphoric effect. It is also a drug of addiction.

LSD makes the user hallucinate, causing psychological and physical problems (e.g. distortion of space and distance). A few people have walked out of a window because they believed they could fly.

Opiates (*heroin, morphine, opium, pethidine*) are all drugs of addiction and can be taken several ways, including intravenously. Heroin is the most commonly used drug of this group. It makes the user feel happy and excited – the effects wear off within about four hours and withdrawal is felt with irritability, anxiety, yawning, running eyes and nose, restlessness, diarrhoea and vomiting, limb pains and stomach cramp.

Help
- If you – on your own behalf or that of someone else – need help, telephone 01–289 1123 or 01–603 8654 (24-hour emergency service).
- Information and referral on illegal and prescribed drugs is offered by:

> Release
> 1 Elgin Avenue
> London W9 3PR
> 01–289 1123 or 01–603 5864

> South Wales Association for the Prevention of Addiction
> 111 Cowbridge Road East
> Cardiff CF1 9AG
> 0222–26113

- The Church of Scotland operates a counselling and support group for drug addicts and their families (especially teenagers):

> Simpson House
> 52 Queen Street
> Edinburgh EH2 3NS
> 031–225 6028

- Tranquillizers are mainly benzodiazepines, which include Alivan, Librium and Valium. Dalmane and Mogadon (sometimes called sleeping pills or 'hypnotics') are tranquillizers in large doses. Tranquillizer dependency is mostly found among women. If you are prescribed tranquillizers, discuss with your doctor the effects they might have and ask exactly how long you should take them for. For information and support with tranquillizer dependency, contact:

Tranx
2 St John's Road
Harrow
Middlesex HA1 2EZ
01-427 2065

South Wales Association for the Prevention of Addiction
111 Cowbridge Road East
Cardiff CF1 9AG
0222-26113.

- See also 'Glue Sniffing' below.

EPILEPSY

When an epileptic is having a fit:
- He may have an 'aura' (a 'feeling') before getting a fit.
- He falls to the ground, sometimes lets out a short cry. For up to one minute he is quite motionless and rigid, not breathing, and his mouth and lips turn blue.
- Then convulsive jerking movements begin and he may bite his tongue.
- Finally, muscles relax and he may remain unconscious for a few minutes or more.

What to do
- Do not try to control the jerking – clear a space so he does not hurt himself.
- Do not put anything into his mouth.
- When convulsions cease, put in the recovery position (see 'Unconsciousness', page 167).
- Do not try to wake him. Stay with him until fully recovered.
- There is no need to send for an ambulance (unless he has several fits one after the other or has injured himself).
- Advise him later to tell his doctor.

Help

British Epilepsy Association and Epilepsy Research Fund
Crowthorne House
Bigshotte
New Wokingham Road
Berks RG11 3AY
0344-773122

National Society for Epilepsy
Chalfont Centre for Epilepsy
Chalfont St Peter
Gerrards Cross
Bucks SL9 0RJ
02407-3991

The Epilepsy Association of Scotland
48 Govan Road
Glasgow G51 1JL
041-427 4911

FITS OR
CONVULSIONS

Children's convulsions

These are usually due to a high temperature in children up to four years old. Symptoms include:
- high fever, sweating
- he will become rigid and the muscles of his arms, legs and body will relax and contract so that he jerks and twitches
- his face may grimace with his teeth clenched and he may hold his breath
- his back and spine may be arched.

What to do
- *Do not put anything into his mouth.*
- Loosen constricting clothing around neck and chest.
- Put him on the floor in a clear space – do not restrict.
- Stay with him in case he vomits or injures himself.
- Treat as for an unconscious casualty (see 'Unconsciousness', page 167).
- Cool by removing bedclothes and clothes and then sponge with tepid water, starting from head and working downwards and let him dry. Do not allow him to become chilled.
- Call the doctor.

GLUE
(SOLVENT)
SNIFFING

Substances sniffed include aeroplane glues, aerosols, enamels, glues, lacquers, lighter fuel, nail polish remover, paint thinners, plastic cements in building kits and spot or stain remover. They have an intoxicating effect and may lead to unconsciousness or sudden death.

Sniffers are commonly between the ages of twelve and sixteen and may well give it up when they are legally old enough to buy more socially acceptable substitutes such as alcohol.

For advice telephone the youth counselling section of your local social services department or the health education unit. Alternatively, contact:

> Kick It
> 6 Church Street
> Wolverton
> Milton Keynes MK12 5NJ
> 0908–368869

See
'Sniffing Glue and Other Solvents' (send 60p (inc. p.&p.) to 1 Elgin Avenue, London W9 3PR)

HEART
ATTACK OR
CORONARY
THROMBOSIS

A *heart attack* is linked with changes in the lining of the walls of the coronary arteries which become narrowed and thickened. These arteries supply the heart with blood. A *coronary thrombosis* is a sudden blockage of a narrowed artery by a clot. Sometimes there is no clot only extreme narrowing of the arteries; this is *arteriosclerosis*. The blockage of the blood supply to the heart muscle (myocardium) causes the area of muscle served by that particular blocked artery to die (infarct); this is called a *myocardial infarction* or heart attack.

Factors which may contribute to a coronary thrombosis

● *Diet*: a diet high in animal fats may lead to a higher blood cholesterol level. A high blood cholesterol level leads to the greater risk of fatty substances being deposited in the lining of the coronary arteries which will narrow the artery and reduce the blood supply to the heart. These deposits of fatty substance are called atheroma.

● *High blood pressure*: the higher the blood pressure the greater the risk of developing coronary artery disease.

● Smoking.

● A family history of coronary heart disease.

● Lack of exercise.

● *Obesity*: overweight may be the result of a diet high in animal fat and lack of exercise.

● *Tension, anxiety, stress*: it does seem that there is a higher incidence of coronary heart disease among people who suffer from these.

Signs and symptoms

● Uncomfortable pressures, squeezing or pain in the centre of the chest may spread to the neck, left shoulder or arm.

● This feeling builds up gradually: the pain may be no more than a dull ache and is often mistaken for indigestion although it may, alternatively, be severe.

● There may also be sweating, shortness of breath, a weak rapid pulse, nausea and dizziness and the patient may feel cold and clammy.

What to do

● Loosen tight clothing and let patient choose the best position for breathing (probably sitting up); if lying down, the patient should be supported with pillows or rolled-up clothing.

● Calmly reassure him. Do not fuss. Minimize shock (see 'Shock', page 165).

● If heart and breathing stop, resuscitate (see 'Heart Massage', page 162 and 'Artificial Respiration', page 144). *Do not massage a beating heart.*

● If unconscious, put in recovery position (see 'Unconsciousness', page 167).

● Call for ambulance or doctor.

● Some of the research into heart problems is funded by:

British Heart Foundation
102 Gloucester Place
London W I H 4 D H
01–935 0185

HYPO-
THERMIA

The body temperature falls below 35°C (95°F) – you need a special thermometer to record these readings. Babies and the elderly are most at risk.

The conscious casualty becomes slow and dazed. The skin is often puffy and pale or blue and cold to touch all over. The pulse and breathing rate become very slow. Some babies go a red colour even when close to death.

INFECTIOUS You should report these to your doctor. Always consult your doctor before giving any medicines to a child.
DISEASES

DISEASE	USUAL INCUBATION PERIOD	DAY OF APPEARANCE OF RASH	INFECTIOUS PERIOD	COMMENTS
Chicken pox	15 to 18 days (may be as long as 3 weeks)	1st	From a day or so before the rash appears until 6 or 7 days after the appearance of the first spots	Slightly raised temperature, crops of red spots, then fluid-containing vesicles (which look like little blisters). These burst and dry up to form scabs. The rash starts on the front of the body and spreads to the neck and shoulders and is very itchy. Apply calamine lotion or add bicarbonate of soda to a warm bath. After bathing pat dry with a towel.
German measles (rubella)	10 to 21 days (most children develop symptoms 18 days after exposure)	1st	One day before and until 2 days after the appearance of the rash	Headache, sore throat, slightly raised temperature, a rash of small pink spots starting on the face and neck, then spreading to body and limbs. Not serious in itself but may affect the unborn child.
Influenza	1 to 3 days	No rash	Until acute symptoms have subsided	Coughing, sneezing and sore throat, fever, headache and limb pains, feeling generally unwell. Put the patient to bed, give aspirin or paracetamol to bring down the temperature and reduce aches and pains. Plenty of fluids. Keep warm

	10 to 15 days	4th	5 to 6 days before the rash appears and for 4 to 5 days after the temperature is normal	and comfortable. If symptoms are getting worse rather than better in 2 to 3 days, call the doctor.
Measles				Child is miserable with a stuffy head and running nose and raised temperature. Rash starts behind the ears and close to the hair-line and spreads over the face and body, fading within a week. The spots are slightly raised, itchy dusky pink. They are separate at first and then run together to give a blotchy appearance. Small white spots can be seen on the lining of the cheeks. Temperature may rise to 104°F (40°C) with diarrhoea, vomiting, earache or conjunctivitis – these will disappear as the rash spreads. Rash starts to go 5 to 6 days after symptoms appear. Give soluble aspirin or paracetamol for raised temperature, plenty to drink and tepid sponge if necessary (see 'Fits'). If worried, call the doctor.
Mumps	12 to 24 days (majority develop it about 18 days after exposure)	No rash	Day or so before swelling appears until the swelling goes down	Inflammation of salivary glands (under jaws in front of ear and under tongue). Rare in children under five. A mild fever, headache, pains in the neck muscles with swelling in front of and under the ear, usually on one side followed by other side a few days later. Eating and talking are

DISEASE	USUAL INCUBATION PERIOD	DAY OF APPEARANCE OF RASH	INFECTIOUS PERIOD	COMMENTS
				painful. Glands under the jaw also swell in the next few days – swelling may last from 3 to 7 days. Plenty of fluids, soft diet that does not need chewing. Regular cleaning of teeth and rinsing mouth with water. Aspirin or paracetamol for pain. Complications occur in about 1 in 5 men or boys who get mumps after puberty: may result in sterility so they should avoid contact. If patient develops a sore throat, stiff neck or high fever call the doctor at once.
Scarlet fever	2 to 5 days	1st or 2nd	7 to 14 days or until the nose and throat swabs taken by the doctor are negative	Headache, sudden fever, maybe some vomiting and stomach-ache. Sore throat (tonsillitis) may need antibiotics (see doctor). Rash may appear first on side of neck and chest and spread to the rest of the body concentrated around the neck, armpits and groin. Small bright red spots, close together. Rash may be mild. Tongue appears red at one stage (red strawberry tongue). Rash starts to fade after 3 to 4 days and the

				skin may continue to peel for 2 to 3 weeks.
Whooping cough	5 to 14 days	No rash (cough develops about 7 days after exposure)	About 5 weeks from the onset of symptoms	Serious and dangerous if contracted before four months old (mother does not provide immunity for the first few months). *Very contagious. Keep child away from school if you suspect it.* Starts like a cold, with a raised temperature and a cough: continues for a week with cough getting worse, developing into the whoop, which is due to breathing in suddenly through a narrow windpipe which is still partly closed from coughing. Patient may bring up thick mucus or even vomit. He is left breathless and exhausted. Hold the child's head tilted downwards if the coughing is severe to prevent inhalation of vomit or mucus. Coughing fits gradually become less frequent but the illness lasts about two months. *Do not take the child to the surgery.* Telephone the doctor for advice. This is a serious illness.

The unconscious casualty may appear to be dead because the breathing and heartbeat are so slow and weak.

What to do
- Put the patient to bed and cover with loose blankets. Warm him up slowly, but *no hot water bottles or electric blankets.*
- If conscious, warm (not hot) drinks. *No alcohol.*
- Warm the room – the temperature should be between 27 and 30°C (80 and 85°F).
- Call the doctor immediately.

INDIGESTION

Some people think they are particularly prone to indigestion – and others think they only get it when eating certain foods or when eating too fast. There is a burning feeling in the stomach which rises up into the throat – usually about an hour after eating.

An indigestion tablet or 1 tsp of bicarbonate of soda dissolved in water might help. If you are prone to indigestion, it is a good idea to have plenty of exercise and rest and to avoid overeating, especially rich and fatty foods.

If you suffer from frequent bouts of indigestion, consult the doctor.

MIGRAINE
AND
HEADACHE

Many people have headaches from time to time (through too much alcohol, reading in poor light, bad eyesight, stress, etc.).

Migraine
A migraine is a more severe than normal headache, and is accompanied by one or more of the following:
- flickering vision
- feeling of nausea or even vomiting
- a throbbing headache on only one side
- aversion to light and noise
- patient looks pale.

People who suffer from migraine are often over-conscientious and the attack sometimes comes during a period of relaxation following a time of intense activity or anxiety. Regular holidays, relaxation and trying to avoid 'overdoing it' may help. Sometimes certain foods (e.g. cheese, chocolate or alcohol) may bring on an attack.

What to do
- If possible lie down in a darkened room.
- Take two pain-killing tablets (your doctor will be able to prescribe effective pain-killers).
- Place a cold compress on forehead.

Note
- If you are caught suddenly with a migraine in central London, ask to be taken to the City of London Migraine Clinic. You can go, without referral from a doctor, only if a migraine is actually going on:

City of London Migraine Clinic
22 Charterhouse Square
London EC4M 6DX
01–251 3322

Help If you think you suffer from migraines see your doctor. Support, help and information are available from:

> British Migraine Association
> 178a High Road
> Byfleet
> Weybridge
> Surrey KT14 7ED
>   093–23 52468

> Migraine Trust
> 45 Great Ormond Street
> London WC1N 3HD
>   01–278 2676

PRE-
MENSTRUAL
TENSION
This may be due to water retention. Your breasts feel tender and swollen and abdomen bloated. You may become irritable, depressed, sleepy, have headaches or even migraine.

Help See your doctor. For help and information contact (s.a.e.):

> National Association for Premenstrual Syndrome
> 23 Upper Park Road
> Kingston-upon-Thames
> Surrey KT2 5LB
>   (No telephone)

SMOKING See page 385.

STROKES These are caused by an impairment of the blood supply to the brain. If you think of the brain as a telephone exchange and part of the exchange becomes damaged, then all those subscribers controlled by the damaged part would find their telephones out of order. If the part of the brain affected governs speech or movement on one side of the body then the patient will be unable to move that side or speak.

Someone who has had a stroke may suffer from mild temporary clumsiness of hand, leg or speech. A more severe stroke leads to total loss of power of half of the body. A patient may be slightly confused or unconscious.

Slight stroke
- Put the patient to bed and phone for the doctor.
- Stay with him in case he gets worse.

Severe stroke with unconsciousness
- Put in recovery position (see 'Unconsciousness', page 167).
- Phone the doctor.

● After a stroke, patients may suffer from *dysphasia*, a communication problem which affects the ability to speak, write and understand spoken or written words. Contact:

> Action for Dysphasic Adults
> Northcote House
> 37a Royal Street
> London SE1 7LL
> 01–261 9572

SUNBURN
Skin is red, tender and swollen with possible blistering.

What to do
● Put the patient in the shade.
● Gently sponge skin with cold water.
● Give sips of cold water frequently.
● Seek medical advice if there is extensive blistering or your patient becomes unwell.

VAGINAL HEALTH AND DISCOMFORT
The genitals should be kept as clean as possible. Wash the area daily and wear clean underpants every day. Always wipe yourself with toilet tissue from front to back. Avoid sprays, deodorants, talc and strong perfumed soap and bath products – and try to avoid sitting on public toilet seats.

It is normal to have a wetness or secretion from the vagina (it is there to keep the vagina clean and healthy). A clear, slightly milky discharge (pale yellow when dry) is the normal secretion.

Consult your doctor if you have any of these abnormal discharges:
● Severe itching and cheesy discharge – probable cause: *moniliasis*, also known as *thrush*. You are most susceptible to this if you are pregnant or on the pill, anaemic or diabetic or if you have recently been on antibiotics or you are run down.
● Large amount of green extremely offensive smelling discharge – probable cause: *trichomoniasis*, or trich or TM. This infection can be spread by dirty flannels or via sexual transmission.
● Heavy discharge of pus, pain, frequency (passing uring often) – probable cause: *gonorrhoea*. See 'Sexually Transmitted Diseases', Chapter 8.
● Vaginal discharges may occur when the body undergoes physical or hormonal changes which affect the vagina (e.g. pregnancy). They may also occur after sexual activity but even if a woman has never had sexual intercourse she can develop vaginal infection.

See
'Vaginal Health and Discomfort' from the Health Education Council (address on page 197).

VARICOSE VEINS
In the leg veins there are valves which keep the blood flowing back to the heart. When these valves deteriorate the blood tends to pool so the veins become permanently dilated and distended, making them vulnerable and easily ruptured.

What to do
(if a vein ruptures)

- Elevate the leg.
- Press your hand on the bleeding part for ten minutes.
- Apply a dressing.
- Observe for further bleeding.
- Minimize shock (see 'Shock', page 165).
- Transport to hospital.

Public and Private Medicine

THE NATIONAL HEALTH SERVICE   PRIVATE MEDICINE

THE
NATIONAL
HEALTH
SERVICE

The NHS covers all aspects of medical and surgical care except alternative medicines such as aromatherapy, acupuncture, chiropractic therapy, homoeopathy and osteopathy (see relevant organizations – listed in Chapter 20). Even these disciplines may be included if your doctor advises alternative treatment.

- To find the range of National Health Service services, contact your community health council.
- To change your general practitioner if you have moved, apply to a GP in your new area. If you want to change doctors because you are not happy with your present GP, you can apply to another GP and get your previous GP to sign your medical card. Alternatively, send your card to the Family Practitioner Committee with a note saying why you want to change. If you do this you will not be able to see your new GP for fourteen days.

Your GP can remove you from his list without giving any reason but the Family Practitioner Committee will make sure that you get a new GP.

Complaints

- If you have suffered a medical accident (including wrong diagnosis or treatment) for help and support contact: ˙

> Action for the Victims of Medical Accidents (AVMA)
> 135 Stockwell Road
> London SW9 9TW
> 01–737 2434

- If you think you have cause for complaint about any part of the NHS or that you have been treated unjustly through bad administration:

1. You should complain first to the health authority. Write to the administrator of the Authority or the Family Practitioner Committee responsible for the service concerned (address from your community health officer – in the telephone directory – who will help you with your letter).

2. If you are not satisfied, write directly to the:

> Health Service Ombudsman
> Church House
> Great Smith Street
> London SW1P 3BW
> 01–212 7676

PRIVATE
MEDICINE

Many good general practitioners and all family planning clinics regularly test women patients' blood pressure, urine and breasts and do cervical smears. Some women, however, think they get a more thorough health check privately and some large companies make gynaecological checks available for all female staff.

● Insurance plans (e.g. British United Provident Association [BUPA] and Private Patients Plan [PPP]) pay medical costs for an illness or accident but not for general practitioner care:

British United Provident
  Association
Provident House
Essex Street
London WC2R 3AX
  01–353 9451

Private Patients Plan
Eynsham House
Crescent Road
Tunbridge Wells
Kent TN1 2PL
  0892–40111

Bristol Contributory Welfare
  Association
Bristol House
40–56 Victoria Street
Bristol BS1 6AB
  0272–293742

Crown Life Assurance Group
Crown Life House
Woking
Surrey GU21 1XW
  04862–5033

Western Provident Association
Freepost
Bristol BS1 5YT
  0272–23241

● The Hospital Saving Association pay a guaranteed cash benefit whether you are in hospital or convalescing at home. They also pay dental, optical and maternity benefits:

Hospital Saving Association
Hambleden House
Andover
Hants SP10 1LQ
  0264–53211

Further Information

For names and addresses of organizations that are not part of the National Health Service see 'Alternative Medicine', page 578.

*Suggested
further reading*

Many of the free leaflets mentioned throughout this book are available from the Health Education Council which serves England, Northern Ireland and Wales, or from your health visitor. Contact (s.a.e.):

Supplies Department
Health Education Council
78 New Oxford Street
London WC1A 1AH
01–637 1881

If you live in Scotland you have your own range of health publications. Contact (s.a.e.):

Scottish Health Education Group
Woodburn House
Canaan Lane
Edinburgh EH10 4SG
031–447 8044

FIRST AID AND FAMILY HEALTH

A–Z of Family Medicine, Reader's Digest
Carding, David Kellett, *The Family Medical Handbook*, Unwin Paperbacks
Consumers' Association, *The Which? Guide to Family Health*
Playfair, A. S., *Modern First Aid*, Hamlyn
Smith, Bradley and Gus Stevens, *The Emergency Book*, Penguin
Travellers' First Aid, Reader's Digest
● For First Aid and children, see suggestions for further reading for Chapter 9.

ALCOHOLISM

Bauer, Jan, *Alcoholism and Women: the Background and the Psychology*, Inner City Books
Camberwell Council on Alcoholism, *Women and Alcohol*, Tavistock Publications
Kessell, Neil and Henry Walton, *Alcoholism*, Penguin
McConville, Brigid, *Women under the Influence*, Virago Press

BACK PAIN

Consumers' Association, *Avoiding Back Trouble*
Hall, Dr Hamilton, *Be Your Own Back Doctor*, Granada

CYSTITIS

Kilmartin, Angela, *Cystitis: a Complete Self-help Guide*, Hamlyn

DEPRESSION

Nairne, Kathy and Gerrilyn Smith, *Dealing with Depression*, Women's Press
Rowe, Dorothy, *Depression: the Way out of Your Prison*, Routledge & Kegan Paul
Stanway, Dr Andrew, *Overcoming Depression*, Hamlyn

DIABETES

Beer, Gretel and Paula Davies, *The Diabetic Gourmet*, Granada
Stritch, Elaine, *Am I Blue?*, Granada

DRUGS
Foster, Fiona and Alexander McCall Smith, *So You Want to Try Drugs?*, Macdonald (for young people)
Haddon, Celia, *Women and Tranquillizers*, Sheldon Press

HEART ATTACK
Anderson, Dr Ian, *Heart Attacks Understood*, Pan

MENSTRUATION
Dalton, Dr Katharina, *Once a Month*, Fontana
Weideger, Paula, *Female Cycles*, Women's Press

MIGRAINE
Wentworth, Josie A., *The Migraine Guide and Cookbook*, Corgi

STRESS
Consumers' Association, *Living with Stress*

NATIONAL HEALTH SERVICE
Consumers' Association, *A Patient's Guide to the National Health Service*

7 Lifecycle

Without reverting to that old idea of life as merely 'hatchings, matchings and dispatchings', these milestones are what this chapter is about.

Here are the major events of adult life (growth, development and puberty can be found in Chapter 9). From marriage and cohabitation the chapter progresses to motherhood, the possibility of separation and divorce and the certainty of menopause, pre- and eventual retirement and older age. The finale is death, but preparation for it is something that should be considered seriously, so I have included that too.

Marriage and Other Relationships

After adolescence, most girls spend some time as single adults before entering a stable relationship. Some live at home with their parents. Others choose independence.

This can be a difficult decision for someone who has only known home. Where else is there to live? For anyone in such a dilemma the Young Women's Christian Association (YWCA), which has hostels, can be a great help. The national headquarters is at:

Hampden House
2 Weymouth Street
London WIN 4AX
01–636 9722

Young people often want to live by themselves, but some prefer to share a flat with other women or men. Many flat-dwellers think of this as a blissful temporary period of little responsibility other than being able to pay the rent and telephone bills. At the time it is fun. Later, looking back, memories of nothing but cheese to eat (again) and exorbitant bills and problems with flat mates makes it seem less exciting.

Increasingly today, women choose deliberately not to go into marriage; for others, however, the single state in early adult life is a natural preparation for engagement and marriage.

MARRIAGE

*Engagement
Anouncements*

An announcement is generally put in more or less the same papers that were chosen some years earlier for the couple's births. The bride's parents pay for this. The required announcement should be sent to the social editors of the papers concerned and it is preferable if the bride- or groom-to-be endorses the announcement.

A typical announcement might read:

> Mr E. J. Crown and Miss E. P. Cork
>
> The engagement is announced between Edward,
> son of Mr and Mrs Charles Crown of Carlisle,
> and Elinor, only daughter of the late Mr Christopher Cork
> and of Mrs Cork, of Cumnor.

Those who have been living together for some time may prefer to forgo a formal engagement as such and simply announce their forthcoming wedding. Those waiting for a divorce to come through before they can marry do not formally announce an engagement: someone who has been granted a divorce can announce an engagement, as can a widow.

*The legal
requirements*

The choices you have of preparing legally for marriage are:

Banns. In England, where you can marry at sixteen with parental consent, these are 'published' (i.e. read) on three consecutive Sundays after the second lesson at a Church of England service. You should then marry within three months of the last 'publication'. If you and your future husband live in different parishes the banns must be duplicated for both parishes.

● In Scotland, where it is legal to marry without parental consent at sixteen, banns have been replaced by a notice of intention to marry that will be displayed at the register office. You should get a marriage schedule after fourteen days and thereafter you can be married in a register office or in any recognized religious ceremony.

● In Northern Ireland marriages may be either religious or civil. Certain formalities are laid down by the Marriages Act (NI) 1954 and the formalities applicable to the various denominations vary.

Common licence. This is granted upon the authority of a diocesan bishop (apply to your nearest bishop's office). One of you must have lived in the diocese for at least the past fifteen days. The marriage must take place within the following three months.

Special licence. If you cannot meet the requirements for a common licence you can apply for this, granted only by the Archbishop of Canterbury. A special licence is not issued if either party has been divorced. You should apply to:

> Faculty Office
> The Sanctuary
> London SW1P 3JT
> 01–222 5381

Superintendent Registrar's Certificate. This is issued after notice of intention to marry has been displayed at the register office for three weeks: the wedding can take place within the next three months. This certificate – or a licence, see below – is required if you intend to marry in a Nonconformist chapel or Roman Catholic church or Jewish or other ceremony or in a register office: if the officiating person is not an 'authorized person' you will require the presence of the registrar who should be consulted in plenty of time about suitable dates and times.

Superintendent Registrar's Licence (sometimes wrongly called 'special licence'). You have to wait for only one clear day after announcing your intention of marriage. One of you must have lived in the district for the past fifteen days and the other must be living in England or Wales.

Registrar General's Licence. This is the secular equivalent of the special licence. It is usually required only when one of the couple is so ill he or she cannot be moved.

Notes   ● Except in the case of Jews and the Society of Friends (Quakers), in England and Wales the *building* in which the marriage takes place must be registered. With certain exceptions, marriages must be solemnized between 8 a.m. and 6 p.m. and the doors of the building must be left open while the ceremony is proceeding. In a Church of Scotland ceremony, marriage can be conducted anywhere – it is not confined to religious buildings.

● Jewish people need to give notice of their intended marriage to a registrar but the ceremony can take place in a synagogue or private house: they can marry after 6 p.m. For further details contact:

> Jewish Marriage Council
> 23 Ravenshurst Avenue
> London NW4 4EL
> 01–203 6311

● Naval personnel can have banns read by chaplains or commanding officers when at sea or abroad.

● There is no residence requirement in Scotland and persons in other parts of the UK may make postal application to a designated registrar for notice of intention to marry.

● The law on incest, which makes some marriages illegal, differs between England and Scotland.

● If one or both of the parties lives in Northern Ireland, residence in that province must be established for a minimum of seven days.

● A foreign woman marrying a British man does not automatically become a citizen of the UK: she must apply to the Home Secretary for naturalization.

● A British woman marrying a foreign man may retain her British citizenship if she wishes.

● Marriages in foreign countries of British citizens are as valid as those solemnized in Britain (see your local embassy or consulate).

See Nicholls, David, *Living Together: a Guide to the Law on Marriage and Cohabitation in Scotland,* from bookshops or the CAB.

Mothers-in-law It is not easy for a newly married woman to come to terms to the fact that her husband has known his mother all his life. Similarly, it is sometimes difficult for a mother-in-law to accept the fact that now her son 'belongs to someone else'.

Respect is required from both parties. One woman who has an extremely happy relationship with her daughter-in-law advises 'always being ready to help if asked but not to impose'. That advice is fine, but the daughter-in-law has to initiate the help by asking for it.

The relationship can, when successful, be extremely deep and enjoyable. Many women feel closer to their mothers-in-law than to their own mothers.

To make it work, each must respect the other's privacy with the man who is common to both their lives.

The back-up woman This term applies to the woman who has given up her own career, perhaps temporarily, to support her partner. She may or may not be housebound by children. What is definite, however, is that she is there when her partner needs her.

She may be a corporate wife. As her partner rises up the ladder of ambition, she is there to support at every rung. She will entertain the boss and his wife, and she knows how to behave at office functions.

Others describe this woman as 'non-working', which is absolutely untrue. She has given up a lot of her life simply to work behind the scenes for her partner. The back-up woman has many problems. Her friends have to understand that loyalty to her partner and his demands come first. She may be intensely lonely. She may resent the loss of her own identity. She may suffer depression – or turn to alcohol.

If you think that you fit into this category, try not to feel sorry for yourself. Appreciate the fact that you do not have to 'go out to work'. Try to arrange to keep up with your own friends by meeting them during the day. Take up hobbies, sports and activities that get you out of the house. Make the most of daytime television programmes. (See also the suggested reading at the end of this chapter.)

CO-HABITATION Living together might sound ideal to some. There is none of the hassle of the wedding and its arrangements and, if it does not work out, the relationship can be ended without all the fuss of a divorce.

Other people see living together as a natural stage in their lives after which marriage, whether or not to their live-in partner, will follow. Others live together as man and wife for many years and it is this cohabitant who is most likely to need the support of her legal rights.

Common law wife
A woman who lives with a man as his wife without being married to him

can be known as a common law wife. There is no legal time residency. Generally a common law wife has few of the rights of a legal wife:

● She and her partner must be taxed as single people.
● She cannot draw a DHSS retirement pension through her partner's contributions.
● Any children are illegitimate.

She can, on the other hand:

● Get a court order banning her partner from the home.
● Claim a share in the value of their home if she has contributed to it.
● If the father of her children leaves her she can claim for maintenance.

Notes   ● In Scotland, 'cohabitation with habit and repute' is sometimes recognized. As a result of having lived with the same man for a long time, both of you being free to marry and both you and those around you considering yourselves married to each other, you might be able to claim a widow's pension and a share of your late husband's property. You should see a solicitor.

● In Northern Ireland, the position of the common law wife is the same as in England and Wales except that, at present, she cannot get a court order banning her partner from the home.

THE SINGLE STATE   This is generally taken to refer to any adult without a regular partner. She may or may not have dependants: she may or may not be sharing her home ('single state' is not the same as 'living alone').

The category includes the young and those who have never married, by choice or circumstance. There are also the deserted and bereaved, and if you fit into this category see the section on widowhood below. There are people and organizations who understand how you feel and they can offer help and support.

Single mothers have particular problems in trying to bring up children without a partner (some of these are covered in Chapter 9). What do you do, for instance, if you go out to work and your child is sick? In 1984 Sara Holmes, mother of two young sons, made legal history by winning the legal right to work part-time only: the industrial tribunal's finding was that despite changes in the role of women in modern society raising children still tended to place a greater burden on them than it did on men (it is interesting to wonder what would have happened if the case had been brought by a single father).

If the single person is living alone, some of the special problems include loneliness and possible depression (see pages 177 and 590). If you are out at work during the day, there may be no one to let the plumber or electrician in. The financial burden of keeping a home may be immense. On the other hand, there are many advantages. You can do what you like when you like – and you have a lot more time in which to do it.

COMMUNAL LIVING   Although communal living in effect implies two or more adults sharing a home it is generally assumed not to refer simply to a married couple.

Categories who 'live communally' include unattached women sharing with other women and/or men, single women or couples living in another family's home, a family sharing their home with an elderly dependant or, conversely, young couples living in the home of one set of parents. Some people live communally because they enjoy companionship: others are forced by finance or circumstance to share a home.

In order to achieve harmony it is essential to respect everyone else's privacy and it may be a good idea to have a few unstated rules. It may be, for example, that no one else goes into granny's sitting-room without knocking first – or that none of the students in a mixed flat disturbs anyone trying to study.

It is also essential to establish beforehand who pays what share of any bills (electricity, gas, rates). Do not wait until the bill arrives. Since it is impossible to itemize a telephone bill you might find it easiest to install a payphone. Also determine eating arrangements. Some communal households prefer to eat as a unit, others find it easiest for everyone to feed themselves. If you all share such basic commodities as bread and milk, make sure there is always plenty (set up a shopping and cleaning rota).

Everyone involved in communal living has to be prepared to give and take and to accept the foibles of others. But, by the same token, you will benefit substantially from having others around you. There will be companionship when you need it, and you may appreciate having someone there to babysit or let the plumber in when you are out!

Motherhood

by Diana Hastings

THE MENSTRUAL CYCLE
PRE-CONCEPTUAL CARE
SIGNS AND SYMPTOMS OF
   PREGNANCY
FUTURE PARENTS
ANTENATAL CARE
PROBLEMS DURING PREGNANCY
MATERNITY BENEFITS
GROWTH AND DEVELOPMENT
CHILDBIRTH

NATURAL CHILDBIRTH
THE NEW MOTHER
PARENTAL RESPONSIBILITY
SINGLE MOTHERS
ADOPTION
FOSTERING
STILLBIRTH
INFERTILITY
CHILDLESS COUPLES

Note ● For contraception and abortion, see Chapter 8.

THE
MENSTRUAL
CYCLE

Each month – about every twenty-eight days – there is a cycle influenced by the ovarian hormones oestrogen and progesterone. The ovaries lie on each side of the abdomen and produce the hormones and eggs.

A few days after your last period the oestrogen levels in your blood start to rise: this stimulates the lining of the uterus to thicken and grow, ready to receive the fertilized egg. One egg is released from an ovary (ovulation)

Female
reproductive
organs

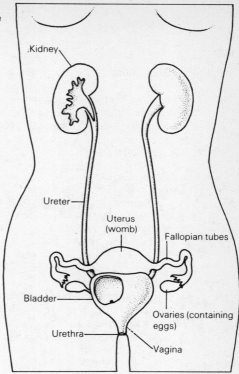

Kidney

Ureter

Uterus
(womb)

Fallopian tubes

Bladder

Ovaries (containing
eggs)

Urethra

Vagina

every 26 to 30 days, usually about half-way between the start of one period and the next – ovulation is therefore around the fourteenth day of your period. You are most fertile during the days either side of ovulation. If sexual intercourse takes place at this time the sperm will travel up through the cervix and along the fallopian tubes. If they come into contact with the egg, a single sperm will bury itself into it (conception). It takes about four days for the fertilized egg to travel down the fallopian tube and into the uterus, where it implants itself into the lining. Here it stays for nine months, developing into a baby.

After ovulation, the hormone levels rise, maintaining and enriching the thickened lining of the womb (uterus), which is there ready to receive the fertilized egg. If conception fails, both hormone levels drop and the lining of the uterus begins to shrink and is shed at about twenty-eight days after the last period. The period, or menstruation, lasts from two to eight days: everyone has her own cycle and the number of days between periods and the number of days that a period actually lasts varies. After a period, the oestrogen hormones start to rise and the cycle starts all over again.

PRE-
CONCEPTUAL
CARE

This aims to help both parents, as far as possible, to produce a happy, healthy start to their child's life. There is advice on the effects on the unborn child of alcohol, allergies, diet, drugs, pollution, smoking, etc.: the aim is for a healthy baby to be conceived and grown in a healthy environment. For more information contact:

> Foresight, The Association for the
>   Promotion of Preconceptual Care
> Woodhurst
> Hydestile
> Godalming
> Surrey GU8 4AY
>   048–68 5743

SIGNS AND
SYMPTOMS
OF
PREGNANCY

Early signs
● The menstrual period is missed (amenorrhoea). If you have regular periods, wait about ten days after the expected date of your period before seeing your doctor. If you have irregular periods, wait and see if there are any other signs, as listed below.

Note
● Amenorrhoea may also be caused by emotional stress, e.g. if you do not want to become pregnant and you are worrying that you may be. These emotions act on the part of the brain which controls the release of the sex hormones. Amenorrhoea may also be caused by some drugs and certain illnesses, e.g. anorexia.
● Breast changes. Some women say that their breasts feel full and uncomfortable. Sometimes there is a throbbing and tingling of the nipples. The nipples gradually become larger as the pregnancy progresses and the dark area around the nipple (areola) becomes larger, darker and swollen. By the eighth week, little raised bumps appear around the nipple in the areola (Montgomery's Tubercles): if you look closely, there may be more veins under the skin of the breast and you may even be able to squeeze a little clear fluid from the nipple. (This is really only a useful sign if it is a first pregnancy.)
● Nausea and vomiting affect about 50 per cent of pregnant women and usually start about two weeks after the first missed period. It is probably due to the increase of sex hormones produced during pregnancy (see 'Morning Sickness', below).
● Frequency of urination (or needing to pass water more often) sometimes happens: this is due to the bulky womb pressing on the bladder.

Examination and tests
● Your doctor will ask you if you have any of the above signs and symptoms. He will probably examine you by listening to your heart and examining your breasts and abdomen. He may gently insert two fingers into your vagina and, with his other hand, press your abdomen. He can feel the shape of your uterus, which is larger if you are pregnant. (If you

feel tense and uncomfortable during the internal examination, concentrate on taking deep breaths in and out to help you to relax.)
● Urine tests for pregnancy can be done by the doctor in his surgery or he may need to send them to a laboratory for testing. You can, alternatively, buy a test which you can do at home. Boots suggest that you talk to the pharmacist in any one of their shops.

Later signs of pregnancy
● The baby's heartbeat can be picked up by ultrasonic Doppler machines in the second or third month: the machine is quite harmless and works on the principle of soundwaves.
● Ultrasound is a machine which also uses soundwaves. They bounce off different parts of your body and produce a picture of your baby in the uterus as early as four weeks after conception. A beating heart can be seen at eight weeks.
● As your uterus – and the obvious bump – grows larger it becomes evident that you are pregnant. At about 18 to 20 weeks you may feel the slight movement of the baby (it is a good idea to write this down so that you can tell the doctor): these flutterings are called 'quickening'. As time progresses, these movements become stronger and you can feel your baby moving and kicking and little lumps and bumps appear and disappear on the surface.

Special tests
These are precautionary measures and are nothing to worry about.
Alpha Fetoprotein Test – a blood test to see if the baby is likely to have spina bifida (a defect of the central nervous system).
Amniocentesis – in women over thirty-five where there is an increased risk of the baby being abnormal (and in women with a positive blood test which suggests an abnormality), at about 14 to 16 weeks into the pregnancy the doctor passes a needle through the abdominal wall into the amniotic fluid surrounding the baby. This is carried out with a local anaesthetic and carries small risk of miscarriage or injury to the baby. The results may take up to three weeks to come through: if any abnormality is shown (Down's Syndrome or spina bifida) you may be offered an abortion.
Blood tests – unless you are anaemic there will be no further blood tests taken after your first antenatal visit (see below) until about the thirtieth week. If you are rhesus negative, the sample will be examined to see if any rhesus antibodies are developing.
Hormone tests – often carried out on either blood or urine to make sure that the placenta is working normally and providing adequate oxygen and nourishment for your baby.

FUTURE PARENTS

Having a baby means that there are going to be big changes in your life. A lot of babies are unplanned and it takes time to get used to the idea of having a baby. Men are sometimes worried by the inevitable responsibility, and even your parents, although they feel proud, may be worried and take a while to adjust to the idea of becoming grandparents.

The most important thing is to take care of yourself and your unborn baby. When your doctor has confirmed your pregnancy he or she will write a letter for you to take to the antenatal clinic or he will arrange to do the care himself. He will also discuss with you where you should have the baby. The following options may be open:

Hospital care. You are referred to the maternity hospital where you will be seen at the antenatal clinic regularly until your baby's birth. It is usually recommended that women over thirty expecting their first babies and those who have had four or more previous children should have their babies in properly equipped maternity hospitals.

Shared care (your doctor and the hospital). Your own doctor looks after you but you go to the hospital towards the end of your pregnancy. They will do any special tests that need to be done and they will book you a bed. You will actually have the baby in hospital.

Home delivery. Your own doctor and the domiciliary (community) midwife do all the antenatal care and the midwife will deliver your baby at home. This type of care is less used now but if you want to have your baby at home discuss it with your doctor (many doctors believe it is safer to have the baby in hospital).

Domino. Your doctor and the community midwife look after you at home until labour starts, and then the midwife takes you into hospital and delivers your baby there. After a few hours' rest she will arrange for you to go home. She will visit you every day giving all the care and advice you need.

General practitioner maternity units. These are small friendly units where your own doctor or the midwife will deliver the baby (part of your local hospital).

ANTENATAL CARE

Care is free under the National Health Service which offers expert advice, early detection of any complications and regular checks to see that you are both progressing normally. After your first visit you will usually be asked to attend: every month until you are 28 weeks pregnant, then every two weeks until the 34th or 36th week, and then every week until you go into labour.

Remember to keep your record card and blood group card safely, and take it with you to every appointment. If you are asked to bring a sample of urine with you, then one passed first thing in the morning is the most suitable.

● On your first antenatal visit to the hospital clinic or a doctor's surgery:

1. The doctor will ask you questions about your general health, any other pregnancies you have had and any past illnesses or operations.

2. He will listen to your heart and chest and examine your vagina and your womb (see above). He will do an internal examination to check that everything is normal and to see if your pelvis is large enough for a normal size baby to pass through. He may do a cytotest (see page 181).

3. You will be weighed, your height recorded, your blood pressure taken and your urine tested.

4. Blood will be taken to find out your blood group, rhesus factor and to check your haemoglobin. This will show if you are anaemic (your blood has too few red cells) – the condition is easily detected and treated. Blood will also be sent to the laboratory to check whether or not you have had rubella (german measles), and blood tests are carried out to exclude the possibility of venereal disease.

5. The doctor will suggest you go to the dentist for a check-up. While you are pregnant, and for one year after, dental treatment is free.

6. You will be invited to attend mothercraft classes, including antenatal exercises and relaxation instruction at the hospital or local health clinic.

7. You will be given a certificate confirming pregnancy so that you can claim maternity benefits (see below). You will be given advice about diet, hygiene and care of your breasts in preparation for breast-feeding – and you will be given a list of things to bring in to hospital and the telephone number to call when labour starts.

8. The doctor will also tell you when your baby is due (but remember that babies have a habit of not coming on time!).

● At subsequent visits to the antenatal clinic you will be asked about your health and your baby's. Do not be afraid to ask questions and ask for the results of any tests that have been done. You should always mention any troubles you are having (even family troubles, if they are relevant). Report any severe headaches, vaginal bleeding, swelling of your fingers or ankles and if the baby stops moving about. (If you feel unwell or you think that something is wrong, do not wait until your next appointment. Contact the doctor or midwife.)

1. You will be weighed – it is important to check that you are gaining weight at the correct rate.

2. Blood pressure will be recorded (it can rise during pregnancy and may be an early sign of complications: if it does start to rise you will probably be advised to rest). Blood tests are done at regular intervals to check that you are not anaemic.

3. Urine is tested, to check for any sugar, infection or protein, none of which should be present.

4. Your abdomen will be felt externally to see which way the baby is lying. In a few cases the baby lies the wrong way round (breech presentation) and the doctor may be able to turn him round the right way (head downwards). He will also estimate how much the baby is growing and whether the size of the uterus corresponds with the number of weeks' pregnancy.

5. The doctor will listen to the baby's heartbeat through a foetal stethoscope, or use the Doppler apparatus (you will be able to listen as well).

● Antenatal classes will help you during pregnancy, labour and with the care of your baby (they are very important and well worth attending).

They are free under the National Health Service (ask the hospital, midwife, health visitor or health centre for details). A few classes are held for expectant mothers during early pregnancy but the majority are held during the last three months, after you have given up work.

1. They may give you advice about diet.

2. They will help with problems like smoking, which has been proved, during pregnancy, to slow the physical and intellectual development of the baby. If you smoke, your baby is quite likely to be at risk – so it is best to give it up and avoid smoky atmospheres.

3. You are taught correct posture and lifting techniques. Pregnancy causes softening of the ligaments, which may lead to backache.

4. You are taught special exercises for use during labour – if possible, the father is encouraged to help you.

5. Advice is given on suitable supporting brassières and care of your breasts.

6. At some classes you can practise with the gas and air machine used to relieve pain in labour. You will be shown around the labour ward and the hospital so that you are familiar with the surroundings.

7. Classes also give you a chance to meet some of the other mothers so you will know someone when you go into hospital.

● Other relevant points during pregnancy

1. *No unprescribed drugs or pills* of any kind should be taken – they can be dangerous to the unborn child, especially during the first three months of pregnancy.

2. If you get *german measles* (rubella) during the first three months of pregnancy it can seriously damage your baby. Most women are tested in early pregnancy to see if they have the antibodies which will protect them from rubella.

3. *Fresh air and exercise* – especially walking – are good for you; you can dance, swim and ride a bicycle during the early months (ask your doctor if it is all right to continue with more strenuous exercise). Daily fresh air and exercise will help you get a good night's sleep.

4. *Rest and sleep* are important. As the pregnancy progresses you will need to take more rest periods during the day. Particularly during the last few months, try and take two hours' rest every afternoon, on your bed or a sofa with your legs raised to the same level as your body. Early nights are a good idea. Eight hours is ideal, but you may find it difficult to get to sleep towards the end of the pregnancy because you cannot get comfortable – see below (Sleep).

5. *Weight gain.* It is normal to put on about two stone (28 lb.) during pregnancy. This is made up of the weight of the fluid surrounding the baby, the placenta, the baby and the extra fat laid down during pregnancy to provide the energy for breast-feeding. The doctor and midwife will watch your weight carefully and advise if you are putting on too much or too little weight. It is best to avoid putting on too much weight in the early months as it may lead to your blood pressure rising during the later stages

of pregnancy, and it will also be more difficult to get your figure back afterwards. Pregnancy, however, is no time to be dieting. You should eat sensibly.

6. Have a *bath or shower* every day but make sure that the water is not too hot or cold (if you cannot bath or shower, sponge down instead).

7. *Care of the breasts:* if the nipples are flat, they should be drawn out every day between the forefinger and thumb (your doctor or midwife may recommend the wearing of special shields to help draw them out). Your breasts will enlarge and from about three months colostrum, a yellow-coloured liquid, is formed: if you express this liquid during the last 4 to 6 weeks of pregnancy it will encourage the flow of milk (ask your midwife to show you – do not try on your own without any guidance). Wash your nipples daily with soap and water to keep them clean and free from the crusts which form from dried secretions.

Notes
- Intercourse during pregnancy – see Chapter 8.
- For advice on diet during pregnancy – see Chapter 13.
- For advice on clothes during pregnancy – see Chapter 14.

PROBLEMS DURING PREGNANCY

Note

- These are symptoms that occur *only* during pregnancy. The same symptoms occurring when you are not pregnant have different causes.

Backache – sometimes the weight of a baby puts a strain on the muscles and joints during pregnancy, but backache at this time might also be caused by a urine infection, so tell your doctor. Try to get as much rest as possible, lying flat on a firm surface.

Constipation – may be due to hormonal changes. Try to prevent it happening by eating fibre and roughage – plenty of fresh fruit, vegetables and salads. Drink plenty of fluids. Do not dose yourself with laxatives or purgatives without first talking to your doctor.

Cramp – often occurs in the back of the calf or thigh during pregnancy (see 'Cramp', page 169).

Depression. During pregnancy, you may feel low and depressed in the first three months even if you really wanted your baby and are thrilled to be pregnant. This is probably due to the change in the hormone balance in your body and will pass, probably by the end of the third month.

Haemorrhoids (piles) – these are swollen veins, little tags or lumps of skin around the anus. They may feel sore or itch. They are caused by hormone changes in pregnancy and the extra weight of the womb. They are made worse by constipation as the straining will encourage their development.

What to do
- Your doctor will probably prescribe some cream or suppositories (small wax cones to insert into the anus).
- If they hurt more at the end of the day, put your feet up.

● If you feel a small bulge or lump in the anus, put a little petroleum jelly (vaseline) or the prescribed haemorrhoid ointment on your finger and gently push the pile back.

● Another remedy is to fill a small plastic bag with ice and hold it on to the piles: this will shrink them and take away the pain.

Piles almost always disappear after the birth of the baby.

Headaches – may be due to eye strain and can be relieved by special glasses, to wear just during pregnancy. They may also be due to constipation. In case of severe or persistent headache, go to the doctor.

Indigestion – usually occurs during the last months of pregnancy (when the ever-enlarging womb causes pressure) by the excess formation of acid in the stomach. (For symptoms, see 'Indigestion', page 192.)

Itching skin. A few women complain of an itchy skin, usually towards the end of pregnancy. This will disappear as soon as the baby is born – until then, use calamine lotion.

Miscarriage – this usually occurs in the first twelve weeks of pregnancy. The first sign is usually bleeding, slight spotting followed by a moderate amount of bleeding rather like a period. Or it may start with heavy bleeding and cramping pains.

However it starts, it may settle down and the pregnancy continue normally, but you should inform your doctor and take his advice.

In about 20 per cent of threatened miscarriages the bleeding and pain becomes worse and the baby is aborted. Call the doctor *at once* and keep anything that has been discharged from the vagina. He will give you something for the pain and examine you.

It may be necessary to be admitted to hospital for 'dilatation and curettage' (D-and-C), to clean out the womb.

Note ● A D-and-C is also used to investigate heavy or irregular bleeding.

● Support and information can be obtained from (s.a.e.):

> Miscarriage Association
> Dolphin Cottage
> 4 Ashfield Terrace
> Thorpe
> Wakefield
> Yorks WF3 3DD
> (no telephone)

Morning sickness – affects about 50 per cent of all pregnant women, commonly starting at about six weeks and continuing until the end of the third month. Sometimes it starts earlier than this and it may even be the first sign of pregnancy.

You may experience a vague feeling of nausea in the morning or afternoon, or there may be actual vomiting. Some women vomit a great deal and are unable to keep anything down: if this happens you should see your doctor.

● For mild cases of morning sickness the following may help:

1. Have a cup of tea and a dry biscuit before getting up. If you cannot take this, have a drink of meat or yeast extract and a piece of dry toast.

2. After this, stay in bed for a little longer than usual and get up slowly. Then have breakfast.

3. Throughout the day, have frequent, light meals. Avoid large, heavy or fried meals.

Sleep. The main ingredients of a good night's sleep include a good bed, comfortable temperature, quiet, and fresh air – even in cold weather, a window open a few inches will help produce good sleep.

● If you have problems getting to sleep try the following:

1. Make your evening meal light and easily digestible.

2. Sleep on a firm mattress – if the bed is too soft and sags in the middle you may get backache.

3. Bedclothes should be warm but light and the added comfort of a hot water bottle on a cold night might help.

If you are pregnant, eight hours' sleep is ideal but you may find it difficult to get to sleep towards the end of the pregnancy because you cannot seem to get comfortable. Sleep may be easier if you follow all the recommendations above – some women find lying on their side the most comfortable position while others prefer to be propped up on several pillows.

Stretch marks – silvery lines which appear on the abdomen during pregnancy. They are harmless and tend to fade a little after birth but there are special lotions and creams to inhibit their appearance (you can use them as soon as you know you are pregnant).

Swelling of the feet and legs – slight puffiness of the feet and ankles is common during the later weeks of pregnancy, especially the first one. It is due to the pressure of the baby in the womb on the large veins and it always disappears after the baby is born.

What to do ● Lie down whenever possible, with your feet raised level with your body.

● Loosen tight clothing around the waist.

Note ● Severe swelling of feet, face and hands during pregnancy may be due to toxaemia.

Toxaemia – is a disease that occurs during the last three months of pregnancy and gets better as soon as the baby is born. Severe toxaemia is rarely seen now: the majority of mothers go regularly for antenatal care and any early signs are treated to prevent it becoming worse.

It is characterized by a high blood pressure, protein in the urine and fluid around the ankles and fingers and sudden increase in weight. If neglected, this is a serious condition and may lead to fits and even to the death of the baby. But do bear in mind that at each antenatal clinic the routine checks of blood pressure and weight and urine test for protein will ensure early detection and effective treatment.

Treatment

● If your weight gain is abnormal, your blood pressure is raised and there are other warning signs, the doctor may advise more rest and a salt-restricted diet.

● He will probably want to see you more frequently or even admit you to hospital for rest and observation until the baby is born (more often, he will advise rest at home first).

These are quite common methods of treatment so do not worry: the best safeguard is the early recognition and treatment of mild toxaemia and it is rare for this to develop into anything more serious.

Urine infections – a frequent desire to pass urine may be present in the first few weeks of pregnancy and then again in the last 2 to 3 weeks. This is perfectly normal and lasts only for a short time. Pain on passing urine, which may smell fishy, may be due to infection of the bladder or kidneys and is not normal, so see your doctor immediately (infection is due to hormonal changes). The doctor will send a specimen of your urine to the laboratory to see if there is an infection and, if so, what kind. He will probably put you on a course of antibiotics.

Infections can be prevented to some extent by drinking plenty of water.

Vaginal discharge. During pregnancy the monthly periods stop and any bleeding or blood-stained discharge should be reported to your doctor (phone him rather than go to the surgery). It may be due to some minor problem or it may be the start of a miscarriage (see above), in which case you may experience some pain as well.

During pregnancy there is also a moderate amount of white or creamy discharge: there is no need to worry about this but if the discharge is yellow or yellowish green and if it starts to itch then you should tell your doctor and he will treat it, making sure that it has cleared up before you go into labour so that it will not damage the baby's health.

Varicose veins. If you have varicose veins, do not wear anything tight around the legs. Support hose can be prescribed by your doctor on the NHS. Put your special stockings or tights on before getting out of bed.

Try to get the weight off your feet as much as possible. Lie flat on bed or couch and raise your feet, with legs stretched straight out and supporting your feet against a wall. Stay like this for 5 to 10 minutes, three or four times a day, to relieve pain by reducing the size of the vein.

MATERNITY
BENEFITS

You are entitled to:

Maternity grant – a lump sum of £25 to help you buy things that you need for the baby. Almost every mother qualifies for this benefit. You need to claim on form BM4 any time from the 14th week before the baby is expected up to three months after birth. You need a Certificate of Expected Confinement form MAT1 or Certificate of Confinement form MATB2 from your doctor or midwife – or you need the baby's birth certificate.

Maternity allowance – this is a weekly allowance and it depends how many national insurance contributions you have paid. Get leaflet N17A and claim form BM4 from the clinic or social security office and return the form to the office between the 14th and 11th week before the baby is expected (even if you are still working).

Dental care and **prescriptions** are free during pregnancy and for one year following.

Spectacles can be obtained at reduced cost if you are on a low income: ask at the optician's.

You can claim for **milk** and **vitamins** if you are receiving supplementary benefit or Family Income Supplement or otherwise have a low income. (See claim form M1.)

Travelling expenses to antenatal departments may be refunded if the total family income is not above a certain level (if you think you qualify, fill in claim form M1).

If you are working, you are entitled to other benefits – see Chapter 11.

PREGNANCY
AND WORK

see Chapter 11.

GROWTH AND
DEVELOPMENT

During pregnancy your baby grows within your uterus for about forty weeks, starting as a tiny object the size of a pinhead. Until the 8th week, it is called an embryo: it is able to move freely because it floats in a bag of amniotic fluid, which protects it from injury. The bag of membranes stretch across the mouth of the uterus and within the closed bag the embryo grows in the dark, warm environment. It does not breathe through its nose, nor does it eat with its mouth: it gets food and oxygen from your bloodstream, through the placenta (afterbirth), which is joined to the baby at the navel (umbilicus) by the umbilical cord. The placenta is attached to the wall of the uterus: the baby's blood vessels and your blood vessels come in very close contact with each other on either side of the placenta but never actually mix.

6 weeks
Embryo does not look human – about 1.25 cm ($\frac{1}{2}$ in.) long. The heart forms very early in development and now beats visibly and audibly; eye socket has formed; arm and leg buds; placenta is larger (and weighs more) than the embryo.

8 weeks

Embryo looks more human – about 2.5 cm (1 in.) long. Large head small thin body; external parts of the ears are forming; legs and arms have tiny fingers and toes; eyes have eyelids (which remain closed until the 24th week). The main organs of the body are formed; heart is beating and blood circulating through the blood vessels.

From now on, all the organs get bigger and their functions become more involved.

12 weeks

Baby is no longer referred to as an embryo but a foetus – about 9 cm (3½ ins.) long and weighs about 14g (½ oz.). Nails on fingers and toes; body has grown and looks less out of proportion, but the head is still much larger; sex organs developing; foetus can swallow the amniotic fluid in which it lives, it will be passed as drops of urine; placenta now weighs about six times the weight of baby.

16 weeks

The baby is about 18 cm (7 ins.) long and weighs about 100g (4 oz.). Heart beats strongly; skin is transparent and looks bright red because the blood shows through; muscles becoming active; head is still larger than its thin body; sex organs have developed sufficiently so that the sex can be determined; placenta weighs about the same as baby.

20 weeks

Baby is about 25 cm (10 ins.) long and weighs about 300g (11 oz.). Skin is less transparent but covered with downy hair; hair is appearing on head and eyebrows; you may be able to feel the fluttering sensations as the baby moves about; internal organs are becoming more mature, but its lungs are still too immature for it to be able to breathe for itself outside the uterus; placenta's growth has slowed down and baby's growth is increasing.

24 weeks

Baby measures about 32 cm (13 ins.) and weighs about 650g (25 oz.). The eyelids have opened but the pupils are covered with a membrane. From now on, fat is deposited in the skin, which is less red but still wrinkled and covered in downy hair; head is still large compared with the body; lungs are still not fully developed and if the baby is born now it will have problems breathing.

28 weeks

Baby is about 38 cm (15 ins.) long and weighs about 1,000g (34 oz.). It can open its eyes (membrane covering the pupils has gone); skin is still rather wrinkled and red and covered with vernix (a white soapy substance which prevents the skin becoming waterlogged); heartbeat can be heard by doctor or midwife; if baby is born prematurely at this stage, it can breathe, cry weakly and move its legs but it would need special hospital care.

32 weeks
Length about 43 cm (17 ins.), weight about 1,800g (4 lb.). Body is getting plumper; lungs developed more and if it were born now it would probably live (still with special care). Usually settles into a head-down position ready for birth.

36 weeks
About 46 cm (18½ ins.) long, weight about 2,500g (5½ lb.). Putting on weight rapidly, fat deposited under the skin and around the shoulders; fingernails reach end of fingers; losing wrinkled appearance and almost ready to be born; head may drop down into the pelvis (this is known as 'lightening').

40 weeks
Length is about 50 cm (20 ins.), weight about 3,300g (7 lb. 4 oz.). Skin smooth, still covered with vernix; hair gone except perhaps a little on the shoulders; hair on head, which is now about one quarter of baby's length; eyes open and usually a slate-blue colour at birth (permanent colour later).

CHILDBIRTH   During your pregnancy the muscles of the uterus have been contracting occasionally (the uterus becomes hard and then relaxes again). You have probably not even noticed that this has happened until late in your pregnancy, when the contractions become more frequent and stronger. You may even think that labour has started but it is only a false alarm.

True labour begins when contractions become regular. With each contraction the cervix dilates (opens up more) and the baby comes down through the pelvis.

● The contractions come slowly at first (about one every half-hour), then they get stronger and come more regularly (about one every 10 to 15 minutes).

● The membranes around the cervix come away: there is a small discharge of blood and mucus (sometimes called 'a show').

● Occasionally the membranes rupture (waters break) and a small amount of fluid is released. This is the *first sign of labour*. The fluid comes from the burst bag of amniotic fluid which has been surrounding the baby in the womb.

● The most common sequence of events is:
(a) start of regular contractions
(b) slight blood loss
(c) waters breaking.

When to go into   ● Regular contractions, one every 10 minutes over the period of one
hospital   hour. (You should assume labour has started even if there has been no show and the membranes have not broken.)

● Slight bleeding is not enough evidence that labour has started, so wait for the contractions to begin.

● If your waters break, this means that the baby is on the way – so go to hospital.

● If in doubt as to whether labour has started, telephone and check with the doctor or midwife or the labour ward sister at the hospital where you are booked in.

Three stages of labour

First stage – from the onset of labour (as above) until the cervix is fully dilated so that it has become large enough to allow the baby's head to pass through. This stage takes several hours: it varies from 4 to 12 hours in a mother giving birth for the first time (a primipara) to 2 to 6 hours for a mother who has already had one or more babies (multipara). During this stage you will be offered an injection of pethidine if the contractions are painful – or an epidural anaesthetic may be available.

It is most important to remember the relaxation and breathing exercises that you have been taught in antenatal classes. Having someone with you – your husband or a friend or relative – is very helpful.

Note

● Pethidine will not put you to sleep or delay the birth. It will just make you more comfortable – it sometimes takes about fifteen minutes to work so tell the midwife when the contractions are getting uncomfortable (do not leave it until they are really bad). If given at the correct time, pethidine will not have any effect on the baby. If it is given too late and has an adverse effect on the baby, then there are drugs to reverse this.

● If you are offered an epidural block, it will be done under the supervision of a doctor. A needle is inserted into the lower part of the back into the spinal canal, close to the nerves which carry the pain sensations from the uterus to the spinal cord above. It anaesthetizes the vaginal nerves (perineum) and the leg nerves so that there is a feeling of numbness and you cannot move your legs properly. Once the needle is in position, a fine soft plastic tube is passed down through the needle – this stays in position throughout labour and more anaesthetic fluid can be injected as a top-up to prevent you feeling any pain when the uterus contracts.

● The doctor usually puts an intravenous drip into a vein in your arm. This is to give you some fluid if you feel sick or faint after the spinal anaesthetic injection has been given. One disadvantage of this method is that it is so effective that during the second stage of labour you may not be aware of the contractions and therefore you will have to be told when to push – sometimes the doctor may need to use simple low forceps to deliver the baby.

Second stage – from the dilatation of the cervix until the baby has been delivered. When the cervix has opened up you feel the urge to push the baby out. At this stage you will probably be offered the gas and air machine (Entonox). In a normal birth the head comes first and strong contractions push the baby out. The head and shoulders turn sideways to fit in with the shape of the birth canal. Once the head is born, the rest follows without too much effort on your part.

Notes

● Using the gas and air machine cannot make you unconscious and no one will hold the mask over your face – or make you use it. You hold it and are in control all the time. It is a very safe and effective way of treating any discomfort. You will be shown how to use the Entonox (a mixture of nitrous oxide and oxygen) during your antenatal classes. All you do is to hold the mask over your mouth and nose and take several deep breaths, then put the mask down until you want it again. Remember to start breathing through the mask as soon as you feel the contractions start.

● If you are having your baby at home, the midwife will bring the gas and air machine to your home.

Third stage. Once your baby is born there is no longer any need for the placenta or the umbilical cord, so the midwife ties off the cord in two places and cuts it, about 2.5 cm (1 in.) from the baby's navel, between the ties. (This does not hurt as there are no nerve endings in the cord.) The other end of the cord is still attached to the placenta, which then comes away from the wall of the uterus and is delivered with just one or more contractions.

NATURAL CHILDBIRTH

The aim is to keep the birth of your child as natural as possible. It involves a conditioned response that enables the active participation of you and your partner in the delivery of your baby. The method originated in the Soviet Union and in 1932 Dr Grantly Dick Read introduced his own method of concentrated relaxation during labour. The course of instruction lasts about three weeks and involves you and your partner.

● You have first to get rid of all the old ideas you had about labour – and learn what labour is really like.

● You learn a new pattern of breathing and relaxation techniques, which you practise daily. This allows you to control your own labour rather than it controlling you.

● A series of conditioned responses reduces the perception of the pain of the contractions.

● There are exercises to practise daily which tone up the muscles for labour.

● If you would like more information, contact:

National Childbirth Trust
9 Queensborough Terrace
London W 2 3 TB
01–221 3833

The Leboyer
birth method

This is named after a French doctor who believes that peace and calm at the moment of birth are essential. He feels that the lack of a peaceful atmosphere will have an effect on the development of the child so the transition from uterus to outside world should be slow and non-frightening. To help create this atmosphere, the room should be quiet and darkened. As soon as the baby is delivered it is placed gently on your abdomen with the cord still attached. Once breathing is established, the cord is clamped and cut and the baby is bathed in warm water and put to your breast.

Note   ● All coverage of your baby is given in Chapter 9 – but read the rest of this section first as it applies to you, as mother.

THE NEW   1. You may stay in hospital for seven to eight days after the birth;
MOTHER   alternatively, you may be able to go home a few hours after the birth.
● Some new mothers get a cramp-like feeling in the lower abdomen – a little like a contraction. This is known as after-pains, and it can be helped by pain-killing tablets such as paracetamol.
● There will be a red vaginal discharge called lochia. It will turn brown and yellow as it gets less.
● Your periods may return as early as six weeks after the birth, but they usually take three to six months. Failing to have a period, or breast-feeding, will *not* stop you becoming pregnant.
● It is important to do your postnatal exercises regularly, to get back the muscle tone in your abdomen and the pelvic floor.
2. The postnatal examination – about six weeks after the birth – is very important indeed. It is only natural to feel that you have been examined enough over the last few months and now that you feel so well – why bother? But you should think of it as an essential and a natural conclusion to the care that was started when you were first pregnant – so keep the appointment. Do tell the doctor if you have any problems. Do not be embarrassed.

Your doctor will check to see whether your reproductive organs have returned to their normal condition. The nurse will weigh you – ideally your weight should be nearly, if not exactly, what you were pre-pregnancy. Your urine will be tested and your blood pressure measured. The doctor will examine your legs for varicose veins – and your abdomen to see if the muscle tone is returning to normal. He will do an internal examination.

PARENTAL   Apart from Northern Ireland – where the child is still the responsibility
RESPONSI-   of the father – married parents share legal guardianship.
BILITY

Fathering   In the early months, plenty of support and understanding is required. The hormonal changes in a pregnant woman may lead to nausea, tiredness, great happiness one moment and despair the next.

Sexual desire may stay unchanged or lessen – her feelings should be respected and fears that her loss of interest in sex is permanent are unfounded. If she gave up work she may feel lonely and uninteresting, so plenty of understanding conversation will help.

The prospective father should try to learn and understand as much about the pregnancy and birth as he can. Most hospitals welcome fathers at the birth – providing the mother wants him to be there. If he has been to at least one of the preparation classes, it will help him to understand what is going on. It is also comforting for the mother to have him there with her. (Most fathers who have been at the birth of their child say they would not have missed it for anything!)

SINGLE
MOTHERS

In England and Wales, you are sole legal guardian unless you have the child adopted or it is taken into the care of a local authority because you are incapable of looking after it. The father can be responsible for supporting the child voluntarily or through an affiliation order. You can apply for an order before the birth or up to three years afterwards. If the father does not admit paternity, you will have to prove it. You can require him to have a blood test but this cannot be positive proof. (If you do not have a solicitor ask your Citizens' Advice Bureau to help you find one.) The court can order the father to make regular payments and/or a lump sum of up to £500. The father has no automatic rights over your child (even if his name is on the birth register) but he may apply for custody. A custody order could give him equal or even sole rights but this is rare and he is more likely to be granted access, allowing him to see the child on a regular basis.

Notes

● In Scotland, your solicitor can appeal to the sheriff court for an order of 'affiliation and aliment': you can do this three months before the expected birth or any time afterwards. If you are married to someone else you will have to prove that your husband cannot be the baby's father. If you have had several partners and do not know who the father is you will not get legal support from any of them.

● The important point to note in Northern Ireland is that the father cannot apply for custody.

See

'One-parent Families' in Chapter 9.

ADOPTION

No one can be adopted under eighteen weeks or over eighteen years old (nor can anyone who has been married, even if under eighteen). If a child has been adopted once it can be adopted again.

You can adopt a child provided you are over twenty-one and have looked after it, to the satisfaction of the local authority, for three months. The consent of the child's parents is required but may be dispensed with in certain circumstances. An adoption can only be effected by a court order, not privately. In practice, there are few babies available for adoption these days but there are a number of older children in care who need adoptive families. Babies are, wherever possible, placed with parents of the same race. Partners cohabiting cannot jointly adopt.

Notes
- In Scotland, the child must reside with you for a minimum of six weeks.
- Although the law on adoption in Northern Ireland is broadly the same as in England and Wales, there might be difficulties as there is no legislative equivalent to the relevant Act in England and Wales (English Children's Act 1975).
- If you want to have a baby adopted or if you want to adopt, contact the adoptions office of your local DHSS or an adoption service:

> British Agencies for Adoption and Fostering
> 11 Southwark Street
> London SE1 1RQ
> 01–407 8800
>
> or

Scotland
> 23 Castle Street
> Edinburgh EH2 3DN
> 031–225 9285
>
> Scottish Adoption Advice Service
> c/o Dr Barnado's
> 21 Elmbank Street
> Glasgow G2 4PB
> 041–339 0772
>
> Scottish Adoption Association
> 69 Dublin Street
> Edinburgh EH3 6NS
> 031–556 2070

See 'Adopting a Child: a Brief Guide for Prospective Adopters' and 'Step-children and Adoption: Information for Parents and Step-parents Following Divorce', both from British Agencies for Adoption and Fostering, 'How to Adopt', Consumers' Association.

FOSTERING You do not have to be rich or have a large house to be a foster parent – all you need is time, tolerance, a sense of humour and a love of children.

Most foster-care is supervised by the DHSS (in Scotland, by regional social work departments), and in some instances voluntary organizations such as Barnardo's approve foster parents.

For further information on having your child fostered or on how to become a foster parent, contact:

> National Foster Care Assocation
> Francis House
> Francis Street
> London SWIP IDE
> 01–828 6266

- If you want to see a comprehensive list of scores of youngsters waiting for fostering, contact:

Fosterfacts
34 John Adam Street
London WC2N 6HW
01–839 4036

STILLBIRTH   The Stillbirth and Neonatal Death Society defines stillbirth as a baby who
is born lifeless after 22 weeks of pregnancy (the DHSS definition classifies
stillbirth as occurring from 28 weeks of pregnancy and earlier loss as a
miscarriage or spontaneous abortion). Neonatal and other baby deaths
include babies who die from any natural causes after delivery while still
in hospital, including infants known to be terminally ill before discharge
from hospital.

Stillbirth is a tragedy that you cannot believe has happened to you.
You think you will never get over it. There are, however, others who
have suffered similar catastrophes and you will receive sympathy and
strength from contacting:

Stillbirth and Neonatal Death Society
Argyle House
29–31 Euston Road
London NW1 2SD
01–833 2851

INFERTILITY   Most women who have sexual intercourse two or three times a week
usually becomes pregnant within a year. Do not worry if you do not
become pregnant immediately you have started trying for a baby.

In 1978 Louise Brown was the first 'test-tube baby', born as a result
of *in vitro* fertilization (IVF) and since then new reproduction techniques
have raised many ethical questions.

Surrogate mothers are those who offer to conceive on behalf of women
who cannot become pregnant. Again, ethical and emotive issues are
raised.

If you are unable to become pregnant, the first step is to talk to your doctor.
- Possible causes of infertility include:
1. Your partner has insufficient sperm.
2. You may not ovulate.
3. Your fallopian tubes are blocked.
4. The cervical mucus secreted by the glands of the cervix is abnormal
and prevents the sperm passing through to the uterus.
- Investigations include:
1. Your partner is seen by a specialist. A sample of seminal fluid is
analysed to see how many sperm are present and if they are normal or
abnormal.
2. You are examined by a gynaecologist who specializes in infertility
problems. You will be tested to see if you ovulate and if your fallopian
tubes are open. This is done by laparoscopy: under an anaesthetic, a
very thin telescope-type instrument (a laparoscope) is passed into the

abdomen through a tiny incision made just below the umbilicus. The gynaecologist is able to see if everything is normal and, at the same time, take a sample of the inside of the uterus to see if ovulation is taking place. A sample of the secretion in the cervix is taken after sexual intercourse has taken place and is then examined under a microscope to see if living sperm are present – in some cases the secretion is too sticky or contains a substance which is harmful to the sperm and only a few dead sperm will be seen.

Treatment

- Drugs or other treatments can be given to your partner to improve the sperm count and the quality of the sperm.
- A fertility drug can be used in cases where the woman does not ovulate (the outcome may be a multiple birth).
- Blocked fallopian tubes can sometimes be unblocked surgically.
- The cervical mucus problem can be helped by treatment with oestrogen.

CHILDLESS
COUPLES

If you cannot have children, support can be obtained from:

> National Association for the Childless
> 318 Summer Lane
> Birmingham B I 9 3RL
> 021–359 4887

Separation and Divorce

MARRIAGE BREAK-UP   DIVORCE
SEPARATION

MARRIAGE
BREAK-UP

Every couple has problems at times. Even those who appear idyllically happy to the outside world have rough times in private. It is rare for people to live on an even keel without any troubles.

If you have problems, talk them over. You may have an understanding friend in whom you can confide.

If you prefer an anonymous ear, marriage guidance counselling is always available to you. Counsellors are not trained simply to 'glue' marriages together; sometimes it is appropriate to help people through the pain of parting. This is especially useful in the case of divorce. A sympathetic counsellor can help people recognize feelings of pain, rejection and failure, and offer support. This is particularly important where children are involved as so often they become the pawns in the hands of warring parents.

A break-up of a partnership is very like a bereavement and people who have lost a loved one are helped enormously by coming to someone who understands the pain and anger of being left. The counsellor will be supportive but objective. (For further information about the work of marriage guidance counsellors, see pages 257–60.)

SEPARATION   If you and your husband are living apart it is not necessary to have a court order to make it 'legal' but in case of difficulty over children, maintenance, property, etc., you can apply to a court even though you are not divorced (talk to your solicitor).
● Tell your tax office as soon as you separate.
● Let the tax office see any separation agreement. Tell them about any changes which might affect your tax.

See   Leaflet IR 30 'Separation and Divorce', from any Inland Revenue or PAYE office.

If one partner chooses to move out – or to live separately in a house – against the will of the other, this is desertion. After two years, desertion is grounds for divorce.

DIVORCE   'Irretrievable breakdown of marriage' is now the only grounds for divorce in the British Isles. Except in special cases (which your solicitor will explain) no petition for divorce may be presented until one year has elapsed since the date of the marriage (this time regulation does not apply in Scotland).

Grounds for divorce   You can cite 'irretrievable breakdown of marriage' if:
● your husband has committed adultery;
● your husband has behaved in such a way that you cannot reasonably be expected to live with him;
● your husband has deserted you for at least two years continuously;
● you have lived apart for at least two years and your husband and you both agree to divorce;
● you have lived apart for at least five years. You do not need your husband's consent but he may oppose the divorce if he can show that he will suffer grave hardship as a result.

Procedure   There are two methods of applying for a divorce: the ordinary method for which you will need a solicitor and the quick cheap 'do-it-yourself' method.
1. With a solicitor, your petition will be filed:
● in England and Wales, at a divorce county court or at the Divorce Registry in London
● in Scotland, at the local sheriff court or at the Court of Session in Edinburgh
● in Northern Ireland, in the county court or the Family Division in the Royal Courts of Justice, Belfast.
These courts also deal with claims for ancillary relief, applications for custody, care and control of children. Defended cases are more complicated.

Solicitors are required, at the time a petition for divorce is filed, to lodge a certificate to say if they have discussed with the client the possibility of reconciliation. If the court feels at any point in the proceedings there is a possibility of reconciliation, welfare officers may be brought in to help effect it.

An ordinary divorce which requires the services of a solicitor will cost more than a do-it-yourself one and take six months or more to obtain.

2. *Do-it-yourself divorce* is also possible in certain circumstances (i.e. you have been separated for at least two years, there are no children of the marriage and the divorce is uncontested): if in doubt, talk to your Citizens' Advice Bureau. You can get petition forms from your relevant divorce court (see above) and you will be told what to do. You will need your marriage certificate.

A do-it-yourself divorce usually costs about £40 and takes about two months to obtain.

Your divorce   When a divorce judge is satisfied that breakdown of marriage has been proved, a *decree nisi* is granted. While this is in operation, the court can cancel the divorce either because both parties have changed their minds or because some irregularity has been discovered.

After about six weeks, the petitioner can apply for a *decree absolute* (this is not granted unless you ask for it). Now the marriage is over and both parties can remarry.

Note   ● Women in Northern Ireland with religious objections to divorce can petition the same courts for judicial separation which will give them the same order for property and financial support as in divorce.

A few relevant terms include:

Custody – the right to look after children. Do not assume this will automatically be given to you as mother but you are likely to get it if the children are still very young.

Injunction (in Scotland, **Interdict**) – if either party is in fear of the other he/she can apply to the court for a court order to prevent such specific things as taking children away or breaking into the home. Failure to comply with an injunction can lead to imprisonment.

Maintenance – financial arrangements for you and/or your children. These can take the form of regular payments (which can continue until you remarry) and/or a lump sum. In addition, an order will usually be made in respect of your property. In Scotland, the regular weekly or monthly sum given to support children is called aliment. Scottish divorce courts have no power to make orders about property – i.e. the house. You can claim a lump sum payment if your spouse has capital assets.

Help   Contact your local Citizens' Advice Bureau or local marriage guidance council (national address on page 260) or the Samaritans (national addresses on page 593) or:

Catholic Marriage Advisory Council
15 Landsdowne Road
London W I I 3 A J
01–727 0141

Divorce Conciliation
and Advisory Service
38 Ebury Street
London SW I W OLU
01–730 2422

National Council for
the Divorced and Separated
13 High Street
Little Shelford
Cambridge CB2 5ES
(no telephone)

Scottish Catholic Marriage
Advisory Council
18 Park Circus
Glasgow G3 6BE
041–332 4914

Menopause

The menopause usually occurs between the ages of 45 and 55. It is a gradual process which ends a woman's fertility. Changes involve glands producing various hormones which act upon the ovaries, which then stop producing eggs. The womb no longer sheds its lining each month and thus there are no more periods.

The menopause may last for up to five years and covers many symptoms and body changes, most of which are due to the falling production of the hormone oestrogen. Continuous function of the ovaries is necessary for menstruation and the production of oestrogen. If you have your ovaries surgically removed then the menopause will follow.

Signs and symptoms

- more frequent periods or long gaps between
- hot flushes and sweats – especially in bed at night
- irritability and tiredness
- decreased vaginal secretions leading to dryness and possible difficulty during intercourse.

For some women there are no symptoms at all and their periods just stop. A woman is past the menopause two years after her last period if she is under fifty and one year if she is over fifty.

The following symptoms should be brought to the attention of the doctor:

- irregular bleeding or spotting between periods or after intercourse
- bleeding after the menopause
- heavy periods which leak through several pads.

Problems

- *Hot flushes.* A sudden feeling of heat over the chest, neck and face, with a reddening of the skin which may be noticeable to anyone near you, and sweating. This may occur only a few times a day or it may occur several times in an hour. Also, the intensity of the flush may vary. At night it is likely to wake you up. Cotton sheets, and night-clothes, a single blanket instead of a duvet may help. Try taking a cool shower or bath or sponge down before going to bed.

Flushes are always worse in the hot weather, under stress or anxiety, and after alcohol and hot coffee. If they are severe, consult your doctor.

Many women have no hot flushes, others have them on and off for up to ten years or even longer. If you have them they commonly last for two years with phases lasting a few weeks and then a lull before the next phase.

● *Weight gain.* Most of us put on some weight in middle age because we are not doing so much and therefore we burn calories more slowly. This doesn't mean that you inevitably become fat. You need to know your ideal weight and balance your food intake with the amount of energy that you burn. Use up energy by moving around faster or exercising and take in less calories.

● *Change in moods.* Some women become irritable and short-tempered, partly due to the fall in the level of oestrogen, which has a mild tranquillizing effect. Feeling tired, depressed, tense – any one of these is not necessarily caused by the menopause. Take a good look at how much you are doing, what is going on at home and see if the cause is there.

● *Irregular periods.* If they are more frequent or heavier or there is bleeding in between periods, see your doctor. It is probably a good idea to keep a diary of your periods once you are over forty.

● *Pregnancy.* It is advisable to use contraceptives for two years after your last period if you are under fifty and for one year if you are over fifty.

● *The contraceptive pill.* Take advice from your doctor about what age to stop taking the pill and use another form of contraception. Generally, the risks of taking the pill increase after the age of forty.

● *Sex.* There is no reason why you should not enjoy a normal sexual relationship. In some women the vaginal passage tends to become dry and rather tight – a lubricant jelly used before intercourse may be all that is necessary. If this doesn't help, see your doctor. There is a great deal that can be done to help you so there is no need to suffer unhappiness and discomfort.

● *Headaches.* There are numerous causes of headaches including migraine, sinusitis, nervous depression, various kinds of medicine, dieting or irregular meals – none of which is necessarily related to the menopause. So it is better to see your doctor if you have headaches so that the cause can be established.

Hormone replacement therapy There is a lot of argument about this treatment. Those in favour say it keeps women looking young, it preserves sexual function, it may prevent heart attacks and breast cancer and it may help reduce depression, tingling of the fingers, tiredness, dizziness, weakness and loss of sexual desire.

There is also evidence that oestrogen therapy taken for a long time thickens the womb lining causing irregular or heavy bleeding and cancer of the womb in some women.

Most experts agree that it is effective in the treatment of hot flushes, sweats and dryness of the vagina and if taken at the start of the menopause and continued over many years may prevent or slow down the process of the thinning of bones which occurs in old age.

Most doctors give oestrogen in combination with progestogen – taken like the contraceptive pill for a certain number of days then stopped which allows the womb to shed its lining every month and causes periods to start again. For more information talk to your doctor who will base his advice on your previous medical history.

Retirement

Although women usually retire earlier than men, they live longer. The chances are, therefore, that they are likely to spend their last years alone.

Retirement is no longer the short period between the end of work and the end of life. It can last for twenty-five years or more and even intelligent and otherwise well-adjusted people can find its onset traumatic.

Plan ahead Although the value of planning ahead for retirement has been recognized for more than twenty years, no more than 10 per cent of working women at present receive any help with preparation for their retirement period. Even in the comparatively few enlightened companies who do provide retirement planning courses, the take-up by women on such courses is significantly lower than that of the men. As a result, organizers of such courses sometimes tend to overlook women's problems and needs.

Problems ● *Money*. Women frequently have less money than men in the same age group; they frequently come late into company pension schemes (or not at all). Not all women are entitled to full DHSS retirement or widows' pensions and some women may have been shielded from financial responsibilities by their husbands, often with disastrous results.
● *Care of ageing relatives*. This usually falls on women, and this is especially demanding for single women.
● *Age* is supposed to be unkind to women (or many think it is).

What to do Older women, especially those by themselves, have to be positive about creating and filling new social frameworks.

Margaret Scott-Knight, a retirement and pre-retirement specialist with DPS Consultants, suggests:
● Look around you and find out what is going on.
● Develop new interests – pursue, explore and experiment.
● Be a 'joiner'.
● Cultivate new friendships and nurture old ones. Friends are important in retirement, especially to those living alone.
● Entertaining does not have to mean expensive dinner parties.
● Get back into the habit of letter writing.

● Think about volunteering – voluntary work is much more interesting and rewarding than its image suggests. Every kind of skill and expertise is needed.

Help ● The Pre-Retirement Association of Great Britain and Northern Ireland (PRA) consists of over thirty affiliated organizations which help and advise on planning ahead for retirement and for specific guidelines on courses, health, leisure and living arrangements.

> Pre-Retirement Association of Great Britain
> and Northern Ireland
> 19 Undine Street
> London SW17 8PP
> 01–767 3225

Belfast	02322–21324
Cardiff	0222–754515
Glasgow	041–332 9427
Gwent	049–55 3699

● DPS. retirement consultants, hold courses especially concerned with the needs of women whether they are attending in their own right or as accompanying wives. Partners are encouraged to attend courses together: but DPS stresses that all women should be aware of the vital importance of financial knowledge and planning. Courses include: creative use of leisure, financial planning, health, lifestyle, occupational pensions and national insurance, and personal relationships; security and technological change are also included in the programmes.

For details of retirement and pre-retirement courses contact:

> DPS Consultants
> 66 Preston Street
> Faversham
> Kent ME13 8PG
> 0795–531472

● Other study possibilities include the University of the Third Age (U3A), which offers courses of study and activities to retired people and those out of work. Details from:

> U3A London
> 137 Langton Close
> Wren St
> London WC1X OHD
> 01–833 4747

or, for U3As outside London, s.a.e. to:

> 6 Parkside Gardens
> London SW19 5EY

● Other useful addresses include:

> Scottish Retirement Council
> 212 Bath Street
> Glasgow G2 4HW
> 041–332 9427

See The monthly magazine *Choice* is specially designed for the over-50s. Subscription details from your newsagent or:

> *Choice*
> 2nd Floor
> Whitehall
> East Grinstead
> Sussex RH19 1ZC

'Looking after Yourself in Retirement', Health Education Council.

Widowhood

This is a time of crisis. Even if you are prepared for the death of someone you love, when it happens it may be some time before you come to believe it – and before you can come to terms with it.

Immediately, however, there are things to do. You may be lucky enough to have someone by you who can give you all the help you need at this time. If not, for advice on what to do, and for comfort, contact Cruse. This is an organization of people who know what you are going through. They know what has to be done. They can guide you through this particularly difficult time and, later, they will be able to help you to adjust to a new way of life.

At any time of night or day, telephone 01–940 4818. The main headquarters of Cruse is at:

> Cruse House
> 126 Sheen Road
> Richmond
> Surrey TW9 1UR
> 01–940 4818

and
Edinburgh   031–229 6275
Glasgow   041–332 1299

Your benefits The payments made to you will depend on your age, the number of children, and the national insurance contributions your husband paid. They will cease if you remarry or live with a man as his wife. Benefits are made regardless of other income and are taxable. See leaflets IR23 'Income Tax and Widows', from the registrar, or any inspector of taxes.

● **Widow's allowance.** This is paid for twenty-six weeks after your husband's death. The basic rate may be increased in certain circumstances. You need claim form BW1 – see leaflet NP35 from the social security office. If you were already receiving retirement pension, see leaflet NP32A.

● **Widowed mother's allowance.** If you are pregnant with your late husband's child and/or you have children under nineteen receiving full-time education, this is paid after the ordinary widow's allowance ends. See leaflet NP36.

● **Widow's pension.** This is usually paid automatically after the widow's (or widowed mother's) allowance ends. You must have been forty or over when your husband died (or forty or over when your widowed mother's allowance ceased). See leaflet NP36.

● As far as *tax* is concerned, you should tell the tax office as soon as you can that you have been widowed. Tell them what benefits you are getting. See leaflet IR23 'Income Tax and Widows'.

● If your husband died *without leaving a will* – see page 240.

Help　Later problems may include acute physical and emotional loneliness. Financial hardship can also be felt. A widow, for instance, has no automatic right to sickness or unemployment benefit. She may take home less pay than a married woman as her pension is added to her salary so she is taxed more highly. If she was under forty and childless when widowed, she receives no pension at all.

● The National Association of Widows fights against these and the many injustices to which widows are subjected, and acts as the catalyst for social life. Details from:

> National Association of Widows
> Voluntary Service Centre
> Chell Road
> Stafford ST16 2QA
> 0785–45465

● *War widows.* It is a staggering fact that there are still many thousands of women who were widowed during the First World War. They, and their counterparts more recently bereaved in wars, can contact:

> War Widows' Association of Great Britain
> Kerries
> South Brent
> South Devon TQ10 9DD
> (No telephone)

How much pension a war widow receives depends upon her age, her husband's rank and the number of children. Information (leaflets MPL151 and MPL152) from:

DHSS
North Fylde Central Offices
Norcross
Blackpool FY5 3TA

Older Age

Although it is generally accepted that the advent of old age is later now than it was in the past, when it happens to you is really up to you. A sudden shock or trauma – say the death of someone close to you – may escalate the feeling that you are getting old. A medical condition may cause you to look older to others and possibly feel older too.

But many older women say that although their bodies look different from the way they did a few years ago, they themselves, 'inside', so to speak, feel the same.

Alas, loneliness, isolation and unhappiness are facts of life for many old people. It is up to everyone to give them help and encourage conditions which allow elderly people to continue to make a real and worthwhile contribution to the community in which they live.

Help The elderly should be aware of the following facilities available to improve their quality of life:

● Volunteer hostesses, Granny Sitting schemes, Good Neighbour schemes (contact Age Concern or DHSS).

● Day-care provision, luncheon clubs and day centres (contact DHSS).

● Volunteer transport schemes.

● Mobile library.

● Meals on wheels (WRVS – via your doctor).

● Domiciliary hairdressing and chiropody facilities.

● Help with gardening and decorating (often through youth employment schemes).

● Extra financial aid available through the DHSS.

● Keep-fit classes, swimming club and other activities.

● Special concessions at some cinemas, shops, etc.

● Special help with taxes (see inland revenue leaflet IR4 'Income Tax and Pensioners').

● Special aids to make life more agreeable at home: send a large s.a.e. for a catalogue of their living aids to:

F. Llewellyn & Co.
Carlton Works
Carlton Street
Liverpool L3 7ED
051–236 5311

● *Housing.* 'Old peoples' homes' 'rest homes' and 'residential homes' are not allowed to advertise night attendance. 'Nursing homes', by contrast, are inspected frequently by medical and nursing officers and must maintain all appropriate facilities day and night. For details of registered nursing homes ask your doctor or contact:

Registered Nursing Home Association
75 Portland Place
London WIA 4AN
01–631 1524

Useful addresses All the organizations below will advise where you can get help on your rights or any other problem: you can also contact your local Citizens' Advice Bureau or the social services.

● Age Concern publishes a quarterly journal, *New Age*, and provides a centre for policy, research, information and social advocacy on all subjects.

Age Concern
Bernard Sunley House
60 Pitcairn Road
Mitcham
Surrey CR4 3LL
01–640 5431

Age Concern Scotland
33 Castle Street
Edinburgh EH2 3DN
031–225 5000

Age Concern Wales
1 Park Grove
Cardiff CFI 3BJ
0222–371821

● The Centre for Policy on Ageing encourages better provision for all elderly people and is concerned with those working with and for older people.

Centre for Policy on Ageing
Nuffield Lodge
Regent's Park
London NWI 4RS
01–722 8871

● Confidential counselling for any problem is offered by:

Counsel and Care for the Elderly
131 Middlesex Street
London EI 7JF
01–621 1624

● The Employment Fellowship sets up centres for worthwhile activities such as light contract work or toy-making.

> Employment Fellowship
> Drayton House
> Gordon Street
> London WC1H OBE
> 01–387 1828

● Friends of the Elderly provides grants and allowances, e.g. nursing home fees, and runs its own residential homes. Contact:

> Friends of the Elderly
>   and Gentlefolk's Help
> 42 Ebury Street
> London SW1W OLZ
> 01–730 8263

● Help the Aged runs day- and work-centres, offers health care and initiates housing care.

> Help the Aged
> 32 Dover Street
> London W1A 2AP
> 01–499 0972

● Line 81 offers general advice and information.

> Line 81
> PO Box 7
> London W3 6XJ
> 01–992 5522

● Practical support for those caring alone for elderly dependants is given by:

> National Council for Carers and Their Elderly Dependants
> 29 Chilworth Mews
> London W2 3RG
> 01–262 1451

● General information and advice is available from:

> National Federation of Old Age Pensioners' Associations
> 91 Preston New Road
> Blackburn
> Lancs BB2 6BD
> 0254–52606

● Pensioners' Link is a national organization which links pensioners to resources, advice, health, education and activities.

> Pensioners' Link
> 17 Balfe Street
> London N1 9EB

See   'Home Care of the Elderly', Health Education Council.

Death

Some people will have suspicions, confirmed or not, of imminent death, particularly in the case of terminal cancer. Perhaps you – or someone you know – are lucky enough to be offered hospice care. This will be in a small unit specially set up to understand the needs of dying people and their relatives.

The most modern development of this idea is to send staff from the hospice into the home to give the family an opportunity to share in caring for a dying person. In this way death can come as a logical conclusion to life – to die well is a great achievement.

A very readable book on this subject is: Richard Lamerton. *Care of the Dying*, Penguin.

DEATH AT HOME

What to do

- If a death occurs at home you should immediately contact:
(a) the doctor
(b) near relatives
(c) the relevant minister of religion.
- If there are suspicious circumstances, call the police immediately (999) and do not touch or move the body or anything in the room.
- If you have to cope with the death of someone you do not know (and whose doctor, relatives and minister of religion you do not know), contact the police.
- The doctor will give you advice and issue:
(a) a medical certificate showing the cause of death
(b) a formal notice stating he has signed the certificate and telling you how to register the death.
- If he thinks fit, the doctor will report the death to the coroner.
- You must then register the death (see below).
- Find out if there is a will. If so, who is responsible for dealing with it? Are there specific instructions for funeral or cremation, or for body organ donations?

DEATH IN HOSPITAL

What to do

- The hospital or police will tell the nearest relative and arrange for him/her to come to the hospital to identify the body and take away personal possessions.
- Tell the hospital if any organs or the body are to be donated.
- The hospital will keep the body until you arrange for it to be taken away.
- The doctor will give a medical certificate and formal notice or he will report the death to the coroner.
- You must register the death (see below).

● Find out if there is a will. If so, who is responsible for dealing with it? Are there specific instructions for funeral or cremation or for body organ donations?

See 'What to Do When Someone Dies', Consumers' Association

Body organ donations **Body donation:** Unless you think there might be a post-mortem (in which case the coroner has to give special permission for donation), as soon as you can:

1. Telephone HM Inspector of Anatomy: 01–703 6380 ext. 3738 or 3743.

In Scotland, telephone the Department of Anatomy at the Universities of Aberdeen, Dundee, Edinburgh, Glasgow or St Andrew's.

2. Tell the doctor.

Eyes must be removed within six hours so it is necessary to act with speed.

1. Tell your family doctor.

2. Telephone the nearest eye hospital.

Kidneys must be removed within half an hour of death, so cannot usually be used in case of home deaths.

REGISTERING A DEATH ● If the death has not been referred to the coroner (see below), go to the Registrar of Births and Deaths as soon as possible (normally within five days). Take with you:

(a) medical certificate showing cause of death

(b) the dead person's NHS medical card

(c) any pension order book, or allowances received from public funds

● The registrar will want to know:

(a) full names and surname(s) of the deceased

(b) date and place of birth (and country, if abroad)

(c) if married, the date of birth of surviving spouse

(d) whether or not deceased was receiving a pension or public allowance

(e) deceased's usual address

(f) date and place of death.

Notes ● In Scotland, the registrar also wants to know:

(a) the occupation of the deceased

(b) the full name and occupation of the dead person's father and the full name and maiden name of the dead person's mother

(c) the name and address of the deceased's NHS doctor.

(d) about the birth, marriage and insurance certificates if they are available.

● The registrar will give you two certificates: one for disposal of the body (give this to the funeral director) and the other for social security (give it to the local DHSS office to claim the death grant and/or widow's benefit). You can get more copies of these certificates if you think you may need them for the will. He will also give you leaflets on those and other benefits, and form PR48 dealing with the procedure for wills.

THE
CORONER

Do not be upset if the coroner – a doctor or lawyer – is brought in: he is involved in about 20 per cent of all deaths. If you want to notify the coroner of a death which you think should be investigated you can do so. If you cannot find his number in the telephone directory ask your doctor or the police how to contact him.

The coroner can authorize a post-mortem without the consent of the relatives, but they can ask that a doctor be present. If death was from natural causes he will issue a 'pink form' which he will either send direct to the registrar or give to you to take to him.

If the cause of death cannot be attributed to natural causes an inquest may be held. This is a public inquiry, sometimes with jury, organized by the coroner. Relatives can attend and if the death was caused by a road or other accident it is important to have a lawyer present.

If required, the coroner will give permission for a body to be taken out of England and Wales.

Note

● In Scotland, the Procurator Fiscal investigates unexpected, unexplained, violent or suspicious deaths.

THE FUNERAL

Do not start making final funeral arrangements until you have found the dead person's will (see below) and established what he or she wanted for the funeral, and you are sure that the death will not be reported to the coroner.

When you can make arrangements, go to a funeral director who is a member of the National Association of Funeral Directors. He will give you an estimate. Find out what this includes (e.g. church or cemetery fees) and also find out the date by which the sum should be paid.

If you have special requirements (say, a non-religious ceremony) tell the funeral director. Some people, for instance, ask for simple readings rather than hymns and prayers. You will not be allowed to bury the body wherever you want: strict local planning regulations and hygiene codes determine where a burial can take place.

To pay for the funeral you might have to take out a sum from the deceased's savings bank or building society accounts, as any bank accounts of the deceased will be frozen unless they are joint accounts. You can also claim the death grant (see leaflets NI49 and NI196 from DHSS). If you are on supplementary benefit you might get a cash grant (see leaflet SB1).

The National Association of Funeral Directors recommends that you tell the funeral director as soon as possible how much you can afford.

Note

● The Association has a code of practice covering the services provided by members. If you are unhappy with the funeral direction – though not with floral or gravestone services – you can afterwards contact, in complete confidence:

National Association of Funeral Directors
57 Doughty Street
London WC1N 2NE
01–242 9388

Cremation The funeral director will advise and help with the organization of a cremation.

If a cremation is required the following will be needed:

- an application form signed by the next of kin or executor
- two cremation certificates, from the family doctor and another doctor
- a third certificate signed by the medical referee at the crematorium.

It is important to make clear what should be done about the ashes.

Other business The following items of the deceased should be returned as soon as possible:

- Giro cheques, order books and payable orders, also child benefits (to the social security office).
- Passport (to the nearest passport office).
- Driving licence (to DVLC, Swansea, Glam SA6 7GL).
- Car log-book (for change of ownership to be recorded).
- Season tickets (and any refunds claimed).

And you should tell:

- All the deceased's medical advisers (doctors, nurses, dentist, any hospital he/she was attending).
- Employer and trade union.
- Children's teachers (if any relative has died).

See 'What to Do After a Death . . . Practical Advice on Times of Bereavement', Scottish Information Office on behalf of Scottish Home and Health Department.

THE WILL A will says what you want to happen to your possessions after death and whom you want to be guardian of your children. It can also set out your wishes about burial or cremation.

Your will must obviously be signed by you when you are in sound mind. You must name at least one *executor* (see below) and clearly state your wishes and who are the beneficiaries. Any amendments to your will can be written separately as a codicil.

Anyone over eighteen (sixteen in the armed forces) may make a will, and there are a number of landmarks in your life at which making a will becomes a matter of common sense:

1. Marriage (your partner will not as a matter of course inherit if you die intestate, and in Scotland marriage does not automatically cancel previous wills).
2. You become a parent.
3. You buy a house (this is especially important if you are moving from England to Scotland as you will then become subject to Scottish law under which children have automatic rights which are unknown in English law).

4. You inherit money.

Notes
● In Scotland, although a typed will needs two witnesses, a will hand-written in your own hand, and signed by yourself, will be valid but it might be challenged.
● Do-it-yourself wills are not encouraged by the legal profession. If you want to do your own will, printed forms can be bought but they might not conform to the law and the will may be challenged.
● Remember to make sure that people can easily find the will (lodge a copy with your solicitor or your bank, and keep one copy at home with other important papers). Tell someone where your will is.

The executor
The executor (there are usually two) winds up the dead person's estate. If you find yourself as an executor you should:
● Locate the will and find out the deceased's wishes about burial or cremation.
● Arrange the funeral.
● Find out what has been left and what debts are owed.
● Apply for permission to wind up the estate (this is called 'grant of probate'), from the local probate registry – see the telephone directory.
● Distribute the estate.

No will
If someone dies *intestate* (without leaving a will) the following happens in England and Wales:
● The surviving spouse is entitled to personal 'chattels' (personal belongings, apart from business, money and securities) plus the first £42,000 of the money and life interest in half the rest of the estate.
● Children receive the other half of the interest when they achieve their majority. At the death of the above-mentioned parent they receive his/her share too.
● If there are no surviving children, the spouse receives the first £85,000 of the estate and the other life interest in half of the remainder goes to the deceased's parents and/or siblings.
● If the deceased left no children, parents or siblings the surviving spouse receives the whole amount.
● A surviving partner who was not legally married to or who was divorced from the deceased receives nothing if he died intestate.

Notes
● In Scotland, the remaining spouse – if there are no children – gets the house plus up to £10,000 of its furnishings, cash up to £25,000 and half of the remaining movable estate. If there are children, the entitlement is £15,000 cash plus house and furnishings up to £10,000 value and one-third of the movable estate: the remainder goes to the children. Divorced women are entitled to nothing from an intestate estate.
● In Northern Ireland, a spouse's inheritance rights if there is no will are as follows:
1. The surviving spouse is entitled to the personal chattels plus £40,000

plus either half of the rest of the estate if there is one child or one-third if there is more than one child.

2. Child(ren) receives one-half or one-third of the residue in equal shares.

3. If there are no surviving children, the spouse receives the personal chattels, plus £85,000, plus half the residue. The other half of the residue goes to the parents or, if they are dead, to brothers and sisters or their issue.

4. If the deceased left no children or relevant next of kin, the spouse receives the whole estate.

5. Half-blood relationships count as whole blood for the purposes of distribution on intestacy.

6. A surviving partner who was not legally married or who was divorced from the deceased receives nothing under these provisions (but see below).

● In the case of grievance over lack of adequate provision, whether under a will or on intestacy, the spouse should apply to the court for an order under the Inheritance (Provision for Family and Dependants [NI] Order 1979), for which separated and divorced women and a surviving partner who was not married to the deceased can also apply.

See 'Rights of Succession: a Brief Guide to the Succession [Scotland] Act 1964' from Scottish Information Office, 'In the Event of Death' from Scottish Association of Citizens' Advice Bureaux.

Help A particularly difficult time is the first anniversary of death. If you know a bereaved person who is coming up to this anniversary, do remember this is a potentially traumatic period.

An organization which helps the parents of dead or chronically ill children is:

> National Secretary
> Compassionate Friend for Bereaved Parents
> 5 Lower Clifton Hill
> Clifton
> Bristol BS8 1DT
> 0272–292778

Further Information

Suggested further reading

MARRIAGE AND COHABITATION; YOUR RIGHTS

Coote, Anna and Tess Gill, *Women's Rights: a Practical Guide*, Penguin

Fitch, Janet, *Married to the Job: Wives' Incorporation in Men's Work*, Allen & Unwin

Mostyn, F. E., *Marriage and the Law*, Oyez

Nichols, David, *Living Together: A Guide to Marriage and Cohabitation*, Scottish Citizens Advice Bureau

Street, Henry (consultant ed.), *You and Your Rights*, Reader's Digest

PREGNANCY AND BIRTH

Bennet, V. Ruth, *A Pocket Book on Pregnancy*, Octopus

Boston Women's Health Collective, *Our Bodies, Ourselves*, Penguin

Bourne, Gordon, *Pregnancy*, Pan

Brook, Danaë, *Naturebirth*, Penguin

Consumers' Association, *Pregnancy Month by Month*

Dale, Barbara and Johanna Roeber, *Exercises for Childbirth*, Frances Lincoln

Decker, Albert and Suzanne Loebl, *We Want to Have a Baby*, Penguin

Holme, Richard, *Pregnancy and Diet*, Penguin

Kitzinger, Sheila, *The Experience of Childbirth*, Penguin
Pregnancy and Childbirth, Michael Joseph

Llewellyn-Jones, David, *Everywoman*, Faber & Faber

Odent, Michel, *Entering the World*, Penguin

Russell, Dr Keith P., *Expectant Motherhood*, Eastman's

PARENTHOOD

Dowrick, Stephanie and Sybil Grundberg (eds.), *Why Children?*, Women's Press

Kitzinger, Sheila, *Women as Mothers*, Fontana

Roeber, Johanna, *Parenthood: a Father's Guide*, Frances Lincoln

Shakespeare, Penny, *The New Mother's Handbook*, Voyager

Singer, Peter and Deanne Wells, *The Reproduction Revolution*, Oxford Paperbacks

Whiteford, Barbara and Maggie Polden, *Fitness after Birth*, Frances Lincoln

MISCARRIAGE

Oakley, Ann, Dr Ann McPherson and Helen Roberts, *Miscarriage*, Fontana

INFERTILITY

Pfeffer, Naomi and Anne Wollett, *The Experience of Infertility*, Virago Press

ADOPTION

Livingston, Carole, *Why Was I Adopted?*, Angus & Robertson

SEPARATION AND DIVORCE

Consumers' Association, *On Getting Divorced*

Dineen, Jacqueline, *Going Solo: Starting Out Again After Separation*, Allen & Unwin

Harper, W. M., *Divorce and Your Money*, Allen & Unwin

Lowe, Robert, *Questions of Divorce Law*, Hamlyn

MENOPAUSE

Anderson, Mary, *The Menopause*, Faber & Faber

Cooper, Wendy, *No Change*, Arrow (about hormone replacement therapy)

Evans, Dr Barbara, *Life Change: a Guide to the Menopause, Its Effect and Treatment*, Pan

Reitz, Rosetha, *Menopause: a Positive Approach*, Allen & Unwin

Stoppard, Dr Miriam, *50 Plus Lifeguide*, Dorling Kindersley
Weideger, Paula, *Female Cycles*, Women's Press

RETIREMENT
Consumers' Association, *Approaching Retirement*
The *Choice* retirement library (address on page 231) contains titles such as:
Eves, Edward, *Money and Your Retirement*
Gore, Irene, *Age and Vitality*
Kemp, Fred and Bernard Buttle, *Looking Ahead: a Guide to Retirement*
Loving, Bill, *The Choice Guide to Retirement*

WIDOWHOOD
Taylor, Liz, *Living with Loss*, Fontana

OLDER AGE
Agate, John, *Taking Care of Old People at Home*, Allen & Unwin

From Age Concern (send s.a.e. for details to address on page 234):
 Davies, Eira, *Let's Get Moving*
 Seabrook, Jeremy, *The Way We Are*
 Macdonald, Barbara and Cynthia Rich, *Look Me in the Eye: Old Women,
  Aging and Ageism*, Spinsters, Ink
Stoppard, Dr Miriam, *50 Plus Lifeguide*, Dorling Kindersley

DEATH
Barbanell, Sylvia, *When a Child Dies*, Pilgrim Book Service
Consumers' Association, *Wills and Probate*

8 Sex and Personal Relationships

Sex is always thought of as the taboo subject which nevertheless interests everyone – and I mean *everyone*. I therefore spoke to **Dordie Daniels**, a marriage guidance counsellor and sex therapist, and she has contributed greatly to this chapter.

Sex is more than simply bed. It also affects the whole structure of relationships between people. Here you will find factual information and revealing insights from people whose job it is to help us towards a better understanding of the nature of sex and personal relationships.

How It All Begins

Humans are profoundly sexual beings from the first days in the womb. The male hormone testosterone is secreted by the developing testicles of a male embryo. At first the testicles are inside the abdomen: from about the third month of pregnancy they make their way down the body until they come to rest in the scrotum, the special sac which lies outside the body between the legs. There they are at a lower temperature than the rest of the body: this is favourable for production of sperm later. (If the testicles fail to come down after birth, an operation to correct this should be done before the child is five years old.)

While still in the womb, the female's ovaries develop a lifetime's store of about 400,000 ovocytes (cells). These are not yet ova (eggs) but have the potential to develop into them. They will lie dormant until puberty.

Many a new mother must have experienced surprise on seeing her baby son's tiny penis sometimes become erect when he is at the breast. Babies of either sex, indeed, are soon aware of their bodies. They discover mouths, toes and feet, the torso, all the orifices of the body and the genitals. They make the discovery early that some places more than others give pleasure when touched.

As they get older children often play games to discover more about themselves and the opposite sex. Little girls may state firmly that they are going to marry their fathers when they grow up. Little boys will court their mothers. They absorb their parents' attitudes to being male, female, father, mother and their behaviour towards each other. They also absorb their parents' attitudes towards their bodies. Some children learn to associate the whole genital area with 'dirt'. For some it is unmentionable. Few parents are able to tolerate their offspring handling their genitals in front of others so, for the children for whom it is pleasurable, touching the genitals can become imbued with guilt. Later sexual attitudes may become associated with such remembrances.

Those deprived in early childhood of love and closeness with parents are likely to have difficulty in accepting their own bodies and tend to have a diminished sense of their own value. This can be a barrier to forming satisfying, trusting and reliable relationships when horizons widen to include the world outside the family.

Touching is something a baby first learns from its mother, and then from others in the family. Some people, as adults, find touching unacceptable, something they avoid doing except when necessary. Some find even shaking hands difficult. It cannot be denied that some children, right from the start, seem to have more liking for the cuddles and caresses of their parents and friends than do others. However, when children are nurtured in families where cuddling and touching are allowed and enjoyed, it is likely that they will grow up feeling good about their bodies and their sexuality. In another family, a child may receive much care in the form of good food, clothing and cleanliness but experience little in the way of physical closeness which will encourage the development and enjoyment of the sense of touch. Such children grow up uneasy and suspicious of touch by other human beings – although some make up for this to some extent by their experience of having animals as pets which they will happily handle and stroke.

At puberty young people start to become acutely aware of the changes in their bodies. They are often highly conscious of their appearance and the whole body image in relation both to their own and the opposite sex (see '10 to 16 Years – Adolescence' page 275ff.).

Young men may experience nocturnal emissions ('wet dreams') during, or as a result of, sexual dreams. They will find, sometimes to their embarrassment, that their penis has become hard simply through thinking about or looking at a girl or even at the thought of any sexual activity. Girls, too, become fairly easily aroused and are aware that their vagina becomes moist. In both sexes, arousal causes an extra blood supply to flow to the genital area which becomes sensitive and enlarged.

The girl's clitoris, like the boy's penis tip, contains a mass of nerve-endings and is acutely sensitive to touch. Breasts may become sensitive and the nipples, now a deeper colour, become erect. Boys and girls tend to become acutely aware of the other sex and deeply self-conscious in their new awareness of themselves as sexual people. In their contacts with the opposite sex their feelings become heightened, tumultuous and powerful.

It is important that young people have access to good information on contraception, and it is immensely helpful if they are given the opportunity for open and frank discussions about their feelings and attitudes towards sexuality. Such discussions, when led by an open and non-judgemental adult, can help them to share thoughts and feelings, greatly reduce their sense of isolation and encourage a sense of responsibility.

Conflicts can arise as young people struggle to establish their own identity. Some of this conflict may be about their sexual aggression and if boys and girls can be helped to acknowledge the power of their sex drive rather than to ignore it, they can move more easily towards adult life. Parental attitudes about everything – amount of freedom, 'standards', religion, money and marriage – are likely to be questioned and if this can be done openly in the family the adolescent has at least a chance of working out some independent attitudes and feelings. If such attempts are met with a rebuff or a conspiracy of silence the young person may seek other means by which to work things out.

Some Common Questions

Is it true that women 'go off sex'
around the time of their period?
As far as sexual desire and satisfaction are concerned, some studies have shown that for many women this is most intense in the period just before, during and after menstruation. Other studies have shown that women's interest and sexual responsiveness starts to rise when ovulation occurs half-way between periods and oestrogen levels are high. Controversy remains.

Do women go off sex after the menopause,
when their periods have stopped?
Some women feel the ending of their fertility is a great loss. To others, not having to worry about an unwanted pregnancy is a burden lifted from them. They can begin to relax and enjoy their sex life with greater freedom.

The slowing down of the hormone supply can, apart from stopping the monthly periods, cause swings of mood, hot flushes and dryness in the vagina and nostrils. If these effects are causing you distress or affecting your sexual relationships, seek help from your doctor. It may be worth investigating with him the possibility of hormone replacement therapy.

Desire for sexual activity does not cease even if the frequency with which couples have sex may lessen. Nowadays the post-menopause period of a woman's life can be quite a long time and many couples go on enjoying their sexual relationship until the partnership ends. Menopausal or after, there is no reason why an active sex life should not continue into old age.

What can you do if, perhaps in middle age,
your partner wants sex more often than you do?
If there is a problem over this, you would probably find it a help to see a sex therapist or a doctor specializing in psycho-sexual counselling (e.g. at your family planning clinic).

Any tips for older lovers?
Do not give up! Erections may not come quite so fast now, but if no disease or alcohol excess is present they will come. What is the hurry? *Take your time.* Both partners may need stimulation for a little longer than before and it may be that erotic books and pictures can help here. If lubrication is insufficient, use a sterile lubricating jelly specially made for this purpose.

Should women always have an orgasm
during intercourse?
Women might want to – but even highly orgasmic women do not always come during intercourse. Some women find that manual or oral stimulation by their partners or themselves helps to keep their arousal high and leads to climax during intercourse. Other women, however, never experience orgasm during penetration but do through manual and/or oral stimulation around the clitoris and genital area.

Is sex always serious?
Unlike other animals, we are given the choice to use sex as we want. By practising birth control we can have sex without producing babies. Irresponsibility in this area can lead to an unwanted pregnancy. In many such cases it is the child who suffers the most.

On the other hand, although it should be considered seriously, responsible sex can also be fun, playful, and full of pleasure and variety when there is trust and confidence between the partners.

Is it his job to turn me on?
Your sexual response is largely your own responsibility and you have the power to improve it.

Start by looking closely at your whole body in a mirror. Then discover where everything is in your genital area. Sit on your bed with your legs wide open, with a small mirror propped up between your legs, or on the floor in front of a full-length mirror. Using both hands, gently draw back the outer lips of your genitals. Can you identify each part there? Touch and explore yourself and gently find out what feels pleasant and exciting.

Get to know what arouses you so that you can help your partner know this and guide him in doing what pleases *you*. You and your man will find yourselves 'turned on' if you take the initiative sometimes. Let him know when it is not intercourse you want, but touching, caressing, stroking and cuddling. Be alert to the fact that he may feel the same sometimes.

Why don't men understand?

It *does* sometimes seem as if there is an unbridgable gap between the sexes and some of this is due not just to the gender difference but because cultural conditioning has played a profound part in the way men see themselves and what they think women and society expect of them (e.g. not to show feelings).

Perhaps it is beginning to be more widely understood that there is male and female in each of us and we need to learn how to come to terms with and accept both aspects of our nature. It is probably true that women may be generally more in touch directly and intuitively with their feelings. Many men have been taught to keep their more tender feelings out of sight. Anger is often similarly suppressed.

Loss of control is feared by many people, and this can cause 'blocks' in sexual relationships. This fear to some extent acts as a safety-valve but it can also prevent us from coming to terms realistically with good and bad feelings on any level. By learning and practising honesty it should be easier to manage our feelings. In sexual as well as other aspects of relationships, it is important to be willing to share feelings with partners and be to open to accepting their right to have them too.

Can you become pregnant if he does not come inside you?

Yes, you can. If after making love any seminal fluid is spilled near the vagina, it is quite possible for sperm to swim up the moist vagina towards the egg. Less sperm will complete the journey but it is likely that some will manage it. Sperm can live for up to two days in the woman's body.

Can masturbation seriously damage your health?

About 98 per cent of the population masturbates from time to time – perhaps feeling guilty, but we do it none the less. Contrary to what is sometimes thought, nothing terrible happens and we experience a sense of relief from sexual tension and a feeling of well-being from an intensely pleasurable activity.

Most people masturbate occasionally even when they are part of a stable relationship. Studies show that of women who are not yet having orgasms, some have never masturbated.

What is an orgasm and how do you achieve it?

Orgasm, if pursued as an end it itself, can prove very elusive. Hundreds of thousands of words have been written about it and in spite of this, to quote John Bancroft, 'of all the various sexual responses, orgasm remains the most mysterious and least well understood'.

It is probably the most intense physical pleasure known to human beings and perhaps to all animals. It comes as a result of erotic stimulation, excitement and arousal which, if continued, lead on to a peak of intense feeling at which point some trigger causes the abandonment of control with spasms of intense pleasure, perhaps even ecstasy, followed by a sense of release.

Experience and research show that not only do people vary in this sexual response, but that any one person will find that each experience of orgasm is different.

Some women have never experienced an orgasm at all and some never experience it during intercourse but do so in love-making or masturbation. If a woman wishes to become orgasmic, it is essential for her to learn how to get in touch with her body, her senses and her sexuality and become comfortable with it. It has been found that a programme of relaxation exercises and focusing on body exploration and touching has, together with proper information, helped women towards a deeper awareness of their bodies and their own sexuality both with or without a sexual partner.

Does it make any difference how often you make love?
It does seem as if practice makes if not perfect, certainly more pleasurable and satisfying sexual experiences. Each partner learns what they themselves like and what their partner likes and how to trust and experiment and maintain interest in themselves and each other as sexual people.

Contraception

Remember:
- Pregnancy *can* occur without the woman having an orgasm.
- Breast-feeding does *not* prevent pregnancy.
- Pregnancy *can* occur without male penetration (sperm can make their own way through the vagina and they live for up to two days in the vagina, womb or fallopian tubes).
- First intercourse *can* result in pregnancy.
- *Any* position of intercourse can result in pregnancy.
- Withdrawal (see below) *can* lead to pregnancy.
- Douching (washing) afterwards does *not* prevent pregnancy.
- Contraception should be continued until a woman has not had a period or any bleeding for two years if she is forty-five to fifty or one year if she is over fifty.

Your GP or family planning clinic should prescribe or insert the following:
Combined pill (almost 100 per cent effective), includes triphasic and biphasic pills – all contain oestrogen and progestogen. Taken regularly, it stops ovulation (the release of an egg each month). Easy and convenient to use, it does not interfere with love-making, often reduces the amount of period bleeding, pain and pre-menstrual tension. Less suitable for those over thirty-five or with a family history of strokes, heart attacks or raised blood pressure. Other risks are still being investigated. Does not work if taken over twelve hours late or when there is sickness or diarrhoea.

Mini-pill (98 per cent effective) – progestogen-only pill, useful for older women as there is less risk of blood pressure and clotting. Easy to use, does not interfere with love-making, might make monthly cycle irregular.

Intrauterine device or IUD, IUCD, loop or coil (96 to 98 per cent effective) – a small plastic or copper device inserted into the womb which is designed to prevent an egg settling. It lasts two to three years (copper IUD) or longer (plastic Lippes Loop IUD). Does not interfere with love-making, effective immediately on fitting. Disadvantages include possibility of heavier period bleeding, pelvic infections and possibility of coil coming out spontaneously.

The following method is available from a GP or family planning clinic – it is also available from a chemist but fitting should first be made at doctor's surgery or family planning clinic:
Diaphragm or *cap* (97 per cent effective – must be used with spermicide cream, jelly, pessary or foam which inactivates sperm). This is a soft rubber device inserted into the vagina before intercourse to prevent sperm entering the cervix. It can be inserted up to three hours before and must be left in six hours after intercourse. May protect against cervical cancer. Check every six months (or after weight loss or gain or after pregnancy) that diaphragm is the correct size.

The following method is available from a chemist or family planning clinic:
Condom or sheath, rubber, french letter or johnny (97 per cent effective) – a thin rubber sheath worn over the penis, easy to obtain and use and can protect both partners against sexually transmitted diseases. Disadvantages include possibility of rubber splitting and some men may find loss of sensitivity during intercourse. (Approved sheaths carry a British Standards Institution kitemark.)

You need trained advice to help you effectively with:
Safe period – checking temperature, cervical mucus (Billings method) or calendar, so as to ascertain when you are least likely to conceive (85 to 93 per cent effective with careful use of sympto-thermal method). Daily recording of temperature, change in mucus and other signs of ovulation are necessary. No use of hormones or mechanical devices. Suitable for couples with religious or personal objections to other methods.

Note The safe period method is not always safe. You should not rely on it if:
- your periods are irregular
- you have just had a baby
- you are approaching or at the menopause
- you are travelling abroad (when your periods might be affected by change in climate or routine)
- you are ill or emotionally upset
- you are taking any drug, especially pain-killers which could interfere with your temperature.

Think seriously before considering:
Female sterilization – a permanent method of birth control. The fallopian tubes are closed so that the eggs cannot travel from the ovaries to the

uterus. Sterilization is effected by an operation through a small direct cut in the abdominal wall (laparotomy) or, more usually, via a delicate telescope (laparoscopy). The tubes are blocked by tying and removing a small section (tubal ligation) or by sealing (diathermy) or by the use of clips or rings. Female sterilization is effective immediately. It gives women complete freedom from fear of pregnancy: a few notice heavy periods.

Male sterilization or vasectomy – the vas deferens, tubes through which sperm travel from the testes to the penis, is cut or blocked so that sperm no longer enter the ejaculate fluid. The only effect is that there is no sperm in the ejaculate – sterilization does not affect libido or erection.

● It is recommended that other contraceptive devices are used until up to twenty ejaculations after sterilization as some sperm may be left in the tube leading to the penis.

Not recommended is:

Withdrawal method – the man withdraws his penis from the woman's vagina just before ejaculation. A small amount of sperm is sometimes released before ejaculation, and sperm near the vagina can still find their way into it.

Other methods:

Morning-after contraception, post-coital attention – must be prescribed by a GP or clinic. This is for emergency use only, after the failure of your usual method or if no method was used. You will be given either special doses of the pill (within three days) or an intrauterine device (within five days).

Injectable contraceptive or the jab (almost 100 per cent effective) – a single injection of progestogen injected into a muscle, approved by a doctor only for a few women, short term.

See   Various leaflets from the Family Planning Information Service.

Help   ● For advice on contraception and planning your family see your GP or local family planning clinic (look under Family Planning in Yellow Pages). Family Planning advice and services are free. You can also contact the Family Planning Information Service (FPIS) which provided the facts and figures used in this section. It is run jointly by the Family Planning Association and the Health Education Council:

> Family Planning Information Service
> 27–35 Mortimer Street
> London WIN 7RJ
> 01–636 7866

Regional administrators:

Belfast	0232–25488	*Cardiff*	0222–387471
Birmingham	021–454 8236	*Glasgow*	041–333 9696
Exeter	0392–56711	*Liverpool*	051–709 1938

● Advice on contraception for disabled people is available from:

(a) National Association for Mental Health (MIND): 01–637 0741

(b) Association to Aid the Sexual and Personal Relationships of the Disabled (SPOD): 01–486 9823

(c) Sexual and Personal Relationships of the Disabled, 286 Campden Rd, London N7 0BJ, 01–607 8851.

● Information on contraceptive advice in many languages can be obtained from:

> International Planned Parenthood Federation (IPPF)
> Dorland House
> 18–20 Lower Regent Street
> London SW1Y 4PH
> 01–839 2911.

● Information for travellers on what contraceptives and clinics are available world-wide can be obtained from IPPF, as above.

● Free advice and clinics especially for young people are available at the sixteen Brook Advisory Centres around the country. Their main work is contraception and birth control and anyone – regardless of how young – is welcome. All discussions are completely confidential. The centres also provide pregnancy testing (this can be done fourteen days or more after you have missed a period).

The head office of Brook Advisory Centres is:

> 153a East Street
> London SE17 2SD
> 01–708 1234

Telephone numbers of clinics around the country include:

Birmingham	021–455 0491
	021–643 5341
	021–554 7553
	021–328 4544
Bristol	0272–736657
Coventry	0203–412627
Edinburgh	031–229 3596
Liverpool	051–709 4558
London	01–580 2991

Hygiene and Sexually Transmitted Diseases

HYGIENE   INFESTATIONS
INFECTIONS

Much of the information in this chapter came from the Health Education Council, who produce excellent leaflets (address on page 386).

HYGIENE   Circumcision is not essential but lack of personal cleanliness in men who have not been circumcised can lead to disease in both partners. The foreskin must be pulled back fully every day to wash the penis tip. If the man does not do this, after repeated intercourse you may feel irritation and inflammation of the genital passages that could, in time, contribute to the onset of cervical cancer.

If you use the diaphragm, always clean it thoroughly after use using cold water and unscented soap.

Certain religions completely ban any sexual contact during menstruation. Some other people have intercourse during this time as they find it particularly stimulating (and mistakenly think that a woman cannot conceive while menstruating). It is important that internal tampons (if used) be removed – and important, too, to remove the last tampon at the end of a period.

INFECTIONS   Infections can be transmitted by all kinds of hetero- and homosexual activity. Some people who are not sexually active also develop conditions which, in all cases, can best be investigated at a clinic.

You and your sex partner should go to a clinic if you have any of the following symptoms:

● an itching, soreness or discharge from vagina, penis or anus which is unusual for you

● a sore lump or rash on genital area, anus or in the mouth

● increased frequency of passing water or discomfort in doing so.

Specific diseases   **Gonorrhoea.** Women: sometimes an unusual anal or vaginal discharge, burning when passing water, symptoms of fever – or no symptoms at all.

Early diagnosis and treatment means that gonorrhoea can be cured quickly and completely with out-patient treatment.

Syphilis. Men and women: at first a painless sore will appear on or around the sex organs which will clear up on its own. The sore is often inside the vagina or rectum where it is unseen. The next stage are body rash, mouth sores, lumps, flu-like symptoms and a general feeling of ill-health.

Before the discovery of antibiotics syphilis was often thought of as an incurable disease. Now it can be treated safely, usually by a course of penicillin, and it is essential that someone who has it goes for help before permanent damage is done to all parties concerned.

Help   You cannot diagnose or treat yourself. You should go straight to a special clinic (see below). You do not need a doctor's permission. Everything will be conducted in complete confidence.

To find a clinic look up V D or Venereal Disease in the telephone directory or phone or visit the casualty department of your local hospital. Posters are also displayed in some public places. Venereal disease clinics operate under such names as:

● Department of Genital Medicine

● Department of Genito-Urinary Medicine

- Department of Venereology
- Special Clinic
- Special Treatment Centre
- STD Clinic.

You will be given an appointment, which may take up to an hour as the doctor will do a physical examination. You must be prepared to tell the doctor what symptoms you have had and for how long, what sex partners you have had in the past three months, if you have had anal and/or oral-genital contact and if you are allergic to any drugs.

Until you are free of infection you must not have sexual relations.

INFESTA-
TIONS
Note:

- Not all infestations need be sexually transmitted.

Genital warts. Usually sexually transmitted, they appear up to nine months after exposure to infection. Removal requires special techniques.

Herpes genitalis. Also usually sexually transmitted; it is thought that these are related to mouth and face sores. Genital sores can cause extreme discomfort and there may be difficulty in passing water. Treatment varies: there is no known antibiotic to kill the virus but there are ways of treating an affected area which relieve pain and help healing (see your doctor or go to a special clinic).

Pubic lice (also called crabs or nits). These live in the pubic hair and sometimes in all other hair except on the scalp. If you notice eggs or lice on underclothes or feel itching if the lice bite, you need a special shampoo or lotion from your chemist, doctor or one of the special clinics mentioned above.

Scabies (also known as 'the itch'). These are tiny mites which burrow into the skin, usually around the sex organs, backside, wrists and ankles. Treatment consists of a special lotion put on the entire body from neck to toe and leaving it without bathing: diagnosis and treatment can quickly be carried out from one of the special clinics mentioned above.

- See also 'Vaginal Health and Discomfort', page 194ff.

See 'Gonorrhoea', 'Syphilis', 'Viral Infections and Infestations' and 'What You Should Know about Sexually Transmitted Diseases', all from the Health Education Council.

Sex During Pregnancy

It is perfectly all right to enjoy a full sex life during pregnancy, although towards the end of your pregnancy it may become rather difficult due to your shape and size.

If you have had previous miscarriages it may be advisable not to have intercourse during the first three months – talk to your doctor about it.

After the birth of your baby it is usually recommended that you wait six weeks before having sexual intercourse. However, providing that you do not experience any pain during intercourse and the lochia has ceased (a bloody discharge from the uterus passed through the vagina after the birth of your baby), there is no reason why you should not resume a full and normal sex life as soon as you feel ready.

Abortion

The Abortion Act 1967 says it is not illegal to have an abortion if two doctors agree in good faith that it is necessary under at least one of the following conditions:

● Your life is at greater risk by continuing the pregnancy than by terminating it.

● Your physical or mental health is more likely to be injured by continuing with the pregnancy than by terminating it.

● The physical or mental health of any existing children you have is more likely to be injured by your continuing with the pregnancy than by terminating it.

● There is a reasonable chance that the baby may be abnormal or deformed.

If you want an abortion see your family doctor. He must be able to state in accordance with the Act that you are unfit to continue with the pregnancy. Two doctors independently must see and examine you before an abortion can be carried out – *before you are twenty-eight weeks pregnant.* Your doctor can refer you to a NHS hospital, a non-profit-making charitable organization or a private clinic.

In Scotland the 28-week time limit does not apply although doctors would not necessarily co-operate after that time. In Northern Ireland, abortion is available only in exceptional circumstances (contact the Ulster Pregnancy Advisory Association in Belfast, telephone 0232–667345).

What is an abortion?

In the first three or four months of pregnancy there are simple ways of terminating it vaginally which involve gently stretching the neck of the uterus and emptying its contents. The earlier the termination, the more simple the operation. You will feel fully recovered within an hour or two and you can usually leave the hospital or clinic the following day.

From the fourth month onwards, simple techniques are no longer possible and you will have to stay longer in hospital. One method involves the introduction of substances to bring on labour: this usually lasts between 12 and 36 hours, after which the pregnancy comes to an end naturally.

After an abortion

● Blood loss following an abortion varies. It may finish after a few days or it may dribble for some weeks.

● If you are too energetic for forty-eight hours or so afterwards you may bring on heavy bleeding.

● As it is impossible to sterilize the vagina before the operation and as the neck of the uterus remains open for a while afterwards, there is always a slight risk that infection might occur. To reduce this, patients are advised to avoid using tampons or other internal protection and to avoid sitting or lying in a hot bath for a week afterwards.

● Intercourse should be avoided for at least two weeks.

● After a fourth month (or later) abortion, lactation may occur two or three days after the operation and the breasts remain painful for about three days. A firm bra should be worn and pain-killers can be taken.

● If you experience undue or sudden pain, continuing or excessive bleeding, rises in temperature or you feel ill you should go to your doctor *immediately*.

Help ● The British Pregnancy Advisory Service offers help with establishing pregnancy, advice on abortions and subsequent arrangement for them. They have their own clinics. Free leaflets (s.a.e.) and information from the head office:

> British Pregnancy Advisory Service
> Austy Manor
> Wootton Wawen
> Solihull
> West Midlands B 9 5 6 BX
> 056–42 3225

Other telephone numbers – most with 24-hour answering service – include:

Birmingham	021–643 1461
Cardiff	0222–372389
Glasgow	041–204 1832
Leeds	0532–443861 or 0532–440685 (Marie Stopes clinic)
Liverpool	051–227 3721
London	01–222–0985 or 01–388 4843 (Marie Stopes clinic)
Manchester	061–236 7777 or 061–832 4260 (Marie Stopes clinic)

● *Breaking Chains* is the bi-monthly newspaper of the Abortion Law Reform Association (ALRA). For details of the publication and of ALRA contact:

> Abortion Law Reform Association
> 88a Islington High Street
> London N 1 8 EG
> 01–359 5200

Help with Relationships

MARRIAGE
GUIDANCE
COUNCIL

The Marriage Guidance Council was originally run by trained voluntary counsellors whose aims were primarily to help people who were having problems in their marriages. The name has stayed the same but the aim has now broadened so that counsellors will help anyone of any age and marital status who has a relationship problem.

Marriage guidance counsellors are still mainly voluntary but they are trained to a high professional standard and the training is continued the whole time they work for the Marriage Guidance Council. They are ordinary people who volunteer and then go through a strict selection procedure during which approximately half are eliminated. Counsellors are chosen for their integrity, their ability to grow and change with training, their own experience of life and the warmth of their personality.

A counsellor's role is to help people sort out their problems. He or she is not there to give advice as such or to make judgements. By listening and encouraging the clients to talk the counsellor helps them to gain the insight necessary to cope.

You generally meet the counsellor at the local Marriage Guidance Office (address in telephone directory, telephone for an appointment). Very occasionally, domiciliary counselling is offered, e.g. when a client is house-bound through physical or psychological disability. You will have an hour's appointment in a comfortable sitting-room atmosphere. You will be able to talk your problem over with someone who is kind, sympathetic and understanding. Everything you say is completely confidential.

At the end of this initial hour you should make another appointment as it can take several weeks to gain the insight necessary to begin to sort out your particular problems. You will see the same counsellor at each visit and you will be asked to pay a 'contribution'. No one is ever refused an appointment if they cannot pay.

How can a marriage guidance counsellor help you? Some people assume that those with problems should sort them out themselves. It is also sometimes thought that there is no point in going for outside help if the husband/partner will not go along too.

The following case history (as described by counsellor Jan Albone) is perhaps the best answer to both assumptions.

Jenny, thirty-eight, is married to John, forty. They have two children (fourteen and twelve). Jenny came to see me on her own. She was very distressed as she had discovered that he was having an affair. She was very unhappy, hurt and angry and at the first interview showed how confused she was.

She thought she had a good sound marriage. John was a shift worker and they had had to struggle in the early days of marriage as his job was interesting but badly paid. She had a part-time job. Together they had got most of the material things they needed and she was obviously a good manager and mother. She could not understand now why John wanted to go to another woman, particularly a 'brassy tart'.

In the first interview I said very little. It was enough that she had a caring listener. She came for six more weeks and we discussed her views of marriage. These were based on her mother's attitude that the important things were home and children and that a husband's role was that of provider. By talking about these attitudes she began to see that she had shut John out of the relationship. We discussed what she needed from a partner and it became clear she needed the warmth, companionship and sexual pleasure that they had had in the early days of the marriage. John needed all this too, but over the years the material side of their life had assumed priority and John's needs had led him to start an affair.

Jenny was helped and supported to be able to talk to John and see him as a real person. She was helped to get her obsessive mother/housewife role into perspective.

The change in her attitude to John – from anger and bitterness to a small attempt to understand herself and him – enabled him to share his needs with her. Over the weeks the situation at home changed and he was able to ease out of the affair, which fortunately had not become too serious.

As counsellor, I should stress I never met John. He was invited, via Jenny, to come but it did not matter that we did not meet.

I was helping Jenny to change and grow. As she changed John was also able to adapt. At any stage Jenny could have cancelled an appointment; there is no commitment on the part of either the client or the counsellor, but she enjoyed the sessions and felt she was given understanding, support and help through an extremely traumatic period.

SEX THERAPY

All marriage guidance counsellors are trained to discuss sex problems in a natural and easy way and as a matter of course.

Sometimes women lose interest in sex. Often in these cases the problem is lack of communication between the partners. Sex itself is, when good, the most perfect communication between two people but so many couples, even today, do not or cannot talk about sex and are therefore unable to ask for what they really want. Or there may be a dysfunction or problem with which they can be helped, either by the Marriage Guidance Council or another organization.

Among the dysfunctions for which help is available are the following:

Men
- premature and retarded ejaculation
- primary impotence (has never had an erection)
- secondary impotence (has had erections but has difficulty in getting them at present).

Women
- dyspareunia (pain on intercourse)
- vaginismus (involuntary spasm of the vagina)
- primary orgasmic dysfunction (she has never yet had an orgasm)
- random anorgasmia (not able to have orgasms with one partner but has been orgasmic with another).

In all cases it is important to have a medical check-up to make sure that no organic cause exists for the problem and that neither of the partners is depressed.

Counsellors and doctors can refer clients/patients to a sex therapist or you can go direct to a Marriage Guidance Council sex therapist. You must commit yourself to at least three months of weekly visits. You need to have a reasonably stable relationship with your partner, and you must both come together to appointments. Remedial counselling (as in the case history described above) requires that the counsellor listens, discusses, suggests and supports. Sex therapy requires a structured treatment programme that must be put into practice between sessions. The sex therapist is an experienced counsellor who has undertaken further and extensive training based on the work done by Masters and Johnson in America.

You and your partner have an initial meeting with the therapist. The problem is discussed and if it is decided that the dysfunction can be treated, you then independently attend verbal history-taking sessions at which you are both asked the same questions. After this you begin the treatment programme. All exercises will be carried out by a couple in the privacy of their own home (the exercises are not observed by the counsellor).

You are told to refrain from intercourse until given permission but at the same time you are given instruction in the giving and taking of sensual enjoyment. No one is ever asked to do anything they could not do, but there is gentle progression week by week to eventual happy enjoyable intercourse.

The following case history (described by Jan Albone) provides an example of the sex therapist's work.

> James and Clare, both twenty-six, had been married for six years. They had had intercourse together since they were eighteen. Their problem was that Clare had never had an orgasm and was now refusing to have intercourse at all as it was uncomfortable and unsatisfactory. Clare was very articulate. James was the 'strong silent type' with a strong sex drive.
>
> They entered the treatment programme and both enjoyed the touching and stroking exercises without intercourse. Clare found these very stimulating, especially when they were instructed to touch each other's genitals very gently.
>
> They came one day with grins from ear to ear. She had managed to have an orgasm through him touching and stroking her genitals. Before coming for treatment there had been very little love play. She had not been able to ask for it – in fact she had not realized that this was what she needed to get turned on.
>
> It took several more weeks of instruction for her to be orgasmic on intercourse. The therapy enabled them to communicate about sex and what had been a quick act of intercourse with a certain of pleasure for him but none for her became enormous fun for both and much more uninhibited. Not only did their sex life improve but their general relationship was so much better because they were really communicating.

● More information, and details of publications, can be obtained (send s.a.e.) from:

National Marriage Guidance Council
Little Church Street
Rugby CV21 3AP
0788–73241

In Northern Ireland, you may like to contact:

76 Dublin Road
Belfast BT2 7HP
0232–223454

LESBIAN LINE

by the Lesbian Line Collective

We at Lesbian Line believe that every woman should have the right to live as she wants: to choose her own sexuality, her own friends and lovers, her own lifestyle.

If you are unsure of your sexual orientation, *trust your feelings.* A lot of people are only too anxious to convince you that what you feel is not real. *Only you know how you feel.*

It can be lonely, it can seem as though you are the only woman in the world who wants to have a relationship with another woman. It can mean rejection by your friends and family – a particular problem for young lesbians living in their parents' home. But there are friendly, comfortable places where lesbians can meet.

Help

Lesbian Line is a London-based national phone-line for lesbians, operated entirely by lesbians, offering help, advice and information. There are also lesbian lines in many other cities with better access to local information and therefore of more help to women living in their area.

A frequent caller is the woman living in a small rural community who has no contact with other lesbians and wants to know where she can meet women like herself. There are women who have drink or drug problems, who have been beaten up by men, who want to know good doctors, dentists, car mechanics . . .

We have files on many organizations that function both as campaigning bodies and as valuable contact and support groups for, for instance, black lesbians, disabled lesbians, young lesbians, lesbian mothers. If you want to know what is happening in your area, have a particular problem, feel lonely or worried or just want a chat, please ring us. We will do our best to help.

Lesbian Line
BM Box 1514
London WC1N 3XX
01–257 6911

(Mon. and Fri. 2 to 10 p.m. Tues., Wed. and Thurs. 7 to 10 p.m.)

● There are many other lesbian lines/contact groups all over the country, some of which are listed below. For details of your local lesbian line, please ring 01–837 8602 or any of these numbers:

Belfast	0232–222033 (Thurs. 8 to 10 p.m.)
Birmingham	021–622 6580 (Wed. and Fri. 7 to 10 p.m.)
Edinburgh	031–557 0751 (Sun. 8 to 10 p.m.)
Glasgow	041–248 4596 (Mon. 7 to 10 p.m.)
Manchester	061–236 6205 (Mon. to Thurs. 7 to 10 p.m.)
Newcastle	0632–612 277 (Thurs. to Fri. 7 to 10 p.m.)

● Counselling help for couples or individuals in relationships where one partner is homosexual or bisexual and the other is 'straight' is available from:

Sigma
London WC1N 3XX
01–837 7324 (24 hour service)

and from homosexual support groups in:

Edinburgh	031–556 4049 (Mon. to Sat. 7.30 to 10 p.m.)
Glasgow	041–221 8372 (Mon. to Sun. 7 to 10 p.m.)

Further Information

Suggested further reading

Brothers, Joyce, *What Every Woman Should Know About Men*, Granada

Brown, Paul and Carolyn Faulder, *Treat Yourself to Sex: a Guide to Good Loving*, Penguin

Comfort, Alex, *The Joy of Sex*, Quartet
More Joy of Sex, Quartet

Consumer's Association, *The Which? Guide to Birth Control*

Crabtree, Tom, *The Search for Love: a Guide to Your Relationships*. Cosmopolitan

Heiman, Julie, Joseph and Leslie LoPiccolo, *Becoming Orgasmic*, Prentice-Hall

Kitzinger, Sheila, *Woman's Experience of Sex*, Penguin

Kurtz, Irma, *Crises: a Guide to Your Emotions*, Cosmopolitan

Macdonald's Guidelines, *Sex and Life*, Macdonald

Shapiro, Howard I., *The Birth Control Book*, Penguin

Wittig, Monique and Sande Zeig, *Lesbian Peoples*, Virago Press

9 Your Child

This chapter discusses the typical growth and development of a child from birth to sixteen. Your child will develop at his or her own pace and may well reach these milestones sooner or later than the ages given.

First there are guidelines for feeding and caring for children and adolescents, set out in chronological order. The second half of the chapter lists some useful information and looks at common problems.

I believe strongly in going to specialists for their advice. This chapter was contributed by Diana Hastings, who shares her own experiences and passes on advice from other experts on child care too.

The chapter is intended to be used for quick reference. If there is a topic in which you are particularly interested, the suggestions for further reading and the names and addresses of various organizations may help you to find the extra information you require.

Care and Feeding from Birth to Adolescence

Notes
- The feeding plans for babies are suggestions only. 'Jars' are mentioned because they are a useful guide to the amount of food to give, whether you have prepared it yourself or bought jars, tins or dehydrated food.
- 1 jar equals approx 3 tbs of food.
- If your child has any feeding problems, see your health visitor or doctor.
- To avoid confusion with the mother, the baby/child is referred to as 'he' throughout.

BIRTH   At birth, babies weigh on average 3.1 kg (7 lb.) and measure 50 cm (20 ins.). They tend to look rather wrinkled and they are covered with vernix, a sticky coating which washes off.

As soon as the baby is born, early body contact between you is very important. Once he has cried and is breathing normally and the cord has been cut, the midwife will clear any mucus from his nasal passages and wrap him in a shawl. Then you will be able to cuddle your baby and put him to the breast and the close bond between you will begin.

The birth is very tiring for your baby as well as for you. You both need a good rest.

During the next few days and weeks:

● At first your baby may lose some weight, but he will have regained his birth weight at around ten days old.

● The stump of the cord at the navel withers away and falls off at about seven days.

● The midwife will help you with feeding, bathing and generally looking after him.

Going home If your baby was born in hospital, providing everything went normally you will probably be able to go home two days or even a few hours after the birth. Then the community midwife will visit you twice a day for the first three days and then daily until the baby is ten days old – or even longer if you need help with feeding or any other problems.

Your baby will probably react to the change of environment from hospital to home and may be restless or irritable for a day or so. You are probably tired and things may seem difficult. You need someone to help you with shopping, cleaning and cooking for the first two to three weeks. The thing that really matters is for you to get to know and love your baby.

If you want to meet other new mothers, contact the Home-Start Scheme. There are twenty-five schemes around the country and you can get help, advice and companionship from people who realize what you are going through. For details of the nearest Home-Start Scheme contact (s.a.e.):

Home-Start Consultancy
22 Princess Road West
Leicester LE1 6TP
0533–554988

Birth registration If the parents are married only one signature is needed to register the birth, which must be registered in England and Wales within forty-two days.

In Scotland, the birth must be registered within twenty-one days but this can be done either in the district in which the birth took place or where the mother lives. In Northern Ireland, the birth should be registered within forty-two days either in the district where the birth took place or where the mother lives. (Registrars visit maternity hospitals and most mothers register babies then.) Births can also be registered by close relatives.

Regardless of where they live, if the parents are unmarried and the father wants to have his name entered in the register, either both parents must go to the register office or the father can get a special form to sign. If she later obtains an affiliation order (see page 221), a mother can re-register a birth.

Announcements The desired announcement should be sent or telephoned as soon as possible to the Births column of the selected national or local newspaper. There is a charge for this and a typical announcement might read:

Garner – to John and Anne, at the Middlesex Hospital on 5 January 1985 – a daughter, Maria.

An announcement from a single mother could read:

Garner, to Anne, at the Middlesex Hospital on 5 January 1985 – a daughter, Maria.

Health visitor The health visitor will call at your home within the next week or two. She is trained as a nurse with obstetric experience and will be able to help with mothercraft and child care. You can also see her at your local child health clinic or the doctor's surgery – so if you have a problem then talk to her and ask for her advice (it is sometimes difficult to remember all the questions you wanted to ask, so write them down on a piece of paper).

Money From the moment he is born, your baby can have a current or deposit account with a bank or building society (although you will have to open it for him!). He can also hold Premium Bonds. See also 'Child Benefits', below.

Breast-feeding *During the first few days* colostrum is produced. Put him to the breast for a few minutes when he wakes, which is about every three hours, or even more frequently. The milk is produced on about the third day.

After about ten days he is usually taking full feeds. Some babies suck rapidly and take all they need in up to seven minutes. Others suck slowly and need to pause to get up wind.

Most babies need a night feed for the first few weeks.

For successful breast-feeding you should

- Eat a well-balanced diet just as you did when you were pregnant.
- Drink plenty of fluids.
- Avoid medicines such as laxatives unless given to you by your doctor.
- Cut down on alcohol and smoking.
- Sit down comfortably in a calm and peaceful atmosphere.
- Nurse him against your breast, touch his cheek with your breast and he will instinctively move his mouth towards the nipple.
- Make sure he takes the nipple and the coloured area around it into his mouth.
- Hold your breast away from his nose.
- Give multi-vitamin drops, obtainable from the clinic or a chemist.
- Have plenty of rest – this is important.

There may be some difficulties at first, so do not be disheartened. It takes time to learn how to breast-feed.

Your baby is getting enough food if he is a happy contented baby and is gaining about ½ lb. a week in weight. But he is not getting enough if he cries a lot and is generally miserable, if he wakes up two hours after a feed, crying and if he demands two feeds during the night. If he is not getting enough food although he is normally a happy contented baby, it may mean that you are producing less because you are busier and coping with the rest of the family and he is demanding more because he is growing.

Try to have more rest if possible and increase the milk by putting him to the breast more frequently – just as you did when you first started breast-feeding. The more he sucks the more milk you will make. It may take as much as two weeks before your baby is really happy and contented again and gaining weight.

If you are having problems, take the baby to the health visitor or clinic.

Bottle-feeding   If you do not want to breast-feed or you are unable to, there is no need to feel guilty or to think that you are failing as a mother – you certainly are not. For you, bottle-feeding is best.

Make sure everything is sterilized (in Milton solution or sterilizing tablets). You will also need:
● 8 to 10 wide-necked bottles with caps or covers and teats – milk from teats should come out in fast drops: if the hole is too small, enlarge it with a red-hot needle
● a measuring jug
● a knife for levelling off the powder
● a spoon for mixing
● a cleaning brush
● a container for sterilizing solution large enough for everything to be completely submerged. Bottles must be full of sterilizing solution – no air bubbles. Hold teats on the bottom with an upturned egg cup
● water which has been boiled and cooled
● baby milk powder.

Amount of feed:
● 75 ml (2½ oz.) per pound per day – e.g. a 10lb. baby needs (10 × 75 ml) 750 ml or 25 oz. in twenty-four hours.
● Divide this into five feeds per day (for a 10lb. baby, 150 ml or 5 oz. per feed).
● If he finishes the bottle to the last drop he can have more if he wants it.
● If he is sick give a little less.
● If he cries between feeds he may be hungry or thirsty – in the first week he will probably want only milk but after that he may take 60 ml (2 oz.) of tepid boiled water.

To make up a feed:
● Use the instructions on the packet. Never add more powder. Allow the powder to lie naturally in the scoop before levelling with the knife. An over- or under-concentrated feed will damage your baby.
● You can make up the feeds for the whole day but keep them in the fridge.
● Warm bottles before feeding your baby. Do not keep feeds warm for more than three hours as they may begin to grow germs. Test the temperature of the feed by letting a few drops flow on to the inside of your wrist: it should feel warm, *not* hot.
● Keep everything spotlessly clean. Turn teats inside out to clean them

and use a bottle brush on the bottles. Immerse in solution for at least as long as instructed and then just shake the solution out of the bottles – do not wash or rinse. Sterilizing solution must be changed every twenty-four hours.

When feeding:
- Hold the baby close to you.
- There is no need to give extra vitamins – they are already in the feed.
- If he is not happy and is crying a lot, do not keep changing from one brand of milk to another. It is probably not the milk but some other reason, so take him along to the clinic or the doctor.
- Never leave a baby with a bottle.

1 MONTH   Your baby watches you and responds to your voice. He can grasp with his fingers and hold his head up for a few seconds, watch a toy when held within his vision, and enjoy a colourful mobile. He sleeps a lot and cries, but quietens when you pick him up. He is startled by sudden noise. He seeks out the nipple, sucks and swallows. Needs plenty of sleep.

2 MONTHS   Now your baby can lift his head when lying on his tummy. He begins to follow people with his eyes and focuses, he listens to a bell or rattle and follows the sound. He smiles at you when you talk to him, and loves to be talked to, sung to, smiled at and touched. There is no change in feeding but he enjoys orange juice, rose hip syrup or blackcurrant syrup, diluted as instructed on the bottle.

3 MONTHS   Can push himself up on his arms when lying on his tummy, kicks well. Tries to grasp objects which he can hold if placed in his hand. Follows people and searches for sound with his eyes. Pulls at his clothes. Smiles, gurgles or squeaks with delight. From three to four months you may need to start mixed feeding if he is obviously hungry and weighs about 12 lb. If he is contented with his milk feed and is gaining weight, then there is no need to start him on solids just yet.

Feeding   Weaning (at three months or later):
- At first try 1 or 2 tsp of strained boiled carrot or strained mashed potato and gravy or baby cereal – give only one new taste at a time and watch for upsets before increasing the amount or variety.
- Do not add salt or sugar.
- Make sure there are no lumps – make a purée. Utensils must be sterilized.
- Give small amounts – progress gently and cut down the amount of milk you give. Eventually you will be able to replace the milk feeds with the strained food and give cooled boiled water or diluted fruit juice to drink.
- Aim to replace one milk feed with solids by the fifth week of weaning.

4 MONTHS   When you put the baby in a sitting position, he holds his head up well and looks around. He can lift his head and chest when on his tummy

and enjoys playing with his hands and clapping them together. He will reach for a rattle or toy, hold on to it and shake it about. He can pull his clothes over his face, laugh and show pleasure. He shows interest and excitement in everything going on around him, especially in food.

Feeding *Early morning*: breast and vitamin drops or 200 ml (7 oz.) bottle.

Mid-morning: breast or 200 ml (7 oz.) bottle.

Lunch: 1 to 2 tsp of meat and vegetables plus a drink (cooled boiled water or fruit juice).

Tea: 1 to 2 tsp of dessert, drink (cooled boiled water or fruit juice).

6 p.m.: breast or 200 ml (7 oz.) bottle.

10 p.m.: breast or bottle if required.

5 MONTHS The baby has full control of his head, loves playing with his toys and splashing about in the bath. When he drops a toy he looks to see where it has gone. He smiles at himself in the mirror. It is time to start encouraging your baby to join in with family meals.

Feeding *Early morning*: vitamins if breast-fed.

Breakfast: 1 to 2 tsp of cereal or fruit. Breast or 180 ml (6 oz.) bottle. Use 1 oz. milk from feed bottle to make up cereal.

Lunch: jar or 3 tbs of meat and vegetables plus jar of dessert. Drink of cooled boiled water or fruit juice.

Tea: jar or 3 tbs of savoury food, breast or 90 ml (3 oz.) bottle.

Bedtime: breast or 240 ml (8 oz.) bottle.

Note ● If he is gaining weight too fast reduce the amount of food you are giving.

6 MONTHS The baby can hold his bottle. He holds out his hands to be pulled up, rolls from front to back. He may show fear of strangers by wrinkling up his face and looking worried. He babbles and coos to music, blows bubbles and laughs. The lower front teeth appear and he begins to chew. He may show likes and dislikes over food.

You can now use boiled cows' milk (if you do, you should give vitamins) and there is no need to sterilize utensils. If he wants to feed himself with his fingers – a messy business – make it easier by cutting food into cubes or slices.

Feeding *Early morning*: vitamins if breast-fed.

Breakfast: jar or 3 tbs of cereal or scrambled or poached egg. Breast or 180 ml (6 oz.) bottle.

Lunch: jar or 3 tbs of meat and vegetables, jar of dessert. Drink of cooled boiled water or fruit juice (1 cup).

Tea: 3 tbs egg custard, jelly, jar of savoury or half mashed banana. Breast or 90 ml (3 oz.) bottle.

Bedtime: breast or 240 ml (8 oz.) bottle.

7 MONTHS He can sit up unsupported for a few minutes before rolling over. He sleeps less and can roll from his back on to his front, and answers to his name and says 'ba', 'da', 'ka'. He loves to bang toys on the table or floor and tries to touch his image in the mirror. He will imitate what you do – e.g. sticking out your tongue, coughing. He puts everything in his mouth. He feeds from a cup and likes feeding himself with a biscuit.

Feeding *Early morning*: vitamins if breast-fed or drinking cows' milk.

Breakfast: 1 jar or 3 tbs cereal or scrambled egg, 1 slice wholemeal toast and butter, breast or milk drink (180 ml, 6 oz.).

Lunch: 3 tbs mashed fish or minced meat or cheese plus ½ jar (1 to 2 tbs) vegetables and 1 jar or 3 tbs dessert. Drink in a cup.

Tea: bread and butter with savoury spread or honey, sponge finger or biscuit.

Bedtime: breast or cup of milk (about 180 ml, 6 oz.).

8 MONTHS The baby can sit unsupported, leaning forward to keep his balance. He shouts for attention and responds to no, says 'dada' and 'mama', and tries to crawl. The upper front teeth appear.

Feeding He now eats junior proprietary food or more coarsely chopped food.
(8 to 10 months) *Breakfast*: vitamin drops, 1 jar or 3 tbs porridge or cereal or 1 boiled, poached or scrambled egg and toast and butter, cup of milk (180 ml, 6 oz.).

Lunch: 1 jar or 3 tbs of main meal plus 1 jar vegetables – or well-chopped meat and vegetable. 1 jar or 3 tbs dessert or peeled apple or banana. Drink.

Tea: 1 jar or 3 tbs savoury or 1 slice bread and butter or sponge finger. Cup of milk (180 ml, 6 oz.).

Bedtime: breast or cup of milk (180 ml, 6 oz.).

9 MONTHS The baby can pick up small objects between finger and thumb. He can sit up without falling sideways and begins to crawl or manages to move about by rolling over and over. He helps to hold a cup when drinking.

10 MONTHS The baby can pull himself up into a sitting position and then on to his feet. He stands holding on to the furniture and smiles at himself in the mirror. He can pull himself forward on his tummy. He points to objects that he wants. He has discovered how to get attention by pulling off his clothes and likes to help you dress him, holding out an arm for his cardigan. He loves clapping his hands and waving goodbye and understands simple questions like 'where is mummy?'.

11 MONTHS   He is becoming a very good crawler, and stands well, with one foot raised ready for walking. He loves to cover his face and play 'peep bo' and can place an object in a container. He loves to drop toys on purpose for you to pick up – this causes great hilarity. He uses a few recognizable words, and loves picture books. He feeds himself with his fingers.

Feeding   *Breakfast*: cereal or boiled, poached or scrambled egg. Wholemeal toast
(*11–18 months*)   and butter. Cup of milk.

Lunch: junior main meal or meat and vegetables. Dessert or fruit. Drink – water or orange juice.

Tea: junior supper. Bread and butter with honey or cheese. Cup of milk.

Bedtime: cup of milk – flavoured if preferred.

12 MONTHS   The baby can walk holding your hand. When sitting, he may shuffle around on his bottom. He will kiss you when asked and knows about three words with meaning. He can drink from a cup himself and loves noisy toys.

Sleep   He needs 12 to 14 hours at night and 1 to 2 naps during the day.

● Travelling with a baby – see 'Useful Information and Common Problems', page 280.

15 MONTHS   The baby now walks on his own and crawls up stairs. He can build a tower with two bricks if you show him how and loves to sit on your lap looking at picture books. The back teeth begin to appear. He understands nearly everything you say and chatters back in his own language, which includes words like 'mummy', 'daddy', 'pussy' and 'dog' – uses four or five clear words. He pushes a pram or other mobile toy around and climbs on to furniture. He can feed himself but has difficulty getting food on to the spoon. May tell you when he is wet. Very interested in his excreta – this is normal, take no notice of it.

18 MONTHS   He is very active and exhausting and it takes all your time to keep up with him. He walks well, runs, jumps, climbs the stairs holding on to the banister. He can throw a ball, build a tower with three bricks and scribble with a pencil. He pulls or pushes toys and likes constructive play toys. He recognizes favourite nursery rhymes and repeats the last word.

Dressing   He can take off his gloves, socks, shoes and unzips fasteners. He puts on his coat. He copies you when you are cleaning or sweeping. He asks for food and drink, and joins two words together and repeats things you say. He may have some bladder control.

● Teeth – see 'Useful Information and Common Problems', page 280.

2 YEARS   At this age he can walk up and down stairs on his own and walk on tiptoe. He loves looking at books, turning the pages singly. He can dress himself with simple clothes. He talks incessantly and knows his full name, plays near others but on his own. He can feed himself and hold a pencil in his hand, not in his fist, and draw lines. He may be dry during the day and at night if lifted during the evening. He likes cookery sets, dolls, toy sweepers and teddy bears and enjoys threading games, drums, whistles, hammering and pull-and-push toys.

After 2½, he notices the differences between boys and girls and usually remarks about it in a loud voice in front of shockable adults – treat this as normal. He answers questions simply and truthfully and is inclined to be bossy and sometimes difficult. He becomes negative – this may simply be because it is easier for him to say 'no' than 'yes'.

Dawdling is one of his most annoying tricks – another is pretending he has not heard you. He takes ages to eat his food, and goes on and on making a noise he knows is irritating. He asks questions all day long – when you answer he asks another, and another . . . He is obsessional – e.g. stories must be repeated exactly, word for word.

Suddenly your 'little angel' becomes a 'little monster'. He is torn between his dependence on others and wanting to become independent, which he may express in the form of temper tantrums when he does not want to do as you tell him. But he is also feeling insecure with his increasing independence and may turn to things which represent security – e.g. a blanket. Insecurity may show itself in feeding, speech, sleeping and toilet problems. During these tantrums he may even kick and bite you. He is not trying to inflict pain but trying to get what he wants. He cannot see things from anyone else's point of view.

This sort of behaviour may make you feel anxious and unable to cope – if so, get some help and advice from your health visitor or doctor.

Feeding Meal times should be regular and snacks between meals avoided as they
(2–5 years) are often of high carbohydrate content and not good for the teeth or weight. Most toddlers love ice-cream, crisps, biscuits and sweets. Save them for special treats and give immediately after meals rather than in between.

He needs three meals a day and an extra drink on waking and at night before going to bed. Cut his food into manageable pieces and he may be able to feed himself. He needs a varied diet with plenty of protein, meat, fish, eggs (three per week maximum as the yolks are rich in fat) and cheese, fresh vegetables and fruit. He needs some carbohydrate in the form of cereal, bread, butter and a pint of milk a day.

He may become faddy with foods. Some children refuse to eat meat, regardless of whether or not their parents are vegetarian. Contact the Vegetarian Society, address on page 385.

He should be encouraged to sit at the table and wait until others have finished eating. He will learn to feed himself with a spoon and then go on to a knife and fork.

● Potty training – see 'Useful Information and Common Problems', page 280.

3 YEARS His strong will and temper tantrums continue but gradually he becomes more sociable and learns to share and to take turns. He dresses and undresses fully (except shoelaces). He can ride a tricycle.

He likes to help – e.g. setting the table – and can be trusted with some china. He asks questions all the time and knows and loves singing favourite nursery rhymes. He can count to ten and draw pictures. Favourite games include dressing dolls, modelling with plasticine and simple two- or three-piece puzzles, tracing books and gyroscopes. Adores you and wants to be like you, imitating everything you do.

Mother and toddler groups These are groups of adults, usually mothers, who meet perhaps once a week and bring along their toddlers. The mothers get a chance to meet new people and talk for a couple of hours, while the children play in the same room. There are usually toys and play activities suitable for babies, toddlers and pre-school children and a cup of tea for you. You can find out about your nearest group from the local newspaper, library or information centre.

4 YEARS He is lively, active and imaginative. A boy may mimic his father and exaggerate about the strength of daddy and just about everything else. A girl may mimic her mother – 'a little madam'.

The child climbs and jumps, repeats nursery rhymes and is generally very lovable. He asks 'why?' and questions everything. He listens to reason as long as he is being treated as a grown-up and acts accordingly. He does not respond well to answers like 'because I told you so'.

Sex-play between children is common and natural – they may even handle each others' genitals. Try to show no interest or anxiety.

This is also an age of showing independence – e.g. 'look what I can do'. Showing off is natural and goes on from four to seven years. He needs encouragement to develop his skills.

Pre-school education **Playgroups.** These are usually run by playleaders who have undertaken special courses. They are held in halls, private houses or wherever there is space, and a fee is charged.

They provide an opportunity for children from three to five to play with paint, sand, water and many other activities which may be difficult to do at home. There are toys which fire the imagination and clothes for dressing up, numerous jigsaws and building toys for concentrated effort. There are things to climb on, picture books to look at and friends to play with.

They give you a chance to meet some new friends and leaving the child for two or three hours gives him a chance to become a little more independent and increases his confidence.

Nursery schools. These are generally maintained by the state and are free. They are staffed by qualified teachers and assistants holding the National Nursery Examination Board (NNEB) certificate. However, there may not be one available in your area. There are, for instance, no day-long state nurseries in Northern Ireland and availability of other forms of pre-school education is lower than elsewhere in the British Isles: for details of what is available near you contact your local DHSS.

There are also private fee-paying schools. These offer more structured learning for three- to five-year-olds than playgroups do. Here they can play with their new friends, listen to stories and music, start to read if they are ready and draw and paint pictures.

Nursery schools are a natural way of loosening close ties between mother and child but he must be secure in your love to be willing to be parted from you. He enjoys make-believe play where he recreates things he has seen or done. He can become totally engrossed in his make-believe world. He may still have problems expressing everything in language but he can do it in play. This is a good introduction to school (it is helpful if he can dress and undress himself without help and if he is confident in managing his toilet needs before he goes to school).

Contact your local education authority for more information or:

> Pre-School Playgroups Association
> Alford House
> Aveline Street
> London SE11 5DH
> 01–582 8871

or, in Scotland, Glasgow 041–221 9388.

● Queries about education of children up to nine years old can be answered (s.a.e.) by:

> British Association for
>   Early Childhood Education
> Montgomery Hall
> Kennington Oval
> London SE11 5SW
> 01–582 8744

Sleep The four- to five-year-old needs 12 to 14 hours' sleep at night and will usually have dropped his sleep during the day. He needs to be tucked up in bed with his favourite toy after a warm bath. Giving him a cuddle and reading him a suitable story will help him unwind and fall asleep.

Discipline Smacking should not hurt: the occasional tap on the buttocks between the ages of three and five may well be necessary, but in the older child there should be no need for smacking.

5–10 YEARS At five years, your child must start full-time education.

At seven years he will be able to have a deposit account in National Savings and Trustee Savings Banks and draw money on his own signature.

A child of five is active, full of energy, persistent, careful, generous, friendly, sociable and very proud of his drawings and paintings. He talks clearly and asks masses of questions. He will also pull his younger sibling's hair, tease the cat and tear things up ... He destroys in order to build up his own self-confidence. These energies need to be directed into more constructive pastimes by an inventive, patient parent.

Starting school   Starting school is a big event. Although he now enjoys the company of other children he is still dependent on his parents. When he goes to school he will probably transfer this dependence to his teacher. Even if he has been to a playgroup he may still find separation from you for a whole day difficult – the large buildings and masses of strange children may be overwhelming so he may develop mild anxiety symptoms such as sickness, headache, disturbed sleep or nightmares.

Most children look forward to starting school. It is a happy and enjoyable place and they benefit from making new friends (who change frequently). They learn by doing and the activities are changed often, with plenty of time to release all that physical energy.

He is likely to be tired at the end of the day and need a good night's sleep (11 to 12 hours). He has been learning and concentrating and mixing with other children. Most children are exhausted when they get home – sometimes all they want to do is to sit in front of the television with a drink and a snack, but after a very short while they are ready to go into action again.

The hours between the end of school and bedtime should include some time spent outside in the fresh air and some time spent on hobbies or other special interests. Any homework should be completed early in the evening so there is time for play before bed. He will need somewhere he can do all this without being disturbed (this also means the rest of the family can get on with what they want to do).

Clothing for school, unless a uniform is worn, should be kept for school only and be easily washable, comfortable and allow freedom of movement. There is an education social worker who can be contacted through your school (or ask your health visitor) who may be able to help with the cost of clothing, uniform grants, maintenance allowance, cost of school meals or transport if there is a need.

School health services   The records from the child health clinic are passed on to the school health service when a child begins school.

His first medical examination is generally shortly after he enters infant school and you are invited to attend. In some areas this is carried out the year before he goes to school and you are invited to take him along to the nearest clinic. At this examination the doctor takes a full history, does a medical and dental examination. His immunizations are checked: if they are not up to date the school nurse will arrange for them to be done. If there are any problems, extra follow-up examinations will be arranged

Throughout his school life a nurse visits the school each term to check on minor illnesses, cleanliness and signs of infestation such as head lice. She also keeps the immunizations up to date. She will probably send you a questionnaire which you should fill in and return to the school.

Visits are also made to the school by the dentist every six months. He or she examines the children and will offer treatment at a nearby dental clinic. He also teaches good dietary habits and dental hygiene.

Diet A child needs a well-balanced diet with plenty of protein and minerals for growth and carbohydrates for energy (some very physically active children need more carbohydrates than others).

For detailed information about fats, carbohydrates, minerals, vitamins, etc., see 'What Your Body Needs', page 379ff.

The best guide to how much food a child needs is his appetite. He may eat very well indeed for a few days and then very little for a while – this is quite normal. It is better not to force him to eat or to restrict his food intake in either of these phases as it balances out in the long run.

He should have three meals a day:

1. *Breakfast* should be substantial – never skipped or rushed. It does not have to be a cooked breakfast: cereal and milk is excellent. If he really dislikes eating in the morning give him a piece of fruit or cheese to eat at playtime.

2. *Lunch.* If he comes home to lunch it should be ready so he does not have to rush. If he takes a packed lunch it should be nourishing and sustaining but not too much carbohydrate – perhaps a sandwich made of wholemeal bread filled with cheese, hard boiled eggs, peanut butter or meat, or a meat pie with raw carrots and nuts followed by fruit or yogurt.

3. *Evening meal.* If possible all the family should eat together – and not too near his bedtime (if the family usually eats late he may have to eat separately).

● *Snacks* mid-morning and when he gets home from school, a glass of milk and a piece of fruit.

During each day a child should have at least:

● 1 helping of meat, fish or poultry
● 1 or 2 helpings of cooked or raw vegetables
● 2 pieces of fruit
● 3 or more helpings of wholemeal bread, wholegrain cereals or potatoes.

He should have one pint of milk a day (if he dislikes it as a drink, use it to make soups, sauces, jellies or puddings). Avoid carbohydrates in the form of crisps, sweets, soft drinks and biscuits.

Vitamin A, C and D preparations should be given (these are available for younger children, under the Welfare Foods Scheme from the clinic).

At meal times try to create a nice happy atmosphere. Table manners can be learnt by example – too much nagging over manners destroys the pleasant atmosphere. If he eats a little of everything you give him you may not have too many problems with 'food fads'.

Teeth   During their sixth year children start to lose their milk teeth and the first of the permanent teeth – the six-year molars – push their way through.

7 YEARS

By this age the child is well settled into the competitive busy life of school. He can concentrate for much longer and is quick and keen to learn. He reads and writes well, makes up and writes imaginative stories and enjoys nature and history. This is a time when he saves up his weekly pocket money to buy something special. He really enjoys life. He is becoming less dependent on adults. He loves to ride about on bikes, to run, climb, play ball, anything physically strenuous.

There are likely to be questions about sex and these should be answered simply and truthfully.

Teeth   The permanent front teeth – incisors – usually appear, first in the lower jaws. Girls often shed teeth earlier than boys.

9–10 YEARS

He still accepts what you say. He likes to learn and enjoys the company of his friends and is probably part of a gang or 'secret society'; or he may join the Cubs or the Brownies. Generally he is interested in many activities and seems happy and emotionally stable. He takes himself very seriously and likes to work things out for himself. He adapts to new situations, concentrates on what he is doing and enjoys life to the full. He is self-confident and takes criticism well. He does not usually say he does not care or blame someone else when things go wrong. He cares about other people and gets on well with his own age group, adults and younger children.

He may show his emerging independence by objecting to being told when to come in and when to go to bed. He may fluctuate between childish and adult behaviour: this is the prelude to adolescence and is sometimes frustrating for parents. He still needs you, your standards and values and the limits you have set. He starts to set his own standards and if he wants to do something well he will work at it. He is less dependent on your praise but he still likes it.

At school he is studying a wide range of subjects and prefers the company of his own sex and forms firm friendships.

Teeth   Still getting permanent teeth – see 'Useful Information and Common Problems', page 280.

10–16 YEARS – ADOLESCENCE

This is a complex stage of development when physical, mental and emotional changes take place.

At the onset of puberty, physical development comes before the emotional. This period is a challenge for the child, teachers and parents.

During this period he moves to a secondary school and will need advice about a future career. Get this at an early stage so he can take the right exams and gain the necessary qualifications to follow the career of his choice.

Medical examinations by the school doctor are repeated at fourteen and include a fitness test for employment.

At twelve years, your child can buy a pet. At thirteen he can work (see below): at fourteen he can be fingerprinted and own a shotgun. At fifteen he can be sent to a corrective training centre. With his parents' consent he can join the armed forces (in which case he can make a will). And he can see a '15' film.

At sixteen a girl can legally consent to sexual intercourse. There is no specific legal age for boys for heterosexual relationships but for homosexual ones the legal age is twenty-one.

Both boys and girls can, among other rights, get married (with parents' consent, unless in Scotland), apply for a passport (if married or in the armed forces), fly solo in a glider, work underground, buy fireworks and leave school (after Easter following the sixteenth birthday or at Whitsun or at the end of the summer term).

Working

Taking a job (e.g. a paper round) should not be allowed to interfere with school work. Work may not begin before 7 a.m. or continue after 7 p.m. and not for more than two hours on any school day or Sunday. It must not involve heavy carrying or lifting.

Physical growth

Hormones are the secretions of the internal endocrine glands. The most important of these, the pituitary gland, lies in the middle of the brain. Before puberty only very small amounts of sex hormones are present in the body. At puberty there is an increase in the female hormone (oestrogen) and male hormone (testosterone). These are produced in the ovaries (in girls) or in the testes (in boys). The pituitary stimulates these glands to produce the sex hormones in girls which makes the breasts enlarge (see below) and the menstrual cycle begin. She develops body hair and female curves. In boys the testes enlarge, the voice deepens and facial and body hair grows.

Young people grow at an accelerated rate in height and weight. This growth varies greatly in boys: many start at ten to twelve or as late as sixteen, some have almost completely developed physically before the growth spurt begins – or vice versa (neither is abnormal). The average boy grows rapidly from about twelve and reaches his fastest rate at fourteen and then drops back to pre-growth-spurt rates. Girls begin on average two years earlier.

The heads, hands and feet reach adult size. The arms and legs grow faster than the trunk, giving a temporary feeling of awkwardness. Children may feel their hands and feet look too large or that they are 'all legs'. *Be careful how you comment on appearance – thoughtless remarks can hurt.*

Changes in the shape of girls produce typical female contours with wider hips while boys develop thicker and larger bones, more muscle tissue and broader shoulders – generally they become and will remain stronger than girls. They develop larger hearts and lungs.

Acne (spots) is a skin condition which appears on the face and upper parts of the body – and can cause great distress (see page 280).

Sexual development

Boys
- Testes and scrotum become larger.
- Pubic hair appears.
- Penis becomes larger.
- Voice deepens as the larynx grows and the vocal cords become longer: it can take two years for him to get full control over this (voice breaking) and there can be sudden jumps from high pitch to low.
It is not helpful to make fun of him.
- Hair appears under his arms and on his top lip.
- Sperm production increases with occasional ejaculation during sleep (wet dreams).
- Pubic hair becomes darker.
- Prostate gland enlarges.
- Increase in the size of dark area around the nipples – sometimes there is enlargement of the breast itself which will cause anxiety, but it will go away. Reassure him that he is not turning into a woman.
- He may also show slightly rounded hips but normally this goes away as well.

Girls
- Bud development of breasts.
- Rounding of hips.
- Soft downy pubic hair.
- Increase in size of uterus and vagina, labia and clitoris.
- Pubic hair becomes darker and thicker.
- Hair under the arms.
- Breasts develop more, nipples become darker and the size of the areola (the dark area around the nipple) becomes larger.
- Menstruation starts.
- Breasts mature more and there is increased growth of hair under the arms. Many worry that breasts are too big or too small and may try to hide this under loose-fitting jumpers or stand with rounded shoulders – or may display them in tight-fitting jumpers.
- Worry about the size of hips or the physical side of menstruation is common.
- About a year after her first period she is able to conceive.

Menstruation. This is a simple explanation to introduce your daughter to the menstrual cycle:

Once a month the body prepares for having a baby. The pituitary gland excretes a hormone through the bloodstream to the ovaries which release an egg – the ovum. This travels down the fallopian tubes to the womb or uterus. The uterus prepares a special lining, mainly of blood, to receive the ovum which, if it has been fertilized by the male sperm, will grow into a baby. If it has not been fertilized the uterus does not require the lining so it comes away and is passed through the vagina as a monthly period.

The period may last from three to seven days. At first it may not happen regularly but will eventually occur roughly every twenty-eight days until the age of about forty-five or older.

It is important to teach your daughter how to manage her periods. Introduce her to small sanitary towels or tampons. Advise her to change them regularly – at least four times a day. Towels and tampons should be disposed of according to the instructions on the packet. A warm shower, bath or all-over wash every day keeps her fresh and clean. She can safely go swimming if she wears a tampon (otherwise, it is better if she does not swim). She needs plenty of sleep, fresh air and exercise. If she gets mild cramps then a pain-killer may help. If the pain is severe, see your doctor.
● For menstrual problems – see below.

Sexual relationships
● First sexual relationships may be homosexual – the 'crush' involving someone of the same sex (this is more common among girls than boys and it usually involves an older person).
● A heterosexual crush is also usually on an older person – pop stars or footballers.
● Some heterosexual interest is shown in the same age group. Adolescents go out together in groups and then they gradually pair off. There are often frequent changes of partner. When a relationship finishes there is loss of face, despair, unhappiness and sometimes even a suicide attempt. These relationships are all-important and social life revolves around them, so when one comes to an end the loving support of the family is needed. These wounds soon mend with the arrival of the next boyfriend or girlfriend but support is needed in the meantime.

Diet
Plenty of protein, meat, cheese, eggs and fish, fresh fruit and vegetables. If they are really hungry between meals, instead of giving carbohydrates choose snacks of fruit or nuts. If possible, avoid snacks altogether and give substantial well-balanced meals, two or three glasses of milk a day and plenty of other fluids. Girls may worry about their weight and even develop anorexia nervosa (see page 389f.).

Sleep and exercise
During this period of rapid growth adolescents need seven hours' sleep per night. Fresh air and exercise are also very important.

Mental development
Adolescents like to be with others of their age group, wear the same clothes, same hairstyles and use the same expressions. Many feel they are unattractive or inadequate – so give them reassurance.

There may be a lot of criticism of you, the way you live, the world in general, and strong verbal support for various causes but perhaps little active support. Vandalism may be due to boredom.

Try and instil the need for independence, self-reliance and a strong sense of their own value. Recognize and encourage their need for independence and privacy but let them know you will be there if they need you. Realize that growing up cannot happen overnight and that they should be able to take for granted security and stability at home.

Let them form relationships – 'best friends' and boyfriends and girl-friends – without feeling unloved and jealous of them yourself; there are bound to be painful and difficult times and perhaps a longing for the days when you were 'just a family'. There are also times when you feel that they are reliable and grown-up – and the next moment they are behaving like children.

It is encouraging to realize that most parent–adolescent conflicts are over minor problems (like not coming in at the right time, choice of clothes or hairstyle or not helping at home). These are not devastating problems. With a bit of give and take they can be solved, but mood swings are difficult to live with.

Regular pocket money and freedom to spend it as preferred encourages independence.

Relationships between father and daughter will influence her attitude to men. The happiest relationships occur when he takes an interest in her hobbies and activities and they become great friends. This helps her gain a friendly and confident attitude towards the opposite sex.

Parents should try not to criticize their children's clothes, hairstyles or opinions or make them feel foolish. Constructive criticism given with gentleness and tact may have the desired effect, but problems sometimes occur when the adolescent has had a better education than his parents and the parents feel they cannot compete.

Physical symptoms, such as giddiness, hunger or loss of appetite, indigestion, headaches, may be caused by stress, and a doctor should be consulted.

The best parental influence is by example. Adolescents need loving, caring parents they can trust. Eventually they will form a new and more adult relationship with you.

Note ● Many students and schoolchildren ring or visit the Samaritans (see page 593) for support. As with adults, this is completely confidential. Some ring about their own distress; others call about that of a friend or parent.

Useful Information and Common Problems

Note ● There are no main cross-references in this section. Some points shared with adults – e.g. asthma – are covered in Chapter 6. If you cannot find what you are looking for here, refer to the main index at the end of the book.

ACNE Most common between the ages of 15 and 25. It is thought to be caused by an imbalance of hormones which causes an increase in the secretion from the sebaceous glands which become blocked; a blackhead prevents the free flow of sebum out through the hair follicle. This becomes inflamed and produces a pus-filled pimple. The condition may temporarily become worse during menstruation or under stress (e.g. examinations or changing jobs).

What to do ● Wash the area thoroughly with clean hands (not a flannel) using medicated soap several times a day. Rinse well and dry with a soft towel.
● Do not touch the skin or squeeze the pimples or you may be left with permanent scars.
● Wash your hair frequently as it tends to be greasy in people who have acne, and dandruff will make the condition worse.
● Take plenty of outdoor exercise, get adequate rest and have a well-balanced diet with not too much fat and very little chocolate, nuts and

sweets. Sunshine will help the healing process but be careful not to overexpose the skin to the sun as it is more sensitive than usual.

● Consult your doctor if acne is severe: there are tablets and a variety of lotions which will help.

BABY-SITTERS AND NANNIES

Baby-sitters

If you are leaving your child with a sitter:

● Make sure she knows where to contact you if there is a problem – write down the telephone number.

● Tell your child that you are going out and that you will be back. Tell him who is sitting and make sure it is someone he knows. If he does not know her then ask her to come a little earlier and give them time to get to know each other.

● Leave a list of emergency numbers – including your doctor's number.

● Make sure that you know how much to pay the baby-sitter. If she has not got her own transport and it is late at night make sure she gets home safely.

● Make sure she knows what to do if the child wakes up (e.g. a drink might settle him or a favourite cuddly toy).

● Leave her something to eat and show her where the kitchen, coffee, tea, etc., are and how to operate the various pieces of electrical equipment.

● Give her an idea of what time you will be back.

Nannies

To find a nanny, look in a local or national newspaper or a magazine like *Nursery World* and *The Lady*. Some of the most highly qualified, though expensive, nannies are those with Norland or Princess Christian training:

>Norland Nursery Training College
>Denford Park
>Hungerford
>Berks RG I 7 OPQ
>   0488–82252

>Princess Christian College
>26 Wilbraham Road
>Fallowfield
>Manchester M I 4 6JX
>   061–224 4560

● Nannies and baby-sitters can also be found through such agencies as:

Au Pair Bureau (Piccadilly)
87 Regent Street
London W I R 7HS
    01–930 4757

British Employment Agency
Sussex House
22 London Road
Horsham
Sussex RH I 2HA
    0403–65571

Childminders
67a Marylebone High Street
London W I M 3 A H
  01–935 2049/9763

Nanny Service
Oldbury Place
London W I M 3 A H
  01–935 3515

Consultus
17 London Road
Tonbridge
Kent TN I O 3 A B
  0732–355231

Occasional and Permanent Nannies
15 Beauchamp Place
London S W 3 I N Q
  01–584 0232

Country Cousins
98 Billinghurst Road
Broadbride Heath
Horsham
West Sussex R H I 2 3 L F
  0403–65188

Universal Aunts
250 King's Road
London S W 3 5 U E
  01–351 5767

West End Nannies
68 Great Portland Street
London W I N I A J
  01–580 3113

BED-WETTING
(Enuresis)

This is normal in babies. Most children are dry by two and a half years and bed-wetting is a nuisance at five years. Some children wet themselves during the day as well.

Treatment is not usually offered under the age of four and a half. During this time it may help to withhold drinks before the child goes to bed and to lift your child on to the toilet before you go to bed.

The *buzzer* treatment can be used from five years on. You will be shown how to set up the equipment, which consists of several layers:

● a waterproof sheet
● a metal mesh
● a separate sheet
● another metal mesh
● top sheet.

Your child sleeps on a sheet which separates him from the detector or metal mesh, which is connected to an alarm buzzer. The wet urine completes the circuit and the alarm sounds. This wakes the child, who gets up and goes to the toilet. The amount of urine he passes become less and less until he either wakes up before he passes urine or he sleeps through the night without passing urine. Your GP will refer your child for treatment when he thinks it is necessary.

See 'Bed-wetting', Health Education Council.

BOW LEGS

A lot of babies look as though they have bow legs. This is partly due to longer muscles on the outer side of the leg than on the inner side, so although they look bowed the bones are actually straight.

The legs usually look straight by three years, but if you are worried that they might be abnormal then talk to your doctor or health visitor about it.

CHILD
BENEFIT

This is paid for all children under sixteen – or under nineteen and still studying full-time at school or college. For more information see leaflet CH 1 from the local social security office.

If you are bringing up a child on your own you may be able to get increased benefit: see leaflet CH 11. Claim forms are available from your local social security office and payment is made by an order book which you cash at the post office.

CHILD-
MINDERS

A child-minder is someone who looks after children under the age of five in her own home. She is paid for doing this.

The social services department will help you find a registered child-minder (this means that she has been visited by the department and is approved by them). She usually looks after three or four children, including any of her own under five. The cost varies – so ask the social services department. Discuss the hours with the minder and then keep to the times, and let her know if they change or if you are going to be late.

Settling your child with the child-minder

- Visit her together so he is familiar with the surroundings.
- Make his first stay with her a short one and increase to the required time as he gets used to it.
- Give him a favourite toy to take with him.
- If he is in nappies, provide a good supply and all the changing equipment.
- Provide a change of clothes and outdoor clothes so that they can go for a walk.
- For a young baby, the minder may ask you to bring his food.
- Make sure she has your work address, phone number and your family doctor's name, address and phone number.
- Tell her what illnesses and immunizations he has had.
- Do not take him if he is ill – phone her and let her know what is happening.
- He may well cry when you leave him and behave badly when you collect him. This is quite normal – he has probably been quite happy all day. The child-minder will tell you if she thinks he is unhappy or not settling. Do not spend ages talking to her when you collect him as she is busy with her own family and the other children.
- Give him time to get used to being parted from you.
- It is not a good idea to change from one child-minder to another unless you really have to: continuity is the best care.

If you want to become a child-minder

- If you receive payment for looking after one or more children who are not related to you for two hours or more per day you should, by law, register with your local social services department.
- Someone from the department will probably come to your home and ask you to fill in some forms.
- You must have a safe, warm place for the children to play.
- Your kitchen and toilet facilities must be adequate.

● The department will want to make sure that you are prepared to give all your time and care to the children, that you will look after them well and take them out for walks. They need to be sure that you really like children.

● They may ask you about your own health, whether you have had a recent chest X-ray. If you have not, they may ask you to have one.

● You will be asked to sign a statement about previous child care.

When you become a registered child-minder

● The social services department will put your name on the vacancy list and you can advertise your services.

● They will visit you from time to time.

● You may get the chance to go on a course.

● They may lend you some toy kits, first aid kits and safety equipment.

● You should charge a minimum £12 a week for full-time care – you can charge more if necessary (e.g. if more meals are provided).

● Full time may mean 8 a.m. to 6 p.m. or even longer depending on the parents' working hours.

● Check with the parents:

(a) where they can be contacted

(b) when holidays are going to be taken

(c) the number of hours required and when they will collect their child (the National Child-minding Association has a useful contract form for this)

(d) that they know you cannot look after the child when he is ill

(e) whether or not you are expected to take the child to the clinics or a playgroup

(f) what immunizations and illnesses the child has had

(g) the doctor's address and phone number (record these in a book – the NCMA has another suitable form for all this information).

● As a registered child-minder you may be entitled to $\frac{1}{3}$ pint free milk for each child each day.

● In some areas there are group meetings where you can meet other child-minders.

● For more information contact:

> National Child-minding Association
> 236a High Street
> Bromley
> Kent BR1 IDE
> 01–464 6164

CHILDREN'S BOOKS

What should you read to your child, and at what stage of his development?

See

Jim Trelease, *The Read-Aloud Handbook*, Penguin

Peter Braithwaite and Bing Taylor (eds.), *The Good Book Guide to Children's Books*, Penguin

CIRCUM-
CISION

In Jewish Law, at the age of eight days, male infants are taken to be circumcised in a religious ceremony (Berit Milah) presided over by a Mohel, an official experienced in performing the rite. The child is held by his godfather during the operation.

Circumcision is the cutting off of the sleeve of skin which covers the head of the penis, the foreskin. It is rarely performed on babies for medical reasons – usually for religious or social reasons.

If your baby is not circumcised, leave the foreskin well alone. Pulling it back may cause small splits which, when they heal, leave scar tissue which may fix the foreskin to the penis and later on this will make it impossible for natural retraction.

COLDS AND
COUGHS

See Chapter 6.

COLIC

Sometimes called three-month colic or evening colic.

Colic usually starts in the first three weeks of life and stops at about three months. It usually occurs during the evening at about the same time every day.

The baby cannot settle after his late afternoon or early evening feed and either screams as soon as he has finished feeding or wakes up about an hour later. He cries, is miserable and draws his knees up to his stomach.

Nothing helps very much. He may stop crying for a short while when you wind him, pick him up or lay him on his stomach. If you offer him a feed he takes it, then suddenly pulls away and starts crying again. This may last for anything up to three hours and then it stops as suddenly as it started.

● If you think your baby is suffering from colic or appears to be in pain, inform your doctor. He may prescribe something to help relieve the colic.

CON-
VULSIONS
AND FITS

See Chapter 6.

COT DEATHS
(OR SUDDEN
INFANT
DEATH
SYNDROME)

This refers to the unexpected death of a baby in his cot. He may die quietly during the night even though he seemed perfectly well only a few hours before.

It was thought that a chest infection might be the cause and, indeed, a sudden, very acute viral infection of the respiratory tract *may* be the cause. But there is still a great deal of research going on.

> British Guild for Sudden Infant Death Study
> Pathology Department
> Royal Infirmary
> Cardiff CF2 1SZ
> 0222–492233

● Bereaved parents can contact others who have undergone the same loss themselves:

Compassionate Friends
5 Lower Clifton Hill
Bristol BS 8 1BT
    0272–292 778

4 Duntocker Road
Bearsden
Glasgow G6 1 4NP
    041–942 2327

CRADLE CAP   Cradle cap or scurf is very common in babies – it is unsightly but not harmful. It is the accumulation of a greasy product of the skin on the scalp.

What to do   ● Wash the head regularly with soap or shampoo, including the 'soft spot' which is covered by a very tough membrane and will not be harmed by being washed and cleaned.
● There are products which can be bought at the chemist which will remove cradle cap. Follow the instructions carefully.
● If it persists or spreads to the eyebrows see your doctor or go to the clinic.

CRISIS   If everything gets too much for you and you cannot cope talk to your doctor or health visitor. If you need support you can telephone:
● National Children's Centre, 0484–41733 (for details of your nearest 'parents' help-line')
● National Children's Homes, 01–226 2033 (for details of your nearest Family Network Centre)
● You can also contact the Organization for Parents Under Stress (OPUS), which has phone-in groups in England and Scotland. To find your nearest group, contact:

OPUS Information Officer
26 Manor Drive
Pickering
North Yorks YO18 8DD
    0751–73235

CRYING   Crying in a very young baby is usually a sign of hunger or thirst. If food or drink is rejected then he may be in pain or discomfort or just need to be held in your arms for a while. Picking him up and giving him a cuddle almost always stops his crying. Rocking movements in your arms or in his pram might also help.
    Crying in some older babies can be because they are wet or dirty or their bottoms may already be sore. Tiredness can also make a baby fretful and some regularly cry before going to sleep. Wrapping your baby in a soft blanket gives him a sense of security and he may go to sleep. Cuddling, walking up and down with baby in your arms or the gentle movement of the pram moving often stops him crying.

Older babies may also cry because they are bored or lonely. Put him somewhere he can see you working. He may cry because of a particular noise he dislikes (e.g. the vacuum cleaner) or he may cry at new experiences (e.g. being sat on a tricycle or a swing). He will more than likely cry when you stop him touching the electric plug socket or going too near the fire (i.e. a cry of frustration). All these are quite normal.

● If you feel you need help, there is a support group for mothers with crying babies:

> Cry-Sis
> 63 Putney Road
> Freezywater
> Enfield
> Middlesex EN3 6NN
> 0992–716645
>
> 21 Falkland Gardens
> Edinburgh EH12 6UW
> 031–334 5317

DAY NURSERIES

These are provided for mothers who have to go out to work. They should take no more than 40 to 50 children, divided into small groups and looked after by trained staff. There should be plenty of toys, with painting, modelling, climbing, pushing and pulling toys and other things to do. They provide all the care your child needs during the day.

There is usually a waiting list and priority is given to single-parent families and mothers in essential services like nursing and teaching.

There are also private day nurseries which must be registered with the local authority.

Your local library will have a list of day nurseries, playgroups and nursery schools – or contact your local education authority.

DISABLED CHILDREN

● The Church of England Children's Society's work includes support to families who are caring for their own handicapped children through counselling, holiday care, day care, playgroups and parents' groups. They give children who need long-term residential care the personal family-type care:

> Church of England Children's Society
> Old Town Hall
> Kennington Road
> London SE11 4QD
> 01–735 2441

● Similarly, the Church of Scotland operates a home in Stonehaven for mentally and physically handicapped children up to mid teens:

Church of Scotland Board on Social Responsibility
121 George Street
Edinburgh EH2 4YN
031–225 5732

● *In Touch* is a magazine for parents of mentally handicapped children. It provides an excellent forum for contacting parents of children with more uncommon conditions and syndromes:

In Touch
10 Norman Road
Sale
Cheshire
061–962 4441

● Some useful addresses of support groups:

Association of Parents of Vaccine
 Damaged Children
2 Church Street
Shipston-on-Stour
Warwicks CU36 4AP
 0608–61595

Down's Children's Association
4 Oxford Street
London WIN 9FL
 01–580 0511

Scottish Down's Syndrome
 Association
5 Marine St
Glasgow G51 1JL
 041–427 6681

Scottish Society for Autistic
 Children
Room 2
12 Picardy Place
Edinburgh EH1 3JT
 031–557 0474

Note
● Names and addresses of other organizations are listed under 'Disabilities' in Chapter 20.

EATING
PROBLEMS

Overweight children or teenagers should:
● eat three or four meals a day
● always eat breakfast (cereal and milk or toast and milk drink or a cooked breakfast)
● include two or three moderate helpings of meat, fish or eggs or cheese per day. Baked beans or similar pulses may sometimes be used as an alternative to eggs or meat
● eat plenty of leafy vegetables and salads (limit peas, parsnips, sweetcorn and potatoes to one moderate helping per day)
● eat up to three slices of wholemeal bread a day
● drink up to a pint of milk a day
● eat moderate amounts of apples, pears, bananas, oranges, strawberries when in season
● eat boiled or grilled rather than fried food, with minimum amount of butter or margarine and cooking oil
 They should not:
● miss meals – it will only lead to snacks

- eat fried food and dishes containing extra fat (e.g. pastry, cakes, chips and crisps)
- eat foods with added sugar (e.g. cakes, biscuits, some cereals, ordinary fruit squashes)
- eat snacks (e.g. biscuits, chocolate, ice-cream, fizzy drinks).

Notes
- Small amounts of the 'do not' foods may be taken as an occasional treat (e.g. a weekly packet of crisps, ice-cream or a *small* portion of chips).
- Exercise helps reduce weight.
- For refusal to eat (anorexia nervosa) – see page 389f.

ECZEMA

Infantile eczema is an allergic skin condition. In mild cases, only the inside surfaces of the elbow and knee joints are affected. In severe cases the rash may cover most of the body including the scalp, cheeks and forehead.

There is usually a family history of eczema, asthma or hayfever. Allergy to eggs, fish, cows' milk, some pollens or household dust can sometimes be found – your doctor will investigate possible causes.

There are various creams that can be used which contain hydrocortisone. The irritation can be helped by adding *Ung. emulsificans* to the child's bath: it is soothing and there is no need for soap (you can buy it at the chemist). Dab the skin dry with a soft towel.
- For further information contact:

> National Eczema Society
> Tavistock House North
> Tavistock Square
> London WC1H 9SR
> 01–388 4097

FACTS OF LIFE

'Where do I come from?' How do you answer that question? Some parents feel it will all be taught at school where the mechanical facts will be learnt from charts, films, slides and the teacher. But there is more to sex education than pure facts: there are feelings and attitudes towards the opposite sex and these are learnt by imitation and experience.

Whatever the parents' attitudes are they should remain consistent (e.g. if you have always dressed and undressed in your own room with the door closed it will only cause embarrassment and bewilderment if you suddenly appear naked around the house).

Every child is different and will ask questions at different ages. The following guidelines may help:
- **0 to 18 months:** explores his own body.
- **18 months to 4 years.** If you are pregnant with another child this often stimulates questions. He needs simple answers and not an in-depth sex lecture.
- **4 to 8 years.** Some sex education is probably taught at school – there may be parents' evenings to discuss what is being taught. Strange versions which your child may have heard from other children should be talked

about and gently corrected. When talking about the body it is better to use the correct words which are understood by everybody.

● **9 to 12 years.** Girls are quite likely to have started their periods by this stage and it is very important that they know what to expect. Boys, too, should understand menstruation if they are to be understanding brothers, boyfriends and – one day – husbands. Boys should also understand that wet dreams are normal (your child may be worried, thinking that he passed urine during the night).

Boys and girls need a loving and affectionate home environment where they can ask and have their questions answered freely.

● **12 to 17 years.** Greater freedom, earlier maturity and the legal age of majority being eighteen mean that parents have to decide how they feel about contraception and sex before marriage. A doctor can legally prescribe, without your permission, the contraceptive pill for a girl of sixteen. A young person needs sensible, accurate advice and there are plenty of books and leaflets about sex and contraception written for young people.

Parents may like to read Roger Pilkington's 'Facts of Life for Parents' (30p and s.a.e.) from

> Family Doctor Publications
> BMA House
> Tavistock Square
> London WC1H 9JP
> 01–387 9721

See   Ann Burkitt, 'Learning to Live with Sex' (25p) from:

> Family Planning Association
> 29 Mortimer Street
> London W1A 4QW
> 01–636 7866

FINGER AND THUMB SUCKING

This is harmless as long as it stops by age six. If it goes on after this age it may cause deformity of the teeth. Suggest to the child that it is a babyish habit and try and stop it gently without any fuss.

GIFTED CHILDREN
by Dr Joan Freeman, former director of the Gulbenkian Research Project on Gifted Children

Giftedness is, like beauty, partly in the eye of the beholder. Where one child will be seen as gifted, another with exactly the same abilities will not. Boys, for example, are more likely to be identified as gifted than equally endowed girls. It all depends on parents' and teachers' outlooks – and comparisons with other children around.

Children do not have to have a high intelligence score (IQ) to be gifted, but it certainly helps as that is how most are identified for special education and research. Average IQ is 100 and anything above 130 (about 3 per cent of the population) is usually taken to indicate very high intellectual ability.

Children may be gifted across the board or in specific ways. Some kinds of high-level gifts (e.g. sports and music) may be much admired by schoolteachers whereas those gifted in, say, mathematics or languages, may find themselves isolated as 'swots'.

Gifted children are no different in physical appearance, personalities or sleep patterns but they do seem to have exceptional memories, concentration, curiosity, sensitivity and often early development milestones like walking and talking.

My research has shown that keeping children in education along with others of different levels of ability does not have a bad emotional effect on the gifted as long as teachers are aware and flexible. Inadequate teaching can bore and disillusion any child and, as intellectually gifted children often have a voracious appetite for ideas and information, they do need access to plenty of mental sustenance to build up and fulfil their true potential. Parents may have to fill in with family activities or perhaps by forming a group with parents of other gifted children.

Perhaps the single most helpful thing which parents can do for their highly able children is to develop a close, loving relationship with them. The next important items are both material provision for learning and the examples parents set in their own lifestyles. In these ways, parents are the best placed to give children the confidence and mental freedom to search and experiment with learning, discover their own interests and enjoy a lifetime of creative endeavour.

For information and support contact (s.a.e.):

> National Association of Gifted Children
> 1 South Audley Street
> London WIY 5DQ
> 01–499 1188

HEAD LICE (NITS)

The head louse lives on the scalp, particularly at the back along the nape of the neck and at the sides behind the ears. The louse can be seen and the eggs (the nits) are small, white and regular in shape, firmly attached to the hair.

The child complains of itching and is constantly scratching his head, which may bleed and become infected. It is a very common condition among schoolchildren and it is no disgrace to be infested providing you get treatment. The head louse will live in clean or dirty hair. Your child should not, however, go to school until he has been treated.

What to do Wash the hair in a special shampoo which you can buy from the chemist. Apply the solution as per instructions and remove the nits with a fine-tooth comb.

● If you think you may have bed-bugs (which are on the increase) contact your health visitor. These pests are a problem and you need professional help.

See ● 'What to Do about Head Lice', Health Education Council.

HOLIDAYS

Details of special events are given on national and local television and radio and in newspapers and magazines. Information on special events for children can be obtained by telephoning: 01–246 8007.

If you want ideas for what older children can do, telephone: Kidsline, 01–222–8070 (weekdays, 9 a.m. to 4 p.m. during holidays, 4 to 6 p.m. during term).

HOMOSEXUAL
BEHAVIOUR

Some boys and girls pass through a homosexual phase in their adolescent development. The majority pass from homosexual experimentation to heterosexual feelings. Some of them become very anxious during this stage that they are homosexual and that they will stay that way for ever. They may not want to talk about it. It is important that they understand that this may be only a phase of adolescence. Some, of course, will be homosexual and go on to form adult relationships.

HOSPITALS

There are plenty of books specially written for children about going into hospital. As you read a book to your child you too will be able to find out what goes on in a children's ward. The hospital will probably give you an admission booklet which tells you what to bring in for your child, what happens in hospital, visiting, suitable toys, etc.

Prior to admission the child has probably been an out-patient and so the staff may have shown you both around the ward so that he has an idea of what it is like. The staff on children's wards are specially skilled in the care of children. They will make you feel welcome and generally you will be allowed to visit and stay as long as you like. The staff are pleased to have you there to wash, feed and amuse your own child – and probably others too.

Some hospitals have units where mother and child can stay. The mother takes a large share of the care of her child. Priority is given to mothers of:
- 6 months to 4-year-old age group
- mentally subnormal children of all ages
- breast-fed babies
- physically handicapped children
- very sick children
- those a long way from home.

To help your child settle into the ward

- His favourite toy or teddy labelled with his name should go with him.
- If he uses a dummy – even if you think he is a little old for it – then make sure it goes with him.
- Tell the nursing staff if he uses special names for going to the toilet, so that they know what he is talking about.
- Tell them if he has any strong likes or dislikes or allergies to food, feeding regimes for babies or how far you have got introducing him to solids.
- Make sure they know if there is anything he is particularly frightened of or if he has nightmares or sleepwalks.
- While he is in hospital visit him frequently and send lots of letters, cards and postcards. Encourage other friends and relations to do the same.
- Tell the staff whether he sleeps in a cot or bed at home.
- If he has a nickname make sure the staff know what it is.

● When you leave him make sure he knows you are coming back and when that will be.

Schooling will be continued while he is in hospital for short periods each day.

Play is very important and if he is occupied he will be happier. Some hospitals have play supervisors who organize the children's play. This usually takes place in a playroom which is separate from the rest of the ward so that it does not disturb children confined to bed.

● If you want a private hospital specially for children and women, contact:

> Portland Hospital for Women and Children
> 209 Great Portland Street
> London WIN 6AH
> 01–580 4400

● Counselling and information can be provided by:

> National Association for the Welfare
>   of Children in Hospital
> Exton House
> 7 Exton Street
> London SE1 8VE
> 01–261 1738

> National Association for the Welfare
>   of Children in Hospital (Scotland)
> 15 Smith's Place
> Edinburgh EH6 8HP
> 031–553 6553

● Help and support is also available from:

> Invalid Children's Aid Association
> 126 Buckingham Palace Road
> London SW1W 9SB
> 01–730 9891

LOVE AND SECURITY

Love means giving your child lots of time, attention and friendship. He will need sympathy, understanding and plenty of patience. You need to give him guidelines so he knows how to behave, and when he goes wrong he needs firm but loving discipline to get him back on the right track.

Never make fun of him or be unkind in your criticism. If he has failed in some aspect of his life try not to compare him with his friends – or his brothers and sisters – and certainly do not discuss his failures in front of him with your friends or relations.

Every child needs to be told that you love him. Even when he is at his most revolting he needs to know that you still love him despite his dreadful behaviour.

A strong, loving relationship with your child built up over the early years is less likely to come apart during adolescence. Children are more likely to grow apart from their parents when there has been an unhappy atmosphere in the home with favouritism, arguing, constant criticism and scoldings.

Remember you will never spoil a child with love.

MASTURBA-
TION

In *childhood* this often takes the form of rocking, flushing of the face and a look of great concentration, then the child goes limp and dazed. Any interruption of the pleasure is resented. No harm will come from this activity. If it embarrasses you, keep the child busy and this will reduce the incidence.

In *adolescence* most boys and some girls masturbate. Some may feel guilty and anxious about it but there is no reason why they should – it offers a sexual outlet when 'real' sex is unavailable. There is no indication that it increases the difficulty of later adjustment to normal sexual relationships.

MENSTRUAL
PROBLEMS

Irregular periods: girls usually settle down to a regular cycle every 28 days after 2 to 3 years from the start of menstruation. Irregularity may occur during stress of any kind or during rigorous dieting or a series of crash diets. It may also be due to illness or any kind of infection.

If periods used to be regular but become irregular, see the doctor. If they are irregular and always have been so, then it is probably not significant but it would be a good idea to see the doctor to confirm this.

Feeling unwell during periods: for minor stomach-ache, cramps or head-aches try taking a soluble aspirin. You may find that going to bed with a hot water bottle or going for a walk helps. If your period makes you feel ill and miserable see your doctor.

Putting on weight just before or during periods: breasts, thighs or stomach may feel slightly swollen due to fluid retention. Normally the excess weight goes as soon as the period is over.

NAPPY RASH

Almost all babies develop nappy rash at one time or another. It need not mean that you have been neglectful. The skin is sensitive and needs extra care. The rash may be due to ammonia produced by the bacterial fermentation of urine. Nappies are changed frequently during the day but at night there may be enough ammonia to burn the skin and a change may be needed during the night.

The rash is a collection of small red pimples and patches of rough red skin. Some of the pimples may become slightly infected and if the rash is severe raw spots may appear.

What to do

Make sure the area is kept clean and dry and apply some cream (which you can buy from the chemist). If it does not clear up quickly it is best to get expert advice from your doctor or clinic.

ONE-PARENT
FAMILIES

You are head of a one-parent family if you are looking after a child or children and you are a single mother or separated, divorced or widowed.

If you do not have a partner with whom to share the problems of parenthood, your child needs special support and love. You are not the only mother bringing up children alone. There are many others – and fathers too. Gingerbread offers an opportunity for you to get together with other lone parents in a local group so that you can give each other help and support. It also offers advice on welfare rights and holidays for one-parent families. Some groups also provide after school and holiday day care centres and hostels and housing co-operatives.

The national headquarters is at:

Gingerbread
35 Wellington Street
London WC2E 7BN
01–240 0953

They can also be contacted at:

Belfast   0232–231417
Cardiff   0222–384877
Edinburgh   031–553 3970
Glasgow   041–248 6840

● Other organizations to which you might like to turn are:

One-Parent Families
255 Kentish Town Road
London NW5 2LX
01–267 1361

Scottish Council for Single Parents
13 Gayfield Square
Edinburgh EH1 3NX
031–556 3899

Notes ● If you have any housing problems you can talk to your housing aid centre, Citizens' Advice Bureau or a solicitor. See also the most helpful: 'One-Parent Families: Help with Housing' published by the Department of the Environment.
● You should find out all your tax allowances. See leaflet IR29 'Income Tax and One-Parent Families', from your tax office or CAB.

POSTNATAL
DEPRESSION
– BABY
BLUES

The *baby blues* is a period of mild depression which can occur about three or four days after your baby is born. Almost half of all mothers go through this and it lasts only a day or two.

Postnatal depression usually starts after you have left hospital. You may feel deep despondency, tearfulness, tension, a feeling that you cannot cope with the baby, fears for your own health and the baby's health. You may feel irritable or exhausted or experience pain, poor appetite, difficulty in sleeping and loss of interest in sex.

If this is how you feel and it has been going on for a couple of weeks or more, you should consult your doctor. He will help you and you will find that the bad days gradually get fewer and eventually disappear.

● You may find talking to someone who has had postnatal depression helps a great deal. Contact:

Association for Post-Natal Illness
7 Gowan Avenue
London sw6 6rh
01–731 4108

POTTY TRAINING

Bladder and bowel control occur any time from eighteen months, but if you leave it until the child is two years old you may find the whole process easier. There are bound to be occasional accidents so try to keep calm and not get too upset. Be patient, loving and show consistent understanding.

What to do

● You need a strong comfortable potty with a rigid base to stop it tipping sideways (you need one with a splash guard for a boy). When you buy the potty get your child to help you choose it.
● Keep it in the same place at home so he knows exactly where it is – preferably on a washable floor and in a comfortable warm room so that he does not associate using the potty with feeling cold.
● Put him on the potty for a few minutes after meals and once every 3 to 4 hours. You will soon be able to estimate how often he needs the potty.
● Trainer pants have towelling linings and a plastic outside with elasticated legs. These are quite easy to pull up and down. He will be able to manage them himself – teach him to pull them right down to his ankles. The alternative is to use towelling pants with a pair of plastic pants on top.
● When you succeed in potty training during the day, then replace his nappy at night with the trainer pants. As long as you leave him in nappies at night he will assume that they are there to be used.
● If possible start training in the warm weather so that he can run around with less clothing on – and you will not worry so much about accidents that occur in the garden.
● When he has used the potty get him used to:
  (a) being cleaned and eventually cleaning himself with soft toilet tissue
  (b) washing his hands well.
● Always say 'well done!'

Problems

● Refusal: if you put him on his potty and he screams and yells or just sits there politely and does nothing then proceeds to do it as soon as he is off the potty, forget it for now and try again in a few weeks' time with plenty of patience and tact.
● Do not make an issue of his not using his potty. Do not leave him sitting there for more than ten minutes.
● If a baby is potted regularly from birth after every meal, the touch of the potty against his skin will very likely cause the bowels to open. This is without any conscious effort on the baby's part. When he reaches the age of two years his mother may be very upset to find that she has to start all

over again retraining her toddler, who only now begins to have conscious control over his bladder and bowels.

● Make sure that everyone in contact with your child has the same views on potty training and that there is no difference of opinion. *You* are potty training the child.

Notes ● Your child is potty trained when he tells you every time he wants to go to the toilet and in enough time to avoid accidents, and he can also tell you correctly when he does not want to go.

● If you let a boy go to the toilet with his father – or a girl with you – he will understand how to use the toilet seat. To make it easier for the child, buy a trainer seat which is a small seat that fits on to the toilet seat. The child will probably need a rigid step to reach it.

SCHOOL PROBLEMS

Bullying and teasing

If your child is a bully it is likely that he is being bullied by other children, his brother or sister, parents or a teacher. You must look out for the cause. The bully should be punished but corporal punishment usually does more harm than good.

If your child is being bullied he may be unable to stand up for himself, be timid and easily resort to tears. He may be very tall or very small – in other words a little bit different from the others. Encourage him to stand up for himself. Arrange for him to have classes in judo, wrestling, boxing or karate – this will build up his self-confidence and enable him to deal with a bully.

Children will tease any child that they consider different – e.g. those with different accents, those who are fat, clumsy, tell tales, show off, know everything and the child who is not very bright, who is deaf or wears glasses. Children can be very unkind to each other. The only thing a parent can do is not to be over-protective at home. Help the child to stand up for himself.

Does not like school

Tears when he starts school are neither unusual nor abnormal and a positive attitude from parents before he starts will help.

In the mornings he may complain of headaches or stomach-aches. You have to decide whether these are genuine or not – a guide is how he looks and what his temperature is. If he has a severe headache he is unlikely to look well: if he has a raised temperature he probably *is* unwell.

If this problem becomes worse you may need the help of a child psychiatrist and your doctor, working with the schoolteachers.

The longer he stays away from school the more difficult it becomes to get him back.

Changing from one school to another rarely works.

Laziness
Possible causes
- he may not get on with his teacher
- he may find the subject(s) boring
- he may find work too easy
- he may be influenced not to work by friends
- he may be a slow thinker and unable to think at all when the teacher tries to hurry him
- he may be so keen on sport that he neglects his work
- he may have unknown defects such as poor vision or poor hearing
- he may be over-active and unable to concentrate

The school and parents must find the cause and put it right.

Reading difficulties
These may be due to prolonged absences from school, a reduced intelligence level, defective eyesight or hearing. These problems need to be recognized and remedial teaching may help.

> National Association for Remedial Education
> 2 Lichfield Road
> Stafford ST I 7 4JX
> 0785-46872

Dyslexia (word blindness) commonly follows lateness in learning to speak. Many children affected are clumsy, have difficulty telling right from left, are often ambidextrous or left-handed. They tend to write slowly and hesitantly and leave too small or too large a space between letters and to write at an angle. They reverse letters (e.g. 'p' for 'b') and confuse letters of similar shapes. They may also read from right to left (e.g. 'was' becomes 'saw').

The treatment is good remedial teaching and some may lose their disability altogether as they get older. For help with dyslexia contact:

> British Dyslexia Association
> Church Lane
> Peppard
> Henley-on-Thames
> Oxon RG9 5JN
> 0491-7699

> Scottish Dyslexia Association
> Centre for Continuing Education
> Dundee University
> Perth Road
> Dundee DD I 4HN
> 0382-23181

SHOES   It is very important that the shoes you buy for your child really do fit properly and that they are comfortable.

When buying shoes ask the fitter to assess the size of shoes required but remember that the different makes of shoes will vary in size so he may take a size 9 in one make and need a size $9\frac{1}{2}$ in another. Too wide a fitting is almost as bad as too narrow: if the foot is too loose in the shoe the toes may become bruised or the heel blistered from rubbing. Too small or too narrow a pair of shoes may mean that the toes can be cramped, causing blistering and corns. Lace-up shoes give the best instep fit.

Check your child's feet every three months. Good shoe shops will do this for you without your having to buy a pair of shoes. To check at home sprinkle some talcum power into his shoes, put them back on and get him to walk about for a few minutes. Then remove the shoe and look at the print of the foot in the powder. If the toes are too near the end of the shoe, then the fitting should be checked.

Ideally a child should not wear the same pair of shoes every day, but shoes are expensive and this is not always possible. Leave shoes to air overnight so that moisture can evaporate. Do not leave the socks in overnight.

If you cannot buy real leather shoes, do not go for plastic. Buy canvas 'plimsoll type', which allow the feet to breathe.

● The Children's Foot Health Register is a guide to shops which have undertaken to stock children's shoes or sandals in four widths of fittings and in whole and half sizes. Trained staff in these shops measure both feet and fit the shoes carefully at the time of sale. A list of shops is available (s.a.e.) from:

Children's Foot Health Register
84–8 Great Eastern Street
London EC2A 5ED
     (no telephone)

See

'Children's Shoes' from (s.a.e.):
Shoe and Allied Trades Research Association (SATRA)
SATRA House
Rockingham Road
Kettering
Northants NN16 9JH
     0536–516318

SLEEP PROBLEMS

Difficulty in getting to sleep. Try giving the child a warm bath, followed by wrapping in a familiar warm blanket with a soft toy beside him or, as he gets older, reading a suitable story or singing a nursery rhyme before turning out the light. Some children are frightened by the dark so leave on a small night-light. As the child gets older he can read to himself before going to sleep.

Early morning waker. If your two-year-old wakes very early, try getting him a low divan bed instead of a cot so that he can get out of bed and play with his toys on the floor and leave the rest of the household to sleep until a more civilized hour.

Waking during the night. Babies often open their eyes and move their limbs and heads and then go straight back to sleep, so resist getting up to see if he is all right as you may wake him. If he does wake up, give him a drink to comfort him.

As he gets older, if he wakes up during the night he may be getting too much sleep during the day. Leave some toys in his cot and his night-light on and if he wakes he will probably amuse himself, happily talking to himself and not crying. Some children do this quite normally.

If your child is half asleep he may cry or shout out and be obviously frightened by something. Reassure him and stay with him for a while until he is settled. Sometimes such night-time upsets can be prevented by censoring frightening stories or television before bed.

Nightmares are rare (they sometimes happen when children have high fevers). Your child looks wide awake but is not conscious of what he is doing or saying. He is probably sitting bolt upright in bed screaming at something in the corner of the room – something that you cannot see. He may be terrified, angry or crying. Even when you hug him or talk to him he may not recognize you. Put on the lights (this will help you cope with the situation). Talk to him in a quiet, soothing and reassuring voice. There is no need to wake him up, when the terror goes away he will just go back into normal sleep.

He may laugh, speak clearly or just utter incoherent babble in his sleep. There is no need to wake him up or tell him about it in the morning.

● If there are sleep problems that leave you exhausted and at the end of your tether, see your doctor.

SPEECH PROBLEMS
Your doctor will refer these to a speech therapist. For contact with parents of others with problems contact:

Association for All Speech Impaired Children
347 Central Markets
Smithfield
London EC1A 9NH
01–236 3632

National Association for Stammerers
86 Blackfriars Road
London SE1 8HA
(no telephone)

STEALING
A child must learn what is his and that he must not take things that do not belong to him. It helps if he has his own toys and books and somewhere to keep his own things. This means that when other members of the family want to borrow something they have to ask his permission first. He will learn best by example.

Stealing is not really a problem in the under fives but at school it may be that he is being influenced by friends or that he is just showing off.

He needs love and understanding and an investigation into the cause of his stealing.

STICKY
EYES

In babies, a yellow discharge in the inner corner of one or both eyes may be normal, or due to a blocked tear duct or infection.

What to do

● Wipe the eye carefully with cotton wool soaked in cooled boiled water, wiping away from the nose. Use each piece of cotton wool once only.
● Redness or swelling is a sign of infection. See your doctor.
● Eyes that water all the time may have blocked tear ducts, so see your doctor.

STRANGERS

Children are at risk from evil-minded, sick individuals who assault, rape and murder. This can happen at any time and any place. Being near home is just as dangerous as being in an area where nobody knows the child.

Children must learn to say no to strangers. They must *never* accept gifts, sweets, etc., get into a stranger's car or go anywhere with a stranger, even if he says 'Your mother asked me to collect you from school.'

It is a good idea to teach your child to trust people in uniform – police officers, park keepers, bus conductors, traffic wardens. If they are frightened or need help or are in trouble or lost they should feel that they can go to these people and that they will help them.

TEETHING
AND TEETH

A child who is teething dribbles, has his fingers constantly in his mouth and is generally irritable. Teething does *not* cause a rise in temperature, bronchitis or a rash – if your child is unwell see the doctor.

Dummies or comforters should be kept clean and never dipped in or filled with sugar, honey or anything syrupy. This can cause decay to the teeth as they come through. Teething rings should be kept clean.

Teeth should be cleaned carefully for him until he can manage to do it himself – at least twice a day using a soft brush and fluoride toothpaste.

Fluoride is an essential nutrient for development of normal teeth and a deficiency leads to poor dental health. If the natural fluoride in your

APPROXIMATE DATES OF YOUR BABY'S TEETHING PROCESS

TOOTH	APPEARANCE IN MONTHS
UPPER JAW	
Central incisors	6–8
Lateral incisors	8–11
Cuspids or canines	16–20
First molars	10–16
Second molars	20–30

APPROXIMATE DATES OF YOUR BABY'S TEETHING PROCESS

TOOTH	APPEARANCE IN MONTHS
LOWER JAW	
Central incisors	5–7
Lateral incisors	7–10
Cuspids or canines	16–20
First molars	10–16
Second molars	20–30

water supply is low, give children whose teeth are still growing fluoride tablets.

Visit the dentist every six months once your child is about three years old.

TELLING LIES

Up to the age of three a child will make up stories about people or creatures that he has met or things he says he has done. These are just 'pretend games' and not lies as such. Telling the truth develops slowly and the best method of teaching is by example: make sure you are honest and truthful.

The four-year-old, particularly, may boast or exaggerate the truth. Perhaps if you say that unless he tells the truth you will never know when to believe him he will realize that telling the truth is a good idea.

TRAVELLING WITH A BABY OR YOUNG CHILD

Plan ahead:

1. If you usually use terry nappies then buy some disposable nappies. These are all-in-one type with absorbent layers and a waterproof backing or the pad type which you insert into a pair of plastic pants.

2. You will need enough prepared feeds or food and drink for the journey.

3. Mothercare's suggested items to take with you on a journey include:

- carrycot or basket
- sheets, blankets, towels
- brush and comb and bottle brush
- store, pour and measure jugs
- sterilizing unit and sterilizing tablets
- changing-mat
- bibs and pack of 3 face-cloths
- feeding beaker, spoon and fork
- cereal bowl
- food heater and car bottle heater
- nursery apron
- changing-mat, top and tail bowl and moistened wipes
- teether, safety rattle and cuddly toy
- baby cream, cotton wool balls and swabs.

If there is room, the following might also be taken: pram, highchair, harness, travel cot, bath and stand and bouncing cradle.

During long car journeys take rest periods when everyone – including the driver – can relax. Older children love to play 'I-spy', to sing songs or to listen to you telling them a story. When you want a bit of silence and a rest from entertaining, encourage them to colour or draw or make animals and shapes out of pipe cleaners, depending on how you are travelling (e.g. car or train).

Safety in cars
- Never allow a child to travel in the front seat of a car sitting on an adult's lap. Even a small jolt can throw a child against the windscreen, causing serious or even fatal injury.
- A child belted into the front seat is safer than a child loose in the back. It is the driver's responsibility to ensure that children under fourteen wear seat belts when travelling in the front of a car.
- Never put children in the very back of an estate car.
- Babies under seven months should travel strapped into carrycots placed on the back seat (across the car) with the baby's head towards the centre of the car. The carrycot should be restrained with straps bearing the BSI mark BSAU 186:1983.
- Older babies, seven months to four years, should travel in a car seat bolted firmly to the back seat structure of the car (check that the seat you buy bears the BSI kitemark BS3254 or ECE Regulation 44, identifiable by a capital E).
- Four years and over should wear a seat belt with child restraints bearing the BSI kitemark BS3254 or ECE Regulation 44, identifiable by a capital E.
- There should be special locking devices fitted to the car doors so children cannot open them from the inside.
- For further information, see the BSI information sheet 'Children's Safety in Cars'.

Travelling by air
Babies
1. Restrict hand baggage to one bag (containing baby's needs).
2. Take Paddi pads (easier to change on board than disposable nappies).
3. Take ample baby food/milk (will be heated up on board by crew and, at least at Gatwick, the restaurant will provide hot water).
4. Take wet wipes/tissues.
5. Take a change of clothes – and a few toys.

Note:
- Flights can sometimes be delayed for a period of time. Although there are nursing mother rooms provided at all UK airports this is not always the case overseas.

Children
1. Take little hand baggage for yourself – and if possible none for the child.
2. Take a favourite toy, but clearly label it with name and address.
3. Take new colouring books and crayons (not felt-tip pens) and pads of paper and pencils.
4. Take playing cards, comics, travel games and boiled sweets (chocolates can be messy).

5. Take wet wipes/tissues and plasters/antiseptic cream/junior aspirin.
6. Take a change of clothes (if room).
7. Dress young children comfortably for the flight (a track suit or similar).
● For children's escort service – see Chapter 17.

TROUBLE WITH THE LAW

A child under the age of ten cannot be charged with any criminal offence as the law presumes conclusively that such children cannot be guilty of crime. Children under ten who get into serious trouble may, however, be taken before a court in certain circumstances as being in need of care or control.

Children in England and Wales aged between ten and sixteen inclusive can be summonsed or charged with criminal offences, when they have to appear before a special juvenile court. The court will require the child's parent or guardian to attend also and it has power to order the parent or guardian to pay any fines, costs or compensation instead of the child. Although the court case may be reported in the press, they are not allowed to publish anything which might identify the child.

Often, especially if the crime is not particularly serious, the police decide to give youngsters an 'official caution' rather than take them to the juvenile court. The caution is a warning as to future conduct and if the child gets into trouble again and is taken to court, the magistrates can be told about the previous caution.

After the seventeenth birthday, a person is presumed to be an adult for the purposes of criminal proceedings and will be dealt with by the magistrates' courts.

In Scotland, children under sixteen appear in court only when offences such as murder or assault to the danger of life are in question. Generally, children (in some cases up to the age of eighteen) who have committed lesser offences, who are truants or who are in need of care or protection appear before a Children's Hearing. The key figure in the system is the Reporter to whom referrals are made by the police, teachers, special workers or members of the general public. Following his own investigations, the Reporter may make referrals to the social work department: or, on the grounds that the child is in need of compulsory measures of care, he may refer the child to a Children's Hearing. The panel of people who sit at these hearings comes from a wide range of occupations and income groups and it is the panel's task to decide on the measures of care which are in the interest of the child. The panel has a wide range of options but it does not have the power to impose corporal punishment or fine the child or his parents.

● The Children's Legal Centre represents the rights of children in relation to the law:

Children's Legal Centre
20 Compton Terrace
London N1 2UN
01–359 6251 (2 to 5 p.m.)

- Justice for Children can advise on juvenile court procedure:

  Justice for Children
  35 Wellington Street
  London WC2E 7BW
  01–836 5917

- Child Molestation:

  Child Watch
  60 Beck Road
  Everthorpe, Brough
  North Humberside HV15 2JS
  04302–3824

Further Information

Other useful addresses (see also Chapter 20)

Child Poverty Action Group
1 Macklin Street
London WC2B 5NH
01–405 5942

Mother's Union
24 Tufton Street
London SW1P 3RB
01–222 5533

National Association of
    Youth Clubs
Keswick House
30 Peacock Lane
Leicester LE1 5NY
0533–29514   ·

National Deaf Children's Society
158 West Regent Street
Glasgow G2 4RJ
041–221 2620

National Society for the
    Prevention of Cruelty to Children
67 Saffron Hill
London EC1N 8RS
01–242 1626

Royal Scottish Society for
    Prevention of Cruelty to Children
Melville House
41 Polwarth Terrace
Edinburgh EH11 1NU
031–337 8539

Suggested further reading

BABIES AND CHILDREN: GENERAL

Boston Women's Health Collective, *Ourselves and Our Children: A Book by and for Children*, Penguin
Bowlby, John, *Child Care and the Growth of Love*, Penguin
Clegg, Averil and Anne Woollett, *Twins*, Frances Lincoln
Crowe, Brenda, *Living with a Toddler*, Unwin Paperbacks
    The Playgroup Movement, Unwin Paperbacks
Jolly, Dr Hugh, *Book of Child Care*, Sphere
    Common Sense about Babies, Unwin Paperbacks
Leach, Penelope, *Baby and Child*, Penguin
    The Parents' A to Z, Allen Lane
Messenger, Maire, *The Breast-feeding Book*, Frances Lincoln

Nash, Barbara, *The Complete Book of Baby Care from Conception to Three Years*, St Michael

Stanway, Drs Andrew and Penny, *The Baby and Child Book*, Pan

Stoppard, Dr Miriam, *Your Growing Child, 3 to 11*, Octopus

Thompson, Brenda, *The Pre-School Book*, Unwin Paperbacks

Winnicott, D. W., *The Child, the Family and the Outside World*, Penguin

ONE-PARENT FAMILIES

Barber, Dulan (ed.), *One-Parent Families*, Hodder & Stoughton

Davenport, Diana, *One-Parent Families*, Pan

COOKING

Griggs, Barbara, *Baby's Cookbook*, Granada

Hull, Sylvia, *Cooking for a Baby*, Penguin

Templeton, Louise, *First Foods for Healthy Children*, Frances Lincoln

HEALTH

Barnes, Belinda and Irene Colquhoun, *The Hyperactive Child: What the Family Can Do*, Thorsons

Douglas, Jo and Naomi Richman, *My Child Won't Sleep*, Penguin

Encyclopedia of Child Health, Frances Lincoln

Shisler, Jack, *Childhood Illness*, Unwin Paperbacks

HANDICAPPED CHILDREN

Carr, Janet, *Helping Your Handicapped Child*, Penguin

Hannah, Charles, *Parents and Mentally Handicapped Children*, Penguin

McCormack, Andrina, *Coping With Your Handicapped Child*, Chambers

LEARNING DIFFICULTIES

Fanham-Doggery, Sylvia, *Learning Disabilities*, Fontana

Horsby, Dr Beve, *Overcoming Dyslexia*, Dunitz

GIFTED CHILDREN

Freeman, Dr Joan, *Clever Children: a Parents' Guide*, Hamlyn

Gifted Children: Their Growth and Development in a Social Context, MTP Press

SEX EDUCATION

Althea, *A Baby in the Family*, Dinosaur

Claesson, B. H., *Boy, Girl, Man, Woman*, Penguin

Cousins, Jane, *Make It Happy*, Penguin

Heleger, Stan, *Peter and Caroline*, Tavistock Publications

Mayle, Peter, *Where Did I Come From?* Macmillan

Rayner, Clare, *The Body Book*, Piccolo

10 A Guide to Education

Education is without doubt an emotive issue in a parent's life and, when children are old enough to make decisions for themselves, in their lives too.

Here is a simple guide to what education in Britain is about. Information was supplied by a former public school headmaster, the Independent Schools Information Service (ISIS) and the National Union of Teachers (NUT), organizations responsible for higher and further education and those with knowledge of education throughout England and Wales, Northern Ireland and Scotland.

Notes
- Learning up to the age of five, emotional and other problems in starting and coping with school and special help for gifted children and those with learning problems are all covered in Chapter 9.
- Between the age of five, when formal education in Britain begins, and the age of eighteen, there are two systems of education in England, the *maintained* system (so called because all the running costs are covered by public funds) and the *independent* system.
- The variations in education in Wales, Scotland and Northern Ireland are set out in 'Regional Differences' below.
- While parents naturally feel an equal responsibility to all their children this does not necessarily mean they should all go to the same kind of school. A school should be chosen to suit the ability and temperament of each individual child.

The Maintained Sector

ORGANIZA-
TION
Educational policy, as far as schools are concerned, is controlled in England by the Department of Education and Science (DES), under a senior Cabinet minister, and in Wales by the Welsh Office. The two bodies usually move in step. Their policy is administered by the local education authorities (LEAs) which are based on the non-metropolitan counties and on the districts of the metropolitan counties. The inner London boroughs have their own joint LEA. Each LEA has its own Chief Education Officer (CEO) or Director of Education.

The work of the schools is monitored (not controlled) by Her Majesty's Inspectors (HMIs). As their name implies, they are independent of the DES and in theory responsible directly to the Crown.

Stages of education

Broadly speaking there are three stages:
PRIMARY: age 5 to 11
SECONDARY: age 11 to 18
HIGHER: from the age of 18
but this clear-cut division is blurred in two ways:

● Some LEAs have established a *middle school*, straddling across the primary/secondary range. Those schools with an age range of 8 to 12 are normally regarded as being an extension of the primary school, but where the range is 9 to 13 the school is more like a junior secondary school in its approach.

From the parents' point of view this diversity of practice may present at any rate a temporary difficulty if they have to move when the child is at a crucial age.

● There is some confusion between the terms *higher* and *further* education. Present practice is to confine the term 'higher education' to academic, normally full-time, courses on which pupils embark after taking the General Certificate of Education (GCE) at Advanced Level at the age of eighteen. 'Further education' is much broader and covers all full-time and part-time education for pupils over the school leaving age (sixteen), together with training for the use of leisure.

Most of the maintained schools (the *county* schools) are owned as well as maintained by the LEAs. However, there is a significant number of schools, especially in the primary sector, (*voluntary* schools) which are maintained by the LEAs but which remain the property of the voluntary bodies – usually denominational – which originally provided the buildings. These voluntary schools retain certain elements of independence which are less obvious in *controlled* than in *aided* schools.

Religious education

In England and Wales the law says that all children in maintained schools, whether county or voluntary, shall start the day with an act of corporate worship and shall receive religious instruction – unless their parents specifically opt out for them. In county schools the act of worship is non-denominational and the religious instruction is in accordance with an agreed non-denominational syllabus. In voluntary controlled schools the instruction is based on the same agreed syllabus, but provision may be made for not more than two periods a week of denominational instruction. In voluntary aided schools both worship and instruction are a matter for the governors to decide – subject to the right of withdrawal. Governors of aided schools are also responsible for admissions to the school (subject to any agreement with the LEA) and have to publish the criteria they use for deciding on admissions whenever applications exceed the places available.

PRIMARY
SCHOOLS

Almost all primary schools are co-educational. Except in very small schools there is a division between infants (the first two or three years) and juniors. Sometimes the two stages occupy different schools but more commonly they work as different departments in the same building.

There was a period when revulsion against cramming for the old 11-plus examination, combined with enthusiasm for new so-called 'activity' methods, led many teachers in junior schools to discount traditional skills. A nationwide survey in 1978 showed that the pendulum had swung back and that parents need not fear that children would not be taught the 'three Rs' properly.

In rural areas the nearest primary school may be the small village school, perhaps with a couple of teachers in charge of all age groups. A small intimate community has its own advantages at this age and a dedicated head- or class-teacher can do much to make up for the inevitable limitations.

SECONDARY
SCHOOLS

Maintained secondary schools are usually – though not always – co-educational. The selective system of admissions remains in a few areas where there is still a distinction between the *grammar* school and the *secondary modern*, but the great majority of LEAs now organize all their secondary education on *comprehensive* lines.

A comprehensive school caters for children of all grades of ability except those unable to benefit from a normal education for whom special schools are provided. In most comprehensive schools, pupils are *streamed* after the first or second year: even in schools which on principle are not streamed there is a certain amount of 'natural selection'. A pupil who opts for, or is selected for, a second language will undoubtedly find him/herself working with a small group of academic peers. Continuation at school beyond the legal school leaving age is also a form of self-selection.

Examinations

The traditional grammar school prepared most of its pupils to take GCE. The comprehensive school fulfils this function and also provides courses for the Certificate of Secondary Education (CSE), originally designed for less able children. Now it is possible for the same pupil to take some subjects in GCE and others in CSE, but in autumn 1986, in England and Wales, a new General Certificate of Secondary Education (GCSE) will replace GCE O-level and CSE examinations.

STAYING ON

The more able pupils, who may have higher education in mind, will wish to stay on for two years after the compulsory leaving age in order to take GCE A-level. If a comprehensive school is to have a sixth form that is viable in the sense that it can provide an adequate choice of subjects without uneconomic use of manpower, then it must have a very large base. The logic of this was accepted by some LEAs which built schools up to two thousand in size or, alternatively, organized existing schools on different sites into a monolithic complex.

Such large schools are now out of fashion and school rolls are falling anyway. Alternative methods have been developed for dealing with the needs of those who stay on. In some areas all the teaching is concentrated in a *sixth form college*; elsewhere *tertiary colleges* have been set up. These, unlike sixth form colleges, are regarded as colleges of further education rather than as schools and they offer vocational as well as academic subjects.

PARENTAL
RESPONSI-
BILITY

Lip-service is universally paid to the principle of 'parental choice' but this is limited, for practical reasons.

A practising Roman Catholic (much more rarely, an Anglican) may find a voluntary secondary school within reach where she may claim some priority of admission for her child. Some authorities may allow a certain amount of choice between their own schools, though your child may not be allotted to your first choice if the school is oversubscribed.

In general, children will go to a school near their home. It is therefore important to look into local education facilities before moving house. Parents can find out about prospective schools from their local education authority (phone number in the Telephone Directory): a recent require-ment is that every school must provide information about its objectives and its achievements.

Whatever the local set-up, wise parents should 'do their own home-work' by calling on the head, finding out what the school has to offer and by finding out the obligations of pupils and parents (is there an active parents' association?). See 'Visiting suitable schools', page 315.

There does not seem to be any consistent principle of school uniform in Britain. Most schools still have their policies, though individual head-teachers and staff will decide, sometimes after consulting parents.

Once a pupil has started at a school, parents are well advised to keep in close touch with the class teacher or whoever is immediately responsible for the pupil's welfare. It is a good idea to join the parents' association and few engagements should be allowed to take priority over a parents' evening.

REGIONAL
DIFFERENCES

I asked Stuart Skyrte, Press Officer of the National Union of Teachers, for his thoughts on education in England today.

England

Parents visiting schools in inner cities or large towns in England today might begin to understand the meaning of the term 'multi-racial society'. In infant, primary, middle or secondary schools, children from a wide diversity of ethnic backgrounds can be found playing, working and learn-ing together.

Many children born in Britain have parents who were born elsewhere and whose first language at home may not be English. Teachers consider this a challenge rather than a problem and, provided that funding is available for in-service training and language help, schools can only gain from this experience.

Teachers believe that the way in which children from different ethnic backgrounds adapt to each other, tolerate and respect each other, is a pointer to a future Britain in which racism is eliminated. A small but growing number of schools in inner city areas is adopting anti-racist codes of behaviour for children and teachers in order to prevent or eradicate racist activities in schools.

Government money is available under Section 11 of the Local Government Act 1966 to enable local education authorities to fund specific projects and employ special teachers and advisers to help develop multicultural education and overcome disadvantage.

Northern Ireland School education in Northern Ireland is administered centrally by the Department of Education and locally by five education and library boards.

In Northern Ireland, clergy have right of access which might be used for denominational instruction (in voluntary schools, worship and religious education are controlled by the management authorities).

The system is virtually the same as that in England except that secondary schooling is on selective rather than comprehensive lines. At the secondary level all schools come within the state system.

The Northern Ireland GCE and CSE examinations correspond to the equivalent exams in England and are accepted as such for university and other entrances.

Scotland Janet Rae says that, in Scotland there are two main categories of schools:
1. The *public sector*, known as the local authority schools, funded by central government and the ratepayer.
2. *Independent* schools, which are private and do not receive any funding from central government.

Overall responsibility for Scottish education rests with the Secretary of State for Scotland, who acts through the Scottish Education Department.

Scotland has its own Schools Inspectorate. The inspectors are responsible to the Secretary of State for Scotland. Most Scottish schools are non-denominational but by law separate Roman Catholic schools exist within the public system at both primary and secondary level.

In the public sector, Scottish children enter co-educational primary schools at the age of five in the area in which they live.

There are no intermediate schools in Scotland and at the age of twelve children transfer to secondary schools, the majority of which are comprehensive. During the first two years they are introduced to a wide variety of subjects to discover their individual interests and abilities. During the second year most schools group their pupils into sets.

SCE O-grade examinations are normally taken in the fourth year and they are followed by Highers, generally in the fifth year (consequently these are not so advanced as GCE A-levels). The more able pupils take four or five Highers: a requisite number of Higher passes qualifies for admission to any Scottish and almost any English university although a few Scottish comprehensives and some of the independent schools also offer GCE A-level with particular thought for candidates who might wish additional qualifications for entrance to English universities.

Sixth-year pupils who have demonstrated an ability to pursue independent study and who have passed Highers in their selected subjects are eligible for the Certificate of Sixth Year Studies.

Scotland: curriculum and examination changes

First examinations in new courses of study in English, mathematics, science and social and vocational skills will take place in some schools in 1986. They will run in tandem with existing O-grade examinations.

As a result of the Munn and Dunning Reports, 1977, a new qualification, the SCE Standard Grade, will eventually replace O-grades in all courses of study. This will be given to successful candidates on a scale 1 to 7, reflecting the level of syllabus study: *Foundation* will give recognition to the low achiever, *General* will apply to the middle-ability range, and *Credit* will be more demanding than the existing O and a challenge for the able pupil. Highers will continue for those pupils who need the qualification for further study and the Certificate of Sixth Year Studies will also continue, although both will gradually be revised to take account of the new SCE Standard Grade.

The new 16–18 Certificate absorbs the former Scottish Certificate of Vocational Studies and is based on a collection of modules (learning units of forty hours' study). These can be accumulated in schools, colleges of further education or as part of the Youth Training Scheme: pupils can take a mixture of modular courses, Highers, SCE O-grades or the new SCE Standard. And employers will be able to specify the combination of modules they require when recruiting staff.

The transition from old to new certificates is going to take several years and it is advisable for parents to keep abreast of developments. You can contact your local education authority or get information and such leaflets as 'Scottish Education' and '16–18 Certificate' from:

> Scottish Information Office (Room 2/88)
> New St Andrew's House
> Edinburgh EH1 3TG
> 031–556 8400 ext. 5123

Another useful aid, which is also helpful on holidays, jobs, law, money management and welfare benefits, is 'Young Scot' (50p + s.a.e.) from:

> Scottish Community Education Council
> Atholl House
> 2 Canning Street
> Edinburgh EH3 8EG
> 031–229 2433

Wales

Although education in England and Wales is very similar, one significant difference is that in a number of schools in Wales the Welsh and English languages are both used as media for instruction. Most of these schools are in the traditionally Welsh-speaking and largely rural areas. Designated bilingual schools continue to be established in the anglicized industrial areas of the country to cater for children whose parents wish them to be educated in both languages.

See 'Education in Britain', Central Office of Information reference pamphlet 7, HMSO.

The Independent Sector

BOYS' SCHOOLS
GIRLS' SCHOOLS
HOW TO CHOOSE

PAYING
EXPERIMENTAL AND
FOREIGN SCHOOLS

The two ladders – maintained and independent – are no longer as separate as they used to be. Many parents choose to send their children to a maintained primary school before switching to the independent sector, or vice versa. At the other end of the scale movement either way is becoming more common. Both boys and girls can, and do, transfer to the sixth form of a public school after taking O-levels at a comprehensive school. Conversely – and not only for financial reasons – boys or girls from independent schools can choose to take A-levels from a sixth form college or college of further education.

BOYS'
SCHOOLS

'Traditional' public school education is based on the *preparatory* school (8 to 13) and the *public* school (13 to 18). Transfer from preparatory school to public school is usually by way of the *common entrance examination* which is a qualifying rather than a competitive hurdle. There is a growing number of *pre-preparatory* schools for parents who want their children to start on the bottom rung of the independent ladder. Many independent secondary schools have their own junior or preparatory departments. Some of the boys' schools now accept girls in the sixth form.

There are over 2,500 registered independent schools in Britain catering for pupils of all ages. The best known are probably those commonly known as the public schools, which are in membership of the Headmasters' Conference (HMC): practically the same group of schools forms the Governing Bodies' Association. There are more than two hundred schools whose headmasters belong to HMC. All have high, sometimes very high, academic standards and flourishing sixth forms. About a third of the schools are wholly or mainly day schools. These may well have their normal entry at the age of eleven, through their own entrance examination.

There are also many other independent schools which have reached the standards required by the Independent Schools' Joint Council (ISJC) and which offer good value for money. It follows that while individual schools are selective – and in view of their average size they could be nothing else – the system as a whole is comprehensive in that there are schools in it which will cater for every type of pupil.

GIRLS'
SCHOOLS

Here the overseeing committees are the Girls' Schools' Association (GSA) and the Governing Bodies of Girls' Schools' Association (GBGSA).

The age structure is generally slightly different in girls' schools. There are some girls' prep schools and the pupils have their own common entrance examination but the age of transfer is much more flexible and the examination may be taken at 11, 12 or 13.

HOW TO
CHOOSE

1. Once parents have decided on independent education the first question is: *day or boarding?* Proximity is important. If a pupil is to take a full part in out-of-school activities, a long double journey each day makes heavy demands on time and energy. And if the school is primarily a boarding-school, it is important to make sure that proper provision is made for the day pupil.

It is difficult to generalize. It may be suggested that where there is a good day school within reach and where the child has a normal home background, preferably with one or more siblings, he (probably) and she (perhaps more probably) can gain most of the advantages that the independent school has to offer without losing the advantages of home life. On the other hand, there are a very few pupils who do not benefit from even a limited period of living in a community. These children can usually be identified and should be sent to board only if there is no reasonable alternative.

2. *Co-education or single-sex?* Although most public schools are single-sex, co-education, especially but not only at sixth-form level, is becoming more common. Schools which have a nearby 'sister' school – whether or not officially founded as such – with which sixth-form facilities can be shared, possibly make for the best of both worlds.

3. Choice between *schools of similar type* is more difficult. There are many reasons why parents should choose to send children to one school rather than another. Many schools are specifically identified with a religious denomination, and parents will, of course, be concerned with a school's academic standing (although it is arguable that standards of behaviour nowadays count for more with parents). Other factors include family connection, geographical location and – to a lesser extent – such considerations as whether a school has (or has not) a Combined Cadet Force, a classics department or plays rugger or soccer.

Parents starting from scratch should note:

● It is never too early to start planning education – as long as you remember that you must be prepared to switch plans if necessary.

● Much may be learned from old pupils of recent vintage and from friends with children at a particular school. The satisfied parent, indeed, is the best advertisement a school can have.

- Do not hesitate to shop around and send for prospectuses.
- Make sure you go to see as many 'possible' schools as you can.
- Remember that freedom of choice for parent implies freedom of choice for school as well. Schools may close their entry lists years in advance. If you send your child to a preparatory school then the head will advise you what schools would or would not be suitable for the particular abilities and needs of the child.

Help
- There are plenty of central sources of information to help you choose a school. Pre-eminent is the Independent Schools Information Service (ISIS) but even they can give you only factual information about what is available. They are not in business to say that this school is better than that school. ISIS deals with more than 100,000 inquiries a year, mostly from parents. Details of the nearest regional director can be obtained from the main address below.

ISIS publications include *Choosing Your Independent School*. 'Assisted Places Schools', 'Boarding Is Fun', 'Girls in Boys' Schools', 'Scholarships and Grants', 'School Fees', 'Schools' Handbook' and the annual 'Boarding Schools' Directory'. For information on all these and other services send two first-class stamps to:

> Independent Schools Information Service
> 56 Buckingham Gate
> London SW1E 6AH
> 01–630 8793/4

- For a list of preparatory schools in a particular area contact:

> Incorporated Association of Preparatory Schools
> 138 Kensington Church Street
> London W8 4BN
> 01–727 2316

- You can also get help with information on schools from:

> Gabbitas-Thring Education Trust Ltd
> 6 Sackville Street
> London W1
> 01–734 0161

> Truman & Knightley Educational Trust
> 78(HQ5) Notting Hill Gate
> London W11 3LJ
> 01–727 1242

Visiting suitable schools
There is no substitute for the personal visit. Make sure that before you visit the school you are properly briefed. Carefully read the prospectus and any other literature that has been sent to you.

You can learn much from your own observation. Look out for:

- the general cleanliness of the buildings (not only the entrance hall!)
- the presence or absence of graffiti and litter
- signs of life in the classrooms and corridors (pin-up boards, pictures, maps, perhaps flowers)
- the general demeanour of the pupils (cheerful, courteous, reasonably neat – or dull, slovenly, slouching).

When you see the head ask yourself if he is genuinely pleased to see you or really rather bored. Does he seem keen on his job and does he know what makes a boy or girl tick?

Ask the head some (not all!) of the following questions:

CURRICULAR

- how big are classes in the middle of the school?
- how is the choice of subjects arranged in the middle of the school?
- what is the policy on homework (prep)?
- and on the taking of early O-levels?
- how big is the sixth form?
- and what choice of subjects is there in it?
- how many leavers went up to university last year and what proportion does this represent?

EXTRA-CURRICULAR

- what are the facilities for games?
- and for music?
- and for art?
- and for swimming?
- and for domestic subjects?

FINANCIAL

- how inclusive is the inclusive fee?
- are pupils fully covered by accident insurance?

PERSONAL

- what are the dormitories like (boarders only)?
- how much free time does the child have in the evenings? (boarders only)
- and over the weekend? (boarders only)
- are the children encouraged to read?
- what is the policy on television?
- what provision is made for 'pastoral care' (in the broadest sense)?
- and for career guidance?
- and for 'education in citizenship'?
- what is the policy for sex education?
- is there any liaison with neighbouring boys'/girls' schools?
- what methods of incentive and punishment are employed?
- what are the lines of communication with parents? (This covers PTA, parents' evenings, reports, accessibility of heads and staff, etc.)
- what are the rules for school uniform?

● how compulsory are compulsory games?

Remember, heads are busy people. Concentrate on points of special interest or importance.

If you are shown round the school and have a choice, ask to see some or all of:

● the library (does it give the impression of use?), the laboratories, computer centre, the changing rooms, a typical day-room (boarders only), the sick-bay (and ask about the school doctor – boarders only), and the chapel.

Finally, ask the head for the names and telephone numbers of two or three parents living within range whom you can contact for candid opinions.

PAYING

Boarding fees for each pupil currently run at an average of £15,000 for prep school (five years at £3,000 p.a.) and £25,000 for public school (five years at £5,000 p.a.). This sum, of course, does not include school uniform and extras such as music lessons.

The decision to embark on independent education is a serious one and should normally be made early in the child's life. Broadly speaking, a parent may be able to secure help from internal or from external sources.

Internal sources of income

Within the family, parents can take out *educational endowment insurance* which, if done early enough, will considerably ease the financial burden. Grandparents (not parents) can *covenant* any help given so that tax relief may be claimed (see Chapter 1).

Help can also be given by an investment specialist. Parents need an investment of about £10,000 and contact should be made as soon as possible (at birth) and at least five years before the first fees are required. Such capital could produce £20,000 over the following five years.

For help with school fees investment advice ask ISIS for its list of recommended school fee firms (address above).

External sources of income

● The endowed public schools offer a wide range of *scholarships* (for academic merit) and *bursaries* (for cases of real need), details of which are given in the *Public Schools' Year Book* and the *Girls' Schools Year Book*. Except for the top scholarships, such awards can be expected to cover only a proportion of the cost.

● Parents below a certain income limit may be within reach of one of the schools at which the government takes up *assisted places*. Also, local authorities are allowed to help towards the cost of boarding where boarding is essential rather desirable.

● Parents serving overseas may be eligible for help from their own firms or from the government.

● Boys with good voices may win places as choristers at cathedral choir schools, perhaps subsequently winning music scholarships at large public schools.

Details of scholarships and grants may be obtained from ISIS (address above).

EXPERI-
MENTAL AND
FOREIGN
SCHOOLS

There is what is called an *alternative* educational system which some parents might like to consider. Schools in this category extend from experimental schools to highly esteemed foreign schools, some of which are listed below (they .offer variously the diploma of the International Baccalaureate or American college placement qualifications as well as, in some cases, British qualifications):

American School in London
2 Loudoun Road
London NW8 ONP
01–722 0101

American School of Edinburgh
29 Chester Street
Edinburgh EH3 7EN
031–225 9888

American School of Aberdeen
Craigton Road
Cults
Aberdeen AB1 9QD
0224–868 927

Dartington Hall
Totnes
Devon
0803–862567

French Lycée
35 Cromwell Road
London SW7 2DG
01–584 6322

Steiner Schools Fellowship
Orlingbury House
Lewis Road
Forest Row
Sussex RH18 5AA
0342–82 2115

Higher Education

UNIVERSITIES   POLYTECHNICS

If little is said here about universities and similar institutions of advanced study it is because secondary schools – whether maintained or independent – are generally so much better placed to give advice.

Facilities for career guidance are available through the careers officer employed at most schools.

The Independent Schools Careers Organization (ISCO) to which most of the mainstream boys' independent schools are affiliated also offers useful career guidance.

As a result of such guidance the pupil may leave school after O- or A-levels to begin professional or technical studies. If he/she decides to go on to university this postpones choice of career but a decision still has to be made on the course of study. Should the pupil follow an interest or read something specifically vocational? It should be borne in mind that some subjects (such as law) straddle the division and that other subjects (such as history) can be vocational for a schoolteacher and cultural for someone else.

Ratios of graduate unemployment might influence choice of study. Figures for the percentage of graduates in each discipline who failed to find full-time employment within a few months of leaving university (from the *Sunday Times*, 11 September 1983) included the following:

			PERCENTAGE UNEMPLOYED
Medicine	0.1	Chemistry	16.9
Architecture	3.2	Economics	17.0
Law	5.2	English	22.3
Music	10.6	Art and design	22.5
Civil engineering	11.5	Combined sciences	24.4
Maths	11.8	Sociology	24.9
Education	12.8	Drama	37.5
Business studies	14.9	Philosophy	40.4
Physics	15.7		

The only safe generalization is that someone going to university without any specific career in mind is better advised to tackle a demanding discipline rather than one of the arts subjects. In order to promote the sciences, the Engineering Council and the Equal Opportunities Commission have together conceived 'Women Into Science and Engineering' (WISE). Among the information they offer are ideas for those who opted for the arts in their early teens and want now to pursue scientific fields. Details (s.a.e.) from:

WISE
Education Section of Equal Opportunities Commission
Overseas House
Quay Street
Manchester M3 3HN
061–833 9244

UNIVER-
SITIES

There are forty-six universities or institutions with university status in Britain. They are independent and self-governing bodies but by far the greater part of their income comes from public funds. Similarly, over 90 per cent of full-time university students – excluding pupils from overseas – receive grants which cover their living expenses in whole or part.

There are currently about 304,000 full-time university students (including about 46,000 postgraduates). Universities have absolute control of admissions. Decision is normally based on track record and head-teachers' reports, sometimes supplemented by interview, and it may be dependent on specific performance in A-level examinations. Oxford and Cambridge still have their own examinations but all applications for full-time first degree courses are centralized through the Universities Central Council on Admissions (UCCA). Instructions on how to apply are found in the UCCA handbook available from schools and from:

Universities Central Council on Admissions
PO Box 28
Cheltenham
Glos GL50 1HY
0242–519091

Note • Oxford and Cambridge entrance scholarships and exhibitions are in the process of being phased out. 'Oxbridge' still retains an attraction to many but the day has long gone when a student at a 'provincial' university was in some sense regarded as a second-class citizen.

The University of Buckingham The University of Buckingham (still often called by its earlier title, the Independent University) receives no direct grant from public funds, though its students are now eligible for the usual university grants of tuition and maintenance from local authorities. Its degree courses, in such subjects as law, economics, business studies and accounting, take two years of four terms each instead of the usual three years of three terms each. Information from:

The University of Buckingham
Bucks MK18 1EG
0280–814080

Open University The Open University provides part-time university education 'at a distance' by the use of correspondence, occasional attendance at tutorial sessions, radio and television programmes and short residential summer schools. There is no upper age limit and there are no entry qualifications. Degree and other courses are offered in a vast range of subjects.

Hilary Cox recently gained a degree (BA) from the Open University and she says:

> I found I had to spend about 12 to 15 hours per week on my work – that was direct study and reading on the subject. Reading around it needed more time. In addition there were 10 essays a year and they took several hours each. My tutors were good at getting them back to me, in about 10 to 14 days. The radio and TV programmes were fun and a lot of help, though they are on at atrocious times. It is best if you can record them to play back at convenient times and to use for revision. Attendance at the day schools was invaluable. I would say that you need a sympathetic and tolerant family: I don't know how anyone with a family *and* a full-time job could cope – something would have to give! It's a marvellous feeling to have finished and graduated after all this time (I won't say how long).

The Open University has over 75,000 students. For those with no previous or recent experience of further education it offers a variety of introductory courses and for those embarking on a first degree there is a broad 'foundation course' to begin with before specialized work is started. Details of the Open University can be obtained from:

The Open University
PO Box 48
Milton Keynes MK 7 6AA
0908–74066

Open University Scottish Office
60 Melville St
Edinburgh EH3 7HF
031–226 3851

National Extension College The National Extension College offers courses to help prepare you for a return to study (some courses include 'How to Write an Essay', 'Word Power' and 'Writing for Everyone'). Details from:

National Extension College
18 Brooklands Avenue
Cambridge CB2 2HN
0223–63465

Students' Unions Your college may have an active union. The main headquarters are:

National Union of Students (NUS)
461 Holloway Road
London N7 6LJ
01–272 8900

You can contact the Mature Students' Union through your local branch of the NUS, or by telephoning Blackpool (0253) 293911.

POLY-TECHNICS The thirty polytechnics offer an education that is essentially vocational and professional in its intentions. This means that a wide variety of courses is offered. Percentages of all (full- and part-time) enrolments in polytechnics in 1982 included:

	PERCENTAGE
Ancillary health	2.9
Adminstrative, business and social studies	32.5
Language and literature	3.6
Science and maths	16.0

There are opportunities to study at a range of levels and thus to secure qualifications at postgraduate, first degree and the various sub-degree levels which include the Higher National Diploma (HND), the Diploma of Higher Education (DipHE) and a great many professional certificates and diplomas.

There are about 300,000 enrolments in polytechnics, of whom just under half are full-time students. About one third of these take 'sandwich courses'. At sub-degree level, a great many of the HND courses are sandwich, which means three years rather than the full-time two years. At first degree level, this also adds a year to the usual (three-year) schedule. There are also 'thin' sandwich courses where the time spent in placement is shorter and parcelled out in smaller chunks. There are also part-time modes of attendance: part-time day, part-time day and evening, part-time evening. These modes offer particular attractions to women contemplating a return, or first entry, to higher education.

Minimum entry qualifications for a first degree course are usually five GCE passes (at least two of which should be A-level) or ONC/OND, various BTEC awards and the Scottish Certificate of Education. For sub-degree qualifications, the formal entry requirements are five GCEs (of which one must be at A-level with a second at least studied to A-level) or the equivalent in terms of ONC/D or BTEC awards. Polytechnics are also prepared in certain circumstances to consider mature applicants without conventional academic qualifications but with relevant work experience.

Applications for entry are handled by the polytechnics themselves. You can get a leaflet on the colleges and *Polytechnic Courses Handbook* from:

> The Committee of Directors of Polytechnics
> 309 Regent Street
> London WIR 7PE
> 01–637 9939

Further Education

CITY AND GUILDS
CORRESPONDENCE COLLEGES
BUSINESS, SECRETARIAL AND
 LANGUAGE STUDIES

TUTORING
HELP FOR STUDENTS
EVENING WEEKEND AND
 OCCASIONAL CLASSES

It is difficult to summarize these facilities for two reasons:
1. The provision covers such a wide field and depends so much on the policy of the LEAs which are mainly but not entirely responsible for it. (In England and Wales, in 1980 they were responsible in round figures for 30 designated *polytechnics* (discussed above), 600 other major colleges, 6,000 adult education centres and 30 residential establishments. Perhaps because the system is so diverse and so diffuse its value to the community is not always recognized. Those who have been associated with the *colleges of further education* (CFEs) know what a variety of courses, full- and part-time, for work and for fun, they are able to offer under one roof. Conversely, some of the courses at the polytechnics – an instance at random would be the course in architecture at the Oxford 'Poly' – have acquired a far more than local reputation.

The Ulster Polytechnic is being merged with the University of Coleraine:

in Scotland there are no polytechnics by name but five higher education institutions are comparable in character and aims.

2. There have been so many structural changes in the last quarter of a century. One major development came in 1964 when a Council for National Academic Awards was established, with powers to validate and monitor degree courses at institutions other than a university and subsequently to award its own degrees. Two years later the ten major institutions of further education, the *colleges of advanced technology* (CATs), were either made universities in their own right or incorporated as colleges of universities already in existence. More recently, at a lower level, the system of technical qualifications based on the Ordinary and Higher National Certificates and Diplomas, and the certificates of the City and Guilds of London Institute, has been reviewed.

Beside the polys and the CFEs which cater for a broad range of subjects, there are specialized institutions for those seeking qualifications in fields as diverse as teaching, agriculture or art and design. The DES funds a small number of vocational colleges, many professional associations run their own training establishments, voluntary organizations and commercial enterprises account for many more, including the schools which teach English to foreigners and the correspondence colleges.

There is also a wide range of activities, much of it sponsored by voluntary organizations, which comes under the comprehensive heading of 'Youth and Community Service'.

Provision, therefore, is made – though of course not to the same extent in every part of the country – for everyone from the sixteen-year-old seeking a career qualification through the middle-aged woman wanting self-improvement to the senior citizen seeking a new interest in life.

CITY AND GUILDS
The largest technical body in Britain offers comprehensive full- and part-time courses in over 200 subjects around the country. For details of what is available contact your local library, adult education authority or (s.a.e.):

City and Guilds of London Institute
76 Portland Place
London W1N 4AA
01–580 3050

CORRESPON-
DENCE
COLLEGES
The advantages of studying 'by post' include: the possibility of part-time studying after work and the probability of being able to study at home, undisturbed by others and by travelling to and from the place of study. Those tied to the home also find correspondence courses attractive, as do those 'cramming' or resitting GCE and other examinations.

Many of the main correspondence colleges are members of the Council for the Accreditation of Correspondence Colleges (CACC). Application for admission is made to the relevant college – but you can get a list of all colleges (offering courses in everything from law to journalism, massage and canine studies) from (s.a.e.):

Council for the Accreditation of Correspondence Colleges
27 Marylebone Road
London NW1 5JS
01–935 5391

BUSINESS,
SECRETARIAL
AND
LANGUAGE
STUDIES

Courses in business and computer studies and languages may be taken at colleges of further education, polytechnics and many universities, but these subjects as well as secretarial skills are also offered by a wide range of private colleges. Look in your local Yellow Pages under 'Commercial Schools', 'Language Schools' and 'Secretarial Training'. (Yellow Pages for other parts of the country are available in public libraries.)

The disadvantage is that such private education may be expensive. Before embarking on it, be sure that you find out as much as you can about the college you are thinking of attending. Look carefully at the prospectus and course content to see if it offers what you need. Try to discover from former or current students what the standards are.

TUTORING

Individual tuition in any subject is likely to be expensive too. Personal recommendation is probably the best way to find a good tutor if you need one, but again the Yellow Pages lists sources of tutoring. In special cases such as music, try consulting the teachers at local colleges and schools; they may know of suitable tutors.

Tutoring that you undergo voluntarily can work wonders: do not think of it as a substitute for work though! On the subject of tutors, many a desperate parent has called in a tutor to try to 'get' a child through some important exam and been disappointed when the stratagem has not worked. The problem sometimes is that the child may not have been keeping up in class and now, relying on the tutor, does even less.

HELP FOR
STUDENTS

● Help with knowing what courses are available where can also be obtained from (s.a.e. in each case):

Compendium of Advanced Courses in Colleges
of Further and Higher Education
London and Home Counties Regional
Advisory Council for Technological Education
Tavistock House South
Tavistock Square
London WC1H 9LR
01–388 0027

Council for National Academic Awards (CNAA)
344–54 Gray's Inn Road
London WC1 8BP
01–278 4411

● Especially of interest to *mature students* who lack normal entry requirements for universities of Birmingham, Leeds, Liverpool, Manchester and Sheffield:

>Joint Matriculation Board
>Manchester M I 5 6EU
>061–273 2565

● Help with *accommodation* can be obtained from a university, polytechnic or college's own accommodation office or from its students' union. In London you can also get help from:

>Student Accommodation Services
>44 Langham Street
>London W I N 5RG
>01–637 0248

● To find out about *grants* available for students contact can be made with:

>Department of Education and Science
>(Room 1/27)
>Elizabeth House
>York Road
>London SE I 7HP
>01–928 9222

There are also covenants for students (see Chapter 1). The Inland Revenue issues a standard deed of covenant form for students (only those aged eighteen or over). 'Form IR47: Student Covenants' is available free from local tax offices. There are also two 'student covenant kits' you can buy:

>*Which?* Student Covenant Kit
>Consumers' Association
>Castlemead
>Gasgoyne Way
>Herts SG14 1LH

and

>Student and School Fees Covenant Kit
>Bourke Publishers
>PO Box 109
>London SW5 9JP

● Higher-level fellowships which enable you to be at least partially supported during study or research include:
● Travelling Fellowships offered by the Winston Churchill Memorial Trust. In 1965 £3 million was subscribed to provide 100 awards annually. All UK citizens, of any age and in any occupation, are eligible. Applicants propose a study project related to their trade, profession or interests and, if selected, they are expected to make their own arrangements to achieve their objectives. Different categories are offered awards each year: to find out if you fit into a current category contact:

Winston Churchill Memorial Trust
15 Queen Anne's Gate Terrace
London SW7 5PR
01–584 9315

● The Leverhulme trustees offer annually a number of fellowships and grants to individuals in aid of research. These are intended for the assistance of senior persons, particularly those who are prevented by routine duties or like cause from undertaking a research programme. No subject is excluded from consideration. Awards are limited to residents of the United Kingdom and the amount of each depends on the nature of the work but does not usually exceed £5,100. Closing date for applications is normally mid-November and awards must be taken up between the following 1 June and the next 1 May thereafter. Applications should be made on Form F2 (available from 1 September annually from):

Research Awards Advisory Committee
The Leverhulme Trust
15–19 New Fetter Lane
London EC4A 1NR
01–822 6952

EVENING, WEEKEND AND OCCASIONAL CLASSES

Your local library will have full particulars of what is available near you.

In inner London, the ILEA co-ordinates part-time day and evening classes. Among the many thousands of different courses available there are some organized specially for women ('Feminist Theory', 'Women's Rights', 'Women's Computer Workshop', 'Self-defence', 'Motor Car Maintenance' and 'Woodwork for Women').

Enrolment is usually in mid-September. Women who are under eighteen or over sixty, unemployed or receiving family income supplement or supplementary benefit, and students in basic education classes, literacy, numeracy, mother tongue English, English as a second language and linked skill courses – and the blind, deaf and mentally handicapped – pay only a nominal fee. As well as special classes for disabled people, the ILEA encourages those with handicaps to attend all courses. Anyone with a special problem should contact the principal of the adult education institute or college where the class will be held to see if there would be difficulties.

The annual brochure of classes, *Floodlight*, is available from newsagents and from:

Inner London Education Authority
Room 80
County Hall
London SE1 7PB
01–633 1066

Each local authority around Britain is responsible for its own programme of part-time and evening classes. Many universities offer part-time and evening classes as do some agricultural colleges.

The National Institute of Adult Education (NIAE) advises on all aspects of continuing education, maintains contact with international bodies, promotes conferences and undertakes developments and publications. Some of their special courses include such diverse subjects as cartoon drawing in Cambridge to karate in Abergavenny. Prospectus from:

> National Institute of Adult Education
> 19b De Montfort Street
> Leicester LE1 7GE
> 0533-551451

> Scottish Institute of Adult Education
> 30 Rutland Square
> Edinburgh EH1 2BW
> 031-229 0331

Information on other opportunities can be obtained from:

> Workers' Educational Association
> Temple House
> 9 Upper Berkeley Street
> London W1H 8BY
> 01-402 5608

> WEA
> Scottish Council
> 212 Bath Street
> Glasgow G2 4HW
> 041-332 0176

Adult Literacy and Numeracy

It is estimated that 6 per cent of the adult population are functionally illiterate, which means that their limited reading and writing skills seriously affect almost every aspect of their lives. Similarly, as many as one in three adults in Britain cannot deal with simple subtraction, multiplication, division or with percentages.

The Adult Literacy and Basic Skills Unit (ALBSU) was established in 1980 to act as a central focus for dealing with this problem. For help with literacy or numeracy you can approach your local library, local adult education institute or, in complete confidence:

> Adult Literacy and Basic Skills Unit (ALBSU)
> Kingsbourne House
> 229-31 High Holborn
> London WC1V 7DA
> 01-405 4017

Scottish Adult Basic Education Unit
Atholl House
2 Canning Street
Edinburgh EH3 8EG
031–229 2433

There are about 23,000 trained literacy and numeracy volunteers. If you would like to have details of how to become a volunteer contact:

Broadcasting Support Services
252 Western Avenue
London W3 6XJ
01–992 5522

Further Information

The Advisory Centre for Education (ACE) gives free advice, by telephone, to any parent whose child is at a state school. They produce many useful books and leaflets for parents, including *Where to Look Things Up*, a guide to sources of information on education, and Felicity Taylor's *Choosing a School*. *ACE Bulletin*, published six times a year, contains much information of interest to parents. Contact:

ACE
18 Victoria Park Square
London E2 9PB
01–980 4596

Suggested further reading

Buzan, Tony, *Use Your Head*, BBC Publications
Consumers' Association, *A Parent's Guide to Education*
Miller, Ruth, and Anna Alston, *Equal Opportunities: Careers Guide*, Penguin
Pedley, Robin, *The Comprehensive School*, Penguin
Preparing to Study, Open University Press

11 Your Job

Some people think that those who go out to work are necessarily more exciting than those who stay at home. This is a myth. Haven't you come across 'workers' who seem to have nothing to do all day and who have nothing to talk about in the evening? And, by the same token, how about those people who are housebound and yet are always cheerful and able to contribute to the conversation?

This chapter examines your feelings about work and gives ideas for setting about getting a job and for making that job more worthwhile. Here are the ins and outs of establishing your own business – and guidelines to coping with unemployment.

I am inspired by the determination of others. I hope you are too.

Thinking About Work

DO YOU
REALLY
WANT TO
WORK?

Before rushing into a work commitment, it is a good idea to assess the pros and cons of working.

Advantages of working
- money coming in
- more freedom away from domestic ties
- self-confidence
- chance to use talents
- chance to meet new people.

Disadvantages of working
- less free time
- less freedom for domestic matters
- increased expenditure: transport to and from work; help with house, children and garden; extra expense for food (more convenience foods); extra expense for your wardrobe; possibly an increased tax level
- less chance to pursue activities and see friends.

ALTERNA-
TIVES TO
WORKING
FULL TIME

Perhaps you do not want to commit yourself to a full-time paid job. Why not think about *voluntary work?* There are so many organizations that need your help, from fund-raising to spending a few hours in a second-hand shop (some voluntary work ideas are set out in Chapter 20).

Particularly if you have children you might prefer to think about part-time work or job sharing.

Part-time work is legally defined as working less than thirty hours a week. You will probably find that you are not covered by company sick pay and you may be excluded from maternity leave, pension schemes and agreements on redundancy.

Part-time work is difficult to find. Unless you are lucky enough to find a job in a school (teaching, catering, etc.,) you will probably find that the only available part-time jobs require you to work during school holidays – exactly when you need to be home. The best way to find part-time work is to keep your ears and mouth open and have as many people as possible looking on your behalf.

Part-time work and part-time earnings affect your social security benefit rights and the contributions you have to pay to the national insurance scheme, just as full-time work and earnings do. See: 'Part-time Work and Social Security Benefits', form NI242 from your jobcentre or MSC office (see below).

Job sharing is already being used with great success by a few businesses. From the employer's point of view it means the job is always covered. If one person is ill or on holiday, the other partner in the team may be able to take over full-time.

Some of the individual employment rights and benefits do not apply to anyone working less than a certain number of hours per week. Before considering job sharing you should read: 'Job Splitting Scheme: What You Should Know about Working in a Split Job', Department of Employment (from your jobcentre or MSC office).

WORKING
FROM HOME

The advantages of working from home include the flexibility of being able to work when you want, the convenience that enables you to combine household responsibilities with work and the financial savings (no commuting costs, for instance).

The disadvantages include possible loneliness and the fact that no one might be responsible for you. Increasingly companies are, for instance, setting up computer terminals in employees' homes so that they can work 'out on a technological limb' and these home workers probably enjoy most of the benefits of their office colleagues. But there are other people who work at home – 'piece workers' who pack Christmas stockings or work in the garment industry, for instance – who are simply paid for the work they do and have no company emoluments.

Any home worker in the garment industry who thinks she is underpaid can contact the Wages Inspectorate (see below). Regardless of the work done, anyone with a problem can go to the nearest Citizens' Advice Bureau for help.

FREELANCING   Some women decide, after working in traditional office environments, deliberately to freelance. The advantages to the worker are as outlined above – and there are also advantages to others. Publishing houses may, for instance, save on overheads by employing a freelance designer and the customer saves time and money by having a freelance hairdresser come to her home.

The disadvantages to the freelance worker are stated above. It is also essential that the freelance continually 'touts for business'. She can never relax and forget about 'selling herself'. Word of mouth from satisfied customers may not suffice. In order to get enough business it is essential to keep up to date with new trends and products in your business, read any magazines which may be useful and to find out from others in your profession which advertisements have reaped business, and follow that advice.

Agents   Most actors and many writers work through agents (as, too, do those in some other professions). The agent does the selling of the client so she does not have to find her own projects. Getting an agent is rather a Catch-22 situation. It is sometimes difficult to get a good agent until you are well known and you cannot sometimes achieve that fame until you have been helped by a good agent ...

The agent gets business and collects all incomes. The agent's share (usually 10 per cent gross) is deducted and the money passed on to you. In return, the agent guarantees that you will deliver the goods, be they performing in a play or writing a book.

Having an agent should bring you business. It also means you can be friends with, say, your publisher without having to argue about money because all that is handled by the agent. If you are famous you can protect your privacy as everyone knows they can contact you via your agent.

Do make sure, however, you have a good agent. Ask friends in the profession whom they recommend.

RETRAINING   If you have not worked for some time, you might consider a refresher course.

● '*Cosmopolitan* Returners' Information Leaflet' gives details of colleges with returner programmes. It is available (s.a.e.) from *Cosmopolitan* (address on page 338).

● The *Manpower Services Commission* (MSC) is generally known for the Training Opportunities Scheme (TOPS) courses for both men and women. MSC is aware that women, especially those seeking to return to work after a period of domestic responsibility or those trying to enter non-traditional areas of work, may have special training needs that are not necessarily met by the standard TOPS division.

Among MSC's special programmes for women are the Wider Opportunities for Women (WOW) programmes, which are designed to meet the specific training needs of women who have decided to return to work (lack of confidence and skills, etc.). In the main, MSC prefers you to find out about courses via jobcentres, but you can also get details from a regional office, telephone:

Basingstoke	0256–29266
Birmingham	021–632 4144
Bristol	0272–291071
Cardiff	0222–388588
Edinburgh	031–225 8500
Leeds	0532–446299
London	01–836 1213
Manchester	061–833 0251
Newcastle	0632–326181

You can get details of WOW and other courses specifically for women and a publication list from (s.a.e.):

> Training Division
> Room W406
> Manpower Services Commission
> Moorfoot
> Sheffield S1 4PQ
> 0742–753275

WORKING IN A MAN'S WORLD

Geraldine Rees became the first woman to complete the gruelling Grand National when she rode Cheers in 1982. She feels that girls in this male-dominated sport have to prove themselves to be extremely tough and their ability often has to be well above average before they are given an opportunity.

Her special advice to would-be lady jockeys is:

- Get as much early experience (e.g. mucking out stables) as you can.
- Never be disheartened. Racing is a series of ups and downs.
- Complete dedication is necessary. There is not much time for other interests or social life.

Geraldine keeps fit by riding three lots of horses each morning and with as much swimming and skiing as possible. She does not have a problem keeping her ideal riding weight although as she loves food, especially chocolate, she restricts herself to high-fibre foods when she feels it is necessary.

She retains her femininity when riding by:

- always wearing pearl earrings
- although not having time to put on much make-up, she always has mascara, even when working in the yard
- if her hair gets untidy, she tucks it up into a jaunty peaked cap
- and, on racing days, she always tries to wear something (usually trousers) feminine.

EXECUTIVE STATUS

People at the top frequently, though not necessarily always, work much harder than others. And women who are there already have worked much harder than many men.

What is stopping *you* from going further? Remember, to a large extent you make your own 'luck'. If you want to get ahead you need to:
- formulate a plan
- boost your self-confidence
- look for promotion
- advertise your ability and achievements
- follow success.

It is essential to be continually on the lookout – for improving your experience and therefore your capabilities for new responsibility. Your company might have a well-organized programme specially designed to provide such education. If, on the other hand, you are not lucky enough to have such opportunities presented on a plate, you should consider taking a course.

- The Industrial Society runs regular programmes on management development, communications, personal marketing and women and money (some are run in conjunction with *Cosmopolitan*). For details of all the Industrial Society courses send a large s.a.e. to:

> Women's Management Development Courses
> Industrial Society
> 3 Carlton House Terrace
> London SW1Y 5DG
> 01–839 4300

or phone the Industrial Society in:

Scotland 041–332 2827
Central and West Region 0926–881261
(also covering Northern Ireland
and Wales)

- 'An Introduction to Assertiveness', a one-day course run by the Polytechnic of Central London. Details from:

> Short Course Unit
> Polytechnic of Central London
> 309 Regent Street
> London W1R 8AL
> 01–580 2020 ext. 233

- Henley Management College's residential management course lasts nine weeks. Details of this and other courses (and financial help available if required) from:

> Henley Management College
> Greenlands
> Henley-on-Thames RG9 3AU
> 049–166522

● 'More Time' is a results-management workshop showing you how to work more effectively, and thus achieve better results. The course is expensive – details from:

> More Time
> 10–14 Macklin Street
> London WC2B 5NG
> 01–242 1696

● Women in Management (WIM) is a voluntary group helping individuals to realize their career potential and persuading employers of the need to identify, develop and make use of the skills and talents of women, particularly in non-traditional areas. Membership of WIM is open to employers, individuals and anyone concerned with equal opportunities for women. A related concept, EM Courses, provides one-day and longer intensive courses on 'Building Personal Effectiveness', 'Secretarial Development' and similar topics. Details of both WIM and EM courses from:

> Mapledale Avenue
> Croydon
> Surrey CRO 5TA
> 01–654 4659

● If you work at a senior level and would like to meet women in different professions send s.a.e. to:

> Network
> 16 Percy Street
> London W1P 9FD
> 01–580 5773

(nationwide group with branches in London, Glasgow and Manchester)

> City Women's Network
> 58 Coleman Street
> London EC1R 6VE
> (no telephone)

(aimed primarily at those working in or near the City)

Working Woman, edited by Audrey Slaughter, is a new monthly glossy magazine for the businesswoman. Subscription details from:

> Working Woman
> 79 Farringdon Road
> London EC1M 3JY
> 01–430 0471

Good London clubs for businesswomen, which provide suitable meeting places, and are good 'bases' for those who are not always in London, are:

Consul Club (American Express cardmembers only)
4 Suffolk Place
London SW1Y 4HX
  01–839 1571

Institute of Directors
116 Pall Mall
London SW1Y 5ED
  01–839 1233

Maxim's
Panton Street
Haymarket
London SW1Y 4DL
  01–839 4809

WAGES In most cases pay is agreed between employer and employees or their representatives. For those employed in retail shops and stores (except chemists and butchers), catering (except canteens and boarding houses), hairdressing, clothing and toy manufacture and laundries (except dry-cleaning and self-service launderettes), wages are fixed by law.
● If you are employed in one of these professions and you think you have cause for complaint, or if you want to know to what money and holidays you are entitled, contact the Wages Inspectorate nearest you:

Wages Inspectorate
Red Lion Square
London WC1R 4NH
  01–405 8454

Birmingham	021–643 8191
Brighton	0273 23333
Bristol	0272 291071
Cardiff	0222–388 588
Edinburgh	031–443 8731
Glasgow	041–248 5427
Hemel Hempstead	0442 3714
Ipswich	0473 216046
Leeds	0532 438232
Manchester	061–832 6506
Newcastle upon Tyne	0632 327575
Nottingham	0602 417820

TRADE UNIONS One in three of all trade union members is a woman and the majority of new recruits are women. Membership of a union offers support. Some of the points that are campaign issues include:
● better training opportunities (women account for only 3 per cent of all apprentices, and many of these are in hairdressing)
● no sexual discrimination and the opportunity to do jobs that are

generally thought to be 'masculine' (at the time of writing 58 per cent of women in 'manual' jobs are doing hairdressing, cleaning and other personal service work and 55 per cent of women in 'non-manual' jobs are in clerical work)

● equal pay (women's average weekly earnings are only 66 per cent those of men)

● promotion possibilities

● better conditions for part-time workers (currently 41 per cent of all working women)

● nursery facilities (less than 1 per cent of under-fives currently have places in local authority nurseries)

● the plight of young black and Asian workers (although there is evidence to suggest that those who were actually born in Britain obtain higher level jobs than their parents)

● better conditions for part-time workers.

Trade unions are also specifically concerned that new technology could affect the role of the working woman. On the one hand, technology in some manufacturing has deskilled and downgraded some of the more skilled jobs done by women (e.g. quality control in food processing plants). On the other hand, however, new technology could revolutionize home working with a dramatic increase in the numbers using their homes as workplace – an important point to women with families.

If you want to know more about union membership, the Trades Union Congress (TUC) suggests you ask others at your workplace. If there is no union you can send details of the type of work you do to:

Trades Union Congress
Congress House
Great Russell Street
London WC1B 3LS
01–636 4030

How to Get a Job

JOB-FINDING SERVICES   THE INTERVIEW
APPLYING FOR A JOB

One of the best methods of making sure you get the job you really want is to have as many relevant qualifications as possible (if necessary, learn how to type).

Secretarial colleges help former students find jobs. Daily papers (especially *The Times*'s 'La crème de la crème'; the *Guardian*'s 'Creative and Media Appointments' on Mondays and the *Daily Telegraph*) advertise not only specific jobs but also agencies or recruitment consultants. Some of these include national chains of agencies.

JOB-FINDING
SERVICES

● Some agencies specifically deal with recognized professions. Graduate Appointments, for instance, helps recent graduates through five different divisions: accountancy, media, sales and marketing, secretarial and technology (marketing and public relations). Details from:

Graduate Appointments
7 Princes St
London W I R 7RB
01–629 7262

● Analysts and consultants assess the type and level of job which is most suitable for you and help with finding employment. Among the analysts offering specific help for those returning to work as well as potential first-time workers are:

Career Analysts
Career House
90 Gloucester Place
London W I H 4BL
01–935 5452

Independent Assessment and Research Centre
57 Marylebone High Street
London W I M 3 AE
01–486 6106

National Advisory Centre
on Careers for Women (NACCW)
Drayton House
30 Gordon Street
London WC I H 0AX
01–380 0117

Vocational Guidance Association
7 Harley House
Upper Harley Street
London NW I 4RP
01–935 2600

(Branches in Cheltenham, Glasgow, Liverpool, Manchester and Northampton).

● Graduates can contact the Association of Graduate Careers Advisory Services (AGCAS). You can contact the careers service of your university, college or polytechnic or:

AGCAS
Careers Service
The University
Leeds LS 2 9JT
0532–31751

● Capital Radio in London offers a free job-finding service for school and college leavers by telephone and in the foyer:

> Capital Radio Jobfinder Service
> Euston Tower
> Euston Road
> London NW I 3DR
> 01–439 2222

● *Cosmopolitan*'s 'Careers Advisory Service' will answer written queries. Contact them at:

> 72 Broadwick Street
> London W I

● The *Sunday Telegraph*'s 'Jobhunters' Information' covers specific openings in accountancy, banking, computing, engineering, executive recruitment, insurance and the city, law, medicine, nursing and allied professions, science, selling and sales management and working overseas. Each guide costs £1.30 post free (overseas orders add £1), cheques payable to the *Sunday Telegraph*, from:

> JobScope Jobhunters' Information
> WC99
> London WC I A I AA

● If you have specific questions you can write to (s.a.e.):

> *Daily Telegraph* Careers Information Service
> 121 High Street
> Berkhamstead
> Herts HP4 2DJ

● The newly established Women at Work Unit is building a unique databank of information on what jobs are available where and relevant statistics and features of the work involved. For further information contact:

> Women at Work Unit
> Department of Management Sciences
> UMIST
> PO Box 88
> Manchester M60 I QD
> 061–236 3311.

APPLYING
FOR A JOB

The basic contents of a job application letter (which should be typed) are as follows:

(date)

Dear Mr Smith,

I wish to apply for the position of personal secretary advertised in today's *Daily Telegraph*.

For the past five years I have been senior assistant to the director of public relations at Lees-Rice Ltd.

I am twenty-six years old. I have five O-levels and a City and Guilds Diploma in business studies. I am married with no children.

I look forward to hearing from you and, I hope, subsequently to talking with you.

Sincerely,

Notes

- When applying for a job, be short, sweet and accurate.
- Do not expound on your private life.
- Do not send a photograph of yourself.
- For details about layout, envelopes, forms of address and so on, see 'Letters', page 363.

THE
INTERVIEW

- Dress so that you feel comfortable. Do not wear brand-new clothes for the first time.
- Interviewers disagree on what are suitable clothes. Some like not being able to remember what the candidate was wearing – others prefer to bring dress into considering the candidate's overall suitability.
- Make sure you take with you:

(a) pens, pencils and paper

(b) copies of your *curriculum vitae* (c.v.) – this should be short, crisp and as full of impact as possible, it must be typed and clean

(c) names, addresses and telephone numbers of any referees

(d) any supporting material (publications, etc.). Have all the above suitably contained. Do not use a shopping bag or totebag. If you do not have a brief case or wallet buy a cardboard A4 wallet.

- Feel comfortable at the interview itself. If you are looking directly into the sun, either twist the chair slightly or ask if you can move. Sit comfortably, with your legs crossed if you feel more at ease (do not slouch or lean lazily over the back of the chair with your legs anyhow). Make sure your case or wallet is immediately to hand. Remember hands, eyes and legs all speak. Do not flirt. If you are nervous, say so at an opportune moment. Most interviewers are impressed by honesty.
- Selling yourself involves imparting maximum information in the minimum time. When you are asked why you want the job, say so honestly. You have of course rehearsed the gist of this many times in front of a mirror. When it comes to the actual delivery, the interviewers must be impressed by your spontaneity.
- Similarly, when asked about yourself, come up with a newsy personal verbal paragraph that does not repeat word for word the more formal content of your c.v.
- At lunch-, or other meal-time, interviews:

(a) Do not over-drink. A good maxim is to order what your interviewer has, and then sip only a small amount of it.

(b) If you never drink at all, say so and order a soft drink.

(c) When it comes to ordering food avoid anything that takes a long time

340 · YOUR JOB

to cook, anything that you have never eaten before and anything that is impossible to eat neatly (e.g. spare ribs in a sauce).

Again, a good maxim is to follow your interviewer. If he/she orders dessert, you do the same. Since it is difficult to eat and talk simultaneously try consciously to take only small bites of food at a time. Do not talk with your mouth full.

● Before you leave an interview, make sure you know what your job (if offered) would be, its promotional prospects, details about the company's pension, health and other responsibilities, any sports facilities, your holiday entitlement, travel potential (if relevant) and your salary and other 'perks'.

After an interview   Unless you have specifically agreed with the interviewer that he/she will get in touch, write a short letter as soon as you get back, telling the interviewer that you enjoyed talking, you very much want the job (if you do!) and you look forward to hearing from him/her. Send the letter first class.

If you are offered the job   Think carefully before accepting. Some points to bear in mind:
● Did you really like the prospect of the job itself?
● Were you impressed by everyone you met?
● Did people seem to like their work?
● Is the remuneration satisfactory?
● Is the future potential satisfactory?
● Do you have enough information to make a considered decision?

Working Mothers

HOW TO ORGANIZE YOUR LIFE   PREGNANCY AND WORK

I have no children; Diana Hastings, who has two, describes her experience of being a working mother:

I had my first child when I was twenty-nine and I stayed at home with her until she was two years old. Then I was offered my job back, on a part-time basis.

My husband was really supportive and encouraging and all seemed to be going well until a friend told me that my place was in the home, my child would suffer and so would my husband. I would never manage to keep a home and job working satisfactorily – one or both would suffer. Suddenly I felt guilty, and since then I have heard or sensed many people voice this opinion.

Before I went back to work I took my daughter to the day nursery and left her there, first for a couple of hours and then for an afternoon and eventually for the whole day. She loved it and it looked as though there were going to be no problems. On the first day of my job, I left her at the nursery screaming her head off. They had warned me that this might happen, and to take no notice of it, and she would soon settle, but I still sobbed all the way to the station and sat on the train to London Bridge with waves of guilt surging over me. As soon as I got to work I phoned the nursery, expecting to be asked to come and collect her. A cheerful voice said she had stopped crying as soon as I had left and she was thoroughly enjoying herself. Feeling totally drained of all emotion, I then started work.

Collecting my daughter in the afternoons was another problem. She would either burst into tears or become utterly unco-operative – but this soon stopped. She loved the company of the other children and attached herself very firmly to one member of staff and talked incessantly about her at home.

My daughter is now, incidentally, a very friendly outward-going child. It is difficult to tell whether this was her natural personality or whether it was helped by her social contact with so many children when she was young. I also went back to work again two years after the birth of my second child and the pattern was similar, except that I left her with a child-minder rather than in a day nursery.

● For suggestions about care of your child while you are at work, see Chapter 9.

HOW TO ORGANIZE YOUR LIFE

The better the organization of your own life at home and with your family, the more smoothly the entire operation of your going back to work will be.

Planning

Think of everything in terms of prior planning for smooth running.

● Make lists. Take a few moments daily to write down things that must, should, be done, on a daily, weekly and monthly basis. Things written down are more likely to be remembered, and therefore attended to. It is also extremely satisfactory to be able to cross out things as you do them.

● At a Woman of the Year lunch recently, Shirley Conran – superwoman *par excellence* – swore that her best friend was her all-purpose organizer file. It is always better to have all notes centralized. You can buy your choice of small ring wallet and whatever fillers you want – diary pages, address book, note sheets in various colours – from most stationery shops.

● Work carefully through your daily time schedule. Do you, for instance, at the moment spend an average of two hours a day on housework? Check that your allotment of time is realistic.

● Try not to rush at the beginning of the day. A quickly gulped cup of black coffee is not going to stand you in good stead for the rest of the day – and dirty dishes left on the table will look even more sordid when you come back at night.

● Similarly, try not to rush at the end of the day. Take time to think about what you are going to wear tomorrow and put everything out ready. Relax for a few minutes before going to bed. Good sleep is essential.

● Schedule time alone. You need it. This is your time to organize your life, and to 'catch your breath'.

● Schedule time with your partner and family. You need it – and they need it too.

● Schedule time for sport and exercise. Your body needs it.

● Try to decorate the house so that it is as easy to run as possible – washable paint on the walls and carpets which do not show marks, for instance.

● Organize the household so that everyone knows his/her job and/or schedule. This is where Shirley Conran's book *Superwoman* will undoubtedly help you – it is full of hints and tips for super-organization.

Give family members their own regular jobs but do not put too much pressure on them. Their time is valuable too. Remember, children sometimes love to help. Check the appliances you have and those you might think of buying (e.g. microwave oven, dishwasher). Is each time-saving, easy to manage, easy to clean, permanently available? See 'Electrical Appliances', page 435.

● Install a bulletin board in a central place with a 'master calendar', lists of telephone numbers, shopping lists and suggested errands.

● Use the telephone to your advantage. It saves time, and therefore money, to telephone rather than to go and see someone. It can similarly save time over letter-writing. Make sure all telephones have long extension cords or invest in a British Telecom approved cordless phone so that you can keep an eye on the cooking while you are on the phone. Have notepads and pencils by each instrument.

● Plan shopping trips beforehand so that you can do as many errands as possible on one journey. Try to plan what you are going to eat for a week at a time and shop accordingly. Keep up the stocks of basic items (toilet paper, soap, washing powder). It is a good idea to cook double the amount of some foods and freeze the remainder so that you do not have to spend precious hours slaving over a hot stove. Ask others' to help with errands, and wherever possible, shop from places that deliver or use mail order.

● Try to organize appointments (doctors and dentists) so that several members of the family go at once.

● Save time on the post. Look at mail only once. Discard anything that does not need a reply. Either respond to something that needs a reply immediately or file it, making a note to remind you to reply to it on a specific day.

● Do not over-stretch yourself outside your work and family. Do not take on outside commitments if they will take away from your family time.

● Remember that other family members' daily schedules will not necessarily be the same as yours. Make adequate arrangements for schoolchildren arriving home before you.

Working mother's organization   You will probably have to pay for good help to look after the children so you will need to be paid enough to cover this. Whether you leave your child in a nursery or crèche or have someone in your own home to look after the child, make sure you introduce them to the person who is going to look after them gradually. Give them time to get to know and like each other before you actually leave and go to work. When you leave, tell your child when you will be back – and make sure you are.

It is generally regarded (by the social services) as unsatisfactory if a child not yet in his teens is left in a house alone. If you are not back when your children come home from school and there is no friendly neighbour to look after them until your return, here are some ideas to help ensure their safety:

(a) they must go straight home and telephone you at work when they get in

(b) leave a spare key with a neighbour in case they lose theirs and make sure neighbours know they are on their own

(c) no cooking until you get home (leave them a snack and a friendly note)

(d) no friends to come around until you get home

(e) suggest that they do their homework as soon as they get home and you will look at it as soon as you get back – or, if they have a hobby, they could get on and do that and when you get home you will see what they have been doing. It is important to show an interest in the end product

(f) leave phone numbers for the doctor (and anyone else they could contact in an emergency) prominently by the telephone

Plan for school holidays a long time in advance. If you cannot yourself take enough holidays to cover school holidays:

(a) look around in plenty of time for someone who can look after your children

(b) ask at local colleges and schools for responsible students wanting to earn pocket money

(c) think about camps – like computer camps – for older children

(d) some areas have school schemes or holiday play schemes: contact your local authority or the social services for more information.

See 'Holiday Play Schemes' (50p) from:

> Scottish Community Education Council
> Atholl House
> 2 Canning Street
> Edinburgh EH3 8EG
> 031–229 2433

and Julie Kaufmann, *Self-help Day*, Gingerbread.

You cannot always take time off to be with sick children. Before the situation arises you should make contingency plans:

(a) make arrangements with a neighbour, relative or near friend

(b) contact a local nursing service

(c) ask your family doctor's advice.

PREGNANCY AND WORK

● NB. Other aspects of pregnancy are covered in chapter 7. Check with your doctor that there is no risk to your health in the work that you do. If there is it may be possible for you to change your work routine in some way.

Early in your pregnancy ask your personnel department about your maternity rights (see below). If you have worked for your present employer for two years at the time you are due to leave to have your baby you should be able to get maternity pay and maternity leave.

Try not to get overtired. If you do feel tired or unwell when you are at work talk to the nurse, supervisor or a union representative. It may be possible to arrange to lie down or put your feet up during the lunch break.

Make sure your posture is good. When standing try not to lean back. Stand up straight with your feet slightly apart. When you are sitting try not to slouch: put a cushion in the small of your back and sit up straight. It is important how you lift things when you are pregnant. Hold whatever you are lifting close to your body and lift by straightening your legs so that they do the work and not your back.

What you eat is important. You should be able to take nourishing food with you as a packed lunch or get suitable food in the canteen. Have a good breakfast before you go to work – both you and the baby need it. If you are suffering from morning sickness then leave more time in the morning to get up slowly. If you still feel sick when you get to work then tell someone and see if it is possible to sit down for a while.

When you get home try not to overdo things – if possible get some help with the housework. Go for a short walk if you can: it will help you unwind and relax and the exercise is good for you.

Normal healthy pregnant women give up work at about eleven weeks before the baby is due and from then on you can claim your maternity allowance – but the best thing is to ask your doctor for advice about when to give up work.

Your rights
- You have the right to take time off work to attend antenatal appointments and to be paid by your employer for it, whether you go to a hospital clinic or to your doctor's surgery. You have this right regardless of how long you have worked for your present employer (see leaflet EP4). You should give your employer plenty of notice about the appointment before. Get your appointment card stamped or signed.
- If you leave work earlier than eleven weeks before the expected birth you lose the right to have your job back again. Whether or not you want it back, you should tell your employer how long you intend to work.
- After the baby is born you can have your job back as long as you return within twenty-nine weeks of the week in which your baby was born and you have written to your employer at least three weeks before you went on leave telling him your intention.
- For more information about maternity leave go to your local jobcentre or employment office and ask for information concerning Employment Protection (leaflet no. 4).
- See also, 'Maternity Benefits', page 215.

Starting a Business

BEFORE YOU BEGIN   FINANCIAL ASPECTS
TERMINOLOGY

Three years ago Judith Davenport's fish company, Channel Foods, employed five members of staff; now they have seventy. The joy of winning an EEC grant was last year's reward; diversification from simple smoked mackerel into delicatessen pâtés and mousses is this year's project.

> It is an exciting growth business, full of character and smells! Its fascination stems from being the last 'hunting' food industry; fish, unlike cattle and corn, do not grow to order, do not stop in one place. There is always a fear that tomorrow the catch will no longer be there – as happened with herring off Scotland. There is an element of danger and chance that brings out the buccaneering spirit in this industry.

BEFORE YOU BEGIN

- Do you really want to start a business?
- Are you able to face risk and challenge without getting upset?
- Do you persevere when things go wrong?
- Are you healthy and strong enough to cope with the demands of your intended business?
- Are you, in all honesty, someone who does not tire easily?
- Do people seek your advice and do what you suggest?
- Will your family be supportive?

The answer to all the above should be 'Yes' before you explore further the viability of starting a business ...

Finding out about starting a business

1. Check the suitability of your intended business:
- Is there a market for it? Is the location right (is parking convenient, are there one-way streets, low bridges)?
- If you intend to work from home, is it easy to find? If you need casual sales (e.g. a furniture shop), what kind of customers can you expect to attract?
- What competition is there? Is your trade likely to be seasonal?
- What would happen in the case of a telephone strike, a postal strike or an electricity strike? Is your stock/equipment likely to be short-lived and to need updating?

2. Contact the government's Small Firms Service run by the Department of Trade and Industry. There are thirteen Small Firms Centres around Britain (Belfast, Birmingham, Bristol, Cambridge, Cardiff, Glasgow, Leeds, Liverpool, London, Manchester, Newcastle, Nottingham and Reading). There are also over eighty Area Counselling Offices at which experienced business people are available for consultation. To find out the centre nearest to you, telephone Freefone 2444. The information service is completely confidential and free – as is individual counselling if you are starting a business or in the first year of operation.

The Small Firms Service can help you with business efficiency and put you in touch quickly with the right people in local authorities, government departments and relevant professions. It also identifies national and international sources of information which you might need.

The headquarters of the Small Firms Service is:

> Small Firms Centre
> 2–18 Ebury Bridge Road
> London SW1W 8QD
> 01–730 8451

● Information for those in rural areas, whether running office-type businesses or small crafts-workshops, can be obtained from the Council for Small Industries in Rural Areas (COSIRA), an agency of the Development Commission. COSIRA can provide business management information and advice, technical advice and help with finance.

You can ask COSIRA for help if you live in a town with less than 10,000 inhabitants. To get in touch with the COSIRA organizer for your county contact the Small Firms Service (Freefone 2444) or COSIRA's head office:

> Council for Small Industries in Rural Areas
> 141 Castle Street
> Salisbury SP1 3TB
> 0722–336255

● Some local enterprise business centres also offer free advice and counselling. Those in the Hull area, for instance, can contact:

> Hull Business Advice Centre
> 24 Anlaby Road
> Hull HU1 2PA
> 0482–27266

and those in Devon can contact:

> East Devon Small Industries Group
> 115 Heathpark
> Honiton
> Devon EX14 8BR
> 0404–41806

For a detailed list see Colin Barrow, *The Small Business Guide*, BBC Publications.

● Information can also be obtained from:

Scotland

> Highlands and Islands Development Board
> Bridge House
> 27 Bank Street
> Inverness IV1 1QR
> 0463–234171

Scottish Development Agency
Small Business Division
Rosebery House
Haymarket Terrace
Edinburgh EH12 5EZ
031–337 9595

Northern Ireland   Industrial Development Board for Northern Ireland
64 Chichester Street
Belfast BT1 4JX
0232–233233

Wales   Small Business Unit
Welsh Development Agency
Treforest Industrial Estate
Pontypridd
Mid Glam CF37 5UT
044–385 2666

or any area office:
Bangor   0248–52606
Swansea   0792–586715
Wrexham   0978–61011

● Black people can contact:

Black Business Development Unit
Polytechnic of the South Bank
Manor House
58 Clapham Common Northside
London SW4 9RZ
01–223 8977

Read the following   Department of Health and Social Security publications:

NP15   'Employer's Guide to National Insurance Contributions'
N1208   'National Insurance Contribution Rates'
N141   'Guide for the Self-Employed'
NP18   'Class 4 Contributions'
N127   'People with Small Earnings from Self-Employment'

Department of Trade and Industry publications:
Maurice Gaffney, 'Running Your Own Business: Planning for Success'
L. A. Richard and T. J. Terry, 'Elements of Bookkeeping'
    'Starting Your Own Business: the Practical Steps'
Alexander Wilson and G. W. Lockhart, 'How to Start Exporting: a Guide
    for Small Firms'
In Business Now, a free newspaper available from: In Business Now,
    Freepost, London SW1P 4BR

Board of Inland Revenue publications:
'Starting in Business'
'The Business Expansion Scheme'

4. Courses on running your own business last from one day upwards. One-day courses in the City of London on the financial aspects of starting your own business are offered by the CASH Course (see page 50). Short courses are also available at the Industrial Society. Details (s.a.e.) from:

Industrial Society
3 Carlton House Terrace
London SWIY 5DG
01-839 4300

Longer courses are offered by the Manpower Services Commission: the New Enterprise Programme is designed specifically for people who are determined to set up a new business which has the potential to grow into a sizeable venture. The courses last sixteen weeks, at the business schools at the universities of Durham, Glasgow, London, Manchester and Warwick. All are sponsored by the MSC, which bears the full cost of the courses, including financial support for any family members. The Small Business Course caters for those who are interested in a more modest venture which will still employ others as well as themselves. Courses, usually about six to ten weeks long, are run for the MSC by universities and other bodies around the country.

See   'A Firm of Your Own: a Key to the Future' and 'Planning to Start Your Own Business', Manpower Services Commission.

Talk to   as many people as possible who have gone through the process of starting their own businesses (try to talk to some who have failed, and assess why they did not manage to succeed).

TERMIN-
OLOGY   **Business expenditure** – your accountant will be able to advise on what is justified. You will probably not be allowed to claim tax relief on business entertaining, the whole of the car and (if working from home) all your heating and telephone bills. See your accountant or tax inspector.

Capital expenditure – in broad terms, this is expenditure of which the benefit is not used up in the course of a year (by contrast, 'revenue expenditure' recurs year after year). Ask the tax inspector to give advice on capital expenditure (and ask him for pamphlet CA1, 'Capital Allowances on Machinery or Plant').

Franchising (business format variety) – this is the fastest-growing sector in the small business world: in the UK, franchises take only about 1 per cent of the retail market but in the US the figure is 6 per cent. To obtain a franchise (the right to sell someone's product or service) you pay a lump sum and/or royalty payments: in return, you should receive help in the form of advertising and expertise from the company concerned.

A list of potential franchise firms and what they do for those holding their franchises, as well as information about franchise consultancies, is set out in: Colin Barrow, *The Small Business Guide*, BBC Publications.

Before taking on a franchise you would be well advised to consult your bank manager, solicitor and any other financial and legal advisers. You may, also, be interested in taking a course in franchising:

Thames Polytechnic
School of Business Administration
Riverside House
Beresford Street
London SE18 6BH
01–854 2030

Lastly, anyone contemplating taking any type of franchise is strongly advised to contact the British Franchise Association – to whom, also, any complaints should be addressed.

British Franchise Association
Grove House
628 London Road
Colnbrook
Slough SL3 8QH
02812–4909

Limited company – as a legal entity separate from its members or shareholders it can sue and be sued. A limited company has limited liability. Advantages include a greater credibility with suppliers, and tax losses can be carried forward in case of change of activity. Disadvantages include the expense of setting up, the detailed record keeping required, the higher accountancy fees because of the requirement of audited accounts and the fact that capital gains can be taxed twice (once on capital gains and again when funds are paid out as dividends).

Your accountant or solicitor can incorporate a limited company for you but check first how much it will cost. For further information about setting up a company and on company registration agents who specialize in company formation (at a minimum of around £100) contact the Small Firms Business Service (Freefone 2444).

If you want to check whether a company name has already been used or if you need information on companies, directories are published by:

CBD Research
154 High Street
Beckenham
Kent BR3 1EA
01–650 7745

City Business Library
Gillett House
55 Basinghall Street
London EC2V 5BX
01–638 8215

See   'Seeking Company Information: United Kingdom Sources', Department of Industry.

Partnership – all partners share the profits and each is responsible for all the company's debts, not merely his or her investment in it. Similarly, each partner is responsible for tax demands if one or more partners fails to pay his/her share. Carefully consider various points before setting down in writing the amount of capital to be provided by each partner, each partner's role, the apportioning of each partner's share of profits/losses, the duration of the partnership, arrangements for arbitration, for bringing in new partners or getting rid of unsatisfactory ones, how the bank accounting is to be operated and what happens in case of death or serious accident or illness. A letter signed by all partners establishing all necessary requirements will suffice to set up a partnership.

Sole trader – the simplest form of business establishment. The sole trader enjoys the advantages of full control of business and all profits. There is no specific cost involved in being a sole trader.

Workers' co-operative – working together without forming a company or partnership. For information contact the Co-operative Development Agency (CDA). It is government sponsored and can give you advice – and pass you on to one of eighty local offices around the UK (the CDA does not have money to lend). Contact:

> Co-operative Development Agency
> 20 Albert Embankment
> London SE1 7TJ
> 01–211 4633

or their Belfast office: 0232–665368

or:

> Scottish Co-operative Development Committee (SCDC)
> Templeton Business Centre
> Templeton Street
> Bridgetown
> Glasgow G40 1DA
> 041–554 3797

> Wales Co-operative Development and Training Centre
> 55 Charles Street
> Cardiff CF1 4ED
> 0222–372237

FINANCIAL ASPECTS
● The Small Firms Service or others to whom you have talked will advise you on the possible financial pitfalls and legalities of starting your own business.
● Make sure you read the Board of Inland Revenue's pamphlet 'Starting in Business'.

- If you need a loan talk first to your bank manager. The Small Firms Service will also tell you about possible loan schemes. See also the Department of Industry's 'Loan Guarantees for Small Businesses: Guide for Applicants'.
- You should tell your tax inspector (complete and send him form 41G at the back of 'Starting in Business'). If you have given up previous employment, send him the form P45 given to you by your last employer.
- Consider engaging an accountant, but regardless of whether or not you are going to manage the accounts yourself, keep accurate and neat records of income and expenditure from the very start.
- You will probably find it easier to have a separate bank account. Talk to your bank manager.
- If you want to trade under a name other than your own, talk to your accountant or solicitor.
- National Insurance contributions:

(a) if you are self-employed you will probably pay a weekly flat-rate Class 2 contribution (NI stamps from the post office) and earnings-related Class 4 contributions (assessed at a percentage, about 6 per cent, of annual profits by the Inland Revenue – see leaflets NI41 and NP18)

(b) if you are still working for someone else at the same time, you will also be liable for Class 1 contributions (see NP18).

- You need a good address to be shown to be doing a good job. It is not professional to be selling computers from 'Chez Nous'. It is professional to be offering your service from a post office box (ask at your post office – it costs under £1 a week and protects your anonymity, although anyone can find your exact address if they go to the post office to ask). Or rent office services from a reputable organization.
- For details of competitions for enterprising small and new businesses and other incentives, look at 'Your Own Business – Briefing' in *The Times*.

Useful contacts

- The Alliance of Small Firms and Self-Employed People gives its members advice and information on a wide range of matters. Contact:

> Alliance of Small Firms
>   and Self-Employed People
> 42 Vine Road
> East Molesey
> Surrey KT8 9LF
>   01–979 2293

- The Institute of Small Business publishes many useful periodicals:

> Institute of Small Business
> 13 Golden Square
> London WIR 4AL
>   01–437 4923

- If you are a director of your company, you can get information and advice from (and belong to the club of):

Institute of Directors
116 Pall Mall
London SW1Y 5ED
01–839 1233

● If you have an idea and want someone to develop it – or vice versa –
contact:

Ideas and Resource Exchange (IREX)
Snow House
103 Southwark Street
London SE1 0JF
01–633 0424

● If you want to meet other executive women, see Network, page 334.

Problems at Work

Not everyone is happy at work. Are you being unfairly treated?
● If you are in or out of work and if you have any problems (unfair
treatment, sexual discrimination, doubts about pay, etc.) you can contact
the Inquiry Point of the Advisory, Conciliation and Arbitration Service
(ACAS) nearest you:

Advisory, Conciliation and Arbitration Service
11–12 St James's Square
London SW1Y 4LA
01–214 6000

Birmingham	021–643 9911
Bristol	0272 211921
Cardiff	0222–762636
Glasgow	041–204 2677
Leeds	0532–431371
Liverpool	051–427 8881
Manchester	061–228 3222
Newcastle upon Tyne	0632–612191
Nottingham	0602–415450

● For information if you think you are being *badly paid* contact:

Low Pay Unit
9 Poland Street
London W1V 3DG
01–437 1780

● If you think there is *racial discrimination* involved contact:

Commission for Racial Equality
Elliot House
10–12 Allington Street
London SW1E 5EH
01–828 7022

● For *sexual discrimination* see Chapter 5.
● Complaints from individuals that employers have broken the law about unfair dismissal, sex discrimination or equal pay (or other matters) are heard by *industrial tribunals*.

If you think you have cause for complaint you can contact your local Citizens' Advice Bureau. Or send a completed complaint form (obtainable from a jobcentre or from an unemployment benefit office) to:

Central Office of the Industrial Tribunals
    (England and Wales)
93 Ebury Bridge Road
London SW1W 8RE
    01–730 9161

or

Central Office of the Industrial Tribunals
    (Scotland)
St Andrew's House
141 West Nile Street
Glasgow G1 2RU
    041–331 1601

Unemployment

REDUNDANCY   DISMISSAL

REDUNDANCY   This happens when your job disappears: your firm may close down altogether or your particular role is no longer needed. (Note, being sacked for sub-standard work is not the same as being made redundant.)

You should be able to claim redundancy payment if you have worked:
● a minimum of two years (104 weeks) in a job for at least sixteen hours a week or
● a minimum of five years (260 weeks) in a job with the same employer for at least eight hours a week.

You cannot claim if you are over sixty, self-employed, doing domestic work for close relatives or if you were employed by your spouse or in certain jobs.

How would you cope if you were made redundant? This is how Janet Drummond (who now runs her own successful promotions company) felt:

Disbelief, bitterness, anger, helplessness, fear of the future, grief . . . should you suddenly become unemployed you will undoubtedly feel some, or all, of these emotions. However the redundancy comes about it is hard not to feel *personally rejected*.

Grief is the most important emotion to work through. You have lost something very important in your life. *Do* grieve – in private, and for a limited period only. *Don't* waste time or energy on bitterness and anger – that is negative and you need positive energy to work on your unknown future.

Other moods will follow in the days and weeks following your departure – lack of self-worth (you may find yourself afraid of social gatherings as well as job interviews), loneliness (you will miss all your former work colleagues so keep in touch with them and other friends as much as possible). You may have a vague feeling that the world is still busy revolving and you are not. Your depression may make you lethargic and getting up in the morning when you have nowhere to go will be difficult.

Jenny Kirkpatrick, General Secretary of the National Association of Probation Officers, says, 'Many people are more affronted by unemployment among young men than young women. Society believes men "deserve" work and that women "take it from the men" and the problem becomes more acute with someone even slightly older.'

It all sounds very depressing but it can be exhilarating. Draw on your resources of self-discipline and self-motivation. Your work now is to plan your new life, so draw up a schedule. Make action lists – and use them. Keep busy job hunting or starting a new business (do not spend your time mowing the lawn, taking the dog for a walk or having endless cups of coffee or something stronger). It will be rough but ultimately tremendously rewarding.

You can beat redundancy – do not let it beat you!

Help

● As soon as you are informed of redundancy, you should go your unemployment benefit office and ask for leaflet RPL (redundancy payment leaflet) and P45 (income tax form). If you need help, ask your union representative or Citizens' Advice Bureau. See also CAB's leaflet, 'What to Do about Redundancy'.

● You will be advised by the jobcentre or unemployment office if you qualify for any special training schemes. If you want information on rent and rate rebates ask your local Housing Office. (Note: if you are buying property on a mortgage it is a good idea to let your Building Society know as soon as possible.)

● Talk to those around you. Share your feelings but do not become a bore. Let people know you are looking for work.

● Consider taking a MSC course.

DISMISSAL

Dismissal means you have been 'sacked'. Your employer has terminated your employment with or without notice. You are also dismissed if a fixed-term contract is not renewed or if your employer refuses to allow you to return to work after you have had a baby, assuming you have taken all the correct legal steps (see page 137).

Reasons for fair dismissal include redundancy and reasons relating to the employee's conduct or qualifications for the job. Reasons for unfair dismissal include discrimination, trade union membership or activities or non-membership of a trade union.

If you think you have been unfairly dismissed, apply to your industrial tribunal (see 'Industrial Tribunals' in Chapter 5). This application must be made within three months of leaving work. If they rule that you have been dismissed unfairly, you will be reinstated (treated as if dismissal had never happened), re-engaged or you will be awarded compensation.

If you need further information, go to your local Citizens' Advice Bureau or contact your nearest office of ACAS (see page 137). See also: 'Unfairly Dismissed?' from the Department of Employment.

For information on mature re-employment contact:

> Recall
> Leatherhead Institute
> Surrey KT22 8AH
> 0372 379093

Further Information

Suggested further reading

ORGANIZATION
Conran, Shirley, *Superwoman*, Penguin
   Superwoman in Action, Penguin
  and Elizabeth Sidney, *Futurewoman*, Penguin
Garner, Lesley, *How to Survive as a Working Mother*, Penguin

STARTING YOUR OWN BUSINESS
Barrow, Colin, *The Small Business Guide*, BBC Publications
de Bono, Edward, *Opportunities: a Book of Business Opportunities*, Penguin
Consumers' Association, *Starting Your Own Business*
Kinnaird, Hugh, *How to Be Your Own Boss*, Blackwell

WOMEN AT WORK
Aldred, Chris, *Women at Work*, Pan
Gill, Tess and Larry Whitty, *Women's Rights in the Workplace*, Penguin
Huws, Ursula, *Your Job in the Eighties: a Woman's Guide to the New Technology*, Pluto Press
Jones, Brenda, *Cosmopolitan's Guide to Getting Ahead*, Cosmopolitan
Lewenhak, Sheila, *Women and Work*, Fontana
Montague, Anne and Amanda Webb, *More Careers*, Observer
O'Malley, Mary, and others, *Sweatshop: a Woman's Guide to Self-Employment*, Friday Publications
TUC, 'Working Women: a TUC Discussion Book for All Trade Unionists'

UNEMPLOYMENT
Coyle, Angela, *Redundant Women*, Women's Press
Melville, Joy, *A Survivor's Guide to Unemployment and Redundancy*, Corgi
Nathan, Robert and Michel Syrett, *How to Survive Unemployment*, Penguin

12 Some Etiquette Points

Etiquette is not 'how to mind your Ps and Qs'. To most of us it is how to write a letter, answer the telephone and do things in a way that does not embarrass other people.

Etiquette is also how to give good parties. Nothing should irk – a good party, indeed, is generally judged by the absence of anything that goes wrong and that statement applies equally to a casual supper for two and to a formal wedding.

Here are the tips and ideas you need for etiquette in the 1980s.

Entertaining

PARTIES As party-giver Diana May says, 'In the legal sense, there are two parties to every party: there is the giver of hospitality and the taker and both should fulfil their "contract", as embodied in the invitation, to the best of their ability. The host must follow up an invitation with a decent standard of hospitality. A guest has, by being paid the honour of receiving an invitation, certain obligations such as replying, turning up, acting cheerfully and saying thank you.

The host should strive for a mixture of people she really likes. In general – unless it is a ladies' lunch – it is a good idea to have a balance of gender, interests and backgrounds. Whether a formal dinner party with a particular number at places allocated round a table or a larger, more informal, buffet, the fun of the party will be the spontaneous relationships that emerge between various people.'

Invitations Invitations are often verbal these days, but there are good reasons for maintaining written arrangements, printed or handwritten. It allows formality and it means the recipient can consider the request (do you really want to go or not?). You can consult with your partner and look at your diaries – and, if necessary, assemble your excuses. Written invitations with telephone numbers are useful as they can be left with the baby-sitter (but, if you are the guest, remember to take your invitation with you if there are travel details on it).

In general, if you receive a formal printed invitation you should reply in similar vein.

● 'Mr and Mrs John Smith request the pleasure of the company of Miss Jane Bloggs' requires a 'Miss Jane Bloggs thanks Mr and Mrs John Smith . . .' reply.

● 'Ann Smith is having a party' (with 'Jane' handwritten at the top) requires a 'Jane is delighted to come to Ann's party' reply.

A telephone invitation is generally answered at the time. If you have to check with your partner or there is some other reason why you cannot answer immediately, it is courteous to telephone back as soon as you can.

Refusals A telephone or face-to-face invitation may be particularly embarrassing. If you genuinely do not want to go, what do you say? It is better to be firm now than be embarrassed later. Let the host down now, gently but firmly, by explaining that your husband is busy or that you have a holiday coming up and you have so much to do.

Adult parties **Breakfast**
Breakfast parties should generally be avoided except as a rare event and unless you know that everyone you are inviting at least has one eye open in the morning, or you hold it at a civilized starting hour on a Sunday morning. Breakfast parties should not be confused with 'brunch', the amalgam of breakfast and lunch; brunch parties can sometimes continue throughout the day.

Lunch
This is a good way to entertain friends. It is not as time-consuming as dinner and need not necessarily involve lots of drinks. This is a good time to gossip, albeit briefly. Pubs provide inexpensive good food.

Dinner
These are usually mixed parties – they can be expensive and time-consuming but conversations should be worthwhile and people will remember the occasion.

It is a good idea to tell guests beforehand:

● What time they are meant to turn up (an invitation for 8 p.m. can mean precisely that in some parts of the country, but 8.30 to 9 in London).

● What to wear ('casual' is not enough – it can mean anything from black tie to sweater and jeans and is much harder on the men than on the women).

● Who else is going to be there (so that guests can do their homework).

Drinks
There are two sorts of drinks parties:

● Small intimate groups which are a good way of getting to know new acquaintances – everyone should have the chance to sit down.

- Large 'have to have them' occasions to which a few friends might be invited to 'help out' – although such an invitation is not doing anyone a favour and your friends will not thank you for being invited to 'put some life' into the event.

A drinks party is less expensive than dinner. As an indication:

- I bottle of sherry serves about 12 glasses
- I bottle of whisky serves about 20 tots
- I bottle of wine (70 cl) serves about 6 glasses.

Remember, too, to have more than adequate supplies of mixers for parties: people may prefer to drink the mixers on their own.

Children's parties These are a special issue – and whole books have been written about them. Basically the rules of hospitality are the same and children should learn them early on.

Have the party at home. It is so much more fun than just going to a hamburger bar, however flashy their giveaways. If you are desperate, hire a proper children's entertainer (consult friends or the Yellow Pages).

A little thought can produce a list of workable games. A theme is a great thing as it makes the party special. It can be carried through invitations, optional fancy dress, table decorations and take-home favours.

Some ideas to try include:

- 'colour' party (say, all in red)
- rainbow party
- space party
- tramps' ball (arrange for fish and chips to be brought in for everyone to eat from the bags)
- witches' feast.

ORGANIZA-
TION
You, as host, have invited your guests and you know how many are coming. If you are still waiting to hear from people, check whether or not they are coming – and remind anyone likely to forget.

Preparation Work out your finalized menu and prepare a shopping list – long term (dry goods) and last minute (fresh meat and vegetables). Aim to cook ahead if you can and freeze some things.

Make lists of things to do (flowers, housework). Do potatoes the night before and soak in cold water with some milk added. Check what you are going to wear. Set the table in plenty of time.

On the day, remember to allow plenty of extra time in case an old friend calls for a long chat or you have to remake a mousse (the failed one will do for leftovers tomorrow night). Try to be ready at least fifteen minutes before your guests are expected in case they come early.

Serving If you stand and 'present' food, it should be presented from behind the left of each guest and cleared from the right. Drink should be poured from the right of each guest. Port is always passed clockwise – some people like to try not to let it touch the cloth as it goes around.

The leading hotel school in Lausanne describes ways of serving food as follows:

American style – 'plated', with each person's food brought from the kitchen already on the plate

English style – the dish is presented to the host who then serves everyone else

French style – the dish is presented to the host, who serves himself, and thereafter to each guest

Russian style – everything is brought to the table on serving platters and served by a waiter to each guest individually.

Clearing Some people 'scrape and stack' (noisily scrape and pile used plates one on top of another) at home and even in public. If you do this in private, try to avoid doing it at the table when you have guests as it offends many people (particularly Americans). It is a simple matter to stand up and carry each plate at least away from the table (say to a sideboard) before stacking. If there are several guests someone will probably offer to help you.

TABLE SETTINGS Nothing looks nicer than a suitably dressed table. It should be the right height and size, and the chairs should be comfortable and the right height. The lighting should be neither too bright nor too dim and the table should be set attractively (with cloth, or mats, and napkins, salt, pepper and butter if required, centrepiece, china, all cutlery set exactly in military precision).

Colour This is important. White cloths, white napkins and white china with no colour relief is formal and cold. Try to give some inviting warmth to the table (e.g. some bright flowers to act as contrast). Think of the colour of the cloth or mats, the napkins, the centrepiece and the china. Since the food is not always on the table at the start of the meal, try not to rely on the food to provide the only colour.

As with clothing, do not introduce too many colours. Try to limit 'obvious colours' to a maximum of two. If you have a yellow cloth and your china is predominantly blue patterned, do not have central flowers unless they are white, or the same shade of yellow or blue.

Try for variety. Make each meal slightly different. Do not bore yourself, your household and your guests with the same setting meal after meal. You might not have different china. You can change the colour of cloth, napkins (especially if they are paper) and centrepiece from meal to meal. Try changing the entire centrepiece so that variety is achieved through colour and shape and content: try switching from lunch's central flowers to supper's central bowl of fruit. Variety can be achieved by the smallest alteration: tying a differently coloured length of wool around napkins, as makeshift napkin 'holders', changes a table setting.

Cloth or mats. This is a matter of preference. The beautifully ironed white damask cloth has an unsurpassed elegance but it is impractical for everyday. If you do choose a table cloth it is a good idea to make sure it completely covers the table and that table mats, if used, are placed on top of the cloth only if they are complementary (do not put patterned mats on top of a checked cloth). The cloth itself must be spotlessly clean and in good condition.

Table and place mats should be spotlessly clean and in good condition. Do not use an odd assortment of mats. Place mats too should be large enough to hold the entire setting so that knives placed outside the mat do not 'rock' on the table underneath.

Napkins. Today, paper napkins are generally thoroughly acceptable – and definitely preferable from a hygiene point of view unless you can afford to launder fabric napkins after each meal. It must be admitted, though, that disposable paper napkins are uneconomic for a large family. Try, if possible, to buy several-ply soft tissue napkins rather than the 1-ply harder paper variety. Budget-minded shoppers will appreciate that supermarkets and chemists have good-value large packs of table napkins. 'Seasonally decorated' napkins can sometimes be purchased at a discount after the holiday concerned.

Centrepiece. This really livens up a table. Make sure it is not too tall as people want to be able to see across the table. Some ideas for central decorations include candles, flowers, fruit bowl.

Condiments. These include salt and pepper and butter or margarine. It is obviously preferable not to put the original containers on the table and if you want to limit the amount of fat taken, people help themselves to more butter or margarine if a larger amount is placed in front of them than if it is put out on small dishes.

Place settings
If there is more than one course, you are doing your guests a favour by putting all cutlery out before the meal starts. It is embarrassing, as a guest, to sit down to what looks like only one course so you have a large second helping – only to find another four courses are to be brought on, with their different utensils.

Check that each place setting is conveniently placed to its neighbours.

Make sure that each place setting has:

- mat (if used)
- butter plate (if used), to left or upper left of where main plate will go
- first course plate (if put out before meal starts)
- napkin (placed on butter plate, on mat or in glass)
- cutlery
- glass or glasses, to upper right hand of where main plate will go.

Do a final check that:

- all cutlery is placed exactly, with vertically placed items exactly vertical and horizontally placed items exactly horizontal
- all china, if patterned, is placed with pattern facing the person

- all place settings are complete and identical.

For a simple supper each person might need a knife, fork, and soup spoon. For a more complicated dinner, each person might need a butter knife, a knife, fork, dessert fork, dessert spoon. If you are a guest, start from the outer utensils and work inwards (or watch what your host does).

Help If you want to learn more about table etiquette, contact:

> Ivor Spencer's School for British Butlers
> 12 Little Bournes
> Alleyn Park
> London SE21 8SE
> 01–670 5585

RESTAURANT ENTERTAINING

If you are the host, try to get to the restaurant first. If you are entertaining a man let the head waiter know that it is you who are the host. If you are seated at a table that has one 'banquette' (sofa) seat and one ordinary chair, suggest that the person who has the most baggage (e.g. umbrella, pile of books) take the banquette seat.

You, as host, should be in a position to attract the waiter's eye. When the menu comes check carefully to see if service is included (if you ask the waiter at the end of the meal he will invariably say 'no' even if it is). It is a good idea to give your guest some idea of what you are going to have to eat.

Do not be afraid to tell the waiter or the restaurant manager if your meal is too slow coming or if there is something wrong. If you need more wine poured and you cannot reach for the bottle, ask for it. Do not be 'loud' but do not be a 'mute presence'. You will get much better treatment on this visit and on future meals if you show confidence.

Try to avoid having the bill brought to you at the table. It is difficult to check each item while talking to your guest. At a suitable time excuse yourself from the table and go over to the cashier.

If there is any error in the bill and you need to discuss the matter, be honest and suggest your guest go on his way so that you can argue it out in peace.

OVERNIGHT GUESTS

The problem of tradition really only comes to the forefront when you have people staying. What happens in the bedroom?

A good maxim is never assume that people want to share a room. Just because John and Jane appear to have been good friends for years it does not mean that they want to share a small (and perhaps lumpy) double bed in your house. On the other hand you should not embarrass them by turning out of your bed so that one of them can have it.

Honesty is the best solution. No one today would be shocked by being asked, outright, where they would like to sleep. If you cannot ask one of the guests tactfully beforehand, offer alternatives when they arrive: 'There is a double bed in there – and the sofa downstairs is very comfortable. What would you prefer?'

Note   ● If your daughter brings home her new boyfriend, do not ask her outright. It is up to her to decide if she wants to sleep alone, but you should be aware that, even if she does seemingly go to her own room, she can also tiptoe where she wants once you have gone to bed and you simply cannot impose regulations.

BEING A   If you are not sure about dress, ask. If in doubt, remember to dress 'under'
GUEST   rather than 'over'. Find out what time you are really required and try to arrive on time.

Try to remember your table manners. Do not talk with your mouth full (take small mouthfuls so that if you are asked a question there is not an embarrassing pause while you swallow). If asked if you would like a second helping and you would, say so.

If you are stuck at a party with the most boring person around:
● Pretend you have seen an old friend in the middle of 'that crowd over there'.
● Be quite honest – say you both need to talk to some other people.
● Say you have to rush for the lavatory.
● Or (if you are ruthless) grab the nearest passer-by, introduce him or her to the bore and melt away quickly.

If you spill something:
● Do not try to cover the spill up – if it is serious enough the host will find out later who did it.
● Immediately admit what has happened and see if you can do anything about it.
● If they say you cannot do anything do not get in the way and pester.

If you are staying overnight, either find out what time roughly you are expected both to arrive and depart or let the host know your expected times (and days). Try to stick to both arrival and departure within an hour or so.

Staying overnight in someone else's house is an intrusion into their private life. Someone you know quite well by evening can be very different in the morning. If you are a night owl do not assume your host is: if everyone else looks tired excuse yourself and carry on being lively in the privacy of your own room.

Before you go to bed, find out what time breakfast is and what it will consist of: if you eat a big breakfast and you are in a 'make a cup of coffee when you feel like it' household, ask – the night before – if you can prepare cereal 'or something' in the morning. And, in the morning, do not talk to your hosts over the breakfast table unless it is obvious they like conversation at that hour.

Find out what your host likes done with the sheets. In the past all good house-guests in homes with no servants neatly folded all bedding military style. Nowadays many hosts prefer beds 'to be pulled up' or 'left'. Ask.

If you are staying any length of time – one night or more – expect to amuse yourself but always find out what time you will next be expected 'on parade'. Do not go wandering off for a long walk without warning.

Thank yous   All overnight guests should write (see 'Letters' below). A written note after a dinner or lunch is always appreciated – and in some cases is still obligatory.

INTRO-DUCTIONS

Diana May, a friend who knows a lot about etiquette, suggests that rather than concentrating on who is introduced to whom, the introducer should remain unflustered, make sure the names are correct and are given clearly, so that they can be heard by everyone concerned. If it is a mass introduction, gesticulate gracefully as you mention an appropriate name or politely say, 'Do you mind if I go round the circle?' if you are introducing late-comers to an already assembled group.

You generally introduce a man to a woman ('Mrs Jones, this is Mr Smith') and, if the same sex, junior to senior ('Father, this is John Smith').

If necessary, introduce yourself – if in doubt, hold your hand out and say your name, clearly but not too loudly. If you have already met someone, remind him of your name (if he has already remembered it he will not mind the second introduction – if he has not remembered your name he will be heartily relieved that you have saved him embarrassment). *Never* assume that others have remembered your name.

Letters

HOW THEY SHOULD LOOK   **LETTERS FOR ALL OCCASIONS**
OPENING AND CLOSING

HOW THEY SHOULD LOOK

Format

All business correspondence should have the sender's address and other contacts (telephone, with dialling code, and telex if relevant) clearly at the top of the paper. Where all this is sited is a matter of design choice. If you have the details printed it should be done well: a well-typed address on good quality paper looks more professional than smudgy printing on cheap paper.

Personal correspondence can also be written on printed ('headed') paper. If you are writing on a plain sheet make sure your address and telephone number are clearly written at the top of the first page.

Envelopes

These should be clearly written. Remember, the postman starts reading from the bottom line up.

How you address the envelope reflects your opener inside:
- A 'Dear Sir' inside becomes 'The Editor of the Dalkeith Daily' on the envelope.
- A 'Dear John Smith' is, outside, 'John Smith Esq.' or, increasingly, 'Mr John Smith' or 'John Smith'. It is now generally thought that 'Esq.' is pretentious and should be reserved only for lawyers; you should also note

that if you are writing to someone overseas 'Esq.' might not be recognized, the letter could be filed under 'Esq.' and never reach the intended recipient.

● Similarly, Ann Doe's envelope is addressed to 'Mrs John Doe', 'Ms Ann Doe', 'Miss Ann Doe' or 'Ann Doe', reflecting how you have addressed her inside.

Typed or handwritten?

If possible, type job applications and all business letters (including complaints) on one side of the paper only. If you cannot type, at least write clearly. If you type personal letters it is a good idea to write opener and closer by hand.

Do not type letters of condolence or thank you notes or Christmas cards.

OPENING AND CLOSING

The date should be clearly written at the top of the letter. How you start the letter itself is a matter of choice:

● Business letters often start with a formal 'Dear Sir' or 'Dear Madam'. Some people prefer to write to those they do not know personally with a 'complete name' opener, e.g. 'Dear John Smith' or 'Dear Ann Doe'.

● Do not presume and open 'Dear John' unless you *do* know him.

● If he is in the army and you do not know his rank, better to be up than down.

● If you know Ann Doe is married and working under her husband's name you can address her as 'Mrs Doe'. If she is married but Doe is her professional name you can address her as 'Miss Doe'.

● If you do not know whether Doe is her married name or not better simply to address her as 'Dear Ann Doe', as 'Ms' sometimes offends.

Closing a letter is less complex. Most people have their own preferred ending of 'Yours faithfully', 'Yours sincerely', 'Sincerely' or 'Yours'. It does not really matter much today which you use.

● If you are writing formally, you have a choice of 'Yours faithfully' (most formal), 'Yours sincerely' or 'Sincerely' (which covers everything from most formal to quite friendly).

● If you are writing on business to a man or woman you know, 'Yours' is more personal than 'Sincerely'.

● If you are writing to someone you really know well and who is roughly your age, a simple 'Love' or 'With love' is becoming increasingly popular. Use of 'Love' implies a confidence on the part of the sender.

● If you are writing to someone you know well who is in a different age group, 'Affectionately' or 'Fondly' cover most eventualities. You should then sign your whole name (more formal) or your Christian name (less formal). Do not, under any circumstances, sign yourself 'Mrs John Doe'. If your signature is illegible, clearly type or write your name beneath the scrawl ('Ann Doe'). Put 'Ann Doe, Mrs' if the recipient does not know you.

Note

● It is presumptuous to assume that the recipient knows who 'Mary' is. Give some indication such as 'Mary (Brown)'. The same applies to Christmas cards – unless you have an unusual name.

Specific and realistic forms of address

With reference to:

The *Queen* (or the *Duke of Edinburgh* or the *Queen Mother*) – address the envelope to 'The Private Secretary to Her Majesty The Queen', etc.

A *royal prince* – address the envelope to 'His Royal Highness, The Prince Charles, Prince of Wales' (or whichever) and open the letter with 'Your Royal Highness'.

A *royal princess* – address the envelope to 'Her Royal Highness, The Princess of Wales' (or whichever) and open the letter 'Your Royal Highness'.

A *royal duke* – address the envelope to 'His Royal Highness, The Duke of Timbuctoo' and open the letter with 'Your Royal Highness'. Address his duchess in similar form.

A *duke* – address the envelope to 'His Grace, The Duke of Somewhere' and open the letter with 'Your Grace', 'Dear Duke of Somewhere' or 'Dear Duke'. Address his duchess in similar terms and address his mother with an envelope reading 'The Dowager Duchess of Somewhere' or 'Gloria, Duchess of Somewhere' (this is a personal choice) and open the letter as for a duchess.

A *marquess* – address the envelope to 'The Marquess of Mummerset' and open the letter with 'My Lord Marquess'. Address his marchioness in similar terms.

An *earl* – address the envelope to 'The Earl of Gloriousness' and open the letter with 'Dear Lord Gloriousness'. Address his countess in similar terms.

A *viscount* – address the envelope to 'The Lord Discretion' and open the letter with 'Dear Lord Discretion'. Address his viscountess in similar terms.

A *baron* – address the envelope to 'The Lord Facit' and open the letter with 'Dear Lord Facit'. Address his wife in similar terms.

A *baronet* – address the envelope to 'Sir Thomas Thumb, Bart' and open the letter with 'Dear Sir Thomas'.

A *knight* – address the envelope to 'Sir Andrew Aguecheek' and open the letter with 'Dear Sir Andrew'. Address his wife as 'Dear Lady Aguecheek'.

A *married woman* – 'Mrs Jones', 'Mrs Ann Jones' or (in some circles) 'Mrs John Jones' on the envelope: open with 'Dear Mrs Jones'.

A *divorced woman* – 'Mrs Ann Jones', or whatever name she is now using, on the envelope: 'Dear Mrs Jones', or whatever name she is now using, inside.

A *widow* – it is now increasingly a matter of personal choice. If you do not know whether she still wishes to retain her husband's name as 'Mrs John Jones' address her as 'Mrs Jones'.

LETTERS
FOR ALL
OCCASIONS

Business

Whatever the reason for a business letter, how it looks is all-important. Follow all the guidelines above. Typical basic contents are:

(date)

Dear Mr Smith

As Director of Fantastia Flores Ltd, you must be aware of the great potential interest in your products among typical housewives in rural areas.

I am in charge of Tarrant Hinton's annual garden fete to be held 23 July 1985. We anticipate printing about 5,000 brochures about this event and there will be at least 10,000 related posters and handouts.

Would Fantasia Flores like to join in this important opportunity and have their name exclusively on the cover of each brochure and on each flier?

May I telephone your secretary on [ten days hence] to make an appointment to come and see you?

Sincerely

Notes
- Make it short, pleasant and accurate.
- Make him feel good.
- The ball is in your court – you will telephone in ten days' time but that is long enough for him to come back to you with an immediate no.
- Job applications are dealt with in Chapter 11.

Complaints

(date)

Dear Locks Grocery Store

I wish to complain most strongly that the enclosed packet of Cleany washing tissues has – as you can see – only 21 tissues instead of the advertised 'average 35'.

I look forward to hearing from you within the next few days. You can reach me at the telephone number at the top of this letter every day after 11 a.m.

I trust I shall not be forced to take this matter further.

Sincerely

Notes
- Be firm and to the point.
- Tell the recipient where you can be reached and when.
- Give a deadline for an answer (in this case, in 'the next few days').
- Indicate that you know your rights and will not hesitate to take the matter further.

Condolences

(date)

Dear Mrs Green

I just want to let you know how shocked and sorry I am to hear of Dr Green's death.

He was always so kind to me – just an ordinary patient with whom he always had time to chat about our mutual interest in budgerigars. He was a very special person. It was an honour to have known him.

Please do not answer this. My thoughts are with you at this time.

Sincerely

Notes
- Must be handwritten.
- Short, sweet and with a personal remembrance.
- Make it clear that you do not expect a reply.

Thanks

1. *After hospitality*

(date)

Dear Mrs MacDonald

That was such a *lovely* dinner last night. I enjoyed every single morsel and how did you know that a well-done steak with tomato sauce was one of my favourite foods?

It was really stimulating to meet Dr Jekyll and Mr Hyde: they are both such interesting people and it is fascinating to note how similar they are in fact.

Frank and I much look forward to inviting Professor MacDonald and yourself to our house before too long. Frank joins me in all good wishes.

With our thanks
Sincerely

Notes
- Must be handwritten.
- Try to include something personal – a mention of food or other guests – so that it does not appear as a form letter.
- Send it as soon as you can – ideally first class, posted the following morning.

2. *Other thank yous*

(date)

Dear Mr Baker

The Tolpuddle Martyrs have asked me, on their behalf, to thank you for taking the trouble to come to talk to us all last night.

I, personally, learnt a lot about underwater campanology. The other members of the committee have similarly expressed enthusiasm and appreciation for your delivery.

Thank you on behalf of us all.

Sincerely

Notes
- Such a letter can be typed.
- Again, it should mention something specific and it should be sent as soon as possible.

Present Giving

This is an art that some people are born with. Fortunately, it is also a skill that can be acquired.

Some golden rules to remember:
- Unless you know someone's house well do not give anything that fits into the category of 'furnishing'.
- Do not leave price tags on.
- Do not write in books. The recipient might want to change the gift.
- Be wary about 'unusual gifts'.
- Be careful about food. Some foods are always 'safe' but it is not a good idea to arrive with something that must be eaten immediately. This could be embarrassing and it might, also, be taken as an affront to the host's ability to provide suitable fare.
- Magazine subscriptions might seem like a good idea but make sure the recipient really wants the publications in question.

Tipping

If in doubt – do not.

You do not tip the owner of a restaurant – and you do not, similarly, tip the owner of a hairdressing salon.

Women are notorious undertippers. A few points:
- Only tip when service warrants it. If you have been badly treated, do not tip and say why you are not tipping.
- Try to forget the 10 per cent rule and go above it, say to 15 per cent if you are specially pleased.
- In a restaurant, check that 'service' is not already included: service is really the same as gratuities but generally service implies that the money is divided among all the employees, even those behind the scenes.

- If you want to write in a tip on a bill, check that the money will actually go to the person who has served you.
- If tipping by handing over notes or coins, do so discreetly.
- Try to have the money already to hand (no fumbling).

Wedding Etiquette

BEFORE
ON THE DAY
THE RECEPTION
WHO PAYS FOR WHAT?

TIPS FOR GUESTS
WEDDING PRESENTS
CALAMITIES

If a traditional church wedding is planned, everything can be organized in a few days and the whole occasion will still be utterly memorable. Many prospective brides, however, have much longer in which to plan the big day. The guidelines below assume that at least six months are available.

BEFORE

6 to 5 months before

- Check the date with the minister, book the church and the music.
- Select and ask best man, bridesmaids and other attendants.
- Think about accommodation for them and close family members and, if necessary, make local hotel reservations.
- Start thinking about your dress, and those of your bridesmaids (for suggestions for wedding fashions, see Chapter 14).
- Decide on what hospitality you plan to offer at the reception and book the caterers.
- If a marquee is required, book that.
- Book flowers (for the church, bouquets and reception).
- Book a photographer.
- Book cars (to and from church, and if required for departure from the reception).
- Think about the honeymoon and, if necessary, make definite reservations.
- Think about your wedding present list (see below).
- Make an appointment to visit your doctor or a family planning clinic.

4 to 3 months before

- Confirm arrangements with the minister and arrange for the banns to be called. Finalize the order of service. Check if confetti is allowed.
- Order wedding stationery. You can generally find a wide range of what you need at a stationery shop or at your local printers (look in Yellow Pages). Invitations usually consist of a folded A5 card with black

or silver engraving or printing on the front. Accepted standard printing is:

Mr and Mrs John Jones
request the pleasure of your company
at the marriage of their daughter
Emma Jane
to
Mr Graham Crunch
at St James's Church
Carshalton
on Friday 23 July 1985
at two o'clock
and afterwards at
Catherly Manor

RSVP
99 Milton Avenue
Yardley
Birmingham B II OBP

Notes
- The recipient's name is then handwritten at the top of the invitation.
- The hosts are usually, as above, the bride's parents. Variations on this wording include:

(a) if the bride's mother is alone: Mrs John (or Jane) Jones ... her daughter.

(b) if the bride's father is alone: Mr John Jones ... his daughter.

(c) if the bride's mother has remarried and she and her present husband are hosts: Mr and Mrs James Brown ... her daughter Emma Jones.

(d) if the bride's father has remarried and he and his present wife are hosts: Mr and Mrs John Jones ... his daughter Emma.

(e) if divorced parents get together momentarily to host the wedding: Mr John Jones and Mrs Jane Jones (or, if she has remarried, Mr John Jones and Mrs James Brown) ... their daughter.

- if some guests are to be invited only to the reception, the invitation could read:

Mr and Mrs John Jones
. . .
at a reception at Catherly Manor ...
following the wedding ...

and it is customary to include a short note explaining that, for instance, the church is small.

- You will also need a printed order of service, reception accessories (if required) such as printed napkins and favours such as matchbooks.
- Buy wedding rings.

- Think about accessories for your dress:

  (a) hair (make an appointment for the day)
  (b) hair covering (flowers? veil? hat?)
  (c) shoes
  (d) underwear

- Check that your mother, and your mother-in-law to be and other close family members, are happy about their outfits, and that the colours will not clash.
- Start planning the trousseau.
- Check menus with the caterers.
- Think about the cake, which will taste much better if it has had several months to mature.
- Check passports and necessary visas are in order for the honeymoon.
- Start writing the invitations.

6 weeks before
- Post invitations.
- Ask someone who has known you a long time to make the speech at the reception.

4 weeks before
- Go over the route to and from the wedding and plan exact timing.
- Think about wet or cold weather contingency plans:

  (a) a supply of umbrellas
  (b) light wraps if necessary
  (c) if the reception is to be held outside, a supply of cardigans and sweaters.

- Check through invitation replies and, as soon as you can, give caterers written confirmation of anticipated numbers.
- If you are making the cake, put on marzipan, which takes a couple of weeks to harden.
- Plan the cake's table:

  (a) table and cloth
  (b) cake stand
  (c) cake knife

and, if required, order boxes for cake to be sent to those unable to attend. As refusals to the wedding come in, start writing names and addresses on the boxes.
- Check, item by item, all necessary clothes and accessories for all in the wedding party.
- Contact your local paper.

1 week before
- Have a detailed rehearsal of the wedding ceremony.

● Put the main icing on the cake.
● Try on your complete outfit. If you are doing your own make-up, try it out.
● Plan where you are going to display your presents: make sure that they are insured and arrange for a guard while you are all at the service.

ON THE DAY ● Remember to leave plenty of time for hair appointments especially if you have a weekend wedding.
● The groom gives the ushers a list of close family members and who should be specially seated and where – traditionally, bride's family and friends sit on the left, and groom's family and friends are on the right of the main aisle.
● The best man should check he has the ring (or rings).

At the church
● Ushers should arrive forty minutes before the service is due to start to show guests to their seats. Orders of service can be either already placed on seats or handed out by ushers.
● The groom and best man should arrive twenty minutes before the bride.
● Guests, ideally, should plan to arrive about twenty minutes before the bride.
● Bridesmaids should arrive five minutes before the bride.
● The bride's mother usually arrives just before the bride, and is escorted to her seat.
● The bride and father should not be late. They should even try to arrive just ahead of time so that the veil, etc., can be readjusted and so that photographs can be taken.

The service
● The bride proceeds up the aisle on her father's right arm, followed by her attendants. The groom steps out of the front right-hand seat, his best man to his right. The minister greets them.
● The chief bridesmaid steps forward and takes the bride's bouquet.
● If she has not already done so, the bride switches her engagement ring from her left to right hand.
● The ceremony lasts about thirty minutes: the minister will have a detailed description which he will have gone through with you carefully. This will be the exact ceremony that will be used.
● For the signing of the register the following leave the main body of the church:

  1. minister
  2. bride on the groom's left arm
  3. bride's mother with groom's father
  4. groom's mother with bride's father
  5. bride's attendants
  6. best man

- After the signing, the wedding party returns to the main body of the church for the final procession:

  1. bride/groom
  2. young attendants
  3. chief bridesmaid/best man
  4. other attendants
  5. bride's mother/groom's father
  6. groom's mother/bride's father

- The best man is responsible for making sure everything is left neat and clean after the service. After the final photographs, therefore, he should check around that no handbags or orders of service, etc., have been left – and he is the last to leave the church.

Register office
- A register office wedding overcomes the need for some of the requirements listed in the above arrangements. On the day itself the bride, specially dressed but not in full white with long train, the groom and a few family and friends, should arrive ten minutes before the ceremony is due to start. (No one should arrive more than fifteen minutes beforehand or confusion is likely to occur with other, earlier, ceremonies).
- The attendant registrar will clearly guide the bride and groom through the order of ceremony.
- The register office ceremony will last about seven minutes (confetti may not be allowed). Afterwards, there may be a full-scale reception as outlined below.

Subsequent weddings
Second and subsequent marriages tend to be somewhat lower key than first marriages. Sometimes a service of blessing in a church, for instance, follows a register office ceremony. If you want a religious involvement in your forthcoming wedding, it is a good idea to talk to your vicar at the earliest opportunity.

Be tactful when compiling the guest list as you do not want to embarrass anyone associated with previous partners (of the man you are planning to marry as well as you). Try to plan the reception so that it does not appear as a carbon copy of earlier marriages: you do not want some guests to think they have 'been there before'.

THE RECEPTION
Professional caterers will advise you on what type of meal to offer at what time of day. If you want to avoid the cost of professional help, bear in mind that it is almost impossible for the bride herself, however good a cook, to do her own reception catering as there is so much else to be done before and on the day. If you do decide to go for alternative catering, why not ask a friend to do a simple meal, or make arrangements with a travelling fish and chip van to call?

If you decide on buffet food, do check that all food is easily eaten without a knife and without subsequent drips.

As far as drinks are concerned, you may decide to go for champagne throughout. Alternatives include: a selection of drinks on arrival followed by champagne just for the toasts; an open bar (expensive); a pay bar (not very friendly); wines throughout (if you choose this, go for good wines). Whatever you decide, make sure that plenty of soft drinks and water are also available.

On arrival someone should be on hand to direct people to cloakrooms and to take coats. The reception line will probably consist of:

- bride's parents
- groom's parents
- bride and groom (and possibly attendants).

If a Master of Ceremonies announces guests, he calls the man's name first (Mr and Mrs David Jones) but probably the woman will go first down the line (Mrs Jones followed by Mr Jones).

At some point someone (usually the best man) calls for attention. Speeches should all be short:

1. a friend of the bride (usually an older man) toasts the couple
2. the groom replies, thanks the bride's parents for the wedding and toasts the attendants
3. the best man replies on behalf of the attendants, and reads out any messages that have arrived.

Note Many people have to talk in public at some time during their lives and it can be a nerve-racking experience. Here are a few tips: be confident and be brief; do not be afraid of using notes; play safe – do not risk anything that might offend.

The cake cutting is announced by the best man. If the icing is hard it is a good idea to have the first cut already half-made. The bride's hand is under the groom's as they both cut the cake. After their initial cut the cake is quickly removed to be cut professionally behind the scenes.

It used to be the custom for all guests to remain until the bride and groom had changed into their going-away clothes and departed. The bride might throw her bouquet to signify that the catcher would be next to get married. Nowadays, many wedding receptions continue on as discos or other parties. Sometimes the bride and groom stay nearly to the end. It is, anyway, perfectly acceptable for guests simply to slip away when they wish.

WHO PAYS
FOR WHAT? Nowadays there is a generally a civilized agreement between all parties concerned as to who pays for what. Sometimes the groom's parents offer to pay for at least part of the reception. Sometimes the bride pays for all her own clothes. Traditionally, however, responsibilities were divided like this:

Bride's father:
- Press announcements (engagement, wedding).
- All printing.
- Bride's dress and (sometimes) attendants' dresses.

- Photographs.
- Flowers for the church and reception.
- Transport (except for groom and best man).
- Reception.
- Cake.

Bride:
- Ring (if required) for the groom.
- Present for the groom.
- Trousseau.

Groom:
- Bride's engagement and wedding rings.
- Presents for the bride, attendants and best man.
- Church/legal fees.
- Music, etc.
- Flowers for the bride, attendants and close family members.
- Transport for himself and the best man to the ceremony and for bride and himself from ceremony to reception.
- Honeymoon.

TIPS FOR
GUESTS
by Diana May

The bride and groom have invited you to join them on their special day not as disinterested spectators but to contribute to the atmosphere of love surrounding them. They have done you the honour of inviting you so it is for you to reciprocate by filling the role of the perfect guest.

When you receive the invitation note the date in your diary and reply in writing to the address at the bottom of the card (usually to the bride's parents). If you are of the parents' generation and do not know the couple's taste too well, you could enclose a friendly note asking if they could send you a present list and also asking (if the invitation does not state it) whether men should wear morning suits.

Nearer the time deliver your chosen present, well labelled. Plan the outfits you and your partner (and children) will wear. Plan for a sudden cold or wet spell (thermal vest or brollies). Does your man need to hire a morning suit or, if he has his own, can he get into it comfortably without alterations? Is it a 'hat' occasion? If so, choose something stunning but comfortable to wear (the champagne can be relied upon to give you that wedding headache, after all). If you are of either family party, liaise to ensure that not everyone is in navy with white accessories.

If it is going to be a large wedding, it makes sense to slip the invitation into your handbag to show at the reception afterwards (also you may need the reassurance of the church's name in writing as you get lost for the third time in an unfamiliar county). Small church weddings will be less formal but still be ready with your answer to 'Which side?'. If one side is likely to be conspicuously empty, opt out of kindness for that side but go where the ushers direct (if there are any) and do not hog the front rows unless you are family. Resist the temptation to do too much waving and gossiping: that can wait for the reception and you are, after all, in a place of worship.

Do use discretion about throwing confetti or rice (do not do it if the church asks you not to – and never throw computer punch dots). Similarly, use discretion about cameras: certainly camera lights and video-recorders in the church are a major intrusion so do not use them without checking first.

Register office etiquette is mostly a matter of common sense. Arrive in good time, behave sensibly but cheerfully (it is just as exciting for the couple as a church wedding) and observe the office's rules about confetti and cameras. Do get lots of photos outside, particularly if the couple have not arranged for an 'official' photographer.

Enjoy the reception and the flummery of speeches and cake-cutting. There should be plenty to drink but use moderation as other guests have not come to see you make a spectacle of yourself. As for departure, say brief thanks as you go but as a point of courtesy write a letter of thanks to the newly-weds or their parents soon afterwards. If any of those photos come out really well and differ from the official posed pictures, it would be nice to send copies.

WEDDING PRESENTS Many guests prefer not to be tied to a particular list and give a present of their own choosing. Others find it easier if the bride has a 'list' at a store, or a printed list that she can send to guests.

If you want to give a present and there is no bride's list, think carefully before deciding on your gift. Many brides today have already had their own homes or lived away from their parents. There is a good chance that the recipient of your gift already has her own toaster. And if she is an experienced cook do not give her a basic introductory cookbook.

If you are getting married, going to a shop that has an established 'brides' bureau' will save you a lot of time and inconvenience. You should not end up with six toasters – and you should get the china that you actually want. Someone at the shop will show you around and note which items you would like. Anyone who wants to give the bride a present can then choose, perhaps, just one of the chosen place settings from that store. The list should not be sent unless requested. Presents should be sent in plenty of time before the wedding so that the bride can write her thank you before the wedding and gifts can be displayed on the day. If presents are taken on the day, they should be handed to someone responsible at the reception. Each gift should have the card from the donor clearly displayed and the donor's name and address should also be attached inside the box or parcel.

CALAMITIES • In case of a death, with indefinite postponement, an announcement and individual notices should be given: 'Because of the death of Mr William Shakespeare, Mr and Mrs John Jones regret they are cancelling/postponing the marriage of their daughter ...' (if a new date is already arranged, put it in).

- Cancellation for another reason: 'Mr and Mrs John Jones announce that the marriage of . . . will not now take place.'
- Whatever alteration does arise should be imparted to guests, some of whom may already have long-distance travel plans, at the earliest opportunity. If the wedding is cancelled completely then gifts should be returned to donors as quickly as possible.
- If the engagement is broken, regardless of by whom, the ring is generally today considered to have been given unconditionally. You should perhaps return it only if it has been a family ring.

  Similarly, personal gifts (but not household articles) are deemed to have been given unconditionally.
- Wedding or engagement presents are normally made conditionally and should be returned to the donors as soon as possible.

Christenings

This generally takes place some time after the baby is about six weeks old. Most parents prefer their child to be christened in a church with which they have an association. If you, as new parents, are not yourselves church-goers, you should find out the name of the vicar (see the notice-board outside the church) and make an appointment to see him. He will explain everything to you.

In the Church of England you will need at least the accepted minimum of two godparents for the child (two godfathers for a boy and two godmothers for a girl). They should all be baptized, confirmed and practising members of the Church. There are no godparents in the Church of Scotland baptismal service.

The Church of England service will probably take place either during a morning service or, privately, during the afternoon. In the Roman Catholic Church, baptism can take place privately at any time agreed with the priest or during a Mass. Unless there are unusual circumstances, baptism in the Church of Scotland takes place in the face of the congregation. The Church of Scotland has definite guidelines on baptism and parents are advised to contact the parish minister.

Further Information

Suggested further reading

Beyfus, Drusilla, *The Bride's Book*, Allen Lane
Coleridge, Nicholas and Napier Miles, *The Long Weekend Book*, Stourton, Coleridge and Miles
Donald, Elsie Burch, *Debrett's Etiquette and Modern Manners*, Pan
Woodman, Mary, *Wedding Etiquette under All Denominations*, Foulsham

13 Body Beautiful

Body Beautiful shows you how to make yourself healthy, fit and happy with yourself.

It is not all handed to you on a plate. You have to work at being fit and healthy. You may have to diet and you should certainly exercise. Your posture and what you do to your face and the rest of the body can similarly enhance the real you, and make you feel better within yourself.

Much of the valuable dietary information here has been provided by nutritionist Moira Pinder. She cares about what you eat, and so should you. I also spoke to Barbara Attenborough, cosmetic consultant to Boots.

This chapter is for self-enhancement, whatever your age.

Nutrition

10 hints for health

1. Eat a wide variety of foods.
2. Avoid being overweight.
3. Eat less fat and fried foods.
4. Eat less sugar and sugar-rich foods.
5. Eat more fruit and vegetables (including potatoes).
6. Eat wholemeal bread and cereals.
7. Use salt in moderation.
8. Drink less alcohol.
9. Take regular exercise.
10. No smoking!

There is no getting away from it – you are what you eat, and a faulty diet can give rise to all sorts of health problems.

If you are living on white bread, sugar, fried foods, cakes and sweets you are never going to feel really healthy and full of energy. There is nothing wrong with eating some of these foods sometimes – but if they form the basis of your daily eating pattern it is not the way to good health.

Eat sensibly, take plenty of exercise and feel the difference it makes to your energy level. If you feel terrific you will look terrific!

Nutritional topics today are 'news' and attract great interest in newspapers, magazines and books. So much conflicting advice is given, however, that there is still confusion about which foods should be eaten to keep healthy and which foods should be cut down or avoided altogether.

The following guidelines are based on advice given in recent reports on obesity and on fibre by the Royal College of Physicians, a report by the National Advisory Committee on Nutrition Education (NACNE) and reports from the Department of Health.

The NACNE panel of doctors, nutritionists and education experts made recommendations for the future that include:

● most people should – on average – cut their fat intake by about a quarter, sugar consumption by half and salt by about a quarter

● most people in Britain are getting ample protein, vitamins and minerals

● fibre intake should be increased by about a half

● average alcohol intake should fall to an average of 20 g a day maximum (less than two glasses of wine).

WHAT YOUR BODY NEEDS

Proteins Intake of protein is essential in a growing child to build new tissue and it is also required by adults to replace cells which are constantly being worn out.

Animal protein (meat, fish, eggs, cheese and milk) should be included as part of a varied diet. It tends to have a high fat content and if it is necessary to restrict your fat intake then emphasis should be placed on lean meat, poultry, white fish, skimmed milk, low fat cheeses and yogurt.

Vegetable protein sources include nuts, peas, beans (baked, kidney, haricot, etc.), lentils and bread. Nutrition experts are increasingly stressing the value of these vegetable proteins in the diet: as well as being good sources of protein they are high in fibre and they also contain iron and B group vitamins. They have a low fat content and they are an economical way of making meat 'go further', e.g. chilli con carne or lamb casserole with haricot beans.

Fats These provide a concentrated source of calories (energy): 1 oz. of fat contains twice as many calories as 1 oz. of sugar. Fat gives you energy and supplies warmth.

As well as the 'visible fats' (butter, margarine, lard, oils, cream) other fats are found in meat, cheese, oily fish and milk. And pastry, cakes, chocolate and ice-cream are all high in fat content.

More and more, research strongly suggests that a high percentage of fat in the diet is a factor in the development of coronary heart disease and obesity (see below). It is sensible to adopt a few simple measures to reduce your fat intake:

- Grill meat rather than frying it.
- Spread butter or ordinary margarine (their fat content is the same) thinly, or switch to a low fat spread.
- Use single cream instead of double (its fat content is about half).
- Watch the amount of foods you are eating which have a high and not always obvious fat content, such as chocolate, doughnuts, cream buns, etc.

Dietary fat and coronary heart disease

Death rates from coronary heart disease in the United Kingdom (especially Scotland) are among the highest in the world. Reports from many international and national committees suggest that the incidence of coronary heart disease can be lowered by the reduction of total dietary fat although the role of cholesterol and fats is controversial. It may be helpful to define what some of these fats are.

Cholesterol – a fat-like substance which is naturally present in the body. If the level of cholesterol rises too high the arteries become clogged up and the flow of blood can be impeded. This occurs particularly in the arteries which lead to the heart. Egg yolk, liver and kidney are rich sources of cholesterol, as are full-cream dairy products.

Polyunsaturates – fats which are liquid or very soft at normal room temperature (e.g. sunflower oil). These do not raise the level of cholesterol in the blood. Not all vegetable oils and margarines are high in polyunsaturates, however, so you should check labels carefully before buying.

Saturated fats – fats which are hard or solid at room temperature (butter, suet, lard, hard margarine and meat fat). They may raise the cholesterol level. Other saturates include the fat in full-cream milk and in cream and cheese, and some vegetable fat (generally, if it is solid at room temperature it is a saturated fat).

It should be noted, of course, that diet is only one factor that contributes to coronary heart disease. Smoking, obesity, heredity, lack of exercise, stress and strain have all been cited as factors that put an individual at risk. Surveys have shown that those who take regular vigorous exercise are less likely to suffer from heart trouble. In the light of present knowledge, the best dietary advice would be to:

- Avoid obesity.
- Reduce salt intake.
- Reduce total fat intake by eating less butter, margarine, lard, cream, cakes, pastries, fried foods and fat meat and try to veer towards white fish, poultry, skim milk and low fat spreads.
- Change from saturated fats for cooking (e.g. lard) to polyunsaturates (e.g. sunflower oil) and, where possible, switch from butter to polyunsaturated margarine.

Note • Do not use skim milk for young children as it is too high in protein and salt and low in Vitamins A and D.

Salt NACNE recommends a lower intake of salt for almost everyone. This can most practically be achieved by using only a little salt in cooking, not adding any extra salt at the table and by not eating excess quantities of processed foods which have a high salt content – e.g. tinned meats, pâté, salami and so on.

It has been found that a low incidence of high blood pressure is associated with lack of obesity, a high level of physical activity, a diet low in animal fats and a low intake of salt.

Carbohydrates Carbohydrates, like fat, contain energy-giving calories. Sometimes carbo-
(CHO) hydrate calories seem to be 'used up' more quickly than fats so, perhaps, your starch-only breakfast does not 'last' as long as a cooked meal. Carbohydrates, unlike fat, are not considered dangerous as far as your heart is concerned.

More than 50 per cent of the average daily calorie intake comes from carbohydrates, of which there are two main groups:

Sugars, mostly sucrose (cane sugar), found in foods such as jams, preserves, cakes, sweets, chocolates, puddings, sweetened drinks.

Starches such as bread, potatoes, cereals, rice, pasta and root vegetables.

Sucrose is an 'empty' source of calories. It is one of the few foods which comprises only one nutrient – CHO. Fruit includes types of sugar but in a much less concentrated form as a high water content is also present. The different types of sugar are outlined on pages 477–8.

NACNE recommends a total intake of no more than 2 oz. of sugar per person per day, including that used in cooking and in beverages. Expert opinion is united about the fact that if we cut our sugar intake there would be less obesity and related diseases and less dental decay. As a nation we consume far too much sugar and NACNE recommendations should be followed. Consumption of starchy CHO, on the other hand, is to be encouraged. Bread (especially wholemeal), potatoes, cereals (especially those with a high fibre content), rice, pasta, pulses and root vegetables should be included in a healthy diet. Bread and potatoes should even be included in a calorie-reduced diet, provided they are not fried, as they are useful in providing 'bulk' which lowers feelings of hunger.

Minerals From a dietary source, there are two substances which are most necessary in small amounts:

Calcium – this, with phosphorus, forms strong bones and teeth. Milk and cheese have the highest calcium content and other sources include bread, pulse vegetables, green vegetables, hard drinking water and sardines and other small fish with bones that can be eaten. For the ordinary adult, one pint of milk provides all the calcium needed per day.

Iron – this is needed to form healthy red blood cells to carry oxygen around the body. Iron deficiency anaemia (IDA) is most commonly found in women of child-bearing age: it causes tiredness and apathy. Richest sources of iron are liver and kidney (2 oz. of liver provides a day's iron requirement) and it is also found in bread, pulses, dried fruit and green vegetables and corned beef and other meats and eggs (but beware the fat content of some of these foods, see above). Iron is also found in cocoa and chocolate – but do not use this as an excuse for consuming too much of either!

Vitamin C is needed to make sure that iron is properly absorbed from the digestive system. With Vitamin C, even a fairly low intake of iron can be sufficient.

Vitamins The body needs a regular intake of vitamins, which many people supplement by taking tablets (much to the delight of the pharmaceutical companies). There is no evidence to suggest that taking extra vitamins in the form of tablets will make you healthier or give you more resistance to infection. Indeed, excess consumption of Vitamins A and D, which can be stored in the liver, can be toxic. As far as Vitamins B and C are concerned, the body simply excretes any surplus in the urine.

With a good healthy daily diet that includes lots of fresh food, you should not need any surplus intake except perhaps in winter or when you travel.

Vitamin A is necessary for the growth of all living cells, for good sight and for protection against infection. It is found particularly in dairy products, liver, carrots, green vegetables and fatty fish.

The **Vitamin B** group (including niacin, riboflavin and thiamine) is needed to convert food into energy and, without Vitamin B, you become weak. It is also needed for the nervous and digestive systems. As with Vitamin C, it is not stored by the body so a regular intake is required: you can find Vitamin B in breads and cereals, dairy products, liver and other meats, green vegetables and Bovril and Marmite.

Vitamin C is needed for the growth of cells, for healthy gums and healing of broken bones and wounds and – if you follow a certain school of thought – to ward off head colds (though many say there is no convincing account of it preventing or curing colds). The best sources are citrus fruits (grapefruit, lemon, orange) and blackcurrants – but remember that many fruit juices bought as such contain added sugar. You can also find Vitamin C in salads, green vegetables and potatoes but the goodness can easily be destroyed by cooking or prolonged soaking beforehand. Increasingly, nutrition experts urge the importance of eating as many vegetables as possible either raw or barely cooked.

Vitamin D is needed for absorption of calcium by bones and teeth and most people get enough by the skin's exposure to ordinary sunlight. It can also be obtained by eating dairy produce or sardines or other oily fish.

Fibre Fibre is the indigestible part of plants and cereals which forms the 'skeleton' of the plant – cabbage stalks and the outer husk of wheat, for instance. It used to be thought that since these parts could not be digested they were not necessary for a healthy diet, but now medical opinion is agreed that a high fibre intake is *essential* for good health. In Third World countries where a high fibre diet is the norm, diseases such as constipation, diverticulitis and bowel cancers are rare. It is also thought that a fibre-rich diet may provide some protection against coronary heart disease but this is by no means certain.

Ideally you should eat a mixed diet including cereal, fruit and vegetable fibres – that is to say, do not live entirely on wholemeal bread or on cabbage stalks! There is no need to restrict your diet in this way as fibre-rich foods are plentiful and varied. They include peas, beans, lentils, potatoes, carrots, parsnips, apples, pears, bananas, dried fruits, tomatoes, bran, wholemeal bread, wholemeal flour and nuts. Eating a fibre-rich diet can also be useful when slimming – fibre is the only component of our food that contains no calories. Also, whole foods need more chewing so we tend to eat more slowly and, as a result, consume a smaller amount.

Here are some tips to help you increase your intake of fibre, whether you are dieting or not:

● Eat wholemeal bread (this has the highest fibre content, followed in descending order by granary, wheatgerm and white).

● Use wholemeal flour to replace some or all of the white flour used in cooking.

● Eat wholemeal pasta and brown rice.

● Eat the skin of potatoes ('baked potato skins' are now a speciality in some American restaurants).

● Eat 'digestive' and bran biscuits in preference to others.

● Eat nuts, dried fruits and raw vegetables.

● Eat fibre-rich breakfast cereals, preferably those without sugar added, and add extra bran or wheatgerm, available from your local health food shop.

● Eat plenty of fresh fruit, plus skin wherever possible.

See   'Fibre in Your Food' (in English or in Welsh) from the Health Education Council.

HEALTH   Many people have become disillusioned with what industry has done to
FOODS   foods in the form of such additives as sugars, preservatives and artificial colours (check the contents listed on the outside of an innocuous-looking pot of marmalade). Some, therefore, opt for 'natural', 'health' or 'organic' foods.

These terms may be misleading as they suggest that some foods are 'good' and some 'bad', whereas it is often the combination of foods that makes a good or bad eating pattern. Over the last few years there has been a large growth in the number of wholefood health food shops which are excellent places in which to find wholemeal bread, muesli, a wide variety of dried fruit, wheatgerm and other things that might not always be easy to find. But – a word of warning – some 'health' foods are put on the market with rather exaggerated claims about their qualities. These should be viewed with some caution. More and more supermarkets sell those 'healthy' foods you need and usually at a much lower price.

CON-
VENIENCE
FOODS

As life becomes increasingly busy, the demand for ready-cooked foods and dishes which you simply 'heat and eat' grows. Some people are worried that these foods are of diminished nutritional value but, especially where frozen fruit and vegetables are concerned, there should be no loss of Vitamin C because usually only the best quality fruit and vegetables are frozen immediately after harvesting.

Some processed foods contain a high percentage of salt and it would obviously be unwise to consume them to the exclusion of fresh foods. You cannot control the amount of salt used, for instance, in take-away hamburgers while you can limit the amount in those prepared at home. The use of some additives is unavoidable in the modern food industry but this is under strict control.

The rule is that convenience foods should not be eaten to the exclusion of all others but, as part of a varied diet, they need not be harmful.

VEGETARIAN-
ISM

Some people feel healthier when they do not eat meat – and even eggs and dairy products. Many vegetarians eat fish. Some of the different categories of vegetarians are:

Lacto vegetarians – they eat milk and dairy products but exclude all meats, poultry, fish and eggs.

Lacto-ovo vegetarians – as above, but with the inclusion of eggs.

Vegans – they consume no animal products at all: their diet is based totally on fruits, vegetables and cereals.

The first two types of vegetarian diet can supply most of the essential nutrients, provided they include a wide range of cereals, pulses, nuts, vegetables and – where allowed – eggs.

Iron can be in short supply in all vegetarian diets; it must be provided by pulses, vegetables, dried fruit and dark green vegetables (e.g. spinach). Iron from fruit and vegetables, however, is less easily absorbed by the body than iron from meat sources and it is important to have a good intake of Vitamin C, which helps its absorption – usually this is no problem in a vegetarian diet where plenty of fresh fruit, vegetables and salads are eaten anyway.

Special care must be taken with vegan diets to ensure an adequate intake of nutrients. Vitamin B12 is found only in foods of animal origin so that on a vegan diet a supplement of this must be taken in the form of special vegan food (e.g. Tastex or Barmene). Calcium intake may also be low because of the absence of milk and cheese, and the required calcium will have to be provided by vegetables, pulses, nuts and cereals (sesame seeds are a good source).

You can get literature and help from the Vegetarian Society and the

Vegan Society (you can also consult the Vegetarian Society if your child or toddler refuses to eat meat).

> Vegetarian Society
> Parkdale
> Dunham Road
> Altrincham
> Cheshire WA14 4QG
> 061–928 0793

> Vegan Society
> 47 Highlands Road
> Leatherhead
> Surrey KT22 8NQ
> (no telephone)

SMOKING   Cigarette smokers absorb into the lungs:

Nicotine – a habit-forming drug which constricts small blood vessels and raises blood pressure
Carcinogenic tars – when isolated from cigarette smoke, these tars have been shown to cause cancer in experiments on animals
Carbon monoxide – in pregnancy, the resulting carboxyhaemoglobin passes into foetal circulation.

Cigarette smokers are more prone to:
- cancer of the lung
- chronic bronchitis and emphysema
- chronic laryngitis
- coronary thrombosis and arterial disease.

Gastric and duodenal ulcers take longer to heal; pregnant women may produce smaller babies, with a higher incidence of foetal abnormalities; and there is an increased risk of spontaneous abortion and premature labour.

It is estimated that two out of every five heavy smokers will die before the age of 65. The mortality rate increases with the number of cigarettes smoked. It is also estimated that one in eight of all heavy smokers will die of a primary lung cancer growth.

Help   If you want to give up smoking, you can try hypnotherapy, acupuncture or other possible 'cures' but the only way really to give up is to be determined. You cannot simply 'cut down': you must stop altogether.

There are chewing gums and tablets from the chemist which may help. If you find these ineffective talk to your doctor and he may be able to prescribe tablets which will reduce your craving for nicotine.

You can get information from:

> Action on Smoking and Health (ASH)
> 5–11 Mortimer Street
> London W1N 7RH
> 01–637 9843

Health Education Council
78 New Oxford Street
London WC1A 1AH
01-637 1881

Scottish Committee, Action on Smoking and
Health
Royal College of Physicians
9 Queen Street
Edinburgh EH2 1JQ
031-225 4725

Dieting and Weight Loss

WHY LOSE WEIGHT? DIET IN PREGNANCY
RESTRICTING FOODS DIETING PROBLEMS

If you follow a healthy diet based on the guidelines above, and eat
moderately, the problem of being overweight should not arise. However,
it is only too obvious, if you look around, that many people in Britain
appear to do the reverse.

WHY LOSE WEIGHT? Obesity is probably the most common nutritional disorder in this country
today. More has been written about the problems of being overweight
and the possible remedies than any other nutritional topic. The health
risks of being overweight are well documented. You run more risk of
developing various diseases such as high blood pressure, heart disease,
orthopaedic problems (because the weight-bearing joints in the body, e.g.
knees, hips, etc., are under strain), and mild diabetes. Recent research has
shown that even those with a mild degree of obesity are at risk from
these ailments.

Advice abounds from the pages of magazines and books on to how
to lose weight successfully. Why then is permanent weight loss so difficult
to achieve? To be successful you must make a change in dietary habits:
it's not enough just to go on a crash diet (unless you have only a few
pounds to lose). Short-term rapid weight loss on a crash diet tends to
be a loss of water rather than a reduction in body fat. Keep a food diary
for a week and write down *everything* you eat and when. It should pinpoint
if you are missing meals, when you are nibbling and make you aware
of just what you *are* eating. However, most people, while being aware
of these health factors, want to lose weight in order to *look* better, so
that they can get into their clothes and be able to run for the bus without
getting hopelessly out of breath.

The chart below will give you a rough idea of what you should weigh.
Remember, however, that it is only a guide. As long as you are not

obsessed by your weight, you are the best judge as to how many pounds you need to lose, simply by looking in the mirror.

DESIRABLE WEIGHT IN POUNDS AND *KILOGRAMMES* (IN INDOOR CLOTHING), WOMEN AGES 25 AND OVER

HEIGHT (IN SHOES)			SMALL FRAME		MEDIUM FRAME		LARGE FRAME	
ft	in	cm	lb	kg	lb	kg	lb	kg
4	10	147.3	92–98	41.7–44.5	96–107	43.5–48.5	104–119	47.2–54
4	11	149.9	94–101	42.6–45.8	98–110	44.5–49.9	106–122	48.1–55.3
5	0	152.4	96–104	43.5–47.2	101–113	45.8–51.3	109–125	49.4–56.7
5	1	154.9	99–107	44.9–48.5	104–116	47.2–52.6	112–128	50.8–58.1
5	2	157.5	102–110	46.3–49.9	107–119	48.5–54	115–131	52.2–59.4
5	3	160	105–113	47.6–51.3	110–122	49.9–55.3	118–134	53.5–60.8
5	4	162.6	108–116	49 –52.6	113–126	51.3–57.2	121–138	54.9–62.6
5	5	165.1	111–119	50.3–54	116–130	52.7–59	125–142	56.8–64.4
5	6	167.6	114–123	51.7–55.8	120–135	54.4–61.2	129–146	58.5–66.2
5	7	170.2	118–127	53.5–57.6	124–139	56.2–63	133–150	60.3–68
5	8	172.7	122–131	55.3–59.4	128–143	58.1–64.9	137–154	62.1–69.9
5	9	175.3	126–135	57.2–61.2	132–147	59.9–66.7	141–158	64 –71.7
5	10	177.8	130–140	59 –63.5	136–151	61.7–68.5	145–163	65.8–73.9

See 'Obesity', available from
Flora Project for Heart Disease Prevention
25 North Row
London WIR 2BY
01–408 2332

If your mirror reflection does suggest you should lose weight, how should you set about it? The only way is to restrict the number of calories you eat (while maintaining the principles of healthy eating), and to exercise regularly.

Calories   A calorie (kcal – officially a kilocalorie) is a measurement of the amount of heat (energy) produced by food when it is digested by the body. EEC terminology means that the unit 'kilojoules' (kJ) – usually shortened to 'joules' – will soon be used instead of calories (kcal).

One calorie is equivalent to 4.2 kilojoules. A standard egg, for example, contains 80 calories (kcal) or 336 joules (kJ).

As a rough guide, most men should lose weight on 1,500 to 1,700 calories per day and most women should lose weight on 1,200 to 1,500 calories per day, although a lot depends on individual metabolic rate (kcal expenditure) and on general levels of activity.

There is no doubt that some people put on weight faster than others and find it more difficult to lose it. If you are putting on weight it is because you are eating too much *for you*. Do not worry about what the average kcal intake should be: it is what *your* body needs that matters.

RESTRICTING
FOODS

Bearing in mind the food groups outlined at the beginning of this chapter, try to:

1. Eat a reasonable *protein* intake but be wary of the fat content:
- cut fat off meat and skim any fat off casseroles
- avoid thick sauces
- grill, casserole, stir-fry or bake rather than fry
- avoid fried eggs
- eat a lower fat variety of cheese e.g. cottage cheese, Dutch cheese
- use skim milk (about half a pint per day).

2. Restrict all *fat* as much as possible:
- good wholemeal bread, plain or toasted, tastes magnificent without any butter at all, but if you cannot deprive your taste buds to that extent at least switch to a low fat spread
- avoid ice-cream, cream, chocolate, pastry and all fried foods.

3. Concentrated carbohydrate (CHO) should be restricted:
- if you must sweeten drinks try a sweetener (be aware that some sugar substitutes may contain sugar, e.g. sorbitol, fructose)
- avoid foods with a high sugar content, e.g. cakes, sweets, desserts, sweet sherry and other sweet drinks, jams and jellies
- include starches in reasonable amounts, say three slices of wholemeal bread and two medium potatoes, including skins, per day.
- eat fresh fruit
- eat only those fruits which are canned in their own juice, never those in a sweet syrup.

Weight loss will be more dramatic for the first one or two weeks of the diet. Thereafter a loss of up to two pounds per week is the target to aim for. Steady and regular weight loss – and weight maintenance at the end of it all – is the object of the exercise (and do not forget to exercise – see page 390!).

If you want to lose only a few pounds so that you can get into last year's dress for this year's Christmas party, give up the gin and tonics and just eat fruit and salads for a few meals ... Serious dieting, however, needs to be on a more long-term and, therefore, more nutritionally sound basis. Not only is it difficult to discipline yourself to eat only, say, pineapple and cottage cheese for two weeks but it is also bad for you. To be successful in losing weight and keeping that weight off you have to recognize which foods you are eating to excess and which foods you should perhaps eat more often and thus change your whole pattern of eating.

Do not be over-ambitious – crash diets do not lead to permanent weight loss. Go slowly with your weight-reducing programme.

Treat 'slimming' foods with caution and read the labels carefully to see how many calories they contain: the calorie content is often quite high. Such foods can be expensive and it may be wiser to spend that money on fruit and salads. In fact they should not be necessary at all if you plan your own slimming programme sensibly.

You may say, 'I cannot afford to go on a diet of fillet steak and caviar and fresh strawberries.' You do not have to. Offal, for instance, is inexpensive and provides good sources of protein, iron and B vitamins. Many vegetables are cheap, and when you eat the stalks as well – to provide fibre – you get even better value for money. Cheaper cuts of meat are perfectly acceptable provided they are cooked without extra fat. Mince and stews are fine – brown the meat in its own fat and skim it off after cooking. Don't thicken with lots of flour – tinned tomatoes, potatoes or lentils can be used in casseroles.

Remember that you will be saving money when dieting by not buying cakes and sweets and between-meal snacks. And you should lower your intake and, consequently, expenditure on alcohol.

Be positive about your efforts to lose weight – it really is worth it to feel and look so much better.

DIET IN PREGNANCY

It is best to avoid putting on too much weight during pregnancy as it may lead to your blood pressure going up in the later stages before the birth, and it is also harder to get your figure back again afterwards. Pregnancy, on the other hand, is no time to be dieting severely.

During pregnancy your body is nourishing a growing baby and storing up energy for the birth and breast-feeding, so you need an especially well-balanced diet. You should try to eat the following:

● Plenty of fresh fruit, salads and vegetables.
● One pint of milk a day (calcium builds strong bones and teeth for your baby).
● Green vegetables every day.
● 3 to 4 eggs per week.
● Liver once a week.
● Fish twice a week.
● Meat and poultry and foods containing vitamins every day.

Notes

● *Carbohydrates* and *fats* are best taken in small amounts as they may lead to excessive weight gain.
● *Fried foods* – if you are suffering from nausea, grill your food instead.
● *Iron* – as well as eating liver and green vegetables, it may be necessary for you to take iron tablets.
● *Protein* – if you do not take enough protein the baby's growth takes place at the expense of your own body tissue. Try to eat a portion of meat, fish, eggs or dairy products at each meal.
● *Vitamins* – ask your doctor or the clinic what amounts you should have.
● See also 'Motherhood' in Chapter 7.

DIETING PROBLEMS

Dieting should not be carried to extremes. Too often it becomes obsessional and this in itself is undesirable. Try to draw a fine balance between enjoyment of food and awareness of your appearance and state of health. There are two well-known diseases which result from overdoing it.

Anorexia nervosa is most common among teenage girls but it can also affect other age groups and males. Sufferers tend to have a distorted picture of their own 'body image', i.e. they may see themselves as being fat when in fact they are of normal weight or even underweight. It can also be a wish to regress to childhood and a desire to avoid adult responsibility.

Sufferers usually refuse to eat 'fattening' food e.g. carbohydrates, sweets, fats. They will often eat foods such as meat, cheese, fruit, salads. Periods of eating very little may be interspersed with binges, and guilt feelings arise as a result of this. Sufferers are often very devious and go to great lengths to hide food and make it appear that they have eaten it. They will also make themselves sick if they feel they have overeaten.

Treatment   It is essential to seek medical help. This is a complex condition often requiring years of help and therapy.

For further information contact:

> Anorexics Anonymous
> Priory Centre
> High Wycombe
> Bucks HP13 6SL
> 0494–23440 (Wednesdays only)

Bulimia nervosa (binge-eating) is associated with extreme anorexic binge-eating and with people who have never been grossly overweight but who have a history of dieting and failing on an endless cycle, and who have discovered that if they vomit they can actually eat and not gain weight.

Bulimia sufferers can sometimes be recognized by a smell of vomit. Constant vomiting can lead to tooth erosion and lack of potassium in the blood which can cause lethargy and tingling fingers and symptoms similar to a heart attack.

Those suffering from bulimia need help. Special research and treatment is available from:

> Eating Disorders Clinic
> Royal Edinburgh Hospital
> Morningside Place
> Edinburgh EH10 5HF
> 031–447 2011

Exercise

POSTURE   YOGA
FITNESS   STRESS
EXERCISING

POSTURE   As well as actually losing weight, it is also necessary to *look* as though you have lost it. *Stand up straight* is the golden rule. Your body will function better all round.

When *standing*:

head – imagine you are suspended by a string pulling up from the centre of the crown

chin – hold it roughly at right angles to the throat (nod the head up and down a few times to find the most comfortable position)

neck – lengthen the back of the neck by holding your chin and shoulders correctly

shoulders – pull them down away from your ears and balance them directly above your hips

arms – let them hang loosely at your sides

spine – stretch the whole of the spine upwards: if you hold your pelvis correctly and keep the back of the neck long, your spine lengthens naturally

knees – try to keep them easy, neither rigid nor bent

feet – stand with your feet slightly apart, your weight evenly balanced between the heels and the balls of the feet (rock back and forth a few times to find the right balance).

When *walking*: keep your head and body balanced as in a simple stand. Keep your movements easy and let your feet use all their tiny joints, with heel down first and then toes. High heels distort posture, so try to wear low heels if you do much walking.

Sitting badly can do terrible things to your back. Sit as far to the rear of a chair as you can, with your hips square to the direction you are facing and your feet flat on the floor. When you are at your desk try to hinge forwards from the hips rather than rounding your spine.

Sleeping: do not use too many pillows (these tend to curve the spine). If you lie face up, try to keep the body symmetrical, with arms away from the chest to prevent inhibition of breathing. If you lie on your side, keep your back in a straight line and try not to become too 'foetal', with legs and arms tucked to the chest. Lying face down overarches the spine (unless you put pillow support under the pelvis). Make sure your bed is firm enough (see 'Beds', page 451ff).

A few tips for helping your everyday posture include:

● When scrubbing, kneel on all fours rather than bending your legs and back.

● When making a bed or cleaning the bath, bend at the knees instead of rounding your spine.

● When eating, lift food to your mouth instead of slouching over the table.

● When pushing a vacuum cleaner or shopping trolley, hold it close to you so your spine is as straight as possible.

FITNESS If you are fit, your heart and lungs can provide more energy more efficiently, enabling your body to work more easily; your muscles are conditioned to be able to work without too much strain; and you look and feel healthier, find it easier to relax, are less prone to minor illnesses and accidents and enjoy a general sense of well-being.

To find out whether or not you are fit, answer the following questions honestly:

1. Are you overweight?
2. Does climbing two flights of stairs leave you breathless?
3. Do you wake up sore in the morning after exercise the previous day?
4. Do you often find it difficult to get to sleep, despite feeling overtired?
5. Do you often feel tired, even though you are doing nothing physically tiring?
6. Do you sometimes feel depressed for no apparent reason?
7. Do you smoke?

If the answer is yes to three or more of the above questions, then you are probably *not* fit and you should do something about it.

EXERCISING

Most people think it is better to exercise for ten minutes daily, or 15 to 20 minutes four or five times a week, than for a whole hour once a week. Many regular exercisers have their own particular 'best time of day': for instance, I prefer to do my workout tape in early morning before breakfast and I run in the early evening.

You should exercise until you are pleasantly tired – the key phrase should be 'train, do not strain'. A good level of exercise produces a sensation of mild breathlessness, but not enough to prevent you from talking.

Your daily routine should be altered to include such little things as:
● Stretching and reaching for things in the house, office or wherever you may be.
● Walking to the next postbox rather than the one nearest to you.
● Getting off at the previous bus or underground stop and walking the final leg home at night.

The best all-round exercise involves repeated easy movements such as brisk walking, running, swimming and cycling. Exercises such as bending and stretching, which increase suppleness, are more useful than mere strength-increasing exercises like push-ups.

A simple daily routine, to be followed automatically at a regular time of day (say, before breakfast or before lunch or when you get back from work), should become a habit like cleaning your teeth. These exercises do not have to be too demanding. Follow a set routine that you do not have to think about – but if you suddenly find you have forgotten where you are in the programme, discipline yourself and start all over again. Put together a co-ordinated programme that suits you and do not overdo it.

Tax yourself – but remember you have to live with your body for the rest of your life so do not abuse it. Start by doing everything, say, five times and, as the days progress, build up the count. Try to do your routine every day: as exercise leader **Stephenie Karony** says, 'For an exercise programme to work you have to be consistent.' Also be consistent in when and where you exercise, and in wearing the correct clothes: simply exercising in what you happen to be wearing anyway just does not work.

Here are some of the exercises that I find most useful.

Warm up your body

Stand up straight, your feet slightly apart, hands together. Bend down and touch the floor and then lift your arms up high – high above your head as far as you can reach. Try to touch the ceiling or the sky above you. Start by doing this five times.

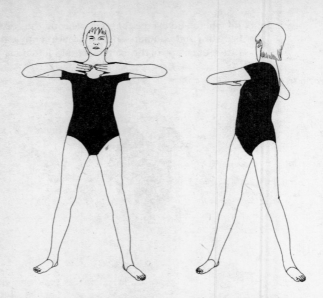

Now, with your fingers touching at shoulder height, turn as far as you can, first to the right and then to the left. Repeat five times.

Firm your bust

Stand or sit, your arms held high above your head. Press the palms of your hands together as hard as you can and hold this position. Let both arms fall to your sides and repeat.

Work on your waist

Stand with your arms out straight, horizontal from the shoulder. Lean over to one side as far as you can, without otherwise moving the body. Now bring the other arm up to meet the upper arm. Lower both arms – and repeat the other side.

Now something for your waist, legs and thighs. Sit straddling a chair back and lean down to touch the floor first one side and then the other. Then lift both legs out level with the seat of the chair and lower them, very slowly, down to the ground.

Slim your hips and buttocks

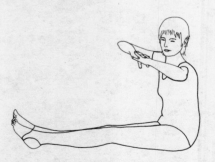

Sit on the floor, legs straight in front of you and your feet flexed, arms locked at shoulder height. 'Walk' forward on your buttocks right across the room. Now walk back again.

Do some pelvic tilts. Lie on your back, knees bent and open. Lift your buttocks right off the ground, squeezing hard as you lift as high as you can. Lower slowly to the ground. Then do the same thing with your

knees together. Then, with your buttocks off the ground, open and close your knees.

Firm your limbs

Think about the flab on your upper arms. Lie on your stomach, head down on your hands. Your elbows should be lying in front of your head.

Slowly push on your arms to raise your head so that your arms are almost straight. Slowly lower, to put your forehead back on your hands. Repeat

five times then do the same thing, bringing your head up as before but coming down only to your elbows, leaving your head up. Relax, your head on the ground and your arms by the side.

Now think about the flab on your thighs. Lie on one side and come up on your elbow. Lift the top leg, straight as high as you can. Slowly lower. Then do the same thing on the other side. If you want to make this exercise harder, lift your upper leg and then lift the other leg up to meet it.

Get air into the body   Sit cross-legged, your arms resting on your knees, your back straight. Slowly roll your head round and round, first one way and then the other.

Still sitting cross legged, take your right hand and put it on your left knee. Reach around behind your back and try to touch your left hand to your right inner thigh. Pull into an even more pronounced twist.

Release your face to the front and then release the rest of your twist. Do the same thing the other side.

Now, still sitting cross-legged and with your hands clasped on the ground behind you, very slowly reach your upper body forward as far down as it will go. Ideally you should be able to get your forehead right on to the ground. Sit like this, completely relaxed for a few seconds.

Recovery   Once again, stand up as tall and straight as you can, your legs apart and your arms by your side. Drop from the waist and let your upper body fall, relaxed. Swing your arms back and forth and gently roll up until you are straight again. Breathe deeply.

Right, do you feel better? If you do not on the first day, you soon will, so remember to go through your routine *every day*. Remember, too, to give your body a few minutes to recover after you finish your programme. Do not sit down straight away.

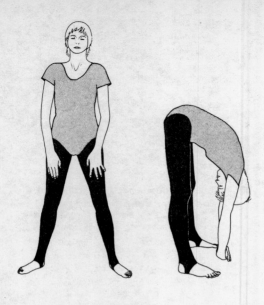

Exercise and weight loss

One of the runners in the 1984 London Marathon was ten-stone Belinda Charlton of Ringwood. Two years before – then weighing 21 stone! – she had watched the marathon and was determined one day to take part.

She started exercising in a big raincoat and walking shoes as she was so embarrassed by her size and her initial training was a mere 30-second run in the New Forest. Within eighteen months she had graduated to 20 miles a week. She found that dieting and exercising together helped her lose weight.

Exercise is essential when you are dieting, not only to help the weight come off but also to firm the surplus flesh. Make sure you check first with your doctor, however, if you want to do serious exercise, like playing squash after years of inactivity.

Exercise does not have to consist of strenuous workouts, marathon running or aerobics. Try walking. Walk instead of taking a bus or car, if there are convenient stairs always use them rather than a lift, take time away from household chores to go for a short walk ... you will soon find ways of including walking in your daily routine.

YOGA

Yoga provides a combination of exercise and relaxation, designed to make body, mind and spirit experience a profound state of well-being. Unlike some other forms of exercise which are comparatively new, yoga goes back some 5,000 years.

The poses bring flexibility, grace and strength to the whole body. Once you know how to do them you can do them by yourself at any time and without any special equipment (you should wear loose clothing – and never try it on a full stomach). It is a good idea, however, to learn initially from an experienced teacher, or at least to consult a good book.

STRESS
The fitter you are, the more easily you can combat stress. Tell-tale signs are:
- sudden overeating or loss of appetite
- sleeplessness
- unusual tiredness
- short temper
- unaccustomed difficulty in making decisions
- difficulty in concentrating
- heavier smoking and drinking.

To avoid excessive stress, analyse its source and see if there is anything you can do to ease the problem – if you are really angry about something, bring it into the open. Stop trying to do more than one thing at a time. Eat a balanced diet, slowly, taking your mind off your work and make sure you relax before you go to bed. Try to exercise every day.

Attention to health and diet should also help to prevent *hypertension*, high blood pressure caused by-
- being overweight
- smoking
- lack of regular exercise
- eating too much salt
- too much stress
- too much alcohol.

Help
There are a great many workout programmes available. You might be able to join a local workout or aerobics class. You can also buy cassette and video tapes to enable you to do the same thing in the privacy of your home.

Do be careful. If you go to a class, check that the instructor is properly qualified and that she (or he) will assess you individually for your ability to cope with various exercises. Professional help, of course, not only encourages you to start but also to stick with a programme. For details of health and exercise facilities look in local newspapers or Yellow Pages.

Caring for Your Skin

BODY CARE   HANDS AND FEET
FACE CARE

Your looks will remain good whatever your age if you are basically fit and healthy. However, there are other ways in which you should look after your body. Cosmetics and various kinds of beauty treatments can do a lot to enhance your natural beauty. Here are a few tips to help you make the most of yourself.

The skin's worst enemy is the lack of time spent in caring for it. A great many women feel guilty about spending time on themselves, but what they do not realize is that a few minutes spent on themselves each day will enhance all aspects of their lives. Make looking after your skin a routine event like cleaning your teeth.

The two major layers of the skin are the *epidermis* (outer layer), which is constantly being replaced by new cells growing from beneath, and the *dermis* (deeper layer), which contains blood vessels, nerves and glands.

The cells on the surface of the epidermis are dead and flake off all the time as microscopic pieces of dried skin. Most of this flaking happens without your even noticing it. Your clothes rub against your skin, you wash daily and perhaps you scratch (albeit unconsciously). If you do not get rid of this layer efficiently, your pores begin to clog – and clogged pores can become spots.

Skin cells gradually travel to the surface, flattening as they do so. Everybody has a different rate of growth but generally cell replacement takes between three and six weeks. The flattened cells make up the skin's surface which is pierced by hair follicles and sweat pores. As a surface cell is removed by daily wear and tear, a new one is born deeper in the dermis.

The thickness of the combined layers of skin varies over different parts of the body. Facial skin, especially that around the eyes, is relatively thin while skin on the palms of the hands and the soles of the feet is much thicker.

Healthy skin produces sebum, nature's own lubricant which is pumped from the sebaceous (oil-producing) glands and keeps the skin soft by forming a protective layer over it. The skin also regulates the body's temperature, it acts as a purifier by getting rid of waste material from the body via the sweat glands and it acts as a barrier against germs and disease. The skin is also waterproof – it keeps essential liquids in and the inessential ones out!

Once you appreciate what a vital and busy organ the skin is, it is easier to understand why it is so important to look after it.

BODY
CARE

The skin on your body does not present as many problems as the skin on your face. Body skin is generally thicker and it is usually protected from the rigours of the weather by clothing. Some people have extremely dry skin, others have dry skin with oily patches and others have skin that is oily all over.

A body-care routine can take place at your regular bath or shower time (it is a good idea to suggest that your family respect your privacy at this time). Try and get into the habit of doing all essential chores while your bath is running: exercise your neck and tummy and pluck your eyebrows (if the skin feels a little tender afterwards soak a pad of cotton wool with cold water and gently pat it over the area).

If you have an oily skin, use a foam bath instead of soap. Most foam baths are detergent-based with added fragrances and are effective cleansers. Using a special glove (there are many different sorts available) massage your body with circular movements to stimulate the circulation and eliminate dead skin cells.

If you have a dry skin, foam baths are best avoided and a bath oil used instead which will cling to the skin to form a moisturizing layer. There are also moisturizing or cream oils (mixtures of oil and detergent) which break down oil and disperse it through the water (this is best for normal or combination skins). As oil is not an effective cleansing agent, you will need to use some soap, but if you have dry skin use a very mild liquid soap on a glove or sponge and make sure it is thoroughly rinsed out of the pores afterwards.

A warm bath is the best place to soften up some of the drier areas of the body – elbows, knees and feet – and get rid of those little hard spots that form on the backs of arms, thighs and buttocks. Wait until you have soaked in the bath for a few minutes and then gently rub the hard skin on your feet with a pumice stone. Use a loofah, gently rubbed in a circular movement, on the other parts of your body and on the rough patches on elbows and knees.

When you get out of the bath, do not leap into your clothes immediately. Pat your body dry and then give yourself an all-over massage with a moisturizing lotion (if you have used a bath oil you will need to use a lotion only on the hard skin on your elbows, feet and knees).

Above all, your bath routine should *relax* as well as cleanse you.

FACE CARE
Skin *type* should not be confused with the *condition* that it is in. The main skin types are dry, oily, combination, sensitive and 'mature' (after twenty-five or so, you naturally produce less sebum). Most people know which skin type they have: if you are in doubt, ask a beauty consultant.

All skins can be affected by such conditions as:
- air travel
- alcohol and tobacco
- antibiotics and other medication
- bad diet
- central heating
- dirt and pollution
- lack of sleep
- prolonged stress
- sunlight – even a pale sun on a winter's day contains harmful UVA light. Your face should be protected (with moisturizer) at all times
- wind.

In some of the above cases (e.g. air travel and alcohol) the skin suffers from dehydration. In other instances (e.g. lack of sleep) the skin loses its 'bloom'.

Your face-care programme should basically consist of cleansing, toning and moisturizing. You should do this twice a day (morning and night) and you should have products that are suitable for your skin type.

Skin problems

Acne – the skin is covered with spots and lumps and a certain amount of scaling. For a woman with acne, 3 to 4 cleanses a day are essential. Do not wear make-up. Give yourself face masks three times a week. Avoid fatty, rich and spicy foods as they can aggravate the situation. (See also 'Acne', page 280.)

Age spots – over-25s may find that they start to get small brown freckle-like marks on the hands, face and elsewhere. These are due to a build-up of melanin (pigment) under the skin, which is constantly being brought to the surface. Use of a special kind of cream will help these marks by gently penetrating the skin tissue and dissolving away the melanin. Ask your beauty consultant for further advice.

Allergies – some people use the wrong product for their skin type, but in many cases it is not the product that is at fault but your diet or your nerves. If you think you are allergic to a particular product, try another one.

Blackheads – these can appear on any area of your face that is too greasy (the nose is the most common). They are caused by excess flow of sebum which has clogged the pores. The little black spot at the end is not dirt: it is melanin, the same substance that helps you turn brown when you are in the sun. The result is a blockage with a build-up of waste material which needs excreting. In most cases, blackheads can be removed by thorough cleansing. You can also help to dislodge them by steaming your face over a bowl (not a kettle) of hot water. Massage your face to stretch the skin but try not to squeeze the blackheads. A face mask will help to loosen them.

Broken veins – everyone has different thicknesses of skin layers and those with the finest skin (a 'fine complexion') are going to be the most prone to broken veins. These can be caused by exposure to harsh weather conditions, drinking very hot drinks, too much alcohol or too many spicy foods.

A good skin-care routine is essential. Try always to protect your face and give it good nourishment.

Cold sores – sometimes known as herpes, these are sores that occur mainly on the lips and around the nose. They are caused by a virus which in most cases lies dormant for years before something triggers it off. If you have cold sores, you should seek medical advice. Try not to touch them.

Enlarged pores – people who have oily skins tend to have enlarged or open pores. It is almost impossible to stop the rate of oil flow but it is a good idea to use a toner and regular face masks (which tighten up the surface skin and free the pores).

Whiteheads – these look like blackheads but because they are under the surface of the skin they stay white because they do not oxidize. Whiteheads may be caused by acidity in the diet or they may be a result of sebum build-up. They are difficult to treat: the most effective method is by professional electrolysis but a good skin-care routine and massage will break them down more quickly.

HANDS AND FEET

Very often it is your hands that people notice first. Hands should be smooth and soft. Handcream, used regularly, can do nothing but good.

When you look after your nails, remember that the base is the living substance and never use metal when pushing back the cuticles. Treat your nails with care. They take about three months to grow from base to end, and split nails or nail ends take a long time to recover.

Both hands and feet need cosseting. Some ideas for your feet include:

- If you have time, treat yourself to a pedicure at a beauty establishment.
- Relax with your feet in a massage footbath. Over 400 tiny invigorating 'stimu-nodes' massage your feet.
- Keep containers of your favourite hand and/or body lotion by your bed, your desk, in the bathroom and in the kitchen and use it regularly.
- Always wear gloves in the kitchen and garden and when doing housework, and outdoors in the cold and wind.
- Tired feet can be refreshed with any brand of footbath or mustard immersed in a bowl of hot water. If you think your feet are swelling up, lie down with your feet about 75 cm higher than your head.
- If your feet feel hurt and bruised consult a chiropodist. If you do not have one near you, see what foot products you can buy to help you.
- Keep shoes and tights, stockings or socks as fresh as possible.

Caring for Your Hair

The average head contains between 120,000 and 150,000 hairs which grow at the rate of approximately half an inch per month. The life of a single hair may be anything up to six years and a healthy head will lose an average of 20 to 80 hairs each day.

Hair is a special arrangement of hard keratin, developed by the reproduction of cells. Beneath the scalp, each hair is protected by a tube-like structure called a follicle. Hairs grow from an upgrowth of the dermis at the base of the follicle called the papilla. The papilla is supplied with small blood vessels which provide the growing hair with nourishment. On the upper or outer portion of the papilla, there is a thin layer of special cells which have the ability to change their supplies of food materials into keratin. Sometimes the papilla degenerates, stopping the follicle producing hair, thus causing thinness and baldness.

Adjacent to the hair follicle is the sebaceous gland which produces sebum, an oily substance that lubricates the skin and hair. Also attached to the follicle and lower layer of the epidermis is an erector muscle: when this contracts, the hair is pulled more upright (e.g. goose pimples).

The hair itself has three separate layers:

1. The *cuticle* is the outer layer, comprising a hard layer of scales overlapping each other – it can be likened to the scales of a fish or the bark of a tree. These scales point upwards in the direction of the hair growth. The prime function of the cuticle is to protect the next layer, the cortex (see below). If the cuticle is loose or open, the hair is porous: The cuticle scales also act as reservoirs to hold sebum and they collect dirt and debris.

2. The *cortex* is the most important and complex part of the hair structure and the natural colour pigments are found in it. The cortex gives your hair its elasticity, pliability, size or diameter, texture and strength.

3. The *medulla* is the inner core which is often broken rather than continuous – it is sometimes entirely missing! Its purpose is still unknown and hair does not appear to suffer when it is absent.

Hair problems

Dandruff – flakes of the skin from the scalp: some scaling is normal but excessive dandruff (a common problem) can be caused by a deficiency in diet, dryness of the skin or improper rinsing after shampooing. Dandruff can be accompanied by a dry or greasy hair condition.

Dry hair – one in three women suffer from dry hair and the problem usually becomes worse as you get older. It is generally caused by an insufficient supply of sebum so that the hair becomes dry and will break and split easily. As the hair dries out, the scales of the cuticle open up, allowing more moisture to escape and making the hairs snag against each other. The hair loses its shine and becomes dull and unmanageable.

Dry hair can also be caused by frequent applications of chemicals to the hair (e.g. bleach, perm, etc.), excessive use of heated rollers and curling tongs, the sun and other climatic elements.

Cleanse with a rich treatment shampoo to give added moisture and lustre: always condition after shampooing.

Fine flyaway hair – hair lacks vitality and sometimes needs shampooing every day to look its best. It can be difficult to handle. Cleanse with a shampoo containing conditioning emollients to give extra body and volume. After styling use a hairspray with extra hold to keep the style in place.

Greasy hair – this is caused by over-activity of the sebaceous glands, a problem which generally arises between the early teens and mid thirties.

Treat with a well-balanced formulation to counteract the greasy buildup. Use an extra-mild shampoo often – or use a dry shampoo between washes. Special care should be taken to avoid massaging the scalp or using very hot water – both will stimulate the sebaceous glands. For conditioning use an oil-free base to restore the natural balance and lustre. Avoid too many greasy foods. A well-balanced diet which includes fresh fruit, vegetables and protein will be reflected in the condition of the hair and scalp.

Tips on hair care
- Shampoo the hair regularly as an accumulation of dirt can cause damage.
- Always use a conditioner after shampooing and give the hair an intensive conditioning treatment about once a month.
- Avoid using heated rollers or curling tongs too frequently (try to use only in an emergency).
- When you set your hair do not wind the rollers too tightly. Hair shrinks as it dries and it can stretch and break easily.
- Do not set the hair dryer too high – use it on medium heat. A setting or blow dry lotion will give the hair extra protection.
- Avoid using inferior brushes or combs that have sharp bristles or teeth as these can split the hair: natural bristle brushes and moulded combs are recommended.
- Have your hair trimmed regularly to prevent split and damaged ends as these cannot be mended.
- During the summer, particularly when on holiday, keep the hair covered from the sun and always rinse it after swimming to remove salt water or chemicals that may be present in swimming-pools.
- Always use the correct preparations for your particular hair condition.

Hair colourants
Be sure to choose the right colouring to suit your skin tone – fairly pale skin tones should go for warm delicate shades, while darker skin tones can take colours with rich red hues. Too dark a shade may look unnatural and can have an ageing effect.

If hair has been straightened or permed recently it is best to wait 2 or 3 weeks before colouring to make sure that the two very different chemical processes do not interact in any way.

It is important to follow instructions very carefully. Leaving colour on too long or washing it off too soon will affect the end result.

Conditioning after every wash is essential to keep hair looking good and in tip-top condition.

There are specialist products for colouring grey hair.

There are two basic types of colourant: temporary and longer lasting. The former coats or clings to the hair shaft rather like a fabric conditioner. Shampoo-in colourants are ideal for adding a little warmth and interest to drab hair or for boosting a previously applied colourant which has begun to fade. They are also a good way of trying out a colour for the first time. Spray-on colourants are used after the hair has been shampooed, conditioned, dried and styled – you just spray your chosen colour where you want it.

Longer lasting colourants: some of these gradually fade after a number of shampoos (up to eight, depending on your hair type) and others slowly grow out – these contain bleaching and colouring agents which penetrate the hair shaft making the hair more porous, thus enabling it to receive the colour. Most of the longest lasting colourants involve the pre-mixing of two solutions – an oxidation dye (the colouring agent) and the developer (peroxide). Remember when using these that you will get areas of growth, so regular retouching will be necessary if you want your colour to remain looking as natural as possible.

If you are a little anxious about treating your hair chemically but would still like a colour change, then take a look at henna, a natural vegetable non-toxic dye which does not contain any chemicals. It gives hair not only more body but also really rich auburn, mahogany or red tones can be achieved.

Complaints   If you are not happy with a *hairdressing salon*, you should contact the salon director. Less than 50 per cent of salons are registered with the Hairdressing Council. If yours is, contact:

> Hairdressing Council
> 17 Spring Street
> London W2 3RA
> 01–402 6367

If the salon concerned is not a member of the Council, you should take further advice from your Citizens' Advice Bureau.

Caring for Your Teeth

Everyone is entitled to two free dental inspections a year on the National Health Service. Some people (young people, those on supplementary benefits and some older people) are entitled to free or cheaper treatment (see form D11 from your post office or DHSS). While you are pregnant, and for one year after, dental treatment is free. Regular brushing is essential during pregnancy because the baby takes some lime from your teeth to build up its bones. Your teeth may therefore become a little soft and more liable to decay. Visit your dentist so that he or she can treat any decayed teeth which may endanger the health of the baby.

Brushing your teeth should remove the harmful food residues and bacteria called 'plaque' which cause tooth decay and gum disease. Change your toothbrush frequently (at least every three months). Buy one with a compact head to reach into difficult areas, soft and firmly packed nylon filaments, a precisely angled neck and a handle with a good grip. Use a fluoride toothpaste.

Correct brushing procedure   Brush gently, up and down one tooth at a time (not across the teeth). Use several short back-and-forth strokes to loosen plaque from the small gap between the base of each tooth and the gum and from between the teeth and then use several longer sweeping strokes to carry the plaque away from the gum line. Be sure to clean the backs as well as the fronts.

Move from tooth to tooth in the following order:

● **upper jaw**

1. Start at inside surfaces, upper left.
2. Move to inside surfaces, upper centre
3. Then to inside surfaces, upper right. Finish off with the chewing surfaces of the upper right molars.

4. Start at outside surfaces, upper right.
5. Move to outside surfaces, upper centre.
6. Then to outside surfaces, upper right. Finish off with the chewing surfaces of the upper left molars.

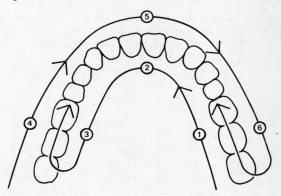

● **lower jaw**

7. Now switch to the lower jaw and start inside, lower right.
8. Move to inside surfaces, lower centre.
9. Then to inside surfaces, lower left. Finish off with the chewing surfaces of the lower left molars.

10. Start at outside surfaces, lower left.
11. Move to outside surfaces, lower centre.
12. Then to outside surfaces, lower right. Finish off with the chewing surfaces of the lower right molars.

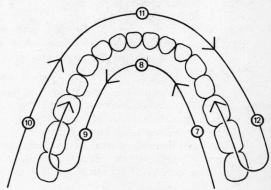

Flossing every day cleans between teeth and under the gums where a toothbrush cannot reach. Never snap the floss hard between your teeth or you could damage the gum. If the floss will not go easily into a gap, gently ease it back and forth to get it past the tight area. If you have any difficulty getting the floss between your teeth, see your dentist.

Odours

Bad breath (halitosis) cannot, alas, be recognized by the sufferer (unless all those around back away!). Prevention is the answer:
1. Regular dental check-ups.
2. Regular brushing of teeth.
3. Gargle (say twice a week) with a medicated (not a green-coloured 'cosmetic') mouthwash.
4. Eat regular meals and avoid too much smoking, coffee or alcohol.
5. If you fear you may have problems:
- eat an apple or carrot
- eat parsley (especially good after garlic)
- ask your best friend, honestly.

Body odour is more or less a thing of the past. Deodorants contain bacteriastats which kill the bacteria that feed on sweat glands, thereby causing body odour. Antiperspirants contain metal salts which restrict the secretion of sweat without actually stopping perspiration. If your usual deodorant/antiperspirant does not work, try switching to another brand or ask your doctor or a dermatologist for advice.

Foot smells can be eliminated by frequent washing of tights and stockings – and of feet. The Shoe and Allied Trades Research Association (SATRA) suggests that it is a good idea not to wear the same shoes day after day as they will not have a chance to dry out. Shoes absorb perspiration and a damp condition will encourage growth of moulds and odours.

To minimize odours:
- Shoes should fit properly.
- Leather shoes should be worn. Leather linings are useful in that they reduce or delay the effects of perspiration on the uppers.
- Loose insoles will absorb perspiration.
- Regularly bathe the feet.

Vaginal odour – *never* use a 'feminine' deodorant. Unperfumed soap and water should suffice: if not, consult your doctor.

Further Information

Suggested further reading

NUTRITION, DIET AND VEGETARIANISM
Brown, Sarah, *Vegetarian Kitchen*, BBC Publications
Campbell, Dr Anthony, *The Natural Health Handbook*, Ebury
Cousins, Margaret and Jill Metcalfe, *High Fibre, Low Sugar, Low Fat, Wholefood Vegetarian Cookbook*, Thorsens
Duff, Gail, *Vegetarian Cookery*, Pan
    Wholefood Cookery, Good Housekeeping/Ebury
Elliott, Rose, *The Bean Book*, Fontana
    Not Just a Load of Old Lentils, Fontana
Handslip, Carol, *The Colour Book of Wholefood Cookery*, Octopus
Kenton, Leslie and Susannah, *Raw Energy: Eat Your Way to Radiant Health*, Century
McCallum, Cass, *The Real Food Guides: Fresh Fruit and Vegetables*, Molendinar Press
    Pulses, Seeds and Grains, Molendinar Press
Marshall, Janette and Sarah Bounds, *Wholefood Cookery Course*, Thorsens
Maryon-Davis, Dr Alan and Jane Thomas, *Diet 2000: How to Eat for a Healthier Future*, Pan
Stanway, Dr Andrew, *Taking the Rough with the Smooth*, Pan
Walker, Caroline and Geoffrey Cannon, *The Food Scandal*, Century
Whittet, Annabel, *Where to Eat if You Don't Eat Meat*, Papermac
Yudkin, John, *Pure, White and Deadly*, Penguin

SMOKING
Jackson, Bobbie, *The Ladykillers: Why Smoking Is a Feminist Issue*, Pluto Press

DIET AND WEIGHT LOSS AND RELATED PROBLEMS
Cannon, Geoffrey, *Dieting Makes You Fat*, Sphere
Chernin, Kim, *Womansize*, Women's Press
Lawrence, Marilyn, *The Anorexic Experience*, Women's Press
MacLeod, Sheila, *The Art of Starvation*, Virago Press
Orbach, Susie, *Fat Is a Feminist Issue*, Hamlyn
Palmer, R. L. *Anorexia Nervosa*, Penguin

EXERCISES FOR HEALTH AND FITNESS
Bury, Bob, *A Pocket Book of Yoga*, Octopus
Consumers' Association, *Avoiding Back Trouble*
    Avoiding Heart Trouble
Polunin, Miriam (ed.), *Health and Fitness Handbook: a Family Guide*, Sphere
Richardson, Sonia, *Yoga and Your Health*, Granada
Ulsden, Arline, *In Great Shape*, St Michael
Woolf, Vicki, *Shape Up for Sex*, Zomba Books

BEAUTY

Hutton, Deborah, *Vogue Complete Beauty*, Octopus

Maxwell-Hudson, Clare, *The Book of Massage*, Ebury

Stoppard, Dr Miriam, *Face and Body Book*, Pan

14 Dress

With a beautiful body it is sometimes immaterial what you wear – or what you don't wear! But, for most of us, what we wear is an important extension of our personality. These days it is far better to wear what suits you than to worry about what is 'right' for the occasion. Whether you prefer feminine frilly clothes or unisex is up to you. As Cyril Kern, Chairman of the British Fashion Council, told me, 'Women and men at many times in history have worn the same clothes so there is nothing new about the androgynous dressing of today. But,' he went on, 'nothing in fashion is for ever!'

This chapter shows you how to work out what is best for you and how to put together a wardrobe, it gives you shopping ideas, and tells you how to look after your clothes.

Above all, I have tried to show that dressing can and should be fun.

Thinking about dress

'Fashion' implies constant updating and attention to the latest fads that might be utterly impractical for daily life. 'Dress', by contrast, is a practical interpretation of what is to be worn and how the various items together constitute the whole (the *wardrobe*). Dress emphasizes the important fact that the *person* and not what she is wearing is the essential factor. The art of dressing satisfactorily requires confidence, experience and style so that clothes become an extension of the wearer rather than being the dominant feature.

One of the chief guidelines to dressing today is that it is essential to feel comfortable at all times. Gone are the eras of tightly pinched waists and impossibly tight hems. The ideal consists of careful pre-planning so that you can forget completely about what you are actually wearing.

ASSESS YOUR
FIGURE

Some people can wear anything regardless of their shape. If they 'wear clothes well' – which more often than not implies a better than average figure coupled with good posture – they can wear anything.

The basic rules include what is obvious:

- *Tall* people look even taller in vertical stripes and in one main garment with no 'break' at the waist.
- Similarly, *short* people will find that horizontal stripes exaggerate their lack of height.
- Big people do not look good in pale colours and lots of frills.

So, be honest with yourself. Wear what *suits* you.

BUDGETING

Try to keep an annual record of everything you spend on clothes, including tights. Is the final figure a shock? Could you have done better? Without working out a basic wardrobe plan you will undoubtedly spend more money and spend it on items that do not take an important role in your dressing schedule.

How much to spend overall is a personal problem which is linked to your lifestyle (business dressing is more expensive than home-based), age (young adults usually spend more than their elders), location (south, north, city or country) and personal connections (entrées into discount shopping) as well as the ceiling imposed by income.

The key to the whole concept is *value for money*. If you wear something enough times, its unit cost per wear comes down and down. Burberry ran a competition a few years ago to find the oldest of their coats still in existence and an 1896 garment won. That represents value for money. The basic formula, therefore, to discover whether or not something is financially worthwhile is: ORIGINAL COST divided by TIMES WORN.

There are some areas in which it is advisable not to skimp – shoes and handbag, for instance. In other cases you really can save. Cleverly chosen dresses from some chain stores often look at least four times their real worth. The more versatile the garments you choose, the more outfits you will have from the basic ingredients. Following the 'value for money' principle will also in the long run save money. Other suggestions for saving money include: shrewd shopping (watch for the sales); borrowing from friends for one-off special occasions; and making your own.

Everyone makes mistakes. The important thing is to realize when you have done so – and to pass the offending garment on to a friend, charity shop or clothes agency. It is also a good idea to remember not to repeat your mistakes.

COLOUR

A basic wardrobe should revolve around three colours which all go together and at least one of which is a 'hub' colour (black, brown, navy, grey, beige, white). 'Red, black and beige' will therefore fit these requirements. 'Red, yellow, pink' will not.

The point of a 'hub' colour is to unite items. It may or may not provide everyday accessories, say black shoes and bag. It probably also provides some of the main clothing, say a coat. A winter 'hub' colour can carry through to spring/autumn, e.g. a black fabric bag, but a summer 'hub' cannot be taken into winter, e.g. white shoes.

'Highlight' colours complement the chosen basics. With 'red, black and beige' a highlight of turquoise – say shoes and skirt – can look stunning with at least two of the chosen basics (black and beige). A wardrobe without 'highlight' colours is boring: so is a monochromatic wardrobe. Highlights provide versatility, an essential ingredient of successful dressing. Colours reflect an image and it is a good idea sometimes to present a different image. Yellows, for instance, are vivacious and bright, whereas blues suggest coolness and calm. Purples indicate a bold superiority and reds are aggressively exciting.

● Colour analysis helps you determine which colours are best for you. For details contact:

Colour Me Beautiful
PO Box 127
London SW11 4RP
01–228 4103

STYLE Some people appear to have style and others do not, and it is very unfair. Partly it is due to the shape and figure of the wearer. You cannot do much about those requirements at this stage. Partly it is the basic clothes – and you can carefully work on your basic wardrobe. Partly, too, it is the way you put them together.

Style is also the confidence which comes with versatility – say a purple polyester shirtwaister that adapts throughout the day, simply worn with flat shoes and no jewellery in the early morning, with low court shoes at lunch and, in the evening, worn with high sandals and long dangling earrings. Versatility is made easier by the simplicity of basic garments. A simple neckline, for instance, is much more adaptable and certainly generally more flattering than fussy frills.

It is also a good idea not to be always 'the first' with a new look. Occasionally be a forerunner but be content to be among the front runners and not the outright winner.

1. *Formality v. informality.* When in doubt, go for understatement. It is better to wear a simple blouse and skirt and find everyone else in black full length than the other way round. If you really are worried about the degree of formality of an occasion, dress down with quality and add accessories. Blue jeans (if well cut) and shirt (if real silk) can more often pass muster if accompanied by, say, a Hermes scarf and heavy gold bracelet.

2. *Do not dress 'old'.* Plain basic colours or clothes too tight or too large can make you look old before your time. You should avoid long jackets, old-fashioned 'fads', sensible shoes, obvious hairstyle and make-up that conflict with your face shape and complexion.

3. *Do not dress too 'young'.* Trying to look too young (wearing blue jeans when you are fifty unless you have a perfect figure) in fact makes you look like the proverbial 'mutton dressed as lamb' and paradoxically emphasizes your age.

4. *Look young naturally.* Bright colours look young, You can also wear contrasting separates, clothes either a perfect fit or one size too large, short jackets, old-fashioned combined with modern trends, comfortable but up-to-date shoes, hairstyle and make-up that complement your face shape and complexion and an overall air of careful planning resulting in relaxed confidence.

CONVERSION TABLES

GARMENT SIZES

British	10	12	14	16	18		
Continental	38	40	42	44	46	48	50
American	8	10	12	14	16	18	20

SHOES

British	3	4	5	6	7	8	9
Continental	$35\frac{1}{2}$	$36\frac{1}{2}$	38	$39\frac{1}{2}$	$40\frac{1}{2}$	42	43
American	$4\frac{1}{2}$	$5\frac{1}{2}$	$6\frac{1}{2}$	$7\frac{1}{2}$	$8\frac{1}{2}$	$9\frac{1}{2}$	$10\frac{1}{2}$

TIGHTS AND STOCKINGS

British	8	$8\frac{1}{2}$	9	$9\frac{1}{2}$	10	$10\frac{1}{2}$	11
Continental	35	36	37	38	39	40	41
American	same as British from $8\frac{1}{2}$ up						

Accessories

BELTS   JEWELLERY
GLOVES   SHOES
HANDBAGS

These can make or mar an outfit but the location must be taken into consideration. Generally, for instance, chic daytime wear should not be accompanied by tennis or training shoes. A good rule to bear in mind is that accessories should either be expensive/classic or inexpensive/fun:
- a 'name' shoulder bag or a bright pink plastic duffle-bag
- classic black shoes or canvas espadrilles.

BELTS   Generally when you buy a dress with its own belt it is the belt that is the giveaway (that is to say, it was an inexpensive purchase). Change the belt and the dress will look twice what you paid for it!

Even if you are not proud of your waist, a simple belt will make your outfit look more expensive (but if your waist really is large, do not go for an obvious and outrageous belt, keep it simple).

A 'basic belt wardrobe' could, at the least, consist of:
- a thick black leather belt with simple gold or black buckle

- a golden metal chain belt.

Keep leather belts either hanging up in your wardrobe or on a hook or loosely rolled, right side out.

GLOVES   These days gloves are not generally worn purely for decoration.

Wash leather gloves in a special glove solution which you can buy at main chemists and department stores. Follow the instructions that come with the glove solution. Allow them to dry – they will look like crinkled prunes – then sprinkle talcum powder on your hands and put the gloves on carefully.

HANDBAGS   Most women find that having one all-purpose handbag prevents that awful feeling of coming to the check-out at the supermarket and finding that you left your cheque book in your other handbag.

Fortunately, the days when the well-dressed woman had to have matching handbag and shoes are now long since past. For everyday, a shoulder bag with a sturdy zip is one of the easiest and most useful styles. For safety, do make sure that when you are in a crowded place you have the bag hanging to the front not the back of you.

Some of the best value bags are to be found in bigger branches of Boots, Marks & Spencer and British Home Stores. Although a Gucci black leather and canvas bag at just under £200 seems an expensive outlay, such a bag will last for years and 'always look good'.

JEWELLERY   The higher the carat, the purer and softer the gold. A 9-carat ring is likely to wear down a 22-carat ring if they touch. Information on gold jewellery and how to identify hallmarks from:

> Gold Information Office
> International Gold Corporation
> 30 George Street
> London WIR 9FA
> 01–499 9201

As a complete contrast to antiques and heirlooms, plastic and coloured aluminium jewellery is marvellously 'direct'. You can find a wide selection at the jewellery counter in most department stores. There are also specialist jewellery shops which you can find in Yellow Pages.

SHOES   Bad shoes hurt. Some people are lucky and can step straight into a pair of shoes and walk from John o'Groats to Land's End but most have difficulty choosing a suitable style which is also a comfortable fit. Part of this problem is the fact that many people tend to know beforehand what they want but then cannot find it. Have you ever tried to buy a pair of flat gold sandals in September? Even a classic pair of low black pumps can be difficult to find in May.

Shoppers therefore often do not enjoy shopping for shoes. Further difficulty is presented by the fact that there may be several shoe shops in the main shopping street. Some of these are owned by the same holding firm and have more or less the same shoes but they are displayed differently enough to warrant inspection of each shop.

Make sure that you go to a shop that is a member of one of the associations forming the Footwear Distributors' Federation. The retailer will then honour the code of practice for footwear.

Good shoe shops should have sales assistants who understand shoes and will not try to make you buy exorbitantly priced and unsuitable purchases. The shoes should extend beyond the foot to give shape. Leather shoes should not gape when you are trying them on: they will stretch later, with wear.

When you have your new shoes home, spray them – depending on the material – with a proprietary leather-protecting spray and leave to dry for a few hours. Then 'break them in', wearing them around the house first for a short time and then for longer. The more comfortably you and the shoes work together, the better you will feel and the better therefore you will be able to work.

Keep two pairs of ordinary everyday shoes to wear on alternate days, thus allowing the resting shoes to 'breathe'. Always put shoe trees in shoes whenever you take them off. Some people think you should then leave the shoe trees in. Others say trees need only be used for half an hour. Covered foam toes-only trees absorb perspiration but they do not hold the shape of the heels as well as the rigid-ended long-tailed trees. If you have problems with smelly feet, use deodorizing insoles. Clean shoes regularly – do not wait for them to become dirty. Damp leather is sensitive to heat so if the shoes are wet avoid harsh drying. Stuff the toes with rolled-up newspaper and allow to dry at normal room temperature in a well-ventilated room. Shoes made with materials other than leather may also suffer from heat: crêpe soles can soften and liquefy and synthetic soling might 'balloon'.

Be prepared, too, for mending. Anticipate when the heels are wearing down and go to a reliable shoe repairer. Very thin or holed soles allow footwear to flex excessively, throwing increased stress on other components. Wetting through thin or holed soles can ruin uppers.

See the shoe sizing conversion table on page 416.

Complaints   If you feel you have cause for complaint over *service* at any shop adhering to the Footwear Distributors' Federation Code of Practice or if you are unhappy with the shoes you bought, first contact the shop manager and, if you are still dissatisfied, contact:

> Footwear Distributors' Federation
> Commonwealth House
> 1–19 New Oxford Street
> London WC1A 1PA

See   'Cleaning Shoes' and other excellent free leaflets from (s.a.e.):

Publications Services
Shoe and Allied Trades Research Association (SATRA)
SATRA House
Rockingham Road
Kettering
Northants NN16 9JH
0536–516318

Underwear

LINGERIE   TIGHTS AND STOCKINGS

As with accessories, underwear can make or mar an outfit. Nothing looks worse than the bulges around a badly fitting bra showing through an outfit (especially if dirty bra straps are also revealed) or the outlines of underpants visible through trousers.

Some people, especially slim people with standard figures, will feel there is little point in investing in anything but chain store bras, underpants and slips. If you do find a style that suits and fits you, buy in bulk as styles change and sometimes front-opening bras, for instance, are not available in winter.

To avoid having bra-straps showing, attach small tapes to the inside of shoulder seams of garments – sewn on at the neck end, with velcro touch-and-close spots at the other.

LINGERIE

It is always worth buying quality bras, slips and nightdresses. The quality of the fabric and the cut and making up of the garment make it feel right.

Find what shape and type of garment you enjoy wearing. You should feel comfortable in it and be able to move freely. When you find such a garment buy several, as garments interchanged and regularly washed last better and look better for longer.

TIGHTS AND STOCKINGS

As with lingerie, it really is worthwhile buying more expensive items. They generally last longer: plain knit – as opposed to mesh – are less susceptible to snagging due to their smoother texture. Your legs certainly look more elegant, too. Sheer tights and stockings need care, so avoid contact with rings, rough skin, fingernails, shopping baskets and other danger points.

One-size tights can be worn by people of average size – although 'average' varies between different manufacturers. Some tights do, however, have sizes printed on the packaging.

Support tights, which are available in fashionable colours and look sheer on the leg, are made in varying degrees of compression (support).

Wash ordinary and support tights and stockings by hand in warm, soapy water. Do not let them come into contact with other garments – even the most neutral coloured tights contain a strong dye which can ruin a white garment if they are washed together. Dry by hanging up by the toes (avoid exposure to direct heat). Heavyweight hosiery and legwarmers may be up to 100 per cent acrylic and can be machine-washed (check washing instructions on packet).

Special Materials

FUR	SILK
LEATHER	WOOL

FUR Furs will retain their 'freshness' better if well cared for:
- Always shake before hanging on a padded hanger. Fasten the buttons.
- Do not enclose in a plastic bag: the fur needs to breathe.
- Hang in a cool dark place.
- Keep away from hair sprays and perfume.
- Wear shoulder bags under not over a coat.
- Fur coats do not like seat belts: if you must drive in a fur coat leave it loose.
- If the coat gets wet, shake off excess water and hang in a cool place with plenty of air and away from direct heat. When it is dry, shake it again.
- Cleaning and repairs should be done by a skilled professional, who might also offer regular summer storage.
- For summer storage all furs should be placed on individual stiff hangers, covered with a cotton sheet and stored in a cool cupboard. After two winter wears the furs should be cleaned by a specialist before storing.

LEATHER Buy the best quality that you can afford. A little extra financial sacrifice will return dividends in giving you longer wear, smartness and greater enjoyment. Only buy branded garments on which the label is sewn and always buy from a shop that specializes in leather. Ask the sales assistant what kind of skin has been used and ask for advice on how to look after your garment.

A leather or suede coat should be kept on a good wooden hanger when not in use: make sure the hanger is the right size (too long and it may 'bag' the upper sleeves and too short and it may 'bag' the shoulder line). If you want to cover the coat use a sheet rather than a plastic bag as it will allow the skins to breathe.

A leather coat can be revitalized with tepid water and washing-up liquid. Rub the leather in circles and polish clean with a dry soft cloth. Or entrust the work to a professional cleaner.

If your coat gets wet, dry gently in a room away from direct heat. It may dry somewhat hardened as a result of the leather fibres sticking together. Stretch the leather, when dry, over the rounded back of a chair or a rounded table edge and work it back and forth to unstick the fibres (make sure the chair or table edge is not sharp).

Brush a suede coat regularly with a soft brush – not a wire brush as it damages the nap. You can keep the colour and appearance fresh by hanging the coat over a warm bath and brushing the nap with a soft brush, but remember that heat ruins leather so avoid close contact with steam (e.g. from a kettle) and do not hang the coat near a radiator.

To remove spots

● Dark spots can occur when rain penetrates the suede's surface. Brush the spots vigorously with a soft brush when the garment is dry.

● Grease marks should be treated appropriately with a suitable brand product available from most suede stockists.

When you need your garment cleaned you should go to a company that specializes in the care of leathers. You can get a list of companies in your area by contacting (s.a.e.) the British Leather Federation (address below) or the Association of British Launderers and Cleaners (address on page 429). If you are dissatisfied with professional cleaning first complain in writing to the cleaning company and ask for a written report on the garment. If you still have cause for complaint, contact the Association of British Launderers and Cleaners (address below).

If you want to know more about leathers and how to look after them, contact:

British Leather Federation
Leather Trade House
Kings Park Road
Moulton Park
Northampton NN3 1JD
0604–494131

SILK

Silk is strong and hard-wearing but it must be treated properly. It should never be allowed to get too dirty as this can cause breakdown of fibres. Among the garments and types of silk that should always be dry-cleaned are silk scarves and ties, silk brocade, chiffon, georgette, organza and taffeta. Wash a silk garment only if it does not fall into one of the above categories and washing is specifically allowed on the manufacturer's instructions. Nevertheless, it is a good idea to do a colour fastness test before washing for the first time. Wet a small unseen section of the garment (interior hem surplus, perhaps) and place it on white fabric. Iron with a cool iron.

Is there any colour running? If not, hand-wash in cool or cold water with a gentle liquid detergent. Rinse well and squeeze out surplus water by rolling in a towel. Dry away from direct heat or bright light and press with a warm iron on the wrong side of the garment when it is slightly damp. If there is any water staining, soak the garment in cold water, dry and iron.

For more information on silk contact (s.a.e.):

European Commission for the Promotion of Silk
50 Upper Brook Street
London W1Y 1PG
01–499 5726

WOOL   'Pure new wool' is any wool that has not previously passed the spinning stage. 'Woollen' is yarn made mainly from shorter fibres and is thick and fluffy with a hairy surface. 'Worsted' is a yarn made only from longer wool fibres to produce a smoother, clearer pattern that can often be printed.

Brush wool clothes before putting away and if you are hanging items make sure hangers fit (see 'Leather' above). Fold sweaters neatly and stack on shelves or in drawers.

● Before you wash any wool garment, turn it inside out to protect the surface and prevent loose fibres (or the tissue you may have left in your pocket) from ending up on show.

● If hand-washing, use lukewarm water and make sure powder or liquid is fully dissolved or mixed before immersing the garment. Do exactly as the detergent instructions tell you: *gently* squeeze the liquid through the garments a few times and remember that a short (2-minute) soak will help to remove dirt. Wool cleans easily: rinse thoroughly first in warm water to remove detergent and then in cold water.

● If machine-washing, first check label to see that this is all right. Then follow the washing-machine instruction book or use a mild wash at 40°C). With a top-loading machine make sure the detergent is completely dissolved before adding the clothes.

● Drying: spin dry for a short spin, coax the garment back to size and shape while still damp and, if possible, dry flat. If you use a clothes line, fold garment over it to avoid stretching and do not peg. Never dry white and light colours in sunlight – and do not dry any item near too much heat.

● Most garments benefit from gentle ironing on the wrong side.

If you want further information on wool contact (s.a.e.):

> Consumer Affairs
> International Wool Secretariat
> Wool House
> Carlton Gardens
> London SW1Y 5AE
> 01–930 7300

If you want to have garments specially knitted, look in the small ads of your local or national newspaper.

Weddings

A wedding dress probably requires more thought – and in many cases more expense – than any other outfit during a lifetime. The dress can be bought, hired, borrowed or made. Some girls have their own dream dress imagined since childhood but few seriously bother to think about the dress until the time comes near. Because the wedding dress is so important, it is advisable to look at as many as possible. Buy all current specialist wedding magazines – they will also help you with planning the occasion (see also Chapter 12).

You can buy your outfit from any of the main department stores (or branches) or from specialist shops which you can look up in Yellow Pages under 'Wedding Reception Services'.

If you are a member of the wedding party (bride's or groom's mother or older sister) do make sure that you know what everyone else is wearing. If others are wearing shades of pink, do not plump for bright orange. Remember that a navy and white combination is sometimes rather ageing. As the mother of bride or groom you are expected to wear something suitably outstanding. And, as such, many brides' mothers have invested in ultra-expensive coat-dresses with matching hats that are never worn again. This may be the one occasion in your life when you will really splurge and do not feel guilty about it. But, on the other hand, if you already have a dress or coat in which you feel comfortable there is no need to feel guilty about not buying a new outfit – why not simply buy a brand-new hat or borrow one? Remember that your back view will be most prominent as you walk up to your front pew seat in the church and during the service. At the reception your front will be seen too. If you plan on high heels for the church try to have a pair of lower heels should you need them as the reception progresses.

Other members of the wedding party should remember that they should not try to outdo either of the mothers. They too will feel happier if they have not spent a lot on outfits that will never be worn again.

Packing for Holidays

Holidays raise problems all their own. Where are you going, and how and for how long? You will probably find that you need as much for a weekend stay at a friend's house as you would for two weeks in a foreign hotel.

The most efficient and experienced travellers:
● Make sure they have one of everything (shoes, dress, etc.) they will need, but do not worry about more unless they know they are going to be completely out of reach of shops.
● They take the same standbys with them wherever they are going overseas – in other words a sweater to the tropics and a thin shirt to Siberia.
● They also make sure they do not run out of basic essentials such as necessary pills and ballpoint pens.
● They make sure they have some good reading with them. You may not be able to find any English newspapers and, if you do, they may be expensive. Take books that are paperback (they make good 'tips', and

you can sometimes swop them). Suggestions for holiday reading are given in Chapter 18.

Packing tips The best method of packing main garments is to fold each vertically, from neck to hem, about 40 cm wide. Lay these long shapes one above the other and roll from one end just like a Swiss roll. Put this in a plastic bag. Other items go in bags too, which means you – and customs officials – can clearly see what you have.

Special People

BIGGER PEOPLE   **SLIMMING PEOPLE**
DIFFERENTLY SIZED PEOPLE **SHORTER PEOPLE**
OLDER PEOPLE   **TALLER PEOPLE**
PREGNANT AND NURSING PEOPLE

BIGGER PEOPLE
Almost 50 per cent of British women take size 16 or over. With careful thought, confidence and flair you too can have fun with fashion.

Try to emphasize your good points and minimize the bad:

1. If you have a large bust, never wear a plain back-fastening bodice: try to wear shirt-style dresses, diagonal stripes, vertical frills, long scarves, long beads, edge-to-edge jackets.

2. Balance big hips with plenty of interest at neck and shoulders and wear classic dresses that skim past waist and hips or suits with long, loose jackets.

3. Tall, large but well-proportioned women are fortunate: go for drama with large prints, swirling skirts, bat-wing sleeves and shawls (never try to fade away and minimize your size with tiny prints and apologetic colours).

4. If you are petite but, frankly, plump, you should try to look neat: choose the narrowest dresses you can find (if you have a relatively small waist, try a princess line), plain if possible or with small, smudgy prints. Avoid separates.

Many local shops specialize in outsize clothes. For sizes 16 to 30 Evans have over eighty-five stores nationwide. To find out your nearest store telephone 01–637 0599.

For mail order (sizes 16 plus) contact:

Fashion Extra
Bridgewater Place
Manchester M60 6AP
061–832 2353

DIFFERENTLY SIZED PEOPLE
Marks & Spencer understand the problem of someone who has, say, a small upper half and bigger lower half. Buy their separates in the required sizes and put together a top and skirt to make what looks like a dress.

You can buy bikinis with differently sized tops and bottoms and matching beachwear in sizes 8–20. Winter clothes are also available in sizes 8–20 from (mail order):

One of Gillie's
Llantrithyd
Cowbridge
South Glam CF7 7UB
04468–357

OLDER PEOPLE

Hilary Wharton, owner of Tyndale Residential Home, told me that older, less mobile or disabled people love pretty things and they like to look smart. Encourage this enthusiasm. Ideas for Christmas or birthday presents include:

- Full length nightie, long sleeves, loose-fitting flowery or lacy (if in doubt about size, go for an 18).
- If they sit a lot, a woolly foot muff is always appreciated.
- Jewellery is always appreciated – and it does not have to be expensive.

Dressing must be considered in the context of an individual's circumstances. To this end an initial assessment by the person involved or a close friend or relative can show the need for simple adjustments to clothing or simple aids and equipment required.

Some adaptations include:

- Velcro touch-and-close fastening instead of buttons or zips.
- Front fastenings, especially on bras.
- Wrap-around skirts (with join down the back for wheelchair users).
- Buttons, if used, sewn on a long shank or two buttons joined together with elastic to make a cufflink.
- Split knickers/incontinence pants.
- Hold-up stockings with elastic tops, or suspenders linked together on a large buttonhole attached to the stocking before being pulled up and then fastened with one hand on to a button on the corset.
- Elasticated shoe laces.
- Try to avoid a demeaning bib – a coloured apron is far less humiliating.

Some available aids include:

- plastic dressing stick (long stick like a coathanger with a curve at the end)
- 'helping hand reacher' (like a long claw)
- button hook
- dressing rail
- plastic stocking 'gutter' (a thin sheet of plastic attached to a string which opens up a stocking so that you can get your foot in).

For details and catalogues of clothing aids send s.a.e. to:

Disabled Living Foundation
380–384 Harrow Road
London W9 2HU
01–289 6111

Equipment for the Disabled
2 Foredown Drive
Portslade
Sussex BN4 2BB
(No telephone)

PREGNANT AND NURSING MOTHERS

Diana Hastings says that the most important thing to remember when you are pregnant is to wear something that is comfortable. Since this is especially a time to look your best you should also wear clothes that make you feel good.

For the first four months of your pregnancy you should be able to wear your ordinary clothes if they are not fitted at the waist. After this look out for garments that have fullness of body, bust and skirt, and adjustable or elasticated waists.

You will need a good supporting bra, even if you do not usually wear one. You can buy maternity underwear at most shops that sell lingerie. If it is your first baby, you should not need a maternity belt or corset as your abdominal muscles should be strong enough, but if you want support look out for pantie girdles with adjustable extra back support.

Nightdresses are also available which will make breast-feeding easy. As your pregnancy progresses, you may need special swimwear: look out for garments with gathered tunic-type tops.

If you usually wear high heels there is no reason why you should not continue to do so until the last few weeks, by which time they may feel uncomfortable. As a general rule, however, wear shoes that feel comfortable.

Similarly, while nursing you will need clothes that disguise the extra weight you are still carrying, make feeding easy and show the least amount of stains and daily wear. You will, during this period, also need nursing bras, either drop front or front opening.

You can get maternity clothes from major department stores, any branch of a childwear shop or from any specialist shop.

SLIMMING PEOPLE

Carole Wesley lost 170 lb. Here are some of her thoughts on dressing as you slim:

I broke a lot of rules as some people say 'wear one colour to look slim'. I certainly did not. I stayed with lots of mix-and-match clothes in strong and soft colours, avoiding pastels.

My main help was my marvellous dressmaker, a friend who every three months went through my entire wardrobe and remade what did not fit. On one occasion she took to pieces an old grey wool skirt that had become a bit nobbly: she remade it inside out and I had the most flattering 'new' skirt.

If you cannot sew, it is essential to know someone who does or you should use a good dressmaker. If you really are on a 'long' slim, do not adjust your clothes too often. Try to do it on a regular basis.

When I had lost 100 lb I actually bought my first new 'usual size' dress.

What a thrill that was! For evenings, I had a long velvet dress with plain neck and long sleeves and it did not matter that it became looser every week.

I bought new (and smaller) underclothes about every three months and simply did the fastening up on a tighter notch, or tied a knot in the elastic, in between.

Accessories are important as you slim. I found I wore simple pearls and gold chains.

And, of course, there is no point in attending to your dressing if you do not look after your skin and exercise as you slim.

SHORTER PEOPLE

You do have some problems that are especially your own. As Freda Williams (5 ft 2½ ins.) says: 'My first thought on buying a new dress or coat is that I *know* I have to cut 3 to 4 inches off the hem (this can prove useful because I can sometimes make a belt or small stand-up collar out of it!). Similarly, all my petticoats need shortening.

'Stockings – I never wear tights – are also too long and I have to turn them over at the top.' Carina has shops specially catering for shorter people (sizes 6 to 16):

> Carina
> 42 Chiltern Street
> London WIM IPL
> 01–486 2712

TALLER PEOPLE

Judy Rich is 6 feet tall. When she came to Britain from her native America in 1975 she could not find a thing to wear – so she started a shop, Long Tall Sally, selling what she and other women like her wanted to buy. Now there are several Long Tall Sally shops stocking sizes 12 to 20 for anyone up to 6 feet and more. The clothes and accessories are specially made up with extended measurements.

'Not only do waistlines have to be lowered but pockets, for example, must be lowered on coats, trousers have to be longer in the rise as well as the legs, bust darts in a blouse or dress have to be in a slightly different position,' says Judy.

> Long Tall Sally
> 21 Chiltern Street
> London WIM IPH
>   01–487 3370 (credit card ordering 01–486 3542)
>
> and

Bath	0225–66682
Birmingham	021–233 4406
Edinburgh	031–225 8330
Manchester	061–832 3331
Tunbridge Wells	0892–34131.

Clothes Care

STORAGE A few tips:
- It takes only a few seconds to hang something up as soon as you take it off – it takes many minutes (and costs electricity) to iron it.
- Do not leave heavy objects in pockets when you hang clothes up.
- Do not use wire hangers – they can distort clothes and allow items to hang too close to each other.
- If you have not got enough hangers do not put clothes on top of each other – the under ones will not get worn. Try, instead, to spend half an hour sorting through what you are likely to wear over the next few months and either get rid of the rest or store them in neatly labelled boxes until the appropriate season.
- Do store knitted garments in drawers, not on hangers, to retain their shape.
- Do not attempt to remove stains by yourself unless you are sure that you know how.
- Do not put a garment away after the season unless it has been cleaned first as any soiling left will become difficult to remove later.

DRY-
CLEANING
HELP Follow the manufacturer's cleaning instructions on garment labels:
- A in circle – materials suitable for dry-cleaning in all processes
- P in circle – materials suitable for dry-cleaning in most processes
- P in circle, line under – dry-clean with care (not 'coin op').
- F in circle – special dry-cleaning process required.

Make sure that you go to a cleaner who is a member of the Association of British Launderers and Cleaners (ABLC). Talk to him about the item you need cleaned (this consultation costs you nothing).

A dry-cleaner offers a whole range of services as well as clothes care:
- Household – curtain, blankets, loose covers, rugs, etc.
- Suede and leather (see leather, page 420).
- Repairs and alterations: if you are losing weight fast, for instance, your clothes can be taken in professionally.
- Express service.
- Flame- and shower-proofing.
- Dyeing.
- Some dry-cleaners will store your clothes while you move house or are away.

If you are dissatisfied with any cleaning service done by an ABLC member you should contact the head office of the company concerned and give full details of your complaint. If you are still dissatisfied, contact the ABLC:

Association of British Launderers and Cleaners
Lancaster Gate House
319 Pinner Road
Harrow
Middlesex HA1 4HX
01–863 7755

Further information

The Dry-cleaning Information Bureau (DIB) will answer all queries about particular cleaning problems and will send you information on cleaning in general and ABLC members near you. Contact (s.a.e.):

Dry-cleaning Information Bureau
Lancaster Gate House
319 Pinner Road
Harrow
Middlesex HA1 4HX
01–863 8658

The ABLC will provide speakers to talk to groups (contact the information officer at the address above).

Further Information

Suggested further reading

Gostelow, Mary, *Dress Sense*, Batsford (a book that you can play with: discover what clothes are best for your lifestyle; get maximum effect for minimum expense and trouble)
Hogg, Kate, *More Dash than Cash*, Hutchinson
Johnson, Lorraine, *The Book of Looks*, Michael Joseph
Ladbury, Ann, *Sewing*, Mitchell Beazley
    Weekend Wardrobe, BBC Publications
Leeming, Jan, *Simply Looking Good*, Arthur Barker
Jackson, Carole, *Colour Me Beautiful*, Piatkus (finding the colours that are best for you and putting together your entire 'look')

Notes

● A variety of services is offered every month in 'Vogue's Address Book' at the back of *Vogue* magazine.
● If you want to make your own clothes, see any books by Ann Ladbury (for dressmaking and tailoring) or Patricia Roberts (knitting).

15 Household

At some point you will have to give attention to the appearance, decoration and equipment in your home. Here are tips on interior design suggested by design consultant Meryll Bradley and Linda Rice of Debenham.

Interior Design

THINKING ABOUT DESIGN   A NEW CHOICE

THINKING
ABOUT
DESIGN

Interior design is a combination of many things – colour and lighting, textures and shapes – all interwoven to transform an empty space into an area which is balanced and functional and which makes a definite statement of style. To the beginner this may seem an overwhelmingly wide subject but, taken step by step, it need not be as frightening as it seems and it can be very satisfying.

Why do I need it?

Your home is probably the biggest single investment you are likely to make. You want it to express your character and personality, to be comfortable to live in and to be admired by visitors and friends. Whether you are moving house, decorating your present one or making alterations to accommodate a growing family, there are already some factors to guide you:

- is your home new or old, urban or rural, large or small?
- what is the function of each room?
- what are your possessions?
- what is your budget?

These are the basics around which any scheme will have to be shaped.

How do I start?

It is never too soon to look around and formulate ideas, but do not rush into anything. Look through magazines and books, keep cuttings and references, visit leading stores and showrooms, collect samples to mix and match at home, note prices and form mental pictures of how you want each room to look.

This should be a stimulating phase. Consciously and subconsciously you are beginning to get ideas for your new home and you will be able to work out how best to spread your budget. Do not go anywhere without a notebook, tape measure and, if possible, a floor plan. Know the height of your ceilings and approximate size of windows.

Carpets and curtains are a major outlay and you should find out all you can about them. Collect samples of wall coverings. Fabrics for curtains, upholstery and bedspreads are often shown alongside wall coverings and are best thought of together: some are specially designed to co-ordinate and this can be very helpful when putting your schemes together. You will have to think about treatment of windows. Collect samples of anything that particularly attracts you – you can decide later if and where to use them.

Colour and lighting are probably the two most useful and least expensive ways of creating effect. The aspect of the room and amount of natural light will influence your choice of colour. Artificial light is a necessity and used imaginatively it can transform a room, giving emphasis to certain areas, drawing the eye to objects which are visually entertaining and giving your colours and textures another dimension. Centre lights may be necessary in some rooms but do little to make them interesting. Ideas for colour are all around. If you live near a big city, notice the display windows of large shops: there is background colour and clever lighting to draw the eye to the objects on display. The most effective windows usually have the least in them: the less effective are overcrowded and have poor lighting. Apply this to your home.

If you live in the country, nature can be an inspiration. A holly berry catches the eye but the background of shiny dark green leaves provides emphasis. A single yellow flower, when studied, will be found to have many different tones of the one colour. When working out your schemes, start with your basic colour, use it in different tones and introduce a complementary colour sparingly. Too many colours can ruin an effect.

Think about paint. You will need to include painted woodwork in your schemes and painted walls in some areas. Ceilings painted in a paler shade of the walls can give a small room a very cosy feeling. High ceilings can be lowered by a subtle deeper tone. It is now possible to get tiny pots of paint so always try out your colours in the appropriate rooms and see how they look by daylight and artificial light: some colours can change quite dramatically and can cause disappointment.

Planning rooms will be made much easier if you have scaled pieces of paper to represent your furniture on a floor plan. The easiest way to do this is on graph paper. You may have such basic essentials as beds, tables and chairs already but, if possible, it is a good idea to wait before buying additional pieces until your room begins to take shape. Then buy carefully: something which is beautiful and of good workmanship will give you pleasure for many years. Pieces that serve a dual purpose can save space – a sofabed, for instance, is a good investment.

There is never enough storage space. Decide where to add cupboards and build shelves. Will you need special housing for hi-fi and other equipment? Remember that your rooms will feel less cluttered if there is somewhere to tidy things away.

A NEW
HOUSE

If you are moving into a new house make sure the electricity supply and telephone are connected as soon as possible. Workmen will need light and power and you need to be able to contact people. If you are planning to change the position of the telephone or have an additional one you should give British Telecom as much prior notice as possible. You will certainly need all telephone work completed before the walls are decorated (and you will need to know a new number before you can get change of address cards printed).

Your team

You may already have a *builder* (see Chapter 2). You should meet him on site and go through each room telling him what you want done. This will include electrical work, plumbing, joinery, plastering and tiling. It will be important to have planned ahead for any rewiring as this is one of the first things to be done. Show him your proposed plan if you are having a new kitchen. Adjusted plumbing and electricity outlets must be allowed for and this is one reason – together with joint requirements of tiling – why it is sometimes a good idea to have your bathroom and kitchen redone at the same time. Remember uneven floors will need hardboard before laying carpets, and doors may have to be eased (carpet-layers do not usually undertake this work).

You should ask the builder for quotations and do the same with the carpet supplier and curtain-maker. Ask if the latter can also supply upholstery and, if so, again get quotations.

Many people have a preconceived notion that *interior designers* are expensive and exotic but in fact a good one will be able to interpret your ideas, help you to execute them and steer you away from making expensive mistakes. They can offer information on builders, curtain-makers, upholsterers and carpet suppliers and will be available to supervise all the work for you. Their services range from a single consultation to organizing part or all of the work.

*Doing it
yourself*

This might be an economy overall and prove very rewarding, but you need time, patience and determination. Unless you are experienced and/or lucky you might make at least one mistake.

It is best to undertake one room at a time, particularly if you are living in the house. Bear in mind the fact that you do not have to opt for mass-produced furniture and fabrics or expensive antiques. There are thousands of artists and craftsmen in Britain who can provide you with an 'original' for your home, be it a hand-thrown ceramic lamp, a piece of custom furniture or a woven fireside rug. The advantage of using individually crafted items – especially if commissioned – is that you can specify materials, colours, sizes, etc.

If you are interested in being put in contact with craftsmen and seeing their work, you can get in touch with:

British Crafts Centre
43 Earlham Street
London WC2H 9LD
01-836 6993

Crafts Council,
8 Waterloo Place
London SW1Y 4BE
01-930 4811

Design Centre
28 Haymarket
London SW1Y 4SP
01-839 8000

Scottish Craft Centre
Acheson House
Canongate
Edinburgh EH8 8DD
031-556 8136

Scottish Design Centre
72 St Vincent Street
Glasgow G2 5TS
041-221 6121

Scottish Development Agency
(Small Business Division)
Rosebery House
Haymarket Terrace
Edinburgh EH12 5EZ
031-337 9595

See *House and Garden, World of Interiors* magazines.

Equipping a House

THE BEST METHOD
DOORS AND WINDOWS
ELECTRICAL APPLIANCES
FIRES
FLOORS
FURNITURE
GAS APPLIANCES

HEATING AND INSULATION
NOISE CONTROL
PAINT
PEST CONTROL
WATER

THE BEST
METHOD

It is tempting to do a bit of shopping here and a bit of shopping there. But this kind of planning may leave you with things that do not go well together, and it is more complicated to deal with many firms, instead of one. The advantages of buying from one place include credit facilities, delivery to your door and the opportunity to ensure a matching style of decoration throughout the house (matching curtains to duvets, for example, and co-ordinating cushions to fabrics). Another big advantage of shopping in one place is that you will also save time and find it less tiring – and you will probably only have to park your car once! On the other hand, provided you are prepared to spend time and, often, great trouble to sort out co-ordination problems yourself, you will obviously get a much wider variety of ideas and products if you 'shop around'.

The best time to shop for anyone who has time – and certainly anyone who is handicapped – is as early as possible in the morning. The lunchtime 'rush' begins about 12.30 and the after-school 'rush' is from 3.30 onwards. And, of course, the most economical time to shop is during the sales.

1. It is important to get the electrical layout decided first:
- centre lights and wall lights
- 5-amp plugs for table and standard lamps
- sockets for TV, hi-fi in living-room – and TV in bedroom(s) (if required) and bedside lights
- kitchen equipment (toaster, fridge/freezer, etc.)
- Always fit double sockets.
- Do not forget telephone sockets – these should be fitted at the same time as electrical sockets so that wiring can be camouflaged as much as possible.

2. Built-in furniture – fitted bathroom and kitchen units – can be fitted after the electrician and plumber and before the main decorating.

3. Choose flooring and carpets about one month before moving in and have them fitted after decorations are complete and just before you move.

4. Fit electrical items (e.g. lights) one day before moving.

5. Move in furniture on the day. If buying from a department store, remember to allow six weeks for suites and units. Ask retailers to hold any stock you have ordered until you are ready for it.

DOORS AND WINDOWS

Doors

Remember all outside doors should be especially strong (see 'Protect Your House', page 560. Remember, too, to think of the postman when you put in a new outside door – do not make the letter box difficult to reach.

Double-glazing

This is a matter of personal consideration. Factors that you should bear in mind include:
- *Safety.* There have been fatal cases of children and others unable to get out of a double-glazed room during a fire. On the other hand, unwanted intruders may be unable to get through double-glazing.
- *Effectiveness.* Salesmen state elimination of draughts, reduction of heat loss and lower fuel bills to be among the many advantages of double-glazing. Sound-proofing is improved, which can be an important consideration.
- *Cost.* It is possible that at the moment a double-glazed household might only save £30 or so on the annual heating bill. Double-glazing might cost up to £3,000 to install (although you can do it for less yourself). Double-glazing, therefore, is not always cost-effective (see 'Heating and Insulation' below).

For a list of recommended suppliers (and any after-sales complaints), contact:

Glass and Glazing Federation
6 Mount Row
London W 1 Y 6DY
01-409 0545

Curtains

As well as privacy, curtains can provide warmth, especially if they have thermal linings. Before buying, investigate the different kinds of lining available, particularly if you want to block all light out of a bedroom, for example.

To avoid having to pull on the curtain fabric to open and close them, it is worth the extra outlay to buy rods with draw-strings.

Rufflette have a full-colour booklet on different ways to dress windows. You can get this free from (s.a.e.):

> Rufflette
> Sharston Road
> Manchester M22 4TH
> 061-998 1811

For information on net curtains – how to buy them and look after them, send an s.a.e. to:

> Curtain Net Advisory Bureau
> 68 Knightsbridge
> London SW1X 7LN
> (no telephone)

Blinds

These have become more fashionable in recent years. They are often less expensive than curtains. Sometimes blinds and curtains are used together, with blinds providing extra insulation or with curtains purely as decoration either side of the window.

Among the types of blinds available are:

● *Austrian or Roman blinds* – fabric twice the width of the window can be drawn up through lines of tape sewn down the drop of the blind at regular intervals across the width.

● *Roller blinds* – made from stiffened fabric and available in plain or patterned fabric with a choice of decorative edging. Many blinds are now available with co-ordinating wallpaper or fabric. Purchased roller blinds are wipe-clean with a damp cloth.

● *Venetian or slatted blinds* – these have separate horizontal slats which are difficult to clean.

All large chain stores have a wide range of blinds. There are also many specialist shops which offer a wide range and can be found by looking up in your local Yellow Pages under 'Blinds'.

ELECTRICAL APPLIANCES

Notes

● For safety see 'Electrical Problems and Accidents', page 562.
● Disabled people should be aware of the free leaflet 'Making Life Easier for Disabled People' available from any Electricity Board showroom or:

> Electricity Council
> 30 Millbank,
> London SW1P 4RD
> 01-834 2333

Costs   Electricity can be expensive, especially if the house and hot water pipes are not well lagged and if appliances are not used correctly. Electricity is measured in units, the cost of which varies around the country – your area's unit rate (cost per kWh) will be clearly marked on your electricity bill or you can ask at your Electricity Board shop or show-room.

As an approximate indication, this is the cost of using some electrical appliances:

blender – 1 unit makes 500 pints of soup

coffee percolator – 1 unit makes 75 cups

convector heater (2kW) – half an hour for 1 unit

cooker – one week's meals for a family of four costs about 20 units

dishwasher (cold fill) – one full load, about $2\frac{1}{2}$ units

fan heater (2kW) – half an hour for 1 unit

freezer – $1\frac{1}{2}$ units per cubic foot per week

fridge (compressor type) – one day for 1 unit

immersion heater – 3 gallons of piping hot water for 1 unit

iron – two hours' use for 1 unit

kettle – 12 pints for 1 unit

microwave – four chicken pieces for 1 unit

television (colour, 22 ins.) – 6 to 9 hours' viewing for 1 unit (black and white TVs use about half as much electricity)

tumble dryer – 30 minutes for 1 unit

washing-machine (automatic) – average weekly wash for family of four, 9 units.

See   'Electricity and You: a Guide to Running Costs' from the Electricity Council, address above.

If you can run all your expensive items (e.g. washing-machine) at night and if you heat with night storage heaters, one method of saving money is with the Economy 7 tariff. This provides electricity at two rates. In most Electricity Board areas the cost is slightly more during the day and (on Economy 7) considerably cheaper for seven hours during the night, when you could be running your dishwasher, etc. Further details from your electricity showroom.

Some tips   ● Wherever possible, use the oven to capacity: a casserole or roast in one dish, vegetables in another and baked sweet in another.

● When cooking large items, turn the oven off ten minutes before completion.

● It is less expensive to make toast in a toaster than under a grill.

● Try to use the washing-machine only for full loads.

● Spin-dryers get clothes 'damp dry' very economically.

● Showers use less hot water than baths.

● Never wash hands or dishes under a running tap – plug the basin or fill a container for your wash.

● Boil only the amount of water required (but make sure the element is covered).
● Steam is more effective than boiling water. You can cook vegetables in a pot with a well-fitting lid: they do not have to be covered with water completely but make sure there is enough to prevent the saucepan from boiling dry.
● Fluorescent lamps offer the same amount of light for half the running cost of ordinary bulbs.
● Drawing curtains and closing doors reduces heat loss.

Buying appliances When buying any electrical appliance you should check its safety and economy. Remember, an *appliance* should be used but a *gadget* is something that was attractive when first purchased but might, after a bit of use, put away in a cupboard and hardly brought out again. Apart from essential items such as an iron, what you have out on display is invariably going to be used the most.

Blender, heater-blender, mixer and processor
● *Blenders* have one main function – powerful liquidizing. They are ideal for making soups, sauces, breadcrumbs and mayonnaise.
● *Heater-blenders* have more power than ordinary blenders and they can also heat and blend simultaneously. They are expensive machines but they are superb for soups and sauces and (without the heater) for making mayonnaise and for decurdling.
● *Mixers*, which beat, blend, cream, knead and whisk and perform many other functions, can be large, powerful machines with their own supporting bases or small with bowls and stands (these can be hand-held if required).
    Mixers are considered by many to be the most useful machine for family cooking. There are many attachments but – if you are busy – it may paradoxically seem easier not to bother with fitting them and washing them up afterwards.
● *Processors*, by contrast, are ideal for quickly puréeing, salad-making and slicing. They are good for pâtés and doughs but not all are ideal for soups as some models do not pulverize satisfactorily. Some have bowls and blades that should not go in the dishwasher (check the manufacturer's instructions).

Coffee-makers
When buying a *filter coffee machine*, things to check include:
● Is the cold water reservoir clear or coloured? (If the former, and your water is hard, the reservoir will become dirty-looking with use.)
● Will the heater plate really keep the jug warm?
● Do you need a coffee-maker that will keep coffee warm for some time? (If so, look out for a coffee-maker which has a vacuum flask instead of the usual glass jug.)
● Is the jug easy to pour?

● Is the filter holder attached to the lid? If not, is it easy and quick to remove without spilling the filter paper and used grounds?
● Has it got an automatic pre-setting timer?
● Do you need a wall-mounted machine to save using work-top space?

Percolators may have jugs made of aluminium, stainless steel or a ceramic material. Some people find coffee made this way tastes slightly acid, but percolators are handy – and the jug is easy to pour. If you use a percolator remember not to put the basket, even when empty, in a dishwasher as any remaining grounds will mar the cleaning of other items in the machine. One advantage of a percolator is that it can generally be stored out of sight.

Care Unless the manufacturer's instructions specifically say otherwise, never immerse any part of any coffee-maker in water. Disconnect the appliance before any cleaning operation or if any water comes into contact with any part other than the main jug (percolator) or reservoir (filter machine). If you live in a hard water area, de-scale when needed: buy de-scaler from your supermarket or electrical shop and follow the written instructions.

Deep fryer

Electrical fryers are safer than frying in an ordinary deep pan on a stove. They are thermostatically controlled and many have lids with fitted charcoal filters to reduce smells during frying.

As with coffee-makers, never let any part of the appliance come into contact with water unless specifically allowed in manufacturer's instructions. Disconnect before cleaning.

Dishwashers

Contrary to popular opinion, a dishwasher is useful for one or two people. As long as you have enough china and cutlery, used items can be put in the machine and rinsed a few at a time. When the machine is finally full it can be run on full cycle.

Most dishwashers are front-loading to leave the top for a work surface. Those who find bending difficult and those who have no under-shelf space might prefer a model which can be placed on the work-top.

A dishwasher should not be used to wash: pans and cutlery with wooden, plastic or bone handles, hand-painted porcelain, thick glass or painted or cut glass, narrow necked vessels, thin plastic, wooden items or anything that the manufacturer specifically says must not be put in the machine.

See the booklet of instructions supplied with each different machine for a list of problems and how to cope with them.

Dryers

● *Spin-dryers* or *spin-rinse dryers* (spin-dryers with pumps). These are the most efficient methods of extracting water from clothes although items are left only 'damp dry'. They are made in circular or cabinet form and take up little floor space.

● *Tumbler dryers.* These dry clothes completely but excess water should be removed first by hand-wringing or by spinning in the washing-machine.

● Spin-drying in some automatic washing-machines is very good – check spin speed before purchase. Some models incorporate a tumbler dryer.

● *Drying cabinets* and *dryer airers.* Both are rather makeshift constructions but less expensive than other appliances – excess water should first be removed.

Electric ovens
(For choice of cooking method, see 'Kitchen' below.)

The types of *hobs* available are:
● *Ceramic* hob – the heated areas are marked in the flat, smooth surface and the elements underneath are spiral-wound electric heating elements.
● *Disc ring* hob – the disc has a flat top with a shallow indentation in the centre. The spiral heating element is covered by the disc and sealed into the hob by a stainless steel band. Discs do not glow when in use.
● *Radiant ring* hob – the element is contained in a spiral tube which glows red when at full heat (some rings have a dual circuit for heating either the whole ring or just the centre portion).

The types of *ovens* available are:
● *Convection* oven – heating elements on both sides behind removable side panels.
● *Radiant/convection* ovens – uncovered elements fitted in top and/or bottom of the oven and the top element usually doubles as the grill. This can mean a slight difference in cooking times and temperatures for a cook used to a convection-only oven.
● *Forced air (fan)* ovens – provide even more uniform heating. Generally, a circular heating element in the back of the oven is positioned round a small fan which circulates the heated air.
● *Microwave* ovens – operate on electromagnetic energy, which will cook, defrost and reheat individual items of food or complete plated meals quickly, safely and economically as the energy is completely absorbed and used by the moisture in the food.

A few points to remember when using a microwave oven:
1. Never put anything metallic in the oven unless the manufacturer's instructions specifically say it is all right (this forbidden list includes metal containers and utensils and paper-covered wire ties).
2. Never run the cooker when it is totally empty.
3. It cooks single portions amazingly quickly (about four minutes for a baked potato) but takes longer to do a large quantity (twelve baked potatoes cooked together in a microwave take as long as conventional oven cooking). No obvious quality is lost.
4. Some things (cabbage and other vegetables) really do taste better

microwaved – and cooking smells are not so apparent when cooking such things as fish.

5. Leftover coffee reheated in the microwave does not taste as if it is second-time-round.

A microwave oven is a boon to people living by themselves and families where people need/want to eat at different times: vegetables and sauces can be pre-cooked, covered with clingwrap and reheated immediately before serving with no loss of taste. It is useful for young people, the infirm and elderly (there is no direct exposure to heat), the blind (some microwaves can have calibrated dials fitted in braille) and for busy people everywhere.

A selection of literature on different types of microwave ovens is available (s.a.e.) from:

Microwave Oven Association
16a The Broadway
London SW19 1RF
01-946 3389

The Microwave Cooking School
Apple Tree Cottage
2b South Hill Park
London NW3 2SB
01–794 8567

Freezer, fridge/freezer and fridge

● 'Chest' type, top-opening freezer, from 100 litre capacity upwards. Disadvantages include defrosting and the difficulty of finding items buried at the bottom.

● 'Cabinet' upright, front-opening freezer, from 50 litre capacity (small work-top standing model). Easy to see what is there. Disadvantage is that more air is allowed in each time you open the door.

Both the above freeze food. They can be kept in a garage or somewhere else cool, thus keeping down running costs.

● Combined fridge/freezer. One cabinet which freezes food lies above – or below – one that chills it. This appliance is generally kept in the kitchen so running costs of the freezer section might be higher than with other freezers.

● The conventional fridge is front-opening. It chills food and there is generally a frozen food storage compartment (evaporator) which also makes ice. The length of time for which commercially frozen food can be stored will depend upon the star marking on the packet.

● Instead of a frozen food storage compartment, a larder fridge has a thin vertical or horizontal cooling plate (evaporator) fitted towards the top or back of the cabinet.

With all the above it is important to check the food freezer symbols. Make sure when buying a new machine that you know what star symbols your machine will accept (see manufacturer's instructions). When putting food into the appliance, similarly take note of the star rating for that item.

Freezer tips
- Put waxed paper under ice trays to prevent them from sticking.
- Put crisps in a plastic bag in the freezer to prevent them from becoming soggy.
- Put cheese in the freezer for ten minutes to make it easier to grate.

Iron

When buying an iron:

Decide if you need a dry iron, a steam iron (which can be used as dry iron) or a steam iron with added spray (which can also be used as dry iron).

Dry irons are generally smaller and lighter than steam irons and less expensive to use. A crisp result depends on ensuring that clothes are not too dry before they are ironed.

Steam irons are more expensive than dry irons but they produce a better 'finish' if clothes are overdried.

You will probably find that if several people are going to use an iron without looking after it properly, a basic dry iron will be most handy.

Select an iron that feels comfortable and balanced. Try the handle for grip and comfort. Check on the size of the soleplate – slimmer ends are better for ironing clothes, broader soleplates are easier for table linens. Non-stick soleplates may scratch easily.

If you use a steam iron, unless the manufacturer's instructions say you can use tap water, always fill with demineralized or distilled water. Never use defrosted freezer water as it may contain food particles. If you have to clean the soleplate with an iron cleaner, be careful not to clog the vents.

Notes
- All irons take longer to cool down than to heat up.
- Never use an electric iron connected to a lighting circuit.

Washing-machine

Front-opening machines are more convenient than top-loading ones, but they take up slightly more space. Some people prefer twin-tubs, one of the advantages of which is that a second load can be washing while the first, removed to the other tub, is spin-drying.

Most washing machines use the textile care labelling code of the Home Laundering Consultative Council (HLCC). You can find this code in each machine's instructions and on packets of washing powder.

Information and complaints
- For information on electricity and its use, contact the Electricity Council or the Electrical Association for Women (addresses in Chapter 19).
- For complaints about the electricity service, see Chapter 19.
- If you want information about manufacturers' products, send a large s.a.e. to the marketing services department of the relevant company. Their addresses will be in Yellow Pages.

- For complaints about an appliance, see 'Sale of Goods Act', page 136.
- If you have any problems with repairs or servicing see 'Services', page 136. If you are unhappy with repairs done to an appliance purchased from an Electricity Board shop, contact the shop manager and, if still dissatisfied, the manager of your Area Electricity Board. If you purchased a British appliance made by a member of the Association of Manufacturers of Domestic Electrical Appliances (AMDEA), you can contact:

> Association of Manufacturers of Domestic Electrical Appliances,
> AMDEA House
> 593 Hitchin Road
> Stopsley
> Luton
> Beds LU2 7UN
> 0582-412444

FIRES   A coal fireplace is inexpensive to install if you already have a chimney, and economical to run. One with a back-boiler can heat your water and even run radiators. Your hearth must extend at least a foot in front of the fire and six inches on either side: it must be at least two inches thick. For further information, see 'Real Fire Heating' from (s.a.e.):

> Solid Fuel Advisory Service
> Hobart House
> Grosvenor Place
> London SWIX 7AE
> 01-235 2020

Regional offices:

Belfast	0232-667924
Cardiff	0222-481652
Doncaster	0302-66611
Edinburgh	031-664 1461
Gateshead	0632-878822
Harrow	01-427 4333
Nottingham	07737-66111
Warrington	0942-673127

For information on all types of fires – including woodburning and peat stoves – contact:

> Wood and Solid Fuel Association of
>   Retailers and Manufacturers (WARM)
> PO Box 35
> Stoke-on-Trent ST4 7NU
> 0785-44311
> and
>   Exeter 0392-58214

Guarding a fireplace is best done with a 'fire curtain'. It looks like chain mail and keeps sparks in without taking away the joy of looking at – and feeling – the fire.

There are still craftsmen/blacksmiths who will make fire grates, fire-dogs and other items to order. For addresses contact any of the crafts organizations listed on page 433.

Your coal merchant should adhere to the Approved Coal Merchants' Scheme, the trade's code of practice. If you are dissatisfied, you should first complain to the merchant and, if you still think you have cause for complaint, you should contact your Citizens' Advice Bureau or:

Approved Coal Merchants' Scheme
2 Turnpin Lane
London SE10 9JA
01-853 0787

If you need a chimney sweep, you can get a list of people in your area from (s.a.e.):

Domestic Coal Consumers' Council
Gavrelle House
2 Bunhill Row
London EC1Y 8LL
01-638 8914/29

National Association of Chimney Sweeps
PO Box 35
Stoke-on-Trent
Staffs ST4 7NU
0782-44311

Coal is a nationalized industry. If you have any complaints contact:

FLOORS ● *Fitted carpets* – give warmth and colour, plus continuity to rooms. Costs range from £3 per square metre up – you get the quality you pay for. It should be professionally laid – remember to ask for any offcuts for possible repairs later. Among the best-known traditional types of carpets are Axminster and Wilton; other types are tufted, fusion-bonded, needlefelt, etc.

When you are thinking of buying it is a good idea to choose a carpet which is already protected with a fluorocarbon protective seal (if you have this done later it will cost at least £1 per square metre). Check whether or not the price you are quoted includes underlay, fitting and door-risers.

For further information on carpets or for any complaints, the relevant trade association is:

British Carpet Manufacturers' Association
Royalty House
72 Dean Street
London WIV 5HB
01-734 9853

- *Rugs and small carpets* – advantages include portability; you can change a rug from one part of the room to another and take it with you when you move house. Disadvantages include possible slipping: make sure each rug has a non-slip backing or pad.
- *Tiles* – cork tiles are warm, resilient and hard wearing.
- *Vinyl* – a quick and relatively inexpensive way of covering bathroom or kitchen floors, practical and durable. Best laid on to well-prepared flat surfaces (e.g. screed, or hardboard on top of floorboards).
- *Wood flooring* – looks good, but sometimes is more difficult to clean than fitted carpets. There is also the added disadvantage that if the wood is laid in small tiles, some may distort slightly.

If you need information on flooring or have a specific problem, contact (s.a.e.):

Contract Flooring Association
23 Chippenham Mews
London W9 2AN
01-286 4499

FURNITURE Some companies are specifically associated with individual rooms (e.g. bedrooms or living-room seating). For co-ordinating furniture for the whole house, you might be interested in these ideas:
- Large department stores usually have good in-store displays and will deliver anywhere in Britain.
- If you want to choose at your leisure you will have to contact individual furniture companies and ask for their catalogues. Some firms, e.g. Habitat, who have stores throughout Britain, have their own specialist catalogues.

Complaints The following organizations have a furniture code of practice. Labels must be attached to all items sold or information must be available giving dimensions, construction details and care and cleaning instructions. Retail members must also quote realistic delivery dates or inform customers when these cannot be met. If you have any problems contact:

National Association of Retail Furnishers (NARF)
17–21 George Street
Croydon CR9 1TQ
01-680 8444

GAS Advantages of gas include quick warming-up time and a visible flame
APPLIANCES – which some people prefer. The oven is zoned so that it is hotter at the top than the bottom. Dishes requiring different cooking heats can

therefore be put in the oven at the same time. Disadvantages include dirtier cooking, more cleaning required and direct heat in the oven (not always wanted).

Costs One therm of gas – which is roughly the equivalent of 30 units of electricity – costs about 40p and will provide:

cooker – grill on full for 7 hours, oven Mark 2 for 36 hours, oven Mark 7 for 20 hours

fire – high setting 5 hours, low setting 10 hours

fridge – run for 7 days

water-heater – 5 baths, 25 showers, 72 washing-up bowls

Some tips ● Cooker:

(a) no need to pre-heat the grill except for fast browning

(b) keep flames on hotplates right under saucepans which should have lids on

(c) try to avoid opening the oven door while cooking.

● Heating:

(a) Reducing room thermostats by 2°C (4°F) can lower consumption in a gas-heated house by up to 10 per cent for the average household.

(b) Make sure your heating system is properly controlled – e.g. by fitting cylinder, radiator and room thermostats and clock control programmer and make sure the cylinder jacket fits snugly (consult your local gas showroom).

Special customers British Gas offers several services to help anyone who is elderly or disabled to get the most from their gas appliances: special tap handles, for instance, can be provided to help those with hand disabilities or brailled or studded taps are available for those with failing sight. Disabled people should also ask for the booklet 'Gas Consumers' Council's Guide to Special Services and Benefits for Elderly and Disabled People' from any gas showroom. A home service adviser can call on customers in their homes: contact them through the showroom.

For further information on gas appliances, contact your local gas board (under Gas in the telephone directory).

For safety see 'Gas Problems', page 569.

See 'Helpfuel Services from the Gas People', British Gas.

HEATING AND INSULATION

Central heating

● *Electricity* (off-peak storage radiators). This is the least expensive system to install. There is minimal disruption during installation (wiring is easily threaded under the floor or run on the surface), and medium annual running costs. Fuel availability is generally fine, but there may be some restrictions on loading in remote areas. Power cuts are less likely to affect off-peak supplies. Reliability of equipment is very good (no moving parts) and there are virtually no servicing requirements. The equipment is very safe unless tampered with, and there is no possibility of fumes. Off-peak systems cannot easily be controlled to suit varying requirements. Radiators are slim and no boiler is required. Extra storage radiators can be added if an extension of the system is required. Warranty: usually installed by local electricity board or contractors with one year's guarantee.

● *Gas.* Moderately expensive to install and needs a week or so of disruption (floorboards and carpets lifted, hot and cold water, except cold tap in kitchen sink, disrupted). This system has the least expensive annual running costs, the equipment is usually reliable and needs minimal servicing. Natural gas is available in about 75 per cent of British homes (not Northern Ireland): bottled gas can be used but it is much more expensive. Safety is good if equipment is installed and used correctly. It can be easily controlled for maximum efficiency and economy, and has aesthetic appeal (the units are compact and versatile). If an extension is likely to be required later, the boiler capacity and pipe sizes should accommodate this at first installation. Warranty: usually one year's guarantee given by installer.

● *Oil* is the most expensive system to install, involving disruption during installation as for gas, and it has the most expensive running costs. Fuel is generally available provided tanker access is possible and the equipment reliability is generally good. However, the controls are slightly more complex and slower to respond than those in gas systems. It needs regular servicing (usually twice a year) to maintain optimum efficiency and economy. Its aesthetic appeal is as for gas, but the boilers are less compact and sometimes noisy. Ease of extension and warranty: as for gas.

● *Solid fuel.* Medium expense to install, involving disruption during installation as for gas. Annual running costs are inexpensive. Indigenous coal supplies will last for many years but there are some local variations in availability of different types of solid fuel. Simple non-electric controls on many appliances aid reliability. Minimal servicing of appliances on an annual basis, but flues and chimneys must be kept clear and swept regularly. There is generally a slower response to controls than for gas or oil (some boilers are better than others but none is fully automatic) and aesthetic appeal and ease of extension is as for gas. Warranty: as for gas. (The Solid Fuel Advisory Service (see page 442) operates a one-year guarantee scheme, but responsibility for guarantee remains with installer.)

● For further information contact:

Heating and Ventilating Contractors' Association
ESCA House
34 Palace Court
London W2 4JG
01–229 2488

or the addresses in the 'Fires' section, page 442.

Cavity wall insulation

Generally, walls account for 35 per cent of the total immediate heat loss from a home. Cavity wall insulation can eliminate up to 75 per cent of this loss and effect up to a 26 per cent saving in annual fuel bills.

Insulating material is mechanically injected into the cavity formed between the inner and outer walls of your home: this results in captive air acting as a barrier to heat loss. The house will be warmer and there will be fewer draughts from the walls as the warmth is evenly distributed and condensation is reduced. Some homes are not suitable for cavity insulation. Check that yours is – and check that anyone undertaking cavity insulation for you follows the code of practice of the National Cavity Insulation Association. For details and for names of companies in your area send an s.a.e. to the address below.

Draught proofing

Up to 15 per cent of the immediate heat loss from your home can be saved with effective draught proofing of doors and windows. This is an inexpensive and efficient method of insulation that can be done for a tiny fraction of the cost of double-glazing (see 'Doors and Windows', page 434).

External wall insulation

This is especially important for properties with solid walls that were built prior to the 1920s. External wall insulation can prevent up to 72 per cent of the heat loss through the walls and this can result in an overall saving of up to 25 per cent on fuel bills.

Loft insulation

If you want to insulate your loft you might be entitled to a government grant of £69, or 66 per cent of the cost of materials and labour (whichever is the smaller); pensioners can sometimes claim £95 or 90 per cent. As the grants include labour, employing a contractor becomes a really economic proposition. You can get details of grants from your local council office or from a contractor.

● The headquarters of the Draught Proofing Advisory Association, the External Wall Insulation Association, the National Association of Loft Insulation Contractors and the National Cavity Insulation Association are at:

PO Box 12
Haslemere
Surrey GU27 3AN
0428–54011

LIGHTING   Lighting can be decorative or functional – the ideal is to combine the two. Consider these points:

● When you enter a room in the dark the switch by the door needs to illuminate the basic parts of the room. In the past the door switch controlled a main central light but increasingly it turns on table lamps or bedside lights.

● The next consideration is to highlight features in the room – pictures, a collection of items on a shelf or a display of flowers or items on a table.

● Lighting can be cruel to uneven walls or bad plastering. 'Uplighters' – powerful spots that can illuminate a dark corner, perhaps set behind a pot plant – can be especially revealing.

● Office, kitchen and other functional lighting needs to be in the right place for the job. It must not cast a shadow. Most functional lighting should also look attractive but this is not the first consideration.

● Outside 'protection' lights should also be essentially functional.

NOISE CONTROL

Noise is measured in *decibels* (dB), 120dB is so loud that it can cause pain. Decibel ratings of common noises include:

30	rustle of paper
40	residential area at night
50	inside average home
60	loud conversation at 3 feet
70	heavy traffic outside
100	food blender at 2 feet
110	power mower at 4 feet
120	jet aircraft going overhead at 500 feet

Surprisingly, outside noises are not much lessened by height. If you live on the 20th floor you will still hear street noises.

Noise reception is affected by the size of window, the type of glass (generally speaking, the thicker the glass the better) and the sealing quality of the window. It is also affected by 'reflection' (noise bounces off one wall to another). If your house is particularly noisy and you want to apply for a grant to help with double-glazing and noise insulation, contact the local authority.

If you feel strongly about noise control contact:

Noise Abatement Society
PO Box 8
Bromley
Kent BR2 0UH
01–460 3146

PAINT

Whatever needs painting, there is a correct way to prepare the surface and a correct set of paints to use. Try to cut corners and you may end up with poor results or even a disaster.

All major paint manufacturers have comprehensive ranges of the different types of paint, as well as colour cards of each range. Some of them have sample pots of paint so you can try the effect before committing yourself.

Lead in paint All paint containing more than 1 per cent soluble lead must be clearly labelled – the label includes a prominent dark diagonal cross. Paint containing 0.5 per cent lead must also be labelled.

Try to use low-lead paint wherever possible, and never use any paint labelled 'contains lead' on surfaces in reach of children. Be careful when redecorating, as the old paint may contain lead. Do not burn it off with a blowlamp (it causes fumes) or rub it down with dry sandpaper (this may put lead-rich dust into the air). Instead, use a stripper that blasts a jet of hot air. There are also liquid paint strippers but these are harder to handle.

For further information and queries on all type of paint – and if you have any complaints – contact:

> Paint Manufacturers' Association
> Alembic House
> 93 Albert Embankment
> London SE1 7TY
> 01–582 1185

See 'Lead in Paint', Department of the Environment (from the Citizens' Advice Bureau).

PEST **Rodents**
CONTROL Rodents are the pests most likely to be a nuisance. The rat population is never less than 50 per cent of the human population in a given area and often more than that. The mouse population is likely to be double the rat population ...

A rat will gain entry to a house through a hole that is big enough to put your thumb in. A mouse will gain entry through a hole the size of a pencil. In addition to the obvious health hazards, rodents are a major cause of structural fires since they gnaw most materials including electric cables.

Insects
Insects can be a special nuisance. In addition to animal fleas, fly infestations, mosquitoes and cockroaches (associated with 600 or so species of salmonella), ants, wasps and others may require control.

If you are worried about any of the above, telephone your local DHSS and ask for the pest inspector. He will come, as soon as he can, free of charge.

WATER If your water is hard, it might be good to drink but you need to use more soap when washing, and shower heads and other water fitments can clog up.

A water softener removes the hardness-forming impurities, calcium and magnesium salts. This will lessen fuel and repair bills because radiators, boilers, pipes and kettles remain free of the scale which is often responsible for inefficient heating and blockages. It also makes cleaning baths and sinks easier, prevents cutlery from 'streaking' if you drain it and is better for your skin and hair.

To find out more about water softeners, contact any industrial and domestic water treatment specialist (see Yellow Pages).

Individual Rooms and What to Put in Them

BATHROOM
BEDROOM
DINING-ROOM

KITCHEN
LIVING-ROOM

BATHROOM
Bathrooms are much softer and warmer in design these days. If you are completely modernizing, a visit to one of the many bathroom shops around the country will give you an idea of the many interesting styles, colours and fittings available. Accessories will play an important part and if you have space an easy chair would not be out of place.

If you are updating an existing small bathroom, a foil paper could be interesting; continued over the ceiling it will reflect light and give a feeling of space. Mirrors, preferably tinted, will also do this. Replace dated chrome fittings with more modern ones and include towels in your colour scheme. Unless you have a very young family a foam-backed carpet is not impractical: carried up the side of the bath it could do much to transform a cold, outdated room into one of modern comfort.

Bath linens
The Association of British Launderers and Cleaners advise buying the best quality you can afford as they have to stand up to hard wear. Ensure that towels have a selvedge on both sides or a double hem so that they will not fray when washed.

Always launder terry towels before use as they are made up from a foundation fabric into which spun yarns are looped. After several washes this fabric will tighten and hold the loops firmly but until then loops are liable to be pulled out easily.

● For a list of firms which specialize in bathroom design and equipment, look up 'Bath Equipment' in your local Yellow Pages.

BEDROOM
Bedrooms should be allowed to reflect the personality of their occupants. Do not over-furnish, and provide as much storage space as possible. Sometimes bedrooms have to double up: a young child's room is also a playroom, a teenager's room is his retreat, and so on.

Few people nowadays can afford to set aside a whole room for the occasional visitor. It should ideally be adaptable to other uses – a sewing room, a television room but not, all being well, a dump room. If carefully thought out, the spare room can be attractive for all its uses – but above all it should be warm and welcoming for guests.

Beds   Standard bed sizes:

single	76.2cm × 1.90m (2ft 6ins. × 6ft 3ins.)
single	91.4cm (3ft)
double	1.37m (4ft 6ins.)
queen size	1.52m (5ft)
king size	1.83m (6ft)

It is an investment to buy the best quality possible. Check in as many shops as you can and remember that the only way to try beds is by lying on them, often in full view.

A new bed will feel hard at first, particularly in comparison to older beds. It should last a minimum of five years and, possibly, most of your life (there may be life expectancy – for the bed not you – on the label). Turn the mattress every three months, upside down and top to bottom so that in each year it has completed four positions, top to bottom and left to right.

What to look for when buying a bed:

● Does it fit your room and your bedding?

● If you are buying a king or queen size bed, are there enough legs or will it 'squeak'?

● Consider the construction: divan with drawers for storage or bunk-bed (space saving) or stacking (single beds that become a double).

● Are the edges of the bed firm?

● What kind of base springs does it have?

● What kind of mattress does it have: pocket springs (most expensive, but last longest and give best support), open spring and wadding, polyester foam (budget), or is it an orthopaedic bed with heavier gauge wire in the springs and perhaps a board in the base? The quality of the mattress ticking usually indicates overall quality – orthopaedic mattresses often have striped ticking, best quality of all have damask.

● Most important, does the bed have the resistant label (a green square with a match and cigarette within) indicating that it is resistant to sparks and flames?

See   'A Shopper's Guide to the Furniture Safety Labels', Department of Trade leaflet from the CAB.

Orthopaedic beds provide excellent support to keep the spine relaxed and flexible and to help lift pressure off bones, muscles, tendons, nerve endings and joints. Look for advertisements for orthopaedic bedding specialists in the national newspapers or contact:

> Orthopaedic Bedding Design Centre (OBDC)
> Dunraven House
> Weighton Road
> London SE20 8BR
> 01-778 9931

See   'Back Complaint or Bed Complaint?' from OBDC (s.a.e.).

Sofa beds convert from daytime seating to night-time bedding.
- The relevant trade association for all types of beds is:

National Bedding Federation
251 Brompton Road
London SW3 2EZ
01–589 4888

Bedding The introduction of the *duvet* from mainland Europe has made a great impact in Britain. Bed-making with duvets is considerably time-saving and easy. A duvet gives a cosy feeling to a bed – although the traditional sheet and blankets preclude the possibility of feet and other parts of the body sticking out and getting cold. The bedding market in Britain today is divided into 40 per cent preferring duvets and 60 per cent preferring sheets and blankets, although many switch from duvets in winter to traditional bedding in summer.

It is important when buying duvets or pillows to check the filling. Many people do not realize they or their children are allergic to natural fillings ('plumage', 'feathers') and wake up snuffling or 'blocked up'. The types of filling available are:

1. Natural fillings (in descending order of quality and cost):
- *down* – fine fluff from the breast of a goose or duck
- *down and feathers* – mixture of down and small curly feathers (the minority)
- *feathers and down* – mixture of down and small curly feathers (the majority)
- *feathers* – virtually all feathers, with a tiny amount of down.

Check that your naturally filled duvet or pillow conforms to British Standard 5335: 1983. This eliminates the risk of it being filled with old feathers, chopped feathers or poultry feathers.

2. Man-made fillings: a high proportion of quilts contain a branded filling, such as 'Terylene Supersoft' or 'Terylene P3' from ICI. An unbranded filling may not carry a guarantee: it may contain low-grade cut fibre that was not specifically designed for use as a quilt filling and it may become lumpy and uneven after use or washing.

Note - If you are over 160cm (5ft 10ins.) you should buy an extra-long duvet. Your duvet should always be 45cm wider than your bed but the minimum size for one adult is 250cm and for two adults 295cm regardless of the width of the bed. Do not be mean when buying a duvet: it can never be too long.

When *blankets* are preferred, the choice available includes:
- *Acrylic fibre* – machine washable, least expensive, not as warm as other varieties. Cellular construction (i.e. with obvious holes to trap heat) gives warmth and lightness when used over a top sheet and under another blanket or bedcover.
- *Pure wool* – most expensive and most warm, might need dry-cleaning. (Some people may be allergic to wool.)

The Association of British Launderers and Cleaners suggests buying branded articles as they are more likely to be made from a well-constructed foundation fabric which will stand up to normal wear and washing. Beware of blankets made from rayon or cotton mixture as they are neither moth- nor shrink-proof and may 'fluff' when washed.

An important heat saver is the *thermal underblanket*, either an electric blanket or an acrylic sheepskin-type blanket which wraps over the mattress underneath the flat sheet and is fully washable.

Easy-care *sheets* are most popular and consist of a mix of polyester and cotton. The higher the percentage of polyester, the 'harder' the feeling of the fabric. A wider range of designs and colours is available: pastel dyes are less expensive than dark ones. Some people still prefer pure cotton sheets but these require ironing and do not have the ease of laundering of polycotton.

Sheet sizes (these vary between manufacturers):

(mattress width)	(sheet size)
75cm	162 × 265cm
90cm	200 × 265cm
105cm	210 × 265cm
120cm	235 × 265cm
135cm	250 × 265cm
150cm	265 × 265cm
165cm	280 × 265cm
180cm	295 × 265cm

Pillowcases should be up to 9.5cm wider and 15 to 20cm longer than the pillow. Corded hems are stronger than hem-stitched pillowcases, which tend to break before the pillowcase is worn out.

The Association of British Launderers and Cleaners suggests you should beware of buying cheap sale sheets and pillowcases which contain a large percentage of dressing to disguise a poor quality fabric: after the first wash they will become thin and flimsy. Test for excessive dressing by rubbing sections of the sheet together. If a white powdery dust falls out, do not buy.

See 'Fabric and Garment Care' from the Association of British Launderers and Cleaners, address on page 429.

DINING-ROOM

China

Once you find the type of china you like, it is a good idea to buy not only enough for your present needs but, if you can afford it, a few spares – manufacturers have a habit of discontinuing even 'everyday' china.

Cutlery

Types of cutlery available include:
- *Silver* – expensive but has the best investment potential. Disadvantages

include the necessity of cleaning it with silver polish; it is a soft metal, and therefore unpractical for everyday use.

● *Silver plate* – the thickness of the silver on base metal determines the price, which may range from below the price of good stainless steel to a high price for a thick coating of silver. Disadvantages include the necessity of cleaning with silver polish and the fact that a dishwasher can wear away the coating.

● *Stainless steel* – prices range from inexpensive to about the same as silver plate. No real disadvantages.

See also   'Table Settings', page 359.

KITCHEN   Today many kitchens are almost as much a family room as the living-room. Modern designs make much better use of space, are labour saving, attractive and comfortable. If you are lucky enough to have the space, a dining area could adapt to a homework area for a child, and a comfortable place for family and friends to join you when one of you is committed to the cooker and sink.

Units

If you are fitting your kitchen yourself rather than working with a kitchen specialist, a few things to check include:

● Check that all units really are the same size (many items are not exactly as described and a few millimetres difference can be crucial).

● Inspect the hinges – do they adjust?

● Are the drawers manufactured in one piece or in sections (the latter might collapse later)?

● Is the drawer movement smooth?

● Are shelves adjustable for maximum space usage?

● Do wall cupboards take full-size plates?

● Are the doors laminate or melamine? (Melamine is cheaper, thinner and inferior.)

● Does the work-top height suit you?

For details of wooden kitchen units, contact:

> Kitchen Furniture Manufacturers' Section
> British Woodworking Federation
> 82 New Cavendish Street
> London W1M 8AD
> 01–580 5588

See also   'Kitchen Extensions and Rebuilding', page 57ff.

Cookers

See also   'Electrical Appliances' and 'Gas Appliances' above.

Oven temperature conversion chart:

FAHRENHEIT (F)	CELSIUS (C)	GAS MARKS	
150	70		
175	80		
200	100		
225	110	$\frac{1}{4}$	Very cool
250	120	$\frac{1}{2}$	Very cool
275	140	1	Cool
300	150	2	Cool
325	160	3	Warm
350	180	4	Moderate
375	190	5	Fairly hot
400	200	6	Fairly hot
425	220	7	Hot
450	230	8	Very hot
475	240	9	Very hot

Most people adhere rigidly to their favourite cooking method – electric, gas or solid fuel. Others prefer, say, an electric oven with a gas hob. Each form of heat has its advantages:

● *Electricity* takes longer to heat to the required temperature but it provides even heat – and it is clean.

● *Gas* provides instant heat but it is not always even. It is not as clean to use.

● *Solid fuel* relies on no 'provided services' and is a superb standby in times of power cuts and other shortages. There is also something comforting about the 'friendliness' of an Aga or Rayburn. The disadvantages of solid fuel include the physical labour needed continually to 'mind' the beast and the consequent dirt. Oil-burning cookers rely on electricity so are not immune from crises.

Details of solid fuel heaters/cookers can be obtained from the Solid Fuel Advisory Services in most areas of the country. Find them in Yellow Pages under Coal, or Solid Fuel Advisory Service or National Coal Board. If all else fails contact the London head office on 01–235 2020 which will put you in touch with your nearest service.

Buying a cooker

● Check that the floor is level (if it is not, you will need a cooker with adjustable legs).

● Check that there is space around for cleaning.

● Do you want an eye-level grill? You can see more easily, but the grill area may be smaller than on a low-grill cooker. If you have shaky hands you should go for a low-grill. Either way, make sure you have a convenient heat-resistant surface on which to rest the grill pan.

See 'Choosing an Electric or Gas Cooker', 75p from *Good Housekeeping* magazine.

Notes
- Never leave saucepans on the hob with handles facing forward.
- Never dry teatowels by hanging them over a grill or hot oven.

LIVING-ROOM

This is the centre of the home, the room used by all the family and most seen by visitors and friends. It will have many different functions and moods, lighthearted or serious, casual or formal. Cater for as many occasions as you can. How many people do you want to be able to sit down, and in what arrangement (grouped, or round a focal point such as fire or television)? A three-piece suite can be cumbersome and dominate a small room: a sofa with several smaller chairs would be more adaptable. Do you want to emphasize any architectural feature, say an alcove with shelves and concealed lighting for display purposes? Remember that books are decorative and interesting.

Seating

Work out what you need. In the showroom check the springs of all the pieces you try. Sit in each: is it comfortable for you and all other tall/short people? Most important, make sure all pieces have the resistant label (see page 451).

The look of a sitting-room and the uses to which it is put can be changed by purchasing two 2-seater sofas to face each other on either side of the fireplace with tables or storage units at either end.

Remember – open shelves in a sitting/dining-room act as dividers without cutting out all vision.

Banquettes may be permanent built-in seating (e.g. a window space with upholstered cushions) or a set of movable sections that join together to form a seating unit in a line, L-shape or U-shape, according to space. These can be fun but need quite a lot of space to work properly.

Chairs can be upholstered in the old way with springs, horsehair and felt: this is covered with canvas and calico and the chosen fabric which may be anything from velvet pile to bright cotton. Less expensive modern chairs may be upholstered with rubber webbing and a foam block or chips and then softened with Dacron beneath a covering of the chosen fabric.

Upholstery

A good piece of furniture may deserve restoration by a competent upholsterer. This can cost several hundred pounds per item but it could still be less than half the price of a replacement piece.

If you want to learn how to upholster, look at evening classes available nearby (ask your library or local education authority). It may take you some months to finish the piece and you must be prepared to cart it to and from the class.

Modern or less expensive pieces of furniture can sometimes be re-covered at home using staple guns and hand tools from a DIY shop.

Spots, Stains and Smells

1. Speed in attending to the stain/mark is almost as important as the technique itself.

2. Be careful: some of the ideas below might have worked for those who recommended them – they might not always work for you.

3. Many liquids used in the home contain chemicals which may be harmful to textiles. If you spill anything that may contain a chemical, do not allow the liquid to dry into the fabric – wash it immediately or send it to the cleaners. Some of the liquids that might cause damage to textiles are: acid from batteries, bleach, deodorants, disinfectants, polishes, stain removers.

Ballpoint (biro) pen:
- washable items – sponge with undiluted liquid detergent and then rinse with cold water
- dry-cleanable items – dab lightly with a cloth soaked in methylated spirits and take to be cleaned as soon as possible
- or use Ballpoint Pen Stain Devil.

Blood:
- soak washable items in cold salted water
- older or obstinate stains may be loosened by soaking in a cold solution of biological detergent
- on carpets: sponge with cold water and blot with paper towels; then shampoo.

Candle wax: on a carpet or fabric, cover with brown paper and lightly iron. Repeat several times with fresh paper. Alternatively, use Ballpoint Stain Devil.

Chewing gum:
- on clothes – put garment in fridge so that the gum, when hardened, can be cracked and picked off
- or use Glue and Chewing Gum Stain Devil.

Coffee:
- washable items – small stains can be dabbed with liquid detergent in warm water; large stains can have the same mixture poured over them. Wash thoroughly afterwards.
- dry-cleanable items – dab with a clean pad soaked in water and take to be professionally cleaned (if the coffee had sugar in it, tell the cleaner)
- coffee stains on a carpet – use carpet shampoo: put some solution on a cloth and dab gently in a dark corner – say under a chair – to test colour fastness and then, with solution-wetted cloth, dab (not rub) from outside of stain in
- or use Coffee and Tea Stain Devil.

Felt tip pens: the ink has a different base from other inks and the Association

of British Launderers and Cleaners suggests that no home remedy should be attempted.
- take dry-cleanable items to be professionally cleaned
- wall coverings can be sponged with washing-up liquid or with methylated spirits
- or use Felt Tip Pen Stain Devil.

Fruit juice:
- washable items – soak in Biotex or rinse in cold water and launder in the usual way. If the stain changes on drying, seek professional help
- dry-cleanable items – most articles can be dabbed with a clean damp pad (test with an area which will not show)
- or use Fruit and Wine Stain Devil.

Grease:
- washable items – treat with grease solvent or washing-up liquid (butter can also sometimes remove a thick grease or tar)
- dry-cleanable items – dab the fresh stain with stain removal fluid, starting in a large circle outside the stain and working in (always keep a pad of clean cloth underneath). Take the item to be dry-cleaned
- some items can be covered with blotting paper and the mark pressed with a hot iron
- or use Grease and Oil Stain Devil.

Ink:
- washable items – wash the garment (washable ink).
For permanent ink, dab with methylated spirit using a small pad and then wash in detergent or rinse in cold water, soak in milk and then rub with lemon juice and wash in the usual way.

- dry-cleanable items – dab with stain removal fluid (see 'Grease' above) and take to be dry-cleaned
- or use Mould and Ink (or Ballpoint Pen) Stain Devil.

Nail varnish: dip cotton wool in methylated spirits and rub the stain, or use Tar and Paint Stain Devil or nail varnish remover.

Paint:
- emulsion paint marks – sponge in cold water and then launder if possible
- oil-based paint marks – dab fresh paint with white spirit and sponge in cold water (or try paint-brush cleaner)
- or use Tar and Paint Stain Devil.

Rust:
- washable items – moisten with lemon juice (do not let it dry) and rinse quickly in water with a little ammonia. Rinse. (Never use liquid bleach as this will not remove the stain and is certain to rot the fabric eventually)
- dry-cleanable items – take to be professionally treated
- or use Rust and Iron Mould Stain Devil.

Scorch marks: removal depends on degree of burning – slightly scorched natural fabrics may be cleaned by brushing with a stiff clothes brush to remove burnt fibre ends. Man-made fibres will harden and damage may be irrevocable.

Spirit marks: use Ballpoint Pen Stain Devil.

Tea: dilute the stain before it dries using hot water or Coffee and Tea Stain Devil. If you cannot soak, dab frequently with a wet pad. If the stain persists, seek professional help.

Wine: dab with soda water as soon as possible. White wine stains may fade. If possible, pour white wine on top of red wine stains and then dab with soda water. Alternatively, use Fruit and Wine Stain Devil.

See ● 'Fabric and Garment Care' from (s.a.e.):

> Association of British Launderers and Cleaners
> Lancaster Gate House
> 319 Pinner Road
> Harrow
> Middlesex HA1 4HX
> 01–863 7755

'The Complete Home Valet' from branches of Sketchley.
● For information on Stain Devils, and a list of stockists, contact (s.a.e.):

> DDD
> 94 Rickmansworth Road
> Watford
> Herts WD1 7JJ
> 0923–29251

Other objects

Bathtubs: regular use of bath foam helps keep a bathtub more or less clean. Keep a bath brush handy and, when the water is running out after a bath, brush foam into bath surrounds. Other ideas: Jif or Duraglit (for fittings). Yellow stains on bathtubs: make a paste of peroxide and cream of tartar, leave it on the mark for a few hours and rub well.

Brass and copper: dip a lemon half into a mixture of salt and vinegar and add lots of elbow grease as you rub. Do not leave the solution on too long as the chloride in the salt can lead to corrosion.

China:
● remove tea stains from cups by rubbing them with a cloth dipped in vinegar and salt
● a little vinegar mixed with inexpensive washing-up liquid helps attack grease.

Cookers: if your oven has a catalytic lining, dirt and grease are carbonized when cooking at high temperatures and you simply need to wipe the oven from time to time with a damp cloth. If your oven does not have a catalytic lining, clean it when new with a solution of bicarbonate of soda and water. After each use of the oven you then simply wipe the interior. Ammonia in an enamel bowl placed in the oven overnight will loosen grease and dirt.

Glass:
● drinking glasses – use biological washing powder to remove 'scum'. Cut glass and thick-bottomed glasses should never be put in a dishwater
● decanters – use denture cleaner (Steradent) or vinegar swirled around with marbles or sand
● mirrors and windows – use cold tea.

Ivory: methylated spirits or bicarbonate of soda and lemon juice mixed into a thin paste.

Lavatories: scrub with bleach. To remove stains from difficult under-rim areas, make a paste of flour and bleach and leave this on the offending area overnight.

Leather: use milk or, for white leather handbags, sal volatile.

Paintwork: clean paintwork with a little soap in warm water, or a cleaner such as Flash. Use cold tea for varnished paint.

Saucepans: soak in biological detergent (Biotex or Ariel).

Silver: tarnishing results from the reaction of silver to various compounds, e.g. gas from burning of coal, gas, oil or petrol; eggs, fish, peas and other foods; newspapers and blankets; rubber (rich in sulphur, rubber gloves can tarnish silver even through several layers of protecting cloth).

Ideally, antique silver should never be subjected to modern cleansers or the 'quick method' outlined below. Silver plate powder, available from silver/jewellery shops, should be used, with an old soft toothbrush. (Storage of silver, incidentally, is much facilitated by the use of tarnish-proof bags. These are available from big department stores.)

For everyday silver, the quickest cleaning method is to dissolve a handful of washing soda crystals in hot water in a clean aluminium pan, say a preserving pan. Put the silver in for about four minutes, swirling occasionally. Remove, rinse thoroughly and rub dry with a clean tea towel.

It is recommended that the following products are used for cleaning:
● long-term silver polish – for all silver, but especially useful for removing heavy tarnish and stains
● long-term silver foam – for intricate and ornate silverware
● silver dip – for silver cutlery and other small items
● long-term silver cloth – for silver kept on show or in frequent use.

Stainless steel: most cutlery can be cleaned in a dishwasher but do not let any piece come into contact with another metal (e.g. silver spoon). Similarly, do not let stainless steel come into contact with silver dip cleaners, lemon juice, vinegar, salt, bleach, undissolved detergents or wire wool. If stains appear, use a proprietary stainless steel cleaner.

Tiles: use household spray polish.

Vacuum flasks: fill with hot water and 1 tsp of bicarbonate of soda, soak overnight and rinse well. Bad stains should be removed with warm water and a little vinegar. Rinse well.

Wood: scratches can be covered by Topps (pale, medium or dark) or, if teak-coloured, with iodine. Try rubbing a stain with a light oil or a cut nut.

SMELLS   *Bathroom smells*: burn a match.

Breath smells (garlic/onion): eat parsley and keep a breath spray in your car and handbag.

Cigarette and tobacco smells: leave a saucer of vinegar in the room, out of sight (also relieves possible 'eye sting').

Kitchen smells:
- Fish – empty tea leaves from pot into saucepan, cover with water and let stand for half an hour. Rub vinegar on your hands to remove smell.
- Frying – avoidance techniques only (e.g. not using too high a flame and, where possible, using a wok rather than a deep fat fryer).
- Garlic cloves – store in a pot with a lid. Rub bicarbonate of soda on your hands to remove garlic smell.
- Onions – clingwrap before putting in the fridge. Rub salt on your hands to remove onion smell.
- Rubbish – mothballs in the garbage/dustbin will neutralize smells (and stop insects).
- Saucepan odours – remove by filling the pan with a small amount of vinegar in water and leaving it for several hours.

Further Information

Suggested further reading

INTERIOR DESIGN
Conran, Terence, *The Bed and Bath Book*, Mitchell Beazley
Dickson, Elizabeth and Margaret Colvin, *The Laura Ashley Book of Home Decorating*, Octopus
Healey, Deryck, *Living with Colour*, Macmillan
Manser, Jose, *The Kitchen and Bathroom Book*, Pan

EQUIPPING A HOUSE
Downing, Beryl, *Where Can I Get?*, Penguin
Lansbury, Angela, *The A to Z of Shopping by Post*, Exley Publications

Kitchens: from the wide range of cookery books relating to specific items of kitchen equipment, I would recommend the following:
Allison, Sonia, *Sonia Allison's Food Processor Cookbook*, Fontana
Barry, Michael, *Food Processor Cookery*, ICTC
Good Housekeeping Step by Step Microwave Cookery Book, Ebury Press
Norman, Cecilia, *Cecilia Norman's Microwave Cookery Course*, Granada

Tenison, Marika Hanbury, *Magimix Cookery*, ICTC

HOME CARE
Bremner, Moyra, *Supertips to Make Life Easy*, André Deutsch
Conran, Shirley, *Superwoman*, Penguin
Evans, Lizzie, *1,000 Handy Household Hints*, St Michael
Evetts, Echo, *China Mending: a Guide to Repairing and Restoration*, Faber &
    Faber
McGlone, Jean, *A Pocket Book of 500 Household Hints*, Octopus

16   Food and Drink

If you do not possess a single cookbook you are a *very* unusual person. So, assuming that you do have at least one, this information is different: there are no recipes – but there are lots of ideas about where you can get them. This chapter is about stocking a basic store cupboard and being aware of the kinds of food we eat.

The second part of the chapter is on food's partner, drink. Information includes what to look for on the label of a wine bottle and just why champagne is so special.

The subject of food and drink is a lifetime's obsession for some, daily consideration for most and a recurring annoyance to a few. Below are a few ideas for the busy woman who cares about quality, her budget and the meals she cooks.

What You Buy

BASIC STORES   FRUIT AND VEGETABLES
EGGS   BREAD
DAIRY PRODUCTS   PRESERVES
MEAT   TINNED GOODS
POULTRY AND GAME   DRIED GOODS
FISH   COFFEE AND TEA

I heard a story the other day of a British actor who, straight after landing in Los Angeles from Heathrow, went to stock up on food supplies at the nearest supermarket and wandered round in a post-flight daze. Only at the check-out did he realize that he had not had to think about what he was buying as everything was in the same place as in his local branch of the same supermarket back home!

BASIC STORES   It is recommended that the *basic household store* cupboard should always have stocks of:
condiments
eggs
flour
milk
sugar
tea and coffee.

In order to cope with emergencies (unexpected entertaining, or being cut off by snow) an *emergency store* cupboard should contain:

tinned fruit
tinned beans and other vegetables
tinned meats (chopped ham, pork and more expensive meats such as chicken)
tinned sardines, pilchards and other fish
tinned and packet soup
tinned evaporated milk
various packages and mixes for sauces, cakes, cheesecakes
cook-in-sauce products
pulses – rice – pasta
instant mashed potatoes
biscuits
crisps and nuts
milk powder.

EGGS

Egg sizes range from 1 (largest – minimum weight 70 g) to 7 (smallest – maximum weight 45 g). When recipes specify '1 egg' you should use size 3 or 4.

If kept in a cool place (a fridge or in a temperature approximately 7 or 8°C (45°F) eggs remain fresh for as long as two months. Store them with the blunt end uppermost in the egg container or rack so that the yolk, which deteriorates more quickly, is kept surrounded by the white. As eggs absorb smells and strong flavours they must not be stored near strong smelling foods.

Use any cracked eggs immediately in cooked dishes. If you want to freeze eggs, separate the whites and yolks of fresh, undamaged eggs.

For further information contact:

Egg Information Bureau
Union House
Eridge Road
Tunbridge Wells
Kent TN4 8HF
0892–33987

DAIRY
PRODUCTS

Dairy products are high in goodness (calcium, protein, riboflavin): milk and milk products make a valuable contribution to everybody's diet as they contain a wide variety of nutrients. They are versatile as part of a 'balanced diet'. They do, however, have a high fat content (see page 380).

Milk

Pasteurized (silver top) – about 86 per cent of all milk sold retail has been pasteurized: milk is heated and kept at a temperature of not less than 71.7°C (162°F) for at least fifteen seconds and then immediately cooled to not more than 10°C (50°F). This kills harmful bacteria and improves the keeping quality.

Pasteurized Channel Islands, Guernsey, Jersey or *South Devon* (gold top) – 'creamier' than silver top, with a higher fat content.

Pasteurized homogenized (red top) – milk is warmed and then forced through a fine aperture causing fat globules to break down into smaller particles. The smaller globules remain widely distributed and do not rise to the surface, so there is no 'cream'. It is particularly suitable for young children, invalids and the elderly as the smaller globules of fat are easily digested. After homogenization, the milk is then pasteurized.

Pasteurized kosher (blue/silver top) – from a dairy that has been blessed by a rabbi. For everyday use.

Pasteurized kedassia (purple/silver top) – for use only during Passover.

Sterilized (blue top) – milk is first homogenized and then heated to a temperature of not less than 100°C (212°F) for 20 to 30 minutes and then allowed to cool. It should keep unopened for at least seven days – and for several weeks in a fridge.

Ultra Heat Treated milk (UHT) – 'long-life' milk is homogenized and packaged and then retained at a temperature of not less than 132.2°C (270°F) for at least one second. Milk thus treated will keep if unopened for several months – once unopened, it should be used within 2 or 3 days.

Untreated (green top) – the produce of brucellosis-free accredited herds.

Untreated Channel Islands, Guernsey, Jersey and *South Devon* (green/silver tops) – as above.

Condensed and *evaporated* milks – must contain at least 9 per cent milk fat and 31 per cent milk solids.

Dried milk – must state the number of pints of liquid milk.

Skimmed milk – most of the fat has been removed, as have the fat-soluble Vitamins A and D, but the amount of protein, calcium and riboflavin are unchanged.

Cream
All containers of cream must be marked with the net weight. Types of cream (with percentage of legal minimum butterfat) regularly available are:

Clotted cream (55 per cent) – heated to about 82°C (180°F), cooled for 4½ hours and the crust skimmed.

Extended life double cream (48 per cent) – heated to 82°C (180°F) for fifteen seconds, cooled, homogenized, vacuum sealed, heated to 115°C (239°F) for twelve minutes and cooled.

Fresh extra-thick double cream (48 per cent) – heavily homogenized to increase viscosity.

Fresh half cream (12 per cent) – pasteurized by heating to 79.5°C (175°F) for fifteen seconds, cooled to 4.5°C (40°F).

Fresh single cream (*pasteurized*, 18 per cent) – may be homogenized, then treated as above.

Fresh soured cream (18 per cent) – pasteurized cream incubated with a special culture of harmless bacteria until desired acidity is reached.

Fresh whipping cream (*pasteurized*, 39 per cent) – pasteurized as above.

Sterilized cream (*tinned*, 23 per cent) – homogenized, filled into cans and sealed, heated to 115°C (240°F), for twenty minutes and cooled rapidly.

Ultra Heat Treated (*long-life*) *creams*: half (12 per cent), single (18 per cent) and whipping (39 per cent) – homogenized, heated to 132°C (270°F), for one second, cooled immediately, aseptically packed in foil-lined containers.

When buying cream, check the 'Sell by ...' date. Fresh creams should keep in a refrigerator for two or three days in summer or three to four days in winter once the date stamp expires. Extended life cream will last two or three weeks (unopened) in a fridge. Sterilized cream should keep for up to two years. Purchased *frozen* creams (single double, whipping) have been pasteurized at 80°C (176°F) for fifteen minutes, cooled and immediately frozen. They must be kept frozen until the stated time before use.

If you freeze cream note that:

- half, single and soured creams do not freeze successfully
- whipping cream freezes best if half-whipped before freezing
- double cream freezes better if mixed with milk (1 tbs milk, 150ml cream) and then partly whipped
- when whipping thawed frozen cream, take care as it tends easily to overwhip.

For further information on butter and cream contact:

Milk Marketing Board
Thames Ditton
Surrey KT7 OEL
01–398 4101

Scottish Milk Marketing Board
Underwood Road
Paisley PA3 ITJ
041–887 1234

Butter and margarine

Butter contains 81 per cent milk fat, 16 per cent water, 2 per cent salt (except unsalted butter) and artificial colouring. Interestingly, it has the same number of calories as ordinary margarines (185 kcal per 25 g). There are traditionally two kinds of butter:

1. *Sweet cream butter* – the fresh cream is pasteurized and cooled before being placed in cream ageing tanks for at least twelve hours at a consistently low temperature.

2. *Lactic butter* – the cream is ripened at 18 to 21°C (65 to 75°F) by growing in it a pure culture of lactic bacteria. These produce flavourings in the

butter in a process similar to the making of yogurt. After this the cream is pasteurized.

For further information on butter contact:

> Butter Information Council
> Tubs Hill House
> London Road
> Sevenoaks
> Kent TN3 1BL
> 0732–460060

Margarine may be blended with up to 10 per cent butter; it must have added vegetable, animal fish oil, vitamins and not more than 16 per cent added water. Basic margarine has the same amount of calories as butter but you can also buy 'low fats' which contain fewer calories per gram.

Cheese

Smaller pieces of cheese dry out more quickly than larger. This may occur with pre-packed cheese so avoid any packs that are hard and dry in appearance and which have evident cracks and colour variations.

When storing cheese at home, the cut surface should be closely covered with clingwrap and/or aluminium foil. Cheese should then be kept in a cool place.

1. *Hard pressed* cheeses include:
- Cheddar (golden or orange-red)
- Cheshire (orange-red or white)
- Derby (often honey-coloured)
- Double Gloucester (orange-yellow)
- Leicester (deep orange).

All are aged when bought, from four weeks (Derby) to as much as eighteen months (Cheddar). Once cut, these hard cheeses do not improve with keeping so it is better to buy as often as possible. Ideally keep them in a plastic container in a cool larder. If this is not possible keep them in a fridge but remember to remove them at least an hour before eating as the cool temperature masks the flavour. If you are freezing leftover hard cheeses which sometimes crack and crumble when frozen, grate before freezing.

2. *Lightly pressed cheeses* include:
- Caerphilly (white)
- Lancashire (creamy white)
- Wensleydale (white).

These may be sold when as young as two weeks.

3. *Blue cheeses* include:
- Stilton (should never be scooped as it encourages the cheese to dry out – cut with the knife, point at centre, held horizontally)
- Cheshire
- Wensleydale.

4. *Unusual British cheeses* include:
- Cheddar mixed with beer/garlic/pickles, etc.
- Cotswold (Double Gloucester with chives)
- Huntsman (Double Gloucester with Blue Stilton)
- Lymeswold (a soft blue cheese)
- Sage Derby (Derby with sage juice)
- Windsor Red (Cheddar with red wine).

5. Some *soft cheeses* may require ripening. Keep them for a few days prior to eating until the required ripeness is achieved. Store leftover soft cheeses in the fridge to prevent further ripening. Put soft cheeses into the freezer at best point of ripeness.

6. *Cream cheeses* have especially short lives as they are made from fresh cream. Do not freeze cream or cottage cheeses.

For further information on cheese send a large s.a.e. to:

English Country Cheese Council
5–7 John Prince's Street
London W I M O AP
01–499 7822

Yogurt

This is made from a skimmed milk base to which extra skimmed milk powder is added. Fat-free yogurt contains less than 0.5 per cent milk fat: low fat yogurt contains no more than 1.5 per cent milk fat. However, with the exception of plain yogurt, all fruit- and nut-flavoured yogurts have large quantities of sugar added to them together with the fruit, so don't be misled into thinking that flavoured yogurt is 'slimming'.

Excellent information on all dairy products is available (large s.a.e.) from the Dairy Produce Advisory Service at the Milk Marketing Board (address on page 466).

MEAT There is little difference between fresh and frozen meat although frozen lamb has a less delicate flavour than fresh and looks different (the lean is paler and does not have the bloom of fresh meat while the fat is whiter and crumbles more easily). Nutritionally, both fresh and frozen meats are comparable: the only difference after cooking is the content of the B vitamins although this loss can to some extent be rectified by using the liquid which collects while the meat is thawing to make gravy.

It is also worth remembering that the bigger the cut of meat, generally the better the flavour and the better the overall value. Good value cuts include braising steak (beef), shoulder (lamb), whole hand or picnic (pork).

Raw meat may contain, along with many harmless bacteria, some stray micro-organisms that could cause disease. In addition it may acquire other bacteria during handling and cutting up. It is therefore essential to eat meat when it is in prime condition and, generally, as soon as possible after purchase.

Cuts of beef

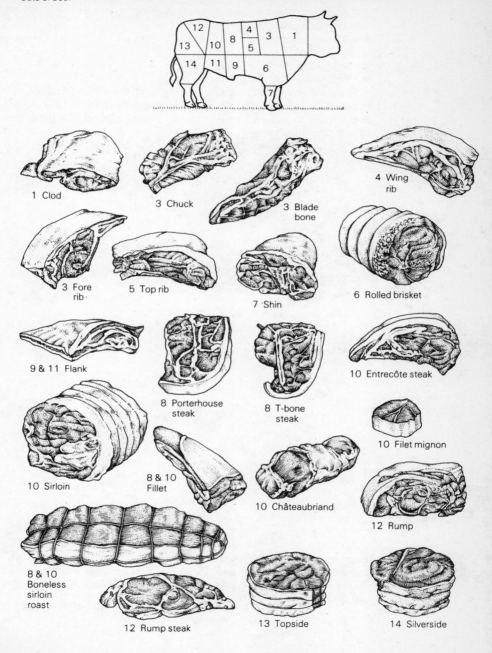

1 Clod

3 Chuck

3 Blade bone

4 Wing rib

3 Fore rib

5 Top rib

7 Shin

6 Rolled brisket

9 & 11 Flank

8 Porterhouse steak

8 T-bone steak

10 Entrecôte steak

10 Sirloin

8 & 10 Fillet

10 Châteaubriand

10 Filet mignon

12 Rump

8 & 10 Boneless sirloin roast

12 Rump steak

13 Topside

14 Silverside

Cuts of lamb

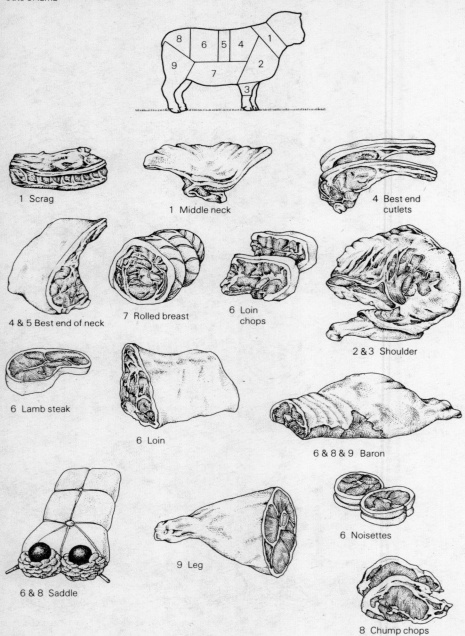

1 Scrag

1 Middle neck

4 Best end cutlets

4 & 5 Best end of neck

7 Rolled breast

6 Loin chops

2 & 3 Shoulder

6 Lamb steak

6 Loin

6 & 8 & 9 Baron

6 & 8 Saddle

9 Leg

6 Noisettes

8 Chump chops

Cuts of pork

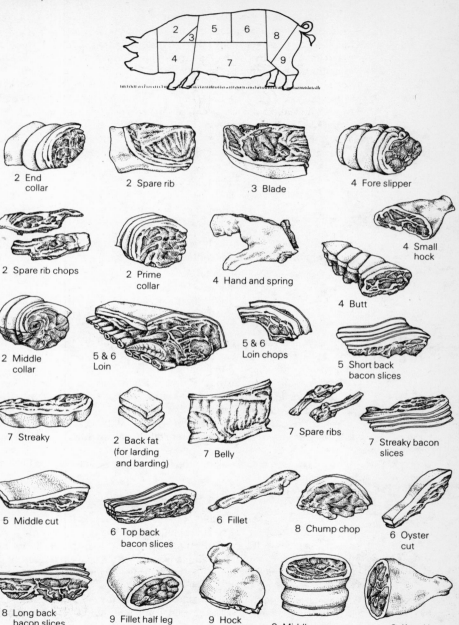

2 End collar

2 Spare rib

3 Blade

4 Fore slipper

2 Spare rib chops

2 Prime collar

4 Hand and spring

4 Small hock

4 Butt

2 Middle collar

5 & 6 Loin

5 & 6 Loin chops

5 Short back bacon slices

7 Streaky

2 Back fat (for larding and barding)

7 Belly

7 Spare ribs

7 Streaky bacon slices

5 Middle cut

6 Top back bacon slices

6 Fillet

8 Chump chop

6 Oyster cut

8 Long back bacon slices

9 Fillet half leg

9 Hock

9 Middle gammon

9 Knuckle

Meat products

Beef sausages have by law to contain at least 50 per cent beef and pork sausages must have a minimum 65 per cent pork. Many local butchers' home-made sausages today contain what nutritionists may think is too much fatty meat. By contrast, many commercial sausages appear tasteless and also have a high fat content.

Meat pies, which must contain at least 25 per cent meat, are attractive to the busy shopper. When buying pies, remember that the bigger sizes contain a smaller percentage of pastry or other starch. And, when buying frozen pies and other main courses, bear in mind that the stated number of portions seldom satisfies that number of adult appetites.

For further information on all meat products, contact:

Meat Promotion Executive
5 St John's Square
Smithfield
London EC1M 4DE
01–251 2021

● Many people feel strongly about factory farming. If you would like further information on this contact:

Animal Aid
7 Castle Street
Tonbridge TN9 1BH
0732 364546

POULTRY AND GAME

Chicken and turkey offer good value for money and are the basis of many easy and versatile dishes. They are also attractive to health-conscious appetites, as they are low in fat and low in calories.

Frozen poultry must be thawed slowly, left in film wrapping and allowed to defrost for at least twenty-four hours (chicken) or forty-eight (whole turkey). It should never be thawed in warm water.

Poultry requires special attention when cooking because of the risk of salmonella. Never eat any meat that still shows any hint of pink.

FISH

When buying fresh fish look for the following signs of freshness:
● pleasant smell
● slippery shiny-bright skin
● tight scales which are not coming off
● reddish or bright pink gills.

Fish does not improve with keeping and even a few days' storage will mean less flavour. If you do want to store fresh fish for up to twenty-four hours, keep it surrounded and covered with icecubes (regularly replenished) in a covered container in the fridge. If you want to store fresh fish for longer, freeze it.

If you are going to freeze fish make sure that they are really fresh. Fish in a supermarket may once have been frozen and should never be refrozen. Gut all fish before freezing.

Buying frozen fish represents excellent value, combining convenience with, in many cases, no apparent loss of flavour – especially if you thaw it in a little cold milk.

Skinning fish

- *Flat fish* – lay the fish on a board with dark skin uppermost. Make a slit across the skin just above the tail. Slip your thumb into the slit and gently loosen the skin. Hold the fish firmly by the tail and pull the skin quickly towards the head (salt on the fingers improves the grip). Cut it off. Although the white skin on the other side is usually left on you may remove it in the same manner.
- *Round fish* – usually cooked with the skin on but you can remove it prior to cooking. Use a sharp knife to loosen skin around the head and gently draw it down towards the tail. Cut off, and repeat on the other side.

Fish products

- *Fish paste* must contain 70 per cent of any fish and *fish spread* must contain the same amount of the named fish: both make good cupboard standbys to serve on toast for nibbles or starters.
- *Smoked fish* keeps for several days (look for the date label). Packets of smoked mackerel fillets are good value, time-saving and versatile as they can be used as a starter or main course.

FRUIT AND VEGETABLES
Fresh produce

The best way to buy both fruit and vegetables is fresh. If you use a super-market you can generally buy pre-packaged as well as serve-yourself goods.

Look out for unusual fruit and vegetables and ask if you want to know what they are, how to cook them and how to test for ripeness.

Fruit generally does not keep long at room temperature. The following are all best eaten on the day of purchase:

- strawberries, raspberries and all currants (you can blend overripe soft fruit into a purée with a bit of olive oil to make a fruit mayonnaise salad dressing)
- all stone fruit (with the exception of plums and nuts)
- bananas (unless bought slightly green, in which case store in a brown paper bag in a cool larder: alternatively, you can keep bananas if you put them in the fridge – their skins will turn brown but they will be quite all right inside).

The following will keep longer:

- apples and pears will keep for up to two weeks if kept cool
- all citrus fruits keep well, ideally in a cool larder (up to a week) or in the vegetable box of the fridge (up to two weeks).

Notes

- Peaches will ripen quickly if you put them in a box and cover them with newspaper.

- If you need only half an avocado, leave the stone in the remainder and cover it all with clingwrap.
- If you need only part of an apple, wrap the rest firmly in clingwrap.
- If you need only a few drops of lemon juice, simply prick one end and squeeze out what you need.
- If you have lemon over, cut it into slices and freeze individual slices for a real English 'g-and-t'.
- Fruit salads: to everyday fruit (apples, oranges, bananas) add a tin of exotics (e.g. lychees). Or marinate sultanas and other dried fruit in whatever liqueur or leftover wine is handy and mix that in with the fresh fruit.

Vegetables

When buying vegetables try not to overbuy as 'fresh tastes best'. And look out for such recent arrivals as white aubergines, kuuchai and jumboo (all from Thailand).

Green vegetables and salad plants must be dry or they will rot if stored for even a couple of hours. All should be bought as fresh as possible and they should be stored loosely wrapped or in a covered plastic box in the fridge. Do not store for more than three days in the fridge.

Watercress should be used within twenty-four hours of purchase.

Root vegetables may be stored for up to three days only when indoors: if you remove the tops of carrots they will keep firm a little longer. For longer storage keep dry in soil or sand or in an outdoor shed and remember to keep potatoes out of the light.

Onions do not keep for ever. They sometimes tend towards mould on the inside. Before slicing an onion, put it in the fridge for a while to prevent tears.

Broccoli, purchased clingwrapped, should keep for nearly a week. It is a versatile standby: small raw florets can be colourful in a salad or enliven pasta, and those long stalks can be sliced longways and cooked and eaten like asparagus.

Frozen fruit and vegetables

Commercially frozen produce is frozen so quickly after picking (in many cases just a few hours) that the taste is retained in a way that may not be achieved even with home-frozen produce. Remember that 'oven chips' are a useful standby for hearty appetites or unexpected guests.

Buy the largest packets of produce you can store in your freezer. Snip the corner of the packet and use what you require at one meal carefully resealing the packet.

BREAD

All bread over 10 oz. must be sold by weight. White bread must contain vitamins, iron and chalk for calcium content, brown or wholemeal must have at least 0.6 per cent fibre and may have up to 5 per cent soya or rice flour added, wheatgerm should have 10 per cent processed wheatgerm, milk bread must have 6 per cent milk solids and protein bread should contain 22 per cent protein. Wholemeal bread is made from wholemeal flour without the addition of any other flours.

TYPES OF BREAD

Bran enriched bread – white, brown or wholemeal flour with added bran.

Brown or wheatmeal bread – baked from 85 to 90 per cent extraction flour.

Enriched bread – usually white bread with high levels of fat, sugar, milk and egg (e.g. bun loaves).

Germ bread – baked from white or wheatmeal flour with added wheatgerm.

Malted wheat bread – special formulated flour mixture, such as granary, which includes kibbled and whole grain, which has been malted.

Low density bread – white or brown flour, almost twice the size of ordinary breads of the same weight.

Malt bread – usually baked from proprietary prepared mixtures.

Milk bread – white flour, with 6 per cent full cream milk solids.

Soda bread – unyeasted dough with buttermilk and bicarbonate of soda as raising agent (often Irish).

White bread – baked from 70 to 75 per cent extraction flours.

Wholemeal/wholewheat bread – baked from 100 per cent extraction flour, sometimes stoneground.

TYPES OF LOAF

Labelling can also refer to *shape* of the bread. Here are some of the most popular loaf types.

Barrel or *pistol, rasp* or *landlady's loaf* – circular, ridged tin loaf.

Bloomer or *twist* – crusty loaf (London and South East), slashed diagonally on top.

Cob – round loaf, often with sprinkling of crushed wheat on top.

Coburg – crusty, dome-shaped with two cuts on top to form a crown.

Cottage – two round loaves one on top of the other.

Currant loaf – fruit bread with regional variations (e.g. Welsh bara brith, Irish barmbrack, Scottish Selkirk bannock).

French stick – long baguette, or baton.

Plait – open-baked plaited dough.

Sandwich loaf – flat tin loaf, often sliced.

Split loaves (slit along the top) can be split tin, farmhouse, Danish – open baked for a firm crust all round.

Vienna – horseshoe or stick shaped, enriched with milk and highly glazed thin crisp crust.

Bread may be stored in a clean bread bin or crock, wiped out daily with a dry cloth, or in a cool larder. It should be covered to prevent it drying out. Generally the fridge is not the best place to store bread; a loaf kept for one day in a fridge is similar in staleness to a three-day-old loaf. Bread freezes well and slices can be taken out as required.

Bread can be revitalized by damping the outside of the loaf and putting it into a very hot oven for up to twenty minutes.

For a selection of information and recipe leaflets using bread send a large s.a.e. to:

Flour Advisory Bureau
21 Arlington Street
London SW1A 1RN
01–493 2521

PRESERVES These include fruit jams and jellies – and vegetable preserves such as various types of chutneys and pickles. All must have a label containing a list of ingredients. Jam must have, for instance, a minimum 25 per cent of fruit content for blackcurrant and 38 per cent for strawberry. Marmalade must have at least 20 per cent of citrus fruit.

Remember that jams are good for such desserts as traditional trifle and steamed puddings and jellies make an interesting accompaniment to roast meats.

TINNED A few standbys are recommended, particularly for times when fresh
GOODS produce is not available. Certain tinned foods are thought by many really to have the better taste.

Notes ● When opening tins, remember to wipe the top before opening, to prevent accumulated dirt from getting inside, and to wash the opener afterwards.
● Serve own label petit pois – much less expensive than brand names and just as good – with a garnish of well-cooked bacon pieces and lemon juice.
● Use condensed soups as bases for casseroles and other dishes.

DRIED GOODS **Pasta**
Unless you run an Italian restaurant it is really not worth while making your own. If you are in a large city you might have a fresh pasta shop near you and some supermarkets sell fresh pasta in the delicatessen department. Dried pasta in a variety of shapes is available everywhere.

When cooking pasta, check the time instructions on the packet (dried pasta requires longer cooking than fresh). Use as large an uncovered pot as you can and the secret is to put the pasta into a lot of boiling water, with a teaspoon of oil and a little salt. Do not overcook – plunge the pasta into cold water if you are not going to use it immediately. Leftover pasta can be frozen, reheated in the microwave or served cold, with a dressing.

Cereals
Once opened, cereals should be stored in an airtight container or the pack should be properly resealed to prevent softness. Store in a cool dry place.

Sugar

Sugar is bad for you: it is fattening, can seriously damage your health and is disastrous for your teeth. The prominent role that sugar plays in the eating habits of the British is demonstrated very clearly by looking at the extraordinary range available:

● Brown sugar

There is a widely held belief that brown sugar is 'better' for you than white. This is a fallacy, so do not be misled into thinking that you are doing yourself a favour by eating brown instead of white sugar.

Brown sugars vary analytically, but of greater significance are the differences in crystal sizes, colour and the quality and strength of the cane sugar aroma and taste. In the main, brown sugars are used as additives after cooking – on cereal, for instance. They do not dissolve well in coffee and tea.

Demerara – raw cane sugar, originally that produced in a single location but in recent years any West Indian raw cane sugar having a large crystal size and characteristic light brown colour, taste and smell.

Muscovado – raw cane sugar to which extra molasses has been added: sugar content is typically 96 per cent.

Soft sugar – a legally specified term. Both words should appear in the product name.

● Golden syrup

High purity sugar liquors from the cane sugar refining process are blended, partly decolorized and inverted, then evaporated. Lyle's Golden Syrup contains 74 kcals per 25 g. Golden syrup is thought by some to be the perfect addition to porridge – and it is used in 'nursery' desserts such as treacle tart (sic) and steamed syrup pudding.

Both syrup and treacle will mix more easily if slightly warmed beforehand: they should never be refrigerated.

● Molasses

The molasses sold in retail packs is almost invariably derived from cane sugar. Typically it contains 55 kcals per 25 g.

● Treacle

This is a blend of refinery sugars with cane molasses – it contains approximately 65 kcals per 25 g.

● White sugars

White sugars, especially caster and granulated, are often used in cooking, and cube sugar is sometimes preferred for addition to coffee or tea.

Caster sugar – white sugar refined from raw sugar, as for granulated, but the crystallization process is modified to produce smaller crystals.

Cubes – moistened granulated sugar is pressed into moulds and oven-dried to produce cubes.

Granulated sugar – white sugar produced by refining raw sugar: sieving removes coarse and fine sugar to give a product of uniform crystal size.

Icing sugar – a white sugar, usually granulated, is milled. Retail products usually contain a quantity (legal max. 1.5 per cent) of an anti-caking agent, e.g. calcium phosphate.

Preserving sugar – white sugar with a large crystal size so that, because of the reduced surface area, the crystals dissolve more slowly than other white sugars and the risk of burning on the bottom of the saucepan is lessened.

White sugars will remain stable and free-flowing almost indefinitely if they are kept in dry storage conditions at a relatively stable temperature. If sugar becomes damp it will 'cake' (in a process similar to the making of cube sugar). The finer the grain the quicker this will happen.

Brown sugars should be stored at ambient temperatures with medium humidity and similarly they should last for a long time: in dry conditions they may cake but they can be restored to their original consistency by placing in a bowl and covering with a damp cloth overnight.

For recipes using sugar contact:

> Tate & Lyle Customer Services
> Lion House
> High Street
> Croydon CR9 3NH
> 01–686 5656

Flour

Types of flour generally available include:

Granary bread flour – a proprietary strong bread flour containing malted wheat grain and malted flaked wheat in addition to malt flour. The characteristic flavour comes from malted wheat.

Plain flour – produced from the centre of the wheat berry with all outer husk and wheatgerm removed.

Strong bread flour – produced from stronger higher protein wheat to give the necessary structure to bread products.

Wheatmeal flour – a brown flour containing some bran but with the wheatgerm and the rest of the bran from the original wheat removed. It is now customarily produced by adding bran to a white flour.

Wholewheat flour – contains all of the original wheat berry with nothing added and nothing taken away. It can be a strong or soft flour.

Self-raising flour (SR) – usually a 'weak' flour, it has a relatively low proportion of gluten and is therefore suitable for cakes and biscuits; it has an admixture of raising agents: bicarbonate of soda and an acid phosphate.

For information on flour and making your own bread contact (s.a.e.):

Flour Advisory Bureau
21 Arlington Street
London SW1A 1RN
01–493 2521

Condiments

Checklist for a basic store cupboard:

salt	ginger, ground
salts – celery, garlic, onion	herbs, mixed
peppers – black, white	marjoram
lemon juice	mint
wine vinegar	nutmeg, ground
bay leaves	oregano
bouquet garni	paprika
chives	parsley
cinnamon	sage
cloves	spices, mixed
curry powder	thyme

For information on herbs and spices contact (s.a.e.):

Spice Information Bureau
6 Cavendish Square
London W1M 9HA
01–636 2461

COFFEE AND TEA

Coffee

For those who like the real thing, nothing tastes better than coffee brewed from freshly ground beans, so if you grind your own don't do too much at a time. Likewise, if you buy freshly ground coffee, just buy a few days' supply and keep it in an airtight container. Pre-packed ground coffee in unopened vacuum or gas-flushed packs has a longer life but will begin to lose flavour after some months.

You can make coffee in a variety of jugs, plunger pots, drip filter machines and so on. Select the right 'grind' for the method you use, e.g. medium fine for filters, coarse for jugs. The water should be freshly drawn from the cold tap and just off the boil (about 94°C or 200°F).

Beans for ground coffee are mostly of the Arabica variety. Try blends from different countries and different roasts – light, medium, full and high.

French coffee is sometimes a mixture of coffee and chicory (at least 51 per cent coffee – check the label).

Instant coffees are also made from Arabica beans, but mainly from another variety of coffee called Robusta, which can be grown at lower altitudes than Arabica. There are spray-dried (powder), freeze-dried grains and granules and only by trying them and comparing prices can you find the best choice. As with ground coffee, be sure to use water that is just off the boil – boiling water or, worse still, boiling the coffee after making, detracts from the taste.

Liquid coffee extract, pre-sweetened, is now not much used for drinking but acts as a coffee flavouring for milk shakes and iced coffee.

There are de-caffeinated varieties of both ground and instant coffee.

For further information contact:

London Coffee Information Centre
21 Berners St
London WIP 4DD
01–580 4043

Tea

The United Kingdom is the world's biggest importer of tea, taking 25 per cent of the tea exported by countries such as Sri Lanka, India, Kenya, Malawi and, the oldest tea-growing country, China.

Types of tea include:

Black tea – produced by allowing the plucked and withered leaves to ferment or oxidize before drying at a high temperature. It is the familiar and most popular type in Britain.

Oolong tea – partially fermented and then steamed, giving a lighter greeny-brown leaf.

Green tea – less familiar here, but highly regarded in Central Asia and the Far East. It is produced by steaming the leaves without prior fermentation.

Tea is graded by leaf size and characteristics in terms which are probably fully understood only in the tea trade itself. The main sizes are:

- leaf tea (mainly large whole leaves)
- broken (broken large leaves)
- fannings (smaller whole leaves)
- dust (broken smaller leaves – as in tea-bags)

First introduced into the UK in the fifties, tea-bags, because of their convenience of use and disposal, now account for over two-thirds of our consumption. The same types of tea are used in popular packet and bag brands, but the smaller leaf size in the bag allows quicker infusion and thus a shorter brewing time. You should still allow three minutes with a tea-bag to extract the flavour effectively. If this makes too strong a cup or pot for your taste, use more water, don't cut the time. With packet tea, five minutes is the right brewing time, followed by a stir.

For both packet and tea-bag tea, use freshly drawn water from the cold tap, brought to a vigorous boil. Pre-heat the pot or cup with very hot water.

The popular brands at your local supermarket or corner store are ideal for everyday use: they are blends of many different teas. There are also, at a somewhat higher price, special blends such as Earl Grey, with its scent of the citrus oil of bergamot, and 'English Breakfast', a full rich flavoured blend. For variety and interest try the teas from a particular area: delicate

Darjeeling, fragrant Nuwara Eliya, smoky and pungent Lapsang Souchong and light Keemun with Chinese food.

For more information contact:

The Tea Council Ltd
Sir John Lyon House
5 High Timber Street
London EC4V 3NJ
01–248 1024

Caffeine

The US Food and Drug Administration reports these figures for the range of typical caffeine content of coffee, tea, cocoa and colas:

150 ML (5 FL.OZ) CUP	CAFFEINE IN MILLIGRAMS
ground coffee	40–180
instant coffee	30–120
tea	25–110
cocoa	2–20
(12 fl.oz)	
cola	30–46

Freezing

When buying frozen foods, remember that all large sizes are usually good value for money (the larger the size, the more saving in packaging and distribution). Buy frozen foods last. Ideally put them into an insulated bag or wrap them in newspaper. Keep them out of the sun and take them home to the freezer as soon as possible.

Packing and labelling
In all cases except liquids, as much air as possible must be excluded. When freezing liquids, make sure there is at least 1 cm ($\frac{1}{2}$ in) clear headroom to allow for expansion.
  Suitable wrappings/containers include:
● aluminium foil (either heavy gauge, or several thicknesses of ordinary foil)
● heavy gauge polythene bags
● rigid plastic boxes with lids
● waxed cartons
● shaped foil dishes.
  Some small individual items (fruits, cauliflower florets, beans, mushrooms and small mince pies) are sometimes open-frozen so that they can be used later as required and not as part of the whole frozen unit. Items should be put in a single layer on a plastic tray in the top of the freezer.

When they are completely frozen, they should be removed with the aid of a spatula and packaged in the normal way.

No frozen food should be exposed. Foods left uncovered are liable to freezer burn and drying (this is especially important in the case of meat). All packages must be well sealed, with twisted wires or with special freezer tape. All packages should be labelled.

Recommended
maximum storage
times

BAKED GOODS	
Bread	4 weeks
Parbaked	4 months
Cakes	6 months
iced	2 months
Pastries	2 months
unbaked	6 weeks
Scones, etc.	6 months

DESSERTS	
Ice-cream	1 month
Mousses, etc.	2 months

FISH	
Fillets, steaks, whole	6 months

FRUIT AND VEGETABLES	
Fruit	
juice	4–6 months
purée	6–8 months
sliced, whole	12 months
Mushrooms	3 months
Vegetables (average)	12 months

MEAT	
Meat	
cooked	1 month
dishes	2 months
pies	3 months
Beef joints	8 months
mince, cubes	3 months
Lamb, pork, veal joints	6 months
cutlets, cubes	3 months
Offal	1–3 months
Pâté	1 month
Sausage	1–3 months

POULTRY AND GAME

Chicken	12 months
Duck	4–6 months
Goose	4–6 months
Turkey	6 months
giblets/liver	3 months
Game	6–8 months
Hare, rabbit	6 months
Venison	12 months

OTHER

Pancakes	2 months
Pastry	6 months
uncooked	3 months
Pizza	2 months
unbaked	3 months
Sauces, stocks, soups	2–3 months

See   'Food Freezing – the Golden Rules', the Electrical Association for Women (address on page 566).

Alcohol

WINE

CHAMPAGNE

SPIRITS

SHERRY

WINE

by Adrian Talboys, wine buyer for Safeway Food Stores

Since the Weights and Measures (Sale of Wine) Order 1976, carafe sizes have been standardized:
¼ litre, ½ litre, ¾ litre, 1 litre or ½ pint and 1 pint. Written indication must be given – say, on the wine list – about how much a carafe holds.

Similarly, since 1983 there are two standard glass of wine sizes, 73 ml and 125 ml. In pubs and wine bars, however, you cannot rely on the quality of wine.

When judging how far wine will go, a few points to remember include:
- *table wines* – 8 to 9 drinking glasses per 75 cl bottle
- sweet wines go further than other table wines
- decanted wine with sediment does not go as far as bottled
- *port* – 10 glasses
- *sparkling wines* – 9 glasses per 75–80 cl bottle.

Labels

Look at the label when buying. Some points of wine label terminology include:

Appellation contrôlée (French) – a guarantee by law that the wine comes from the district or region stated on the label and that it meets certain standards of quality.

Auslese (German) – a sweet wine that is made from grapes that have been left on the vines longer than usual.

Cave (French) – a cellar.

Chai (French) – a cellar in Bordeaux, ground-level.

Château (French) – not always a castle, this word is also used to denote a vineyard in Bordeaux and other parts of France.

Claret – the English name for a red wine that comes from Bordeaux.

Clos (French) – a specific vineyard.

Cru (French) – the produce of a particular vineyard or part of a vineyard.

Cuvée (French) – a special cask. *Cuvée clos* means an enclosed cask and refers to a way of making sparkling wine.

Demi-sec (French) – a fairly sweet rather than fairly dry wine.

DOC (Italian) – *Denominazione de origine controllata*, meaning that the wine comes from the region stated and meets a specific standard.

Eiswein (German) – 'ice-wine'. A very fine wine that has come from frozen grapes left so long on the vine that there may be snow in the ground when they are picked.

Grand cru (French) – the best wine of a region.

Hock – English name for a wine that comes from the Rhine region of Germany.

Kabinett (German) – a high quality, usually dry wine.

Marque deposé (French) – registered trademark.

Mis en bouteilles à la propriété (French) – 'bottled in our cellars'.

Mousseux (French) – sparkling wine.

Négociant (French) – wine shipper.

Pétillant (French) – wine with a slight sparkle.

Qualitätswein (German) – a quality wine which has come from one of eleven special wine-growing areas.

Sec (French) – a dry wine (except in the case of champagne when the word *'brut'* denotes dryness).

Sekt (German) – sparkling wine.

Spätlese (German) – 'late harvested' and, therefore, sweet grapes producing sweet wine.

Spritzig (German) – wine with some natural sparkle in it.

Spumante (Italian) – sparkling wine.

Tafelwein (German) – table wine: an ordinary inexpensive wine for everyday use.

VDQS (French) – vin délimité de qualité supérieure, another quality control similar to *appellation contrôlée*.

Vin du pays (French) – locally made wine.

Vin ordinaire (French) – everyday table wine.

Vino da tavola (Italian) – table wine.

Glasses Wine glasses come in all shapes and sizes and can be bought cheaply from a supermarket or at high cost from a hand-cut-crystal specialist. While it is pleasant to have several sets of glasses for different types of drink, it is perfectly possible to choose a basic shape that accommodates any drink. Such adaptable shapes include: 'tulip', tall, fairly slim with a slightly curving rim; and 'Paris goblet', the all-purpose round-bowl pub-type glass.

When buying glasses, take size into account. Generously sized glasses need generous amounts of wine whereas small glasses seem mean and skimpy. Glasses holding 6 to 8 oz are a good compromise (and can be used for other drinks).

The best wine glasses are clear glass and, ideally, as thin as possible. The stem should be long enough to take your hands so that warm fingers are kept away from the bowl. Many glasses have bowls that curve gently inwards towards the rim so that they direct some of the bouquet up but, at the same time, retain some in the glass for the rest of your enjoyment.

Wine glasses should be half to two-thirds filled to allow space to swirl the wine to savour the bouquet.

Buying wine If you have a query about a particular wine go to the outlet it was purchased from and make inquiries. Some wine-producing countries operate special wine information offices such as Food and Wines of France and the Italian Trade Centre.

A specialist shop – often called an off-licence – is licensed to sell alcoholic beverages for consumption off the premises. One of the main advantages of shopping at a retail wine and spirit shop is that you have a wide range of wines and spirits from which to choose and there is always someone you can ask for advice. You have to be eighteen to buy in a retail wine and spirit shop but you can take a child in with you.

Headquarters of some of the main retail wine and spirit merchants are:

Peter Dominic
IDV Ltd
1 York Gate
London NW1 4PG
01–935 4446

Gough Brothers
Durham House
12 Upper Green West
Mitcham
Surrey CR4 3YE
01–640 5131

Oddbins
73 Wapping High Street
London E1 9 PL
01–488 9066

Victoria Wine
Brook House
Chertsey Road
Woking
Surrey GU21 5BE
048–62 5066

Most supermarkets stock a good range of wines, clearly displayed. You can compare prices between well-known brands and own-label bottles but there is generally no one whom you can ask for detailed advice. Supermarkets are overcoming this to some extent by putting more information on shelf tags and on the bottles.

Note ● If you want to buy wine as an investment – say for a christening present to be enjoyed when the baby grows up – wine expert **John Morley** suggests a case of 1982 château-bottled Bordeaux, from a wine club or a reliable off-licence.

Serving wine White wine should be served chilled (drier wines) or cold (sweeter wines). The average bottle will take two hours to chill in the fridge, three hours to become really cold. Never leave white wine in the fridge for longer or it will lose flavour. If you are in a hurry put the wine glasses into the fridge to cool as well. *Never* put still wine bottles into the freezer.

If you serve more than one white wine at a meal, serve the driest first and proceed to the sweetest (if you try to reverse the order the dry wines will appear to taste vinegary).

Most red wines should be allowed to reach room temperature before serving. They need opening at least two hours before serving – in the case of fuller red wines like burgundy, claret, chianti or rioja it is best to open the bottle at least three or four hours before serving so that their full character can emerge.

Never be tempted to warm a bottle of red wine under a running tap or stand it near a fire in order to bring up its temperature – half the bottle will be cooked and the rest still cold. If you are in a hurry, warm a carafe or decanter by running warm water over the outside and then decant the wine into that before serving it.

Storing wine Few people have a proper wine cellar as such, but if you have a sudden windfall, if you have entertaining days ahead or you simply enjoy wine, it is a good idea to have a selection of wines from which to choose. A last-minute dash to the shops does not give you time to make a careful choice. It is better to browse around the shelves and choose several bottles to keep so that you have them when you need them.

Wine that is to be used within a day or two of purchase can be stored anywhere, although it makes good sense to keep red wine in a room that is basically fairly warm (say the kitchen) and white wine somewhere cool (say the garage or a cupboard under the stairs).

Wines being stored for any length of time need an even and correct temperature. It is important to remember that violent fluctuations in temperature affect wine the most. The ideal temperature for long-term storage for both red and white wines is 55°F (12°C). Make sure that an apparently cold place stays that way – a cupboard, for instance, might have a hot water pipe running up to it. The damper the conditions the better – a damp dark cellar is ideal.

If the storage place has too much light, make sure the wines are in closed boxes or have covers over racks. To keep them in perfect condition, bottles of wine should be stored on their side so that the wine flows against the cork and keeps it moist. This will prevent the cork from drying out and letting air into the bottle. Wine racks for long-term storage can now be bought relatively inexpensively. Alternatively, you can turn the box in which a consignment of wine is packed on its side.

Wine should be kept still, so do not keep it anywhere it will be knocked or shaken (wine stored in boxes on the floor may be disturbed by floorboards as people pass to and fro). Anything chemical or vegetable with a strong smell should be kept away from it.

Complaints   If you have cause for complaint you should first talk to the wine club or shop (or restaurant) where you got the wine. If you are dissatisfied with the outcome, you can contact your local trading standards officer or write to:

> Wine Standards Board
> 68½ Upper Thames Street
> London EC4V 3JB
> 01–236 9512

CHAMPAGNE   Champagne is a sparkling wine usually made as a *cuvée*, a blend of wines from thirty or more villages in the Champagne region and of the pressings of some or all of three types of grape, two reds (Pinot Noir, which gives body and long life, and Pinot Meunier, which produces a wine with freshness and youth) and a white (Chardonnay, which supplies lightness, elegance and freshness). A champagne made exclusively from the white grapes is known as Blanc de Blancs. A rose champagne is made either by adding an amount of 10 to 20 per cent of red wine (often from Bouzy) to the blend just before bottling, or by allowing the skins of the black grape to come into contact with the juice, or the grapes are allowed to ferment for a short time before being pressed so that a naturally pink wine is produced.

The production of champagne is controlled by the Comité Inter-professionnel du Vin de Champagne (CIVC) in Épernay, about 90 miles north-east of Paris. There are about 57,600 acres in full production with another 12,500 acres being added in the next decade (fruit from these vines will not be used in production for another 5 to 7 years). Each 4,000 kilos of grapes produces 2,500 litres of juice (or *must*) that can legally be made into champagne: any surplus cannot be called champagne. Harvesting begins 100 days after the flowering and the wine from each harvest cannot, by law, be sold as champagne for at least one year for non-vintage wines and three years for vintage wines. No other sparkling wine can legally be called champagne.

The following information must appear on every bottle of champagne:
- the appellation 'CHAMPAGNE'
- the name of the brand or the producer
- the registered number given by the CIVC preceded by initials which provide information about the producer
- the capacity of the bottle.

There may also be an indication of the location of production (which is, of course, always in the Champagne district), the *millésimé* (or vintage year), details of the cuvée and the sugar content. The degree of sweetness indicated can be rather misleading since today's champagne terms give the dryness in comparison to the very sweet wine from which champagne as we now know it evolved. A dry champagne today, therefore, is not very dry; an extra-dry is dry.

Degrees of sweetness of champagne, working from the sweetest to the driest, are usually:
- demi-sec
- sec or dry-sec
- extra-dry
- brut
- ultra brut (completely sugar-free – and ideal for those watching their weight).

A leading champagne house suggests:
- You should buy champagne at least two weeks before you want it – in an ideal world you would always have some in stock.
- For technical reasons, the best champagne size is the magnum – if you can afford it. Quarter-bottles are decanted from larger bottles so lose on perfection.
- Buy as good a champagne as you can afford. It is worth buying from an off-licence or small purveyor, as large stores deal in bulk and cannot give each bottle the care it deserves.
- When you get the bottle home, store it in a cool dark place until the day you need it.
- Always store wine on its side. This will keep the cork moist and prevent oxidization.

Non-vintage champagne should retain its elegance and quality for up to five years after shipment. Beyond this period you might notice a slight yellowness in the wine – although it is still extremely drinkable. Vintage champagne will keep for at least ten years on average, depending on the quality of the harvest.

Serving champagne
Champagne should be served cold, not iced (about 45°F). Put the bottle in the bottom of the fridge for a couple of hours. If you need to save time do *not*, under any circumstances, freeze champagne. Half-fill a metal or plastic bucket with ice and water and plunge the bottle in that. It will not harm the wine and is much faster than any other method.

To open the bottle:
- Take off the metal capsule.
- Hold the bottle in one hand and with the other undo the wire muzzle.
- Keep a thumb on the cork, hold the bottle in one hand and gently turn the bottle round the cork (not the other way round). The cork will come out easily. Never let the cork rush out with a bang as this will bruise the wine and cause a lot of wasted froth.
- After removing the cork, hold the bottle at the same angle for about five seconds to allow pressure to equalize.
- Wipe the brim of the bottle mouth.

To pour champagne you should ideally hold it with your thumb in the punt (the indentation in the bottom of the bottle). Pour 1.5 cm ($\frac{1}{2}$ in.) of champagne into each glass before filling two-thirds.

The ideal glass is one with a fine stem and elegant base. A tulip or egg-shaped bowl is best but a tall flute is suitable. The flat 'ice-cream container' is not suitable as it allows bubbles to evaporate too quickly. The glass should not be chilled with ice.

If you have any champagne left over it can be stored, at least for a few days, without losing any effervescence. You need a special champagne retainer cap.

More people these days – especially the young – are serving champagne as an aperitif.

For further information about champagne, the wine, the region and the people, contact (s.a.e.):

The Champagne Bureau
34 Dean Street
London WIV 5AP
01-437 3526

SPIRITS
The range of spirits is vast, so for this book we investigated only gin, vodka and whisky.

Gin
Classic British distilled gin (from the French *genièvre*, juniper) is a strong spirit distilled from grain and flavoured with the berries from which it

takes its name. Pure grain spirit is distilled in copper three times. During each distillation a head stillman carefully noses out the crystal-clear 'middle run' from the 'foreshot' that precedes it and the 'feints' that follow. During the final distillation, juniper berries, angelica root, coriander seed and rare spices are combined with alcohol vapours to give the gin great clarity and brilliance. Most gins are colourless, although some have a pale straw tinge. Dutch gins have a pronounced flavour which makes them unsuitable for cocktails. The Anglo-American gins may be drunk neat or with a mixer of, for example, bitter lemon, lemonade or tonic water. Some people like them with plenty of ice and a slice of lime or lemon.

Vodka

The word 'vodka' comes to us from Poland as one of the many white spirits distilled in Northern Europe from a variety of basic products.

When made in Poland and Russia it is distilled from cereals or potatoes and often retains a flavour derived from the basic products. However, the modern British vodka is a very highly rectified neutral alcohol, often derived from molasses, which is filtered through carbon after distillation to achieve the highest possible degree of purity. It has therefore little taste.

Whisky

The word 'whisky' comes from the Gaelic for 'water of life'. The main types are:

Scotch whisky – distilled and matured in Scotland.

Irish whiskey (this is the conventional spelling) – distilled and matured in Ireland. The old Irish whiskey (licensed to distil in 1608) is Bushmills.

Bourbon – distilled and produced in the US from a mash of not less than 51 per cent corn grain.

Rye – distilled and produced in Canada or the US, in the US from a grain mash which is not less than 51 per cent rye grain.

A Scotch whisky blend contains roughly 70 per cent grain spirit and 30 per cent malt whisky. It is much lighter in taste and character than a malt and is often a pre-dinner drink. Scotch liqueur whisky is made from a mixture of Highland malt whisky, heather, honey and herbs, it is sweet in taste and the most famous is Drambuie. This is generally a post-prandial drink.

Malt is the individual flavour of the whisky produced by over 115 malt distilleries in Scotland. The necessary ingredients of water, peat and barley give each malt a distinctive taste but the final character of the whisky is shaped and its quality is determined by the stills, onion-shaped copper vessels from which the basis of the drink is distilled. Connoisseurs drink this any time – you might prefer it after a meal.

When buying whisky note the size of the bottle (most bottles in Britain are 75 cl) and the strength (in Britain this is 40 per cent volume, in mainland Europe 43 per cent). Other information on the label will include the names of the distiller and blender. Note that cut-price brands may have smaller bottles or weaker whisky, but this will be indicated on the label.

No whisky can legally be sold until it has matured for three years. The age of a standard blend is five years; of a standard malt about twelve years. The age on the bottle refers to the maturity of the youngest whisky in a blend: whisky is matured in wooden casks of American oak and does not age in the bottle so an unopened bottle should last indefinitely. Make sure bottles are properly closed as the air affects the quality of whisky.

Serving whisky   The most popular glass shape for serving whisky is the tumbler. For malt whisky, a shaped glass which will retain the bouquet is recommended. Whisky can be drunk neat or with sparkling or still water or mixers such as soda water and ginger ale, even coca-cola or lemonade. Ice is generally abhorred in Scotland (by contrast, a 'Scotch on the rocks' on the other side of the Atlantic is a tumbler filled with large ice chunks and whisky simply poured in to fill up the cracks).

Further   ● For details of tours of distilleries in Scotland contact Aberdeen Tourist
information   Board (0224–632727), Highland Scottish Omnibuses (0463–233371) or Lothian Region Transport (031–554 4494).
● For details of the Scotch Whisky Festival usually held in Aviemore in November contact the Strathspey Thistle Hotel in Aviemore (0479–810681) or the Stakis Coylumbridge Hotel near Aviemore (0479–810661).
● For 'Scotch Whisky: Questions and Answers' and general information on Scotch whisky contact (s.a.e.):

> Scotch Whisky Association
> 17 Half Moon Street
> London w1y 7rb
> 01–629 4384

SHERRY   Sherry takes its name from the area where it is exclusively produced, Jerez ('herreth') in southern Spain.

The different types are:
Dry sherry (*Fino*) – at its best when served well chilled for an aperitif, or drunk as table wine with seafood and delicately flavoured fish. Choose a tall broad-flute glass, fill it about one-third full and gently swirl the sherry to release its delicate fragrance.
Medium sherry (*Amontillado*) – perfect for parties, and as an accompaniment to soups, salads and cheeses. It is often drunk in a glass with a shallower, broader bowl.
Cream sherry – can be drunk as an aperitif or after a meal, delicious at room temperature, chilled or on ice (on the rocks). Although often served in Britain in a small thimble glass it can also be served in a rounded-bowl glass.

Sherry can also form the basis of cocktails.

For general information on sherry, or if you have any cause for complaint, contact (s.a.e.):

> Sherry Institute of Spain
> 23 Manchester Square
> London WIM 5AP
> 01–487 5826

Further Information

Suggested further reading

My personal favourites among books about food – always to hand in the kitchen – are:

Reader's Digest, *The Cookery Year* (an amazingly good all-round cookbook)

Simon, André L. and Robin Howe, *A Dictionary of Gastronomy*, Rainbird (good for quick reference)

Masefield, G. B., *et al.*, *The Oxford Book of Food Plants*, Oxford University Press (what they are and what they look like)

I also enjoy reading and get valuable ideas and information from anything written by Caroline Conran, Josceline Dimbleby, Prue Leith, Madhur Jaffrey, Delia Smith and Katie Stewart. For information on wines I turn to anything by Hugh Johnson or Michael Broadbent.

17 Travel

The first time I flew I was so scared I ate grapes non-stop, and before my first really long flight I was so worried I might be overweight (luggage, at least) that I cut off most of the inside seams of my clothes!

That was years ago and now I have been round the world many times, writing and lecturing. I honestly think that the more you know about travel the more relaxed you are going to be.

This chapter, therefore, has tips from British Airways and many other experts on what to expect from air, land and sea travel.

Travellers' Information

Notes
- Never leave valuable possessions (passport, tickets, credit cards, money) in your hotel bedroom, never keep them in a back pocket, never leave them unattended on a beach or in a car.
- Leave the numbers of all items (including credit cards and travellers' cheques) at home as well as carrying a copy.
- Carry valuables in your hand baggage – never in checked cases.

UP-TO-DATE INFORMATION

Whether travelling by air, rail, sea or road you can get up-to-date information by calling the following numbers:

Air information	01–246 8033
Rail information	01–246 8030
Road information	01–246 8031
Sea information	01–246 8032

General information is also given for many areas, including: Bangor, Belfast, Birmingham, Blackburn, Bristol, Cardiff, Cheltenham, Colchester, Edinburgh, Glasgow, Gloucester, Guildford, High Wycombe, Leeds, Liverpool, London, Luton, Manchester, Medway, Newport, Oxford, Portsmouth, Southend, and Tunbridge Wells. Within these areas, dial your own main code (e.g. 0254 when in Bradford) and then 8021.* If in doubt, consult your local telephone directory or your operator.

Most travel agencies, certainly the large ones like Thomas Cook, are happy to give timetable advice on air, sea or rail arrivals and departures in many countries. Otherwise contact the airline concerned, sea company or British Rail direct.

Other useful telephone numbers

AIRPORT INQUIRIES

Aberdeen	0224–722331
Birmingham	021–767 5511
Edinburgh	031–344 3295
Gatwick	0293–31299
Glasgow	0293–31299
Heathrow	01–759 4321
Term. 1	01–745 7702
Term. 2	01–745 7115
Term. 3	01–745 7412
Leeds and Bradford	0532–509696
Liverpool	051–494 0066
Luton	0582–36061
Manchester	061–489 3000
Newcastle	0632–860966
Stansted	0279–57641

For airline numbers, see 'Air Travel', page 504.

FERRY AND SEA CROSSING INQUIRIES

Dover	0304–206560
Felixstowe	0394–604346
Hull	0482–701787
Newhaven	0273–514131
Parkeston (Harwich)	0255–502141
Poole	0202–685261
Portsmouth	0705–819156
Southampton	0703–23844
Weymouth	0305–785101

For ferryboat operators, see 'Ferries' p. 511.

BRITISH TOURIST BOARDS

General information on all aspects of travel and holiday in Britain is available from the national tourist boards:

English Tourist Board
4 Grosvenor Gardens
London SW1W 0DU
   01–730 3400

Scottish Tourist Board
23 Ravelstone Terrace
Edinburgh EH4 3EU
   031–332 2433

*Exceptions: in Birmingham, Edinburgh, Liverpool, London, Manchester and Glasgow dial 246 8021.

Northern Ireland Tourist Board
High Street
Belfast BT I 2DS
0232–246609

Welsh Tourist Board
Brunel House
2 Fitzalan Road
Cardiff CF 2 1UY
0222–499909

GOING ABROAD

Passports and visas

Make sure your passport is up to date and that you have the necessary visas. If you need a new passport it can sometimes take up to six weeks to get one in spring or summer: in the winter seven to ten days is average. A personal visit to the passport office, particularly for a renewal, may speed things up.

Ask your travel agent (or the embassy or consulate of the country to which you are going) if a visa is required. If you are going to more than one country which needs a visa this can be a lengthy business as each office, open only on certain days and sometimes with long, slow-moving queues, may keep your passport for several days. You will need plenty of time and a stock of spare passport photographs.

Should you require a passport or visa in a great hurry, most large travel agencies can help.

Inoculations

Ask your travel agent what you might need. Start thinking about this in plenty of time as you might have to leave time between jabs and you should not, anyway, travel too soon afterwards. The normal period of effectiveness of vaccination for listed diseases is as follows:

Cholera – 6 months
Polio – 5 years for booster
Tetanus – 5 years for booster
Typhoid – 3 years for booster
Yellow fever – 10 years

Phone your GP to arrange immunization (give him time to order the appropriate vaccine if necessary).

You should check whether or not you need a course of anti-malaria tablets: these should be started at least two days before you reach the malaria-prone area and continued after you leave it (check instructions on packet or with your GP).

If you find at the last moment you need assistance, you can contact the British Airways Medical Unit at Heathrow (01–750 5616) or the British Caledonian Medical Unit at Gatwick (0293–27890) who both operate a 24-hour emergency medical service.

Money

If you are going to mainland Europe you will find Eurocheque encashment cards handy. With this card you can cash up to £50 a day on your ordinary cheque book: the money will be given to you in local currency at the going rate.

Charge cards and credit cards can be used to pay bills abroad.

If you are going further afield all branches of the clearing banks can provide you with foreign currency or travellers' cheques. These are usually denominated in sterling or currencies such as US dollars,

Deutschmarks, Swiss francs, French francs or Japanese yen and they are the safest way of carrying cash when you are abroad. Because payment is guaranteed by your bank they are usually accepted by most foreign banks, and in many countries hotels, shops and supermarkets will accept and encash them. When you collect your travellers' cheques you will be required to sign each one – they are usually issued in denominations equivalent to £10, £50 or £100 – in the presence of the cashier. When you go to cash them at a bank abroad you will be required to endorse them again and may have to produce your passport for identification. This provides a great deal of security for you and the banks.

Insurance   If you are travelling abroad it is essential to be fully insured to cover such calamities as death or illness. Form E 1 1 1 available from the DHSS does provide you with a partial extension of the NHS in some EEC countries: always take it with you on a European trip.

Check that your travel insurance policy covers:
- luggage (usual cover up to £1,000 maximum) and money
- cancellations and curtailments
- delays and missed connections
- medical insurance (usual cover up to £1,000,000)
- personal accident and personal liability

See   'P.S. Thank Goodness for Holiday Insurance!' from (s.a.e.) British Insurance Association, address on page 39.

TRAVEL   Even the most seasoned sailor can be seasick at times. If a ferry crossing
SICKNESS   suddenly becomes rough, you should go to the purser and ask for medication unless there is some reason (e.g. pregnancy) that precludes you taking anything. By contrast, few people today are actually airsick. If you know you are a bad traveller, go to your chemist before you travel and ask for advice.

As with those who suffer from carsickness, people have their own particular remedies. Some travel better on an empty stomach. Others find they should not read while travelling. The best thing is to try and take your mind off the flight, voyage or journey – and the possibility that you might be sick.

If you have children who are invariably carsick, take comfort in the fact that most sufferers grow out of it. Adults prone to carsickness often travel better in the front passenger seat, and it is an unexplained fact that drivers are not carsick, perhaps further evidence of the suggestion that sufferers should have something else on which to concentrate. Some people think that a chain hanging from the car to the ground lowers static electricity and prevents carsickness.

DUTY FREE   Passengers under seventeen are not entitled to tobacco and drinks
GOODS   allowances. Of goods obtained, duty and tax paid, in the EEC each traveller is allowed to bring back:

1. Cigarettes   300
   or cigarillos   150
   or cigars   75
   or tobacco   400g
2. Drinks   1.5 litres over 38.8 proof
   or   3 litres not over 38.8 proof
   Table wine   4 litres
3. Perfume or   75g (3fl. oz.)
   toilet water   375cc (13fl. oz.)
4. Other goods   £163 worth

Note ● EEC countries are Belgium, Denmark, France, Greece, Irish Republic, Italy, Luxemburg, Netherlands, United Kingdom, West Germany; Spain and Portugal are expected to join soon.

Goods obtained duty and tax free in the EEC, or duty and tax free on a ship or an aircraft, or goods obtained outside the EEC:

1. Cigarettes   200
   or cigarillos   100
   or cigars   50
   or tobacco   250g
2. Drinks   1 litre over 38.8 proof
   or   2 litres not over 38.8 proof
   Table wine   2 litres
3. Perfume   50g (2fl. oz.)
   or toilet water   250cc (9fl. oz.)
4. Other goods   £28 worth.

Note ● If you are buying on board you can generally pay in pounds, American dollars or Canadian dollars and the currencies of the countries of embarkation and disembarkation: some airlines also accept credit cards and traveller's cheques.

Air Travel

TERMINOLOGY   BABIES AND CHILDREN
FARES   THE FLIGHT
TRAVEL AND HEALTH   COMPLAINTS
PREPARATIONS   AIRLINE NUMBERS
AT THE AIRPORT

TERMINOLOGY   **Bucket shop** – an unlicensed retailer, bonded by no trade association. He buys seats from airlines in bulk and sells individually, below usual price.

Bumping – deliberate overbooking on flights may mean that at least one person cannot fly and has to be compensated (see 'Complaints' below).

Charter seats – can sometimes be purchased individually shortly before a flight. You can buy these direct from the travel company.

Consolidators – travel agents who buy seats in bulk at discount and pass them on to other agents. The public can buy consolidation fares from some specific companies.

Fares code

A – advance purchase (APEX: Advanced Purchase Excursion, must be purchased some time before travel, depending on destination. Cancellations are usually not allowed.)	F – first class
	J – super executive
	N – night fare
	O – one way
	P – PEX, instant ticket
	Q – no stopovers
	R – return
C – club/exchange	S – standby
D – discount/special	Y – economy
E – excursion	

Flight identification – all flights have an airline prefix followed by the actual flight number – see identifying prefixes at end of this chapter.

Maximum Permitted Mileage (MPM) – full-fare passengers with MPM can deviate from their most direct route by up to 20 per cent without paying more.

Maximum validity code on tickets:

T – 14 days	Z – 60 days
U – 25 days	XX – 90 days
V – 30 days	ZZ – 120 days
W – 35 days	ZX – 180 days
X – 45 days	XXZX – 270 days

Travel agent – a travel agent will sort out your air flights beforehand and arrange tickets. If you need a ticket in a hurry most large agencies will arrange for you to pick up the ticket at the airport of departure. He can also arrange accommodation. Check that your travel agent is a member of the Association of British Travel Agents (ABTA – see below).

Unaccompanied minor (UM) – children travelling alone up to the age of twelve must be classed as unaccompanied minors.

FARES   To plan the best route it is advisable to consult a travel agent who has the schedules of all the airlines and can arrange an itinerary to suit your requirements. Bear in mind that not all routes are flown on a daily basis so some flexibility in travel dates may be necessary (this also applies to using the best flights to arrive at your destination at a reasonable time of the day).

Fare types vary from airline to airline but the following will act as a guide:

First class – usually year-round fares and not subject to seasonal changes.

They are unrestricted in that bookings can be changed at any time or interchanged with other airlines without any financial penalty.

Business class – again, usually year-round fares with no restrictions on changing bookings, routes or interchanging with other carriers.

Full economy – usually subject to seasonal variations, normally peak fares in the summer and off-peak or basic during the winter. These are normally unrestricted fares as far as changes are concerned.

Apex – these fares have many restrictions: reservations, payment and ticketing must be made at least twenty-one days in advance of travel, there are minimum/maximum stay restrictions on the use of the tickets and any change in return booking once travel has commenced is subject to a charge of £25 or US$50 (this charge also applies if a passenger cancels the booking within the twenty-one-day period).

Standby – tickets available at the last-minute if there are any spare seats. They are one-way only and carry many restrictions (they cannot be exchanged with another carrier or issued if you already have a booking in another class on the same service). In the event that a seat does not become available after all a full refund is made.

Notes

● All the above fares except standby have 50 per cent discounts for children under twelve years – and infants under three pay 10 per cent of the full adult fare.

● Infants pay 10 per cent of the standby fare but must be accompanied by an adult at least eighteen years of age – no child discounts apply.

● If you can make a last minute decision to travel, reductions on package holidays are advertised in the national press.

● If you look around in advance you will find special deals advertised in the national press.

Paying for your flight

Most airlines and travel agents will accept charge or credit cards for payment. It is always wise, however, to check with an airline beforehand in case they have limits on the amount they will accept against a card.

Since currency exchange rates change frequently, it is sometimes an advantage to purchase tickets overseas. To avoid confusion, airlines do not always change their exchange rates with the same frequency so the advantage in purchasing tickets elsewhere may be quite small.

TRAVEL AND HEALTH

by Dr P. J. C. Chapman
Chief Medical Officer, British Caledonian

All major carriers have medical departments or medical advisers who are used to dealing with any type of problem. It is essential that in case of any illness the carrier should be consulted as long as possible before the flight.

Ear pressurization: the eardrum has air on either side of it to accommodate pressure changes. When the aircraft climbs and the pressure decreases, a small amount of air passes out via the Eustachian tube and the pressure each side of the drum is equalized. On the descent, when the pressure rises again, the corresponding amount of air passes up the tube and back into the cavity.

Sometimes there is a severe catarrhal condition in the nose at just the point where the tube opens, and the presence of mucous secretions and swellings of the soft tissues may block the end of the tube. In these cases pain (which can be severe) and even damage to the eardrum can occur. The only complete answer to this is not to fly if you have a really bad cold.

If you do notice pressure building up inside your ears as the aircraft descends, try blowing your nose hard.

Pregnancy: time limits for flying when pregnant are thirty-six weeks for short-haul (European) flights and thirty-four weeks for long-haul (intercontinental) flights. However, all pregnant women should get the advice of their GP before contemplating any journeys by air.

When actually on board you (whether pregnant or not) should walk about now and again during long flights in order to get the blood flowing. Very loose clothing should be worn.

PRE- PARATIONS

Making your booking

● Check the date and number of your flight and times of departure and arrival.
● Know how long beforehand you should be at the airport and make sure the airline has a contact telephone number for you.
● Specify if you want special food on board or require special help (e.g. a wheelchair).
● Do you want hotel accommodation? (Some airlines provide a full hotel booking function and they may have preferential rates for their passengers in some hotels – check on this.)
● Arrange for car hire at the other end if required.
● Make arrangements for children.

Some time before your flight

Check passport and visas, inoculations, money and insurance; see 'Going Abroad', page 495.

Luggage

First-class passengers are normally allowed to check 30kg of baggage each: other passengers have to limit themselves to 20kg. The exceptions to this are that some airlines are introducing the two-piece allowance for any flights for first class and business class, and all airlines allow anyone flying to and within the US to check any two bags.

Always ensure that all baggage carries your name and address. The information should be placed on a label or piece of paper inside each case. (Do not give full name, address and telephone number on the outside of the case as this alerts potential burglars.)

More or less any suitcase can be opened and you should avoid putting anything of value into a checked bag. Put stickers over the locks and string or straps around each case in an attempt to delay a would-be thief, if only for a few minutes. Bright luggage straps make your suitcase easy to distinguish from all the others in the luggage arrival hall.

You should have only one piece of hand baggage other than your handbag (which can generally be any size and weight). Make sure it can accommodate duty free bottles, magazines, etc., bought at the airport.

Always have basic make-up, any necessary medications and a change of clothing in your hand baggage. (It is a good idea to put a swimsuit in, too, in case you are stranded somewhere without baggage, but with a pool!)

2 to 3 days before leaving home

1. Within 72 hours of your flight, it is a good idea (though not essential) to confirm it with the travel agent or airline.
2. Make a checklist:
● driving licence (if hiring a car)
● keys
● money: cash/charge/credit cards/cheque book/travellers' cheques
● passport
● ticket.
3. Check that your house is secure (see Chapter 19).

AT THE AIRPORT

You should aim to arrive at a British airport an hour and a half before departure for an international flight and one hour beforehand if you are flying within Britain. Some airlines refuse to allow you to check in until two hours before the flight. Generally, the earliest people checking in have the shortest queue and their choice of seat – but they may find their luggage is last to arrive at the other end.

If you are going to be returning to the same airport within a short time, it often makes sense to drive there. If you are returning within a couple of days you can use the airport's own short-term carpark. Otherwise it is often less expensive to use one of the many commercial carparks near the airport sign-posted 'Off-airport parking'. You leave your car with the keys, and you and your luggage are driven to the departure terminal. On your return, after you have claimed your luggage and cleared customs you can call the garage who will pick you up and take you back to your car.

Once you have checked in, you will be free until it is time to go through security and passport checks and boarding pass check. It is always advisable to have a light snack at the airport before departure as you may have to wait for in-flight service (e.g. if the flight is delayed).

Membership of an 'airline club' means you have a special lounge in which to sit, prior to departure, at some airports, but you need to fly a lot to make membership worthwhile.

EXECUTIVE CLUB

The British Airways Executive Club offers its members, for an annual subscription of £55 specially tailored reservations and airport services, a range of discounts on car hire and hotels, and free worldwide travel insurance.

Other benefits include the use of more than sixty executive lounges at airports around the world; special check-in service at many airports; an express reservations service at key business destinations; emergency cash facilities against personal cheques and a free subscription to *Executive World* magazine.

BABIES AND CHILDREN

Marion Porter (Marketing Manager, USA, of British Airways) says:

> Treat a flight like a car journey and stock up with the same sort of provisions. Take plenty of things children can do on their own, and a favourite toy. Tire toddlers out beforehand so they will sleep more. Pushchairs are marvellous for taking children on and off planes – and on longer flights earphones are a godsend.

You should check beforehand with the airline to find out if the following are provided:

- sky cots/bassinettes
- cows' milk
- baby food
- paddi pads, bottles and nappy-changing trays.

Ask if you can take a collapsible baby carrier/pushchair into the cabin with you.

On many long-haul flights 'funpacks and comics' are provided free of charge and special meals are available (if requested at time of booking). All soft drinks on board should be free of charge.

See
'Travelling with a Baby or Young Child', page 302, and 'Flying with Children', from Cathay Pacific.

Children's escort service
- Request the service when you make the booking: fill out a special form which you will be given.
- Children can be met by prior arrangement.
- If an overnight transit stop is required at Gatwick or Heathrow, an escort will accompany them.
- After check-in the escort will accompany the child right into the aircraft.
- If there are more than ten unaccompanied minors on a long-haul flight, an escort will be provided throughout the flight, free of charge.
- Children under six years old cannot travel unaccompanied. A special escort can be provided to accompany the child throughout the journey at a cost of 50 per cent of the one-way fare.
- Escort services are available for disabled children.

THE FLIGHT

As soon as you get on board, make yourself comfortable. Make sure you have reading material and toilet requisites to hand. Take off boots or shoes and undo any tight belts.

Some experienced travellers take their own food. If you prefer a kosher or vegetarian meal, ask for this when you make the booking. This special meal is free (and on some airlines tastier, and served more quickly, than ordinary meals). The inexperienced traveller should be warned that she might be very hungry by the time the meal arrives. Where a flight departs near a mealtime, the airline will serve the relevant food.

Whatever you eat, do not eat too much. And remember that alcohol has a quicker effect in the air. It is very tempting – when there is nothing else to do – to drink your way through a flight. Because of the altitude and the dry cabin pressure you need an amazing amount of water, fruit juice, tea or coffee, but not alcohol.

Some people swear that continual intake of soft drinks and regular exercise together combat jetlag. Try to get up and move around the cabin every half-hour or so on a long flight. If you cannot, at least cross and uncross your legs, roll your head round and stretch every limb.

COMPLAINTS

● *Travel agent goes bust*: make sure *before* booking that your travel agent is a member of ABTA, whose members adhere to a Code of Conduct and who put in a large sum in bondage against eventualities. If you have a cause for complaint contact:

Association of British Travel Agents
55–7 Newman Street
London WIP 4AH
01–637 2444

● *Airline goes bust*: you have no protection unless you are on a charter or a package through an ABTA agent (contact your travel agent).

● *Booking mistake*: if your travel agent delayed in making your required reservation and by the time he did so there were no vacancies, then he is responsible. If necessary, contact ABTA.

● *Surcharges*: these occur through increased cost of fuel and fluctuations in sterling. If you receive a surcharge after your booking was confirmed you are entitled to a detailed breakdown of the costing of the surcharge.

● *Dissatisfaction with the airport*: contact the Airport Consultative Committee or the manager of the airport concerned.

● *Bumping*: airlines often intentionally overbook on flights simply to cover themselves against those passengers who made reservations and did not turn up. If too many passengers turn up, there are various forms of compensation for the extra. In the US, 'auctions' are sometimes held on board with extra passengers holding out for the largest compensation possible for getting off the plane. In the UK, British and a number of foreign airlines operate a voluntary compensation scheme: if you are 'bumped' you are entitled to 50 per cent of the value of the overbooked ticket (maximum £100) if the airline cannot get you to your destination within four hours of your scheduled departure (within six hours for long-haul flights and within two hours on intra-British flights).

● *Delayed flight*: if a stopover is required it is unlikely that the airline would be held responsible – unless, say, the company's employees (not air traffic controllers or similar) went on strike. In practice, however, many airlines do quickly provide accommodation and refreshment.

● *Dissatisfaction with an airline*: you should write direct to the customer relations manager of the relevant airline in the first instance. If you are still dissatisfied, write to:

Air Transport Users' Committee
129 Kingsway
London WC2B 6NN
01–242 3882

● *Missing luggage*: you have no claim against a tour operator or travel agent, only against the responsible airline. Always report loss at once to the airline: they will ask you to fill in forms to register contents, etc. If the baggage is not found the airline will pay you by weight (about £11 per kilo) and you will do much better to claim against your insurance company. Some travel insurance policies also give compensation as soon as baggage goes astray.

● *Your accommodation is not as described*: if there is obvious deviation from what the brochure described you will be entitled to compensation from the tour operator. If you are unhappy, take as many photographs and notes as you can and get names, addresses and telephone numbers from other dissatisfied guests and contact your travel agent as soon as you get back (in extreme cases you could make contact while you are away with the nearest British consulate); if you continue to be dissatisfied contact ABTA.

● *Injury while abroad*: you need good travel insurance to compensate for such trivial mishaps as wine being spilt over a dress through to real catastrophes. The tour operator will in most cases not be responsible for any mishap and it may be impossible to sue a foreign person or hotel.

● *Theft abroad*: you should be prepared for possible loss of passport and other valuable documents as well as money and, sometimes, items that are highly desirable in the country concerned. If items are stolen from your hotel room you may get compensation from the hotel (a good reason for staying in an international hotel chain). If your passport and other documents are taken, inform your nearest British consulate immediately.

AIRLINE NUMBERS (London)		

Other numbers are available from your travel agent, local telephone directory or directory inquiries.

		airline flight prefix
Aer Lingus	01–437 8000	EI
Air Canada	01–439 7941	AC
Air France	01–499 8611	AF
Air India	01–493 4050	AI
Air New Zealand	01–370 5411	TE
Air UK	01–293 38100	UK
Alitalia	01–602 7111	AZ
American	01–629 0195	AA
Austrian	01–439 1851	OS
Britannia	0582–424155	BY
British Airways	01–759 5511	BA
British Caledonian	0293–51888	BR
British Midland	0332–810741	BD
Cathay Pacific	01–930 4444	CX
Dan Air	01–638 1747	DA
Delta	01–828 5905	DL
Eastern	01–491 7879	EA

		airline flight prefix
Iberia	01–437 9822	IB
JAL	01–629 9244	JL
KLM	01–493 1231	KL
Lufthansa	01–408 0322	LH
Olympic	01–493 7262	OA
Pan Am	01–759 2595	PA
People Express	0293–38100	PE
Qantas	01–995 1364	QF
Sabena	01–437 6950	SN
SAS	01–734 6777	SK
Singapore	01–439 8111	SQ
South African	01–437 9621	SA
Swissair	01–734 6737	SR
TAP	01–828 2092	TP
Thai	01–491 7953	TG
TWA	01–636 5411	TW
United	01–734 9281	UA
Virgin Atlantic	01–493 5998	VS
World Airways	0293–33525	WO

Rail Travel

PASSENGER INFORMATION   HOLIDAYS
FARES   COMPLAINTS

The advantages of rail travel include an outstanding safety record, freedom to work or move around when in transit and the relaxation of not having to drive yourself. The disadvantages include the fact that you might not always find convenient routes and timetables. The comfort of the journey itself and the standard of cleanliness and catering service depend somewhat on the region.

The best times to travel are weekdays, out of office rush hours. It is better to avoid weekends during the summer and to try not to get involved with beginning and end of school terms and half-terms and such annual events as Chelsea Flower Show. If you do have to travel at peak time it is worth booking a seat (£1) at a station, by post or through a travel agent.

PASSENGER
INFORMATION

Main London stations

Charing Cross	01–928 5100
Euston	01–387 7070
King's Cross	01–278 2477
Liverpool Street	01–283 7171

Paddington	01–262 6767
St Pancras	01–387 7070
Victoria	01–928 5100
Waterloo	01–928 5100

FARES   Fare structures mean that it is cheaper to travel off-peak. An 'Awayday Return' (second class, valid only on day of issue and generally not on a train which reaches the terminus before 10 a.m.), a 'Weekend Return' (forward Friday to Sunday and returning Saturday to Monday of the same weekend) and an 'InterCity Saver' (valid for a month, with some restrictions on the forward journey) are much cheaper than an 'Ordinary Return' ticket (valid, outside London, for three months).

Special services are available for some travellers:

● Senior citizens have a choice of railcards which for an annual fee give most basic train fares at half price, reductions on Golden Rail holidays and on some Motorail journeys, and the right to take up to four children for £1 each. There is also a Rail EuropSenior, which entitles the holder to reduced-rate tickets for journeys to and from and within most countries in Europe.

● Full-time students of any age and young people up to age twenty-three can buy a Young Person's Railcard entitling them to half-price travel (second class) for most of the year. An InterRail card for anyone under twenty-six, costing little more than £100, allows free second-class travel on the railways of most West European countries, Scandinavia and Morocco as well as half-price tickets in Britain and on Sealink.

● Family railcards entitle children under sixteen at time of purchase of the card and accompanied by at least one adult to travel for a flat £1 each. Adults travel half-price on most second-class tickets and get reductions on Golden Rail holidays and Motorails.

● A Disabled Person's railcard entitles both the holder and one accompanying adult to travel half-price on many fare structures. From 12 May 1985 discounts are expanded. See 'Disabled Persons Railcard Discount Travel' from any BR station.

Note   ● Ask at any British Rail station for details of how to qualify for a railcard or write to:

> British Rail
> PO Box 28
> York YO1 1FB

● Animals in containers measuring not more than 18ins. in any direction can normally be transported free. Larger animals are charged by weight (per kilo). There is a charge for unaccompanied animals. Animals are carried in the guard's van. It is best to make prior arrangements with British Rail.

● If you live outside Britain, a BritRail Pass gives very good value. Details from any main British Rail European office.

Notes
- Seats for non-smokers constitute 50 per cent of InterCity carriages and up to 75 per cent of shorter-distance and local trains.
- It is a good idea to stock up from the station refreshment facilities before leaving or take your own supplies as not all trains offer a buffet or restaurant service.
- British Rail undertake to get you to your destination in one piece. If you are delayed and miss an important appointment, that is not their fault.
- If you travel a lot on business, consider British Rail Travel Key card, which gives you discounts on rail travel, hotels and car hire. Details from:

> Travel Key
> 222 Marylebone Road
> London NW1 6JJ

HOLIDAYS

Rail holidays include all-inclusive packages of rail travel, accommodation and food or self-catering and, in some cases, car hire. Contact:

> Golden Rail Holidays
> PO Box 12
> York YO1 1YX
> 0904-28992

As well as the Rail EuropSenior and the InterRail cards mentioned above, there are often bargain rail travel offers available to all age groups. Contact British Rail travel centres.

People under twenty-six who want information on European rail travel can contact:

> Eurotrain
> 52 Grosvenor Gardens
> London SW1W 0AG
> 01-730 8519

or

> Transalpino Ltd
> 71-6 Buckingham Palace Road
> SW1W 0QU
> 01-834 9656

COMPLAINTS

First complain to the stationmaster and if you are still dissatisfied contact the Transport Users' Consultative Committee of the relevant region.

British Railways Board
Rail House
Euston Square
London NW1 2DZ
 01-262 3232

London Midland Region
Euston House
Eversholt Street
London NW1 1DF
 01-387 9400

Eastern Region
Railway Station
York YO1 1HT
0904-53022

Scottish Region
Buchanan House
58 Port Dundas Road
Glasgow G4 0HG
 041-332 9811

Southern Region
Waterloo Station
London SE1 8SE
01–928 5151

Western Region
125 House
1 Gloucester Street
Swindon
Wilts SN1 1DL
0793–26100

The headquarters of the Central Transport Consultative Committee is at:

First Floor
Golden Cross House
Duncannon Street
London WC2N 4JF
01–839 7338

LONDON
UNDER-
GROUND

The London Underground system is currently experimenting with a complete no-smoking ban in all trains.

If you have any complaints about the Underground – or if you would like a map of the system – contact:

Public Relations
London Regional Transport
55 Broadway
London SW1H OBD
01–222 5600

Bus and Coach Travel

BOOKING
FARES

SCOTLAND
COMPLAINTS

The advantages of coach travel include less hassle in booking and checking-in, and a speedy service which is cleaner and less expensive than travelling by train. The disadvantages are primarily the cramped conditions and the fact that, on some routes, it is not as quick as travelling by train. Coaches are liable to be delayed, too, by road works and traffic.

National Express provides the most comprehensive network of services. Every day it links 1,500 cities, towns and villages in England and Wales, and during the summer and at all holiday peak times extra services are run. The holding company is the National Bus Company which is made up of some fifty operating companies including National Express. While no other operator provides a network of this size, there are, none the less, many coach operators providing inter-city and local express coach services. National Express carries 13.5 million passengers a year.

All National Express coaches have the front two-thirds of the vehicle reserved for non-smokers. All seats have an individual reading light and personal ventilation, and many recline. Luggage can be stowed in a separate compartment before the journey begins. Toilets and refreshments are available on some coaches but it is a good idea to be comfortable before you get on board. On longer routes there are recognized stopping points – often motorway service areas – so that passengers can use the facilities and stretch their legs.

'Rapide' routes are a new style of travel service. Specially designed single- and double-decker coaches have reclining seats, individual air ventilation, video film entertainment and a steward service for light refreshments and snacks. Toilets are also provided on the coaches, which operate fast services – usually non-stop by motorway – between major cities.

BOOKING

If you need special assistance it is recommended that you ask for it when making your booking. Wheelchairs will be carried free of charge. Those with hearing disabilities are given a 'sympathetic hearing scheme' card. Guide dogs are carried free of charge with a ticket-holding owner.

Many bus and coach stations have facilities for nursing mothers: ask about these when making your booking.

On the 'Rapide' services to Ireland and on all continental (and some services within Britain) routes pre-booking is essential. On other routes, pre-booking saves time and trouble. You can book at any agent (travel agent, bus and coach station and some shops) displaying the National Express sign. You can also book by telephone at over forty main centres (see your telephone directory for local numbers).

The following booking centres accept Access and Visa (if at least five clear days' notice is given):

	information	booking office
Birmingham	021–622 4373	021–622 4225
Liverpool	051–709 6481	051–709 6481
London	01–730 0202	01–730 3499
Manchester	061–228 3881	061–228 3881
Ramsgate	0843–581333	01–730 3499

FARES

- Single (valid any day of the week).
- Day return (out and back, same day).
- Boomerang (midweek return, out and back on any Tuesday, Wednesday or Thursday within three months).
- Period return (valid any day of the week for three months). You can buy it with a return open booking.
- Special fares: one-third off single, day and period returns (not Rapide) is available for anyone under seventeen, students with a valid International Student Identity Card and women over sixty (and men over sixty-five).

For further information contact your travel agent or the headquarters of the relevant company:

National Bus Company
25 New Street Square
London EC4 3AP
01–583 9177

National Express
Victoria Coach Station
172 Buckingham Palace Road
London SW1W 9TN
01–730 3453

SCOTLAND   The Scottish Transport Group consists of the Scottish Bus Group and Caledonian MacBrayne, which provides sea ferry services on the Clyde and to the Western Isles (see 'Ferries' below).

The eleven bus companies forming the Scottish Bus Group are:

- Central Scottish – based in Motherwell
- Clydeside – based in Paisley
- Eastern Scottish (Scottish Omnibuses) – based in Edinburgh
- Fife Scottish – based in Kirkcaldy
- Highland Scottish – based in Inverness
- Kelvin – based in Glasgow
- Lowland – based in Galashiels
- Midland Scottish – based in Falkirk
- Northern Scottish – based in Aberdeen
- Strathtay – based in Dundee
- Western Scottish – based in Kilmarnock

They operate a total fleet of over 3,200 buses and coaches which cover some 120 million miles a year and carry 314 million passengers. They provide an extensive rural network within Scotland and a year-round express service linking major Scottish cities with the rest of Britain, and 'Scottish Citylink' with routes like Aberdeen–Leeds–Kettering.

Additionally there are special all-in holiday coach tours in the UK and short tourist excursions from major centres (details from the bus companies) and coaches can be used for private hire.

You can make reservations with any travel agent or by contacting:

Scottish Coach Travel Service
298 Regent Street
London W1R 6LE
01–580 4708/636 9373

Travel Centre
Buchanan Bus Station
Glasgow G2 1NQ
041–332 9191

St Andrew's Square Bus Station
Edinburgh EH1 3DU
031–556 8464

COMPLAINTS

- If you are delayed, and miss an important appointment, this is not the coach company's fault.
- Any suggestions or complaints on inter-city coach travel can be sent to the customer services manager of the relevant company.
- If you are unhappy with your local town or rural bus company contact the local traffic commissioner (address from the local council offices). In London, contact:

London Transport Passengers' Committee
26 Old Queen Street
London W1H 9HP
01–222 8777

Ferries

BOOKING   HOVERCRAFT
SCOTTISH FERRIES

Ferry travel is less expensive than flying and you avoid the hassle associated with many airports. It is easier to take your car and there is no maximum baggage allowance: many thousands of people, indeed, take day trips to France to take advantage of duty free allowances and the opportunity to shop for some items that are less expensive there.

BOOKING

As with most forms of transport, it is worth shopping around to find out which route and what fare will suit you best. Before making your reservation look carefully at all available brochures.

Make your reservation as early as you can. Especially at peak times of year some sailings get booked up a long time ahead. If anyone needs special attention (e.g. disabled people or unaccompanied minors) or anyone needs special foods during the voyage, make this known when you make your reservation.

You should find with major ferry companies that a mother and baby room, video entertainment and a special children's play area are available on cross-Channel voyages. All new ships have special cabins and toilets and lifts for disabled passengers and older ships are being adapted. If you have any problems on board go straight to the purser in the information office.

Main ferry companies include:

Belfast Car Ferries
47 Donegal Quay
Belfast BT1 3ED
0232–220364

Brittany Ferries
Wharf Road
Portsmouth PO7 8RU
0705–827701

Fred Olsen Travel
11 Conduit Street
London W1R OLS
01–409 0536

Olan-Line
Sheerness
Kent ME12 1SN
0795–666666

Sally Line Ltd
Ramsgate Harbour
Ramsgate
Kent CT11 83P
0843–595522

Sealink Travel
Eversholt House
Eversholt Street
London NW1 2EJ
01–387 1234

Townsend Thoreson
Arundel Tower
Portland Terrace
Southampton SO9 4AE
0703–32131

Townsend Thoresen
The European Ferries
1 Camden Crescent
Dover
Kent CT16 1LD
0304–203388

SCOTTISH FERRIES

Caledonian MacBrayne is part of the Scottish Transport Group (see 'Bus and Coach Travel' above). There are thirteen major vehicle ferries and seventeen small ferries providing everything from simple drive-on drive-off service to mini-liner luxury with full restaurant facilities. They also offer a number of summer holiday packages.

You can get details of Caledonian MacBrayne sailings and holidays from your travel agent or by contacting the firm direct at:

The Ferry Terminal
Gourock PA16 1QP
0475–33755

HOVERCRAFT

Travelling by hovercraft is much quicker than by ferry but you cannot move around so easily during the voyage – or is it flight? – and, even on a windless day, you feel as though you are going through a car wash because the hovercraft's windows are usually obscured by spray. In really rough seas, hovercraft cannot operate, but if the service has to be cancelled the operators will transfer reservations to a conventional ferry.

Hoverspeed departures are from Western Docks, Dover. For reservations contact:

Hoverspeed Ltd
The International Hoverport
Ramsgate
Kent CT12 5HS
0843–595555

For those who travel on a fairly regular basis, the Hoverspeed Executive Club offers special facilities and discounts on some hotels. Details from the address above.

You may be interested in longer trips at sea. You can get a full list of who goes where, and what the cost is, by sending a large s.a.e. to:

Passenger Shipping Association
223 Regent Street
London W1R 7DB
01–491 7693

Taking Your Car Abroad

To avoid unnecessary expense and problems, motoring journalist **Roger Bell** suggests:

Plan ahead. Work out from the cross-Channel ferry brochures which operator and route suits your needs best. Prices vary a lot according to the length of the car and the number of people in it.

Have the car properly serviced before you go. Pay particular attention to the tyres, fan-belt, hoses, battery, brake pad/lining wear and ignition system. Try not to use a roof-rack. Heavily laden, it will upset the balance of your car and greatly increase wind resistance while drastically reducing economy and performance.

You will need
- Valid passports and visas for all passengers.
- Current driving licence (not provisional).
- Vehicle registration document/letter of authority.
- Vehicle recovery insurance, from your motoring organization or ferry company (car recovery and passenger insurance can be expensive). Many insurers issue policy-holders with a standard form, European Accident Statement. If you are involved in an accident abroad you can record details on the form without any admission of liability. Under a continental extension of your insurance cover your car will normally be protected on journeys of up to sixty-five hours on any recognized sea route.
- GB sticker (required by law) fixed to the back of the car.
- Red warning triangle (available from accessory shops) – obligatory in some countries, commonly used in most.
- A hire car registration certificate (from your motoring organization) if you are taking a hire car abroad.
- Insurance 'Green Card'. This is not strictly necessary in EEC countries (your normal insurance certificate may suffice, but probably provides only the bare minimum of legal cover – check well in advance). To ensure you have the same level of cover as you have at home you may need to obtain a Green Card regardless of your destination.
- If you need glasses for driving you should always have a spare pair in the glove box.
- Fit a nearside door mirror.
- If you are going to Spain, you will need a Bail Bond from your insurance company (the police tend to put motorists in jail after an accident, whether it is their fault or not).

You should also take
- Spare fuel cap.
- Spares kit, to avoid the inconvenience of searching for parts in unfamiliar surroundings. Sealink will hire you emergency windscreens and, for about 50p a day (depending on the size of your car) a ready-made spares kit consisting of:

plugs, points, condenser, rotor arm, distributor cap, ignition coil, HT lead, headlamp bulb/sealed beam unit, fuses, stop/tail bulb, side bulb, flasher bulb, fuel pump, fan-belt, top/bottom hoses, power steering belt and insulation tape.

● An Autoscope to enable you to have a panoramic forward view of traffic coming towards you when you are driving on the wrong side of the road (it is rather like a wing mirror in reverse).
● If you are going to France, where the French are obliged by law to use yellow lights (visitors are not), you can take stick-on beam convertors so as not to dazzle oncoming traffic.
● Good maps.

Before leaving, make sure you buy petrol as it is probably cheaper here. Do not fill your tank completely because of the risk of spillage. The security of the vehicle and its contents are the responsibility of the owner-driver while it is in the ferry terminal area.

Hotels

If you are on business, choose a hotel in a major chain. You can make reservations through the chain's international networks or through another of its hotels and it will be geared to business life, which should (but, alas, does not always) mean: transport from and to airport, reliable relaying of mail and messages, telex facilities, speedy laundry and all-night room service.

All major chains 'reward' frequent guests with special perks, perhaps complimentary newspapers or welcome champagne on arrival.

Reservations　Try to reserve as far in advance as possible. Hotels may be booked months ahead for such events as the Bristol Wine Fair or Pitlochry Arts Festival. If you make the reservation yourself by telephone, confirm it in writing and ask for confirmation from the hotel. On balance it is a good idea to let the hotel know you are a woman alone. A good hotel will then see that you have a 'good security' room, near the lift.

Warn the hotel if you are going to arrive late (after 6 p.m.). You will probably be asked to guarantee your booking against a major credit card.

Arrival　Check that your room is near the lift or stairs and that there are no ledges outside the window that prowlers could use. Check that fire escape routes are indicated and that the door lock, telephone and all lights work. Make sure you have a comfortable bed and the right type of pillows.

Women alone are much better treated if they tip well on arrival and seem quite happy being alone (even if they are not).

It is a good idea to make a friend of the head porter. He will tell you what is going on in the hotel and nearby, tell you about shopping, arrange car hire or theatre tickets and generally keep an eye on things for you.

Remember, if you eat in your room, to allow plenty of time for room service delivery: twenty-five minutes is average for breakfast or a snack and up to an hour for a main meal.

Try not to use hotel's telephones for outside calls – there is generally a high surcharge. Use the hotel payphone. If you find you get unwanted telephone calls from other hotel guests, ask the operator to put through telephone calls only from specific people.

If you receive any unwanted attention ask for the manager. It is his job to look after you and he is experienced at making every guest feel at ease.

Departure Avoid 'quick check out' facilities as you do not have a chance to check through your bill. Check every item carefully and if you have any cause for complaint first talk to the cashier and then, if you are still dissatisfied, ask to see the manager.

Hotel chains Some main British contact points include

Berni Inns	0272–297161
Best Western	01–940 7566
Capital	01–589 5171
Crest	01–236 3242
Four Seasons	01–499 0888
Gleneagles Hotels	031–228 2881
Hilton	01–631 1767
Hyatt International	01–235 5411
Inter-Continental Hotels	01–491 7181
Leading Hotels of the World	01–583 4211
Marriott	01–836 8521
Novotel	01–724 4000
Prestige Hotels	01–734 4267
Queen's Moat	0708–25814
Ramada Inns	01–235 5264
Sheraton	01–235 0172
Sorova	01–581 1431
Trust Houses Forte	01–567 3444

Holiday Accommodation

Do make sure that you book with a travel agent who belongs to ABTA and that your holiday is arranged with a tour operator who follows ABTA's code of practice. (See 'Package Holidays: Thinking about Booking You Holiday?' from the Office of Fair Trading or ABTA.)

If you have chosen an all-inclusive package trip you probably do not have much further say in where you stay.

If you are going to be responsible for your own accommodation these are some of the points you should consider:

1. Do you need the advantages of staying in a hotel?
● Advantages include all meals, car parking, laundry, possible sports and recreation facilities and the freedom to spend as much time in your room or the hotel as you want all day long.
● Disadvantages may include the cost and the impersonal relationship with employees in some hotels; and some hotels do not have special facilities for children (cots, high chairs and baby-listening devices).

2. Would you prefer to stay in a bed-and-breakfast establishment?
● Advantages may be financial and you may well enjoy a more personal relationship with your hosts.
● Disadvantages include the limited facilities (no regular laundry) and you may feel embarrassed if you have children who cry during the night. There may possibly be no recreation room and if the weather is bad you may wonder what to do all day long. You also have to go out for main meals other than breakfast, unless you come to some arrangement with your hosts about an evening meal.

3. Self-catering in a rented place is becoming increasingly popular:
● Advantages are financial, and the ability to do what you want and eat when you want, generally without having to think about anyone else.
● Disadvantages include the fact that those who do all the work at home may well end up doing as much work on holiday – or even more, as you will not be in your own kitchen!

4. Self-catering in your own caravan has slight variations:
● An extra advantage is that the cook 'knows her kitchen'.
● The disadvantages, however, are cramped space and possibly having to tow the caravan to its site, sometimes much to the ire of other motorists along the way.

5. Camping is also self-catering:
● Extra advantages include the bliss of being 'back to nature'.
● Extra disadvantages include the work of pitching and striking camp, possibly extra-cramped conditions, lack of security while you are away from the tent – and the continual uncertainty, especially in Britain, of the weather!

Further Information

Suggested
further reading

AIR TRAVEL
Barrett, Frank, *A Consumer's Guide to Air Travel*, Daily Telegraph

BUS AND COACH TRAVEL
Gundrey, Elizabeth, *The Good Coach Guide: England through the Big Window*, Century
Pick, Christopher, *Just off the Motorway*, Cadogan Books/Century

HEALTH
'Protect Your Health Abroad' and 'Medical Costs Abroad' from the DHSS.

HOLIDAY ACCOMMODATION
Camping and Caravanning in Britain, AA
English Tourist Board, *Activity and Hobby Holidays*
Guesthouses, Farmhouses and Inns in Britain, AA
Jackson, Michael, *The American Express Guide to London*, Mitchell Beazley
Nissen, Richard, *The Romantic Weekend Book*, Futura
Rubinstein, Hilary, *The Good Hotel Guide*, Consumers' Association/Hodder
  & Stoughton
Self-Catering in Britain, AA

18 Leisure

All the statistics show that we shall have increased leisure time on our hands in the coming years. According to the Henley Centre for Forecasting the biggest growth will be in home computers, outdoor and indoor sports and video watching; but some of the other activities that may enjoy increased popularity in the next few years as some people have more time will include theatre, ballet, opera, seaside activities, eating out, DIY, car maintenance and personal care and beauty.

This chapter is divided into two main parts: first there are tips on their own relevant interests from well-known experts and then there are ideas for you and your family and main contacts for every conceivable activity from politics to walking.

Leisure Activities

READING Some people can spend hours and hours lying on a beach doing nothing. Others store up books specially to take as holiday reading.

What books would well-known people take on holiday with them?

RACHEL BILLINGTON
Wives and Daughters, Elizabeth Gaskell
The Age of Innocence, Edith Wharton
My Ántonia, Willa Cather
A new Graham Greene – or an old one, if it comes to that.
A new Iris Murdoch – or an old one

SHIRLEY CONRAN
Sex Tips for Girls, Cynthia Heime
The Sloane Ranger's Handbook, Peter York and Ann Barr
The complete short stories of Elizabeth Bowen
War and Peace, Leo Tolstoy
Collins' English Dictionary

M. M. KAYE

Albert, Prince Consort, Robert Rhodes James
The Wind in the Willows, Kenneth Grahame, with Shepard's illustrations
The Crystal Cave, The Hollow Hills and *The Last Enchantment* (The 'Merlin' Trilogy), Mary Stewart
The Borrowers Omnibus, Mary Norton
The Secret Garden, Frances Hodgson Burnett, with the original Charles Robinson illustrations

ANDREA NEWMAN

The Weather in the Streets, Rosamond Lehmann
The Parasites, Daphne du Maurier
The King Must Die, Mary Renault
Lolita, Vladimir Nabokov
An anthology of modern poetry

Reading extends personal experience. Just any old reading, however, does not necessarily enhance a knowledge of literature. **Frank Delaney** is well known for his articles and BBC programmes on books and writers; he suggests the following books:

1. *Pride and Prejudice*, Jane Austen
2. *Middlemarch*, George Eliot
3. *The Oxford Companion to 20th Century Verse*
4. *Uses of Literacy*, Richard Hoggart
5. *Madame Bovary*, Gustave Flaubert (to be read in conjunction with Francis Steegmuller's edited *Letters of Flaubert*)
6. *The Group*, Mary McCarthy
7. *Couples*, John Updike (and his 'Rabbit' novels)
8. Anything by Edith Wharton and Eudora Welty
9. *The Glass Bead Game*, Hermann Hesse
10. *The Lost Honour of Katherina Blum* and *Group Portrait with Lady*, Heinrich Böll
11. *The Waves* and *To the Lighthouse*, Virginia Woolf
12. 'To satisfy virtually every sense but you have to read around it': *Ulysses, A Portrait of the Artist as a Young Man* and *Dubliners*, James Joyce and Richard Ellmann's biography of James Joyce

Further information Information on books is available from any local library. Another excellent source is:

> National Book League
> East Hill
> London SW18 2QZ
>   01–870 9055

> National Book League, Scotland
> 15a Lynedoch Street
> Glasgow G3 6EF
>   041–332 0391

Reviews of new books are published regularly in newspapers and periodicals.

The Federation of Children's Book Groups is the national umbrella organization for various parent–teacher groups that hold book fairs and promote an awareness of children's books. Their headquarters is at:

> 10 Lynton Gardens
> Arnold
> Nottingham NG5 7HA
> 0602–205781

Women's Press Book Club You may have noticed that women are increasingly dominant in publishing at the moment. I asked **Ros De Lanerolle**, Managing Director of The Women's Press, why this is so.

'It happens that women are dealing with ideas in a very special way. It does seem to me that so much of the interesting writing is being done by women about everything, from peace and war to history and low-level radiation. Women are expressing a particular passion about global concerns. As four or five women's presses developed, so too did the writing. I find it all very exciting.'

The Women's Press Book Club produces a catalogue and newsletter four times a year. Books are offered at 25 to 80 per cent discount on normal prices and subscribers have to take a minimum of four books a year. For details send an s.a.e. to:

> The Women's Press Book Club
> 124 Shoreditch High Street
> London E1 6JE
> 01–729 7451

Bookshops Some of the best known bookshops around Britain include:

Cambridge:
Heffers — 0223–358351

Edinburgh:
John Grant — 031–556 9698
James Thin — 031–556 6743

Glasgow:
John Smith & Son — 041–221 7472

London:
Foyles — 01–437 5660
Hatchards — 01–439 9921

Oxford:
Blackwells — 0865–249111

If you do not have a bookshop near you you can order books by post from the *Good Book Guide*'s Bookpost service (you can telephone or write with an order and, if you want, charge it to any major credit card). The *Good Book Guide* is published three times a year and keeps you up to date with new titles. Contact:

> *Good Book Guide*
> PO Box 400
> Havelock Terrace
> London SW8 4AU
> 01–720 8182 (24 hours)

ART   As far as an appreciation of painting is concerned, any choice of a few outstanding examples must of course be personal.

Edwin Mullins has introduced many important television programmes on art appreciation. His selection of some of his favourite paintings in the National Gallery is:

Giovanni Bellini (c. 1430–1516), *The Madonna of the Meadow*
Sandro Botticelli (c. 1445–1510), *Mystic Nativity*
J. B. Chardin (1699–1779), *The Young Schoolmistress*
Piero della Francesca (1410/20–92), *The Baptism of Christ*
Francisco de Goya (1746–1828), *Dona Isabel de Porcel*
Camille Pissarro (1830–1903), *Lower Norwood under Snow*
Nicolas Poussin (1594–1665), *Landscape with a Snake*
Rembrandt van Rijn (1606–69), *A Woman Bathing in a Stream*
J. M. W. Turner (1775–1851), *Ulysses Deriding Polyphemus*
Antoine Watteau (1684–1721), *La Gamme d' Amour.*

If you are unable to visit the National Gallery, you may find that there is an art gallery or museum nearer your home.

Major
art galleries
and museums

London

British Museum	01–636 1555
Hayward Gallery	01–928 3144
Institute of Contemporary Arts*	01–930 0493
National Gallery	01–839 3526
National Portrait Gallery	01–930 1552
Natural History Museum	01–589 6303
Royal Academy of Arts	01–734 9052
Science Museum	01–589 3456
Tate Gallery	01–828 1212
Victoria & Albert Museum	01–589 6371

*Membership required

Regions

Belfast	Ulster Museum	0232–668251
Birmingham	Birmingham Museum and Art Gallery	021–235 2834
Bristol	Arnolfini Gallery	0272–299191
Cambridge	Kettle's Yard	0223–352124
	Fitzwilliam Museum	0223–6951

Cardiff	National Museum of Wales	0222–397951
	Welsh Folk Museum, St Fagan's	0222–561357
Exeter	Maritime Museum	0392–58075
	Royal Albert Memorial Museum and Art Gallery	0392–56724
Manchester	The City Art Gallery	061–236 9422
	Manchester Museum	061–273 3333
	Platt Hall Gallery of English Costume	061–224 5217
	Whitworth Art Gallery	061–273 4865
Newcastle	Laing Art Gallery	0632–327724
	Museum of Science and Engineering	0632–326789
Oxford	Museum of Modern Art	0865–722733

Scotland

Edinburgh	National Gallery of Scotland	031–556 8921
	Royal Scottish Academy	031–225 6671
	The Royal Museum of Scotland	031–225 7534
	Scottish National Gallery of Modern Art	031–332 0227
	Scottish National Portrait Gallery	031–556 8921
Glasgow	Burrell Collection	041–632 1350
	Kelvingrove Museum and Art Gallery	041–334 1134
	Museum of Transport	041–423 8000

Many of the above places are nationally owned and admission is free. You should inquire about photography beforehand.

Some of these galleries have excellent and attractive restaurants. Recommended are the buffets at the National Gallery and the Royal Academy of Arts, both in London. Reservations should be made for lunch in the Tate Galley's Whistler-walled restaurant (London, not Sunday), renowned for its wine list (01–834 6754).

MUSIC
Classical music
by Sir David
Willcocks CBE,
former Director
of the Royal
College of Music

Here are twelve works which have long been favourites of mine and which have encouraged me to explore either other works by the composer concerned or works which have the same form. Most of them are 'popular' in the sense that they might well be found in lists of favourite music compiled by 'average' music-lovers – if such persons exist – but I make no apology and I only remain grateful that after more than forty years as a professional musician I still admire and am moved by such works, and am thankful that they have inspired me to seek beauty in countless other pieces of music, some of which I was less able to appreciate at first.

All the pieces listed below were written during the last 350 years and belong to the great corpus of what is known as Western Music. This selection might therefore imply that I have no appreciation of the simple beauty of plainchant which was the music of the church for centuries: nor of the ornate sacred and secular music of the medieval and renaissance composers: nor of the subtle inflections of Indian music and the rhythmic complexities of African music. I have discovered that, having been steeped in the mainstream European classical tradition, I can now respond to and enjoy almost every style of music, including jazz and rock, and that I can be genuinely interested in (even if I occasionally dislike) the work of current avant-garde composers.

Those seeking to develop their appreciation of music may be encouraged by the words of Sidney Smith. 'If I were to begin life again, I would devote it to music. It is the only cheap and unpunished rapture upon earth.'

1. Gregorio Allegri (b. 1582), *Miserere mei* – a setting of Psalm 51 with alternate verses being sung to the ancient plainsong tones. Mozart, as a boy of fourteen, heard it in the Sistine Chapel and subsequently wrote it down from memory.

2. J. S. Bach (b. 1685), the *Brandenburg Concertos* – completed 1721 and dedicated to the Markgraf of Brandenburg. They feature different groupings of solo instruments.

3. Handel (b. 1685), *Messiah* – the greatly loved oratorio which the composer completed in twenty-two days.

4. Mozart (b. 1756), *The Marriage of Figaro* – one of Mozart's operatic masterpieces.

5. Beethoven (b. 1770), *Symphony No. 5* – one of nine symphonic masterpieces, embracing many moods.

6. Schubert (b. 1797), *Die schöne Müllerin*, a song-cycle which is representative of the 600 songs in which Schubert revealed his gift for melody and subtle piano accompaniment.

7. Mendelssohn (b. 1809), *Violin Concerto* – an example of the concertos of the Romantic period which feature a solo instrumentalist (with orchestra) and demand of the player technical virtuosity.

8. Chopin (b. 1810), *Études* – representative of the fine piano works of this composer, these are technically very demanding, contrasted in style and explore the full potential of the piano as a solo instrument.

9. Elgar (b. 1857), *Enigma Variations* – a work for full orchestra dedicated 'to my friends', with each variation a musical portrait, the style of the music reflecting the character and idiosyncrasies of the individual concerned.

10. Stravinsky (b. 1882), the *Firebird Suite* from the score commissioned by Diaghilev for the Russian Ballet in 1910.

11. Messiaen (b. 1908), *La Nativité du Seigneur* – one of many works for solo organ based on biblical texts by a composer of great originality who derives inspiration from his religious faith and from the song of birds.

12. Britten (b. 1913), *Variation on a Theme of Purcell* (The Young Person's Guide to the Orchestra) – another orchestral work in variation form: in this case each variation features a different section of the orchestra or individual instrument and displays its characteristics.

Concert halls and opera houses	London	booking office	credit card booking
	Barbican	01–628 8795	01–638 8891
	English National Opera	01–836 3161	01–240 5258
	Purcell Room	01–928 3191	01–928 6544
	Queen Elizabeth Hall	01–928 3191	01–928 6544
	Royal Albert Hall	01–589 8212	01–930 9232
	Royal Festival Hall	01–928 3191	01–928 6544
	Royal Opera House	01–240 1066	01–240 1911
	Sadler's Wells Theatre	01–278 8916	01–278 8919
	St John's, Smith Square	01–222 1061	—
	Wigmore Hall	01–935 2141	01–930 9232

Outside London
Birmingham

	Town Hall	021–236 388	—

Bristol

	Colston Hall	0272–291 768	—

Cardiff

	Welsh National Opera	0222–32446	0222–396130

Croydon

	Fairfield Hall	01–688 9291	—

Edinburgh

	Queen's Hall	031–228 1155	031–228 1155
	Usher Hall	031–228 1155	031–228 1155

Glasgow

	Henry Wood Rehearsal Hall	041–552 5961	041–552 5961
	Scottish National Opera	041–331 1234	041–332 9000

Manchester

	Free Trade Hall	061–834 0943	—

Newcastle upon Tyne

	City Hall	0632–328 520	—

Suffolk

	The Maltings, Snape	072–885 3543	—

Opera and ballet   I asked **Sir George Christie**, Chairman of Glyndebourne Productions and Founder Chairman of the London Sinfonietta, what his favourite operas are and he immediately cited the three Mozart operas with librettos by Lorenzo da Ponte: *The Marriage of Figaro, Don Giovanni* and *Così Fan Tutte*; and two by Verdi: *Otello* and *Falstaff*. 'I am being unbelievably conventional!' he said.

Appreciation of opera is considered by many to be the zenith of artistic appreciation. If you know nothing about opera but would like to find out about it, Sir George recommends that you should first talk to as many people as possible who do know something. 'Ideally talk to laymen who are enthusiasts because they will be much closer to the ground. Then, having got good guidance, go with your wallet well lined and buy a ticket for something which has been specifically recommended to you.'

● The headquarters for some organizations include:

> Glyndebourne Festival Society
> Glyndebourne
> Lewes
> East Sussex BN8 5UU
> 0273–812321

> Kent Opera
> Pembles Cross
> Egerton
> Ashford TN27 9EN
> 0233–76406

> Royal Opera House
> Bow Street
> London WC2E 7QA
> 01–240 1200

I asked **Merle Park**, now Director of the Royal Ballet School, which ballets had been particularly important to her. This is her choice:
Shadowplay (choreographed by Anthony Tudor)
Romeo and Juliet (Sir Kenneth Macmillan)
Symphonic Variations (Sir Frederick Ashton)
A Month in the Country (Ashton)
Façade (Ashton)
The Nutcracker (Rudolph Nureyev)
Variations on a Theme of Purcell (Ashton)
A Walk to the Paradise Garden (Ashton)

● If you are interested in ballet as a career you should contact:

> The Royal Ballet School
> 155 Talgarth Road
> Barons Court
> London W14 9DE
> 01–748 3123

Rock and pop music
: When asked to define the two terms record producer Noel d'Abo said: 'A good question – I suppose "pop" means the hits of the moment, for the young teenage fans, and rock is more durable and more complex, for the late teens and older.' One way to find out what is happening in this fast-moving world is to read the popular weekly music magazines such as *New Musical Express* (*'NME'*) and *Sounds*. They publish detailed charts – not just the top 50 but US charts, charts of videos, reggae hits, charts from ten years ago, and so on. They carry interviews and reviews and detailed listings of forthcoming gigs, as does the free fortnightly paper *Soundcheck* available at many concerts and at box offices. In the pop world the fortnightly *Smash Hits* covers much of the same ground. *Time Out* and *City Limits* list London concerts.

Rock and pop venues

Birmingham	Exhibition Centre	021–780 4141
Bristol	Hippodrome	0272–299444
Cardiff	St David's Hall	0222–371236
Edinburgh	Playhouse	031–557 2590
Leeds	Queen's Hall	0532–431961
London	Earls Court	01–381 4255
	Hammersmith Odeon	01–748 4081
Manchester	Apollo	061–273 5772
Oxford	Apollo	0865–244544
Portsmouth	Guildhall	0705–824355
Reading	Hexagon	0734–591591
Sheffield	City Hall	0742–735295
Southampton	Gaumont	0703–29772

Jazz
: Jazz enthusiasts usually know what they like and where to find it. For the non-specialist, Peter Clayton's programme on BBC Radio 3 on Saturdays 'Jazz Record Requests' is ideal. Look for 'Jazz Today', in the Radio 3 listings, for new jazz music.

I asked Peter Clayton for a selection of important jazz records. 'Some of these are important in the absolute sense,' he said, 'and others are important to me.' Here is his list, in no special order:

'West End Blues' (Louis Armstrong, 1928)
'Porgy and Bess' (Miles Davis/Gil Evans, 1959–60)
'My Favourite Things' (John Coltrane, c. 1966)
'Epistrophy' (Thelonius Monk and the Giants of Jazz, c. 1972)
'Under Milk Wood', first version (Stan Tracey Quartet, mid 1960s)
'How Long Blues' (Count Basie, piano and rhythm section, late 1930s)
Almost any of the Benny Goodman Trio or Quartet records from 1936 to 1939
'Swing Out' (Henry 'Red' Allen, early 1930s)
'Bundle of Blues' (Duke Ellington, 1933–4)
'Fine and Mellow' (a desolate but wonderful Billie Holliday with all-star backing on CBS television film, 1957)
: *Time Out* and *City Limits* list jazz concerts in London; so do the popular

music magazines. In London, practically every well-known jazz musician eventually appears at Ronnie Scott's Club, 47 Frith Street, London w 1, 01–439 0747.

THEATRE **Patricia Hodge** (famed as the television detective Jemima Shore) comments, 'With theatre, there is a chance to go on and do it every night and there is only you and the audience. With television and films, you are ultimately in the hands of technicians. Personally, I like to do a combination of different media: the variety is stimulating.'

There *is* something special about seeing a performance 'live'. Although from a practical point of view it may require an effort to get tickets. If you have a choice and do not know what to see, ask the advice of friends, because critics sometimes do not view a play as you would and their comments displayed by the theatres in their publicity are, not surprisingly, limited to the good ones.

Here are some of the theatres around the country with booking office telephone numbers (some have separate credit-card booking numbers which you can get from the newspaper or by telephoning Directory Inquiries):

London	*booking office*
Adelphi	01–836 7611
Albery	01–836 3878
Aldwych	01–836 6404
Ambassadors	01–836 1171
Apollo, Shaftesbury Avenue	01–437 2663
Apollo, Victoria	01–828 8665
Barbican	01–628 8795
Comedy	01–930 2578
Criterion	01–930 3216
Drury Lane	01–836 8108
Duchess	01–836 8243
Duke of York's	01–836 5122
Fortune	01–836 2238
Garrick	01–836 4601
Globe	01–437 1592
Greenwich	01–858 7755
Hampstead	01–722 9301
Haymarket	01–930 9832
Her Majesty's	01–930 6606
King's Head	01–226 1916
London Palladium	01–437 7373
Lyric, Hammersmith	01–741 2311
Lyric, Shaftesbury Avenue	01–437 3686
Mayfair	01–629 3036
Mermaid	01–236 5568

National	01–928 2252
New London	01–405 0072
Old Vic	01–928 7616
Palace	01–437 6834
Piccadilly	01–437 4506
Prince Edward	01–437 6877
Prince of Wales	01–930 8681
Queen's	01–734 1166
Royal Court	01–730 1745
St Martin's	01–836 1443
Savoy	01–836 8888
Shaftesbury	01–379 5399
Strand	01–836 2660
Vaudeville	01–836 9987
Victoria Palace	01–828 4735
Young Vic	01–928 6363
Wyndham's	01–836 3028

Headquarters of main theatre companies include:

National Theatre Company	01–928 2252
Royal Shakespeare Company	
(1) Barbican Theatre	01–628 8795
(2) Royal Shakespeare Theatre	0789–292271

Regions
Belfast:

Grand Opera House	0232–241919
Chichester:	
Festival Theatre	0243–781312
Croydon:	
Ashcroft and Fairfield Hall	01–688 9291
Edinburgh:	
King's Theatre	031–229 1201
Royal Lyceum	031–229 9697
Glasgow:	
Citizens'	041–429 0022
King's	041–552 5961
Guildford:	
Yvonne Arnaud	0483–60191
Leicester	
Haymarket	0533 539797
Liverpool	
Everyman Theatre	051–709 4776
Manchester:	
Royal Exchange	061–833 9233
Newcastle upon Tyne:	
Theatre Royal	0632–322061

Nottingham:
Playhouse   0602–45671
Perth:
Perth Theatre   0738–21031
Pitlochry:
Festival Theatre   0796–2680
Sheffield:
Crucible   0742–79922
Stratford-upon-Avon:
Royal Shakespeare Theatre   0789–295623
Windsor:
Theatre Royal   07535–53888

CINEMA   Almost anyone you ask will come up with a list of favourite films. The critic **Philip Oakes** says his choice, on grounds of importance as well as being among his favourites, would be:
1. *Citizen Kane* directed by Orson Welles
2. *La Règle du jeu* directed by Jean Renoir
3. *The Maltese Falcon* directed by John Huston
4. *The Searchers* directed by John Ford
5. *Singin' in the Rain* directed by Vincente Minelli and Gene Kelly
6. *La Peau douce* directed by François Truffaut.

It seemed a few years ago that television had delivered a body blow to the film industry but today the scene is not so bleak. There is still an audience ready to go to a cinema to see good films, particularly if they have been well-publicized and have won some awards. The simultaneous early release of the latest films all over the country, television programmes about new productions and the sub-division of big old cinemas into several small, comfortable 'studios' have all helped. Ironically, television, in showing so many films drawn from the whole of motion-picture history, has created a wide new interest in film as an art form.

To find out what is on in London, look in the national newspapers (London editions) such as the *Daily Telegraph* or *The Times* and in particular in the evening paper, the *Standard*. For complete London listings see magazines such as *Time Out*, *City Limits* and *What's On*. Elsewhere, look in your local daily, evening and weekly papers.

To find out in advance what is to be shown on television, see the *Radio Times* and *TV Times*. Watch for announcements of forthcoming seasons of films from a particular country or by a particular director.

There is probably a film society near you. Details of membership and future programmes can be obtained from most public libraries. If you live in or near London you can join the National Film Theatre (01–928 3232).

Look at the stocks of films held by video libraries near you. The cost of hiring a film has come down dramatically since these libraries began and may be less than the cost of a cinema ticket.

The categories into which films are divided by the British Board of Film Censors are:

U (Universal): suitable for all ages

PG (Parental Guidance): some scenes unsuitable for children, although children will be admitted

15: no one under fifteen years will be admitted

18: no one under the age of eighteen will be admitted.

There are other more restrictive categories for films which are deemed unsuitable for these certificates of 'general admission', such as that which allows a film to be shown in a private club. Some local authorities retain the right to operate their own system of censorship.

EATING OUT

For suggestions on good restaurants throughout Britain, buy the guides published by the following organizations. They are always pleased to have suggestions and comments on restaurants. You should contact:

> Egon Ronay Organization
> Greencoat House
> Francis Street
> London SWIP IDH
>   01–828 6032

> Good Food Guide
> 14 Buckingham Street
> London WC2N 6DS
>   01–839 1222

> Michelin Tyre
> Hotel and Restaurant Guide
> 81 Fulham Road
> London SW3 6RD
>   01–589 1460

See   'Recommended further reading' at the end of this chapter.

FAMILY
ACTIVITIES

Special events are given on national and local television and radio and in papers and magazines. Information on special events can also be obtained by telephoning: 01–246 8007.

Holiday ideas

● In London, you can get information on all Underground and bus travel from London Transport's 24-hour number: 01–222 1234.

● Details of guided London walks from: British Tourist Board (see page 494)

● London Planetarium 01–486 1121

● London Zoo 01–722 3333

● Madame Tussaud's 01–935 6861

Eating out with
Children

At the end of the day – or even in the middle – you might want sustenance.

A child of any age may be taken by parents into a licensed restaurant or hotel. By law, only children over the age of fourteen are allowed in pubs with their parents and then only for soft drinks. In practice, many publicans bend the law slightly and allow children under fourteen to accompany their parents into a lounge bar (this is entirely at the discretion of the individual publican). Ask *before* taking the children into a lounge bar. You will find that in Scotland, for instance, the no-children rule is more strictly enforced.

However, you can legally take children into any room in which alcohol is *not actually sold*. This means that you can perhaps buy your own alcoholic drink in the neighbouring bar and take it to join children in a sitting-room or television room or garden.

The *Good Food Guide*'s 1984 'children's restaurant of the year' was the Hard Rock Café near Hyde Park Corner (01–629 0382). Perhaps more accessible, children of all ages love McDonald's, Pizzalands and any kind of informal eating. Berni Inns take special care of children – and others, too, will find their meals attractive (and their wholemeal rolls addictive). 'Family type' restaurants are going to be more likely to have high chairs and special meals or reduced portions. Increasingly some branches of well-known chains have outside play areas easily seen from within the restaurant: children love climbing in and out of an enormous dinosaur, for instance, while adults eat at more leisure.

Further Information

● In Northern Ireland it is important to remember that there are fewer recreational activities on Sundays than in the rest of the British Isles. You should also remember that pubs are not open on Sundays, although licensed hotels and clubs are.

● In Scotland, information and guiding services are offered by:

> Scottish Tourist Guides Association
> 41 Lilyhill Terrace
> Edinburgh EH8 9DR
> 031–661 3552

● The governing bodies of the arts in Britain are the Arts Councils. They have good information services on what is going on and they tell you about local festivals. Details of all their activities (specify art, community arts projects, drama, festivals, literature and music, etc.) from:

> The Arts Council of Great Britain
> 105 Piccadilly
> London W1V 0AU
> 01–629 9495

The Arts Council of Northern Ireland
181a Stammillis Road
Belfast BT1 5DU
0232–663591

Scottish Arts Council
19 Charlotte Square
Edinburgh EH2 4DF
031–226 6051

Welsh Arts Council
Holst House
Museum Place
Cardiff CF1 3NX
0222–394711

Your Mind

THOUGHT   SPEAKING
MEMORY

THOUGHT
by Edward
de Bono,
author of many
books on logic
and thought

The purpose of thinking is to collect information and to make the best possible use of it.

Because of the way the mind works to create fixed concept patterns we cannot make the best use of new information unless we have some means for restructuring the old patterns and bringing them up to date. Our traditional methods of thinking teach us how to refine such patterns and establish their validity. But we shall always make less than the best use of available information unless we know how to create new patterns and escape from the dominance of the old ones.

Vertical thinking is concerned with proving or developing concept patterns. Lateral thinking is concerned with restructuring such patterns (insight) and provoking new ones (creativity).

Lateral and vertical thinking are complementary. Skill in both is necessary.

MEMORY
by Martin
Gostelow,
a former Brain
of Britain

Not nearly enough is known about the way the memory works but it seems certain that there is no practical limit to its capacity. You will not be knocking out an old fact each time you learn a new one!

Whether you are learning a language for business or holiday or studying for an exam, try to create the conditions in which the memory will work most efficiently for you. Experiments have shown that you will be most likely to retain and recall an event, fact or impression if it is:

1. new to you
2. important to you
3. unusual

4. connected
5. clearly perceived (by sight, sound, etc.)
6. repeated
7. recent.

Some of these factors are obviously mutually exclusive and some may seem to be outside your control, but you can make use of each of them. Here are some ways – you will think of more.

● *Newness*. The first time you open a book to study, be alert, fresh and not distracted. You can create artificial 'newness' by breaking up longer periods of study into 30- or 40-minute blocks separated by short breaks, each block devoted to a different aspect of your work.

● *Importance*. You may be motivated by the prospect of exams or the demands of a job, but in any case devise goals and objectives for yourself and some little rewards for achieving them.

● *Unusualness*. Give ordinary or dull material 'star' treatment in terms of time, place, colour – underline your notes in orange.

● *Connections*. Look for linkages, groups and patterns. Make lists and schematic diagrams. Find relationships with other parts of your subject. Visit the places connected with it.

● *Clarity of perception*. Be fresh and alert. Unless you are a nightowl do not miss out on sleep. Work in a good light – strip (tube) lights can flicker and tire your eyes. Be comfortable and preferably just a bit cooler than usual so that you are less likely to doze. Eliminate distractions and temptations. Make efficient notes using key words, lists, diagrams and underlining. Your own notes will be more help towards retention and recall than anyone else's and they should be selective.

● *Repetition*. Review your material frequently to reinforce its impact on your memory. Do this at gradually increasing intervals – e.g. after ten minutes, an hour, a day, a week, a month. Make cassette tapes of questions and answers or language lessons and play them over and over again.

● *Recency*. Other factors being equal, the events of yesterday are likely to be clearer in your memory than those of last month, so organized revision the day before an exam is worthwhile. If time is really short, use a ruthlessly pruned version of your notes.

If you want to improve your memory, contact:

Improving Your Memory
56 Eastworth Road
Chertsey
Surrey KT16 8DP
09328–63335

SPEAKING
by Eve Snell,
voice teacher

A voice that is warm and mellow and easy on the ear is an asset. Accents or dialects are no longer a drawback – they reflect the speaker's personality. You should aim for clear speech and a voice that is pleasant to listen to. The old style 'elocution' lesson, which taught a forced and unnatural-sounding speech, is to be avoided at all costs, which is why the term 'voice improvement' is preferred today.

Of course, some people do have serious speech impediments, although fewer women than men stammer. Speech therapy can help the sufferer to come to grips with an impediment. Helpful organizations are listed on page 300.

But for those with normal voices, professional help can also be a marvellous boost. A trained voice instructor can devise and show you how to go through your own personal 'voice workout' which includes relaxation, breathing and voice exercises.

Directory of Contacts

POLITICAL PARTIES   OTHER ACTIVITIES
SPORTS

The 300 Group is a cross-party organization which wants to see more women in parliament and in all areas of public life. Contact:

*Some useful
information*

300 Group
9 Poland Street
London W1Z 3DG
01–734 3457

POLITICAL
PARTIES

The Communist Party of
   Great Britain
16 St John Street
London EC1M 4AY
   01–251 4406

The Conservative and Unionist
   Party
32 Smith Square
London SW1P 3HH
   01–222 9000

The Ecology Party
36–8 Clapham Road
London SW9 0JQ
   01–735 2485

The Labour Party
150 Walworth Road
London SE17 1JT
   01–703 0833

The Labour Party Scottish Council
1 Lynedoch Place
Glasgow G3 6AB
   041–332 8946

The Liberal Party
1 Whitehall Place
London SW1A 2HE
   01–839 4092

Plaid Cymru
51 Cathedral Road
Cardiff CF1 9HD
   0222–31944

Scottish Conservative and Unionist
   Central Office
3 Chester Street
Edinburgh EH3 7RF
   031–226 4426

The Scottish Liberal Party
4 Clifton Terrace
Edinburgh EH1 2 5DR
031–337 2314

The Scottish National Party
6 North Charlotte Street
Edinburgh EH2 4JH
031–226 3661

The Social Democratic and Labour
Party (Northern Ireland)
38 University Street
Belfast BT7 1FZ
0232–223428

The Social Democratic Party
4 Cowley Street
London SW1P 3NB
01–222 7999

The Ulster Democratic Unionist
Party
296 Albertbridge Road
Belfast BT5 4GX
0232–58597

The Ulster Unionist Council
3 Glengall Street
Belfast BT12 5AE
0232–224601

The Welsh Liberal Party
15–17 Dumfries Chambers
91 St Mary's Street
Cardiff
0222–22210

SPORTS

For information on any sport contact,
in England:

The Sports Council
16 Upper Woburn Place
London W1H OQP
01–388 1277

Elsewhere, contact:
The National Sports Centre for
Wales
Sophia Gardens
Cardiff CF1 9SW
0222–397571

The Scottish Sports Council
1 St Colme Street
Edinburgh EH3 6AA
031–225 8411

The Sports Council for Northern
Ireland
House of Sport
2a Upper Malone Road
Belfast BT9 5LA
0232–661222

*National
headquarters of
specific sports*

Archery

Grand National Archery Society
National Agricultural Centre (7th
Street)
Stoneleigh
Kenilworth
Warwicks CV8 2LB
0203–23907

Scottish Archery Association
35 Laburnum Grove
Stirling FK8 2PR
0786–65333

Athletics

Scottish Women's Amateur
Athletic Association
18 Ainslie Place
Edinburgh EH3 6AU
031–226 4401

Women's Amateur Athletic
Association
Francis House
Francis Street
London SW1P 1DE
01–828 4731

Badminton
Badminton Association of England
National Badminton Centre
Bradwell Road
Loughton Lodge
Milton Keynes MK8 9LA
0908–568822

Scottish Badminton Union
Cockburn Centre
40 Bogmoor Place
Glasgow G51 4TQ
041–445 1218

Ballooning
British Balloon and Airship Club
Kimberley House
47 Vaughan Way
Leicester LEI 4SG
0533–531051

Bowling
British Tenpin Bowling Association
19 Canterbury Avenue
Ilford
Essex IGI 3NA
01–554 9173

English Women's Bowling
  Association
2 Inghalls Cottages
Box
Corsham
Wilts SNI4 9PP
0225–742852

English Women's Indoor Bowling
  Association
32 St Omer Road
Cowley
Oxford OX4 3HB
0865–779215

Scottish Women's Bowling
  Association
56 Haig Street
Grangemouth FT3 8QF
0324–482731

Scottish Women's Indoor Bowling
  Association
I Underwood Road
Burnside
Rutherglen
Glasgow G73 3TE
  (no telephone)

Camping and caravanning
Camping Club of Great Britain
II Grosvenor Place
London SWIW OEY
  01–828 1012

The Caravan Club
East Grinstead House
East Grinstead
Sussex RHI9 IUA
0342–26944

Canoeing
British Canoe Union
Flexel House
45–7 High Street
Addlestone
Weybridge
Surrey KTI5 IJV
0932–41341

Scottish Canoe Association
18 Ainslie Place
Edinburgh EH3 6AU
031–226 4401

Welsh Canoeing Association
Pen-y-Bont
Corwen
Clwyd LL2I OEL
0490–2345

Canoe Association of Northern
  Ireland
2a Upper Malone Road
Belfast BT9 6LA
0232–661222 ext. 206

Caving
Grampian Speleological Group
8 Scone Gardens
Edinburgh EH8 7DQ
  031–661 1123

National Caving Association
c/o Whernside Cave & Fell Centre
Dent
Sedburgh
Cumbria LA10 5RE
  05875–213

Cricket
Women's Cricket Association
16 Upper Woburn Place
London WC1H 0QF
  01–387 3423

Croquet
The Croquet Association
Hurlingham Club
Ranelagh Gardens
London SW6 3PR
  01–736 3148

Curling
English Curling Association
23 Cross Street
Preston
Lancs PR1 3LT
  0772–54019

Cycling
British Cycling Federation
16 Upper Woburn Place
London WC1H 0QE
  01–387 9320

Dancing – see Movement and
  dance

Fencing
Amateur Fencing Association
The de Beaumont Centre
83 Perham Road
London W14 9SP
  01–385 7442

Scottish Amateur Fencing Union
11 Eyre Crescent
Edinburgh EH3 5ET
  031–557 0335

Fishing
National Federation of Anglers
Halliday House
2 Wilson Street
Derby DE1 1PG
  0332–362000

Salmon and Trout Association
Fishmongers' Hall
London Bridge
London EC4R 9EL
  01 – 626 3531

Scottish Anglers National
  Association
307 West George Street
Glasgow G2 4LB
  041–221 7206

Flying
Aircraft Owners and Pilots
  Association
50a Cambridge Street
London SW1V 4QQ
  01–834 5631

Gliding
British Gliding Association
Kimberley House
Vaughan Way
Leicester LE1 4SG
  0533–531051

Golf
Ladies' Golf Union
12 The Links
St Andrews
Fife KY16 9JB
0334–75811

Gymnastics
British Amateur Gymnastics
   Association
95 High Street
Slough
Berks SL1 1DH
0753–32763

Scottish Amateur Gymnastics
   Association
18 Ainslie Place
Edinburgh EH3 6AU
031–226 4401

Hang gliding
British Hang Gliding Association
PO Box 350
Great Horwood
Milton Keynes MK17 0QS
   (no telephone)

Hockey
All England Women's Hockey
   Association
3rd Floor, Argyle House
29–31 Euston Road
London NW1 2SD
01–278 6340

Scottish Women's Hockey
   Association
18 Ainslie Place
Edinburgh EH3 6AU
031–226 4401

Welsh Women's Hockey
   Association
25 Merllyn Avenue
Connah's Quay
Deeside
Clwyd CH5 4TA
0244–813320

Ice skating
National Skating Association of
   Great Britain
15–17 Gee Street
London EC1V 2RU
01–253 3824

Scottish Ice Figure Skating
   Association
c/o Murrayfield Ice Rink
Riverdale Crescent
Edinburgh EH12 5XN
031–337 3976

Judo
British Judo Association
16 Upper Woburn Place
London WC1H 0QH
01–387 9340

Scottish Judo Federation
8 Frederick Street
Edinburgh EH2 2HB
031–226 3566

Lacrosse
All England Women's Lacrosse
   Association
16 Upper Woburn Place
London WC1H 0QJ
01–387 4430

Scottish Lacrosse Association
95 Dryman Road
Bearsden
Glasgow G61 3RP
041–943 0947

Lawn tennis
Lawn Tennis Association
Barons Court
London W14 9EG
01–385 2366

Scottish Lawn Tennis Association
12 Melville Crescent
Edinburgh EH3 2LV
031–225 1284

Modern Pentathlon

Modern Pentathlon Association
of Great Britain
1a Godstone Road
Purley
Surrey CR2 2DH
01–668 7851

Motor-cycling

Auto-Cycle Union
Millbuck House
Corporation Street
Rugby
Warwicks CV21 2DN
0788–70322

Scottish Auto-Cycle Union
Kippilaw
Longridge Road
Whitburn
West Lothian EH47 0LG
0501–42663

Motor racing

RAC Motor Sports
Association Ltd
31 Belgrave Square
London SW1X 8QH
01–235 8601

Mountaineering

British Mountaineering
Council
Crawford House
Precinct Centre
Booth Street East
Manchester M13 9RZ
061–273 5835

Mountaineering Council
of Scotland
South Tillysole
Cottage
Kinnaird Park
Brechin DD9 6T
(no phone)

Movement and dance

British Ballet Organization
Woolborough House
39 Lonsdale Road
London SW13 9JP
01–748 1241

English Folk Dance and Song
Society
2 Regent's Park Road
London NW1 7AY
01–485 2206

Keep Fit Association
16 Upper Woburn Place
London WC1H 0QG
01–387 4349

Oriental Dancing Association
(belly dancing)
37 The Green
Steventon
Abingdon
Oxon OX13 6RR
0235–834073

Royal Scottish Country Dance
Society
12 Coates Crescent
Edinburgh EH3 7AF
031–225 3854

Scottish Amateur Ballroom
Dancers' Association
37 Tanzie Knowe Drive
Cambuslang
Glasgow G72 8RG
041–641 5073

Netball

All England Netball Association
Francis House
Francis Street
London SW1P 1DE
01–828 2176

Scottish Netball Association
12 Sinclair Street
Milngavie
Glasgow G62 8NU
041–956 4245

Orienteering
British Orienteering Federation
41 Dale Road
Matlock
Derbyshire DE4 3LT
0629–3661

Scottish Orienteering Association
5 The Chenonry
Aberdeen AB2 IRP
0224–44375

Parachuting
British Parachute Association
Kimberley House
47 Vaughan Way
Leicester LEI 4SG
0533–59635

Scottish Sport Parachute
   Association
3 Melford Ave
Kirkintilloeh
near Glasgow
G66 IED
0229 0229
041–776 2895

Riding
British Horse Society
British Equestrian Centre
Stoneleigh
Kenilworth
Warwick CV8 2LR
0203–52241
(also, British Show Jumping
   Association, Pony Club and
   Riding Club)

National Pony Society
30 Mount Pleasant Road
Alton
Hants GU34 INN
0420–88333

Rounders
National Rounders Association
4 Gloucester Close
Desford
Leics LE9 9HQ
04557–3112

Rowing
Amateur Rowing Association
6 Lower Mall
London W6 9DJ
01–748 3632

Scottish Amateur Rowing
   Association
46 Churchill Drive
Bridge of Allan
Stirling FK9 4TJ
0786–833029

Running
Road Runners Club
40 Rosedale Road
Stoneleigh
Epsom
Surrey KTI7 2JH
01–393 8950

Sailing
Royal Yachting Association
Victoria Way
Woking
Surrey GU21 IEQ
04862–5022

Royal Yachting Association
   Scotland
18 Ainslie Place
Edinburgh EH3 6AU
031–226 4401

Shooting
Clay Pigeon Shooting Association
107 Epping New Road
Buckhurst Hill
Essex IG9 5TQ
01–505 6221

National Rifle Association
Bisley Camp
Brookwood
Woking
Surrey GU24 ONY
04867–2213

Scottish Shooting Council
39 Pelstream Avenue
Stirling FK7 0BG
   0786–75769

Skiing
British Ski Federation
118 Eaton Square
London SW1 9AF
   01–235 8227

Scottish National Ski Council
110a Maxwell Avenue
Bearsden
Glasgow G61 1HU
   041–943 0760

Squash
Irish Women's Squash Rackets
   Association
10 Thorndale Park North
Carryduff
Co. Down BT8 8HY
   0232–813343

Scottish Squash Rackets
   Association
18 Ainslie Place
Edinburgh EH3 6AU
   031–225 2502

Welsh Squash Rackets Federation
Trienna
Quarella
Bridgend
Mid Glam CF3 1 1JT
   0656–56752

Women's Squash Rackets
   Association
345 Upper Richmond Road West
London SW14 8QN
   01–876 6219

Surfing
British Surfing Association
Room G5, Burrows Chambers
East Burrow Road
Swansea

West Glam SA1 1RF
   0792–461476

Scottish Surfing Federation
6 Stoneyhill Drive
Musselburgh EH21 6SQ
   031–665 6969

Swimming
Amateur Swimming Association
Harold Fern House
Derby Square
Loughborough
Leics LE11 0AL
   0509–230431

Scottish Amateur Swimming
   Association
Airthrey Castle
University of Stirling
Stirling FK9 4LA
   0786–70544

Welsh Amateur Swimming
   Association
21 Old Vicarage Close
Llanishen
Cardiff CF4 5UZ
   0222–753448

Table tennis
English Table Tennis Association
21 Claremont
Hastings
East Sussex TN34 1HA
   0424–433121

Irish Table Tennis Association
4 Fairhill Gardens
Belfast BT15 4FZ
   0232–77608

Scottish Table Tennis Association
18 Ainslie Place
Edinburgh EH3 6AU
   031–225 3020

Table Tennis Association of Wales
198 Cyncoed Road
Cardiff CF2 6BQ
   0222–757241

Volleyball
English Volleyball Association
128 Melton Road
West Bridgford
Nottingham NG2 6EP
0602–816324

Scottish Volleyball Association
25 Johnstone Terrace
Edinburgh EHI 2NH
031–225 7311

Welsh Volleyball Association
112 St Fagans Road
Fairwater
Cardiff CF5 3AN
0222–562003

Irish Volleyball Association
2a Upper Malone Street
Belfast BT9 5LA
0232–661222

Water skiing
British Water Ski Federation
16 Upper Woburn Place
London WCIH 0QL
01–387 9371

Windsurfing
Windsurfer Class Association of
    Great Britain
The Royal Yachting Association
Victoria Way
Woking
Surrey GU21 IEQ
04862–5022

OTHER
ACTIVITIES

What are sometimes variously called 'crafts', 'hobbies' or 'pursuits' include many interests, such as photography, for which there are no national organizations suitable for the amateur and/or beginner. For information about your chosen activity always inquire first at the local library. It should have details of specialist clubs in your area. A check should also be made of special-interest magazines.

The list below is a selection of activities that do have national organizations. It is appreciated if you send a stamped addressed envelope with any postal inquiry

Animals
People's Dispensary for Sick
    Animals
PDSA House
South Street
Dorking
Surrey RH4 2LB
0306–888291

Royal Society for the
    Prevention of Cruelty to Animals
The Causeway
Horsham
Sussex RHI2 IHG
0403–64181

Antiques
Antiques Collectors' Club
5 Church Street
Woodbridge
Suffolk IPI2 IDS
03943–5501

Archaeology
Council for British Archaeology
112 Kennington Road
London SEII 6RE
01–582 0494

Scottish Council for Industrial
    Archaeology
c/o The Royal Museum
    of Scotland
Chambers Street
Edinburgh EHI IJF
031–225 7534

Art appreciation

National Association of Decorative
and Fine Arts Societies
38 Ebury Street
London SW1W 0LU
01–730 3041

Astronomy

British Astronomical Association
Burlington House
Piccadilly
London W1V 0NL
01–734 4145

Auctions

Headquarters of main auction houses
(some have branches around the UK):
Edinburgh: Lyon & Turnbull
031–225 4627
London: Bonhams 01–584 9161
Christie's 01–839 9060
Phillips 01–629 6602
Sotheby's 01–235 4311

Bee-keeping

British Beekeepers' Association
National Agricultural Centre
Stoneleigh
Kenilworth
Warwicks CV8 2LR
023–552404

Scottish Beekeepers' Association
Richmond Villa
Richmond Avenue
Dumfries DG2 7JS
0387–52773

Bells

Central Council of Church Bell
Ringers
19 Ravensgate Road
Charlton Kings
Cheltenham
Glos GL53 8NR
0242–32454

Birds

Royal Society for the Protection of
Birds
The Lodge
Sandy
Beds SG19 2DL
0767–80551

Scottish Ornithologists' Club
21 Regent Terrace
Edinburgh EH7 5BT
031–556 6042

Cats

Governing Council of the Cat Fancy
4–6 Tennel Orlieu
Bridgwater
Somerset TA6 3TG
0278–427575

Chess

British Chess Federation
9a Grand Parade
St Leonards-on-Sea
East Sussex TN38 0DD
0424–442500

Conjuring

British Magical Society
125 Whitecrest
Great Barr
Birmingham B43 6EX
021–357 5610

Conservation

Association for the Protection of
Rural Scotland
14a Napier Road
Edinburgh EH10 5AY
031–229 1898

Civic Trust
17 Carlton House Terrace
London SW1Y 5AW
01–930 0914

Coastal Anti-Pollution League
Alverstoke
94 Greenway Lane
Bath
Avon BA2 4LN
  0225–317094

Council for the Protection of Rural
  England
4 Hobart Place
London SW1W 0HY
  01–235 9481

Council for the Protection of Rural
  Wales
Ty Gwyn
31 High Street
Welshpool
Powys SY21 7JP
  0938–2525

Fauna and Flora Preservation
  Society
Zoological Society of London
Regent's Park
London NW1 4RY
  01–586 0872

Friends of the Earth
377 City Road
London EC1V 1NA
  01–837 0731

Friends of the Earth (Scotland)
53 George IV Bridge
Edinburgh EH1 1EJ
  031–225 6906

National Trust
36 Queen Anne's Gate
London SW1H 9AS
  01–222 9251

National Trust for Scotland
5 Charlotte Square
Edinburgh EH2 4DU
  031–226 5922

Scottish Civic Trust
24 George Square
Glasgow G2 1EF

  041–221 1466

The Architectural Heritage
  Society of Scotland
436 Manor Place
Edinburgh EH3 7EB
  031–225 9724

Scottish Wildlife Trust
25 Johnstone Terrace
Edinburgh EH1 2NH
  031–226 4602

Dogs
Kennel Club
1–4 Clarges Street
London W1Y 8AB
  01–493 6651

National Dog Owners' Association
39–41 North Road
London N7 9DP
  01–609 2757

Scottish Kennel Club
6b Forres Street
Edinburgh EH3 6BJ
  031–226 6808

Embroidery
Embroiderers' Guild
41a Hampton Court Palace
East Molesey
Surrey KT8 9AV
  01–943 1229

Royal School of Needlework
25 Princes Gate
London SW7 1QE
  01–589 0077

Engraving
Royal Society of Painter-Etchers
  and Engravers
Bankside Gallery
48 Hopton Street
London SE1 9JH
  01–928 7521

Farming

National Farmers' Union
Agriculture House
Knightsbridge
SW1X 7NJ
  01–235 5077

National Federation of City Farms
Old Vicarage
66 Fraser Street
Bedminster
Bristol BS3 4LY
  0272–660663

Women's Farming Union
Cryal's Farm
Matfield
Tonbridge
Kent
  089272–2372

Film-making

Institute of Amateur
  Cinematographers
63 Woodfield Lane
Ashtead
Surrey KT21 2BT
  03722–76358

Fish keeping

Federation of British Aquatic
  Societies
17 Risborough Road
Maidenhead
Berks SL6 7BJ
  0628–25581

Flower arranging

National Association of Flower
  Arrangement Societies of Great
  Britain
21a Denbigh Street
London SW1V 2HF
  01–828 5145

Folklore

Folklore Society
c/o University College London
Gower Street
London WC1E 6BT
  01–387 3611

Gardening

Royal Caledonian Horticultural
  Society
21 Strathalmond Road
Edinburgh EH4 8HP
  031–339 6796

Royal Horticultural Society
Horticultural Hall
Vincent Square
London SW1 2PE
  01–834 4333

Scottish Rock Garden Club
21 Merchiston Park
Edinburgh EH10 4PW
  (no phone)

Gems

Gemmological Association of
  Great Britain
St Dunstan's House
Carey Lane
London EC2V 8AB
  01–726 4374

Genealogy

Scottish Genealogy Society
21 Howard Place
Edinburgh EH3 5JY
  031–556 3844

Society of Genealogists
37 Harrington Gardens
London SW7 4JX
  01–373 7054

Heraldry

Heraldry Society
28 Museum Street
London WC1A 1LH
  01–580 5110

Heraldry Society of Scotland
Limegrove
High Street, Gifford
E. Lothian EH41 4QU
062–081 617

History
British Association for Local
    History
43 Bedford Square
London WC1B 3DP
01–636 4066

Scottish Local History Forum
31 Garlton Court, Gullane
E. Lothian EH31 2HT
0620–842587

Intelligence
Mensa
Bond House
St John's Square
Wolverhampton WV2 4AH
0902–26055

Jigsaws
British Jigsaw Puzzle Library
Old Homend
Stretton Grandison
Ledbury
Hereford HR8 2TW
053183–462

Music hall
British Music Hall Society
47 Woodberry Avenue
North Harrow
Middlesex HA2 6BE
01–863 3459

Pigeons
Royal Pigeon Racing Association
The Reddings
Cheltenham
Glos GL51 6RN
0452–713529

Poetry
National Poetry Society
21 Earls Court Square
London SW5 9DE
01–373 7861

Quilting
Quilters' Guild
Clarendon
56 Wilcot Road
Pewsey
Wilts SN9 5EL
067–263230

Singing
National Association of Choirs
13 Stafford Close
Bulkington
Nuneaton
Warwicks CV12 9QX
0203–315798

National Operatic and Dramatic
    Association
1 Crestfield Street
London WC1H 8AU
01–837 5655

Snooker
Billiards and Snooker Control
    Council
Coronet House
Queen Street
Leeds LS1 2TN
0532–440586

Stamps
British Philatelic Federation
314 Vauxhall Bridge Road
London SW1A 1AA
01–828 4416

British Post Office Philatelic
    Bureau
Lothian House
124 Lothian Road
Edinburgh EH3 9BB
031–556 8661

Theatre appreciation and history
British Theatre Association
9 Fitzroy Square
London WIP 6 AE
    01–387 2666

Scottish Community Drama
    Association
Saltire House
13 Atholl Crescent
Edinburgh EH3 8HA
    031–229 7838

Walking
Pedestrians Association
1 Wandsworth Road
London SW8 2LJ
    01–582 6878

Ramblers' Association
1–5 Wandsworth Road
London SW8 2LJ
    01–582 6878

Further Information

*Suggested
further reading*

READING
The World of Penguin, the publisher's complete catalogue
Harvey, Sir Paul, ed., *The Oxford Companion to English Literature*, Oxford
University

ART
Anything by Sir Kenneth Clark
Gombrich, E. H., *The Story of Art*, Phaidon
Levey, Michael, *A History of Western Art*, Thames & Hudson
Mullins, Edwin, *The Arts of Britain*, Phaidon
Murray, Peter and Linda, *A Dictionary of Art and Artists*, Penguin
Museums and Galleries in Great Britain and Ireland, ABC Historic
    Publication/HMSO

MUSIC
Baines, Anthony (ed.), *Musical Instruments through the Ages*, Penguin
Hartnolls, Phyllis, ed., *The Oxford Companion to the Theatre*, Oxford Uni-
    versity Press
Jacobs, Arthur, *A Short History of Western Music*, Penguin
Kennedy, Michael, *The Concise Oxford Dictionary of Music*, Oxford Uni-
    versity Press
Rosenthal, Harold and John Warrack, *The Concise Oxford Dictionary of
    Opera*, Oxford University Press

CINEMA
Bawden, Liz Anne, ed., *The Oxford Companion to Film*, Oxford University
    Press
Halliwell, Leslie, *Halliwell's Film Guide*, Granada

EATING OUT
Eat Out in Britain for around £5, AA
Foster, Jill and Malcolm Hamel, *The Peaudouce Family Welcome Guide to
    the Best Pubs, Hotels and Restaurants for Parents out with Children*, Sphere

Ronay, Egon, *Just a Bite*, Mitchell Beazley

THOUGHT
de Bono, Edward, *Lateral Thinking*, Penguin
    Wordpower, Penguin

MEMORY
Baddeley, Alan, *Your Memory: a User's Guide*, Penguin

19 Emergencies – and How to Prevent Them

The **999 system** is for emergencies only (fire, ambulance, police, coast-guard):
- Call the operator by dialling 999 or as shown on the telephone label.
- Tell the operator your telephone number (as shown on the telephone label) and the emergency service you need.
- When the emergency authority answers:

(a) tell them the full address where help is needed, and

(b) any other information (including your name, home address and day/night telephone numbers).

Notes
- Speak clearly so that no confusion of details can arise.
- A recording will be made of your call.

For non-urgent calls, the police ask you to look in the local directory for the number of your nearest police station.

Motor Accidents

If you have an accident, however minor:
- *Stop* – by law you must stop and ascertain that:

(a) no one has been hurt

(b) no domestic animals have been hurt

(c) no vehicle apart from your own and no roadside property has been damaged.

- Take down relevant car numbers as soon as possible: in a minor collision it sometimes happens that, if you are alone, the other driver will signal you to stop – and then promptly drive off.
- Check for injury (see 'Car Accidents', page 156).
- Record the accident by writing down:

(a) registration number and make of any cars involved

(b) names and addresses and telephone numbers of the other driver, insurance company of other driver (though he has to tell you this only if anyone is injured), and as many independent witnesses as possible

(c) time of accident, and as many details as you can (you can do this later).

- If possible, photograph the scene and the damage caused or sketch the road layout, skid marks, position of witnesses and anything else you think relevant.

● If requested, you must by law give your name and address to anyone involved in or affected by the accident.

● Do not apologize. Do not admit liability or offer any payment even if you think it was your fault. If you do admit any degree of blame your insurance company could refuse any subsequent claim.

● The police should be called if:

(a) anyone is injured

(b) you think the other driver has committed an offence

(c) you have damaged someone's property and you cannot tell them personally.

Do not feel that you have to talk to the police at this time. You are not obliged to and you may be in a state of shock. If you do decide to make a statement, write it down yourself and keep a copy.

● Report to your insurer as soon as possible, even if you do not intend to make a claim – this is a condition of your policy. Report any statements made at the scene of the accident but do not discuss whose fault it was. Fill in the insurer's accident report form completely.

Stolen vehicle Report the theft to the police immediately and tell your insurer. Be prepared to wait for a reasonable period to see if your car is recovered: many cars which are taken without the owner's consent are found abandoned.

Stolen property Report to the police immediately and tell your insurer. Comprehensive
(from a car) cover should include any loss or damage to clothing, rugs or personal belongings (check with your insurer).

For breakdown and repairs, see Chapter 3.

Suggested 'When It Comes to the Crunch: Do You Know What to Do Next?' from the
further reading British Insurance Association (address on page 39).

Protect Yourself

THINGS TO REMEMBER AT HOME   PROTECT YOURSELF FROM
TRAVELLING   YOUR PARTNER OR FAMILY
LEARN TO DEFEND YOURSELF   OBSCENE TELEPHONE CALLS
RAPE

THINGS TO ● If you live alone it is best not to put your first name or any other
REMEMBER indication that you are a woman on your door or in the telephone book.
AT HOME ● Change all outside door locks when moving into a new home, and if you lose your keys (even if they have subsequently been found).

● Fit and use door-chains when you are in the house. Lock all outside doors when you are home.

● Close the curtains after dark.

● Make sure you have adequate outside lights to leave on when you go out.

● Never allow anyone into the house (repair man, for instance) unless you can first check his credentials.

● Only employ people for whom you have a reliable recommendation.

● Do not allow strangers to come in and use the telephone.

● Ask the local police to send a crime prevention officer to survey your home and make recommendations on how to increase its security (this is a free service). Security companies will also do this for you.

When you go out

● Never leave keys on a string behind the letterbox or under the doormat or behind plants outside the door.

● Do not leave the garden shed unlocked or tools lying around – these can be used to force entry into the house.

● Windows left even slightly open for cats are inviting to humans too.

● Windows near flat roofs or drainpipes are particularly attractive to intruders.

● Leave a light on in a downstairs room – not just in the hall – to give the impression of occupation.

When you come home

● Leave a light on over your front door and have your key ready to open it immediately.

● If you notice anything unusual *do not go into the house or call out*. Telephone the police immediately.

TRAVELLING

● Always remember that women generally support other women. Act if you see anyone in danger.

● Trust your instincts about men – and act on them.

● Always be sure you know exactly how to get to your destination before you start a journey – do not ask strangers for directions.

● Inform friends at both departure and destination points of the times of your journey and your route.

● Always look in the back seat before you get in a car.

● Never pick up hitch-hikers.

● Do not stop to help others who have broken down.

● If you break down when travelling at night on a motorway, many people advise you to lock yourself in and prepare to wait until daybreak (although you will probably be rescued by a police patrol).

● Always note your car's position in a large carpark so you can go straight back to it.

● On public transport, try to sit near the driver, conductor, guard or another woman.

● If pestered, complain.

Walking
- When walking alone at night, choose well-lit, busy routes.
- Try not to walk close to buildings or past unlit alleyways and doors.
- Never walk with both hands in your pockets or carry anything with both hands at once.
- Never daydream as you walk along.
- Avoid waiting alone at an isolated bus stop.
- Never go alone through a subway – wait until there are others to go with you.

Also   Avoid being in a lift alone with a man: if this should happen, stand by the controls.

LEARN TO DEFEND YOURSELF   Ask at your local police station or sports centre if there are any courses in self-defence. If you live within the area covered by the Metropolitan Police, for instance, a special constabulary representative will give courses to any group of between twelve and twenty women (ideally there should be four 2-hour sessions).

> A6 Branch (Self-Defence)
> New Scotland Yard
> Broadway
> London SW1H OBG
> 01–230 2961

Elsewhere, information on self-defence courses is available from:

> National Association of Women's Self-Defence Courses
> 203 Turves Green
> West Hill
> Birmingham B31 4BS
> (no telephone)

Vulnerable points

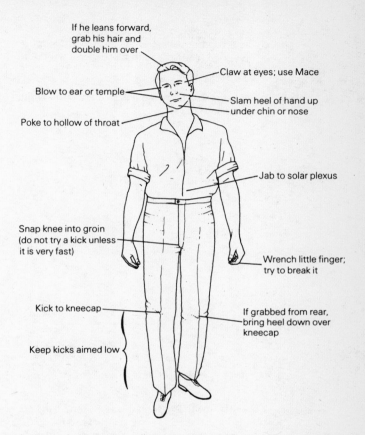

If he leans forward,
grab his hair and
double him over

Claw at eyes; use Mace

Blow to ear or temple

Slam heel of hand up
under chin or nose

Poke to hollow of throat

Jab to solar plexus

Snap knee into groin
(do not try a kick unless
it is very fast)

Wrench little finger;
try to break it

Kick to kneecap

If grabbed from rear,
bring heel down over
kneecap

Keep kicks aimed low

If you are attacked only you can decide whether or not to resist, taking into account all the circumstances. It is no good trying to defend yourself with your car keys when you are confronted by several determined-looking heavyweights. If you do decide to resist:

Defensive stance

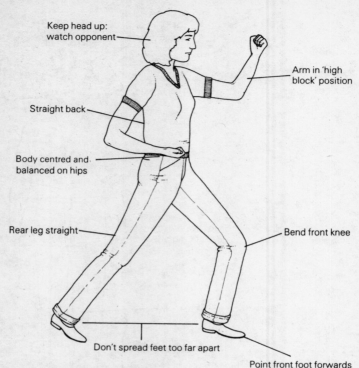

Keep head up:
watch opponent

Arm in 'high
block' position

Straight back

Body centred and
balanced on hips

Rear leg straight

Bend front knee

Don't spread feet too far apart

Point front foot forwards

Point foot either forwards or outwards

- Stand with feet spread, one in front of the other as if you were walking.
- Unless there are several attackers, use your keys as a knuckleduster – but remember, *any weapon you try to use might be taken and used against you.*
- Aim a spray perfume or breath spray at the attacker's eyes.
- Use your belt as a lash.
- If your attacker has a weapon do not try to fight unless absolutely necessary.
- If there is a knife, and you have time, wrap your coat around your arm to act as a shield.
- Always try to deflect the attacker's arms before he hits you – make a fist and sweep, at arm's length, from side to side.

Kicking

Straight back

Maintain 'high block'

Snap the kick out from raised knee

Come out of stance into 'stork' postion

● Kick as hard as you can – your legs are your strongest weapon. If you are standing as recommended above, bring your rear leg up, bent sharply, and snap your kick out from the raised knee.

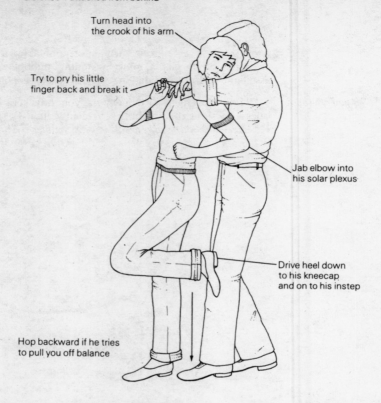

Defence if attacked from behind

Turn head into
the crook of his arm

Try to pry his little
finger back and break it

Jab elbow into
his solar plexus

Drive heel down
to his kneecap
and on to his instep

Hop backward if he tries
to pull you off balance

RAPE

- There is a fair chance (54 per cent) that your assailant will be an acquaintance, friend or relation.
- Fifty per cent of all rapes occur in the home of the woman or the man.
- The rape may be accompanied by other forms of sexual abuse and the use of weapons.
- Section 1 of the Sexual Offences (Amendment) Act, 1976, defines rape as follows:

> A man commits rape if
> (a) he has unlawful sexual intercourse with a woman who at the time of the intercourse does not consent to it; and
> (b) at that time he knows that she does not consent to the intercourse or he is reckless as to whether she consents to it.

In terms of rape in England and Wales, sexual intercourse means penetration of the labia (outer lips) by the penis to any degree – full penetration and ejaculation need not take place in order to constitute rape. It is assumed that no boy under fourteen is capable of intercourse.

In Scotland the definition of rape is stricter and means actual penetration by the man's penis of the woman's vagina although emission of semen into the body is unnecessary. A boy has to be under eight for it to be assumed he is incapable of intercourse.

● Rape can involve sexual and mental humiliation, urination, defecation or spitting on the victim, injury to genitals, multiple rape by one or more assailants and/or intimidation with threats or weapons.

If you are raped

● If he is a stranger, try to memorize your attacker's features, characteristics – anything that might help to identify him.

● Afterwards, *do not take a bath or wash clothing* – or take alcohol or drugs.

● You do not have to telephone the police (see below). If you do, also telephone a friend who can be with you throughout your time at the police station.

● If you do not contact the police, you can go to the nearest hospital for a check-up but many casualty departments will automatically inform the police.

● A doctor will establish proof of intercourse, give antibiotics in case of a sexually transmitted disease and, if necessary, give a 'morning after' contraceptive in the form of four high-strength contraceptive pills taken in two lots of two.

● Telephone your nearest Rape Crisis Centre (see below).

If you do decide
to go to the police

● Report as soon as possible.

● Tell someone else (a friend or the Rape Crisis Centre) what has happened.

● Take someone else with you when you report to the police station.

● Take a change of warm clothing with you as you may have to leave your clothes as evidence.

Police procedure may take several hours.

● You will be asked to dictate a statement which will be written for you. Do not sign it without careful checking.

● You will be asked intimate questions: there is no reason why you should at any time talk to any officer other than the one in charge of your case. You may request that a policewoman question you.

● You will have external and internal examinations by a qualified police surgeon: if you prefer you can request your own GP or a woman doctor.

● You may be asked to look at photographs and/or to accompany the police to the scene of your rape.

● Your anonymity is assured unless in very exceptional circumstances a judge directs otherwise.

Rape
Crisis Centres

There are twenty-six centres around the country ready to provide emergency and on-going support and information about pregnancy prevention after rape, pregnancy tests, abortion and VD. They can help you protect your anonymity. They will explain about police, court and medical procedures and accompany you to VD clinics, doctor, police and court. They can also supply information about applications to the Criminal Injuries Compensation Board as a result of rape or sexual assault.

To find your nearest Rape Crisis Centre telephone the 24-hour service of the London Rape Crisis Centre: 01–837 1600. During office hours contact can be made through:

Rape Counselling and Research Project
London Rape Crisis Centre
PO Box 69
London WC1X 9NJ
01–278 3956

PROTECT YOURSELF FROM YOUR PARTNER OR FAMILY
Battered women

Some women are at risk through battering, abuse or humiliation by their partners. There are now over two hundred refuges to which anyone – married or single, with or without children – can go.

Contact with the local refuge can be made through the local police, social services, Citizens' Advice Bureau or Samaritans. At the refuge to which you are directed, arrangements will be made with schools and nurseries so that your children will not miss any schooling. You can stay at the refuge as long as you like and, if necessary, you will be helped with rehousing. You will also be advised about supplementary benefits and, should you decide to take legal action against the man you have left, you will be put in touch with a sympathetic solicitor.

Women's Aid Federation (England)
London   01–837 9316
Manchester   061–228 1069

Irish Women's Aid
Belfast   0232–662385
Londonderry   0504–65967
Portrush   0265–823195
Strabane   0504–882261

Scottish Women's Aid
Edinburgh   031–225 8011

Welsh Women's Aid
Cardiff   0222–388291

Incest

Incest is sexual intercourse – defined as for rape – with a member of your family (the relations with whom it is illegal to have intercourse vary around the British Isles). The list of banned relationships affects marriage as well as illicit intercourse. The incest victim is often a young girl, and she may be psychologically damaged for life.

The Rape Crisis Centre can advise and refer you to your nearest incest support group or you can contact:

Incest Survivors' Campaign
c/o AWP
Hungerford House
London WC2

OBSCENE
TELEPHONE
CALLS

If you have obscene or other nuisance telephone calls this is what British Telecom suggests:

- Hang up as soon as you can – gently, and showing no emotion (many such callers hope for an emotional reaction and a long chat).
- If nuisance calls, especially silent calls, persist, it is possible the caller is known to you. Random callers are generally put off if they do not get the desired reaction.
- If calls do persist, contact the customer service manager of your local telephone area. He may be able to intercept calls, bar all incoming calls, change your number or try to trace the calls (but, contrary to popular belief, it is very difficult and expensive to do this).

British Telecom suggests these precautions to prevent unwanted calls:

- If an unknown telephone caller asks you what your number is, ask him what number he wants.
- In general, do not give your name and address over the telephone unless the caller is known to you.
- Teach children not to say over the telephone to strangers 'Daddy is not here.'

See 'Nuisance Calls', British Telecom.

Protect Your Property

LOOK AFTER YOUR VALUABLES   **WHEN YOU ARE GOING AWAY**
PROTECT YOUR HOUSE

LOOK AFTER
YOUR
VALUABLES

- Keep a note of serial numbers of all valuable items (e.g. television sets, cameras).
- Put your postcode on those valuables.
- Make lists of all credit card and bank account numbers and all relevant telephone numbers. Keep one copy of the list yourself, put one in the bank and give one to a trusted business associate or friend.

See also 'Cards', page 28.

- Photograph valuable art works, antiques and jewellery.
- Do not chat about your valuables when you might be overheard.
- Do not let anyone know you are going away (see below).
- Keep your cheque book and cheque card separately.
- Try not to keep more money in the house than you need.
- Do not leave handbags and money unattended – and never leave them in sight of people coming in or by your house.
- Remember, a shoulder bag is easier to protect than a handbag: keep it under your arm, to the front of your body and with the zip completely closed. When walking in public places always have your bag over the shoulder *away* from the street. Canvas, leather or plastic money-belts can be worn under your outer garments.

PROTECT YOUR HOUSE

Police records show that most house entries are made through badly secured doors and windows. Your local crime prevention officer (contact him at the police station) can advise on specific precautions for your house.

The main objective is to ensure that all openings to the outside world – doors and french and other windows – should be provided with fastenings with removable keys so that forcible and violent entry is necessary to breach them. In the case of windows this means making certain that the potential thief is forced to break enough glass to get his whole body through and not just his hand.

The main exit must then be provided with a good mortice deadlock and hinge bolts.

If there is a house alarm system it is usual to have a micro switch fitted into the mortice deadlock on the main door.

A few further points include:

● A spyglass 'door viewer' lets you see who is outside, and a door-chain offers protection against the 'foot-in-the-door' thief.

● Windows can be made more secure by the use of double-glazing.

● Make sure that your letterbox is not large enough for anyone to put his hand through and thus open the door from inside.

If you want to investigate the possibility of intruder detection and alarm systems, you can consult Yellow Pages. Make certain that the firm you consult is a member of the National Supervisory Council for Intruder Alarms (NSCIA), the watchdog body for the industry (and refer any complaints to it):

> National Supervisory Council for Intruder Alarms
> St Ives House
> St Ives Road
> Maidenhead
> Berks SL6 1RD
> 0628–37512

Despite all your precautions, however, a practised thief may be determined to get into your house. Remember to keep all outside doors locked when you are at home, check the identity of all callers and never remove the safety-chain until you are satisfied.

Neighbourhood Watch

Some police forces are setting up Neighbourhood Watch or Home Watch schemes. They encourage householders to help one another by keeping a friendly eye on their neighbours' homes, by looking out for suspicious strangers in the locality and by reporting anything untoward to the police. Your local police station will tell you if such a scheme operates in your area.

WHEN YOU ARE GOING AWAY

● Remove all valuables (video, stereo, silver) out of sight.
● Remember to cancel newspapers, milk and other deliveries.
● Ask a trusted friend to check every working day (at least) that no mail or circulars are left sticking out of the letterbox.

- Mow your lawn before leaving home and, depending on how long you are going to be away, ask someone to do it in your absence.

Support
- The person who has experienced loss or distress through any sort of crime can receive comfort and advice from:

National Association of Victims' Support Schemes
34 Electric Lane
London SW9 8JT
01-737 2010

Safety in the Home

BURNS AND SCALDS
DROWNING
ELECTRICAL PROBLEMS AND
   ACCIDENTS
FALLS
FIRE
GAS PROBLEMS

GLASS INJURIES
PLUMBING PROBLEMS
POISONING
SUFFOCATION
QUICK CHECKLIST FOR HOME
   SAFETY

As the British Insurance Association points out, '*your* home is only as safe as *you* make it'. As well as reading carefully all the potential trouble spots – and how to prevent them – mentioned below, it is a good idea to check that your property and its contents are amply insured (see 'Insurance', page 34ff., and 'It Can Happen to You: Some Hints on Home Safety' from the British Insurance Association, address on page 39).

Statistics concerning safety in the home, or lack of it, are staggering ... Every day eighteen people in Britain die from accidents in the home (every day, eighteen people are killed in road accidents). Every year, therefore, more than 6,000 people die from accidents in the home. Many of these accidents could have been prevented.

BURNS
AND SCALDS
Burns occur mainly through direct contact with hot dishes, pans or appliances; gas, oil and electric fires which are not properly guarded; and because flammable clothing catches alight when put in contact with these sources of heat or flames. Burns are also, sadly, often associated with fireworks.

For treatment of burns see page 155.

Prevention
- Make sure all fires are protected by the British Standards Institution (BSI)-approved guards.
- Check that as much clothing as possible is of low flammability or flame resistant, and remember that close-fitting garments are less likely to catch alight than loose clothes.

- Keep matches out of children's reach.
- Don't put anything attractive to touch on a mantelpiece or shelf over a fire.
- Use oven gloves to hold kitchen pans.
- Be wary of the hot surface of the iron.

Scalds occur when hot liquids or steam come into contact with the skin, when pans are spilled, hot water bottles burst or baths or showers are too hot.

For treatment of scalding see page 155.

Prevention
- Keep children out of the kitchen unless supervised.
- Keep pan handles turned away from the front of the cooker.
- Keep spouts of electric kettles away from you.
- Do not expect hot water bottles to last too long. Buy replacement stoppers before any leaks occur. Protect bottles in thick covers when in bed.
- Turn tablecloth corners under to prevent small children pulling the cloth, and its settings, off.

DROWNING
Anyone – particularly a child – can drown in as little as two inches of water. Be careful about:
- garden ponds and swimming pools
- buckets (even half-filled)
- leaving a child unattended in the bathroom.

In case of drowning perform artificial respiration, see pages 144.

ELECTRICAL PROBLEMS AND ACCIDENTS
Electricity boards have the right to disconnect a supply or to refuse to connect a new supply if:
(a) you have not paid your bill
(b) the premises or electrical wiring or appliances are unsafe
(c) the customer is using electricity dishonestly (e.g. bypassing the meter).

If you have been cut off you should make contact as soon as possible with your local electricity showroom or with the relevant department listed on the back of your bill. If you think you are in danger of being cut off through not being able to pay the bill you should also contact your local DHSS office.

Note
You cannot sue the electricity board if lack of power causes business or household inconvenience.

Lack of knowledge about electricity may contribute to some functional problems.

Terminology
Alternating current (a.c.) – electricity generated for public supply is in the form of a.c., which allows the use of transformers to increase or reduce the voltage of the supply. Alternating current changes its 'direction' – positive to negative – at regular intervals (frequency).

Amperage (A) – electrical current is measured in A, sometimes called amps, e.g. current ratings of fuse or flexible cord $\left(amps = \dfrac{watts}{volts} \right)$.

BEAB approved – an appliance which has been *type tested* and certified by the British Electrotechnical Approvals Board that it conforms to the requirements of the appropriate British Standard for Safety: BS 3 4 5 6 for appliances and BS 4 1 5 for radio, TV and hi-fi.

Direct current (d.c.) – electric current which flows only in one direction, e.g. from a battery.

Double insulated appliance – this has additional or reinforced insulation throughout to provide protection against electric shock. Such appliances have only two cores in the flexible cord and must not be earthed. They are marked with the double square symbol (e.g. vacuum cleaners, hair dryers).

Earthed appliance – this has all the accessible metal parts connected to earth via the earthing conductor green/yellow in the three-core flexible cord. This system is one method of ensuring protection against electric shock.

Electron – a basic particle of electricity, having a negative charge.

Energy regulator – an automatic switching device which varies the energy input supplied to a heating element by switching the electricity on and off on a regular basis, thus a variable output from off to full is available (e.g. used to control a cooker's radiant ring).

Hertz (Hz) or **cycles/second** – the unit of frequency of alternating current: the standard frequency in the UK and Europe is 50Hz, i.e. the current goes through a complete change of direction and back again 50 times per second.

Kilowatt (kW) – 1,000 watts.

Neon – a tiny red lamp fitted to a socket, switch or plug and to appliances like a freezer to indicate that electricity supply is available.

Rating plate – a plate fixed to the appliance which gives the model number, wattage, voltage and the name of the manufacturer or vendor. The appliance must be marked if it is BEAB approved. Depending upon the method of electrical protection provided either the words 'this appliance must be earthed' or the words or symbol for double insulation is shown.

Time-switch – this is a switch which is operated automatically by a clock mechanism which may be set to switch on and off at pre-selected times. It may be useful for putting electric blankets on, or for house lights to confuse potential thieves.

Transformer – a device for converting one a.c. voltage to another.

Unit – the measure of electrical supply. One unit is 1 kilowatt hour (kWh). Your electricity bill is based on the number of units used.

Volt – the unit of electrical pressure which causes an electric current to flow in a circuit; the standard electrical pressure for household use in this country is 240 volts.

Watt (W) – the unit of the rate at which electricity is used. Wattage is the general term for the power of a piece of electrical equipment (watts = volts × amps).

Danger Electric shock and possible electrocution may result from:
- broken plugs or sockets, loose wires or frayed flexes
- incorrect wiring of plugs
- faulty appliances
- connecting an appliance which must be earthed to an unearthed appliance (e.g. a lamp holder)
- trying to effect repairs without switching off the electricity
- taking mains-operated appliances into the bathroom
- switching on or off with wet hands
- allowing children to insert metal objects into sockets (*note*: all 13A sockets made to BS1363 are fitted with shutters)
- emptying or filling electric kettles or percolators with the appliance still connected to the electricity supply
- cleaning cookers without turning off the control panel.

What to do in case of electric shock
- *Switch off current.*
- If you cannot do so, pull the insulated cord and wrench the plug from the socket.
- Alternatively, push the casualty away from the electric current with a wooden chair or broomstick (*do not use anything with metal in it*).
- Check breathing and heartbeat and give artificial respiration and/or heart massage if necessary (see pages 144 and 162).
- Get medical help.

Prevention As well as avoiding all the above, here are a few specific tips to prevent electric shock and possible electrocution:
- Have all installations carried out by an approved contractor on the roll of the National Inspection Council for Electrical Installation Contracting (NICEIC), address on page 565.
- Buy appliances carrying the BEAB's mark of safety and follow the manufacturer's instructions carefully.
- While most fused plugs are sold complete with 13 amp fuse, this may be too highly rated for some appliances. Check the instructions, or ask your dealer or a contractor on the roll of the NICEIC which fuse is correct for the appliance.
- Before wiring a plug, remember the colour code:
  Blue to Neutral
  Brown to Live
  Green/yellow to Earth.
- Remember that electric blankets, if not left on the bed all year round, should be rolled or flat-stored and should be regularly serviced at least

Wiring a plug

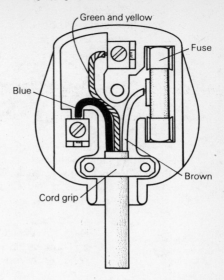

Green and yellow

Fuse

Blue

Brown

Cord grip

once every three years (check with manufacturer's instructions).

● Do not get into bed with an electric pre-heating underblanket still switched on.

● Do not mend electrical appliances or wires with Sellotape.

If an appliance does not work Check the following (from 'Common Sense and Electrical DIY'):

1. Is the plug firmly in the socket?

2. Did you switch the appliance on?

3. Are controls incorrectly set? Return all controls to 'off' and reset machine, particularly cooker – 'auto' to 'manual'; cancel and reset time switches; check thermostat settings.

4. Is the plug or fuse faulty? Check flex is wired to plug correctly and that screws are secure; replace fuse with another, same rating, from an appliance that you know works.

5. Have you checked flex for damage, particularly where it is connected to the appliance? Switch off at socket first.

6. Have you tested the socket? Try plugging another appliance in to it.

Help NICEIC,
237 Kennington Lane,
London SE11 5QJ
01–582 7746

If you have any complaints about electricity, contact your local electricity board. If you are still not satisfied, contact your local

Electricity Consultative Council ('Electricity' in the telephone directory). Each board is autonomous. The Electricity Council has no direct authority over the policy of an electricity board.

(For complaints about electrical appliances, see 'Sale of Goods Act', page 136).

For information you can contact:

Electricity Council
30 Millbank
London SW1P 4RD
01–834 2333

You can also contact the Electrical Association for Women. They run invaluable programmes such as a 1-day course 'Electricity in the Home' which includes meanings of simple electrical terms and symbols, advice on off-peak supplies, meter and electricity bill reading, understanding and changing fuses and plugs, and information on choosing and care of appliances.

Electrical Association for Women
25 Fouberts Place
London W1V 2AL
01–437 5212

See   'Common Sense and Electrical DIY' and 'Electricity for Everyday Living', Electrical Association for Women.

FALLS   These mainly affect old and young people, but even agile adults can trip and slip on highly polished floors or on wet floors in bathrooms or kitchens. They can also fall down stairs or from steps and chairs used as steps.

Prevention
- Try to keep the house tidy and make sure there is no litter on the floors.
- Check that there is sufficient lighting in difficult areas, say around stair bends.
- Use non-slip polishes on floors and put non-slip pads on the underside of rugs.
- To help old people, fix handrails on stairs and beside bath and lavatory.
- Make sure that babies are always secured by safety harnesses when in prams.
- If there is a toddler around, make sure there is a gate at the top of stairs.
- Put safety clasps on windows.
- Double-check that steps or chairs are secure before mounting.

FIRE   *Delay can be dangerous – act quickly*, but take the following actions before
What to do   investigating further:

1. Close the door of the room where the fire is.

2. Alert the household and get everyone out by the safest route. Do not use a lift.

3. Call the fire brigade by dialling 999, then alert neighbours.

4. Try to reduce draughts that may fan the fire. Close all doors and windows.

Also:

5. If you suspect there is a fire behind a closed door, do not open it.

6. Remember, smoke can be as dangerous as flames.

7. If a chip pan catches fire, turn off the heat, smother the flames with a lid or damp cloth and leave for half an hour.

8. If any electrical equipment catches fire, unplug the appliance involved and switch off the electricity at the mains. Then (but not until then) you can use a fire extinguisher.

9. Remember, water is the most suitable extinguishing agent for the majority of fires in the home.

10. If an oil heater catches fire use a dry powder or foam extinguisher immediately, standing at least six feet away in case the fire flares up. Then leave the room, if possible shutting windows and doors behind you. CALL THE FIRE BRIGADE.

11. To use a fire extinguisher, take up a position where access to the fire is unrestricted and from which you can make a quick and safe retreat. Crouching helps the operator to keep clear of smoke. Direct the jet at the base of the flame and keep it moving across the area of fire.

12. If your clothes catch fire, roll on the floor to extinguish flames.

13. If someone else's clothes are on fire the Fire Brigade suggests they should be laid on the floor and rolled in a thick blanket, rugs or a thick coat. The Red Cross and St John's Ambulance Brigade would prefer the person not be rolled on the floor. (See 'Burns and Scalds', page 155.)

If you are cut off by fire

1. Close the door of the room, close any fanlight or other opening and block up cracks with bedding, etc.

2. Go to the window and try to attract attention. If you cannot do this (because of smoke outside), try lying right down on the floor where the air is clearer.

3. If it gets so bad you must escape before the fire brigade arrives, make a rope by knotting sheets or similar materials. Tie one end to a bed or other heavy piece of furniture.

4. If you cannot make a rope, drop as many mattresses, cushions and other items as you can out of the window to break your fall. Get through the window feet first, lower yourself to the full extent of your arms and drop.

5. If the window will not open, break the glass with a heavy object. Try to clear jagged glass from the lower edge and, if possible, place a blanket over the sill before escaping.

What causes fires?

The following can all cause fires:
- cigarettes left burning

- smoking in bed
- children playing with matches
- sparks from open fires
- hot ashes put in cardboard boxes
- chip pans overheating
- badly placed electrical appliances
- faulty electrical equipment and wiring
- paraffin or gas heaters overturning
- flammable materials or tools kept in the house
- arson (wilful criminal damage).

Prevention   As well as avoiding the above, remember:

- Keep flammable liquids such as paraffin, turps, dry-cleaners and paint solvents in approved containers and never store them in under-stair cupboards or near an exit.
- Switch off and remove the plugs of electrical appliances when not in use (apart from those designed to remain switched on). This is especially important when you are going away.
- Unplug the television aerial cable if there is a chance of lightning.
- Have all electrical and gas appliances regularly checked.
- Electrical wiring can be overloaded by the misuse of multi-way adaptors: remember that one appliance, one socket is safest.
- If there is a power failure, turn off all electrical appliances (they might come on again when you are not at home).
- Never cover a lamp – and never run any electrical appliance off a lamp socket.

Try to have in the house:

- smoke detector
- smothering blanket
- fire-resistant chamber into which birth and marriage certificates, insurance policies, passports, wills and other valuable documents can be put
- fire extinguisher – make sure you buy a good one (ideally with the BSI kitemark BS5423) and be prepared to renew it at least every four years or have it serviced regularly. Learn how to use the extinguisher before you need it.

See   'Danger from Fire: How to Protect Your Home', Central Office of Information, HMSO
and an important selection of leaflets (send s.a.e.) from:

> British Fire Protection Systems Association
> 48a Eden Street
> Kingston upon Thames
> Surrey KTI IEE
>   01–549 5855

GAS
PROBLEMS
If you smell gas

1. Put out cigarettes, pilot lights and naked flames.
2. Do not use matches.
3. Do not turn any electrical switches on or off.
4. Open doors and windows.
5. Check to see if a gas tap has been left on or a pilot light has gone out.
6. If not, you may have a leak.

(a) turn off whole supply at the meter (see below)
(b) call your local gas service *immediately* ('Gas' in the telephone directory – or via 999), give them your name and address and tell them that you suspect a leak.

Prevention

● Make sure you know where to turn off the main gas supply. The main tap is near the gas meter: if the meter is in a special meter-box make sure you label the key and keep it in a handy place near the box.

● *To turn off the main gas supply:* turn off all appliance taps and pilot lights and turn the main gas tap to the OFF position – at a right angle to the pipe.
(If you have problems turning off the main supply, do not force the tap. Call your local gas service, who will loosen it, free of charge.)

● Buy appliances (see 'Gas Appliances', page 444) only with an approved label: BSI/QAC Safety Mark or British Gas Seal of Approval.

● Be careful about buying second-hand appliances – if in doubt, check with the gas service.

● Have installations and repairs undertaken only by British Gas or by a member of the Confederation for the Registration of Gas Installers (CORGI).

● Do have all appliances serviced regularly.

● Gas appliances must 'breathe' fresh air so that burning of the gas takes place safely and efficiently. Rooms therefore need ventilators, e.g. air brick, wall, door and/or window ventilators. Do not block them.

● Similarly, chimneys behind gas fires must be completely cleared of any debris. Have a chimney swept before installing a gas fire.

● If you have an old-fashioned open flue type gas water-heater in the bathroom: make sure the room is well ventilated; open the door or window while drawing off hot water; turn off the heater before getting in the bath; and do not run more hot water while you are in the tub.

● If you see any sooty marks, stains or discolorations around a water-heater or any appliance, or if there is an unusual smell, *do not use the appliance*. Turn it off and call your gas service.

● It is illegal to use or allow others to use an appliance you know or suspect to be dangerous. If you suspect an escape you must turn off your main gas supply immediately. (See 'Help Yourself to Gas Safety', available from gas showrooms.)

Help

If you have any complaints contact your regional Gas Consumers' Council (in the telephone directory under 'Gas'. The national headquarters is at:

National Gas Consumers' Council
5th floor, Estate House
130 Jermyn Street
London SW1Y 4UJ
01-930 7431

The headquarters of the British Gas Corporation is at:

59 Bryanston Street
London W1A 2AX
01-723 7030

If you want to know more about how to use gas wisely – and to belong to a network of homemakers, married or single, working closely with other women's organizations – contact:

Women's Gas Federation and Young Homemakers
Gaywood House
29 Great Peter Street
London SW1P 3LW
01-222 3677

GLASS INJURIES   Ordinary glass is brittle. Many forms of glass can, however, be toughened and to make sure your glazing is the safest possible for your particular needs, the Glass and Glazing Federation suggests you contact a local GGF member. Details from:

Glass and Glazing Federation
6 Mount Row
London W1Y 6DY
01–409 0545

PLUMBING PROBLEMS   At the first hint of any plumbing troubles, *turn the water off* (see 'Pipes (Frozen)', page 574).

If you need a plumber   The Institute of Plumbing recommends that you consult only a qualified plumber. Look at the Institute's 'Business Directory of Registered Plumbers', held in local libraries and many water board offices, or send an s.a.e. to:

Institute of Plumbing
64 Station Lane
Hornchurch
Essex RM12 6NB
040–24 72791

The Institute will also send you its detailed leaflet, 'Plumbing in the Home'. It contains a clear diagram of how household plumbing works and suggestions for care and maintenance.

Prevention   ● Locate the main STOPVALVE. This is usually under the sink. If you cannot see it there trace the kitchen cold pipe back to its source. Check that by turning it in a *clockwise* direction you shut the water supply off (you may find some water still coming to the kitchen cold tap even after you have turned the stopvalve off). If you cannot turn the stopvalve, oil the nut below the handle. If you still cannot turn it, call a plumber.

● Do not allow any taps to drip. Change the washers yourself or see your plumber.

● Ensure that the lavatory is working properly. If it continually refuses to fill, or drips incessantly, call a plumber.

● Do not discard any oil or fat down the sink.

● Inspect the cold water storage cistern regularly. If there are any signs of brown-and-white spots or patches – evidence of corrosion – call a plumber immediately.

● Check hosepipes on washing- and dishwashing-machines.

● Central heating should be professionally serviced annually.

● To prevent bursts and freeze-ups in frost, make sure all outside or exposed pipes and cisterns are insulated. If your loft has been insulated, exposed pipes and cisterns there will be even more likely to freeze. Remember, the best protection against freezing is to keep the house warm.

● Never leave fires or heaters in the loft.

Help   If you have any complaints about your local water authority, contact the local office (see 'Water' in the telephone directory).

The Water Authorities Association is at:

1 Queen Anne's Gate
London SW1H 9BT
01–222 8111

POISONING   This often results from children having access to medicines or household cleaners or from eating house or garden plants.

Prevention   Poisoning requires immediate medical attention – dial 999.

● Keep medicines in a locked cupboard out of the reach of children.

● Destroy surplus medicines and tablets by returning them to the chemist or by flushing them down the lavatory.

● Never encourage children to take medicine by calling it 'sweets'.

● Never transfer medicines from their original containers into other unmarked holders or, worse, to soft drinks bottles.

● Check dosage instructions carefully.

● Keep bleach and other household cleaners well out of the reach of children.

● If you transfer such agents to other containers, make sure they are clearly labelled.

SUFFOCATION   This may occur to babies in bed or during or after feeding.

Prevention   ● If a baby is temporarily placed in an adult's bed, watch him or her continuously and make sure no bedding covers the head.

● Never use soft pillows for infants. If a pillow is used, insert it under the head of the mattress.

- Hold a bottle-fed infant throughout the feed and remain long enough afterwards to see that he or she is properly 'winded'.
- Remove airtight rubber or plastic bibs after feeding.
- Do not let children play with plastic bags or in or near freezers or fridges.

QUICK
CHECKLIST
FOR HOME
SAFETY

ENTRANCE
Is it well lit?
Is the doormat 'sunk'?

HALL AND DOWNSTAIRS CORRIDORS
- Is the floor surface non-slip?

LIVING-ROOM
- Are carpets and rugs in good repair?
- Are there sufficient electrical power points for all appliances?
- Is the fire well guarded?
- Is the mirror placed well away from the fireplace?

KITCHEN
- Are all cleaning agents away from children?
- Is the cooker well maintained and working properly?
- Do you wipe the floor immediately after spilling any fat or liquid on it?
- Do you have enough working surfaces at the correct height?

STAIRS
- Is the stair carpet firmly fixed and in good repair?
- Are the banisters firm and strong and sufficient for safety?
- Is the light operated by a return switch for use at top or bottom of stairs?
- Are the stairs free from obstruction?

BEDROOM
- Are fires suitably guarded with fixed guards?
- Are electric blankets in good working order?
- Do they have the BEAB seal of approval?

BATHROOM
- Are medicine and toiletries out of children's reach?
- Are there safety-rails by the baths and lavatories?
- Are there non-slip strips or mats in bathtubs and showers?
- Are lights operated by pull-cords?
- If there are electric wall heaters, are they set high enough?

ELECTRICAL
- Do you have plugs firmly plugged into socket outlets?
- Are you sure you do not have the following:
  fuses that frequently blow?
  wiring over twenty-five years old?
  several fuse boxes?
  wide use of extension leads?

flexes that trail over the floor and under carpets?
wiring extension that has been carried out by amateurs?
- Do you know where the fuse box is?
- Do you know where the main on/off switch is?

Help Further tips on safety, both inside the house and outside, are available from the Royal Society for the Prevention of Accidents. For details of their publications and prices contact (s.a.e.) the society at:

Canon House
The Priory
Queensway
Birmingham B4 6BS
021–233 2461

Emergency Home Repairs

CENTRAL HEATING PROBLEMS   PIPES (FROZEN)
DRAINS (BLOCKED)   SINKS (BLOCKED)
GUTTERS (BLOCKED)   TAPS (DRIPPING)
LAVATORY PROBLEMS   WINDOW REPAIRS

CENTRAL HEATING PROBLEMS

The main problem is caused by air getting into the system and thus into the radiators. This may mean that no water circulates at all. Only the lowest part of each radiator will have any heat.

To remove air from radiators you need a radiator key with which to turn the bleed screw. *Be patient* – do not try to do it in a hurry. Turn the bleed screw very, very slowly, holding a J-cloth around the key. Listen to the air coming out (it will hiss). When water reaches the top of the radiator, retighten.

If air gets into the pipes, release it by undoing the 'vent nipple' near the boiler. As with the radiator valves, close as soon as water begins to flow.

DRAINS (BLOCKED)

There are two tell-tale signs:
1. A sink or lavatory becomes blocked or slow to empty.
2. The outside gulley (ground overflow) becomes blocked – it may just be choked with leaves or hair.

If you cannot immediately determine the cause of blockage, check the manholes. Start with the manhole nearest the house and go on until you find a manhole with no water in it. The blockage is between the last filled manhole and the empty one. (If all manholes are filled, the blockage is between the last manhole and the drain-cleaning cover.)

To clear the blockage, you can:
- use a set of flexible bamboo 'cleaning rods'

- try to move the obstruction with a garden hose, turned on at full pressure
- call a plumber or specialist drain cleaner like Dyno-rod. See 'Drains' in Yellow Pages. Many Dyno-rod numbers operate 24-hours. The main headquarters is at:

> Dyno-rod
> 143 Maple Road
> Surbiton
> Surrey KT6 4BJ
> 01–549 9711

ELECTRICAL EMERGENCIES   See 'Electrical Problems and Accidents', page 562.

FLOOD CLEARANCE   Contact Dyno-rod (address above).

GAS EMERGENCIES   See 'Gas Problems', page 569.

GUTTERS (BLOCKED)   Extra weight of water accumulating in a gutter can cause it to collapse. If necessary – and if possible – check that the top of the downpipe is clear. Try to prevent blocks by regular cleaning out.

LAVATORY PROBLEMS   If the cistern does not fill or if it flushes continuously, take the lid off and check that none of the parts of the flushing system has become disconnected. If all looks in order, manually bend the ball arm gently up and down. If that still does not work, call a plumber.

  If the lavatory is blocked and you do not have a large plunger, try forcing a thin wire clothes hanger around the bend.

PIPES (FROZEN)
- Turn off main inside stopvalve (A on diagram) or, if you cannot find it, outside stopvalve (B on diagram).
- Allow the boiler to go out: should any part of the hot water system be frozen there could be risk of explosion.
- Check that the ice has not cracked the tank before thawing.
- Reactivate the pipe *slowly*. Never use a blow-lamp or other naked flame.
- Apply gentle heat from a hair dryer (lowest setting) or wrap the affected area in rags soaked in hot water.
- Start thawing at the end of the pipe nearest the tap and work away from it.
- Even if water flows from the taps, this does not prove that no other part of the system is frozen.

Burst pipes
- Turn off the water. Go first to stopvalve A on the diagram. If you

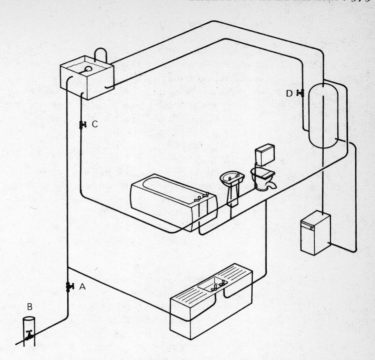

cannot find it – or if the pipe bursts in the garden – turn off stopvalve B on the diagram. If burst is on a pipe supplying water from the storage cistern, turn off stopvalve C: if burst is on a pipe supplying hot water, close stopvalve D.

- Collect some cold water in the bath for washing and wc flushing until supply can be restored.
- Do not open the hot taps as there could be a risk of the hot water cylinder collapsing if the feed and vent pipes connected to it are frozen.
- Turn off the central heating and let the fire in a solid fuel boiler die down.
- Switch off the electric immersion heater.
- Call a plumber.

SINKS (BLOCKED)
- Plug the overflow.
- Half-fill the sink.
- Force a plastic-ended plunger up and down over the drain until the blockage clears (if you do not have a plunger, nail a sponge to the end of a broom handle, cover the sponge with a plastic bag firmly tied around the wooden handle).
- If this does not work, unscrew the U-trap underneath the sink and pull the blockage out from below.

TAPS (DRIPPING) The washer on a tap is a little rubber or plastic-rubber ring. To change the washer:
- Turn off the water supply to that tap (there is usually a stopvalve near the sink, or near the cold or hot tanks).
- Turn tap on fully.
- Put waste plug in sink, in case you drop a small essential part.
- With metal handle taps, remove grub screw and tap top, wrap tap shield with a cloth and unscrew and remove it (many newer taps have a large top which just pulls off).
- Unscrew the large hexagonal nut and lift away the tap mechanism from the base.
- The washer is usually held in place by a small nut or a screw. Remove this, change the washer (the maker's name on the washer should face *down* as the tap is reassembled), replace the nut or screw.
- Reassemble the tap.
- Turn on the water supply and turn off the tap gently. It should not now drip. If it still does, it may need re-seating – probably a job for a plumber.

WINDOW REPAIRS To effect a temporary replacement window pane, take a strong sheet of polythene. Place it on the inside of the window. Put dowel or suitable lengths of wood (parts of broom handles, perhaps) around the inner frame of the window and hold with small nails, thus supporting the plastic.

Help
- SOS Services provide emergency help (electricians, plumbing, etc.). They cover nearly all the UK: you can get details of your nearest 'crisis centre' telephone number from Directory Inquiries or from 01–969 1000 (24-hours). For details of SOS send a large s.a.e. to:

> SOS Services UK
> Tudor House
> 5 Llanvanor Road
> London NW2 2AR

Safety at Work

It is the legal duty of employers to make sure, 'so far as reasonably possible, the health, safety and welfare at work' of all employees. Similarly, it is the duty of every employee while at work to take 'reasonable care for the health and safety' of herself and all other persons. Checking is done by inspectors from the Health and Safety Commission.

If you are injured while you are at work you may be liable for compensation. If you think you have any cause for complaint, go to your local authority or ask the Citizens' Advice Bureau.

The British Safety Council offers industry a comprehensive range of occupational health, safety and fire training programmes. Its objectives include enabling employers to manage safety effectively and employees to work safely and without injury. Full details from:

> British Safety Council
> National Safety House
> Chancellor's Road
> London w6 9rs
> 01–741 1231

Further Information

Suggested further reading

PROTECT YOURSELF

London Rape Crisis Centre, *Sexual Violence: the Reality for Women*, Women's Press

Martin, Del, *Battered Wives*, Volcano Press

Medea, Andra and Kathleen Thompson, *Against Rape: a Survival Manual for Women*, Farrar, Straus & Giroux

Nelson, Sarah, *Incest: Fact and Myth*, Stramullion Co-op

Ward, Elizabeth, *Father Daughter Rape*, Women's Press

PROTECT YOUR PROPERTY

Consumers' Association, *Securing Your Home*

Hasler, Gordon, *Protect Your Property and Defend Yourself*, Penguin

HOME EMERGENCIES AND REPAIRS

Consumers' Association, *Dealing with Household Emergencies*

Ingham, Andrew, *Self-help House Repairs Manual*, Penguin

Reader's Digest Repair Manual

20 Further Useful Information

This chapter contains a miscellany of all the things that we wanted to include in *The Complete Woman's Almanac* and which did not really logically come under any of the other chapter headings. Here you can find out, for instance, about other forms of medicine and about various campaigns and charities. In many cases there has been room only for the organization's address and telephone number, so if you want to know more contact them direct (please always send an s.a.e. when you write).

ALTERNA-
TIVE
MEDICINE

The following are names and addresses of organizations that are not part of the National Health Service.

Anglo-European College of
  Chiropractic
13–15 Parkwood Road
Bournemouth
Hants BH5 2DF
  0202–431028

British Acupuncture Association
  and Register
34 Alderney Street
London SW1V 4EU
  01–834 1012

British Chiropractors' Association
5 First Avenue
Chelmsford
Essex CM1 1RY
  0245–358487

British Herbal Medicine
  Association
Lane House
Cowling
Keighley
West Yorks BD22 0LX
  0535–34487

British Homoeopathic Association
27a Devonshire Street
London W1N 1RJ
  01–935 2163

British Naturopathic and
  Osteopathic College
6 Netherhall Gardens
London NW3 5RR
  01–435 8728

Faculty of Homoeopathy
Royal London Homoeopathic
  Hospital
Great Ormond Street
London WCIN 3HR
  01–837 7821

General Council and Register of
  Consultant Herbalists
1 Meadfoot Close
50 Ilsham Road
Torquay
Devon TQI 2JJ
  0803–22375

General Council and Register of
  Osteopaths
1–4 Suffolk Street
London SWIY 4HG
  01–839 2060

Incorporated Society of Registered
  Naturopaths
328 Harrogate Road
Leeds LSI7 6PE
  0532–685992

Institute for Complementary
  Medicine
21 Portland Place
London WIN 3AF
  01–636 9543

National Federation of Spiritual
  Healers
Old Manor Farm Studio
Church Street
Sunbury-on-Thames
Middlesex TXI6 6RG
  09327–83164

National Institute of Medical
  Herbalists
41 Hatherley Road
Winchester
Hants SO22 6RR
  0962–68776

For further information and leaflets on many different kinds of alternative medicine send s.a.e. to Institute for Complementary Medicine (address above).

CONVER-
SIONS,
WEIGHTS
AND
MEASURES

Length
Imperial/metric
1 in. = 2.54 cm
1 ft = 30.5 cm
1 yd = 91.44 cm
1 mile = 1.61 km
(5 miles is roughly equal to 8 km)

1 cm = 0.39 in.
1 m = 39.37 ins or 3.28 ft
1 km = 0.62 mile

Imperial
12 in. = 1 ft
3 ft = 1 yd
1,760 yds = 1 mile
6,080 ft = 1 nautical mile

Area
1 acre = 0.405 ha (hectares)

1 ha = 2.47 acres

Weight/mass
Imperial/metric

1 oz = 28.35 g	1 g = 0.035 oz
1 lb = 454 g	1 kg = 2.21 lb
1 stone = 6.35 kg	1 tonne (1,000 kg) = 0.98 ton
1 UK ton = 1.016 tonnes	

Imperial
16 oz = 1 lb
14 lb = 1 stone
8 stones = 1 cwt
20 cwt = 1 ton (2,240 lb)

Volume/capacity
Imperial/metric

1 fl. oz = 28.4 ml	1 dl (100 ml) = 3.5 fl. oz
1 UK pint = 0.57 l	1 l (1,000 ml or 1,000 cc) =
1 UK gall. = 4.55 l	1.76 UK pints

Imperial
5 fl. oz = 1 gill
4 gills = 1 pt
2 pts = 1 qt
4 qts = 1 gall.

Paper sizes
A4 = 210 × 297 mm
    (8.27″ × 11.69″)
A5 = 148 × 210 mm
    (5.83″ × 8.27″)

Temperature
To convert Fahrenheit to centigrade (Celsius):
subtract 32 from degrees Fahrenheit, multiply by 5, divide by 9.
To convert centigrade to Fahrenheit: multiply degrees centigrade by 9, divide by 5 and add 32.

● For over temperature conversion chart, see page 455.

Tyre pressures
24 lb/sq. in. = 1.69 kg/sq. cm
26 lb/sq. in. = 1.83 kg/sq. cm
28 lb/sq. in. = 1.97 kg/sq. cm

Speed
Imperial/metric

50 km/h = 31 mph	Imperial
100 km/h = 62 mph	1 knot = 1 nautical mile/h
	66 knots = 76 mph

DISABILITIES Here are some national organizations which offer advice and support: many other disabilities such as migraine are covered in Chapter 6, and you can find the appropriate page via the index.

The Royal Association for Disability and Rehabilitation (RADAR) is the principal umbrella organization for other groups which concern themselves with the problems experienced by physically disabled people. In addition to maintaining contact with other organizations, RADAR provides many of its own services for disabled people and for those who care for them.

RADAR can provide information and advice on all aspects of physical disability (from, 'Where can I hire a wheelchair for two weeks while on holiday?' to 'How can this building be adapted to cater for disabled people?'). RADAR's services include help on social security and social services provision, housing, education, employment, transport and mobility and general welfare. Monthly and quarterly publications are available. For details of these and all other services please send a large s.a.e. to:

Royal Association
for Disability and Rehabilitation
25 Mortimer Street
London WIN 8AB
01–637 5400

Greater London Association
for Disabled People (GLAD)
1 Thorpe Close
London WID 5XL
01–960 5799

Scottish Council on Disability
(SCD)
Princes House
5 Shandwick Place
Edinburgh EH2 4RG
031–229 8632

Wales Council for the Disabled
(WCD)
Lys Ilfor, Crescent Road
Caerphilly
Mid Glam CF8 1XL
0222–869224

These are some of the organizations that make life easier for those with, in some cases, major handicaps:

St Loye's College for Training
the Disabled for Commerce and
Industry
Fairfield House
Topsham Road
Exeter
Devon EX2 6EP
0392–55428

Scottish Centre for the Tuition
of the Disabled
Queen Margaret College
Clerwood Terrace
Edinburgh EH12 8TS
031–339 5408

Thistle Foundation
27a Walker Street
Edinburgh EH3 7HX
031–225 7282

*Aid and
information* A whole variety of aids is available for those with handicaps. Support groups provide information and moral support. Here are some helpful organizations:

Disabled Drivers' Association
Ashwellthorpe
Norwich NR16 1EX
050–841449

Disabled Living Foundation
380–384 Harrow Road
London W9 2HU
01–289 6111

Guide Dogs for the Blind
  Association
Alexandra House
9–11 Park Street
Windsor
Berks SL4 1JR
07535–55711

Mobility Information Service
Copthorne Community Hall
Shelton Road
Shrewsbury
Shropshire SY3 8TD
0743–68383

Talking Books for the Handicapped
  (National Listening Library)
12 Lant Street
London SE1 1QR
01–407 9417

Wireless for the Bedridden Society
81b Corbets Tey Road
Upminster
Essex RM14 2AJ
040–22 50051

See 'Door to Door: a Guide to Transport for Disabled People', Department of Transport, HMSO.

Sports and leisure

British Sports Association
  for the Disabled
Hayward House
Ludwig Guttmann Sports Centre
  for the Disabled
Stoke Mandeville
Harvey Road
Aylesbury
Bucks HP21 8PP
0296–27889

Riding for the Disabled Association
Avenue R
National Agricultural Centre
Kenilworth
Warwicks CV8 2LY
0203–56107

Scottish Sports Association
  for the Disabled
14 Gordon Court
Dalcaverhouse
Dundee DD4 9DE
0382–40263

For details of clubs and holidays for the disabled contact:

Physically Handicapped and Able-Bodied (PHAB)
42 Devonshire Street
London W1N 1LN
01–637 7475

Among travel companies specially catering for the disabled holidaymaker is Threshold Travel – they understand problems of mobility and trying to cope with the customs officials and so on:

Threshold Travel
2 Whitworth Street West
Manchester M1 5WX
061–236 9763

Support groups

Action against Allergy
43 The Downs
London SW20 8HG
01–947 5082

Arthritis Care
6 Grosvenor Crescent
London SW1X 7ER
01–235 0902

Association for Research into
  Restricted Growth
5 Teak Walk
Witham
Essex CM8 2SX
0376–517030

Association for Spina Bifida and
  Hydrocephalus
Tavistock House North
Tavistock Square
London WC1H 9HJ
01–388 1382

Asthma Research Council
St Thomas's Hospital
Lambeth Palace Road
London SE1 7EH
01–928 3099

British Association for
  Rheumatology and
  Rehabilitation
11 St Andrew's Place
London NW1 4LE
01–486 2641

British Association for the
  Hard of Hearing
7–11 Armstrong Road
London W3 7JL
01–743 1492

British Association of Myasthenics
38 Selwood Road
Brentwood
Essex CM14 4PX
0277–218082

British Deaf Association
38 Victoria Place
Carlisle CA1 1HV

British Kidney Patient Association
Bordon
Hants GU35 9JP
04203–2022

British Polio Fellowship
Bell Close
West End Road
Ruislip
Middlesex HA4 6LP
089–56 75515

British Retinitis Pigmentosa
  Society
24 Palmer Close
Redhill
Surrey RH1 4BX
0737–61937

Brittle Bone Society
112 City Road
Dundee DD2 2PW
0382–67603

Chest, Heart and Stroke
  Association
Tavistock House North
Tavistock Square
London WC1H 9JE
01–387 3012

Coeliac Society of the United
  Kingdom
PO Box 181
London NW2 2QY
01–459 2440

Colostomy Welfare Group
38–9 Eccleston Square
London SW1V 1PB
01–828 5175

Edinburgh Cripple Aid Society
28–30 Howden Street
Edinburgh EH8 9HW
031–668 2877

Friedreich's Ataxia Group
Burleigh Lodge
Knowle Lane
Cranleigh
Surrey GU6 8RD
0483–272741

Greater London Fund for the Blind
2 Wyndham Place
London W1H 2AQ
01–262 0191

Haemophilia Society
PO Box 9
16 Trinity Street
London SE1 1DE
01–407 1010

Ileostomy Association of Great
   Britain and Northern Ireland
Amblehurst House
Chobham
Surrey GU24 8PZ
09905–8277

Leukaemia Society
PO Box 82
Exeter
Devon EX2 5DP
0392–218514

Multiple Sclerosis Society
286 Munster Road
London SW6 6AP
01–381 4022

Muscular Dystrophy Group of
   Great Britain and Northern
   Ireland
Nattrass House
35 Macaulay Road
London SW4 0QP
01–720 8055

National Ankylosing Spondylitis
   Society
6 Grosvenor Crescent
London SW1X 7ER
01–235 9585

National Autistic Society
276 Willesden Lane
London NW2 5RB
01–451 3844

National Reye's
   Syndrome Foundation
55 High St
Banbury
Oxon OX16 8ET

Parkinson's Disease Society
81 Queen's Road
London SW19 8LR
01–946 2500

Partially Sighted Society
40 Wordsworth Street
Hove
East Sussex BN3 5BH
0273–736053

Psoriasis Association
7 Milton Street
Northampton NN2 7JG
0604–711129

Royal Association in Aid of the
   Deaf and Dumb
27 Old Oak Road
London W3 7HN
01–743 6187

Royal National Institute for the
   Blind
224 Great Portland Street
London W1N 6AA
01–388 1266

Royal National Institute for the
   Deaf
105 Gower Street
London WC1E 6AH
01–387 8033

Scottish Council for Spastics
22 Corstorphine Road
Edinburgh EH12 6HP
031–337 9876

Scottish Spinal Cord Injury
Association
3 Cargill Terrace
Edinburgh EH5 3ND
031–552 8459

Scottish Spina Bifida Association
190 Queensferry Road
Edinburgh EH4 2BW
031–332 0743

Spastics Society
12 Park Crescent
London W1N 4EQ
01–636 5020

Spinal Injuries Association
5 Crowndale Road
London NW1 1TU
01–388 6840

Tuberous Sclerosis Association of
Great Britain
Martell Mount
Holywell Road
Malvern Wells
Worcs WR14 4LF
06845–63150

EX-SERVICE ORGAN-IZATIONS

The Regular Forces Employment Association works closely with Man-power Services Commission and the Forces Resettlement Branches to assist those from the non-commissioned ranks to find jobs:

> Regular Forces Employment Association
> 25 Bloomsbury Square
> London WC1A 2LN
> 01–637 3918

Here are some of the groups which help those coming out of the services to find jobs and to provide aid and support in many different ways:

British Limbless Ex-Servicemen's
Association
24 Dundas Street
Edinburgh EH3 6JN
031–556 6828

Ex-Services Mental Welfare Society
37 Thurloe Street
London SW7 2LL
01–584 8688 and
3 Cadogan Street
Glasgow G2 6QE
041–221 1303

Royal British Legion
48 Pall Mall
London SW1Y 5JY
01–930 8131

Royal British Legion – Scotland
New Haig House
Logie Green Road
Edinburgh EH7 4HR
031–557 2782

FOREIGN VISITORS AND RESIDENTS

If you are from another country and you need help or further information, contact your embassy, high commission or legation. Here are the main telephone numbers (try to telephone during weekday office hours).

AFGHANISTAN (Embassy of the Democratic Republic of Afghanis-tan): 01–589 8891

AUSTRALIA (Australian High Commission): 01–438 8000

AUSTRIA (Austrian Embassy): 01–235 3731

BAHAMAS (Bahamas High Commission): 01–930 6967

BAHRAIN (Embassy of the State of Bahrain): 01–370 5132
BANGLADESH (Bangladesh High Commission): 01–584 0081
BARBADOS (Barbados High Commission): 01–235 8686
BELGIUM (Belgian Embassy): 01–235 5422
BELIZE (Belize High Commission): 01–486 8381
BOLIVIA (Embassy of Bolivia): 01–235 4248
BOTSWANA (Botswana High Commission): 01–730 5216
BRAZIL (Brazilian Embassy): 01–499 0877
BULGARIA (Embassy of the People's Republic of Bulgaria): 01–584 9400
BURMA (Burmese Embassy): 01–629 6966

CAMEROONS (Cameroon Embassy) 01–727 0771
CANADA (Canadian High Commission): 01–409 2071
CAYMAN ISLANDS (Government Office): 01–408 2482
CHILE (Chilean Embassy): 01–580 6392
CHINA (Chinese Embassy): 01–636 5726
COLOMBIA (Colombian Embassy): 01–589 9177
COSTA RICA (Costa Rican Embassy): 01–373 0197
CYPRUS (Cyprus High Commission): 01–499 8272
CZECHOSLOVAKIA (Czechoslovak Embassy): 01–229 1255

DENMARK (Danish Embassy): 01–235 1255
DOMINICAN REPUBLIC (Dominican Republic Embassy): 01–937 1921

ECUADOR (Ecuadorean Embassy): 01–584 1367
EGYPT (Embassy of Arab Republic of Egypt): 01–499 2401
EL SALVADOR (Embassy of El Salvador): 01–486 8182
ETHIOPIA (Ethiopian Embassy): 01–589 7212

FIJI (Fiji High Commission): 01–584 3661
FINLAND (Finnish Embassy): 01–235 9531
FRANCE (French Embassy): 01–235 8080

GABON (Gabonese Embassy): 01–937 5285
GERMANY, EAST (Embassy of the German Democratic Republic):
    01–235 9941
GERMANY, WEST (Embassy of the Federal Republic of Germany):
    01–235 5033
GHANA (High Commissioner for Ghana): 01–235 4142
GREECE (Greek Consulate General): 01–727 0635
GRENADA (Grenada High Commission): 01–373 7808
GUYANA (High Commissioner for Guyana): 01–229 7684

HONDURAS (Honduras Republic Embassy): 01–486 4880
HONG KONG (Hong Kong Government Office): 01–499 9821
HUNGARY (Hungarian Embassy): 01–235 4048

ICELAND (Icelandic Embassy): 01–730 5131
INDIA (High Commissioner for India): 01–836 8484
INDONESIA (Embassy of the Republic of Indonesia): 01–499 7661

IRAN (Embassy of the Islamic Republic of Iran): 01–937 5225
IRAQ (Iraqi Embassy): 01–584 7141
IRELAND (Irish Embassy): 01–235 2171
ISRAEL (Embassy of Israel): 01–937 8050
ITALY (Italian Embassy): 01–629 8200
IVORY COAST (Ivory Coast Embassy): 01–235 6991

JAMAICA (Jamaican High Commission): 01–493 3647
JAPAN (Japanese Embassy): 01–493 6030
JORDAN (Jordan Embassy): 01–937 9611

KENYA (Kenya High Commission): 01–434 2970
KOREA (Korean Embassy): 01–581 0247
KUWAIT (Embassy of the State of Kuwait): 01–588 8471

LAOS (Laos Embassy): 01–937 9519
LEBANON (Lebanese Embassy): 01–229 7265
LIBERIA (Liberian Embassy): 01–589 9405
LUXEMBURG (Luxemburg Embassy): 01–235 6961

MALAWI (Malawi High Commission): 01–491 4172
MALAYSIA (Malaysia High Commissioner): 01–235 8033
MALTA (Malta High Commission): 01–938 1712
MAURITIUS (Mauritius High Commission): 01–581 0294
MEXICO (Mexican Embassy): 01–235 6393
MONACO (Consulate General of Monaco): 01–629 0734
MONGOLIA (Mongolian Embassy): 01–937 5238
MOROCCO (Moroccan Embassy): 01–581 5001

NEPAL (Royal Nepalese Embassy): 01–229 1594
NETHERLANDS (Netherlands Embassy): 01–584 5040
NEW ZEALAND (High Commissioner for New Zealand): 01–930 8422
NICARAGUA (Embassy of Nicaragua): 01–584 4365
NIGERIA (Nigeria High Commission): 01–839 1244
NORWAY (Royal Norwegian Embassy): 01–235 7151

OMAN (Embassy of the Sultanate of Oman): 01–584 6782

PAKISTAN (Embassy of Pakistan): 01–235 2044
PANAMA (Embassy of Panama): 01–930 1591
PAPUA NEW GUINEA (Papua New Guinea High Commission): 01–930 0922
PARAGUAY (Paraguay Embassy): 01–937 1253
PERU (Peruvian Embassy): 01–235 1917
PHILIPPINES (Philippine Embassy): 01–937 1609
POLAND (Embassy of the Polish People's Republic): 01–580 4324
PORTUGAL (Portuguese Embassy): 01–235 5331

QATAR (Qatar Embassy): 01–373 5182

ROMANIA (Romanian Embassy): 01–235 0388

SAUDI ARABIA (Royal Embassy of Saudi Arabia): 01–235 0831
SENEGAL (Embassy of the Republic of Senegal): 01–937 0925
SEYCHELLES (Seychelles High Commission): 01–439 9699
SIERRA LEONE (Sierra Leone High Commission): 01–636 6483
SINGAPORE (High Commissioner for the Republic of Singapore): 01–235 8315
SOMALIA (Somali Embassy): 01–580 7148
SOUTH AFRICA (South African Embassy): 01–930 4488
SPAIN (Spanish Embassy): 01–235 5555
SRI LANKA (High Commissioner for Sri Lanka): 01–262 1841
SUDAN (Sudan Embassy): 01–839 8080
SWAZILAND (High Commissioner for the Kingdom of Swaziland): 01–581 4976
SWEDEN (Swedish Embassy): 01–724 2101
SWITZERLAND (Swiss Embassy): 01–723 0701
SYRIA (Syrian Arab Republic Embassy): 01–245 9012

TANZANIA (High Commission of Tanzania): 01–499 8951
THAILAND (Royal Thai Embassy): 01–589 0173
TONGA (Tonga High Commission): 01–839 3287
TRINIDAD AND TOBAGO (Trinidad and Tobago High Commission): 01–245 9351
TUNISIA (Tunisian Embassy): 01–584 8117
TURKEY (Turkish Embassy): 01–235 5252

UGANDA (Uganda High Commission): 01–839 5783
URUGUAY (Consulate of Uruguay): 01–589 8735
UAE (United Arab Emirates Embassy): 01–589 3434
USA (American Embassy): 01–499 9000
USSR (Soviet Embassy): 01–229 6412

VENEZUELA (Venezuelan Consulate General): 01–589 9916
VIETNAM (Vietnam Embassy): 01–937 1912

YEMEN, NORTH (Yemen Arab Republic Embassy): 01–629 9905
YEMEN, SOUTH (Yemen People's Democratic Republic): 01–584 6607

YUGOSLAVIA (Yugoslav Embassy) 01–370 6105

ZAIRE (Diplomatic Mission of the Republic of Zaire): 01–235 7122
ZAMBIA (Zambia High Commission): 01–580 0691
ZIMBABWE (Zimbabwe High Commission) 01–836 7755

Note: the following countries do not have any official representation in the British Isles. If you need to make contact, ask the local police or your Citizens' Advice Bureau for information as to who handles their affairs:

Albania	Cape Verde Islands
Angola	Central African Republic
Argentina	Chad
Burundi	Congo People's Republic

Djibouti Republic
Guatemala
Guinea-Bissau
Guinea Equatorial
Guinea Republic
Libya

Madagascar Democratic Republic
Mali
Mauritania Islamic Republic
Mozambique
Niger
Rwanda

GAMBLING

Gambling can be an addiction. If you have gambling problems or you know someone who does, contact:

Gamblers Anonymous
17–23 Blantyre Street
London SW10 8EU
01–352 3060

Another group which offers support to relatives of gamblers is:

Gam Anon
17–23 Blantyre Street
London SW10 0DT
01–352 3060

HOME HELP

Many older people and others who need 'housekeeping skills' done for them at home rely with gratitude and praise on their Home Helps. If you want to know more about this service and whether or not you are entitled to help, ask your doctor or contact your local Home Help Service (via the index of the telephone Yellow Pages).

If you need help or relief on a temporary basis you should talk to your Health Visitor or Citizens' Advice Bureau. The Leonard Cheshire Foundation may also be able to assist with part-time help (and they are always looking for volunteers to provide that help):

Leonard Cheshire Foundation
26–9 Maunsel Street
London SW1P 2QN
01–828 1822

HOMELESS-NESS

If you find you are without a roof over your head you can contact your Citizens' Advice Bureau or one of these organizations:

SHAC (The London Housing Aid Centre)
189a Old Brompton Road
London SW5 0AR
01–373 7276

Shelter National Campaign for the Homeless
157 Waterloo Road
London SE1 8XF
01–633 9377

Scottish Council for Single Homeless
4 Old Assembly Close
Edinburgh EH1 1QX
031–226 4382

Shelter Scottish Campaign for the Homeless
65 Cockburn Street
Edinburgh EH1 1BU
031–226 6347

If you are squatting, you have your own advisory service: telephone 01–359 8814.

**IMMIGRA-
TION**

If you are trying to sponsor a relative to come to Britain or you want to bring a partner here – or if you have any problems relating to immigration and nationality law, contact (s.a.e.):

> Joint Council for the Welfare of Immigrants
> 44 Theobalds Road
> London WC1X 8SP
> 01–405 5527

INVENTIONS

If you want to protect your invention you will need a patent. Ask for the free booklet 'Applying for a Patent' from:

> Patent Office
> 25 Southampton Buildings
> London WC2A 1AY
> 01–405 8721

Help with applying for a patent can be obtained via:

> Chartered Institute of Patent Agents
> Staple Inn Buildings
> London WC1V 7PZ
> 01–405 9450

**LEFT-HANDED
PEOPLE**

There are now many useful inventions for left-handed people, who represent some 20 per cent of the total population. A specialist shop for left-handed people sells a variety of much-needed items from a potato peeler to pruning shears to italic pens and pinking shears. Mail order catalogue (+ two second-class stamps):

> Anything Left Handed Ltd
> 65 Beak Street
> London W1R 3LF
> 01–437 3910

**LONELINESS
AND
MEETING
PEOPLE**

Many, many people are lonely: an opinion poll (published in the *Sunday Times*, 11 December 1983) indicated that it is more common among the 15 to 24 age group, becomes less prevalent during middle age and becomes a problem again later on.

Dordie Daniels comes across many lonely people in her clinic and counselling (see Chapter 8). She encourages young mothers tied with a new baby or unsure of themselves to try and organize at least one evening a week when they can go out and do something they enjoy.

If you are a single parent you will find that Gingerbread offers social as well as supportive help (see page 295). If you are widowed, Cruse will help you regain a social life and offer counselling help (see page 231).

You can be lonely within a secure partnership. If you and your partner cannot solve the problem contact your local Marriage Guidance Council (page 260) where counsellors know how to help you.

Many courses and programmes are available to help people who are lonely gain in assertiveness and self-confidence.

Fulfilling your personal and social life

Career success is often achieved at the expense of a fulfilling personal and social life. One aspect of dissatisfaction may be a lack of satisfying personal and social relationships.

There are, fortunately, a number of ways in which women who find themselves in this position can begin to redress the balance. There are courses, for instance, designed to help participants look at their behaviour and the things that happen to them, and to identify areas in which they would like to make changes. These courses have such titles as 'Assertiveness training', 'Self-development' and 'Relationship workshops'. (You can find out about such courses through advertisements in *City Limits*, *New Society*, *Spare Rib* and *Time Out*.)

For those who want to nurture their physical well-being there are courses on aerobics, massage, meditation, self-defence and yoga. You can also spend time enjoyably in a sauna or Turkish bath.

If you want more information on combating loneliness contact (s.a.e.):

> Skills with People
> 15 Liberia Road
> London N5 1JP
> 01-359 2370

Some organizations which provide opportunities for social meetings are:

National Federation of Eighteen
Plus Groups
Nicholson House
Old Court Road
Newent
Glos GL18 1AG
0531-821210

National Federation of Solo Clubs
Room 8 Ruskin Chambers
191 Corporation Street
Birmingham B4 6RY
021-236 2879

If you are looking for a partner there are advertisements in magazines such as *Time Out* and in the personal columns of most national and local newspapers.

MENTAL
HANDICAPS

When it comes to mental ill-health far too little is understood by the general public. Here are some organizations which do understand:

National Association for Mental
Health (MIND)
22 Harley Street
London WIN 2ED
01-637 0741

National Federation of Gateway
Clubs
117-23 Golden Lane
London ECI ORT
01-253 9433

Open Door (Agoraphobia)
447 Pensby Road
Heswall
Merseyside L61 9PQ
    051-648 2022

Phobics Society
4 Cheltenham Road
Chorlton-cum-Hardy
Manchester M21 1QN
    061-881 1937

Royal Society
    for Mentally Handicapped
    Children
    and Adults (MENCAP)
117–23 Golden Lane
London EC1 ORT
    01-253 9433

Scottish Association for Mental
    Health
40 Shandwick Place
Edinburgh EH2 4RT
    031–225 4446

Scottish Society for the Mentally
    Handicapped
13 Elmbank Street
Glasgow G2 4QA
    041-226 4541

See also 'Anxiety and Depression', page 177, and 'Dieting Problems' (Anorexia nervosa and Bulimia nervosa), page 389ff.

OFFENDERS   National Prisoners' Movement (PROP) is a pressure group campaigning for the improvement of conditions for people in prison:

National Prisoners' Movement
BM-PROP
London WC1N 3XX
    01-542 3744

Other groups are concerned with families and with rehabilitation:

National Association for the Care and Resettlement of Offenders
    (NACRO)
169 Clapham Road
London SW9 OPU
    01-582 6500

Prisoners' Wives and Families Society
254 Caledonian Road
London N1 ONG
    01-278 3981

Scottish Association for the Care and Resettlement of Offenders
    (SACRO)
53 George Street
Edinburgh EH2 2ET
    031-226 4222

PEACE   Whether or not you believe in nuclear disarmament, it is a highly emotive issue, for and against which many women are determined and brave enough to subject themselves to vigils and protests. If you want to learn more about both sides of the story, contact:

> Campaign for Nuclear Disarmament (CND)
> 11 Goodwin Street
> London N4 3HQ
> 01-263 0977

> Women and Families for Defence
> 1 Lincoln's Inn Fields
> London WC2A 3AA
> 01-831 9001

The latter was started by Lady Olga Maitland, to work for peace through defence.

SAMARITANS

Whatever the emergency, you can ring the Samaritans at any time.

A volunteer will listen and try to help you, or you can visit a centre any day or evening all in complete confidence.

There are over 174 Samaritan centres and you can find the nearest one in your local telephone directory. Alternatively, if you prefer to write to a volunteer there are three main correspondence branches:

> PO Box 9
> Stirling FK8 2SA

> PO Box 10
> Northallerton DL7 8XW

> PO Box B8
> Huddersfield HD1 1HR

Offers of help and financial assistance should also be made to your most convenient centre. The head office is at:

> 17 Uxbridge Road
> Slough SL1 1SN
> 0753-32713

VOLUNTARY WORK AND CHARITIES

These organizations all ask for your support. Other charities are listed elsewhere in the book: organizations concerned with sick children, for instance, are in Chapter 9. You can find the appropriate pages by looking up the name of the charity concerned in the index.

1. Delivering 'meals on wheels', driving, disabled welfare, welfare for offenders and their families and many other services. Contact your local branch of the WRVS or:

> Women's Royal Voluntary Service
> 17 Old Park Lane
> London W1Y 4AJ
> 01-499 6040

2. Community work, helping the elderly and mentally or physically disabled people. If you are between 16 and 35, contact your local CSV office or:

> Community Service Volunteers
> 237 Pentonville Road
> London N1 9NJ
> 01-278 6601

3. Help with child welfare:
Child Poverty Action Group (address on page 305).

4. Help with charity shops, fund-raising and general support:

British Red Cross Society
9 Grosvenor Crescent
London SW1X 9EJ
  01-235 5454

Dr Barnardo's
Tanners Lane
Barkingside
Essex IG6 1QG
  01-550 8822

Helping Hand Gift Shops (Help the
  Aged)
2 Warrior Square Terrace
St Leonards-on-Sea
Sussex TN37 6BN
  0424-432263

Order of St John
1 Grosvenor Crescent
London SW1X 7EF
  01-235 5231

Oxfam
274 Banbury Road
Oxford OX2 7DZ
  0865-56777

Save the Children Fund
17 Grove Lane
London SE5 8RD
  01-703 5400

Save the Children Scotland
21 Alva Street
Edinburgh EH2 4PS
  031-225 6683

World Wildlife Fund
Panda House
11–13 Ockford Road
Guildford
Surrey GU7 1QU
  04868–20551

5. For information on a wide range of different charities and voluntary organizations, contact:

> Voluntary Movement Group
> 25 Rickford's Hill
> Aylesbury
> Bucks HP20 2RT
> 0297-82961

6. The main overseeing body of charities in England and Wales is the Charity Commission, to whom any complaints should be addressed at:

14 Ryder Street
London SWIY 6AH
01-214 6000

or

Graeme House
Derby Square
Liverpool L2 7SB
051-227 3191

Note: ● If you want to know how voluntary work affects your social security benefits and the contributions you make, get a copy of leaflet NI240 (about getting benefits) or leaflet NI40 (about paying contributions) from your local social security office.

WOMEN'S RIGHTS AND GROUPS

Catcall
37 Wortley Road
London E6 1AY
(no telephone)
(a non-sectarian forum for discussion, theory and the exchange of ideas by and for women)

Change
29 Great James Street
London WCIN 3ES
   01–405 3601
(succinct reports on overall status of women in the world today)

Fan: Feminist Artists Newsletter
17 Melrose Gardens
London W6 7RN
   01-603 6370
(quarterly publication)

Feminist Library and
Information Centre (formerly
   WRRC)
Hungerford House
Victoria Embankment
London WC2N 6NN
   01-930 0715
(library – list of women's studies and research)

Feminist Review
11 Carleton Gardens
Brecknock Road
London NI9 5AQ

(journal which develops the theory of women's liberation and debates political perspectives and strategy of the movement)

International Women's News
99 The Grove
Isleworth
Middlesex TW7 4JE
(no telephone)
(quarterly, global coverage of women's movement)

Manchester Women's
   Liberation Newsletter
36 Whitechapel Street
Didsbury
Manchester M20 0TX
(no telephone)

Mother's Union
Mary Sumner House
24 Tufton Street
London SWIP 3RB
   01-222 5533
(international organization with local branches)

National Association
   of Women's Clubs
5 Vernon Rise
King's Cross Road
London WCIX 9EP
   01-837 1434
(main headquarters for 700 women's clubs around Britain)

National Federation
of Women's Institutes
39 Eccleston Street
London SW1W 9NT
    01-730 7212
(headquarters of country-based
groups in England, Wales and
Channel Islands)

National Housewives' Register
245 Warwick Road
Solihull
West Midlands B92 7AH
    021-706 1101
(activities, baby-sitting,
general programmes)

National Union
    of Townswomen's Guilds
Chamber of Commerce House
75 Harborne Road
Edgbaston
Birmingham B15 3DA
    021-455 6868
(headquarters of groups of women
in towns all around Britain)

Over Forty Association
    for Women Workers
Mary George House
120–22 Cromwell Road
London SW7 4HA
    01-370 2556
(help with housing and advice,
social club and general support)

Progressive League
Albion Cottage
Fortis Green
London N2 4JD
    01-452 8358
(international co-operation to
banish fear, to end war and to
further education)

Scottish Women's Rural Institutes
42 Heriot Row
Edinburgh EH3 6ES
    031-225 1724

(home and other activities
for women throughout Scotland)

Society of Women Writers
    and Journalists
Old Fyning House
Rogate
Petersfield
Hampshire GU31 5EF
(no telephone)
(support group for
those in the profession)

Sisterwrite Co-operative
    Bookshop
190 Upper Street
London N1 1RQ
    01-226 9782
(feminist and non-sexist children's
books – s.a.e. for mail order details)

Spare Rib
27 Clerkenwell Close
London EC1R 0AT
    01-253 9792
(women's liberation magazine
for black and white women)

Tara Associates
South End House
Church Lane
Lymington
Hants SO4 9RA
    0590-76848
(supplies out-of-print books
on women and society)

Ultra Violet Enterprises
25 Horsell Road
London N5 1XL
    01-607 4463
(publishing service offering
skills and advice to promote
the publication of feminist and
radical writing)

United Kingdom Federation
of Business and Professional
Women
23 Ansdell Street
London W8 5BN
01-938 1729
(divisional and national activities,
seminars and magazine)

WEA Women's Studies Newsletter
Workers' Educational Association
9 Upper Berkeley Street
London WIH 8BY
01-402 5608
(quarterly journal)

Wires (Women's Information,
Referral and Enquiry Service)
PO Box 162
Sheffield S1 1UD
0742-755290
(publishes a fortnightly
national liberation newsletter –
women only)

Women and Education Newsletter
c/o Joy Rose
14 St Brendan's Road
Withington
Manchester M20 9FF
061-973 7624
(twice-yearly magazine)

Women in Media
BM WIM
London WCIN 3XX
01-435 7772
(for accurate portrayal
of women by the media
as well as equality of opportunity
in the media)

Women in Media
7 Winetavern Street
Belfast BTI 1JQ
0232-225426
(network for those in the
profession)

Women in Publishing
PO Box 149a
Surbiton
Surrey KT6 5JH
(no telephone – exchange of
information, open to all in the book
trade)

Women's Centre Newsletter
44 The Grove
(off Prince Street)
Bristol BS1 4QH
0272-22760
(monthly publication: news,
happenings, opinions from, by and
about women and women's groups
in the Bristol area)

Women's Institute for
Freedom of the Press
3306 Ross Place NW
Washington DC 20008
USA
0101-202 966 7783
(publishers of a comprehensive
international *Directory of Women's
Media*)

Women's Media Action Group
A Woman's Place
Hungerford House
Victoria Embankment
London WC2N 6PA
(no telephone)
(campaign to eliminate sexism in
the media)

Women's Press Book Club
124 Shoreditch High Street
London E1 6JE
01-729 4751
(mail order bookclub,
see page 520)

Further Information

Suggested further reading   Inglis, Brian and Ruth West, *The Alternative Health Guide*, Michael Joseph
Stanway, Dr Andrew, *Alternative Medicine: a Guide to Natural Therapies*,
Penguin

DISABILITIES
Nichols, Dr Philip, Ros Haworth and Joy Hopkins, *Disabled: an Illustrated Manual of Help and Self-help*, David & Charles

ASSERTIVENESS
Dickson, Anne, *A Woman in Your Own Right*, Quartet

PEACE
Harford, Barbara and Sarah Hopkins (eds.), *Greenham Common: Women at the Wire*, Women's Press

Index

Mary Gostelow Enterprises is a partnership between Mary Gostelow and Wendy Lees. They were helped by many talented people when *The Complete Woman's Reference Book* was put together.

If you would like details of Complete Woman Ltd and *Outlook* magazine–and further information about other books by those working with Mary Gostelow, please send two first-class stamps to:

> Mary Gostelow Enterprises
> PO Box 135
> Ringwood
> Hants BH24 1JB

NAMES AND ADDRESSES

NAMES AND ADDRESSES

NOTES

NOTES

NOTES

NOTES

NOTES